The Free Movement of Capital and Financial Services

The Free Movement of Capital and Financial Services: An Exposition?

By

Graeme Baber

CAMBRIDGE SCHOLARS

PUBLISHING

The Free Movement of Capital and Financial Services: An Exposition?,
by Graeme Baber

This book first published 2014

Cambridge Scholars Publishing

12 Back Chapman Street, Newcastle upon Tyne, NE6 2XX, UK

British Library Cataloguing in Publication Data
A catalogue record for this book is available from the British Library

ISBN (10): 1-4438-6359-9, ISBN (13): 978-1-4438-6359-9

To my family, especially my mother, for loyalty and support in the preparation for and writing of this work.

[I]n examining the cross-border out-shopping phenomenon, we postulate that those consumers who engage in international (cross-border) out-shopping exhibit low levels of economic patriotism.

—Dmitrovic, T. and Vida, I. (2007), 'An examination of cross-border shopping behaviour in South-East Europe', *European Journal of Marketing*, 41(3/4), 382-395, 386.

CONTENTS

List of Figures

PREFACE

The time has come to review the laws that relate to cross-border capital flows within the European Economic Area. There have been changes in European Law, as a result of the introduction of the Treaty on the Functioning of the European Union. Furthermore, the structure of the Union has developed since the book 'The Impact of Legislation and Regulation on the Freedom of Movement of Capital in Estonia, Poland and Latvia' was published by Cambridge Scholars Publishing in June 2010.

Article 64(3) of the Treaty on the Functioning of the European Union supersedes Article 57(2) of the Treaty Establishing the European Community in providing for the Council to act unanimously, after consulting the European Parliament, in order to reverse the liberalisation of capital movements to or from countries outside the European Economic Area. In the absence of Council action under Article 64(3), Article 65(4) of the Treaty on the Functioning of the European Union permits the Council to unanimously take a decision that declares the restrictive tax measures adopted by a Member State concerning states outside the European Economic Area compatible with the European Union Treaties.

Regulations 1092, 1093, 1094 and 1095 of 24 November 2010 promptly established a European Systemic Risk Board, a European Banking Authority, a European Insurance and Occupational Pensions Authority and a European Securities and Markets Authority, respectively. These organisations are an integral part of the legislative process in European Union financial services law.

The judgment in Case C-101/05 *Skatterverket v A.* [2007] ECR I-11531 provides guidance as to the application of the European Union's free movement of capital rules to countries outside the European Economic Area. In paragraph 37 of this case, the Court of Justice of the European Union held that the taxation by a Member State of cross-border economic activities within the European Union is not always comparable to such taxation if the activities are between Member States and third countries. It will be interesting to watch how the Court develops this principle.

There is increasing convergence of legal standards in financial markets. Some of this is a result of international initiatives, such as that of the G-20 relating to over-the-counter derivative contracts. As a result, capital must, in practice, be able to cross borders as free from restrictions as is reasonably possible. In other words, the issue is larger than the completion of the European Union's internal market – important though this objective is. It involves integration of the financial sector globally.

As there have been developments in European Union and national financial services law since the earlier book, I decided to concentrate this time on this area of the law in particular. Consequently, material that relates to taxation and real property in chapters 2-5 of that publication, and the economic analysis in chapters 6 and 7, have been removed. In addition to Estonia, Poland and Latvia, I have included an examination of an extract of the financial services legislation of Germany and Croatia for compliance with the European Union's free movement of capital rules.

The Federal Republic of Germany joined the European Economic Community on 1st January 1958, at its formation. The European Economic Community was renamed the European Community when the Treaty on European Union came into force, on 1st November 1993. Estonia, Poland and Latvia joined the European Community on 1st January 2004. The European Community became the European Union when the Lisbon Treaty came into effect, on 1st November 2009. Croatia joined the European Union on 1st July 2013. Hence, this book analysis the laws of countries that have been Member States for various lengths of time.

Please feel free to comment on the analysis and comments made in the book. I can be contacted at GraemeBaber@bpp.com, and look forward to receiving your suggestions and feedback.

ACKNOWLEDGEMENTS

The author and publishers wish to thank the following, who have kindly given permission for the use of copyright material:

Elsevier Science Publications B.V. and the Copyright Clearance Center's Rightslink service for: Cardoso and Dornbusch (1989), 'Foreign Private Capital Inflows', figure 26.6, page 1418, *in* Chenery, H. And Srinivasan, T. N. *eds.*, *Handbook of Development Economics, Volume II* (Amsterdam: Elsevier Science Publications B.V.), which is adapted to become Fig. 1-1.

LIST OF ABBREVIATIONS

AIF	Alternative Investment Fund
AIFM	Alternative Investment Fund Manager
Annex I	Annex I to Directive 88/361/EEC
BaFin	German Federal Supervisory Authority
CFSSA	Croatian Financial Services Supervisory Authority
CJEU	Court of Justice of the European Union
ECR	European Court Reports
EEA	European Economic Area, comprising the European Union, Iceland, Liechtenstein and Norway
EFSA	Estonian Financial Supervision Authority
ELLC	Estonian Legal Language Centre
EU	European Union
EUR	Euros
EURATOM	European Atomic Energy Community
FDI	Foreign Direct Investment
IMF	International Monetary Fund
LFCMC	Latvian Financial and Capital Market Commission
LTTC	Latvian Translation and Terminology Centre
Member State	Member State of the European Union
MNCs	Multinational corporations
OECD	Organisation for Economic Co-operation and Development
PAAS	Prior Administrative Authorisation Scheme
PFSA	Polish Financial Supervision Authority
TFEU	Treaty on the Functioning of the European Union
Third countries	Countries outside the European Economic Area
UCITS	Undertakings for Collective Investment in Transferable Securities
WTO	World Trade Organization

Abbreviations for Estonian legislation and regulations

Chapter 3

CIA	Credit Institutions Act 1999
IAA	Insurance Activities Act 2004
IFA	Investment Funds Act 2004
PIA	Payment Institutions and E-money Institutions Act 2009
Regulation No. 19	Regulation No. 19 of the President of the Bank of Estonia of 6 July 1999
SMA	Securities Market Act 2001

Section 4.1

EIFA	Investment Funds Act 2004

Section 5.3.3

EIAA	Insurance Activities Act 2004

Abbreviations for Polish legislation and regulations

Chapter 4

BL	Act of 29 August 1997: Banking Law
IAA	Act of 22 May 2003 on Insurance Activity
IFA	Act of 27 May 2004 on Investment Funds
IMA	Act of 22 May 2003 on Insurance Mediation
IPFSA	Act of 22 May 2003 on Insurance and Pension Funds Supervision and on Insurance Ombudsman
LPF	Act of 28 August 1997 Law on the Organisation and Operation of Pension Funds
OPSA	Act of 20 April 2004 on Occupational Pension Schemes
POA	Act of 29 July 2005 on Public Offers and the Conditions for Introducing Financial Instruments to the Organised Trading System, and on Public Companies
PSA	Act of 19 August 2011 on Payment Services
RIM	Regulation of the Minister of Finance of July 6th 2007 on Detailed Conditions to be Met by the Information Memorandum Referred to in Articles 39(1) and 42(1) of the

	Act on Public Offers, and the Conditions for Introducing Financial Instruments to the Organised Trading System, and on Public Companies
RLDAIP	Resolution No. 389/2008 of the Polish Financial Supervision Authority of 17 December 2008 concerning the list of documents attached to the application to the Polish Financial Supervision Authority on issuing a permit to establish a bank, consent to appoint the members of the bank's Management Board and information about the composition of the board presented to the Polish Financial Supervision Authority by the Supervisory Board of the Bank
RLDEFE	Resolution No. 359/2012 of the Polish Financial Supervision Authority of 20 December 2012 on the list of documents relating to business activity of entrepreneurs or foreign entrepreneurs enclosed with requests for authorisation referred to in Articles 6a(1)(1)(m) and 6d(1) of the Banking Law
RMESBA	Resolution No. 312/2012 of the Polish Financial Supervision Authority of 27 November 2012 on the Mode of Exercising Supervision over Banking Activity
TFIA	Act of 29 July 2005 on Trading in Financial Instruments

Abbreviations for Latvian legislation

Chapter 5

CIL	Credit Institutions Law 1995

Abbreviations for German legislation

Chapter 5

PSSA	Payment Services Supervision Act 2009

Abbreviations for Croatian legislation

Chapter 5

IA	Insurance Act 2006

CHAPTER ONE

BACKGROUND AND METHODOLOGY

1.1 What is the purpose of the research?

On 1st May 2004, ten new Member States joined the EU.[1] The majority of these countries were members of the Warsaw Pact until its abolition in 1990,[2] and three were part of the Soviet Union.[3]

In 1998, the EU entered into accession talks with these countries for membership. The main condition for membership was acceptance and implementation of the '*acquis communautaire*' – the substantial body of Treaty provisions, Regulations, Decisions and Directives and case law already in force in the EU.[4]

One substantial part of the *acquis communautaire* consists of the legislation to create the internal market, which is characterised by the removal of barriers to the free movement of goods, persons, services and capital between Member States.[5] This book concerns the free movement of capital legislation (Articles 63–66) of the Treaty on the Functioning of the European Union (TFEU).

The book investigates the compliance of the financial services laws of Estonia (in depth) and Poland (comprehensively and concisely) with the EU's free movement of capital laws. The conclusions from these studies are then compared with the findings from selected financial services provisions of Latvia, Germany and Croatia. From this analysis, broader conclusions are reached, and their implications for the provision of financial services investigated. This methodology is grounded theory, in so

---

[1] These countries are Cyprus, Czech Republic, Estonia, Hungary, Latvia, Lithuania, Malta, Poland, Slovakia and Slovenia.

[2] The countries from these ten states that were members of the Warsaw Pact are Czech Republic and Slovakia (as Czechoslovakia), Estonia, Latvia and Lithuania (as part of the former Soviet Union), Hungary and Poland.

[3] The countries from these ten states that were part of the Soviet Union are Estonia, Latvia and Lithuania.

[4] See section 1.3.1.

[5] See section 1.2.3.

far as the analysis of the Estonian and Polish financial services legislation and regulations provides observations that are tested on the other three countries, from which general conclusions are made.

Although the author approached this research already familiar with the study of the compliance of national legislation and regulations in Estonia, Poland and Latvia with the EU's rules on the free movement of capital,[6] almost all of the commentary on these three countries is new, due to changes made in the law and to the need for detailed reportage and analysis. The selection of Germany and Croatia was based upon the need to extend the temporal reach of the analysis from countries that acceded to Membership of the EU in 2004.[7] West Germany was one of the founding states of the European Economic Community, whose Treaty was signed on 25th March 1957, and which came into operation on 1st January 1958. East Germany 'joined' the European Economic Community on 3rd October 1990, the date on which it reunited with West Germany to form Germany.[8] Croatia acceded to Membership of the EU on 1st July 2013. At the time of writing, no country has subsequently acceded. Thus, in choosing to analyse the financial services laws of these countries, the whole period of the Community's existence is considered.[9]

1.2 Why legislate to remove cross-border capital restrictions?

It must first be established whether, on balance, it is beneficial for a country or trade block to lift its barriers to cross-border capital flows. Since the free movement of capital is part of the internal market, Member

---

[6] See Baber (2010), *The Impact of Legislation and Regulation on the Freedom of Movement of Capital.*

[7] See note 1, for a list of the countries that acceded to EU Membership in 2004.

[8] West Germany (the Federal Republic of Germany) absorbed East Germany (the Democratic Republic of Germany) as five new Federal States, with a reunited Berlin as a Federal City-State. Thus, the Treaties of West Germany, including Membership of the European Communities, were extended over the whole German territory from the reunification date (3rd October 1990).

[9] The financial legislation of (West) Germany has changed since 1958, in accordance with EU Directives. Furthermore, the Community project started before this, with the signing of the Treaty Establishing the European Coal and Steel Community on 18th April 1951, and the consequent foundation of the European Coal and Steel Community amongst Belgium, France, Italy, Luxembourg, Netherlands and West Germany on 23rd July 1952. This Treaty expired on 23rd July 2002.

States have an additional powerful incentive to remove restrictions to these flows.

1.2.1 Reasons in favour of the free movement of capital

The free movement of capital stimulates cross-border trade and investment, which may increase the rate of economic growth.[10] Investment may also fund training and/or raise the level of exports in the sector concerned, although the latter may cause the terms of trade to deteriorate.[11] Free capital movement across the EU also encourages the formation of companies with subsidiaries and branches in other Member States,[12] and lowers the cost of investment for financial asset providers in such States.[13]

Cardoso and Dornbusch describe the following effects of capital inflows.[14] First, such inflows raise the economy's productive capacity, thereby potentially increasing welfare.[15] There is an increase in national income, whose size is quadratically related to the share of capital in the income accruing to domestic factors of production, and inversely correlated with the elasticity of substitution between capital and other such factors.[16]

Second, capital inflows may smooth consumption in two contexts. 1) Cyclical fluctuations: one can borrow when disposable income is lower than consumption, and repay when income rises. 2) Growth in per capita income: foreign loans can finance investment so that income exceeds consumption and domestic savings increase; later, such savings fund investment and the loans are repaid.

---

[10] The Harrod-Domar and two-gap models incorporate the positive effect of capital inflows on growth, and the Solow growth model has been applied to international capital movements. There are also two groups of optimization models: the representative consumer approach in which the economy is treated as a single unit over time, and the life-cycle approach in which 'younger' consumers earn and save and 'older' consumers do not.

[11] See section 1.2.2.

[12] The free movement of capital therefore complements the freedom of establishment.

[13] The cost of investment includes taxes and administration expenses.

[14] *Handbook of Development Economics*, Volume II, 1989, 1404–1419.

[15] Capital inflows may lower welfare: see section 1.2.2.

[16] The domestic gain is the following fraction of national income: $(1 - \alpha)\,\alpha x^2 / 2\sigma$, where x is the proportionate rise in the capital stock, α is the share of capital in income to domestic factors, and σ is elasticity of substitution. This neoclassical model also predicts a gain to foreign investors.

Third, capital inflows lower the scarcity of capital, thereby raising the factor productivity for domestic factors as a whole. Where such inflows are accompanied by immigration, returns to land increase whilst the income of local capital and labour tend to fall – the effect on factor prices depends on technology and on the relative change in the domestic capital stock and labour supply.

Fourth, if there is a foreign exchange gap, foreign capital goods are too expensive to be purchased by exports and the real exchange rate must depreciate. Capital inflows may alleviate real price rigidity and/or costly adjustments to relative prices, by providing foreign exchange and raising investment for economic growth. In the two-gap model, the capital inflow moves the foreign exchange constraint to the right, thereby raising the growth rate and the ratio of domestic to foreign prices.[17]

1.2.2 Reasons for retaining barriers to capital flows

Capital flows may destabilize macroeconomic conditions within a country. An example is Chile, which implemented a financial liberalization program in the 1970s–1980s. After a period of high growth, the capital account of the balance of payments was opened to medium and long-term international capital movements. There was a large capital inflow, causing the exchange rate to appreciate. Expenditure on imports rose, creating a current account deficit. As the rate of capital inflow declined, a real devaluation of the peso was required to raise the competitiveness of the export sector. Since the nominal exchange rate was pegged to the strong dollar, and since Chile had a law which prevented reduction in real wages, there was initially no devaluation, and output declined rather than prices. The next year, the government devalued the peso, causing a loss of international reserves and lower capital inflows. As inflation was relatively low, there was a real devaluation and competitiveness was regained.[18]

One factor present in Chile's experience is deterioration in the terms of trade, since the exchange rate appreciation made exports and import-competing products more expensive relative to imports.[19] Drs. Raúl Prebisch and Hans Singer believed that the terms of trade had moved against primary products during the early 20th century, a trend which

---

[17] Fig. 1-1 is adapted from Cardoso and Dornbusch, *Handbook of Development Economics*, figure 26.6, 1418.

[18] Edwards (1985), *Economic Development and Cultural Change*, 33, 223–254.

[19] The terms of trade are the price of exports divided by the price of imports.

Fig. 1-1: The two-gap model: a capital inflow shifts the foreign exchange constraint to the right.

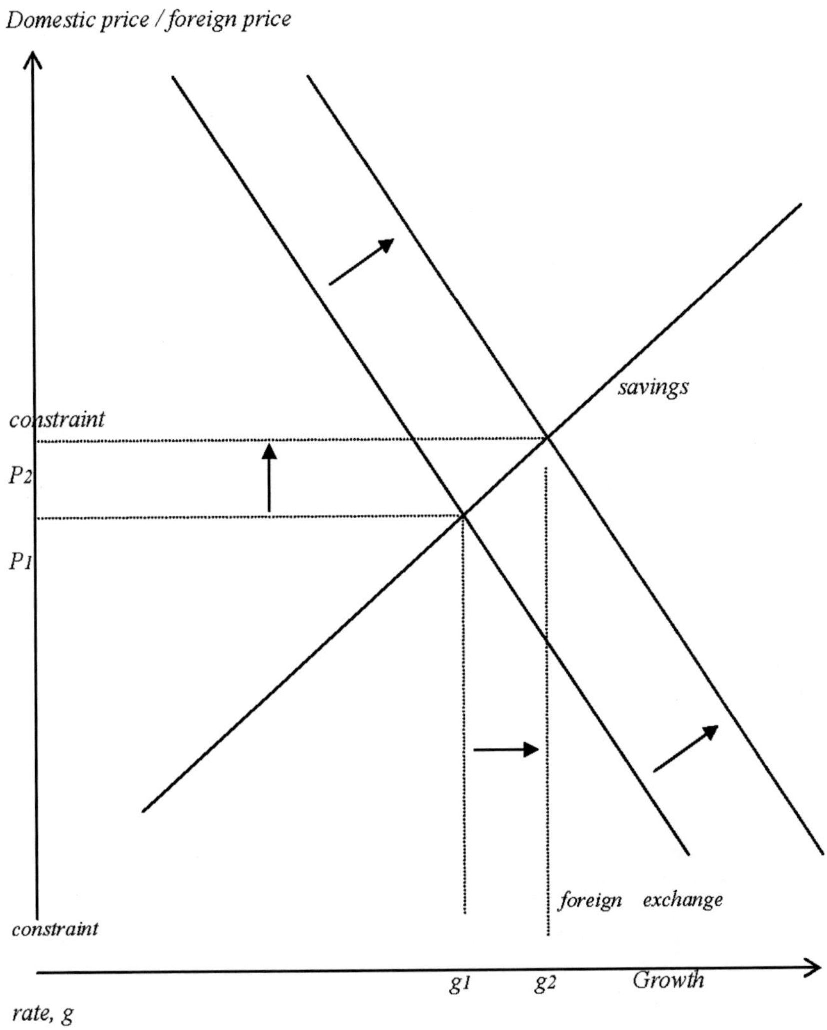

continued into the latter half of the century.[20] A rise in capital inflows to a developing country in these circumstances is counterproductive, stimulating the purchase of imports with the additional burden of debt repayment.

Cardoso and Dornbusch state two cases in which capital inflows reduce welfare.[21] 1) If capital inflows enable the expansion of an industry with monopoly power in the export sector, the terms of trade deterioration due to the rise in the price of exports may, in the absence of an optimum tariff, reduce national income. 2) Tariff or tax distortions may, through general equilibrium effects, cause capital inflows to contract an industry that is already underproductive. These welfare-reducing cases are an exception to the general principle that capital inflows tend to raise national income.[22]

Capital flight–the mass transfer of investment from domestic to foreign assets[23]–is a potential problem for countries in financial distress. The main determinants of capital flight are real exchange rate appreciation and/or currency overvaluation, a high and/or rising inflation rate, the expectation of currency devaluation, and a low domestic interest rate relative to the world interest rate.[24] Controls on capital outflows are essential for countries with these characteristics.[25] Investors may move their assets abroad in

---

[20] Cypher and Dietz (2004), *The Process of Economic Development*, 162–169. Many developing countries have traditionally been net exporters of agricultural products, a trend which changed to some extent with the introduction of import substitution industrialization (ISI). ISI has been partially but not totally successful.

[21] *Handbook of Development Economics*, 1407–1408.

[22] See section 1.2.1.

[23] 'Capital flight' may be narrowly defined as short term capital outflows or broadly defined as the gross value of all capital outflows. The broad definition more accurately describes capital flight because many outflows are long term; for instance, some white South African residents invested abroad after termination of the apartheid regime to safeguard their assets. In estimating capital flight from selected countries from 1979–1982, the World Bank uses a broad definition: gross capital inflows plus the current account deficit less increases in official foreign reserves (Eaton (1989), *Handbook of Development Economics*, Volume II, 1353), leaving gross capital outflows as the residual term. The definition of 'capital flight' used by Cuddington (1986), *Princeton Studies in International Finance*, No. 58, 1–40 is more specific and his investigation covers 1974–1982, but both studies conclude that Argentina, Mexico and Venezuela displayed the highest levels of capital flight.

[24] Cuddington, *Princeton Studies*.

[25] Brazil, Chile and Peru retained some capital controls during 1974–1982, which prevented more extensive capital flight, given their inflation and exchange rate movements in this period (Cuddington, *Princeton Studies*).

response to high domestic taxation or political risk (of expropriation, for instance),[26] or because local financial markets are volatile.

There are also difficulties with debt and FDI. Debtor countries may be unable to make debt repayments, especially after adverse economic shocks. The debt crisis of the 1980s was precipitated by the oil price rises of the 1970s and the worldwide economic recession of the early 1980s. In non-oil producing developing countries, export volumes and prices declined and the current account balance worsened. Real appreciation of the dollar raised the real value of developing countries' debt repayments, since their currencies were pegged to the dollar or to a basket of currencies. In Latin America, repayment problems were so severe that debt restructuring and forgiveness from the commercial lenders under the guidance of the Brady plan and market reforms supervised by the IMF were required to restore economic health.[27]

Governments may incur problems by permitting FDI from MNCs. MNCs may 1) lower domestic savings and investment by smothering competition, extracting profits and providing income for people with a low propensity to save but a high propensity to import; 2) reduce foreign exchange earnings by importing intermediate and capital goods, and by repatriating profits, interest, royalties and management fees; 3) increase income inequalities by widening wage differentials, manufacturing advanced products for the local elites and operating in urban areas; 4) introduce inappropriate products and technologies and 5) use non-arm's length transfer prices in intra-firm transactions.[28]

1.2.3 The internal market

The free movement of capital is one of the four fundamental freedoms provided by the TFEU, the others being the free movement of goods, persons and services. These freedoms are part of the EU's internal market, whose completion by December 1992 also required the removal of internal

---

[26] Cardoso and Dornbusch, *Handbook of Development Economics*, 1423.

[27] Pilbeam (2006), *International Finance*, 377–407. Although their export levels and inflation rates have recovered from the debt crisis, the total external debt in each of the four biggest debtor countries (Argentina, Brazil, Mexico and Venezuela) was higher in 2002 than it was in 1982, when the crisis began.

[28] Cardoso and Dornbusch, *Handbook of Development Economics*, 1413–1414. FDI may provide superior technology to local firms and economies of scale in marketing, and increase competition (ibid., 1407). The benefits and drawbacks are specific to each case.

frontier controls and the approximation of indirect tax rates.[29] Initially the free movement of capital was not intended to apply directly, but to facilitate, by way of Directives, the formation of a common market in financial services.[30] Today, the free movement of capital is stated by Article 63 of the TFEU,[31] and stands on an equal footing with the other freedoms.

Comment

The requirement for Member States to remove barriers to capital flows to and from other States and third countries as part of implementing the internal market (with certain exceptions),[32] renders academic the question as to whether States should retain them. Nonetheless, the arguments in section 1.2.2 are persuasive for countries that wish to borrow to fund investment and which have, or expect to have, high or rising inflation rates and/or real exchange rates. As Poland and Croatia have not yet joined the Euro,[33] they can still experience these conditions.[34]

1.3 The comparison of national law with European Law

1.3.1 Implementing the acquis communautaire

All aspiring EU Member States must implement the body of Treaty provisions, Regulations, Directives and case law that exists at the time of their accession to Membership – 1st May 2004 for Estonia, Poland and Latvia, and 1st July 2013 for Croatia. This is a legal transplantation of EU law onto national law, and has implications of harmonisation of national law with that of other Member States. These issues are discussed below.

---

[29] EC Commission (1985), 'Completing the Internal Market', COM(85) 310 final, 1–2, 9 and 51–54.
[30] Ibid., 32–33. This freedom was referred to as a 'secondary freedom'.
[31] Before 1st December 2009, the relevant provision was Article 56 of the Treaty Establishing the European Community, which was identical to the Article 63 of the TFEU.
[32] See section 2.1.3.
[33] Germany was one of the founder Members of the Eurozone, which introduced the Euro as legal tender on 1st January 1999. Estonia and Latvia adopted the Euro on 1st January 2011 and 1st January 2014, respectively. Poland and Croatia have no target date for joining the Euro.
[34] The European Central Bank sets the monetary policy of the countries that have adopted the Euro as their currency.

Legal transplants

Before the Enlightenment, European laws moved geographically, though usually with peoples – Germans into Poland, Normans into England, English into Ireland, and all of these peoples into foreign territories as part of colonisation. However, this spatial movement of law was perceived by the participants as a growing area of influence rather than as a transplant. Legal rules were considered to be models that could be used or not in specific cases.[35]

Alan Watson considers that the growth of law is primarily to be explained by the transplantation of legal rules. Watson investigates the spread of Roman law across Europe, noting the persistence of Roman legal rules into the present time. He states that the rules of Roman law have been transplanted in bulk into most continental European countries and are the foundation of their legal systems.[36] Watson argues that legal transplants are the main method for legal change in Western countries because the law is conservative and backward-looking. The law is such because the legal profession tends to treat legal rules as ends in themselves, with the sources of law being regarded as given, almost sacrosanct.[37]

William Twining states that most literature on legal transplants is in the 'Country and Western Tradition' of comparative law,[38] and that a broader perspective is required. He perceptively observes that legal diffusion studies have shared origins with 19th century sociology and anthropology, but that such studies have lost touch with literature in other social sciences concerning the diffusion of innovations, language, music, religion and sport, which may enlighten enquiries into legal diffusion. Twining recommends adoption of a global view and a broad notion of law, covering different levels of ordering and relations.[39]

---

[35] Glenn (2006), *Journal of Comparative Law*, 1, 124–130.

[36] Watson (1974, 2nd edition 1993), *Transplants: An Approach to Comparative Law,* cited in Ewald (1995), *American Journal of Comparative Law*, 43, 489–510. These countries are 'civil law' families.

[37] Watson (1985), *The Evolution of Law*, cited in Ewald, *American Journal.*

[38] This tradition concerns positive laws and national legal systems, focuses on Western capitalist societies, is primarily concerned with common law / civil law differences, legal doctrine and private law, and involves description and analysis in preference to evaluation and prescription.

[39] Twining (2006), *Journal of Comparative Law*, 1, 3–26. Such different levels include, for example, the adoption of international norms into national law, such as the incorporation of the European Convention on Human Rights into the United Kingdom Human Rights Act 1998.

Twining's perspective of different levels is applicable to the implementation of EU law in Member States, for such law is of a higher level than the national rules of Member States, since these rules must comply with it.[40] In as far as EU law has direct effect,[41] there is no change in the national law of Member States other than repealing incompatible provisions.

However, a more interactive legal transplantation occurs for Directives than for EU Treaty provisions and Regulations, both because Directives must be transposed into national law and because of the principle of indirect effect.[42] Although the resulting national law must comply with EU law, it is in the context of the Member State's legal system, which may affect the form that the domestic law takes – i.e. the transposed Directive may be transformed in the local environment.

Harmonisation

The TFEU does not refer exclusively to 'harmonisation' of laws. Articles 114(1) and 115 use 'approximation' of laws instead, which conveys a lesser degree of uniformity than harmonisation. Confusion is caused, however, by the use of the term "harmonisation measure" in Articles 114(4) and 114(5), which refer to a measure adopted under Article 114(1).

Article 115 empowers the Council to issue Directives to approximate the laws, regulations or administrative provisions of Member States that "directly affect the establishment or functioning of the common market". The Council must act unanimously on a Commission proposal. By contrast, Article 114(1) authorises the Council acting by qualified majority on a Commission proposal (under the ordinary legislative procedure)[43] to adopt measures to approximate the laws, regulations or administrative

---

[40] In *Amministrazione delle Finanze dello Stato v Simmenthal SpA (No.2)* [1978] ECR 629, the CJEU stated that a national court must set aside a legal rule that conflicts with a provision of EU law.

[41] To have direct effect, an EU provision must 1) be clear and unambiguous, enabling the national court to identify the rights and obligations of individuals, 2) be unconditional, and 3) require no further action from EU and national authorities (*Van Gend en Loos v Nederlandse Tariefcommissie* [1963] ECR 1). The CJEU has extended the principal of vertical direct effect (i.e. rights conferred on individuals against national institutions) to Directives (*Van Duyn v Home Office* [1975] ECR 1337).

[42] The principle of indirect effect states that national courts are required to interpret their national law in the light of the purpose and wording of the Directive, especially if that law is specifically enacted to implement the Directive (*Von Colson v Land Nordrhein-Westfahlen* [1984] ECR 1891).

[43] Article 294, TFEU.

provisions of Member States that "have as their object the establishment and functioning of the internal market".

Article 114(2) does not apply to fiscal provisions, which therefore require unanimity in the Council to be ratified.[44] Since unanimity is difficult to achieve, especially in relation to tax matters, the Council has passed few direct tax harmonisation measures.[45] Consequently EU developments in direct taxation have been by CJEU case law.[46]

Weatherill and Beaumont state that it would "likely to be fruitless" to introduce a single harmonised system, due to the diversity across the Community.[47] They express that replacing national rules by one Community rule is "a discredited option in most circumstances" because the accompanying "elimination" of the Member States' diversity would "stifle tradition and … ossify existing practice, thereby deterring innovation by business".[48] The alternative taken is "to adopt different traditions within a flexible Community framework" and to emphasize "administrative cooperation".[49] Sometimes the Community may use a "minimum standard", which Member States can choose to exceed.[50] This differentiated pace of integration may be "inevitable and desirable" in a heterogeneous Community.[51]

Dashwood, Dougan, Rodger, Spaventa and Wyatt consider whether harmonisation facilitates the working of the internal market,[52] in particular company law and direct tax measures. The rationale of company law harmonisation is that it enables freedom of establishment.[53] Article 50(2)(g) of the TFEU supplies the legal basis for such harmonisation,[54] stating that the European Parliament, the Council and the Commission may "carry out the duties devolving upon them under the preceding

[44] Article 114(2), TFEU. Unanimity is required for the "harmonisation" (not approximation) of indirect taxes (Article 113, TFEU).

[45] Directives 90/434/EEC (the Mergers Directive) and 90/435/EEC (the Parent/Subsidiary Directive) are examples.

[46] See Baber, *The Impact of Legislation and Regulation*, section 2.3, 50–58, for a synopsis of these developments. There have been several more recent CJEU judgments on national direct tax provisions that contravene the free movement of capital, which are not reported there.

[47] (1999), *EU Law*, 556.

[48] Ibid.

[49] Ibid., 556–557.

[50] Ibid., 557.

[51] Ibid.

[52] (2011), *Wyatt and Dashwood's European Union Law*, chapter 21.

[53] Ibid., 677.

[54] Ibid.

provisions [the right of establishment] by coordinating ... the safeguards which ... are required by Member States of companies or firms ... with a view to making such safeguards equivalent throughout the Union."

Dashwood et al. explain that the company law harmonisation measures address the following issues: 1) differences between national rules that cause economic entities to be unfamiliar with those in another Member State, 2) differences between national rules that cause varying requirements for establishment, and 3) national rules or practices inhibiting cross-border establishment.[55] They conclude, as follows.

> "The Commission's approach to company law harmonisation has, however, changed – perhaps more than that of the European Parliament and the Member States. The Commission has sought to utilise company law harmonisation as a means of promoting cross-border business activity to a greater extent than in the past, which accords with the logic of the Treaty basis for harmonisation being the chapter on establishment."[56]

Thus, the Commission may be leading a reversal of the move away from harmonisation that Weatherill and Beaumont observe.[57]

Comment

EU law has been superimposed on the national legal systems of Member States rather than transplanted. This is particularly true for the thirteen States that joined the EU since 2000,[58] because they were required to implement an *acquis communautaire* developed over more than forty years by other decision-makers. In addition, most of these countries have legal systems that were shaped by communist rule during many of these years. By contrast, there was no communist input to the early development of EU law.

Wade Channell states that there are three core problems for post-communist countries in implementing law that support the free market and democratic government:

1. *Lack of Ownership*. Foreign laws are often translated without sufficient attempt to adapt them to the local legal and commercial

---

[55] Ibid., 679. Discussion of the Company Law Directives is outside the scope of this section, which considers the harmonisation of laws within the EU in general terms.

[56] Ibid., 700.

[57] See above in this subsection.

[58] Bulgaria, Croatia, Cyprus, Czech Republic, Estonia, Hungary, Latvia, Lithuania, Malta, Poland, Romania, Slovakia and Slovenia.

culture. Local users of such laws are not consulted and the reform agenda is decided by external donors.

2. *Insufficient Resources.* Law reforms are implemented too quickly and cheaply. The new laws are drafted, often by expatriate experts, passed by the legislature and explained to the legal community, culminating in no meaningful change. There should be wide-ranging public education and institutional reform as a basis for implementation.
3. *Excessive segmentation.* There may be hyper-focus on particular areas, which ignores systemic issues. For instance, judicial education in commercial concepts should be coupled with enforcement improvements.[59]

These issues are of concern in the transposition of EU Directives into Estonian, Polish, Latvian and Croatian law. Since the relevant national rules have been enacted only recently, and since the focus of Chapters 3, 4 and 5 is on compliance of national law with EU free movement of capital rules, the comparison of national law with EU law concerns the content of these rules rather than their implementation.[60]

Whilst there was a move away from harmonisation and towards administrative co-operation, in order to pursue the completion of the internal market, this trend has, to some extent, been reversed.[61] Since the *Cassis de Dijon* judgment,[62] the CJEU has pursued a policy of 'negative integration', in order to bring about the internal market.[63] Furthermore, the EU legislature is increasingly inclined to take a 'maximum harmonisation' approach. For example, the Prospectus Directive[64] and its implementing Regulation[65] provide for a list of requirements for inclusion in a prospectus that relates to an offer for each class of security to the public, or for admission of this class of security to a regulated market.[66]

---

[59] Channell (2005), *Carnegie Working Papers*, No. 57, 4–8.

[60] See section 1.3.2.

[61] See above in the subsection '*Harmonisation*'.

[62] *Rewe-Zentral AG v Bundesmonopolverwaltung für Branntwein* [1979] ECR 649.

[63] 'Negative integration' is the process of bringing national law into line with EU law by the annulment of provisions of the former that are incompatible with the latter. In *Cassis de Dijon*, the CJEU held that a Member State's rules as to the requirements that relate to the minimum alcohol content of alcoholic drinks do not take priority over the requirements of the free movement of goods, because they do not serve a purpose that is within the general interest [paragraph 14].

[64] Directive 2003/71/EC.

[65] Commission Regulation (EC) No 809/2004.

[66] This information is contained in 30 Annexes to Commission Regulation (EC) No 809/2004. For instance, Annex I of the Regulation contains minimum

1.3.2 The methodology used for the comparison

Professor Vernon Palmer indicates that whilst comparative law has one method: "to compare and contrast norms, institutions, cultures, attitudes, methodologies and legal systems", it has many techniques which are called 'methods': "historical, functional, evolutionary, structural, thematic, empirical and statistical comparisons … from a micro or macro" perspective.[67] His four case studies show methods used in various breadth and depth. Although the first two cases concern Sotho law, the techniques used therein can be applied to Member States.

I. Inquiry into Sotho customary law, 1872

A commission of European magistrates put abstract questions to Basotho chiefs and councillors and to two French missionaries about Sotho law and custom. The questions were constructed in English and translated into Sesotho. They comprised Western legal concepts. The answers were translated back to English and revealed differences from English law in content, culture, language, history and religion. Although the method used was simple, inexpensive and ethnocentric,[68] it evoked a reasonable description of Sotho law and custom, and therefore a fairly accurate transfer of legal ideas, even though English and Sotho law in 1872 were very dissimilar.[69]

II. Inquiry into Sotho family law, 1976

Sebastian Poulter's study into Sotho law involved:

1. reading the legal and ethnographic records of Sesotho law and society;
2. reviewing Sesotho family law judgments;
3. assembling an expert panel with judicial experience to discuss unsettled and unclear points of law;
4. conducting interviews with ladies in two villages about women's issues, such as widows' right to land and childbearing.

Poulter found that several versions of the law coexisted. He reconstructed all versions from 1850 to 1976, comparing and contrasting them with the

---

disclosure requirements for the share registration document; Annex IV contains minimum disclosure requirements for the debt and derivative securities registration document.

[67] Palmer (2005), *American Journal of Comparative Law*, 53, 262–263.

[68] The method was 'Eurocentric' and, in particular, 'Anglocentric'.

[69] Palmer, *American Journal*, 266–273.

judgments and panel discussions, thereby presenting a developmental history of Sesotho law over this period.[70]

III. Comparative study of pure economic loss in thirteen EU legal systems, 2003

An international team of tort/comparative lawyers drafted twenty factual hypothetical cases in English that explored different aspects of pure economic loss. This factual approach reduces distortions from the normative terminology of the enquiry's framework system. The three response levels from 'surface to core' are as follows.

1. *Operative Rules*, which state how judges have decided the case, whether doctrine agrees with the judgment, and whether solutions are the same as those in the past or are recent.
2. *Descriptive Formants*, which provide lawyers' reasons in support of the rules, each solution's degree of consistency with legislation and principles, how each solution is reasoned, and whether the solution relies on legal rules and/or public or procedural legal provisions.
3. *Metalegal Formants*, which are broader elements influencing each solution, such as economic factors and policy considerations.

This method yielded insights and knowledge about pure economic loss in the EU. However, it is on too large a scale to apply outside large harmonisation or codification projects.[71]

IV. European Code of Obligations

The Lando Commission, operating from 1982 to 1996, consisted of comparative law academics across Europe. Their objective was to construct a European Code of Obligations, which would form a foundation for a future European Code of Contracts, could be used by Member States, courts and arbitrators to govern their international contracts, and could be a model for legal development and harmonisation. The Commission formed a set of principles from sixteen legal systems using doctrinal works, national cases, codes and statutes, and international and EU legislation and conventions. The notes to each Article neither showed variations in this principle, nor why the Commissioners selected a particular rule; nor did they explicitly compare the laws of one country with another.[72]

---

[70] Ibid., 273–275.

[71] Ibid., 276–281.

[72] Ibid., 285–288. The principles are published in English by the Commission on European Contract Law (Lando Commission) at

Comment

The first method is subjective and investigatory as to Sotho law and custom. Given the limited resources, the study was successful, giving a general picture of Sotho legal practice. The second technique creates an historical record of Sotho law, especially family law. It is thorough and provides triangulation of different sources of evidence. Although conducted by just one researcher, it required substantial resources of his time, and input from other people in order to produce an accurate account.

The third method focuses in detail on one aspect of Member States' laws. It looks at the application of the specific provisions to cases, and at reasons behind the solutions proposed, including non-legal influences. It is the most comprehensive and unbiased technique of the four. However, it required many researchers, detailed analysis and considerable documentation.

The fourth method lacks both depth and objectivity. The Code of Obligations must be fair to all parties, and applicable in and acceptable to every Member State. Unlike the first three techniques, it creates new rules, rather than comparing existing laws on specific criteria. In these circumstances, subjectivity is unavoidable.

Each method is suitable for the objectives of each case study. The first study elicits a knowledge of Sotho law and custom from structured interviews. The second investigation produces a 126 year history of Sotho law from various sources. The third study provides a comprehensive examination of one legal aspect across European systems from in-depth case analysis. The fourth study produces a code that is applicable to all Member States, from an inspection of black letter laws from these countries by European comparative lawyers of different nationalities.

I concur with Professor Palmer's conclusion.

> "There is not, and indeed cannot be a single exclusive method that comparative law research should follow. The tasks of teaching, research, law reform or historical investigation are too varied and contingent to be achieved by a single approach. … [T]he best approach will always be adapted in terms of the specific purposes of the research, the subjective abilities of the researcher, and the affordability of the costs. … [C]omparative law … must be accessible and its methods must be flexible." [73]

---

http://frontpage.cbs.dk/law/commission_on_european_contract_law/PECL%20engelsk/, and are "intended to be applied as general rules of contract law in the European Union" (Article 1:101(1)).

[73] Ibid., 290.

Kötz' functional method and Legrand's critique

Professor Hein Kötz argues for the primary, but not exclusive, use of the functional method in comparative law.[74] Professor Pierre Legrand is its most ardent critic. Legrand proposes an alternative model that is rooted in and emerges from legal culture.[75]

Kötz states that comparative law investigations begin with a question or working hypothesis. From the fundamental methodological principle of functionality flow all the other rules that determine which laws to compare, the comparison's scope, and the creation of a comparative law system. "The question to which any comparative study is devoted must be posed in purely functional terms; the problem must be stated without any reference to the concepts of one's own legal system."[76]

The comparatist must consider statute, custom, trade usage, legal writing, general business conditions and standard-form contracts. He must learn about foreign civilizations, especially those whose law has generated the legal system families.[77] Except in moral and ethical areas of social life, such as divorce and adoption by unmarried people, "[d]ifferent legal systems give the same or very similar solutions, even as to detail, to the same problems of life, despite the great differences in their historical development, conceptual structure and style of operation".[78]

In general, developed countries fulfil the requirements of legal business in a similar way. Consequently, the comparatist can be satisfied if the conclusion of his research is that the systems he has compared produce similar practical outcomes. If he finds substantial differences, however, he must check that the terms of his original question were solely functional and that he has researched sufficiently widely.[79]

The comparatist should prepare separate reports for each legal system before the comparison. No report should contain critical evaluation.[80] To make the comparison, the solutions from the different jurisdictions must be freed from their conceptual context so that they may be seen in the light of their function to fulfil a specific legal need.[81]

Next, we must build a system that is flexible and has sufficiently broad concepts to include the functionally comparable heterogeneous legal

---

[74] Zweigert and Kötz (1998), *An Introduction to Comparative Law*, Chapter 3.
[75] Legrand (2006), *Journal of Comparative Law*, 1, 365–460.
[76] Zweigert and Kötz, *Comparative Law*, 34.
[77] Ibid., 36.
[78] Ibid., 39.
[79] Ibid., 40.
[80] Ibid., 43.
[81] Ibid., 44.

entities. For example, a claim for unjust enrichment may be a claim for restitution, for rescission of contract and a claim in tort in three different legal systems. The comparative law system must find a higher concept for each of the functions of restitutionary claims, such as " 'restitution of payments gone wrong', 'restitution for appropriating the property of others', 'restitution for unjustifiably using another's thing' ".[82]

The comparatist must critically evaluate what he has discovered, stating whether the solutions are equally valid or one is superior. He may form a new solution from elements of different national solutions.[83]

Legrand describes 'functionalism' as "[d]iscarding the contents of experience and values, eliding the concrete law, lacking any critical vocation, betraying a fundamentally technical perspective, and accounting for a view of comparative legal studies as essentially utilitarian".[84] He also states:

> "Kötz's calculative goal is to overthrow difference, to coerce it, to manage it with a view to achieving the reformulation and the re-formation of the local law in terms of what is 'best'. Under Kötz's guardian eye and in the name of 'bestness', disconcerting or distracting singularities will be overlooked, differences will be suppressed".[85]

The problem is Kötz's claim that functionality is the fundamental methodological principle from which flows all the other rules determining the laws to compare, the comparison's scope and the creation of a comparative law system.[86] Kötz has one goal: to compare the content of functionally similar legal rules of different jurisdictions in order to determine, outside the context of national culture, which solution is 'superior', which is not defined. Whilst this is plausible in some contexts, such as a methodology for producing the European Code of Obligations,[87] it is unsuitable in others, especially if the purpose of the study is to explain differences in national laws and/or legal systems. In these instances, legal culture is an integral component of the investigation.

Legrand states that the comparatist's goal is "to re-present a legal culture in ways that have greater interpretive power than is offered by the

---

[82] Ibid.
[83] Ibid., 46–47.
[84] Legrand, *Journal of Comparative Law*, 394–395.
[85] Ibid., 394.
[86] See above in this subsection.
[87] See the subsection '*IV. European Code of Obligations*', above in section 1.3.2.

traditional rule-based model".[88] In the comparative study of pure economic loss,[89] the 'interpretive power' of legal culture is successfully applied. I choose a functional method for reasons set out below.

Reasons for selecting a functional method

Chapters 3 to 5 of the book identify provisions of Estonian, Polish, Latvian, German and Croatian law that do not comply with the EU free movement of capital rules.[90] Thus, I need to know what the national breaches of the free movement of capital are, rather than why they exist. It is therefore pertinent to identify them by comparing national law with EU law on the basis of the CJEU's approach,[91] which is preferable in this research to a literal technique, an historic approach or a method based on the legal culture of the countries concerned.

Two further reasons for applying a functional method concern the status of EU law relative to that of the Member States, which makes the comparison of national law with Community law unique among comparator systems. Firstly, EU law is supreme over the national laws of the Member States in the sense that the latter must comply with it. In *Costa v ENEL*,[92] the CJEU stated:

> "[T]he law stemming from the Treaty [Establishing the European Economic Community],[93] an independent source of law, could not, because of its special and original nature, be overridden by domestic legal provisions ... without being deprived of its character as Community Law and without the legal basis of the Community itself being called into question."

The Court provided explicit guidance in *Amministrazione delle Finanze dello Stato v Simmenthal SpA (No.2)*:[94]

---

[88] Legrand, *Journal of Comparative Law*, 389. Legrand defines 'legal culture' as "the sub-culture that is constituted among law specialists, especially as regards the repository of those elements that partake in the stable, general and unconscious" (ibid., 388).

[89] See the subsection '*III. Comparative study of pure economic loss in thirteen EU legal systems, 2003*', above in section 1.3.2.

[90] See section 1.1.

[91] See Chapter 2.

[92] [1964] ECR 585.

[93] This treaty was incorporated into the Treaty Establishing the European Community, which recently became the Treaty on the Functioning of the European Union.

[94] [1978] ECR 629.

> "[P]rovisions [of the Treaty Establishing the European Economic Community][95] and [directly applicable] measures not only by their entry into force render automatically inapplicable any conflicting provision of current national law but … also preclude the valid adoption of new national legislative measures to the extent to which they would be incompatible with Community provisions."[96]

Secondly, The CJEU applies EU law to Member States and their nationals in the same way, without distinction as to the legal system and culture in each specific State.[97]

The method

For each national provision which applies beyond the borders of the Member State concerned, I ask the three questions below in the order stated.

Is there a capital movement?
Is there a restriction on the free movement of capital?
Is there an acceptable reason for restricting the free movement of capital?

If the answer to the first two questions is 'yes' and the answer to the third question is 'no', then I conclude that the national rule in an unjustified restriction on the free movement of capital, which is contrary to Article 63 of the TFEU (requiring abolition on all restrictions on the movement of capital and on payments between Member States and between States and third countries). Any other combination of answers means that the domestic provision complies with Article 63.

Is there a capital movement?

'Capital movements' are defined by the nomenclature in Annex I to Directive 88/361/EEC.[98]

Is there a restriction on the free movement of capital?

If nationals of other Member States are treated less favourably than those of the home State, the measure in question restricts the free movement of capital, even if it is applied equally to both groups.[99]

---

[95] See note 93.
[96] *Amministrazione delle Finanze dello Stato v Simmenthal SpA (No.2)* [1978] ECR 629, at ECR 643, paragraph 17.
[97] This consistency is present in the '*Commission v Member State*' cases in section 2.1.2.
[98] See section 2.1.1.
[99] See section 2.1.2.

Is there an acceptable reason for restricting the free movement of capital?

The TFEU provides several justifications for restricting free capital movement, which are further developed by the CJEU's case law.[100] Property and direct tax cases have parallel but distinct judicial law.[101] Defences cannot permit arbitrary discrimination or covert restriction of free movement of capital and payments.[102]

Comment

The functional method used differs from that advocated by Professor Kötz in that it is designed to find differences between the EU and domestic free movement of capital rules; the questions asked for the comparison are based on the position of the EU institutions, especially that of the CJEU. By contrast, Kötz's method is intended to find similarities between national laws.[103]

Kötz's technique compares domestic rules on an equal basis in a functional system.[104] By contrast, the functional method in this book assesses the compliance of national provisions with the EU free movement of capital laws.

My method is designed for a narrow application–the comparison of laws concerning the freedom of movement of capital, with a view to ascertaining their effect on cross-border capital movements. Consequently, it is less generally applicable than the functional technique proposed by Professor Kötz.

1.4 Grounded theory

1.4.1 What is grounded theory?

'Grounded theory' is a generic iterative method, in which observations and interpretation of research findings are summarised into theory, and reapplied to further research, which leads to additional interpretation of research findings that are condensed into a modified theory, which is applied to further research, and so on. Kathy Charmaz summarises the approach in this way.

---

[100] See section 2.1.3.

[101] See Baber, *The Impact of Legislation and Regulation*, sections 2.1.4 (43–48) and 2.3 (50–58), respectively, for a summary of this case law.

[102] Article 65(3), TFEU.

[103] See the subsection '*Kötz' functional method and Legrand's critique*', above in section 1.3.2.

[104] Ibid.

> "The method builds a series of checks and refinements into qualitative inquiry through an iterative process of successive analytic and data collection phases of research, each informed by the other and rendered more theoretical."[105]

Grounded theory originates from the 1960s in the work of Barney Glaser and Anselm Strauss.[106] Today, there are several variants of the theory, and flexibility of adaptation to the researcher's circumstances is a key feature. Whilst the strategies of coding, memo writing, theoretical sampling and theoretical saturation are the defining characteristics of grounded theory,[107] it is essential to develop the theory with the research – rather than applying a preconceived set of rules to the latter. Barney Glazer writes thus.

> "When considering the application of an existing GT [i.e. grounded theory], generated by oneself or another person, one needs to ensure that it is credibly relevant and fits to the … population. The modification may be general or specific depending upon the intervention purpose. … Intervention properties will emerge as to how the GT is best applied. Stay open to reciprocal modifications that are earned by generating. This is … extending a [GT] with more fit and relevance."[108]

Charmez comments that grounded theory is an emergent method, in that it begins with a systematic, inductive approach to collecting and evaluating data to generate theoretical analyses, and includes checking categories that emerge from successive stages of analysis through hypothetical, deductive reasoning.[109] She also considers grounded theory methods to be abductive, in the sense that grounded theorists make tentative conclusions through the consideration of all possible theoretical interpretations of their data, and then collect more data in order to check and refine their categories.[110]

---

105 *Handbook of Emergent Methods*, 2008, 155–170, at 156.
106 The seminal publication is Glaser and Strauss (1967), *Awareness of dying*.
107 Charmaz, *Handbook of Emergent Methods*, 167.
108 Glazer (2014), *The Grounded Theory Review*, 13(1), 46–50, at 48.
109 *Handbook of Emergent Methods*, 155.
110 Ibid., 167.

1.4.2 The use of grounded theory in the current context

Chapter 2 ascertains the EU's free movement of capital rules, and situations in which the justifications to contraventions of Article 63 of the TFEU apply, especially those of Article 65(1)(b) and 64(2) of the TFEU, which are summarised in the text of sections 2.1.3 and 2.3.2, respectively. Chapter 3 contains a detailed reportage and analysis of all of the Estonian financial services legislation (and regulations), which contains 263 pages and more than 100,000 words (including footnotes). Chapter 4 contains a comprehensive reportage of all of the Polish financial services legislation (and regulations), with agglomerated evaluation sections. This second detailed Chapter creates a basis for comparison with that of the previous Chapter. Section 4.6 undertakes this comparison, and draws conclusions that are applied to the selected reportage and analysis of financial legislation of Latvia, Croatia and Germany for breaches of Article 63 of the TFEU – in Chapter 5. Section 5.4 makes 5 observations that tend to be consistent across all of the countries whose financial services laws are studied in this book. Chapter 6 develops themes from these observations, makes further conclusions, and suggests strategies that may be taken for a more extensive and efficient use of the free movement of services and of capital across the financial services sector, especially in respect of third countries.

This approach is deductive, in that the EU's free movement of capital rules are applied and ascertained. It is also inductive, in that Chapter 3 starts with a detailed approach, and the observations made from this Chapter and from Chapter 4 are applied as 'theory' to the three countries that Chapter 5 analyses. Section 5.4 develops the theory further, from which Chapter 6 – a Chapter of general application – follows on. Furthermore, the approach is abductive, in that the observations are crystallised into fairly firm theory in the observations made at the end of Chapter 5, through a stage of more tentative theory in Section 4.6 and of reportage and analysis in sections 5.1, 5.2 and 5.3.

Thus, the method is a grounded theory approach, although it does not apply the formal, almost scientific process that the experts advocate. Of the grounded theory strategies, memo writing is the most extensively used. In the analysis in Chapters 4 and 5, memo writing was indispensable to the evaluation – the notes on the memos were incorporated into the analysis sections of these Chapters.

1.5 Concluding comments

Whilst the most of the book contains detailed reportage and evaluation of legal provisions, it also establishes consistent findings both within the laws for a single country, and across the laws for different states. These findings are the basis for a more general analysis and accompanying recommendations, which is original and which, if realisable, may have far-reaching effects for the free movement of services and of capital, especially within the financial services sector. All of this is based on the assumption that the free movement of services and of capital are good things. Although there are problems and risks with the liberalisation of barriers to capital flows – as section 1.2.2 considers – the probabilities of events such as these occurring is reduced by stable exchange rates, low inflation, and steady growth. Whilst the Eurozone offers the first two of these, steady growth cannot be guaranteed – especially as fiscal policy is under the control of the governments of Member States whilst monetary policy is under that of the European Central Bank. Such an unfortunate dichotomy has contributed to high unemployment rates in Spain, Greece and other economies within the EU – which may have consequences for the free movement of workers, even if less so for the free movement of capital.

Thus, at all times it is wise to remember that the EU is part of a global economy, and that the free movement of capital is a better thing in a stable world of free trade and exchange rate stability than in one of trade protection and exchange rate volatility. Fortunately, the advent of international organisations such as the WTO and the IMF contribute to developing the latter rather than the former.

CHAPTER TWO

THE EUROPEAN LEGAL FRAMEWORK

> "[F]or the last two thousand years … human creations … were of overwhelming importance in shaping the future. They acted … upon the minds of generations, sometimes directing, sometimes inspiring, sometimes confining them, always leaving ineradicable signs of their influence on the history of Europeans and of Europe. … The most important of them are to be found in ancient Greece, the world the Romans made, early Christianity, and the barbarian incursions into western Europe in the closing centuries of antiquity. Between them, they constituted the foundations of a future Europe".[1]

Europe as a cultural and geographical concept has survived centuries of territorial struggle between its constituent countries, culminating in the foundation of the European Economic Community (EEC) in 1957. The EEC originally had six Member States: Belgium, France, Italy, Luxembourg, the Federal Republic of Germany and the Netherlands. Today its successor organisation, the European Union (EU), has twenty eight Member States and includes most of the territory of Europe.

The EU contains the internal market, which was introduced into Treaty Establishing the European Community in 1987 by the Single European Act. The internal market "shall comprise an area without frontiers in which the free movement of goods, persons, services and capital is ensured in accordance with the provisions of the Treaties".[2]

Section 2.1 discusses the TFEU provisions on the free movement of capital. Section 2.2 considers the Directives that contain the rules for the provision of financial services to other Member States of the EU – the 'single passport' regime of the 'Single Market Directives'. Section 2.3 considers the rules of EU law that govern the free movement of capital to third countries and the provision of financial services there.

---

[1] J. M. Roberts (1996), *The Penguin History of Europe*, 1.

[2] Article 26(2), TFEU.

2.1 The TFEU: Articles 63-66

Article 63(1) of the TFEU states "[w]ithin the framework of the provisions set out in this Chapter, all restrictions on the movement of capital between Member States and between Member States and third countries shall be prohibited." Article 63(2) of the TFEU states "[w]ithin the framework of the provisions set out in this Chapter, all restrictions on payments between Member States and between Member States and third countries shall be prohibited." The other Articles in Title III Chapter 4 provide exceptions to these unequivocal statements.

2.1.1 How are capital movements defined?

The TFEU does not define 'capital movements'. The CJEU held in *Trummer and Mayer* that the nomenclature in Annex I to Directive 88/361/EEC (hereafter 'Annex I') defines 'capital movements', but that the list contained therein is "not exhaustive".[3] This nomenclature of capital movements includes foreign direct investment, investment in real estate, shares, bonds, long-term loans, money market instruments, credits relating to commercial transactions, insurance premiums, gifts, endowments, dowries and legacies. Furthermore, capital movements cover "all the operations necessary for the purposes of capital movements".[4]

This definition is wide and has included much case law. For instance, liquidation of an investment in real property,[5] a shareholding,[6] and the purchase of real estate by non-residents,[7] constituted 'capital movements' in Annex I. Nonetheless, we must carefully interpret the explanatory notes in the Annex. For example, "bonds" are defined as "[n]egotiable securities with a maturity of two years or more from issues for which the interest rate and terms for the repayment of the principal and the payment of interest are determined at the time of issue".[8] Does this include bonds convertible to shares in less than two years or floating rate notes of more than one year duration? If not, they would probably be classified as "Miscellaneous" capital movements under Title XIII of the nomenclature.

---

[3] [1999] ECR I-1661.
[4] Annex I.
[5] *Trummer and Mayer* [1999] ECR I-1661.
[6] *Commission v France* [2002] ECR I-4781.
[7] *Reisch and Others* [2002] ECR I-2157.
[8] Annex I.

In *Commission v The Netherlands*,[9] the CJEU distinguished between 'direct' investments, which are those "in the form of participation in an undertaking through the holding of shares" that confers the chance of taking part in its management and control, and 'portfolio' investments, which involve the purchase of shares "solely with the intention of making a financial investment" [paragraph 19]. Both are 'capital movements'.

In *Commission v Poland*,[10] the CJEU held investment transactions of Open Pension Funds to be 'movements of capital' within the meaning of Article 63 of the TFEU. The Court stated that, even if the Polish government's argument that the resources allocated to the OPFs were of a public nature was to be accepted, this would be insufficient to exclude transactions using these resources from the scope of Article 63; this is clear from Annex I, which states that the capital movements in the nomenclature contained therein cover "operations carried out by any natural or legal person, including operations in respect of the assets or liabilities of Member States or of other public administrations and agencies".[11]

2.1.2 The CJEU narrowly construes restrictions on the free movement of capital

There are restrictions on the free movement of capital if like situations are treated differently or dissimilar situations the same. In particular, national legislation restricts the free movement of capital if it treats residents of other EU Member States less favourably than those of the home country. This is true, even if the relevant domestic legal provision does not discriminate against residents of, and/or investment in, other Member States.

Commission v France[12]

The French government passed Decree No 93-1298, attaching the following rights to the share it held in Société Nationale Elf-Aquitaine: Article 2(1)–any shareholding exceeding one tenth of the capital or voting rights must first be approved by the Minister of Economic Affairs; Article 2(3)–the government could oppose any decision to transfer or use as security the capital of Elf-Aquitaine's subsidiaries. The Court held that

---

[9] [2006] ECR I-9141.
[10] [2011] ECR I-13613.
[11] Annex I.
[12] [2002] ECR I-4781.

these rules hindered the purchase of shares in Elf-Aquitaine and dissuaded investors in other Member States from investing in this group. They therefore constituted a restriction on the movement of capital.

Commission v Belgium[13]

The Royal Decrees of 10 and 28 June 1994 respectively attached to the share held by the Belgian government in Société nationale de transport par canalisations and in Société de distribution du gaz SA the following rights: Article 3–the Energy Minister can oppose within 21 days of prior notice the transfer, use as security or change in the company's strategic assets if (s)he considers that this adversely affects the national interest in the energy sector; Article 4–the Minister may appoint two government representatives to the Board of Directors, who may propose to him/her the annulment of any Board decision which they consider contrary to Belgium's energy policy. The CJEU held that these rules restricted the movement of capital but upheld them as derogations.[14]

Commission v Portugal[15]

Portuguese Decree-Law 65/94 states that the foreign entities may hold no more that 25% of the capital of Portuguese re-privatised companies, unless the re-privatisation legislation provides otherwise. The Portuguese government claimed that it did not apply this provision in practice and that the provision referred solely to investors who are not EU nationals. The CJEU rejected this argument. It held that the incompatibility of national laws with EU Treaty provisions (including those directly applicable) required amendment by law; administrative practices do not fulfil Treaty obligations because they create uncertainty as to persons' rights guaranteed therein. The Portuguese legislation therefore breached Article 63 of the TFEU.

Commission v Spain[16]

Article 3 of Spanish Law 5/1995 specifies a procedure of governmental prior approval for decisions relating to the privatisation of Spanish commercial entities, including voluntary liquidation, mergers, demergers, changes in the object clause and share purchases. The CJEU held that, although the procedure applied equally to residents and non-residents, it

---

[13] [2002] ECR I-4809.

[14] These derogations are discussed in section 2.1.3, under the subsection '*Derogations in the Commission's cases introduced in subsection 2.1.2*'.

[15] [2002] ECR I-4731.

[16] [2003] ECR I-4581.

constituted a restriction on the movement of capital because it affected the position of share purchasers and therefore was liable to deter nationals from other Member States from investing in the Spanish entities.

Commission v United Kingdom[17]

Article 10(2) of the British Airports Authority's (BAA) Articles of Association specifies a system of Ministerial prior approval for decisions including the voluntary liquidation of BAA or one of its subsidiaries, disposal of an airport or BAA's surrender of control of an airport-owning subsidiary. Article 40(1) of the Articles prohibits a person from acquiring more than 15% of the voting rights in BAA. The CJEU held that both these provisions amounted to a restriction on the movement of capital because they affected the position of share purchasers and therefore were liable to deter investors from other Member States.

Commission v Italy[18]

Article 1 of Italian Decree-Law 192/2001 automatically suspends voting rights attaching to holdings exceeding 2% of the shares of companies in the electricity and gas sectors where such rights are acquired by public entities that dominate their domestic markets and are not quoted on a stock exchange. The CJEU held that since the Decree-Law's purpose was to prevent "anti-competitive attacks" by public organisations operating in these sectors in other Member States, it dissuaded such undertakings from acquiring shares in Italian companies. Therefore the suspension of voting rights constituted a restriction on the free movement of capital.

Commission v Spain[19]

The CJEU held a domestic law, which subjected the acquisition of shareholdings in entities that conduct regulated activities in the energy sector to prior authorisation from the National Energy Commission, to be a restriction on the free movement of capital. This system may deter investors from other Member States from purchasing shares in Spanish energy companies.

Commission v Italy[20]

The CJEU stated that, in order to determine whether the relevant domestic provisions are within the ambit of Article 63 of the TFEU (the

---

[17] [2003] ECR I-4641.
[18] [2005] ECR I-4933.
[19] [2008] ECR I-111.
[20] [2009] ECR I-2291.

free movement of capital) and/or Article 49 of the TFEU (the right of establishment),[21] it must consider the purpose of the national legislation. Domestic measures that apply to the possession by persons of one Member State of holdings in the capital of a company that is established in another Member State, which permit them to exercise a definite influence on the company's decisions and to determine its activities, are within the scope of Article 49. Direct investments, which are those that establish or maintain direct and lasting links between the investor and the economic entity to which capital is provided, are within the ambit of Article 63.

If the relevant national legal provision applies irrespective of the size of the shareholding, it may fall within the scope of both Articles. The CJEU held that Articles 2(1)(a) and 2(1)(b) of Decree-Law No. 332/1994, which empowered Italy's Minister for Economic Affairs and Finance to oppose the purchase by investors of shareholdings representing at least 5% of the voting rights, and to oppose the conclusion of agreements between shareholders that represented at least 5% of the voting rights, respectively, in companies governed by Italian law and operating in the petrochemical, energy, telecommunications, electricity and defence sectors, were restrictions on both the free movement of capital and the freedom of establishment.

Commission v Portugal[22]

Concerning direct and indirect investment.[23] national rules are 'restrictions' under Article 63(1) of the TFEU, if they are likely to preclude or limit the purchase of shares in the relevant entities or to deter investors of other Member States from acquiring such equity. Class A shares in Portugal Telecom, the majority of which must be owned by the Portuguese government or other public sector shareholders, provided for more extensive voting rights than those of the company's ordinary shares. The CJEU held that, although the restrictions apply without distinction to residents and non-residents, they affect the position of a person who purchases shares in Portugal Telecom, and are therefore likely to deter investors from other Member States from doing so.

---

[21] Article 49 of the TFEU states: "… [R]estrictions on the freedom of establishment of nationals of a Member State in the territory of another Member State shall be prohibited. Such prohibition shall also apply to restrictions on the setting-up of agencies, branches or subsidiaries of any Member State established in the territory of any Member State. … ".

[22] [2010] ECR I-6817.

[23] These terms are defined in *Commission v The Netherlands* [2006] ECR I-9141. See section 2.1.1.

The Portuguese state's holding of class A shares is liable to dissuade persons from other Member States from making direct investments in Portuguese Telecom, because they would be unable to participate in the management and control of this company in proportion to the value of their shareholdings. Furthermore, if the Portuguese state refuses to approve an important corporate decision, then this refusal may depress the value of Portuguese Telecom's shares and thus reduce the attractiveness of portfolio investment in the company. Hence, the state's holding of class A shares in Portuguese telecom is a restriction on the free movement of capital.

Commission v Portugal[24]

The CJEU held that the Portuguese state's special rights in Energias de Portugal, which included a right of veto over some company resolutions, the state's exemption from the general assembly's 5% voting limit, and the right to appoint a director of the company, may deter persons in other Member States from making direct investments in the company, and might also discourage portfolio investments. Therefore, these special rights are restrictions on the free movement of capital.

Commission v Portugal[25]

The CJEU reiterated that, with respect to direct and portfolio investment, domestic measures are 'restrictions' within the meaning of Article 63(1) of the TFEU if they are liable to preclude or limit the purchase of shares in the relevant companies, or to deter investors from other Member States from investing in their equity.[26] The Court held that a provision in GALP Energia's Articles of Association that conferred rights upon the Portuguese state to hold golden shares was a government measure. Provisions relating to special rights in the shareholders' agreement were also held to be a state measure.

Although the domestic laws at issue apply to residents and non-residents without distinction, they affect the position of a person who acquires a shareholding, and are therefore liable to discourage investors from other Member States from making such investments. Thus, the Portuguese state's holding of golden shares, together with the special rights that these shares confer on their holder, amounts to a restriction on the free movement of capital.

---

[24] [2010] ECR I-11241.

[25] [2011] ECR I-10889.

[26] See *Commission v Portugal* [2010] ECR I-6817, above in this section.

Commission v Poland[27]

The CJEU found that Article 143 of the Law On Pension Funds, which limited foreign investments by Open Pension Funds to 5% of the value of the assets of the relevant Fund, and listed permissible foreign investments that were a subset of those to which the Law applies, imposed both quantitative and qualitative limitations on Open Pension Funds in respect of investments made abroad. Furthermore, this rule hindered companies established in other Member States from being able to raise capital in Poland via shares in joint investment entities.

Commission v Greece[28]

Article 11(1) of Law 3631/2008 required the Inter-ministerial Privatisation Committee to authorise the acquisition (other than by the Greek government) of voting rights representing more than 20% of the total share capital of strategic public undertakings that have, or have had, a monopoly. Article 11(2) of this law listed evaluation criteria on which the decision for this prior authorisation would be based.

The CJEU reiterated that a national of a Member State with a holding in the equity of a company established in another Member State, that permits him to exercise a definite influence on this entity's decisions and to decide its activities, is fulfilling his right of establishment. Furthermore, domestic legislation that is not intended to apply solely to those shareholdings that enable the holder to exert such an influence and to determine the organisation's activities, but which applies regardless of the size of the holding, may fall within the ambit of both Articles 49 and 63 of the TFEU.[29]

The Court stated that, as the prior authorisation scheme only affects those shareholders who are able to apply a definite influence over the management and control of the relevant entities, Article 49 alone applies to this arrangement. It noted that, even if the effects of the scheme restrict the free movement of capital, these outcomes would be the inevitable consequence of any restriction on the freedom of establishment, and would not require independent inspection in the light of Article 63.

Comment

The CJEU's argument in these cases is that the national rules made potential shareholders in other Member States less likely to acquire shares in the national companies at issue. The Court held that there was a

---

[27] [2011] ECR I-13613.

[28] [2012] ECR I-, not yet reported.

[29] See *Commission v Italy* [2009] ECR I-2291, above in this section.

restriction on the free movement of capital, even when, as in the Spanish case, the national provisions were applied equally to residents and non-residents.

In *Commission v Italy*,[30] the Court held that the national provisions were a breach of both Article 49 of the TFEU and Article 63 of the TFEU. By contrast, it ruled in *Commission v Greece*[31] that only Article 49 of the TFEU applied, and that any consequent restriction on the free movement of capital would be an inevitable consequence from any limitation on the freedom of establishment. The relevant difference was that the Italian rules applied to shareholdings that represented at least 5% of the voting rights in the relevant entity, whilst the Greek provision affected shareholdings of at least 20% of the voting rights.

The Court has not yet stated the criteria on which it decides whether a national provision that restricts the freedom of establishment also limits the free movement of capital. As the free movement of capital is no longer a secondary freedom,[32] it should be on an equal basis with the freedom of establishment – all relevant national rules should be assessed as to whether they breach both freedoms.

2.1.3 Derogations from the free movement of capital

EU law provides several legitimate reasons for restricting the free movement of capital. These include the right to apply national tax law,[33] the prevention of infringement of national law and regulations in the field of taxation,[34] the prudential supervision of financial institutions,[35] formulating procedures for the purposes of administrative or statistical information,[36] public policy,[37] public security,[38] general interest,[39]

[30] [2009] ECR I-2291.

[31] [2012] ECR I-, not yet reported.

[32] Article 67(1) of the Treaty establishing the European Economic Community (now repealed) stated: "Member States shall, in the course of the transitional period *and to the extent necessary for the functioning of the Common Market*, progressively abolish as between themselves restrictions on the movement of capital belonging to persons resident in Member States and also any discriminatory treatment based on the nationality or place of residence of the parties or on the place in which such capital is invested." (emphasis mine).

[33] Article 65(1)(a), TFEU.

[34] Article 65(1)(b), TFEU.

[35] Ibid.

[36] Ibid.

[37] Ibid.

[38] Ibid.

defence,[40] and the prevention and combating of terrorism.[41] The EU case law concerns public policy/public security/general interest, direct taxation, bilateral investment treaties, and the acquisition of real estate. This section discusses the first of these groups of cases.[42]

Public policy and public security

Article 65(1)(b) of the TFEU states "[t]he provisions of Article 63 shall be without prejudice to the right of Member States ... to take measures which are justified on grounds of public policy or public security". These measures cannot be "a means of arbitrary discrimination or a disguised restriction on the free movement of capital and payments" provided by Article 63 of the TFEU.[43]

For Article 65(1)(b) to apply, the measure must be proportionate, i.e. appropriate for accomplishing the objective it pursues without going beyond what is necessary to attain it.[44] More specifically, the CJEU held in *Albore* that the principle of proportionality must be observed for "the requirements of public security" to justify exceptions to Article 63, which means that any derogation be "appropriate and necessary for achieving the aim in view".[45]

---

[39] In *Commission v Portugal* [2002] ECR I-4731, the CJEU held that the free movement of capital may be restricted by national rules that are justified by "overriding requirements of the general interest" and which apply to all persons in the Member State concerned, provided that they are suitable for securing that State's objective and are proportionate.

[40] Article 346(1)(b), TFEU: a Member State can take measures to protect "the essential interests of its security which are connected with the production of or trade in arms, munitions and war material", provided that these measures do not detract from the conditions for competition within the internal market for products that are not intended for specifically military uses.

[41] Article 75, TFEU: The Council of the European Union and the European Parliament are to "define a framework for administrative measures with regard to capital movements and payments" in accordance with the ordinary legislative procedure, which is contained in Article 294 of the TFEU.

[42] The cases concerning the free movement of capital in the context of direct taxation, bilateral investment treaties, and the acquisition of real estate are beyond the scope of this book, other than where the principles contained therein are relevant in this chapter. This section discusses all of the cases that section 2.1.2 considers.

[43] Article 65(3), TFEU.

[44] *Commission v Belgium* [2000] ECR I-7587.

[45] [2000] ECR I-5965.

Public policy, public security, general interest, and prior authorisation

In *Eglise de Scientologie and Scientology International*,[46] Article 5-1(I)(1) of French Law No. 66-1008 stated that if the Finance Minister established that a foreign investment represented a threat to public policy, public health or public security, he/she may, if there is no request for prior authorisation required under Article 3(1)(c) of this law, order the investor to discontinue the investment, or modify or restore the previous position. The CJEU held that Article 65(1)(b) of the TFEU precluded a system of prior authorisation for direct foreign investments which defines the relevant investments as being those that represent a threat to public policy and public security, without providing additional guidance to help the persons concerned to ascertain the specific circumstances in which prior authorisation is required.

The CJEU made the following points.

1. A national provision requiring prior authorisation for a direct foreign investment is a restriction on the free movement of capital.
2. Grounds for public policy and public security must be interpreted strictly because they are derogations from the fundamental principle of free movement of capital.
3. No Member State may determine the extent of these derogations unilaterally.
4. For a Member State to rely on public policy or public security, there must be a "genuine and sufficiently serious threat to a fundamental interest of society" [paragraph 17]. These derogations cannot be used to protect economic interests.
5. Measures justified on public policy and public security grounds must be necessary to protect the interests which they are intended to guarantee, in so far as less restrictive provisions cannot attain these objectives.
6. Whilst a system of prior authorisation is not necessarily contrary to Community Law,[47] the system established in *Eglise de Scientologie* is contrary to the principle of legal certainty because individuals are unable to ascertain the scope of their rights and obligations deriving from Article 63 of the TFEU.

---

[46] [2000] ECR I-1335.

[47] "A procedure of prior authorisation, … which entails, by its very purpose, a restriction on the free movement of capital, can be regarded as compatible with [Article 63 of the TFEU] only on certain conditions." (*Konle v Austria* [1999] ECR I-3099, at ECR I-3134, paragraph 39).

7. For foreign direct investment, a system of prior declaration is inadequate to counter a genuine and sufficiently serious threat to public policy and public security because of difficulties in identifying and isolating capital that has entered a Member State.

Hence, in the case of foreign direct investments, the CJEU requires a system of prior authorisation which specifically makes clear when such authorisation is required, given explicit genuine and sufficiently serious threats to public policy or public security.

In *Analir and Others*,[48] the CJEU considers prior administrative authorisation schemes in the context of freedom to provide services. For a PAAS to be justified, the national authority must show that it is indispensable to the imposition of public service obligations, and that it is proportionate to the aim pursued–i.e. this aim cannot be attained by measures less restrictive of the freedom to provide services, especially a system of declarations. A PAAS cannot legitimize discretionary conduct by the national authorities that may neutralise the effectiveness of EU law provisions, especially those concerning a fundamental freedom.

To be justified, therefore, a PAAS must be founded on objective, non-discriminatory criteria, known previously to those seeking authorisation, thereby ensuring that the national authorities do not exercise their discretion arbitrarily. Additionally, all persons affected by the restrictive measure must be able to obtain a legal remedy.

To summarize, national restrictions protecting discretionary conduct are forbidden. There must be a legitimate objective–to counter a genuine and sufficiently serious threat to a fundamental interest of society. The restrictions must not go beyond what is necessary to attain this objective.

Derogations in the Commission's cases introduced in subsection 2.1.2

In *Commission v France*,[49] the CJEU held that the objective pursued by the national legislation–safeguarding petroleum supplies in a crisis, is a legitimate public interest. The investors are not told "the specific objective circumstances" in which the Minister will refuse authorisation to buy a 10% shareholding in Elf-Aquitaine, or in which the government will prevent the transfer or use as security of the assets of Elf-Aquitaine's subsidiaries [paragraph 50]. Hence, investors do not know their rights and obligations under Article 63 of the TFEU. This system does not fulfil the requirements of legal certainty and goes beyond what is necessary to attain the objective specified because the PAAS includes no precise, objective criteria.

---

[48] [2000] ECR I-1271.
[49] [2002] ECR I-4781.

In *Commission v Belgium*,[50] the Court held that the national legislation's objective–safeguarding energy supplies in a crisis, is a legitimate public interest. The Energy Minister initiates control in each specific case. No prior approval is required. Furthermore, the Minister must exercise his/her power of opposition within time-limits. The regime only concerns companies' strategic assets, especially the energy supply networks, and specific management decisions affecting these assets. The Minister may only intervene if there is a threat that the energy policy's objectives may be obstructed, and must provide a formal statement of reasons for intervention. The national courts may review his/her decision. The scheme therefore guarantees, on the basis of reviewable objective criteria, that the lines and conduits providing the main infrastructures conveying energy products are available. It fulfils the requirements of legal certainty. The Commission has not established that less restrictive measures could attain the objective pursued. The legislation is therefore justified by the objective of protecting energy supplies in a crisis.

In *Commission v Portugal*,[51] the Court stated that Portugal's general financial interests are inadequate justification because they are economic grounds for such restricting free capital movement. In *Commission v Spain*,[52] the CJEU held that the government's objective of providing petroleum or telecommunications and electricity services in a crisis may be a public security justification. The national rules went beyond this objective because the authorities had a particularly broad discretion as to whether to grant prior approval. In *Commission v Italy*,[53] the Court held that the government's objective to safeguard energy supplies may justify restrictions on the free movement of capital under certain conditions. But the national limitation of voting rights of just one category of public enterprises in gas and electricity companies is unnecessary to attain this objective.

In *Commission v Spain*,[54] the CJEU held that the system of prior authorisation is a suitable measure for securing the attainment of the Spanish government's objective, which is security of the energy supply. Furthermore, the Spanish system of prior authorisation is disproportionate to the objective, because it provides the National Energy Commission with the discretion to consider other aims, and because the Spanish government

[50] [2002] ECR I-4809.
[51] [2002] ECR I-4731.
[52] [2003] ECR I-4581.
[53] [2005] ECR I-4933.
[54] [2008] ECR I-111.

have not demonstrated that the objective may not be achieved by less restrictive measures.

In *Commission v Italy*,[55] the CJEU stated that the free movement of capital may be restricted by national measures that are justified by the reasons stated in Article 65 of the TFEU or by overriding reasons in the public interest, to the extent that there are no EU harmonising provisions that provide for the protection of these interests. The Court held that these measures must be proportionate, even in a harmonised area if the Member States retain a degree of discretion. It found that the domestic measures did not connect the criteria and the special powers to which they relate, thus providing disproportionate latitude to the national authorities in using them.

In *Commission v Portugal*,[56] the CJEU reiterated that national measures that restrict the free movement of capital may be justified on the grounds contained in Article 65 of the TFEU or by overriding reasons in the public interest, provided that they are appropriate to attain the objective that they pursue and do not go further than is necessary to achieve it. As public security may only be relied upon if there is a genuine and sufficiently serious threat to a fundamental interest of society, the Court rejected this defence. Furthermore, as neither the domestic law nor Portugal Telecom's articles of association stated criteria to determine when the special powers could be used, the resulting uncertainty confers on the national authorities a latitude in the use of these powers that is so discretionary as to be disproportionate to the objectives specified.

In *Commission v Portugal*,[57] the CJEU held that the Portuguese government's objective of ensuring a secure energy supply in case of crisis, war or terrorism might constitute a genuine and sufficiently serious threat to a fundamental interest of society. However, the government has not stated the precise reasons why it considers that the special rights at issue would render it possible to prevent an interference with this interest. Furthermore, the application of the special rights in Energias de Portugal are not accompanied by any specific criteria that determine the circumstances under which these rights may be exercised. The resulting uncertainty confers on the national authorities, as regards the use of these rights, a breadth that is so discretionary as to be disproportionate to the stated objective.

---

[55] [2009] ECR I-2291.
[56] [2010] ECR I-6817.
[57] [2010] ECR I-11241.

In *Commission v Portugal*,[58] the CJEU held that a justification based on public security could not be upheld, because the Portuguese government does not state the precise reasons as to why it considers that the special rights would make it possible to preclude interference with the energy supply, given its objective of safeguarding a secure energy supply in case of crisis, war or terrorism. The Court also found that the exercise of these rights is not subject to any specific, objective condition or circumstance, and is therefore disproportionate to this aim.

In *Commission v Poland*,[59] the CJEU stated that the need to guarantee the security and stability of the assets administered by a pension fund constitutes a crucial reason of public interest that is capable of justifying limitations on the free movement of capital. The Court held that the qualitative and quantitative restrictions that Article 143 of the Law On Pension Funds imposed on foreign investments by Open Pension Funds were disproportionate to this objective.

In *Commission v Greece*,[60] the objective to justify restrictions on the freedom of establishment is to ensure continuity of Greece's required energy and water supply, the provision of telecommunication services, and the management of its two largest ports. Although the Court held in *Commission v Spain*[61] that an objective linked to the security of the energy supply can be relied on if there is a genuine and sufficiently serious threat to a fundamental interest of society, it is not certain that, at the time of issuing the authorisation, all the instances of real and serious threats to the energy supply may be identified and considered.

The CJEU stated that neither the reference in Article 11(2) of Law 3631/2008 to 'general interest criteria for ensuring the continuity of the services provided and the operation of the networks', nor the evaluation criteria, render it possible to determine the precise, objective circumstances in which the power to oppose the purchase of shareholdings is capable of being exercised, or to provide interested parties with legal certainty as to the cases in which authorisation may be refused. Furthermore, it held that the evaluation criteria did not cover cases of real and sufficiently serious threats to the security of supply. Hence, the prior authorisation scheme grants the administration with a discretionary power, which it is problematical for the courts to control.

---

[58] [2011] ECR I-10889.
[59] [2011] ECR I-13613.
[60] [2012] ECR I-, not yet reported.
[61] [2008] ECR I-111.

Reasons why the CJEU accepted the justification only in Commission v Belgium

In *Commission v Spain*,[62] the CJEU distinguished its judgment in *Commission v Belgium*.[63]

1. The Belgian system was one of "ex post facto opposition", which is less restrictive than prior approval [paragraph 78].
2. The Belgium system specifically listed the relevant strategic assets and the challengeable management decisions in each case.
3. The administrative authorities only intervened in cases in which the energy policy's objectives were threatened.
4. The national legislation required the authorities to give a formal statement of reasons for their decision.
5. The decision was subject to judicial review.

The CJEU reiterated these points in *Commission v Greece*,[64] whilst rejecting the Greek government's claim that the arrangements for subsequent control of decisions by the companies at issue were similar to the scheme at issue in *Commission v Belgium*.

The requirements for a successful public policy/security derogation

Firstly, there must be a genuine and sufficiently serious threat to a fundamental interest of society. In *Commission v Belgium*, the threat is to energy supplies. A crisis is unnecessary–the Court held in *Campus Oil and Others*[65] that public security considerations justifying an obstacle to the free movement of goods include the objective of providing a minimum supply of petroleum products at all times. This reasoning applies to the free movement of capital.[66]

Secondly, the restrictive measures must be necessary for the protection of interests which they are intended to guarantee. This requirement is satisfied in *Commission v Belgium* since intervention "was strictly limited to cases in which objectives of the energy policy were jeopardised" (*Commission v Spain*, paragraph 78).

Thirdly, the measures must be proportionate – i.e. not attainable by less restrictive measures. The CJEU in *Commission v Belgium* states "[t]he Commission has not shown that less restrictive measures could have been taken to attain the objective pursued" [paragraph 53]. The domestic law should state the precise, objective criteria that determine the circumstances

---

[62] [2003] ECR I-4581.
[63] [2002] ECR I-4809.
[64] [2012] ECR I-, not yet reported.
[65] [1984] ECR 2727.
[66] *Commission v Belgium* [2002] ECR I-4809.

under which the special rights at issue may be exercised, in order to prevent the grant of a discretionary, and consequently disproportionate, latitude to the national authorities in the exercise of these rights.

Fourthly, the measures must observe the requirements of legal certainty. They must be specific, objective and known to the parties beforehand. Those in *Commission v Belgium* fulfil this requirement, since they list "specifically the strategic assets concerned and the management decisions which could be challenged in any given case" (*Commission v Spain*, paragraph 78).

Finally, the persons affected by the measures must have access to legal redress. This is so in *Commission v Belgium*, as "intervention must be supported by a formal statement of reasons and [is] subject [to] review by the courts" [paragraph 51].

Article 106(2) of the TFEU

Entities that are entrusted to provide services of general economic interest, or which have the features of a revenue-producing monopoly, are subject to the rules in the TFEU and the Treaty on European Union, especially the rules on competition, in so far as the application of these rules does not hinder the performance of the specific tasks that are allocated to them.[67] The development of trade must not be so affected as to be against the interests of the EU.[68] This article may be relied upon to justify the grant by a Member State, to an entity that is entrusted with the operation of services of general economic interest, of special or exclusive rights that are contrary to the provisions of the TFEU, to the extent that performance of the specific task allocated to this entity can be assured only through the grant of these rights, and provided that the development of trade is not affected to such an extent as to be opposed to the EU's interests.[69]

In *Commission v Portugal*,[70] the CJEU held that the infringement proceedings brought against Portugal were neither concerned with the granting of special or exclusive rights to Energias de Portugal, nor with the classification of this entity's activities as services of general economic interest, but with the lawfulness of attributing to Portuguese government, as a shareholder of this company, special rights in connection with golden shares held by the government in the share capital of Energias de Portugal. Consequently, Portugal could not rely upon Article 106(2) of the TFEU to

[67] Article 106(2), TFEU.

[68] Ibid.

[69] *Commission v Portugal* [2010] ECR I-11241.

[70] [2010] ECR I-11241.

justify the national rules at issue to the extent that they constitute limitations on the free movement of capital.

In *Commission v Portugal*,[71] the CJEU stated that the provisions at issue do not involve the granting of special or exclusive rights to GALP Energia, or the classification of GALP Energia's activities as services of general economic interest, but concern the legality of attributing to the Portuguese government, as a shareholder of this entity, special rights in connection with golden shares that it holds in the share capital of GALP Energia. Furthermore, Portugal has not explained why, in the event of removal of the contested measures, the performance of the tasks of general economic interest that it has entrusted to an entity, would be put at risk. Thus, Portugal cannot rely on Article 106(2) of the TFEU to justify the domestic rules at issue to the extent that they constitute restrictions on the free movement of capital.

In *Commission v Poland*,[72] the CJEU reiterated that a Member State that invokes Article 106(2) of the TFEU must demonstrate that all the conditions for its application are satisfied. The Court held that, while Open Pension Funds perform a task of general economic interest, Poland has not shown to the required legal standard that the conditions for the application of Article 106(2) are fulfilled. In particular, Poland has not demonstrated the extent to which the application of the relevant rules of the TFEU, in this case those concerning the free movement of capital, would hinder the objectives pursued by the Open Pension Funds.

Comment

The five requirements for a successful public policy/security derogation constitute a stiff test, consistent with the CJEU's view that derogations from a fundamental freedom must be "interpreted strictly".[73] The first requirement is specific to the public policy/security justification. Economic and financial objectives are not acceptable under this defence. However, such objectives are relevant to the national right to "take all requisite measures to prevent infringements of national law and regulations, in particular in the field of taxation and the prudential supervision of financial institutions".[74] The lack of EU case law on the 'prudential supervision' derogation is problematical, but it is arguable that this exception includes the right of national financial regulators to uphold their supervisory rules, provided that the measures taken are neither

[71] [2011] ECR I-10889.
[72] [2011] ECR I-13613.
[73] *Eglise de Scientologie and Scientology International* [2000] ECR I-1335.
[74] Article 65(1)(b), TFEU.

discriminatory nor restrictive of free capital movement.[75] The last four requirements extend to derogations from Article 63 of the TFEU Treaty other than public policy/security.

For Article 106(2) of the TFEU to apply, the Member State must demonstrate that 1) the relevant entity is entrusted with the operation of services of general economic interest, 2) the performance of the specific task allocated to this organisation can be assured only through the grant of the special or exclusive rights at issue (that are contrary to Article 63 of the TFEU), and 3) these rights do not adversely affect the development of trade to such an extent as to be contrary to the EU's interests. Neither Portugal nor Poland established all of these points in the cases discussed above.[76]

2.1.4 Against whom may Article 63 of the TFEU be invoked?

Vertical direct effect

In *Sanz de Lera and Others*,[77] the CJEU ruled on the interpretation of Articles 63, 64(1), and 65(1)(b) of the TFEU.[78] It made the following points.

1. Article 63(1) of the TFEU contains a "clear and unconditional prohibition" that requires no implementing measure [paragraph 41].
2. The expression "Within the framework of the provisions set out in this Chapter"[79] relates to the whole of the Title III Chapter 4 (Capital and Payments) of the TFEU, and is, therefore, to be "interpreted in that context" [paragraph 42].
3. As the exercise of the right given to Member States by Article 65(1)(b) may be subject to judicial review, the fact that a Member State may rely on it does not prevent Article 63(1) of the TFEU from bestowing rights upon individuals "which they may rely on before the courts and which the national courts must uphold" [paragraph 43].
4. Consequently, Article 63(1) of the TFEU, in conjunction with Articles 64(1) and 65(1)(b) of the TFEU, "may be relied on

[75] Article 65(3), TFEU.

[76] These are *Commission v Portugal* [2010] ECR I-11241, *Commission v Portugal* [2011] ECR I-10889; *Commission v Poland* [2011] ECR I-13613.

[77] [1995] ECR I-4821

[78] At the time of the ruling, these were Articles 73b, 73c(1), and 73d of the Treaty Establishing the European Communities.

[79] Articles 63(1) and 63(2), TFEU.

> before national courts, and may render inapplicable national rules inconsistent therewith" [paragraph 48].[80]

Thus, Article 63(1) of the TFEU has vertical direct effect.[81] It can be relied upon by individuals in a Member State's national court against that State's central and local government, and its public institutions.

Horizontal direct effect

In *Commission v Federal Republic of Germany*,[82] the Law of 21 July 1960 on the privatisation of equity in the Volkswagenwerk limited company provided for restriction on the exercise of voting rights, and for the Federal Republic of Germany and the Land of Lower Saxony each to appoint two members to the supervisory board. The CJEU held that both of these limitations were an unjustified restriction on the free movement of capital.

The Federal Republic of Germany argued that the 1960 Law was a private agreement that was first expressed in a contract between the Federal State and the Land of Lower Saxony, which led to the adoption of the Law. However, the CJEU stated that the fact that this private agreement between has become the subject of a Law is sufficient to render it a national measure for the purposes of the free movement of capital.

As Professor Catherine Barnard points out,[83] if the CJEU had considered that Article 63 of the TFEU had *horizontal* direct effect, then it would have been able to accept the claim of the Federal Republic of Germany that the 1960 Law was a private agreement – because the Law could be challenged as a restriction to the free movement of capital in the domestic courts of Member States. Instead, the Court held that the law was a national measure, thereby enabling it to be challenged in the national courts – according to *vertical* direct effect.

Thus, Article 63 does not have horizontal direct effect. Individuals are unable to successfully challenge private agreements in the national courts on the ground that they restrict the free movement of capital.

---

[80] The TFEU also noted that both parts of Article 64 of the TFEU are to be interpreted strictly.

[81] As Article 63(2) of the TFEU is worded similarly to Article 63(1), it also has vertical direct effect.

[82] [2007] ECR I-8995.

[83] (2010), *The Substantive Law of the EU*, 567.

2.2 The Single Market Directives

The Single Market Directives state the conditions under which the each Member State's financial regulator can grant authorisation for firms to provide financial services in another State.[84] This is called the 'single passport' regime.[85]

Contracts agreed by telephone and those without significant movement of personnel between home and host Member State are supplied in the home Member State,[86] which is the location of the firm or branch. In these circumstances, there is no need for an authorisation to provide financial services in another Member State, so subsequent cross-border capital movements are unhindered.

2.2.1 Investment firms (Directive 2004/39/EC)

The home Member State designates a competent authority, which is empowered to authorise investment firms to provide one or more of the investment and ancillary services listed in Annex I of this Directive.[87] An investment firm must request an extension to its authorisation if it adds further services. The authorisation enables the firm to supply services throughout the Community, either by establishing a branch or directly from its head office [Article 6].

---

[84] The Single Market Directives apply to the Contracting Parties to the EEA Agreement – the 28 Member States of the EU, Iceland, Liechtenstein and Norway.

[85] In principle, authorised firms can provide services in other Member States without additional legal or administrative requirements. Hence, the authorisation is a 'passport' to these States.

[86] The 'home Member State' is the country in which the company providing services is registered. The 'host Member State' is the country to which this firm wishes to supply cross-border services and/or in which it wishes to establish a branch or subsidiary to provide its services there.

[87] 'Investment services' include the reception and transmission of client orders relating to 'financial instruments', the execution of orders for clients and on own account, portfolio management, investment advice, the underwriting and placement of 'financial instruments', and the operation of Multilateral Trading Facilities. 'Ancillary services' comprise those connected with 'investment services', such as custodianship of clients' 'financial instruments' and foreign exchange services. 'Financial instruments' include transferable securities, money market instruments, units in unit and investment trusts, options, futures, forward rate agreements, derivative contracts for the transfer of credit risk, and contracts for differences (Annex I, Directive 2004/39/EC).

The national authority only grants authorisation if it is "fully satisfied" that the applicant complies with all requirements under the "provisions adopted pursuant to this Directive" [Article 7(1)]. The investment firm must provide all information, including a business and organisational plan, which satisfies the authority that the firm has already set up "all the necessary arrangements to meet its obligations" under the authorisation chapter [Article 7(2)]. Member States cannot impose further requirements for founding a branch or providing cross-border investment services [Articles 31(1) and 32(1)].[88]

Investment firms intending to provide services in another Member State must provide its national authority with this State's name and a "programme of operations" that includes the proposed investment and ancillary services, and the names of "tied agents" [Article 31(2)]. This authority forwards the information to the competent authority of the host Member State [Article 31(3)].

Investment firms wishing to establish a branch in another State must provide its national authority with the name of this State and of the branch managers, the address for obtaining documents in this State, and a "programme of operations" that includes the proposed investment and ancillary services, the branch's organisational structure and the names of "tied agents" [Article 32(2)]. This authority communicates the information to the competent authority of the host Member State [Article 32(3)], and must provide reasons to the investment firm if it refuses to do so [Article 32(5)]. It may only refuse if has "reason to doubt the adequacy of" the firm's administrative structure or financial situation, given the branch's proposed activities [Article 32(3)].

2.2.2 Credit institutions (Directive 2013/36/EU)

Member States must ensure that credit institutions acquire authorisation before starting their activities; they must state the requirements for authorisation and impart these to the European Banking Authority [Article 8(1)]. Applications for authorisation must be accompanied by a "programme of operations", which specifies the institution's structural organisation and types of business [Article 10]. To grant authorisation, initial capital must be and remain at 5 million EUR or more, unless a Member State provides for the credit institution to hold initial capital of between 1 million EUR

---

[88] Article 32(7) permits the host Member State's financial authority to request branch operational and organisational changes that are "strictly needed" for it to enforce compliance with Directive 2004/39/EC and its implementing measures.

and 5 million EUR with accompanying reasons to be given to the European Banking Authority and to the Commission [Article 12]. The authority must give reasons for refusing an authorisation [Article 15], and must inform the European Banking Authority of every authorisation that it grants [Article 20(1)]. It must give reasons for withdrawing an authorisation and must notify the European Banking Authority [Article 20(5)].

A credit institution must inform the national authority of its home Member State of the activities in Annex I of this Directive that it wishes to provide in another State [Article 39(1)].[89] This authority passes this information to the other State's competent authority [Article 39(2)].

A credit institution wishing to establish a branch in another Member State must provide the authority of its home State with the name of this other State and of the branch managers, the address for obtaining documents in the other State, and a "programme of operations" giving the types of business and the branch's organisational structure [Article 35(2)]. The authority forwards the information to the competent authority in the other Member State [Article 35(3)], and must give reasons to the credit institution for refusing to do so, which this institution may challenge in its home State's courts [Article 35(4)]. It may only refuse if has "reason to doubt the adequacy of" the credit institution's administrative structure or financial situation, given its branch's proposed activities [Article 35(3)].

2.2.3 Insurance and reinsurance companies (Directive 2009/138/EC)

The competent authority of the home Member State must grant prior authorisation to undertakings established there to provide direct insurance services or reinsurance services, or to extend their business to other insurance classes [Article 14]. Authorisations are valid across the EU for insurance and reinsurance classes or groups of classes [Article 15]. An authorisation requires a "scheme of operations", which includes particulars of the risks, reinsurance principles, the own fund items that constitute the

---

[89] This Annex specifies a "List of Activities Subject to Mutual Recognition" in other Member States. Items include the acceptance of deposits, lending, financial leasing, money transmission services, the issuance and administration of methods of payment, guarantees and commitments, participation in securities issues, portfolio management and advice, trading on own account or for customers in money market instruments, foreign exchange, transferable securities, futures, options and other derivatives relating to interest rates or exchange rates, and various ancillary activities (Annex I, Directive 2013/36/EU).

Minimum Capital Requirement, set-up costs, and resources intended to finance these costs [Articles 18(1) and 23]. The competent authority's decision to refuse to grant an authorisation is to "state full reasons", and must be notified to the company concerned; this refusal must be accompanied by a right to apply to the courts of the relevant Member State [Article 25]. The withdrawal of an authorisation must "state the full reasons" and be notified to the relevant entity [Article 144(3)].

An insurance undertaking wishing to provide cross-border insurance services in another Member State must inform the home State's competent authority, indicating "the nature of the risks or commitments" it will cover [Article 147]. This authority must communicate to the competent authority of the host Member State a certificate attesting to the required minimum solvency margin, the classes of insurance which the undertaking has been authorised to provide, and the "nature of the risks" to be covered in that State [Article 148(1)]. The home State authority must provide reasons for refusing to communicate this information; the insurance undertaking may appeal against the refusal in the home State's courts [Article 148(3)].

An insurance undertaking wishing to found a branch in another Member State must furnish the competent authority of its home Member State with the name of the host Member State, a "scheme of operations" specifying the types of business and the branch organisation, the name of a person who possesses adequate powers to bind the insurance company to third parties and to represent it in relations with the courts and authorities of the host Member State (the authorised agent), and an address in that State to which documents may be delivered to this agent and from which documents may be obtained [Article 145(2)]. The home State's authority must communicate this information to the competent authority of the host State unless the former has "reason to doubt the adequacy of the system of governance or the financial situation of the insurance undertaking" or the repute, integrity, professional qualifications, knowledge or experience of the authorised agent [Articles 146(1) and 42(1)]. The home Member State's competent authority must give reasons for refusing to so communicate the information; the insurance firm may challenge this refusal in the home State's courts [Article 146(2)].

2.2.4 Insurance and reinsurance intermediaries (Directive 2002/92/EC)

(Re)insurance mediation means undertaking work preparatory to concluding (re)insurance contracts, concluding these contracts, and assisting in their administration and performance [Articles 2(3)-2(4)]. Insurance and reinsurance intermediaries are persons who perform these activities [Articles 2(5)-2(6)]. Such persons that are, or wish to become, established in a Member State, are within the scope of Directive 2002/92/EC [Article 1(1)].

Insurance and reinsurance intermediaries must be registered by the competent authority in their home Member State [Article 3(1)]. If an intermediary wishes to practice in another Member State for the first time, it must inform this authority, which, within one month, must notify the competent authority in the host Member State and the intermediary; the intermediary may start business a month later [Article 6(1)]. The latter authority may publish the conditions under which, "in the interests of the general good", the intermediary may practice in the host State [Article 6(3)].

2.2.5 Institutions for occupational retirement provision (Directive 2003/41/EC)

An 'institution for occupational retirement provision' is an organisation that operates on a funded basis, established separately from any sponsoring company or trade, for the purpose of providing retirement benefits in the context of an occupational activity on the basis of an agreement or a contract agreed between employer and employee, or with self-employed persons, in compliance with the law of the home and host Member States [Article 6(a)]. Each Member State must ensure that every institution for occupational retirement provision in its territory is authorised, or registered in a national register, by the competent authority [Article 9(1)(a)]. Each State must also ensure that the institution is managed by persons of good repute and appropriate professional qualifications and experience, using properly constituted rules for the functioning of any pension scheme of which it has made members sufficiently aware, employing actuarial methods that are recognised by the home Member State's competent authority in order to calculate technical provisions, and adequately informing the members of the pension scheme's conditions [Articles 9(1)(b)-(d) and 9(1)(f)]. A Member State may make institutions for occupational retirement provision situated in its territory subject to additional requirements for operation, with a view to ensuring that the interests of members and beneficiaries are sufficiently protected [Article 9(3)].

If there is cross-border activity, the competent authority of the home Member State must authorise beforehand the institution's conditions of operation, and immediately inform the European Insurance and Occupational

Pensions Authority of this authorisation [Article 9(5)]. The national register shall indicate the Member States in which the institution is operating, and this information shall be notified to the European Insurance and Occupational Pensions Authority for publication on its website [Article 9(1)(a)].

Member States shall permit companies that are situated within their territories to sponsor institutions for occupational retirement provision that are authorised in other Member States; they shall also allow institutions for occupational retirement provision authorised in their territories to accept sponsorship from companies that are located in the territories of other Member States [Article 20(1)]. An institution must notify the competent authority of the home Member State (which has authorised it to provide for occupational retirement) of its intention to accept sponsorship from a company situated within the territory of another Member State [Article 20(2)]. Furthermore, Member States shall require institutions for occupational retirement provision that are located within their territories and are proposing to be sponsored by a company situated in the territory of another Member State, to provide with this notification the names of the host Member State(s) and of the sponsoring company, and the principal characteristics of the pension scheme to be operated for that company [Article 20(3)].

The home Member State's competent authority shall forward all of this information to the host Member State's competent authority within three months of receiving these items, unless the former has "reason to doubt that" the institution's financial situation or administrative structure, or the good repute, professional qualifications or experience of the institution's managers, are "compatible with" the activities proposed in the host State [Article 20(4)]. The host Member State's competent authority shall, within two months of receiving the information, inform the home Member State's authority of any requirements of the host State's social and labour law under which the pension scheme must be managed, asset investment restrictions that the host State applies in accordance with Directive 2003/41/EC, and information requirements that the host State imposes for the benefit of its members and beneficiaries in accordance with this Directive [Articles 20(5), 20(7), 18(7) and 11]. If the home Member State's competent authority receives no communication within that time, or on receiving this notification, the institution for occupational retirement provision may start to operate the pension scheme in accordance with the host Member State's requirements (if any) [Article 20(6)].

2.2.6 UCITS (Directive 2009/65/EC)

Directive 2009/65/EC applies to UCITS that are established within the territories of Member States [Article 1(1)]. 'UCITS' are entities whose sole aim is the collective investment in liquid financial assets of capital raised from the public, which functions on the principle of diversifying risk, and which has units that are repurchased or redeemed out of these entities' assets, at the request of unit-holders [Article 1(2)]. UCITS may be constituted in accordance with contract law as a common fund managed by a management company, trust law as a unit trust, or statute as an investment company [Article 1(3)]. Directive 2009/65/EC does not apply to closed-ended investment funds [Article 3(a)].

UCITS must be authorised in accordance with Directive 2009/65/EC, in order to pursue their business; this authorisation is valid for all Member States [Article 5(1)]. For a common fund to be authorised, the competent authority of its home Member State must approve its management company's application, the rules of the fund, and the choice of depositary [Article 5(2)]. For an investment company to be authorised, the competent authority of its home Member State must have approved its documents of incorporation and the choice of depositary and, if relevant, its management company's application [Article 5(2)]. The home Member State's competent authority shall not authorise UCITS if it finds that the investment company does not comply with the preconditions in Chapter V of Directive 2009/65/EC, or that the management company is not authorised for the management of UCITS in its home State [Article 5(4)]. The home State's competent authority shall not authorise UCITS whose depository has directors who are insufficiently reputable or experienced in relation to the type of undertaking to be managed [Article 5(4)]. This authority shall not grant authorisation if the undertaking is legally precluded from marketing its units in the home Member State [Article 5(6)].

A management company that wishes to pursue the activities, for which it has been authorised, in the territory of another Member State for the first time under the freedom to provide services, must communicate the name of that State to the home Member State's competent authority [Article 18(1)(a)]. The management company must also send to this competent authority a programme of operations that includes a description of its risk management process, the activity of management of UCITS,[90] any

[90] This activity comprises investment management, administration, legal services, accounting services for fund management, valuation and pricing, the monitoring of compliance with regulations, the maintenance of a register of unit-holders, the

additional services that it intends to provide,[91] and a description of the arrangements and procedures taken in accordance with Article 15 of Directive 2009/65/EC[92] [Article 18(1)(b)]. Within one month of receiving this information, the competent authority of the management company's home Member State must forward it to the competent authority of the management company's host Member State [Article 18(2)]. Subject to further informational requirements depending on the circumstances,[93] the management company may commence business in its host Member State [Article 18(2)], provided that it observes at all times the rules of conduct for management companies that are authorised in its home Member State [Articles 18(3) and 14].[94]

A management company that wishes to establish a branch within the territory of another Member State to pursue the activities for which it has been authorised must notify the home Member State's competent authority

---

distribution of income, unit issues and redemptions, the settlement of contracts, record keeping, and marketing (Article 6(2) and Annex II, Directive 2009/65/EC).

[91] In addition to the activity of management of UCITS, the home Member State's competent authority may authorise a management company to manage portfolios of investments that include at least one of the financial instruments that are listed in Section C of Annex I to Directive 2004/39/EC (Article 6(3)(a), Directive 2009/65/EC); see note 87. The management of a portfolio of investment may be accompanied by the non-core services of investment advice, and safekeeping and administration of the units of collective investment undertakings (Article 6(3)(b), Directive 2009/65/EC).

[92] The management company shall legally take the measures that are necessary to ensure that facilities are available in the Member State in which the units in their fund(s) are marketed, for making payments to unit-holders, repurchasing or redeeming units, and rendering the information that UCITS are required to provide (Articles 15 and 92, Directive 2009/65/EC). The management company must also "establish appropriate procedures and arrangements" for the resolution of investor complaints, and to make information available at the request of the UCITS home Member State or the public (Article 15, Directive 2009/65/EC).

[93] These are contained in Articles 18(2), 20 and 93 of Directive 2009/65/EC.

[94] The rules of conduct must implement principles that ensure that every management company (i) acts honestly and fairly in the conduct of its business activities, and with due skill, care and diligence, in the best interests of the UCITS that it operates and the integrity of the market, (ii) possesses, and effectively uses, the procedures and resources that are essential for the correct performance of its business activities, (iii) attempts to avoid conflicts of interests, (iv) ensures that the UCITS that it operates are equitably treated in the event of a conflict of interests, and (v) complies with all the applicable regulatory requirements (Article 14(1), Directive 2009/65/EC).

[Article 17(1)].[95] Member States are to require all management companies that wish to establish a branch in another Member State to provide with this notification the name of the host Member State, the address in that State from which documents may be obtained, the names of the branch's managers, and a programme of operations that contains the activities and services envisaged,[96] the branch's organisational structure, and a description of the risk management process that the management company has put in place, an account of the arrangements and procedures taken in accordance with Article 15 of Directive 2009/65/EC[97] [Article 17(2)]. Within two months of receiving all of the information, the competent authority of the management company's home Member State must communicate it to the host Member State's competent authority, together with details of any compensation scheme that is intended to protect investors, unless the former has reason to doubt the financial circumstances or administrative structure of the management company [Article 17(3)]. If the competent authority of the management company's home Member State refuses to communicate this information to the host Member State's competent authority, then the former must provide reasons for this refusal to the management company within two months of receiving the information; the refusal, or a failure to reply, is subject to the right to apply to the courts in the management company's home Member State [Article 17(3)]. A management company that pursues activities by a branch within the territory of the host Member State is to comply with the rules of conduct that the host State constructs, pursuant to Article 14 of Directive 2009/65/EC [Article 17(4)].[98] The host Member State's competent authority is responsible for supervising this compliance [Article 17(5)]. This authority must, within two months of receiving the information referred to in Article 17(2) of Directive 2009/65/EC,[99] prepare to supervise the compliance of the management company with the rules under its

---

[95] Article 17 of Directive 2009/65/EC starts "In addition to meeting the conditions imposed in Articles 6 and 7". These conditions are the requirements for management companies (rather than UCITS) to be authorised.

[96] These include the activity of management of UCITS and any additional services that the management company wishes to provide – see notes 90 and 91, respectively.

[97] See note 92.

[98] See note 94. Article 17(4) of Directive 2009/65/EC differs from Article 18(3) of Directive 2009/65/EC, in that the relevant rules of conduct in the former are those of the host Member State, whilst the relevant rules in the latter are those of the home Member State.

[99] The information is described above in this paragraph.

responsibility [Article 17(6)]. On receipt of a communication from the competent authority of the management company's host Member State, or on the expiry of two months, the branch may be established and commence business [Article 17(7)].

2.2.7 AIFM (Directive 2011/61/EU)

Directive 2011/61/EU applies to EU AIFMs that manage at least one AIF, non-EU AIFMs that manage at least one EU AIF, and non-EU AIFMs that market at least one AIF in the EU [Article 1(1)]. An 'AIF' is a collective investment undertaking that raises capital from investors with a defined investment policy for the benefit of these investors, and does not require authorisation pursuant to Article 5 of Directive 2009/65/EC[100] [Article 4(1)(a)]. An 'AIFM' is a legal person whose regulatory business is to manage at least one AIF [Article 4(1)(b)]. An 'EU AIF' is an AIF that is authorised or registered in a Member State under the applicable national law, or which has its registered office and/or head office in a Member State although not authorised or registered in a Member State [Article 4(1)(k)]. An 'EU AIFM' is an AIFM that has its registered office in a Member State [Article 4(1)(l)]. 'Managing AIFs' means performing at least the investment management functions referred to in point 1(a) or 1(b) of Annex I of Directive 2011/61/EU[101] for at least one AIF [Article 4(1)(w)]. 'Marketing' means an offering or placement at the AIFM's initiative, or on behalf of the AIFM, of units or shares of an AIF that it manages to or with investors that are domiciled, or with a registered office, in the EU [Article 4(1)(x)].

Member States must ensure that AIFMs are authorised to manage AIFs in accordance with Directive 2011/61/EU, and that they satisfy the conditions for authorisation contained therein at all times [Article 6(1)]. Member States should require an external AIFM[102] to limit its activities to those in Annex I of Directive 2011/61/EU,[103] and the additional management

---

[100] See section 2.2.6.

[101] These are portfolio management and risk management, respectively.

[102] An external AIFM is the legal person that is appointed by, or on behalf of, the AIF to manage it (Article 5(1)(a), Directive 2011/61/EU).

[103] These activities comprise the investment management functions of portfolio management and risk management, and the additional functions of administration (legal and fund management accounting services, customer inquiries, valuation and pricing, regulatory compliance monitoring, maintenance of unit/shareholder register, distribution of income, unit/shares issues and redemptions, contract settlements, and record keeping), marketing, and activities that relate to the assets

of UCITS (subject to authorisation under Directive 2009/65/EC)[104] [Article 6(2)]. However, they may authorise an external AIFM to manage portfolios of investments, and non-core services comprising investment advice, safe-keeping and administration in connection with shares or units in collective investment undertakings, and the reception and transmission of orders in relation to financial instruments [Article 6(4)]. Member States shall ensure that internally managed AIFs[105] are limited to the activities in Annex I of Directive 2011/61/EU.[106] [Article 6(3)].

Member States shall require that AIFMs apply for authorisation from their home Member State's competent authority [Article 7(1)]. The application must be accompanied by information on the persons who are effectively conducting the AIFM's business, the identities of the AIFM's shareholders or members that have qualifying holdings and on the size of these holdings, the remuneration policies and practices pursuant to Article 13 of Directive 2011/61/EU,[107] and on arrangements made for the delegation and sub-delegation of functions to third parties[108] [Article 7(2)(a), (b), (d) and (e)]. The application must also provide a programme of activity, which sets out the AIFM's organisational structure, including information on how the AIFM intends to comply with its obligations under Directive 2011/61/EU [Article 7(2)(c)]. The application for authorisation must also provide the rules of incorporation of each AIF that the AIFM intends to manage, and information on the place of establishment of the

---

of AIFs (services that are necessary to meet the AIFM's fiduciary duties, facilities management, real estate administration activities, advice to companies on capital structure, industrial strategy and related issues, advice and services that relate to mergers and the purchase of entities, and other services that are connected to the management of the AIF and the assets in which it has invested) (Annex I, Directive 2011/61/EU).

[104] See section 2.2.6.

[105] If the legal form of the AIF allows internal management, and if the AIF's governing body decides not to appoint an external AIFM, the AIF itself can be authorised as the AIFM (Article 5(1)(b), Directive 2011/61/EU).

[106] See note 103.

[107] Member States shall require AIFMs to have remuneration policies and practices, for those groups of staff whose professional activities have a material effect on the risk profiles of the AIFMs and or of the AIFs that they manage, that are consistent with, and further, sound and effective risk management (Article 13(1), Directive 2011/61/EU).

[108] Paragraphs 1-3, and paragraphs 4-6, of Article 20 of Directive 2011/61/EU, contain guidelines for AIFMs for delegation and sub-delegation, respectively.

master AIF[109] if the AIF that the AIFM intends to manage is a feeder AIF,[110] on the arrangements made for the appointment of a depositary for each AIF that the AIFM wishes to manage,[111] on the investment strategies, the risk profiles, countries of establishment, and other features of the AIFs that it manages or intends to manage, and any additional information for each AIF in accordance with Article 23(1) of Directive 2011/61/EU [Article 7(3)].[112] The home Member State's competent authority shall not grant authorisation unless it is satisfied that the AIFM will be able to fulfil the conditions of Directive 2011/61/EU, the AIFM has adequate initial capital and own funds in accordance with Article 9 of Directive 2011/61/EU,[113] the persons who effectively carry out the AIFM's business are of sufficiently good repute and are adequately experienced in relation to the investment strategies that the AIFs pursue, the shareholders or members of the AIFM that have qualifying holdings[114] are appropriate taking into account the need to ensure the correct and prudent management

---

[109] A' master AIF' is an AIF in which another AIF invests, or has an exposure to of, 85% or more of its assets (Articles 4(1)(y) and 4(1)(m), Directive 2011/61/EU).

[110] A 'feeder AIF' is an AIF that invests at least 85% of its assets in shares or units of another AIF (the master AIF) or in more than one master AIF if these master AIFs follow identical strategies for investment, or has otherwise an exposure of 85% or more of its assets to the master AIF (Article 4(1)(m), Directive 2011/61/EU).

[111] Article 21 of Directive 2011/61/EU provides information as to the institutional requirements, place of establishment, and conditions of the depositary, and regulations as to its custody of the assets of the AIF or the AIFM.

[112] Article 23(1) of Directive 2011/61/EU requires every AIFM to disclose specified information to investors concerning each of the EU AIFs that it manages, and for each of the AIFs that it markets in the European Union, before it invests in the relevant AIF; it must also disclose material changes in this information to investors.

[113] An AIFM that is an internally managed AIF must have an initial capital of at least 300,000 EUR (Article 9(1), Directive 2011/61/EU). If an AIFM is appointed as external manager of AIFs, the AIFM must have an initial capital of at least 125,000 EUR (Article 9(2), Directive 2011/61/EU). If the value of the portfolio of AIFs that the AIFM manages exceeds 250 million EUR, the AIFM must provide an additional amount of own funds that is equal to 0.02% of the amount by which the value of the AIFM's portfolio exceeds 250 million EUR, but the required total of the initial capital and the additional amount shall not exceed 10 million EUR (Article 9(3), Directive 2011/61/EU).

[114] A 'qualifying holding' in an AIFM is one that represents at least 10% of the capital or of the voting rights in, or which makes it possible to exert a significant influence over the management of, this AIFM (Article 4(1)(ah), Directive 2011/61/EU).

of the AIFM, and the registered office and the head office of the AIFM are situated in the same Member State.[Article 8(1)]. Authorisation is to be valid for all Member States [Article 8(1)]. The relevant competent authorities of the other Member States affected are to be consulted before authorisation is granted to AIFMs who are in the same group as another AIFM, a UCITS management company, an investment firm, a credit institution, or an insurance company, that is authorised in another Member State [Article 8(2)]. The competent authority of the home State shall refuse authorisation if the effective exercise of their supervisory functions is prevented by close links between the AIFM and other (natural or legal) persons, the rules of a third country that govern persons with which the AIFM has close links,[115] and/or obstacles encountered in the enforcement of these rules [Article 8(3)]. The home Member State's competent authority may limit the authorisation's scope, especially as regards the investment strategies of AIFs that the AIFM is permitted to manage [Article 8(4)]. This authority must inform the applicant in writing within 3 months of the submission of a complete application, whether or not it has granted authorisation to the AIFM [Article 8(5)].[116] The home Member State's competent authority may withdraw the authorisation issued to an AIFM in various circumstances, but is not required to provide reasons for this withdrawal.[117]

There are several sets of passporting requirements, depending upon the type of activity[118] and the location of the AIFM and the AIFs.[119] Articles

[115] 'Close links' means a situation in which at least two natural or legal persons are connected by ownership of 20% or more of the voting rights or capital of an organisation, or control within a group of companies (Article 4(1)(e), Directive 2011/61/EU).

[116] The authority may extend period for up to three further months, if it considers this to be necessary due to the particular circumstances of the case, and after having informed the AIFM accordingly (Article 8(5), Directive 2011/61/EU).

[117] These reasons include that the AIFM does not make use of the authorisation within 1 year, expressly renounces the authorisation, has ceased the activity covered by Directive 2011/61/EU for the preceding 6 months, has obtained the authorisation by irregular means, no longer satisfies the conditions under which the authorisation was granted, has systematically or seriously transgressed the provisions adopted pursuant to Directive 2011/61/EU, or falls within any of the cases in which national law (in respect of issues that are beyond the scope of Directive 2011/61/EU) provides for withdrawal (Article 11, Directive 2011/61/EU).

[118] i.e. the management of AIFs and/or the marketing of units or shares of AIFs.

[119] Directive 2011/61/EU provides for the marketing of units or shares of EU AIFs in an EU AIFM's home Member State (Article 31) or in other Member States

32 and 33 of Directive 2011/61/EU consider the conditions for the marketing of units or shares of EU AIFs, and the management of EU AIFs, respectively, by an EU AIFM whose home Member State differs from that of the AIFs. As these requirements are for passporting entirely within the EU, they are considered in the next two paragraphs.

Member States must ensure that an authorised EU AIFM may market units or shares of an EU AIF that it manages to professional investors in another Member State than the home Member State of the AIFM, as soon as the conditions that are stated in Article 32 of Directive 2011/61/EU are satisfied [Article 32(1)].[120] The AIFM shall submit a notification to the competent authority of its home Member State in respect of each EU AIF that it intends to market [Article 32(2)]. This notification is to comprise a notification letter – which includes a programme of operations that identifies the AIFs that the AIFM intends to market and information on where the AIFs are established, the documents of incorporation of each AIF, identification of the depositary of the AIF, information on the AIF that is available to investors, information on where the master AIF is established (if the AIF is a feeder AIF), any additional information in accordance with Article 23(1) of Directive 2011/61/EU for each AIF that the AIFM intends to market,[121] the indication of the Member State in

---

(Article 32), the management by an EU AIFM of EU AIFs established in other Member States (Article 33), the marketing in the EU of a non-EU AIF managed by an EU AIFM with a passport (Article 35) or without one (Article 36), the marketing in the EU with a passport of an EU AIF (Article 39) or a non-EU AIF (Article 40) managed by a non-EU AIFM and conditions that apply to this (Article 41), and the marketing in Member States without a passport of AIFs that are managed by a non-EU AIFM (Article 42). 'EU AIF', 'EU AIFM', 'managing AIFs' and 'marketing' are defined above in this section.

[120] If the EU AIF is a feeder AIF, then this right to market is subject to the requirement that the master AIF is an EU AIF and is managed by an authorised EU AIFM (Article 32(1), Directive 2011/61/EU). 'Master AIF' and 'feeder AIF' are defined in notes 109 and 110, respectively.

[121] This additional information includes, for instance, a description of the AIF's objectives and investment strategy, information on where any master AIF is established, a description of the types of assets that the AIF may hold, the techniques that the AIF may use and all associated risks, any applicable restriction on investment, the circumstances under which the AIF may use leverage, the sources and types of leverage permitted and the associated risks, any restrictions on the use of leverage and any collateral and arrangements for asset re-use, and the maximum level of leverage that the AIFM are entitled to use on behalf of the AIF (Article 23(1)(a), Directive 2011/61/EU). 'Leverage' means any method by which the AIFM raises the exposure of an AIF, whether through borrowing, leverage

which it intends to market the units or shares of the AIF to professional investors, and information concerning arrangements that are made for the marketing of AIFs and (if relevant) on the arrangements that have been established to prevent units or shares of the AIF from being marketed to retail investors [Article 32(2) and Annex IV]. The competent authority of the home Member State of the AIFM shall send the complete notification file to the competent authority of each Member State in which the AIF is to be marketed,[122] within 20 working days of the time at which the former receives this notification, provided that the AIFM complies with Directive 2011/61/EU [Article 32(3)]. Immediately after transmission of the notification file, the competent authority of the AIFM's home Member State must inform the AIFM about the transmission; the AIFM may start to market the AIF in the AIFM's host Member State as of the date of the notification [Article 32(4)]. If they are different, the competent authority of the AIFM's home Member State is to inform the competent authority of AIF that the AIFM may start marketing the AIF's units of shares in the host Member State of the AIFM [Article 32(4)].

Member States must ensure that an authorised EU AIFM may manage EU AIFs that are established in another Member State, either directly or by establishing a branch, provided that the AIFM is authorised to manage this type of AIF [Article 33(1)]. An AIFM that intends to manage EU AIFs established in another Member State for the first time, shall communicate to the competent authority of its home Member State the name of the Member State in which it intends to manage AIFs, and a programme of operations that states in particular the services that the AIFM intends to perform and the AIFs that it intends to manage [Article 33(2)]. If the AIFM intends to establish a branch, then it also needs to provide the address in the home Member State of the AIF from which documents may be obtained, the names and contact details of the branch managers, and the branch's organisational structure [Article 33(3)]. The competent authority of the AIFM's home Member State must, within one month of receiving the complete documentation in accordance with Article 33(2) of Directive 2011/61/EU, or within two months of receiving the complete documentation in accordance with Article 33(3) of Directive 2011/61/EU, send this information to the competent authority of the AIFM's host Member State; the documents are only to be transmitted if

---

embedded in financial derivative positions, or by any other means (Article 4(1)(v), Directive 2011/61/EU).

[122] The competent authority of the home Member State must enclose a statement to the effect that the relevant AIFM is authorised to manage AIFs with a specified investment strategy (Article 32(3), Directive 2011/61/EU).

the AIFM complies with Directive 2011/61/EU [Article 33(4)]. The competent authority of the AIFM's home Member State must enclose a statement to the effect that it authorises the AIFM to manage the specified AIFs, and immediately notify the AIFM about its transmission of the complete documentation to the competent authority of the AIFM's host Member State; on receipt of this notification, the AIFM may commence the provision of its services in the host Member State [Article 33(4)].

2.2.8 Payment service providers (Directive 2007/64/EC)

Directive 2007/64/EC contains rules that concern the transparency of conditions and information requirements for payment services, and the respective rights and duties of payment service providers and payment service users in relation to the provision of payment services as a business activity or regular occupation [Article 1(2)]. It applies to payment services that are provided within the EU [Article 2(1)]. 'Payment services' comprise cash transfers to and from a payment account and all the operations that are necessary for a payment account to function, the execution of payment transactions,[123] the issuance and/or acquisition of payment instruments, and money remittance [Article 4(3) and Annex]. A 'payment service provider' must be a credit institution, an electronic money institution, a post office giro institution, or the European Central Bank, national central banks, and Member States and their regional/local authorities in instances in which they do not act in their capacity as public authorities, or natural or legal persons whose average of the preceding year's total amount of payment transactions does not exceed 3 million EUR per month and whose employees are all free from offences that relate to financial crimes [Articles 4(9), 1(1) and 26(1)]. A 'payment service user' is a natural or legal person that uses a payment service as payer,[124] payee,[125] or both [Article 4(10)].

---

[123] A 'payment transaction' is an act that the payer or the payee initiates, which transfers or withdraws funds (Article 4(5), Directive 2007/64/EC). Payment transactions include direct debits, payment transactions through a payment card, and credit transfers (Annex, Directive 2007/64/EC).

[124] A 'payer' is a natural or legal person who holds a payment account and permits a payment order from this account or, if there is no payment account, a natural or legal person who gives a payment order (Article 4(7), Directive 2007/64/EC). A 'payment account' is an account that is held in the name of one or more payment service users that is used to execute payment transactions (Article 4(14), Directive 2007/64/EC). A 'payment order' is an instruction by a payer or a payee to his

For authorisation as a payment institution, the applicant must submit an application to the competent authority of the home Member State, together with the programme of operations that includes the type of payment service contemplated, a business plan, evidence that the payment institution holds the stipulated minimum initial capital, a description of the applicant's corporate governance arrangements and internal control mechanisms which demonstrates that these arrangements and control mechanisms are appropriate, proportionate, sound and sufficient, a description of the internal control mechanisms that the applicant has established in order to comply with its obligations under Directive 2005/60/EC,[126] a description of the applicant's structural organisation that includes the intended use of branches, agents, outsourcing arrangements and its participation in a national or international payment system, the identity of persons who have qualifying holdings in the applicant, the identity of directors and managers of the payment institution with evidence that they are of good repute and possess appropriate knowledge and experience to provide payment services, the identity of statutory auditors, the applicant's legal status and articles of association, and the address of the applicant's head office [Article 5]. The competent authority of the applicant's home Member State shall grant it an authorisation, if the information and evidence that accompanies the application complies with all the requirements of Article 5, and if the authority's overall assessment of the application is favourable [Article 10(2)]. An authorisation will only be given to legal persons that are established in a Member State [Article 10(1)]. The competent authority shall grant an authorisation only if the payment institution has robust governance arrangements for its payment services business, which include a clear organisational structure with well-defined, consistent and transparent lines of responsibility, effective procedures to identify, manage, monitor and report risks, and adequate internal control mechanisms; these arrangements, procedures and mechanisms are to be comprehensive, and proportionate to the nature, scale and complexity of the payment institution's payment services [Article 10(4)]. The competent authority will refuse to grant an authorisation if it is not satisfied as to the suitability of the shareholders or

---

payment service provider, which requests the execution of a payment transaction (Article 4(16), Directive 2007/64/EC).

[125] A 'payee' is a natural or legal person who is the intended recipient of funds that have been the subject of a payment transaction (Article 4(8), Directive 2007/64/EC).

[126] This is the Directive on the prevention of the use of the financial system for the purpose of money laundering and terrorist financing.

members that have qualifying holdings, taking into consideration the need to ensure the sound, prudent management of a payment institution [Article 10(6)]. The competent authority will only grant an authorisation if any close links between the payment institution and other (natural or legal) persons do not prevent the effective exercise of its supervisory functions [Article 10(7)]. Furthermore, it will only provide an authorisation if the rules of a third country with which the payment institution has close links, or problems involved in the enforcement of these provisions, do not prevent the effective exercise of its supervisory functions [Article 10(8)]. An authorisation will be valid in all Member States, and shall permit the institution to provide payment services throughout the EU, provided that these services are included within the terms of the authorisation [Article 10(9)]. Within three months of receipt of all the information required for the decision, the competent authority is to inform the applicant as to whether or not the authorisation has been granted or refused; it must give reasons for a refusal [Article 11]. The home Member State's competent authority may withdraw the authorisation issued to an payment institution in specified circumstances,[127] and must provide reasons for this withdrawal and make it public [Article 12]. Member States shall ensure that the decisions taken by their competent authority in respect of a payment institution, pursuant to the national rules adopted in accordance with Directive 2007/64/EC, may be disputed before the domestic courts [Article 23(1)].[128]

An authorised payment institution that wishes to provide payment services for the first time in a Member State other than its home State, in exercise of the free movement of services or the right of establishment, shall inform the competent authority in its home Member State [Article 25(1)]. Within one month of receiving this information, the home Member State's competent authority shall notify the host Member State's competent authority of the payment institution's name and address, the names of branch managers, the branch's organisational structure, and the types of payment services that it intends to provide in the host State's

[127] These reasons include that the payment institution does not make use of the authorisation within 1 year, expressly renounces the authorisation, has ceased business for the preceding 6 months, has obtained the authorisation by irregular means, no longer satisfies the conditions under which the authorisation was granted, would present a threat to the stability of the payment system by continuing its payment services business, or falls within any of the cases in which national law provides for withdrawal of an authorisation (Article 12(1), Directive 2007/64/EC).

[128] The competent authority's failure to act may also be contested before the national courts (Article 23(2), Directive 2007/64/EC).

territory [Article 25(1)]. The home Member State's competent authority must co-operate with the host Member State's competent authority, in the former's responsibility for compliance with Title II of Directive 2007/64/EC, in particular to require the payment institution to supply any information that is needed to monitor compliance, to conduct on-site inspections at the payment institution, its agents, branches, or outsourcees, to issue recommendations, guidelines and binding administrative provisions, and to suspend or withdraw authorisation [Articles 25(2) and 21(1)]. The competent authorities of home and host Member State shall provide each other with all essential and/or relevant information, especially in respect of actual or suspected infringements by an agent, a branch, or an outsourcee [Article 25(4)].

2.2.9 Comment

The authorisation and passporting requirements for financial institutions are detailed, especially for AIFMs. Furthermore, they are not always consistent. For instance, Article 11 of Directive 2011/61/EU does not require the competent authority of the home Member State to provide reasons for the decision to withdraw an AIFM's authorisation.[129] By contrast, Article 12(2) of Directive 2007/64/EC requires the competent authority of the home Member State to give reasons for the decision to withdraw the authorisation of a payment institution.[130]

2.3 Free movement of capital to/from third countries

This section considers the rules for the provision of financial services to and from third countries. It also investigates the EU's free movement of capital laws as regards flows to and from these states.

2.3.1 Passporting and third countries

The Single Market Directives tend not to provide a comprehensive passporting regime for the provision of financial services to and from third countries. For instance, Directive 2004/39/EC empowers the Commission to submit proposals to the Council for a mandate for negotiation with a third country, in an instance in which this state does not grant EU investment firms access to its markets that is comparable with that

---

[129] See section 2.2.7.

[130] See section 2.2.8.

provided by the EU to investment companies from the third country [Article 15(2)]. Furthermore, the Commission may also initiate negotiations with a third country that does not grant the national standard of treatment to EU investment firms [Article 15(3)].

With time, the EU is moving towards a position in which firms from outside the EEA are able to provide services within the EEA, and take advantage of the passporting regime to supply these services across the borders of Member States therein. Directive 2011/61/EU provides for the marketing in the EU with a passport of a non-EU AIF that is managed by an EU AIFM [Article 35], of EU AIFs by a non-EU AIFM [Article 39], and of non-EU AIFs by a non-EU AIFM [Article 40].[131] Furthermore, under the Commission's proposed Directive to replace Directive 2004/39/EC, COM(2011) 656 final, companies that provide investment services and activities in third countries may establish a branch in a Member State, and supply these services to other Member States through the free movement of services, provided that the Commission considers that the prudential framework of the relevant third country is equivalent to that of the relevant EU Regulations and Directives [Articles 41-44].[132] Thus, as the EU updates the Single Market Directives, a thorough equivalence regime between the EEA and third countries may develop, under which the free movement of services will be available for the EEA base of the third country firm.

2.3.2 The free movement of capital

Derogations that apply only to capital movements to/from third countries

In addition to the rules in section 2.1, which apply to movements of capital, and to payments, between Member States and third countries, there are derogations that apply specifically to these capital movements. First, the prohibition of the free movement of capital (and of payments) in Article 63 of the TFEU does not apply to restrictions that were in place on 31 December 1993 under EU or national law that were adopted in respect of the movement of capital to or from third countries that involve direct investment, establishment, the provision of financial services, or the

---

[131] There are considerable administrative requirements, especially for a passport under Article 40 of Directive 2011/61/EU.

[132] These are COM(2011) 656 final, COM(2011) 652 final, Directive 2013/36/EU, and Regulation (EU) No 575/2013. Article 41(3) of COM(2011) 656 final does not refer to Directive 2013/36/EU and Regulation (EU) No 575/2013, but to Directive 2006/49/EC, which the former two legal instruments replace.

admission of securities to capital markets.[133] As the supply of financial services is one of the excepted areas, this derogation is of relevance to the national laws that are analysed for their compliance with EU's free movement of capital rules in chapters 3 to 7. However, it is beyond the scope of this work to investigate the history of individual restrictions to capital movements between Member States and third countries. Therefore, this derogation will not be applied each time that the author finds that domestic law imposes a restriction on these capital movements.

Second, the European Parliament and the Council, acting under the ordinary legislative procedure,[134] is to adopt measures on the movement of capital to or from third countries that involves direct investment, establishment, the provision of financial services, or the admission of securities to capital markets – whilst attempting to achieve the objective of the free movement of capital between Member States and third countries as far as possible.[135] Thus, the EU may restrict the free movement capital between Member States and third countries, if it legislates over these areas, provided that the EU institutions carefully take account of the objective of the free movement of capital whilst enacting the legislation. As financial service providers in third countries are not as yet able to fully benefit from the passporting regime,[136] it is necessary for the EU to retain this cautious derogation. This EU provision is relevant to the analysis in subsequent chapters, because the some of the national laws discussed are transpositions of Directives. If domestic rules do not restrict the free movement of capital more than the equivalent provisions of the relevant Directive do, then, to the extent that they restrict the free movement of capital between Member States and third countries, they are justifiable; this is assuming, of course, that all of the provisions of the relevant Directives that hinder the free movement of capital between Member States and third countries are justifiable restrictions under the derogation.

Third, the Council may unanimously, acting under a special legislative procedure and after consulting the European Parliament, adopt measures that constitute a backwards step in EU law as regards the liberalisation of the movement of capital to or from third countries.[137] This derogation only applies only over specific areas, which comprise the contents of the relevant measures. It is only of relevance to the analysis, below, in so far

---

[133] Article 64(1), TFEU. The relevant date is 31 December 1999 for national legal restrictions in Bulgaria, Estonia and Hungary (Article 64(1), TFEU).

[134] Article 294 of the TFEU contains the ordinary legislative procedure.

[135] Article 64(2), TFEU.

[136] See section 2.3.1.

[137] Article 64(3), TFEU.

as it renders any national provisions that breach the free movement of capital legal, in so far as they are in accordance with the EU's derogatory measures.

In the absence of the Council's measures that constitute a backwards step with regard to the free movement of capital, Member States may apply to the Council, who may unanimously adopt a decision, which states that restrictive tax measures that a Member State adopts concerning at least one third country are to be considered compatible with the TFEU and Treaty on European Union, in so far as they are justified by an objective of the EU[138] and are compatible with the correct functioning of the internal market.[139] As this derogation applies to taxation (rather than to financial services), it is irrelevant to the analysis in subsequent chapters.

If, in exceptional circumstances, capital movements to or from third countries cause, or may cause, serious difficulties from the functioning of economic and monetary union, then the Council, acting on a proposal from the Commission and after consulting the European Central Bank, may take safeguard measures in respect of third countries for a period not longer than six months, if these measures are strictly required.[140] This derogation is relevant to Estonia, Latvia and Germany, but not to Croatia and Poland; the latter countries are outside the economic and monetary union. Nevertheless, as the derogation only applies safeguards over a short period of time, it has little bearing on the analysis that relates to movements of capital between the former three states and third countries.

Skatterverket v A.[141]

This case concerned the movement of capital between a Member State (Sweden) and a third country (Switzerland). The CJEU considered the application of the EU's free movement of capital rules to these capital flows, and held the following.

Article 63(1) of the TFEU has (vertical) direct effect.[142] Furthermore, as regards the movement of capital between Member States and third countries, Article 63(1), combined with Articles 64 and 65 of the TFEU,

> "may be relied on before national courts and may render national rules that are inconsistent with it inapplicable, irrespective of the category of capital movement in question".[143]

---

[138] Article 3 of the Treaty on European Union lists the EU's objectives.
[139] Article 65(4), TFEU.
[140] Article 66, TFEU.
[141] [2007] ECR I-11531.
[142] See the title '*Vertical direct effect*' in section 2.1.4.

Thus, the applicability and direct effect of the EU's free movement of capital rules is unaffected by the origin and destination of the capital flow in question, provided that it is across a national border and at least partially within the EU. However, later in the judgment, the CJEU distinguishes the circumstances of capital movements between a Member State and a third country and those of capital flows across a border within the EU, as follows.

> "[T]he extent to which the Member States are ... authorised to apply certain restrictive measures on the movement of capital cannot be determined without taking account of the fact ... that movement of capital to or from third countries takes place in a different legal context from that which occurs within the Community. Accordingly, because of the degree of legal integration that exists between Member States of the European Union ... the taxation by a Member State of economic activities having cross-border aspects which take place within the Community is not always comparable to that of economic activities involving relations between Member States and third countries. ... [I]t may also be that a Member State will be able to demonstrate that a restriction on the movement of capital to or from third countries is justified for a particular reason in circumstances where that reason would not constitute a valid justification for a restriction on capital movements between Member States ... ."[144]

Although this case involved direct taxation, which is beyond the scope of the analysis in the subsequent chapters, the principle that movements of capital between Member States and third countries are within a different legal context to those between Member States is also applicable to cross-border flows that relate to financial services. However, as the CJEU has not ruled on this issue with respect to these services, the forthcoming analysis will treat the context of the free movement of capital similarly, regardless of the origin and destination of the capital movement.[145]

---

[143] *Skatteverket v A.* [2007] ECR I-11531, paragraph 27.

[144] *Skatteverket v A.* [2007] ECR I-11531, paragraphs 36 and 37.

[145] Furthermore, the legal context of the free movement of capital between the EU and various third countries will differ considerably, depending upon factors such as the degree and structure of financial supervision in the third countries, the content, composition, amount and specific destination of capital flows, and the existence and content of co-operation agreements between the EU and specific third countries. These factors are beyond the scope of the analysis in subsequent chapters.

Comment

There is plenty of scope for the CJEU to determine the extent to which the free movement of capital rules apply to capital flows between the EU and third countries, due to the paucity of case law in this area. Unless the capital movement clearly falls within one of the derogations described above in this section, the analysis of Member States' financial services laws in chapters 3 to 7 for possible breaches of Article 63 of the TFEU will take a similar approach to provisions that relate to flows to or from third countries, and those that concern cross-border capital movements within in the EU.

2.3.3 Conclusions

This chapter enables comparison of the laws of Member States with EU law for obstacles to the free movement of capital. It identifies the approach the EU's rules for this free movement, and the derogations that apply to these rules. It describes the principles that the CJEU has applied in its case law, in order to determine whether a particular national legal provision is a non-justifiable contravention of Article 63 of the TFEU.

The chapter describes the authorisation and passporting laws within the Single Market Directives, which should be the basis on which the financial services laws of the Member States are founded. It proceeds to consider the passporting structure and free movement of capital derogations that apply specifically to third countries.

As the book concentrates on financial services, the specific EU case law relating to the free movement of capital and real estate, and to the free movement of capital and direct taxation, is omitted from this chapter. This case law is sufficiently developed to form the basis of a separate substantial work. Chapter 3 compares Estonian financial services legislation on cross-border capital movements with the EU law discussed in the current chapter.

CHAPTER THREE

ESTONIA: LEGAL ISSUES

> "Estonia consists mainly of boulder-strewn lowland, but also includes over 800 islands in the Baltic. It covers 45100 km² (17400 square miles), and until 1945 was noted mainly for its cattle and dairy produce. Its industries now include food processing, electrical engineering and shipbuilding, and its people now have the highest standard of living in the USSR".[1]

Estonia's forward looking adaptability applies equally to its legal translations. The ELLC has translated all the major Estonian Legislation from this Uralic language into English. It translates Estonian laws into Finnish,[2] French and German, as well as into English.

The national regulator for the provision of financial services is the Estonian Financial Supervision Authority (EFSA), which is an independent agency that conducts state financial supervision over activities provided for in the Investment Funds, Securities Market, Credit Institutions, Insurance Activities, Payment Institutions and E-money Institutions, and other, Acts, and in legislation pursuant to these Acts.[3] Its functions include ensuring that its subjects comply with financial soundness requirements under the Acts,[4] guiding subjects to manage prudently,[5] applying the law to protect clients' and investors' interests,[6] ensuring good administrative practice,[7] making proposals for the implementation and amendment, and participating in the drafting, of

---

[1] A. B. Mountjoy *(ed.)* (1987), *Readers Digest Guide to Places of the World*, 216.

[2] There are linguistic and economic reasons for the ELLC to provide legal translations from Estonian into Finnish. Both are Uralic languages. Furthermore, Finland is one of Estonia's main trading partners.

[3] ss.2(1) and 4, Financial Supervision Authority Act.

[4] s.6(1)(1), Financial Supervision Authority Act 2001.

[5] s.6(1)(2), Financial Supervision Authority Act 2001.

[6] s.6(1)(3), Financial Supervision Authority Act 2001.

[7] s.6(1)(4), Financial Supervision Authority Act 2001.

legislation that concerns the financial sector,[8] co-operating with international organisations, foreign financial supervision authorities, and competent institutions of the EU,[9] and joining the financial supervision authorities from other EEA states in financial supervision proceedings as specified in Estonian law.[10]

In the Estonian legislation, 'Contracting State' means a Contracting Party to the EEA agreement.[11] All other foreign countries are 'third countries'.[12] 'Cross-border services' are those provided by a management company, credit institution, payment institution, or e-money institution, in a country in which it or its branch is not registered.[13]

Section 3.1 discusses the Investment Funds Act 2004. Section 3.2 investigates the Securities Market Act 2001. Section 3.3 considers the Credit Institutions Act 1999 and Regulation No. 19 of the President of the Bank of Estonia of 6 July 1999. Section 3.4 concerns the Insurance Activities Act 2004. Section 3.5 reports on the Payment Institutions and E-money Institutions Act 2009.

3.1 Investment Funds Act 2004 (IFA)

Management company

This is a public limited company which manages the assets of a fund.[14] A management company may also manage a portfolio of securities,[15] provide advice on investment in securities,[16] and hold units of shares in a fund for clients.[17] Fund management includes investing the fund assets,[18]

---

[8] s.6(1)(5), Financial Supervision Authority Act 2001.
[9] s.6(1)(6), Financial Supervision Authority Act 2001.
[10] s.6(1)(6^1), Financial Supervision Authority Act 2001.
[11] s.4(1), IFA; s.3, SMA; s.4(4)(1), CIA; s.5(5), IAA; s.3(6)(5), PIA.
[12] s.25(5), IFA; s.13(2), SMA; s.9(5)(2), CIA; ss.29(4)-(5), IAA; ss24(2)-(3), PIA.
[13] s.25(3), IFA; s.19^1(3), CIA; s.24(4), PIA. Investment firms also provide 'cross-border services', which are not defined in the SMA. 'Cross-border insurance activities' are the insurance activities of an Estonian insurance company that relate to insured risks in a foreign country (s.30(1), IAA). 'Cross-border reinsurance activities' are the reinsurance activities of an Estonian reinsurance company, in the context of which this reinsurance firm provides reinsurance to an insurance company that is established in a foreign state (s.30(4), IAA).
[14] s.9(1), IFA.
[15] s.9(2)(1), IFA.
[16] s.9(2)(2), IFA.
[17] s.9(2)(3), IFA.
[18] s.10(1)(1), IFA.

issuing, redeeming, and re-purchasing fund units,[19] issuing documentation to shareholders or unit-holders,[20] communicating necessary information to the shareholders or unit-holders,[21] providing other services to clients,[22] organising the marketing of other units of the fund,[23] keeping account of the fund assets,[24] organising the accounting of a common fund,[25] determining the fund's net asset value,[26] organising the maintenance of a register of the units,[27] calculating the income of the fund,[28] organising the distribution of the income between the fund's shareholders or unit-holders,[29] monitoring the compliance of the activities of the management company and the fund within the Estonian legislation,[30] and activities that are directly related to those specified in this subsection.[31] Furthermore, a management company that does not manage UCITS may provide investment advice and asset management services to third persons for the purposes of fund management, in respect of the class of assets for which the management company has been granted authorisation to manage a fund.[32]

Sections 25 to 33¹: activities of a management company in a foreign state

If an Estonian management company manages an UCITS that is established in another Contracting State, through the provision of cross-border services or the establishment of a branch, then it must comply with specified sections of the IFA.[33] The management company must establish

---

[19] s.10(1)(2), IFA.
[20] s.10(1)(3), IFA.
[21] s.10(1)(4), IFA.
[22] s.10(1)(4), IFA.
[23] s.10(1)(5), IFA.
[24] s.10(1)(6), IFA.
[25] s.10(1)(6), IFA.
[26] s.10(1)(7), IFA.
[27] s.10(1)(8), IFA.
[28] s.10(1)(9), IFA.
[29] s.10(1)(9), IFA.
[30] s.10(1)(10), IFA.
[31] s.10(1)(11), IFA.
[32] s.9(2¹), IFA.
[33] s.25(6), IFA. These sections are sections 51-56¹ (requirements for managers and fund managers), 57-58² (internal control requirements), 69-75 (requirements for the activities of a management company), 85-88 (required own funds for a management company), 144¹ (recording of transactions conducted for the account of UCITS), 144² (report on the issue and redemption of UCITS units), 237-245

an organisational administration, as required according to the legislation of another Contracting State for pursuing the activities of UCITS established there, investing the assets of the UCITS, and carrying out the obligations specified in the prospectus of the UCITS and the fund rules on the basis of the IFA.[34]

As some of the elements of fund management may involve the movement of capital, such as the purchase and sale of units, subsections 25(6) and 25(7) of the IFA are breaches of Article 63 of the TFEU. These provisions can be justified on the ground of taking all requisite measures to prevent infringement of national law and regulations in the field of prudential supervision of financial institutions,[35] provided that they are necessary for the protection of interests that they are intended to guarantee, proportionate, specific, objective, and known to the parties beforehand, and accompanied by legal redress if the provision of cross-border services or the establishment of a branch in another Contracting State is refused.[36] The 'interests' in this case are those of investors in the units of the fund. There are many requirements; if these do not go beyond the passporting requirements in Directive 2009/65/EC,[37] then the CJEU would be likely to consider them to be proportionate.

An Estonian management company that would like to establish a branch in a third country must apply to the EFSA for an authorisation to do this.[38] The management company must also provide the following information to the EFSA: the name of the country in which it is to found the branch,[39] the address of the branch's seat,[40] a business plan for the branch's activities,[41] and specified information about the branch's

---

(management company financial reporting, common fund audit, and information disclosure by a management company), and 248 (risk management) of the IFA.

[34] s.25(7), IFA.

[35] Article 65(1)(b), TFEU. Although the CJEU has developed its case law on derogations in the context of the 'public policy/public security' derogation, four of the five tests are applicable to the 'prudential supervision of financial institutions' derogation. I give reasons for this in the '*Comment*' sub-section of section 2.1.3.

[36] See the subsection '*The requirements for a successful public policy/public security derogation*', in section 2.1.3.

[37] These requirements are described in section 2.2.6.

[38] s.26(1), IFA.

[39] s.26(2)(1), IFA.

[40] s.26(2)(2), IFA.

[41] s.26(2)(3), IFA. The business plan must contain a forecast and analysis of the management company's main economic indicators and the funds that it manages, a description of the company's management structure, the rights, obligations and liability of persons who are involved in management of the funds, and a

managers.[42] The EFSA shall decide to grant or refuse to grant an authorisation for the establishment of a branch within two months of receiving all the necessary information and documents,[43] and is to promptly inform the management company of a decision to grant or refuse an authorisation for the establishment of a branch.[44] The IFA neither requires the EFSA to provide reasons for refusing to grant an authorisation, nor the right for the applicant to appeal against the refusal in the Estonian courts.

The EFSA may refuse to grant an authorisation for the establishment of a branch in a third country if the branch's managers do not satisfy the requirements for managers of management companies provided by the IFA,[45] the documents or information submitted upon application for an authorisation for the establishment of a branch do not satisfy the requirements of the IFA, or legislation enacted on the basis thereof, or are inaccurate, misleading, or incomplete,[46] the management company's resources are insufficient for the supply of the services that are specified in the business plan,[47] the branch's foundation or the implementation of the business plan may harm the interests of the fund, its shareholders, or its unit-holders, or the management company's financial situation, or adversely affect the reliability of its activities in any country,[48] or the third country's financial supervision authority has no legal basis or possibilities for co-operation with the EFSA, due to which the EFSA is unable to exercise adequate supervision over the branch.[49] The EFSA may revoke an authorisation for the establishment of a branch in a third country if any of

---

description, forecast, and analysis of ten specified factors (which include, for instance, the market value, net asset value, and rate of return, of the fund assets) (s.15(1), IFA). The business plan must cover three years or more (s.15(2), IFA).

[42] s.26(2)(4), IFA. This information include each manager's first name and surname, personal identification code (or date of birth), residence, educational and employment history, a description of his/her duties, and documents that certify his/her trustworthiness (s.14(1)(6), IFA).

[43] s.27(2), IFA. The EFSA may require the submission of additional documents and information, if is not satisfied on the basis of the documents and information specified as to whether the applicant has adequate facilities for the management of a fund, or satisfies the legal requirements for management companies, or if any other circumstances relating to the applicant need to be verified (s.14(2), IFA).

[44] s.27(3), IFA.

[45] s.28(1), IFA.

[46] s.28(1^1), IFA.

[47] s.28(2), IFA.

[48] s.28(3), IFA.

[49] s.28(4), IFA.

these grounds become evident,[50] if the management company has communicated false information to the EFSA,[51] the management company has contravened legal provisions of the third country that damage the interests of the shareholders, unit-holders or clients of funds that the former manages,[52] the management company or its branch fail to satisfy the requirements for the issue of an authorisation for the establishment of a branch,[53] the management company does not submit the required reports on its branch,[54] the management company has breached the fund's rules of management contract and the interests of shareholders or unit-holders of the fund may be consequently damaged,[55] the management company or its manager has been punished for an offence that has not been removed from the punishment register pursuant to the Punishment Register Act,[56] the management company has not implemented one of the EFSA's precepts within the period or to the extent prescribed,[57] the risks that arise from the activities of the branch are significantly larger than those emanating from the management company's activities,[58] or the management company's activity licence has been withdrawn.[59]

The EFSA must promptly inform the management company and the financial supervision authority of a third country of a decision to withdraw an authorisation for the establishment of a branch.[60] The IFA neither requires the EFSA to provide reasons for revoking an authorisation, nor the right for the applicant to appeal against its revocation in the Estonian courts.

Establishment of a branch is a 'capital movement' under Title I(1) of Annex I. A national provision that requires prior authorisation is a restriction on the free movement of capital.[61] Prior authorisation for capital movements must be proportionate and be based on objective criteria for

---

[50] s.29(1)(9), IFA.
[51] s.29(1)(1), IFA.
[52] s.29(1)(2), IFA.
[53] s.29(1)(3), IFA.
[54] s.29(1)(4), IFA.
[55] s.29(1)(5), IFA.
[56] s.29(1)(5), IFA.
[57] s.29(1)(6), IFA.
[58] s.29(1)(7), IFA.
[59] s.29(1)(8), IFA.
[60] s.29(2), IFA.
[61] See the subsection '*Public policy, public security, general interest, and prior authorisation*', in section 2.1.3.

legal certainty.[62] Authorisation for the foundation of a branch provides the EFSA with a degree of discretion, for instance, as to whether the documents that the applicant submits are inaccurate, misleading, or incomplete, or whether the third country's financial supervision authority has no legal basis. Hence, unless the EFSA publishes its decisions on authorisations for the establishment of a branch in third countries, with accompanying reasons, and follows these consistently, it does not provide applicants with legal certainty. It is also doubtful that a system of prior authorisation is proportionate for the establishment of branches in third countries whose financial regulatory rules the EU institutions consider to be equivalent to EU law; maybe a system of prior declaration with accompanying informational requirements for Estonian branches to be established in these countries would be satisfactory. Although the revocation of an authorisation is not a 'capital movement' in Annex 1, it affects capital movements, such as the purchase and sale of foreign units by a fund that is covered by the authorisation.

An Estonian management company that intends to establish a branch in another Contracting State must inform the EFSA of this, and submit to it the following information and documents: the name of this Contracting State, the names of the branch's managers, the address of the branch's seat, and a scheme of operations for the branch – which contains information about the services to be provided in the Contracting State and the branch's organisational structure.[63] If the management company is managing UCITS, it must submit to the EFSA the above information and documents, together with a confirmed translation into an official language of the Contracting State in which the branch is situated.[64] The EFSA may refuse to review the above information and documents if they do not satisfy the requirements in the IFA or are incomplete,[65] or if they have these deficiencies and the additional information or documents that the EFSA demands have not been submitted in the prescribed period.[66]

If the Estonian management company is managing UCITS, then the EFSA shall decide to forward, or to refuse to forward, the above information and documents to the financial supervision authority of the Contracting State in which the branch is to be founded, within two months of receipt of all the required information and documents, but not later than

---

[62] See the subsection '*Public policy, public security, general interest, and prior authorisation*', in section 2.1.3.

[63] s.30(1), IFA.

[64] s.30(2), IFA.

[65] s.30(4)(1), IFA.

[66] s.30(4)(2), IFA.

within three months of receipt of the corresponding notice from the management company.[67] The EFSA shall forward the above information and documents to the financial supervision authority of the Contracting State in which the branch is to be established, no later than on the second working day after the decision to forward is made.[68] The EFSA must also forward information concerning the investor protection scheme that applies in Estonia, and, if the management company intends to manage UCITS established in another Contracting State, an attestation from the EFSA which states that the management company has been issued an activity licence according to the provisions of the EU Directive regarding investment funds, and explanations on the scope of this activity licence and the limitations that relate to the types of UCITS managed.[69] A management company that manages UCITS may establish a branch in a Contracting State, if it has satisfied the requirements of the financial supervision authority of the Contracting State in which the branch is situated for the foundation of a branch there, or if the that financial supervision authority has failed to submit these requirements within two months of the receipt of the information and documents.[70]

The EFSA may refuse to forward the information and documents that are required for the foundation of a branch in another Contracting State to that State's financial supervision authority, if the information or documents submitted do not fulfil the requirements in the IFA or are inaccurate, misleading, or incomplete,[71] the management company does not manage UCITS,[72] the resources of the management company are insufficient for the provision of services stated in the scheme of operations of other Contracting States,[73] the establishment of the branch or implementation of the scheme of operations submitted by the management company may damage the interests of the fund, its shareholders, or its unit-holders, the management company's financial situation,[74] or its activities in a Contracting State, or a financial supervision authority of a Contracting State has no legal basis or possibilities for co-operation with the EFSA as a consequence of which the EFSA cannot exercise adequate

---

[67] s.30(3), IFA. The EFSA must promptly inform the management company of the decision.
[68] s.30(5), IFA.
[69] s.30(5), IFA.
[70] s.30(6), IFA.
[71] s.31(1), IFA.
[72] s.31(2), IFA.
[73] s.31(3), IFA.
[74] s.31(4), IFA.

supervision over the branch.[75] The EFSA may issue a precept to forbid the activities of a management company through a branch established in a Contracting State on any of the above grounds,[76] or if the financial supervision authority of that State has informed the EFSA that the management company has breached the requirements contained in the State's legislation and enforced by that financial supervision authority.[77] The EFSA must promptly transmit the precept to the management company, which is required to stop the supply of its services through the branch established in the Contracting State, by the date that the EFSA has specified in the precept.[78]

The foundation of a branch is a 'capital movement' under Title I(1) of Annex I. If the EFSA refuses to review the information and documents submitted by the management company in order to establish a branch in a Contracting State, does not forward the information and documents to the financial supervision authority of this State, or issues a precept in order to prohibit the branch from providing services, then this is a breach of the free movement of capital. For this contravention to be justified on the ground of taking all requisite measures to prevent infringement of national law and regulations in the field of prudential supervision of financial institutions,[79] the restrictive measures must be necessary for the protection of interests that they are intended to guarantee, be specific, objective and known to the parties beforehand, be proportionate, and provide the persons affected with access to legal redress.[80] The IFA does not provide legal redress to persons whose applications to establish a branch in a Contracting State are refused or revoked – it does not require the EFSA to provide reasons for its decision to refuse to review the information and documents, to refuse to forward them to the Contracting State's financial supervision authority, or to issue a precept, and does not provide the management company with a right to redress for this decision in the Estonian courts. Furthermore, the EFSA retains a degree of discretion as to whether to permit the establishment of the branch or to refuse it, i.e. not all the measures are specific, objective and known to the parties beforehand. For instance, the EFSA has a discretion with respect to its decision to refuse to forward the information and documents to the Contracting

---

[75] s.31(5), IFA.
[76] s.32(1)(1), IFA.
[77] s.32(1)(2), IFA.
[78] s.32(2), IFA.
[79] Article 65(1)(b), TFEU. See section 2.1.3.
[80] See the subsection '*The requirements for a successful public policy/security derogation*', in section 2.1.3.

State's financial supervision authority if it considers that the latter has 'no legal basis'.[81] As a consequence, the rules for the establishment of a branch in another Member State breach Article 63 of the TFEU.

An Estonian management company that intends to supply cross-border services in a Contracting State must inform the EFSA thereof, and submit to it the name of the Contracting State to which the management company intends to provide these services,[82] and a scheme of operations, which is to contain information about the services to be provided in the Contracting State.[83] An Estonian management company that manages UCITS shall transmit to the EFSA both this information and a confirmed translation into an official language of the Contracting State.[84] The EFSA may refuse to review the name of the Contracting State in which the management company is to provide cross-border services and the scheme of operations, if they do not satisfy the requirements in the IFA or are incomplete,[85] or if they have these deficiencies and the additional information or documents that the EFSA demands have not been submitted in the prescribed period.[86]

If the Estonian management company is managing UCITS, then the EFSA shall decide to forward, or to refuse to forward, the name of the Contracting State in which the management company is to supply cross-border services and the scheme of operations, to the financial supervision authority of that Contracting State, within one month of receipt of this information.[87] The EFSA must also forward information concerning the investor protection scheme that applies in Estonia, and, if the management company intends to manage UCITS established in another Contracting State, an attestation from the EFSA which states that the management company has been issued an activity licence according to the provisions of the EU Directive regarding investment funds, and explanations on the scope of this activity licence and the limitations that relate to the types of UCITS managed.[88]

---

[81] The European Commission would not be impressed by a decision of this kind with respect to a financial supervision authority of a Member State.

[82] s.33(1)(1), IFA.

[83] s.33(1)(2), IFA.

[84] s.33(2), IFA.

[85] s.33(4)(1), IFA.

[86] s.33(4)(2), IFA.

[87] s.33(3), IFA. The EFSA must promptly inform the management company of the decision.

[88] s.33(3), IFA.

The EFSA may refuse to forward the name of the Contracting State in which the management company is to provide cross-border services and the scheme of operations to that State's financial supervision authority, if the information or documents submitted do not satisfy the requirements in the IFA or are inaccurate, misleading, or incomplete,[89] the resources of the management company are insufficient for the provision of cross-border services,[90] the supply of cross-border services may damage the interests of the fund, its shareholders, or its unit-holders, the management company's financial situation, or the reliability of its activities,[91] or a financial supervision authority of a Contracting State has no legal basis or possibilities for co-operation with the EFSA as a consequence of which the EFSA cannot exercise adequate supervision over the supply of cross-border services in the Contracting State.[92] After forwarding this information to the financial supervision authority of the Contracting State in which the management company is to provide cross-border services, the management company that manages UCITS may start supplying these services there, taking account of the requirements in that State's legislation and its implementation by the financial supervision authority.[93]

The EFSA may issue a precept to prohibit the provision by the management company of cross-border services there, on any of the grounds in the previous paragraph,[94] or if the financial supervision authority of the Contracting State in which the cross-border services are to be provided has informed the EFSA that the management company has breached the requirements in that State's legislation and its implementation by the financial supervision authority.[95] The EFSA must promptly deliver this precept to the management company, whereupon the latter must stop supplying cross-border services in the Contracting State by the date which the EFSA specifies.[96]

Cross-border services are 'capital movements' under Annex I. The information that the management company is required to provide to the EFSA – the name of the Contracting State in which cross-border services are to be provided and a scheme of operations that states the services – is not onerous and does not amount to a restriction on the free movement of

---

[89] s.33(5)(1), IFA.
[90] s.33(5)(2), IFA.
[91] s.33(5)(3), IFA.
[92] s.33(5)(4), IFA.
[93] s.33(6), IFA.
[94] s.33(8)(1), IFA.
[95] s.33(8)(2), IFA.
[96] s.33(9), IFA.

capital. If the management company manages UCITS, however, the informational requirements are greater than for investment funds that are not UCITS – in addition to the information above, the management company must also provide a confirmed translation, and the EFSA must forward to the financial supervision authority of the Contracting State to which cross-border services are to be provided information concerning the Estonian investor protection scheme, an attestation on the issuance of the activity licence to the management company, and explanations on the scope of the licence and the restrictions that relate to the types of UCITS managed. Non-provision of this information amounts to a limitation on the free movement of capital.

These provisions can be justified on the ground of taking all requisite measures to prevent infringement of national law and regulations in the field of prudential supervision of financial institutions,[97] provided that they are necessary for the protection of interests that they are intended to guarantee, specific, objective, and known to the parties beforehand, proportionate, and accompanied by legal redress.[98] The EFSA has a degree of discretion in its decision to forward or refuse to forward the information to the financial supervision authority of the Contracting State in which cross-border services are to be provided, and in whether or not to issue a precept to preclude the provision of these services; for instance, the EFSA may refuse to forward the information or issue a precept on the ground that the financial supervision authority in that State has no legal basis. Consequently, section 33 of the IFA is an unjustified restriction on Article 63 of the TFEU.

If a management company would like to make a public offer of the units of UCITS established in Estonia to investors in another Contracting State, it must submit to the EFSA, before commencing the offer, a notice of offer, in English and in writing, which contains a plan for marketing the units in that Contracting State (the country of destination),[99] the names of the classes of units to be marketed,[100] and a note as to whether the same management company markets the units of the fund in the country of destination as manages the fund in Estonia.[101] The management company must submit a notice of offer, and transcripts of the following documents,

[97] Article 65(1)(b), TFEU. See section 2.1.3.

[98] See the subsection '*The requirements for a successful public policy/security derogation*', in section 2.1.3.

[99] s.33¹(1)(1), IFA.

[100] s.33¹ (1)(2), IFA.

[101] s.33¹(1)(3), IFA.

to the EFSA: the fund rules,[102] the most recent audited annual report of the fund,[103] the latest half-yearly/quarterly report of the fund (if approved after the latest audited annual report),[104] a prospectus,[105] and a document entitled 'Key Investor Information'.[106]

The EFSA is to forward all of these documents to the financial supervision authority of the country of destination, together with its confirmation (in English) that the UCITS conforms to the requirements of the IFA, within ten working days of the receipt of these items.[107] The EFSA is to immediately notify the management company of submission of the documentation to the financial supervision authority of the country of destination.[108] The management company may commence the offer of the units from the day it receives the notice.[109]

The cross-border transfer of units in return for payment by investors constitutes a 'movement of capital' in Title IV of Annex I. Furthermore, the public offer of these units may be a 'movement of capital' under the introductory notes to Annex I.[110] The IFA does not specify grounds on which the EFSA or the financial supervision authority of the host Contracting State might prevent the public offer from taking place.[111]

---

[102] s.33^1(2)(1), IFA.

[103] s.33^1(2)(2), IFA.

[104] s.33^1(2)(3), IFA. The English translation of the IFA states: "the latest semi semi-annual report", which probably is an inadvertent duplication of the word 'semi', but may alternatively be an Estonian way of saying 'quarterly', i.e. a half of a half year.

[105] s.33^1(2)(4), IFA.

[106] s.33^1(2)(4), IFA.

[107] s.33^1(4), IFA.

[108] s.33^1(6), IFA.

[109] s.33^1(6), IFA.

[110] The Annex states: "The capital movements listed in this Nomenclature are taken to cover: – all the operations necessary for the purposes of capital movements: conclusion and performance of the transaction and related transfers. ...". One may argue that the public offer of units is necessary for the sale of the units to take place, and is therefore a necessary operation for the purposes of capital movements. However, the offer is prior to, and (also arguably), remote from, the sale of the units to investors, and might therefore not be considered to be part of the capital movement.

[111] Commission Regulation (EU) No 584/2010, which implements Directive 2009/65/EC, contains the specific conditions of the public offer and the principles of co-operation of the financial supervision authorities that is necessary for this purpose. The management company is to follow the format specified in Annex I to that Regulation for its preparation and submission of the notice of offer (s.33^1(9), IFA).

Consequently, there is only a restriction on the free movement of capital if the informational requirements impose it – which they do, given the substantial amount of data that the IFA requires the management company to submit to the EFSA.

To be justified, the restrictive measures must be necessary for the protection of interests that they are intended to guarantee, specific, objective, and known to the parties beforehand, proportionate, and the persons affected must have access to legal redress.[112] The interests to be protected are those of investors and potential investors in the units. It is reasonable that the investors should be aware of the fund rules, the information in the latest audited annual report of the fund, and the key information. These informational requirements are specific, objective and known to the parties beforehand, and are proportionate in the sense that they are the minimum that is reasonably necessary for potential investors to make an informed decision with respect to the purchase or non-purchase of the units.

However, the IFA does not require the EFSA to provide reasons for refusing to forward information to the financial supervision authority of the Contracting State in which the units are to be offered. Nor does the IFA provide the management company with the right to appeal to the Estonian courts against a decision to refuse to forward the information to the financial supervision authority of the Contracting State in which the units are to be offered. Thus, the management company does not have access to legal redress. Consequently, the informational requirements of section 33^1 of the IFA contravene Article 63 of the TFEU.

Sections 34 to 42^1: activities of foreign management companies in Estonia

A (legal) person who has the right to manage funds or institutions established for collective investment, may manage funds that are established in Estonia, and provide services[113] on the basis of the activity licence that is issued in the country in which it (the person) is founded, by establishing branches or providing cross-border services in Estonia.[114] Mandatory pension funds are not to be managed across borders.[115]

---

[112] See the subsection '*The requirements for a successful public policy/security derogation*', in section 2.1.3.

[113] These services comprise the management of a fund, the management of a portfolio of securities, providing investment advice, and the safekeeping of units of shares of a fund for a client (s.9(2), IFA).

[114] s.34(1), IFA.

[115] s.34(1^1), IFA.

In order to establish a branch in Estonia, a management company of a third country is required to apply for an authorisation from the EFSA.[116] Upon application for an authorisation to found a branch, the applicant is to submit a written petition,[117] the name and address of the management company,[118] information that concerns the managers of the management company and the managers of the branch,[119] information and documents that relate to shareholders who have qualifying holdings in the management company,[120] the scope of the management company's activity licence and information about the agency that issued this licence,[121] the branch's name and business address,[122] an official certificate

[116] s.35(1), IFA.

[117] s.35(2), IFA.

[118] s.35(2)(1), IFA.

[119] ss.35(2)(1^1) and 35(2)(4), IFA. This information comprises each manager's name, personal identification code (or date of birth), residence, educational background, list of places of employment and positions, a description of each manager's duties, and documents that certify the managers' trustworthiness and their compliance with the requirements of the IFA (s.14(6), IFA).

[120] s.35(2)(1^2), IFA. The IFA does not define 'qualifying holding'. This information and these documents include, a description of the company acquired, a curriculum vitae of the acquirer (if a natural person), a list of the acquirer's owners or members (if a legal person), information on the number of shares held by, or the size of the holding and the number of votes of, each owner or member, details (such as the name, registered office, and articles of association) of the acquirer (if a legal person), information on the managers of the acquirer (if a legal person), a confirmation that the persons who manage of the company have not been punished for a selection of offences (such as official misconduct or offence against property), a description of the acquirer's business activities, a description of the interests of persons connected with the acquirer, the last three annual reports of the acquirer, ratings that are required for assessing the financial circumstances of the acquirer, companies connected with the acquirer, and reports that are intended for the public (if the acquirer is a natural person), credit ratings issued to the acquirer (if the acquirer is a legal person), a description of the structure of the acquirer's group, data on the size of the shareholdings of the companies that belong to the group, the most recent three annual and auditor's reports of the group, documents that certify the financial status of the acquirer (if a natural person) during the last three years, information and documents that concern the sources of resources for the acquisition of a qualifying holding or an increase in a qualifying holding (including one that results in gaining control), a business plan and other items of relevance to the gaining (or the exercise) of control (for a management company that becomes a controlled company), and a review of the strategy applied in the management company (s.46(1), IFA).

[121] s.35(2)(2), IFA.

[122] s.35(2)(3), IFA.

that certifies the existence of the management company in its home jurisdiction,[123] a document that certifies the authority of the director of the branch or a copy of a resolution appointing the director,[124] a copy of the company's articles of association,[125] the telephone and fax numbers, e-mail address, and internet home page address, of the management company and of the branch,[126] the management company's audited annual reports for the two most recent financial years,[127] and the branch's business plan – which is to state all the services that it is to provide in Estonia.[128] A management company of a third country is also to provide to the EFSA the permission of the financial supervision authority of the company's home state to establish a branch in Estonia,[129] a confirmation issued by the financial supervision authority of the home state that the management company possesses a valid activity licence in its home country and that it conducts its activities in a correct way and in accordance with good practice,[130] and information from the home country's financial services authority on the financial circumstances of the management company – including the amount of own funds, and a description of the investor

---

[123] ss.35(2)(5), IFA, and 386(2)(1), Commercial Code.
[124] ss.35(2)(5), IFA, and 386(2)(3), Commercial Code.
[125] ss.35(2)(5), IFA, and 386(2)(4), Commercial Code.
[126] ss.35(2)(5), IFA, and 386(2)(5), Commercial Code.
[127] s.35(2)(6), IFA.
[128] s.35(2)(7), IFA. Subsection 35(2)(7) of the IFA requires the branch's business plan to satisfy "the requirements provided for in section 15 of this Act". Section 15 of the IFA refers to "[t]he business plan of a management company", which is to include a forecast and analysis of the significant economic indicators of the management company and the funds that it manages, a description of the company's management structure and of the rights, obligations and liability of persons who are involved in the management of the funds, and a description, forecast, and analysis, of the net turnover and expenditure of the management company by area of activity, the size of the management company's assets, share capital and shareholders' equity, the development of the organisational structure and technical administration of the management company, the organisation of the issue of units, the number and types of funds managed, the market value of the funds' assets, net asset value, rate of return of the funds' assets, the investment policy and structure of investments of the funds, the size and structure of the funds' management expenses, the rates for, and amount of the proceeds from, the issue and redemption fees of units, management fees, depositary's charges, the amount of the fixed overheads, and a list of other services that the management company provides (s.15(1), IFA).
[129] s.35(3)(1), IFA.
[130] s.35(3)(2), IFA.

protection scheme that is applicable to the unit-holders and clients of the funds that the management company manages in the home state.[131]

The establishment of a branch is a 'capital movement' in Title I of the nomenclature in Annex I. The requirement of prior authorisation to establish a branch in Estonia is a restriction in the free movement of capital.[132] As the prior authorisation is accompanied by many informational requirements, it is disproportionate, and, therefore, not justifiable under Article 65(1)(b) of the TFEU.[133]

The provisions of EU legislation that most closely correspond to section 35 of the IFA are Articles 37 and 39 of Directive 2011/61/EU, although they do not specifically mention the establishment of a branch.[134] Member States are to require non-EU AIFMs that intend to manage EU AIFs and/or market AIFs managed by them in the EU in accordance with Article 39 or 40 of Directive 2011/61/EU to acquire prior authorisation from the competent authorities of the home Member State in accordance with Article 37 of Directive 2011/61/EU.[135] Provided that the EU has carefully taken into account of the free movement of capital between Member States and third countries whilst enacting Directive 2011/61/EU, Article 64(2) of the TFEU deems the national provisions to be a justifiable limitation on the free movement of capital – as long as these rules are no more restrictive than the relevant Articles in the Directive.[136] Thus, the requirements of section 35 of the IFA must be carefully compared with the

---

[131] s.35(3), IFA.

[132] See, for example, *Eglise de Scientologie and Scientology International* [2000] ECR I-1335, in the subsection '*Public policy, public security, general interest, and prior authorisation*', in section 2.1.3.

[133] See section 2.1.3.

[134] Article 37 of Directive 2011/61/EU is entitled "Authorisation of non-EU-AIFMs intending to manage EU AIFs and/or market AIFs managed by them in the [European] Union in accordance with Article 39 or 40". Article 39 of Directive 2011/61/EU is entitled "Conditions for the marketing in the Union with a passport of EU AIFs managed by a non-EU AIFM". Section 35 of the IFA may also fall within the scope of the Directive 2009/65/EC (see section 2.2.6). The latter Directive does not provide detailed provisions for passporting to and from third countries; relations with third countries for UCITS are governed by Article 15 of Directive 2004/39/EC, which calls for equivalence in conditions for firms from third countries and those from EEA states (Article 9, Directive 2009/65/EC; Article 15, Directive 2004/39/EC).

[135] Article 37(1), Directive 2011/61/EU.

[136] See the subsection '*Derogations that apply only to capital movement to/from third countries*', in section 2.3.2.

content of Articles 7 and 8 of Directive 2011/61/EU,[137] subject to explicit exceptions from the standard authorisation process.[138]

The EFSA may refuse to grant an authorisation for the establishment of a branch in Estonia of a management company whose home state is a third country, if any of the grounds of refusal provided for in section 18 of the IFA are satisfied,[139] the financial supervision authority of a third country does not sufficiently supervise the applicant,[140] the financial supervision authority of a third country has no legal basis, or is not ready to for adequate and efficient co-operation with the EFSA,[141] the EFSA has reason for believing that it is impossible to verify or ensure the applicant's compliance to the necessary extent with the requirements provided by the IFA or other legislation,[142] or the requirements that are at least equal to

---

[137] See section 2.2.7.

[138] The authorisation is to be given in accordance with Chapter II of the AIFM (Authorisation of AIFMs: Articles 6 to 11), which is to apply subject to specified exceptions, such as the disapplication of Article 8(1)(e) of the AIFM. Article 8(1)(e) requires the head office and the registered office of the AIFM to be situated in the same EEA state. Article 37 of the AIFM also imposes conditions for authorisation that are additional to those in Chapter II, such as that the third country in which the non-EU AIFM is founded is not listed as a Non-Cooperative Country and Territory by the Financial Action Task Force (Articles 37(8)(d), 8(1)(e) and 37(7)(e), Directive 2011/61/EU).

[139] s.36(2), IFA. The EFSA may refuse to issue an activity licence to a management company on one or more of the following grounds: the applicant, managers, fund manager, shareholders, or auditor do not satisfy the requirements provided by the IFA (or legislation that is based on this Act), the resources for the full payment of the share capital of a public limited company being established are not provided, the applicant does not have the required resources or experience to successfully and continuously operate as a management company of a fund, close links between the applicant and another person prevent adequate supervision over the management company, requirements that arise from legislation or from the implementation of legislation of the country in which the persons with whom the applicant has close links is established prevent adequate supervision over the management company, information presented in a business plan is inadequate, the management company's internal rules are not sufficiently accurate or unambiguous for the regulation of the activities of the management company, the applicant has been punished for a specified offence (e.g. an offence against property), and/or the previous activity licence issued to the public limited company has been revoked (s.18, IFA). Section 18 of the IFA does not mention a 'branch'.

[140] s.36(2)(1), IFA.

[141] s.36(2)(2), IFA.

[142] s.36(2)(3), IFA.

those provided for a management company by the IFA do not apply to the activities of a management company of a third country.[143]

The establishment of a branch is a ‘capital movement’ in Title I of the nomenclature in Annex I. A refusal to grant authorisation restricts the free movement of capital. Some of the grounds in the paragraph above, such as that the financial supervision authority of a third country does not sufficiently supervise the applicant, provide discretion to the EFSA as to whether or not to grant an authorisation, which does not provide legal certainty as required by the derogation to the free movement of capital in Article 65(1)(b) of the TFEU.[144] As the applicant management company is situated in a third country, the restrictions to the free movement of capital in Article 36 of the IFA are justified under Article 64(2) of the TFEU, provided that the EU institutions carefully considered the objective of the free movement of capital whilst implementing the relevant Directive (either Directive 2009/65/EC or Directive 2011/61/EU), and that the national measures do not restrict free movement more than the equivalent provisions of the Directive do.[145]

A management company of a Contracting State that would like to establish a branch in Estonia is to inform the EFSA of this intention through the financial supervision authority of that State.[146] The following information and documents are to be submitted to the EFSA: a scheme of the branch’s operations (which shall contain information about all the services provided in Estonia and the organisational structure of the branch),[147] the branch’s business name and address,[148] the names of the branch’s managers,[149] a description of the investor protection scheme that applies to the clients and unit-holders of the funds that the management company manages in the Contracting State,[150] an attestation by the financial supervision authority of the Contracting State that it has issued an activity licence to the management company according to the provisions of the Directive concerning investment funds,[151] and explanations about the

---

[143] s.36(2)(4), IFA.
[144] For there to be legal certainty, the EEA state’s restrictive measures must be specific, objective, and known to the parties beforehand. See the subsection ‘*The requirements for a successful public policy/security derogation*’, in section 2.1.3.
[145] See sections 2.2.6, 2.2.7 and 2.3.2.
[146] s.38(1), IFA.
[147] s.38(1)(1), IFA.
[148] s.38(1)(2), IFA.
[149] s.38(1)(3), IFA.
[150] s.38(1)(4), IFA.
[151] s.38(1)(5), IFA.

scope of the management company's activity licence and restrictions on the types of UCITS managed (if the management company intends to manage UCITS founded in Estonia).[152] Within two months of receipt of this information, the EFSA may take a decision that determines the requirements that the management company is to observe in Estonia, and shall promptly inform the financial supervision authority of the Contracting State of this decision.[153]

The establishment of a branch is a 'capital movement' in Title I of the nomenclature in Annex I. The information requirements in the above paragraph limit the free movement of capital. To be justified under Article 65(1)(b) of the TFEU, the restrictive measures must be necessary for the protection of interests that they are intended to guarantee, be proportionate, observe the requirements of legal certainty, and the persons affected must have access to legal redress.[154] Although the informational requirements are proportionate, the lack of criteria on which the decision of the EFSA is to be taken does not give legal certainty, and the applicant is not explicitly provided with legal redress, i.e. a national provision requiring the EFSA to supply a formal statement of reasons for its decision, and one that enables the decision to be subject to review by the Estonian courts. Therefore, section 38 of the IFA is an unjustified restriction on the free movement of capital.

A management company registered in a third country that wishes to provide cross-border services in Estonia shall apply for an authorisation from the EFSA.[155] In order to apply for this authorisation, the management company is to submit to the EFSA a petition, together with the following information and documents: the management company's name and address,[156] the scope of the activity licence that the third country's financial supervision authority has issued to the management company,[157] information that concerns the authority which issued the activity licence,[158] an official certificate that certifies the existence of the management company in its home jurisdiction,[159] a document that certifies the authority of the director of the branch or a copy of a resolution

[152] s.38(1)(5), IFA.
[153] s.38(2), IFA.
[154] See the subsection '*The requirements for a successful public policy/security derogation*', in section 2.1.3.
[155] s.39(1), IFA.
[156] s.39(2)(1), IFA.
[157] s.39(2)(2), IFA.
[158] s.39(2)(2), IFA.
[159] ss.39(2)(3), IFA, and 386(2)(1), Commercial Code.

appointing the director,[160] a copy of the company's articles of association,[161] the telephone and fax numbers, e-mail address, and internet home page address, of the management company and of the branch,[162] the audited annual reports of the management company for the most recent two financial years,[163] and the business plan that states all the services which the management company provides in Estonia.[164] The management company shall also submit the following information to the EFSA: the permission of the financial supervision authority of the home state to provide cross-border services to Estonia,[165] confirmation of the financial supervision authority of the home state that the management company possesses a valid activity licence in its home country and that the company pursues its activities in a correct way and in accordance with good practice,[166] and information provided by the financial supervision authority of the home state as to the management company's financial situation, including the amount of own funds, a description of the investor protection scheme that is applicable to the clients and unit-holders of the funds which the management company manages in the home country.[167]

The acquisition by residents of units of foreign companies (whether or not they are dealt in on a stock exchange) are 'capital movements' in Title IV of the nomenclature in Annex I. The requirement for prior authorisation by the EFSA in the above paragraph limits the free movement of capital.[168] This restriction is not justified under Article 65(1)(b) of the TFEU, because, together with the informational requirements in the above paragraph, it is disproportionate.[169]

The restriction to the free movement of capital that section 39 of the IFA imposes may be justified by Article 64(2) of the TFEU, provided that

---

[160] ss.39(2)(3), IFA, and 386(2)(3), Commercial Code. This information concerns the establishment of a branch in Estonia, rather than the provision of cross-border services. It is also referred to in section 35(2)(5) of the IFA (see note 124).

[161] ss.39(2)(3), IFA, and 386(2)(4), Commercial Code. See notes 160 and 125.

[162] ss.39(2)(3), IFA, and 386(2)(5), Commercial Code. See notes 160 and 126.

[163] s.39(2)(4), IFA.

[164] s.39(2)(5), IFA. The business plan must satisfy the requirements that are contained in section 15 of the IFA. See note 128.

[165] s.39(3)(1), IFA.

[166] s.39(3)(2), IFA.

[167] s.39(3)(3), IFA.

[168] See, for example, *Eglise de Scientologie and Scientology International* [2000] ECR I-1335, in the subsection '*Public policy, public security, general interest, and prior authorisation*' in section 2.1.3.

[169] See the subsection '*The requirements for a successful public policy/security derogation*', in section 2.1.3.

the EU institutions carefully took into account the objective of the free movement of capital while enacting the relevant Directives (2009/65/EC and 2011/61/EU), and that section 39 of the IFA does not hinder the free movement of capital more than do the equivalent provisions in these Directives.[170] Article 9(1) of Directive 2009/65/EC states that relations with third countries are governed by Article 15 of Directive 2004/39/EC, which considers the access of firms in the EEA to markets in the third country – but not the access of companies in the third country to the EEA. Directive 2011/61/EU does not contain an equivalent provision to the contents of section 39 of the IFA. Hence, this national provision goes beyond the requirements of Directive 2009/65/EC and Directive 2011/65/EU. Therefore the restriction on the free movement of capital that section 39 of the IFA imposes cannot be justified by Article 64(2) of the TFEU.

The EFSA may refuse to grant an authorisation for the supply of cross-border services on any of the grounds in section 18 of the IFA.[171] It may also refuse to provide an authorisation for the supply of these services if a third country's financial supervision authority does not ensure adequate supervision over the applicant,[172] or has no legal basis, possibilities, or preparation for sufficient, efficient co-operation with the EFSA,[173] the EFSA has reason to believe that it is impossible to verify the applicant's compliance to the necessary extent with the requirements of national

---

170 See section 2.3.2.

171 s.40(2), IFA. The EFSA may refuse to issue an activity licence to a management company, or grant it the right to provide services , if the applicant, the managers, the fund manager, the auditor, or the shareholders, do not satisfy the requirements that the IFA (or legislation based on this Act) provides, the applicant has insufficient resources for the full payment of the share capital of a public limited company being established, the applicant does not have the required resources or experience to operate as a management company of a fund of the relevant type with success and continuity, close links between the applicant and another person preclude adequate supervision over the management company, the requirements that arise from legislation (or its implementation) of the country in which the persons with whom the applicant has close links is established prevent adequate supervision over the management company, the information in the business plan is insufficient or inadequate, the management company's internal rules are insufficiently accurate or clear for regulation of the management company's activities, the applicant has been punished for a specified offence (such as an offence against property), or the most recent activity licence issued to the public limited company has been revoked (s.18, IFA).

172 s.40(2)(1), IFA.

173 s.40(2)(2), IFA.

legislation,[174] or requirements that are at least equal to the IFA's requirements for a management company do not apply to the activities of a third country's management company.[175]

The EFSA may revoke an authorisation on any of the grounds in the above paragraph, or if the circumstances stated in section 22 of the IFA become evident.[176] The EFSA may refuse to withdraw an authorisation for the supply of cross-border services, if the clients of a management company of a third country have claims against this company, or if the

---

[174] s.40(2)(3), IFA.

[175] s.40(2)(4), IFA.

[176] s.40(3), IFA. The EFSA may withdraw an activity licence if a management company has not started to manage the fund with one year of the issue of its activity licence or has not managed any funds or assets of funds for a year, false information has been submitted to the EFSA, the management company does not satisfy the requirements for the issue of activity licences, the managers, the fund manager, the auditor, or the shareholders of the applicant do not satisfy the requirements under the IFA (or legislation based on this Act), close links between the applicant and another person preclude adequate supervision over the management company, the requirements arising from legislation (or its implementation) of the country in which the persons with whom the applicant has close links is established prevent adequate supervision over the management company, a management company has frequently contravened the provisions of legislation that regulates its activities, a management company or its manager has been punished for specified offences (such as an offence against property), a management company has published materially inaccurate or misleading information, a management company's activities significantly damage the interests of the fund, unit-holders, clients, or shareholders of a fund that has been established as a public limited company or adversely affect the normal functioning of the securities market, a management company that manages a portfolio of securities, advertises investments, or provides for the safekeeping of a fund's units fails to comply with the prudential requirements of the IFA (or legislation based on this Act) or pay the contributions to the Investor Protection Sectoral Fund that are prescribed in the Guarantee Fund Act, a management company has contravened the rules of a common fund that is managed by the management company if the unit-holders' interests may be damaged as a consequence, a management company has not implemented one of the EFSA's precepts, the amount of own funds of an asset management company does not satisfy the requirements of the IFA (or legislation based on this Act), the management company is involved in money laundering or breaches the legislative procedure for precluding money laundering and terrorist financing, or a management company has contravened the conditions that are provided for in the legislation of the Contracting State or established by the Contracting State's financial supervision authority if it wishes to manage UCITS in that State (ss. 22, 18(1)(4), 18(1)(4^1), 18(1)(5), 9(2) and 30(6), IFA).

revocation of the authorisation damages the fund or the fund's unit-holders or shareholders.[177]

Cross-border services are 'capital movements' in Title IV of the nomenclature in Annex I. The refusal to grant an authorisation, or the revocation of an authorisation, in relation to cross-border services, is a limitation of the free movement of capital. This restriction is not justifiable under Article 65(1)(b) of the TFEU, because grounds for restriction in the above two paragraphs are disproportionate, and do not always provide legal certainty,[178] and because the applicant or authorisation-holder is not provided with legal redress in respect of an adverse decision.[179]

The measures in section 40 of the IFA may be justified under Article 64(2) of the TFEU, if the EU institutions carefully consider the objective of the free movement of capital whilst enacting the relevant legislation (Directives 2009/65/EC and 2011/61/EU), and if the national rules do not limit the free movement of capital between EEA states and third countries more than the equivalent provisions of these Directives.[180] As stated above, Article 9(1) of Directive 2009/65/EC holds that relations with third countries are governed by Article 15 of Directive 2004/39/EC, which does not consider access of companies in the third country to the EEA. Directive 2011/61/EU does not include an equivalent provision to the contents of section 40 of the IFA. Hence, this domestic rule goes beyond the requirements of Directive 2009/65/EC and Directive 2011/65/EU. Therefore the restriction on the free movement of capital that section 40 of the IFA imposes cannot be justified by Article 64(2) of the TFEU.

A management company of a Contracting State that wishes to supply cross-border services in Estonia is to inform the EFSA thereof via that

---

[177] s.40(4), IFA.

[178] For example, the EFSA may refuse to grant an authorisation to a management company from a third country to provide cross-border services to Estonia on the ground that the third country's financial supervision authority has no legal basis for adequate, efficient co-operation with the EFSA. It is the EFSA who decides as to whether the third country's authority has a legal basis. As the EFSA (to my knowledge) has not published criteria according to which they decide whether or not a third country's financial supervision authority has a legal basis, the EFSA has discretion in making this decision. Hence, the grounds for refusal of an application for an authorisation to provide cross-border services do not provide legal certainty to the applicant.

[179] See the subsection '*The requirements for a successful public policy/security derogation*', in section 2.1.3.

[180] See section 2.3.2. As the Single Market Directives apply to the Contracting Parties to the EEA Agreement (see chapter 2, note 34), it is the movement between EEA states and third countries that is relevant in this context.

State's financial supervision authority.[181] The following information must be submitted to the EFSA: a scheme of operations that contains information about the services to be provided in Estonia,[182] a description of the investor protection scheme that applies to the unit-holders and clients of the funds that the management company manages in the Contracting State,[183] an attestation by the financial supervision authority of the Contracting State that it issued an activity licence to the management company according to the Directive regarding investment funds,[184] explanations that concern the scope of the management company's activity licence,[185] and restriction on the types of UCITS managed (if the management company intends to manage UCITS established in Estonia).[186]

Cross-border services are 'capital movements' in Title IV of the nomenclature in Annex I. The information to be submitted to the EFSA, stated in the previous paragraph, is a restriction on the free movement of capital. To be justifiable under Article 65(1)(b) of the TFEU, the requirement to supply this information must be necessary for the protection of interests that it is intended to guarantee, be proportionate, observe the requirements of legal certainty, and provide the applicant with access to legal redress.[187] Whilst this requirement is proportionate and provides legal certainty, it does not supply the applicant with legal redress – the IFA neither contains a provision that enables the applicant to appeal against an adverse decision in the Estonian courts, nor requires the EFSA to provide reasons for refusing to grant permission to the management company to supply cross-border services. Thus, section 42 of the IFA contravenes the free movement of capital under Article 63(1) of the TFEU.

A management company of a Contracting State that would like to manage an UCITS established in Estonia is to submit the following information and documents to the EFSA: a depositary contract and annexes to it,[188] and information about the delegation of arrangements that relate to the investment of the assets of the fund,[189] organisation of the

---

[181] s.42(1), IFA.
[182] s.42(1)(1), IFA.
[183] s.42(1)(2), IFA.
[184] s.42(1)(3), IFA.
[185] s.42(1)(3), IFA.
[186] s.42(1)(3), IFA.
[187] See the subsection '*The requirements for a successful public policy/security derogation*', in section 2.1.3.
[188] s.42^1(1)(1), IFA.
[189] ss.42^1(1)(2) and 10(1)(1), IFA.

issue and redemption of shares or units of the fund,[190] issue of documentation that proves the right of ownership to the unit-holders or shareholders of the fund (if necessary),[191] communication of required information to the unit-holders or shareholders of the fund and the supply of other services to clients,[192] keeping account of the fund's assets and organisation of accounting of a common fund,[193] determination of the fund's net asset value,[194] organisation of maintenance of a register of the units or the shares of the fund,[195] calculation of the fund's income and organisation of the distribution of the income between the unit-holders or shareholders of the fund,[196] monitoring the compliance of the management company's and fund's activities with the IFA and other legislation,[197] and activities directly related to those specified above.[198]

The EFSA may make a resolution, which prohibits a management company of another Contracting State from managing UCITS established in Estonia if the management company does not comply with the requirements of the IFA for this activity (either across the Estonian border or by the establishment of a branch in Estonia, as appropriate),[199] the management company does not hold an activity licence for the management of the UCITS for which the information and documents required by subsection 42^1 of the IFA were submitted,[200] or the information or documents that the management company submits are incomplete or insufficient.[201] Before making this resolution, the EFSA must consult with the financial supervision authority of the other Contracting State.[202]

The acquisition by non-residents of units of national collective undertakings are a 'capital movement' in Title IV of the nomenclature in Annex I. The establishment of a branch is a 'capital movement' in Title I of the nomenclature in Annex I. As an application to manage UCITS in

---

[190] ss.42^1(1)(2) and 10(1)(2), IFA.
[191] ss.42^1(1)(2) and 10(1)(3), IFA.
[192] ss.42^1(1)(2) and 10(1)(4), IFA.
[193] ss.42^1(1)(2) and 10(1)(6), IFA.
[194] ss.42^1(1)(2) and 10(1)(7), IFA.
[195] ss.42^1(1)(2) and 10(1)(8), IFA.
[196] ss.42^1(1)(2) and 10(1)(9), IFA.
[197] ss.42^1(1)(2) and 10(1)(10), IFA.
[198] ss.42^1(1)(2) and 10(1)(11), IFA.
[199] ss.42^1(4)(1) and 34(6)-(8), IFA.
[200] ss.42^1(4)(2), IFA.
[201] ss.42^1(4)(3), IFA.
[202] ss.42^1(5), IFA.

Estonia is to be followed by the provision of cross-border services or the establishment of a branch in Estonia, it is potentially a capital movement. The documentary requirements in subsection 42^{1}(1) of the IFA restrict the free movement of capital. The making of a resolution to preclude the management company from managing UCITS founded in Estonia also limits the free movement of capital.

These restrictions cannot be justified as under Article 65(1)(b) of the TFEU, because the IFA provides no access to legal redress.[203] Hence, they breach the free movement of capital stated in Article 63 of the TFEU.

Chapter 4 Division 9^{1} – sections 173^{1} to 173^15: Merger of UCITS

This Division of Chapter 4 (Common Fund) of the IFA is to apply to the following mergers: merger of UCITS founded in Estonia, if the units of at least one UCITS taking part in the merger are offered in another Contracting State,[204] and merger of one UCITS established in Estonia with another UCITS founded in another Contracting State (hereafter a 'cross-border merger').[205]

UCITS shall enter into an agreement for their merger (hereafter a 'merger agreement').[206] A merger agreement must set out at least the following information: the merger technique and the types of the UCITS that are merging,[207] the reason for the merger,[208] the merger's effect on the unit-holders of both the UCITS to be acquired and the acquiring UCITS,[209] the exchange ratio of the units of the UCITS to be acquired,[210] criteria for the valuation of the UCITS' assets and liabilities on the date of computing the exchange ratio,[211] the method of calculating the exchange ratio,[212] the

---

[203] See the subsection '*The requirements for a successful public policy/security derogation*', in section 2.1.3. As the EFSA has a discretion to decide that the information submitted is 'insufficient' as a ground for a resolution, then there may be a lack of legal certainty. However, the possibility for this is reduced by the IFA's requirement for the EFSA to consult with the financial supervision authority of the other Contracting State, before making the resolution.

[204] s.173^{1}(1)(1), IFA,

[205] s.173^{1}(1)(2), IFA. As subsection 173^{1}(3) of the IFA refers to participation "in a cross-border merger as an acquiring UCITS", and as subsection 173^{1}(4) of the IFA refers to participation "in a cross-border merger as an UCITS being acquired", a 'merger' in this context includes acquisitions as well as true mergers.

[206] s.173^{2}(1), IFA.

[207] s.173^{2}(2)(1), IFA.

[208] s.173^{2}(2)(2), IFA.

[209] s.173^{2}(2)(3), IFA.

[210] s.173^{2}(2)(4), IFA.

[211] s.173^{2}(2)(4), IFA.

merger's planned effective date,[213] and the rules that are applicable to the transfer of assets and the exchange of units.[214]

In order to merge funds, the management company of the UCITS to be acquired is to apply for an authorisation from the EFSA (hereafter 'authorisation for merger').[215] To apply for an authorisation for merger, the management company is to submit a written application and the following documents and information: the merger agreement,[216] the consent of the depositary of each UCITS involved in the merger,[217] an accurate and suitable document that specifies the circumstances of the merger.[218]

The EFSA is to take the decision to grant authorisation for a cross-border merger, if an UCITS founded in Estonia takes part in a cross-border merger as an UCITS to be acquired.[219] On applying for an authorisation for a cross-border merger, the management company of the UCITS to be acquired is to submit the application specified in subsection 173^4(2) of the IFA,[220] which includes the prospectus and essential information of the acquiring UCITS if this undertaking was founded in another Contracting State.[221]

When processing an application for the authorisation of a merger, the EFSA is to verify the information submitted, and assess the extent to which the merger and the information provided is in line with the rights of the unit-holders of the UCITS to be acquired, and with the requirements contained in the IFA and in legislation enacted on the basis thereof.[222] If

---

212 s.173^2(2)(5), IFA.
213 s.173^2(2)(6), IFA.
214 s.173^2(2)(7), IFA.
215 s.173^4(1), IFA.
216 s.173^4(2)(1), IFA.
217 ss.173^4(2)(2) and 173^3(1), IFA.
218 ss.173^4(2)(3) and 173^10(1), IFA. Subsection 173^10(1) of the IFA refers to this document as "information to be provided to unit-holders". This information shall provide explanations of and reasons for the merger, the possible effect of the merger on unit-holders, unit-holders' rights that relate to the merger, terms and conditions of the merger document, key information concerning the acquiring UCITS, and terms and conditions of making payments to unit-holders of the UCITS that is to be acquired (s.173^11(1), IFA). A key information document of an acquiring UCITS is to be appended to the information that is supplied to the unit-holders of the UCITS to be acquired (s.173^13(1), IFA).
219 s.173^5(1), IFA.
220 See the preceding paragraph.
221 s.173^5(2), IFA.
222 s.173^6(1), IFA.

the UCITS to be acquired did not submit, upon application for an authorisation for merger, all the documents and information that subsection 173^4(2) of the IFA specifies, or if these documents and information are incomplete or were not prepared in accordance with the requirements, then the EFSA may order the applicant to remove the deficiencies within ten working days of its receipt of the application.[223] In the case of cross-border mergers, the EFSA must send a transcript of each application for merger to the financial supervision authority of the home state of the acquiring UCITS, immediately after receiving all of the required documents from the UCITS to be acquired (or elimination of the deficiencies).[224]

The EFSA is to notify the management company and the depositary of the UCITS to be acquired of the grant or refusal of the authorisation for merger within 20 working days of the receipt of the application.[225] In addition, the EFSA is to inform the acquiring UCITS and, if applicable, the financial supervision authority of the home state of the UCITS to be acquired of the decision on the grant or refusal of an authorisation for cross-border merger.[226]

If an UCITS founded in Estonia participates in a cross-border merger as an acquiring UCITS, the EFSA must assess, on the basis of a transcript of the application for authorisation for merger (provided by the financial supervision authority of the home state of the UCITS to be acquired) whether the information provided is in line with the rights of the unit-holders of the acquiring UCITS and with the request specified in the IFA or its subordinate legislation.[227] The EFSA must demand any changes with 15 working days of the receipt of the transcript,[228] and is to notify the financial supervision authority of the home state of the UCITS to be acquired immediately of the submission of this demand.[229] An acquiring UCITS must submit changes in the information in a reasonable time, as the EFSA defines it.[230] The EFSA is to notify the financial supervision authority of the home state of the UCITS to be acquired within 20 days of the receipt of these changes, whether the information provided to the unit-

[223] s.173^6(2), IFA.
[224] s.173^6(3), IFA.
[225] s.173^6(6), IFA.
[226] s.173^6(7), IFA.
[227] s.173^7(1), IFA.
[228] s.173^7(2), IFA.
[229] s.173^7(4), IFA.
[230] s.173^7(3), IFA.

holders of the acquiring UCITS is compatible with the requirements of the IFA.[231]

The EFSA may refuse to grant authorisation for merger, if the merger conditions of UCITS do not comply with legislative requirements,[232] the documents and information submitted to the EFSA are incorrect, misleading, or incomplete,[233] the changes made in the information supplied to the unit-holders have not been submitted to the EFSA,[234] the information provided to the unit-holders does not comply with the provisions of the IFA,[235] or no notification has been made upon merger of the UCITS about the offer of the units of the acquiring UCITS in the Contracting States in which the units of the UCITS to be acquired are offered.[236] In addition, the EFSA may refuse to provide an authorisation for cross-border merger if the financial supervision authority of the home state of the acquiring UCITS gives notification that the information that is supplied to the unit-holders of the acquiring UCITS does not satisfy the requirements.[237]

Unit-holders of an UCITS to be acquired and an acquiring UCITS have the right to request redemption or exchange of units for the units of another UCITS with similar investment policy, and managed by the same management company or by any other company with which the management company is connected by common management or qualifying holding.[238] The right to redeem or exchange of these units shall apply to the unit-holders of the UCITS to be acquired and the acquiring UCITS, as of the information provided to unit-holders specified in subsection 173^10(1) of the IFA.[239] The EFSA may request suspension of the issue or redemption of the units of the UCITS, if this is necessary for the protection of the legitimate interests of the unit-holders of at least one UCITS participating in the merger.[240]

---

[231] s.173^7(4), IFA.
[232] s.173^8(1), IFA.
[233] s.173^8(1)(1), IFA.
[234] s.173^8(1)(2), IFA.
[235] s.173^8(1)(2), IFA.
[236] s.173^8(1)(3), IFA.
[237] s.178^8(2), IFA. The national provision refers to “the requirements”. In line with s.178^8(1)(1), considered above, this (probably) means “the requirements provided by legislation”.
[238] s.173^14(1), IFA.
[239] See above in this subsection.
[240] s.173^14(4), IFA.

The acquisition of existing undertakings is a 'capital movement' in Title I of the nomenclature in Annex I. The informational requirements for the merger, and the grounds for refusing authorisation for it, limit the free movement of capital. To be justified under Article 65(1)(b) of the TFEU, the restrictive measures must be necessary for the protection of interests that they are intended to guarantee, be proportionate i.e. not attainable by less restrictive measures, observe the requirements of legal certainty – i.e. be specific, objective, and know to the parties beforehand, and the persons affected by the measures must have access to legal redress – i.e. a statement of reasons and a right of appeal to the national courts.[241] The measures are proportionate and provide legal certainty. However, the persons affected by the measures do not have access to legal redress, i.e. the IFA does not require the EFSA to provide a reason for refusing authorisation, and the participants in the proposed merger are not supplied with a right to appeal against the decision in the national courts. Hence, Division 9^1 of Chapter 4 of the IFA restricts the free movement of capital, contrary to Article 63 of the TFEU.

Chapter 5 Division 6: Merger, Division, Transformation and Liquidation of Fund

Division 6 of Chapter 5 of the IFA provides for the merger, division and transformation of a fund. A fund is not to be transformed into a company of a different type.[242] Furthermore, the division of funds is prohibited.[243]

Funds may be merged according to the provisions of Chapter 31 of the Commercial Code, unless otherwise provided for in Division 6 of Chapter 5 of the IFA.[244] A fund that is entered in the commercial register of Estonia may be merged only with a fund that is established according to the law of a Contracting State.[245]

Division 6 of Chapter 31 of the Commercial Code considers cross-border mergers. A public limited company or private limited company that is registered in the Estonian commercial register may combine with another limited liability company that is established on the basis of a law of another State that is a Contracting Party to the EEA Agreement, which conforms to the requirements of Article 2.1 of Directive 2005/56/EC of

[241] See the subsection '*The requirements for a successful public policy/security derogation*', in section 2.1.3.
[242] s.210(1), IFA.
[243] s.210(2), IFA.
[244] s.211(1), IFA.
[245] s.211(2), IFA.

the European Parliament and of the Council on cross-border mergers of limited liability companies,[246] and whose registered office, location of the board of directors, or principal place of business, is in a Contracting State.[247] The provisions of Chapter 31 apply to the participation in a cross-border merger of companies that are registered, or subject to registration, in the Estonian commercial register, unless otherwise provided by laws that concern cross-border merger.[248]

The merger agreement is to state the business names and registered offices of the companies to be merged,[249] an agreement to transfer all of the assets of the company being acquired to the acquiring company in exchange for a transfer of the acquiring company's shares,[250] the share exchange ratio for the companies and the amount of any additional payments,[251] the terms and conditions of transfer of the shares of the acquiring company,[252] the date as of which the transferred shares are to grant the rights to a share of the profit of the acquiring company and the special conditions that affect this right,[253] the rights that the acquiring company are to grant to the partners or shareholders of the company being acquired,[254] the consequences of merger for the employees of the company to be acquired,[255] the date as of which the transactions of the company to be acquired are deemed to be undertaken by the acquiring company,[256] the remuneration paid to the auditor of the merger agreement,[257] the advantages provided in connection with the merger to the members of the management boards and supervisory boards of the companies or the

[246] Article 2(1) of Directive 2005/56/EC states "For the purposes of this Directive: 1) 'limited liability company', hereinafter referred to as 'company', means: (a) a company as referred to in Article 1 of Directive 68/151/EEC ..., or a company with a share capital and having legal personality, possessing separate assets which alone serve to cover its debts and subject under the national law governing it to conditions concerning guarantees such as are provided for by Directive 68/151/EEC for the protection of the interests of members and others;".

[247] s.433^1(1), Commercial Code.

[248] s.433^1(2), Commercial Code.

[249] ss.433^2(1) and 392(1)(1), Commercial Code.

[250] ss.433^2(1) and 392(1)(1^1), Commercial Code.

[251] ss.433^2(1) and 392(1)(2), Commercial Code.

[252] ss.433^2(1) and 392(1)(3), Commercial Code.

[253] ss.433^2(1) and 392(1)(4), Commercial Code.

[254] ss.433^2(1) and 392(1)(5), Commercial Code.

[255] ss.433^2(1) and 392(1)(6), Commercial Code.

[256] ss.433^2(1) and 392(1)(7), Commercial Code.

[257] ss.433^2(1) and 392(1)(8), Commercial Code.

partners who are entitled to represent the companies,[258] the types of the acquiring company and the company being acquired,[259] the specifics for performance of any right to receive a share of the profit,[260] information that concerns the evaluation of the assets to be transferred to the acquiring company,[261] the dates of the financial instruments that are used to determine the terms and conditions for the merger,[262] and the data that concern employees' participation in the management of the company (if the law provides for this).[263] If the acquiring company is under the jurisdiction of another Contracting State, the shareholder or partner of a company being acquired (which is entered in the Estonian commercial register) who does not agree to the merger resolution has the right, pursuant to the procedure provided in section 404 of the Commercial Code,[264] to transfer the shares thereof, or to demand that the acquiring company acquire the exchanged share(s) of the shareholder or partner for monetary compensation.[265]

In the instance of a cross-border merger of a company that is registered in the commercial register of Estonia, if the acquiring company is under the jurisdiction of another Contracting State, the creditors of the public or private limited company have the right, within two months of receiving the notice specified in subsection 419(4) of the Commercial Code,[266] to

---

[258] ss.433²(1) and 392(1)(8), Commercial Code.
[259] s.433²(1)(1), Commercial Code.
[260] s.433²(1)(2), Commercial Code.
[261] s.433²(1)(3), Commercial Code.
[262] s.433²(1)(4), Commercial Code.
[263] s.433²(1)(5), Commercial Code.
[264] Upon the merger of companies of different classes, a shareholder or partner of the company being acquired who opposes the merger resolution may, within two months of entry of the merger in the commercial register of the registered office of the acquiring company, demand that the acquiring company acquire the exchanged share(s) of the shareholder or partner for monetary compensation. This compensation is to be equal to the sum of money that the shareholder or partner would have received from the distribution of the remaining assets upon liquidation of the company, if the company had been wound up at the time of the merger resolution (s.404(1), IFA).
[265] s.433^7, Commercial Code.
[266] The management board shall publish in the official publication *Ametlikud Teandaaded* a notice that concerns the entry into the merger agreement. This notice is to specify where, or at which world wide web homepage address, it is possible to examine the merger agreement, and the three preceding annual reports, the merger reports, and the auditor's reports of each merging company (ss. 419(4) and 419(1), Commercial Code).

submit a claim for the receipt of a security.[267] Only a creditor who is not able to demand satisfaction of his/her claims, and who provides proof that the merger is likely to endanger the satisfaction of these claims, has the right to receive the security provided in subsection 433^8(2) of the Commercial Code.[268]

If a company that is registered in the Estonian commercial register participates in a cross-border merger as the company being acquired, the registrar is to issue a certificate to the company that confirms that the company being acquired has performed the required pre-merger acts, and that the merger has been entered in the commercial register.[269] In addition, an entry must be made in the commercial register of the company being acquired, which states that the merger is deemed to have taken place pursuant to the law of the Contracting State under whose jurisdiction the acquiring company falls.[270] After receiving a notice about the merger having taken place from the competent authority of the Contracting State under whose jurisdiction the acquiring company falls, the registrar is to make an entry in the commercial register concerning the date on which, according to the notice received, the merger took place, and is to inform the registrar of the Estonian Central Register of Securities (if the shares of the company being acquired are registered here).[271] Having performed these acts, the registrar is to forward electronically all the documents that have been submitted to it concerning the company being acquired to the competent authority of the Contracting State under whose law the acquiring company falls.[272]

If a company that is registered in, or to be registered in, the Estonian commercial register, participates in a cross-border merger as the acquiring company, then the company being acquired that falls under the jurisdiction of the other Contracting State is to submit to the registrar the merger agreement, and an application by the competent authority of that Contracting State, which states that the requirements for merger have been satisfied and pre-merger acts have been concluded, with respect to the company being acquired.[273] In addition, the registrar of the registered office of the acquiring company shall immediately provide notice of the merger entry to the competent authority of the other Contracting State, and shall inform

[267] s.433^8(2), Commercial Code.
[268] s.433^8(3), Commercial Code.
[269] s.433^9(2), Commercial Code.
[270] s.433^9(4), Commercial Code.
[271] s.433^9(4), Commercial Code.
[272] s.433^9(5), Commercial Code.
[273] s.433^9(6), Commercial Code.

the registrar of the Estonian Central Register of Securities (if the shares of the acquiring company are registered here).[274]

An Estonian fund may merge as an acquiring fund with a public limited company of another Contracting State that is not a fund, in compliance with the requirements of the IFA and of the Commercial Code.[275] The management company is to request an authorisation for the merger of the fund and the public limited company from the EFSA, within ten days after the merger resolution has been passed.[276] In order to apply for an authorisation for merger, a management company is to submit a written petition[277] and the following documents and information to the EFSA: the merger agreement,[278] copies of the merger resolutions and the respective minutes of the general meetings of the merging public limited company and the acquiring fund,[279] the merger report,[280] the auditor's report about the merger,[281] information concerning the submission of claims specified in subsection 398(1) of the Commercial Code (or the absence thereof),[282] the opinion of the management company that manages the acquiring fund,[283] the consent of the depositary to the merger (if the fund has a depositary),[284] the reasons why the fund and the public limited company need to be merged,[285] and a business plan that satisfies the requirements of section 194 of the IFA.[286]

---

[274] s.433^9(7), Commercial Code.

[275] s.212(1), IFA.

[276] s.212(2), IFA. In this English translation of the IFA, subsection 212(2) of this Act refers to "private limited company". As section 212 of the IFA is entitled "Merger of fund with another public limited company", subsection 212(2) of the IFA should refer to 'public limited company'.

[277] s.212(3), IFA.

[278] s.212(3)(1), IFA.

[279] s.212(3)(2), IFA.

[280] s.212(3)(3), IFA.

[281] s.212(3)(4), IFA.

[282] s.212(3)(5), IFA. Under subsection 398(1) of the Commercial Code, a court may declare invalid a merger resolution that is in conflict with the law, the partnership agreement, or the articles of association, on the petition of a partner, if the request is submitted within one month from when the resolution is made.

[283] s.212(3)(7), IFA.

[284] s.212(3)(8), IFA.

[285] s.212(3)(9), IFA.

[286] s.212(3)(10), IFA. The business plan of a fund is to set out a description of the fund's management structure, and of the rights, obligations and liability of members of the fund's management board, and a forecast and analysis of all the fund's important economic indicators, including the fund's net turnover and expenditure by area of activity, the size of the assets, share capital, and

The EFSA is to take the decision to grant or refuse an authorisation for merger within two months after the receipt of the written petition, but not later than within one month after the receipt of all of the necessary information and documents.[287] If approval of the amendments to the articles of association is also applied for upon merger, the EFSA shall take, together with the decision to grant an authorisation, a decision on approval of the amendments to the articles of association as provided by section 198 of the IFA.[288] The EFSA is to promptly inform the management company of a decision to grant or refuse an authorisation for merger.[289]

The EFSA may refuse to grant an authorisation for merger if the objectives of the activities and the investment policy of the acquiring fund and the public limited company being acquired differ substantially,[290] the merger agreement contains conditions the occurrence or non-occurrence of which might damage the interest of the fund's shareholders,[291] the merger would contravene the limitations on investment that are provided by the IFA, legislation issued on the basis of the IFA, or the articles of association,[292] other circumstances provided for in section 196 of the IFA arise,[293] or the merger of the fund and the public limited company may harm the legitimate interests of the shareholders for other reasons.[294]

---

shareholders' equity of the fund, organisation of the issue of shares, the market value, net asset value, and rate of return of the fund's assets, the investment policy and structure of fund's investments, the size and structure of the fund's management expenses, the rates of management fees and depositary's charges, and the amount of fixed overheads (s.194(1), IFA).

[287] s.213(2), IFA.

[288] s.213(3), IFA. Subsection 198(1) of the IFA applies the conditions in sections 195 and 196 of the IFA for approval on the foundation of a fund, to the approval of amendments to the articles of association of a fund and the decision to register these amendments. The decision on approval of amendments to the articles of association of a fund is to be added to the petition for entry of amendments to the articles of association of the fund in the commercial register (s.198(2), IFA).

[289] s.213(4), IFA.

[290] s.214(1), IFA.

[291] s.214(2), IFA.

[292] s.214(3), IFA.

[293] s.214(4), IFA. These circumstances are as follows: the fund, or management of the fund, does not satisfy the requirements of the IFA, a public offer of shares of the fund does not comply with the requirements of the IFA or other legislation, the assets of the fund may be, to a significant extent, invested in assets the value of which is hard to assess, the procedure for the disclosure of information that the fund's articles of association provide for is insufficient, the fund manager of the management company does not satisfy the requirements provided by legislation

The acquisition in full of existing undertakings is a 'capital movement' in Title I of the nomenclature in Annex I. The informational requirements for the merger, and the grounds for refusal of the merger, limit the free movement of capital.

To be justified under Article 65(1)(b) of the TFEU, the restrictive measures must be necessary for the protection of interests that they are intended to guarantee, be proportionate – i.e. not attainable by less restrictive measures, observe the requirements of legal certainty – i.e. be specific, objective and known to the parties beforehand, and the persons affected by the measures must have access to legal redress, i.e. the decision must accompanied by a formal statement of reasons and be liable to review by the national courts.[295] Neither the IFA nor the Commercial Code requires the EFSA to provide a statement of reasons for refusing to authorise a merger. Furthermore, neither of these Acts provides for the applicants to apply to the national courts for a review of a decision of the EFSA that refuses the merger. In addition, not all of the reasons for the EFSA to be able to refuse authorisation of the merger observe the requirements of legal certainty. For example, section 214(1) of the IFA states that the EFSA may refuse a proposed merger between an acquiring fund and a public limited company on the ground that the objectives of the activities and the investment policy of these two companies differ substantially. The EFSA has a discretion in the determination of what 'differ substantially' means in this context, which means that this restriction is not specific and objective, as required by Article 65(1)(b) of the TFEU. Hence, the national legal provisions in this subsection restrict the free movement of capital under Article 63 of the TFEU.

---

that regulates the professional activities of the manager, the manager's knowledge, skills, experience and other characteristics are not sufficient to ensure protection of the interests of the shareholders of a fund of the particular type, the depositary does not satisfy the requirements for depositaries provided by legislation or is unable for any other reason to ensure adequate protection of the interests of the shareholders of a fund of the respective type, or the management company's contract with depositary contains provisions that are contradictory, ambiguous, or which preclude the depositary or management company from carrying out their duties in full, or which for another reason do not enable promotion of the best interests of the fund's shareholders (s.196, IFA).

[294] s.214(5), IFA.

[295] See the subsection '*The requirements for a successful public policy/security derogation*', in section 2.1.3.

Chapter 6 Division 2: Public Offer of Units and Shares of Foreign Fund in Estonia

The provisions of Chapter 6 Division 2 of the IFA apply to the public offer of the shares or units of a foreign fund.[296] The provisions of the Securities Market Act concerning the public offer of securities apply to the offer of units of a foreign closed-end fund in Estonia.[297] The provisions of subsections 229 to 233 of the IFA do not apply to an offer of units of an UCITS of another Contracting State.[298]

A foreign fund, or a person who, according to the law of the foreign state in which it is founded, has the right to manage funds or other similar undertakings or institutions established for collective investment (hereafter a 'management company') is required, in order to organise the purchase and sale of units of a foreign fund (hereafter 'marketing'), to enter into a contract in Estonia with a management company, investment firm or credit institution who, or whose branch, is founded in Estonia.[299] A foreign fund is not obliged to enter into a contract in order to market units of a foreign fund, if it has, according to section 35 of the IFA, established a branch in Estonia which, among other things, organises the marketing of units of the foreign fund.[300]

The offer of units of a foreign fund in Estonia is to be registered with the EFSA before the offer is commenced.[301] To register a public offer, a written petition and the following documents and information are to be submitted to the EFSA: a copy of the registration document of the foreign fund that is issued by the financial supervision authority of the home state,[302] a copy of the activity licence of the foreign management company that is issued by the financial supervision authority of the home state, if the fund is managed by a management company,[303] a confirmation of the financial supervision authority of the home country that the activities of the foreign fund comply with the requirements established in the home state,[304] the articles of association and the most recent audited annual report of the foreign management company, if the fund is managed by a

[296] s.227(1), IFA.
[297] s.227(1^1), IFA.
[298] s.227(2), IFA.
[299] s.229(1), IFA.
[300] s.229(2), IFA.
[301] s.230(1), IFA.
[302] s.230(2)(1), IFA.
[303] s.230(2)(2), IFA.
[304] s.230(2)(3), IFA.

management company,[305] the public offer prospectus or another offer document concerning units,[306] a copy of the registration certificate of the prospectus issued by the financial supervision authority of the home state or another document that permits the prospectus to be disclosed,[307] the last audited annual report and the semi-annual report of the foreign fund (if later),[308] the contract entered into with a management company, investment firm or credit institution which, or whose branch, is established in Estonia for marketing units of the fund, except in the case provided for in subsection 229(2) of the IFA,[309] and a description of the organisation of the marketing of units of the foreign fund and transactions that relate to it.[310]

The offer of units of a foreign fund is to be registered if all the conditions provided for in this Division are complied with, including the following: the foreign fund, and the foreign management company if the fund is managed by a management company, are recognised by the financial supervision authority of the home state,[311] the offer prospectus of units of a foreign fund complies with the provisions of sections 220 and 22 of the IFA, and legislation that is issued on the basis of the IFA,[312] the name of the foreign fund complies with the requirements in section 5 of the IFA,[313] a contract is entered into with a management company, investment firm, or credit institution, who or whose branch is established in Estonia, in order to market units of the foreign fund (except in the case

---

[305] s.230(2)(4), IFA.
[306] s.230(2)(5), IFA.
[307] s.230(2)(6), IFA.
[308] s.230(2)(7), IFA.
[309] s.230(2)(8), IFA. There is no obligation to conclude a contract in order to market units of foreign fund, if a foreign management company has (under section 35 of the IFA) established a branch in Estonia, which, amongst other things, organises marketing of the unit of the foreign fund (s.229(2), IFA). See the subsection '*Sections 34 to 42¹: activities of foreign management companies in Estonia*', above in this section (i.e. section 3.1), for section 35 of the IFA.
[310] s.230(2)(9), IFA.
[311] s.232(1)(1), IFA.
[312] s.232(1)(2), IFA. The information that is presented in a prospectus is to be accurate, unambiguous, and not misleading, comply with the requirements of legislation, and contain a clear and understandable explanation about the risk level that is associated with the fund (s.220(1), IFA). Section 22 of the IFA states circumstances under which the EFSA may revoke an activity licence in full or in part.
[313] s.232(1)(3), IFA.

provided for in subsection 229(2) of the IFA),[314] upon the issue of units of the foreign fund, it is ensured that the purchaser receives in the account thereof the number of units that corresponds to the purchase price promptly after payment of this price,[315] upon the redemption or re-purchase of units of the foreign fund and the making of payments for the account of the foreign fund, the receipt of money by the unit-holders of the fund is ensured pursuant to the provisions of the transaction's conditions,[316] organisation of the maintenance of a register of the units of the foreign fund is sufficient to ensure that the interests of unit-holders are protected,[317] and access to information specified in section 245 of the IFA that concerns the activities of the foreign investment fund is ensured.[318]

The EFSA may refuse to register the offer of units of a foreign fund if the offer of the units of this fund does not comply with the requirements of this Division,[319] the offer document does not reflect all the essential rules of the operation of the fund in full, clearly and unambiguously,[320] the offer document contains provisions that are misleading, incomplete, or contradictory,[321] the offer document indicates that the investment of the assets of the foreign fund is not adequately based on the principle of spreading risk,[322] supervision over the activities of the funds in the home state is insufficient or hindered,[323] the financial supervision authority of the home state has no legal basis or possibilities for co-operation with the EFSA,[324] or refusal to register is necessary, in order to protect the legitimate interests of the investors for other reasons.[325]

Units of an UCITS of a Contracting State may be offered in Estonia, if the offer complies with the requirements of the IFA concerning an UCITS, and the following is ensured: the possibility to pay dividends or to make distributions to unit-holders from the Contracting State's UCITS and the ability of unit-holders to require redemption and re-purchase of units and payment of an amount that corresponds to the unit,[326] and disclosure of

[314] s.232(1)(4), IFA.
[315] s.232(1)(5), IFA.
[316] s.232(1)(6), IFA.
[317] s.232(1)(7), IFA.
[318] s.232(1)(8), IFA.
[319] s.233(1), IFA.
[320] s.233(2), IFA.
[321] s.233(2), IFA.
[322] s.233(3), IFA.
[323] s.233(4), IFA.
[324] s.233(5), IFA.
[325] s.233(6), IFA.
[326] s.234(1)(1), IFA.

information about the Contracting State's UCITS pursuant to the procedure, and to the extent that the IFA provides.[327] Units of an UCITS of a Contracting State may be offered in Estonia from the day that the financial supervision authority of the UCITS' home state confirms the compliance of the UCITS with the requirements of that country's legislation.[328] In addition to this confirmation, the following information is to be submitted to the EFSA: the crucial information and prospectus,[329] the fund's rules or articles of association,[330] the most recent audited annual report of fund and the latest half-yearly/quarterly report of the fund (if approved after the most recent audited annual report),[331] the plan for marketing of the shares or units in Estonia,[332] names of any classes of shares or units to be marketed,[333] and a notation with regard to whether the same management company markets the units of the fund in Estonia that manages it in another Contracting State.[334]

Although operations in units of collective investment undertakings is a 'capital movement' in Title IV of the nomenclature in Annex I, this Title comprises transactions in units of collective investment undertakings and the administration of units in collective investment undertakings to the capital market, but not the marketing of units of collective investment undertakings. The capital movements in the nomenclature in Annex I are to include the operations that are necessary for the purposes of capital movements. Therefore, the marketing of units in collective in investment undertakings is to be classed as a 'capital movement', if it is necessary to market the units. 'Marketing' in Chapter 6 Division 2 of the IFA means the organisation of the purchase and sale of units of a foreign fund.[335] Thus, the 'marketing' of units is a necessary operation for the purposes of capital movements, and is therefore classified as a 'capital movement' in Title IV to the nomenclature in Annex I.

The requirements in the above paragraphs limit the free movement of capital. To be justified under Article 65(1)(b) of the TFEU, the restrictive

[327] s.234(1)(2), IFA.
[328] s.234(2), IFA.
[329] s.234(2)(1), IFA.
[330] s.234(2)(2), IFA.
[331] s.234(2)(3), IFA. See note 104.
[332] s.234(2)(4), IFA.
[333] s.234(2)(5), IFA.
[334] s.234(2)(6), IFA.
[335] s.229(1), IFA. To 'market' is to advertise or promote (something), to offer for sale, or to buy or sell goods in a market (Pearsall *(ed.)* (1998), *The New Oxford Dictionary of English*, 1133).

measures must be necessary for protection of the interests that they are intended to guarantee, be proportionate, satisfy the requirements of legal certainty – i.e. be specific, objective and known to the parties beforehand, and the persons affected by the measures must have access to legal redress – i.e. the decision must be supported by a formal statement of reasons and be subject to review by the national courts.[336] Division 2 of Chapter 6 of the IFA neither requires the EFSA to provide a statement of reasons for the restrictive measures, nor gives the applicant a right to appeal against the decision in the Estonian courts. Furthermore, not all of the restrictions provide the applicant with legal certainty. For example, subsection 233(3) of the IFA states that the EFSA may refuse to register the offer of units of a foreign fund, if the offer documents indicate that the investment of the assets of the foreign fund is not adequately based on the principle of spreading risk. This criterion is neither specific nor objective. The EFSA should define risk and its component parts, and should specify a measurable threshold as to the maximum permissible combination of these elemental risks that applicant must satisfy.

Restrictions to the free movement of capital on the provision in Estonia of units of a fund registered outside the EEA may be justified under Article 64(2) of the TFEU, if the EU institutions have carefully taken into account the free movement of capital to the greatest extent possible in enacting the relevant Directives (2009/65/EC and 2011/61/EU) and if the national legislation does not go beyond the limitations to free movement in the Directives.[337] Article 9 of Directive 2009/65/EC states that relations with third countries are to be regulated in accordance with the relevant rules in Article 15 of Directive 2004/39/EC. The latter Article considers the provision of investment services from EEA states to third countries, but not in the opposite direction. The relevant Articles of Directive 2011/61/EU are 35,[338] 36,[339] and 40.[340] Directive 2011/61/EU has more onerous requirements for the marketing of non-EU AIFs in Estonia than

---

[336] See the subsection '*The requirements for a successful public policy/security derogation*', in section 2.1.3.

[337] See the subsection '*Derogations that apply only to capital movements to/from third countries*', in section 2.3.2.

[338] Article 35 of Directive 2011/61/EU is entitled 'Conditions for the marketing in Union with a passport of a non-EU AIF managed by an EU AIFM'. See section 2.2.7 for the definitions of 'AIF', 'EU AIF', 'AIFM' and 'EU AIFM'.

[339] Article 36 of Directive 2011/61/EU is entitled 'Conditions for the marketing in Member States without a passport of non EU-AIFs managed by an EU AIFM'.

[340] Article 40 of Directive 2011/61/EU is entitled 'Conditions for the marketing in the Union with a passport of non-EU AIFs managed by a non-EU AIFM'.

sections 230 and 232 of the IFA. For instance, Article 35 of Directive 2011/61/EU requires there to be suitable co-operation arrangements between the competent authorities of the AIFM's home Member State and the supervisory authorities of the third country in which the non-EU AIF is established,[341] the third country in which the non-EU AIF is established to be absent from the Financial Action Task Force Non-Cooperative Country and Territory List,[342] the third country in which the non-EU AIF is established to have signed an agreement with the home Member State of the authorised AIFM and with each other Member State in which the shares or units of the non-EU AIF are intended to be marketed that complies with the standards in Article 26 of the OECD Model Tax Convention on Income and Capital,[343] and submission by the AIFM to the competent authorities of its home Member State of the documentation and information set out in either Annex III[344] or Annex IV[345] of Directive

[341] Article 35(2)(a), Directive 2011/61/EU.

[342] Article 35(2)(b), Directive 2011/61/EU.

[343] Article 35(2)(c), Directive 2011/61/EU. The Contracting States of the OECD Model Tax Convention are to exchange such information that is relevant for implementing the provisions of this Convention, or to the administration or enforcement of their domestic tax laws (Article 26(1), OECD Model Tax Convention on Income and Capital). Any information that a Contracting State receives is to be treated as secret in the same way in which information is treated under the laws of that State, and is only to be disclosed to specified persons (Article 26(2), OECD Model Tax Convention on Income and Capital).

[344] If an AIFM intends to market shares or units of non-EU AIFs in its home Member State, then it is to submit a notification to the competent authorities of its home Member State that comprises the information and documentation in Annex III of Directive 2011/61/EU, for each of the non-EU AIFs that it intends to market (Article 35(3), Directive 2011/61/EU). This information and documentation consists of a notification letter (including a programme of operations that identifies the AIFs that the AIFM intends to market and information concerning the places in which the AIFs are established), the rules or documents of incorporation, the identity of the depositary of the AIF, a description of the AIF that is available to investors, information on the location of the master AIF (if the AIF is a feeder AIF), a list of 16 items for each AIF (in Article 23(1) of Directive 2011/61/EU) concerning the AIFM, the AIF, and the AIF's depositary, and (if relevant) information on the arrangements that have been established to prevent shares or units of the AIF from being marketed to retail investors (Annex III, Directive 2011/61/EU).

[345] If an AIF intends to market shares or units of non-EU AIFs in another EEA state, then it is to submit a notification to the competent authorities of its home Member State that comprises the information and documentation in Annex IV of Directive 2011/61/EU, for each of the non-EU AIFs that it intends to market

2011/61/EU (as appropriate). Hence, in so far as the funds are not UCITS, the limitations on the free movement of capital that relate to funds from third countries are justified, since the restrictions in the IFA do not go as far as those in Directive 2011/61/EU. However, for funds that are UCITS, the limitations on the free movement of capital that relate to funds from third countries are not justified, as Directive 2009/65/EC does not contain equivalent restrictions.

Chapter 6 Division 3: Cross-border Offer of Occupational Pension Funds

For the offer of a pension fund scheme of a Contracting State in Estonia, the EFSA shall be informed of an offer of a pension fund scheme to the employees of an Estonian entity through the Contracting State's financial supervision authority.[346] The following information is to be provided to the EFSA: an attestation from the Contracting State's financial supervision authority of the person who offers the pension fund scheme that this scheme complies with the requirements of Directive 2003/41/EC,[347] the name of the employer with whom the making of payments into a pension fund scheme was agreed,[348] and a description of the main conditions of the pension fund scheme (including the rules for the investment of assets in the scheme).[349]

The nomenclature in Annex I does not explicitly classify pensions as 'capital movements'. However, it is possible to include pensions in Title XIIIF (Other Capital Movements – Miscellaneous) of the nomenclature, and the list of capital movements in the nomenclature is "not

---

(Article 35(5), Directive 2011/61/EU). This information and documentation consists of a notification letter (including a programme of operations that identifies the AIFs that the AIFM intends to market and information about the places in which the AIFs are founded), the rules or documents of incorporation, the identity of the AIF's depositary, a description of the AIF that is available to investors, information on the location of the master AIF (if the AIF is a feeder AIF), a list of 16 items for each AIF (in Article 23(1) of Directive 2011/61/EU) concerning the AIFM, the AIF, and the AIF's depositary, an indication of the Member State in which the AIFM intends to market the units or shares of the AIF to professional investors, information concerning arrangements that are made for the marketing of the AIFs, and (if relevant) information on the arrangements that have been established to prevent shares or units of the AIF from being marketed to retail investors (Annex IV, Directive 2011/61/EU).

[346] s.235(1), IFA.

[347] s.235(2)(1), IFA.

[348] s.235(2)(2), IFA.

[349] s.235(2)(3), IFA.

exhaustive".[350] Furthermore, the CJEU has held that investment transactions of Open Pension Funds to be a 'capital movement' within the nomenclature.[351] Given that an offer of units of an UCITS is a 'capital movement' by virtue of being an 'operation necessary for the purpose of a capital movement' in Title IV (Operations in Units of Collective Investment Undertakings) of the nomenclature in Annex I, it is only a small additional step to include the offer of units of a pension fund as a 'capital movement' by virtue of the 'operations necessary' clause and the judgment in *Commission v Poland*.[352] The information that the applicant provider of the occupational pension scheme is to supply to the financial supervision authority of its home Contracting State is not onerous, and therefore should not be classified as a restriction to the free movement of capital (as considered in section 2.1.2).

For the offer of an Estonian occupational pension fund in another Contracting State, the management company is to notify the EFSA and to submit the following documents and information to it: the name of that Contracting State,[353] a description of the main rules of the occupational pension fund (including the rules for the investment of assets in the scheme),[354] and the name of the entity in the Contracting State with whom the payments in the occupational pension fund was agreed.[355] If the documents submitted comply with the necessary requirements,[356] and if the management company has adequate funds, organisational capacity, and experience for the offer of the occupational pension fund to be made in another Contracting State, then the EFSA is to communicate the above information to the financial supervision authority of the Contracting State, together with an attestation that the occupational pension fund complies with the requirements of Directive 2003/41/EC.[357] The management company may start to offer the occupational pension fund to the employees of the relevant entity, after receiving through the EFSA the conditions that the financial supervision authority of the specified

---

[350] *Trummer and Mayer* [1999] ECR I-1661. See section 2.1.1.

[351] *Commission v Poland* [2011] ECR I-13613. See section 2.1.1.

[352] [2011] ECR I-13613.

[353] s.236^1(2)(1), IFA.

[354] s.236^1(2)(2), IFA.

[355] s.236^1(2)(3), IFA.

[356] Subsection 236^1(3) of the IFA does not specify what requirements these are. In earlier provisions of the IFA, "requirements" refers to the IFA, and sometimes also to secondary legislation that is based on the IFA.

[357] s.236^1(3), IFA.

Contracting State sets for the offer of the occupational pension fund in that State.[358]

In line with the reasoning above in this section, the offer of units in a pension fund is a 'capital movement' in the nomenclature in Annex I. The requirements of the above paragraph, taken as a whole, restrict the free movement of capital. These limitations are justifiable under Article 65(1)(b) of the TFEU if they are necessary for the protection of interests that they are intended to guarantee, are proportionate, observe the requirements of legal certainty, and the persons affected have access to legal redress.[359] The IFA does not require the EFSA to provide reasons to the applicant for refusing to forward the information to the financial supervision authority of the (other) Contracting State. Furthermore, this Act does not enable the applicant to appeal against a refusal to forward information to the Estonian courts. Therefore, section 236¹ of the IFA restricts the free movement of capital, in contravention of Article 63(1) of the TFEU.

Chapter 6 Division 5: Disclosure

The shareholders and unit-holders of a fund are to be able to examine the documents and information specified in subsection 242(2) of the IFA, at the seat of the management company's branch, at the seat of the management company, investment fund, or credit institution that markets the units of the fund (if established in Estonia), or at the seat of the branch of the aforementioned foreign persons (if founded in Estonia).[360] Upon offering the shares and units of an UCITS of another Contracting State, the documents and information specified in subsections 242(2)(1) to 242(2)(4) concerning the UCITS are to be disclosed.[361]

Subsections 242(2)(1) to 242(2)(4) of the IFA contain the following information and documents: the fund's rules or articles of association,[362] the fund's most recent three annual reports,[363] the last half-yearly report of the fund, if this document is approved after the most recent annual report,[364] and an offer prospectus concerning the shares or units of the

---

358 s.236¹(5), IFA.

359 See the subsection '*The requirements for a successful public policy/security derogation*', in section 2.1.3.

360 s.245(1), IFA.

361 s.245(2), IFA.

362 s.242(2)(1), IFA.

363 s.242(2)(2), IFA.

364 s.242(2)(3), IFA.

fund and a simplified prospectus (if available).[365] The remainder of subsection 242(2) of the IFA comprises the following information and documents: the management company's name and contact details,[366] the fund manager's name,[367] the depositary's name and contact details,[368] a list of the fund's directors,[369] the fund's management contract (if established as a public company),[370] information on the size of the management company's holding in the fund,[371] and the management company's most recent three annual reports.[372]

The disclosure of information in relation to a fund is not a 'capital movement' in the nomenclature in Annex I. Even if it was, the information stated in the above paragraph is not onerous for the fund to disclose, as national law requires the production of most of it. Therefore, disclosure of this information would not restrict the free movement of capital.

Chapter 7 Division 3: Specifications for Investment of Assets of Open-ended Public Fund[373] and of Risk-spreading

The assets of an open-ended public fund may be invested in deposits that mature in no more than one year, at credit institutions.[374] The assets of open-ended investment funds may be invested in deposits at credit institutions of third countries, if the prudential ratios that are applicable to these institutions comply with the requirements – which must be at least as stringent as those that are established by EU law.[375] The EFSA has the right to determine whether a credit institution of a third country satisfies these requirements.[376] An open-ended public fund may not invest more than 20 per cent of the market value of its assets in deposits held with the same credit institution.[377] Other open-ended public funds may invest up to

---

365 s.242(2)(4), IFA.
366 s.242(2)(5), IFA.
367 s.242(2)(6), IFA.
368 s.242(2)(7), IFA.
369 s.242(2)(8), IFA.
370 s.242(2)(9), IFA.
371 s.242(2)(10), IFA.
372 s.242(2)(11), IFA.
373 Open-ended pubic funds include, but are not limited to, UCITS. Hence, Directives 2009/65/EC and 2011/61/EU are both relevant to this Division of the IFA.
374 s.256(1), IFA.
375 s.256(2), IFA.
376 s.256(2), IFA.
377 s.256(3), IFA. The provisions of subsection 256(3) of the IFA do not apply to the bank account of the fund (into which money from the issue of units and the

30 per cent of the market value of the assets of the funds in deposits held at credit institutions that are not specified in subsections 256(1) and 256(2) of the IFA.[378]

The assets of an open-ended public fund may be invested in securities that are freely transferable and that satisfy at least one of the following requirements:[379] the securities are traded on a regulated market in the EEA, or on another regulated market that the relevant EEA state recognises, which operates regularly, and on which the public is able to acquire or transfer securities,[380] the securities are traded on a regulated securities market of a country that is specified in the rules or articles of association of the investing fund,[381] or pursuant to the conditions of issue of the securities, they are to be admitted to the regulated market of a country specified in clause 1) or 2) within one year after issue of the securities.[382]

The assets of an open-ended public fund may be invested in money market instruments not specified in subsection 257(2) of the IFA, which are usually traded on the money market, are liquid, have a value that can be correctly determined at any time, and satisfy at least one of the following requirements:[383] the money market instruments are issued or guaranteed by a state, federated state of a Union, the central bank of a Contracting State, the European Central Bank, the European Investment Bank, or an international organisation of which the Contracting State is a member, shareholder, or partner,[384] the money market instruments are issued by a person who has issued other securities that are traded on a regulated market specified in subsections 257(1)(1) or 257(1)(2) of the IFA,[385] the money market instruments are issued or guaranteed by a management company, investment firm, credit institution, or insurer that is founded in a Contracting State, or if the aforementioned person was established in a member state of the OECD belonging to the Group of Ten (G10) countries – or has been assigned at least an investment grade rating – it can be demonstrated (based on an in-depth analysis of the money

transfer of the fund's assets, and dividends, interest, and other monies, are deposited) and to overnight deposits (ss.256(5) and 99(2), IFA).

[378] s.256(4), IFA.

[379] s.257(1), IFA.

[380] s.257(1)(1), IFA.

[381] s.257(1)(2), IFA.

[382] s.257(1)(3), IFA.

[383] s.257(2), IFA.

[384] s.257(2)(1), IFA.

[385] s.257(2)(2), IFA.

market instrument's issuer) that the prudential rules applicable to the issuer are at least as strict as those laid down by EU law,[386] the issuer of the money market instruments is included among the issuers approved by the financial supervision authority of another Contracting State pursuant to the conditions specified in Article 50(1)(h)(4) of Directive 2009/65/EC,[387] or, in the opinion of the EFSA, the issuer of the money market instruments satisfies the requirements established by the Minister of Finance.[388] Up to 10 per cent of the assets of an UCITS may be invested in securities that are not specified in subsections 257(1) or 257(2) of the IFA.[389] Furthermore, up to 30 per cent of the market value of the assets of another open-ended public fund may be invested in securities that are not specified in subsections 257(1) or 257(2) of the IFA.[390]

Upon investment of the fund's assets in the money market instruments specified in subsection 257(2) of the IFA, appropriate information on the money market instruments is to be made available to the management company, which includes information that permits a suitable assessment of the credit risks related to the specified money market instruments, taking especially into account the provisions of subsections $257^{2}(6)$, $257^{2}(7)$, and $257^{2}(8)$ of the IFA.[391] For the money market instruments specified in subsection 257(2) of the IFA, unless their issuer is the European Central

---

[386] s.257(2)(3), IFA. The EFSA has the right to determine whether the management company, investment firm, credit institution, or insurer that issues or guarantees the money market instruments, complies with these requirements with regard to the application of prudential ratios (s.257(2)(3), IFA).

[387] s.257(2)(4), IFA.

[388] s.257(2)(5), IFA. The investments of an UCITS are to comprise at least one of the following: ... money market instruments other than those dealt in on a regulated market, if the issue or issuer of these instruments is itself regulated for the purpose of protecting investors or savings, provided that they are issued by other bodies belonging to the categories approved by the competent authorities of the UCITS home Member State and that investments in these instruments are subject to investor protection equivalent to that laid down in points (i), (ii) or (iii) of this paragraph, and provided that the issuer is a company whose capital and reserves amount to at least 10,000,000 EUR and which publishes its annual accounts in accordance with Directive 78/660/EEC, is an entity which is within a group of companies that includes one or several listed companies, is dedicated to the financing of the group, or is an entity which is committed to the financing of securitisation vehicles that benefit from a banking liquidity line (Article 50(1)(h)(4), Directive 2009/65/EC).

[389] s.257(3), IFA.

[390] s.257(4), IFA.

[391] s.$257^{2}(5)$, IFA.

Bank or the central bank of a Contracting State, appropriate information is to consist of at least of information on the issue, the offering programme, and the legal and financial circumstances of the issuer prior to the issue of the money market instrument.[392] If the issuer of a money market instrument is the person, Contracting State, regional or local government entity of a Contracting State, or international organisation specified in clauses 257(2)(2) to 257(2)(5) of the IFA, but the money market instrument is not guaranteed by the Contracting State, then the appropriate information shall be, in addition to the information provided for in subsection $257^2(6)$, information on the changes that are related to the aforementioned information, and available, reliable statistical data that permits appropriate assessment of the credit risks that are associated with the investments made in the specified instruments.[393] If the issuer of a money market instrument is the person, Contracting State, regional or local government entity of a Contracting State, or international organisation that is specified in clauses 257(2)(2), 257(2)(4), and 257(2)(5) of the IFA, but the Contracting State does not guarantee the money market instrument, then the appropriate information is also to contain information on verification of the information specified in subsection $257^2(6)$ by third persons who are suitably qualified and independent from the issuer, in addition to the information provided for in subsections $257^2(6)$ and $257^2(7)$ of the IFA.[394]

The value of securities that belong to the assets of an open-ended public fund that are issued by the same person, may make up to 35 per cent of the market value of a fund's assets, if they are issued or guaranteed by: a Contracting State,[395] another country that guarantees conditions for investment with a degree of risk similar to, or smaller than, that of the Contracting States and which is set out in the fund's rules or articles of association,[396] or an international organisation of which at least one Contracting State is a member.[397] More than 35 per cent of the market value of the assets of an open-ended public fund may be invested in securities of a person specified in subsection 259(1) of the IFA, if adequate protection of the interests of the shareholders and unit-holders of the fund is ensured,[398] the assets of the fund comprise securities that are

[392] s.$257^2(6)$, IFA.
[393] s.$257^2(7)$, IFA.
[394] s.$257^2(8)$, IFA.
[395] s.259(1)(1), IFA.
[396] s.259(1)(2), IFA.
[397] s.259(1)(3), IFA.
[398] s.259(2)(1), IFA.

issued or guaranteed by this person during at least six different issues and the value of securities acquired in a single issue totals to no more than 30 per cent of the market value of the assets of the fund,[399] and the fund's rules or articles of association, and the prospectus, set out the issuers, and the relevant issued or guaranteed securities.[400]

The assets of an UCITS may only be invested in covered bonds that are issued by a credit institution of a Contracting State.[401] Up to 25 per cent of the market value of the assets of a fund may be invested in covered bonds that the same person issues.[402] If the value of covered bonds that one person issues is more than 5 per cent of the market value of the assets of an UCITS, then the aggregate value of these bonds is not to total to more than 80% of the market value of the assets of the UCITS.[403]

Subject to two conditions,[404] the assets of an open-ended public fund may be invested in derivative instruments that are traded on regulated markets as specified in clauses 257(1)(1) and 257(1)(2) of the IFA,[405] and derivative instruments that are acquired over-the-counter.[406] The assets of an open-ended public fund may be invested in derivative instruments the underlying assets of which are the following assets, or which price depends on the following factors: deposits that satisfy the requirements of subsections 256(1) and 256(2) of the IFA,[407] securities specified in section 257 of the IFA,[408] share of units of an investment fund specified in subsections 264(1) or 264(2) of the IFA,[409] and securities, financial indices, interest rates, or currency in which the fund may invest by virtue of its rules.[410] The exposure to a counterparty of an UCITS in an over-the-

---

[399] s.259(2)(2), IFA.

[400] s.259(2)(3), IFA.

[401] s.260(1^1), IFA. 'Covered bonds' are non-equity securities that a credit institution continuously or repeatedly issues (s.260(1), IFA).

[402] s.260(2), IFA.

[403] s.260(3), IFA.

[404] These conditions are as follows. The counterparty to the over-the-counter derivative transactions must be a person whose compliance with prudential ratios is subject to financial supervision (s.261(1)(1), IFA). The value of derivative instruments acquired over-the-counter may be reliably assessed each day, and the UCITS can transfer the derivative instruments at any time for a fair price, liquidate its position therein, or close them by an offsetting transaction (s.261(1)(2), IFA).

[405] See above in this subsection.

[406] s.261(1), IFA.

[407] s.261(4)(1), IFA. See above in this subsection.

[408] s.261(4)(2), IFA. See above in this subsection.

[409] s.261(4)(2), IFA. See below in this subsection.

[410] s.261(4)(3), IFA.

counter derivative transaction is not to exceed 10 per cent of the market value of the UCITS' assets, if the counterparty is a credit institution that satisfies the requirements of subsection 256(2) of the IFA.[411] By contrast, the exposure to a counterparty of a public open-ended fund other than an UCITS is not to exceed 20 per cent of the market value of the fund's assets.[412] The exposure to a counterparty of an UCITS in an over-the-counter derivative transaction is not to exceed 5 per cent of the market value of the UCITS' assets, if the counterparty is a person who is not specified in subsection 262(2) of the IFA.[413]

The value of securities that belong to an UCITS' assets and are issued by the same person, deposits placed with this person, and exposures that arise from derivative transactions undertaken with this person are not to total to more than 20 per cent of the market value of the UCITS' assets.[414] The aggregate value of securities, derivative instruments, and covered bonds, which belong to the assets of an UCITS and are issued by the same person, and deposits placed with this person, are not to total to more than 35 per cent of the market value of the UCITS.[415]

The assets of a public fund may be invested in the units of an UCITS,[416] and/or in the shares and units of an UCITS of another Contracting State.[417] In addition, the assets of an open-ended public fund may be invested in other funds that the legislation of Estonia or other countries deems to be open-ended public funds, and which satisfy the following requirements: financial supervision is exercised over the fund pursuant to the requirements of EU legislation – or requirements that are at least as strict as those of EU legislation and co-operation between the EFSA and the authority that exercises supervision over the fund is not hindered,[418] the level of protection for unit-holders pursuant to the IFA is equivalent to that provided for investors in an UCITS and (in particular) the applicant must comply with the requirements of section 72 and subsections 276(3), 276(4), 277(1) and 277(2) of the IFA,[419] the business

[411] s.262(2), IFA.
[412] s.262(3), IFA.
[413] s.262(4), IFA.
[414] s.263(1), IFA.
[415] s.263(2), IFA.
[416] s.264(1), IFA.
[417] s.264(2), IFA.
[418] s.264(2)(1), IFA.
[419] s.264(2)(2), IFA. A management company is to manage the assets of a fund separately from its own assets, the assets of other funds that this company manages, and other asset pools (s.72(1), IFA). For the account of an UCITS and a

of the fund is reported in semi-annual and annual reports, which include a statement of assets and liabilities, an income and expenses statement, and a statement of investments in the fund,[420] and no more than 10 per cent of the fund's assets may be invested in other investment funds.[421] Up to 30 per cent of the market value of the assets of an UCITS may be invested in shares or units of funds that satisfy the requirements in the previous sentence.[422] In addition to the provisions of subsections 264(1) and 264(2) of the IFA, the assets of open-ended public funds may be invested in units of (specified) closed-end funds; upon investment in the shares or units of these closed-end funds, the provisions of the IFA that concern the investment of the assets of an open-ended public fund in securities apply.[423] Up to 50% of the assets of another open-ended public fund may be invested in shares or units of funds that are not specified in subsections 264(1), 264(2), and 264(3^1) of the IFA.[424] The EFSA has the right to determine whether the supervision exercised over the fund in the assets of which investments are made complies with the requirements in clause 264(2)(1) of the IFA, or whether the funds that the legislation of a foreign country classifies as closed-end funds comply with the requirement in subsection 264(3^1) of the IFA.[425] The value of shares or units of an

---

pension fund, it is not permitted to issue debt securities, grant a loan and assume obligations that arise from a contract of suretyship or guarantee contract, borrow from the persons specified in subsections 281(1) and 281(2) of the IFA, and conclude repurchase agreements or reverse repurchase agreements if performance of the obligation is not fully covered by the securities in the fund's assets (ss.276(3) and 276(1), IFA). Securities that, at the time of entry into the transfer deed, do not belong to the assets of an UCITS, are not to be transferred for the account of the UCITS (s.276(4), IFA). A management company may, for the account of a pension fund or an UCITS, take loans, guarantee an issue of securities, and/or enter into repurchase agreements or reverse repurchase agreements, in an amount that totals up to 10 per cent of the market value of a fund's assets (ss.277(1) and 276(1), IFA). The term of a loan taken, or obligation assumed, for the account of an UCITS, is not to exceed three months (s.277(2), IFA).

[420] s.264(2)(3), IFA.

[421] s.264(2)(4), IFA.

[422] s.264(3), IFA.

[423] s.264(3^1), IFA.

[424] s.264(4), IFA. This limitation does not apply to the shares or units of investment funds that are traded on a regulated market specified in clauses 257(1)(1) or 257(1)(2) of the IFA.

[425] s.264(5), IFA.

investment fund are not to add to more than 20 per cent of the market value of the assets of an UCITS.[426]

The shares or debt securities issued by one person and belonging to the assets of an index fund that is an UCITS are not to total to more than 20 per cent of the market value of the fund's assets.[427] The assets of an index fund that is an UCITS may be invested in the securities of a person specified in subsection 266(2) of the IFA, or in securities that are guaranteed by a person specified in subsection 266(2) of the IFA, up to a maximum of 35 per cent of the market value of the fund's assets, if this proves to be justified by the specific conditions of a regulated market in which certain shares or debt securities are very dominant.[428]

The investment of the assets of an investment fund in deposits, securities, money market instruments, and other investments, is a 'capital movement' in the nomenclature in Annex I. The placement of limitations on the types of investments into which an investment fund's assets may be invested limits the free movement of capital.

In order to be justified under Article 65(1)(b) of the TFEU, these limitations must be necessary for the protection of interests that they are intended to guarantee, be proportionate, observe the requirements of legal certainty – i.e. be specific, objective, and known to the parties beforehand, and the persons affected by the restrictive measures must have access to legal redress – i.e. be supported by a formal statement of reasons and be subject to review by the national courts.[429] The IFA does not contain a requirement for the EFSA to provide a formal statement of reasons to an investment fund, for a decision of the former in which it forbids the latter from placing its funds in certain investments; nor does the IFA provide the investment fund with the right to appeal against this decision. Furthermore, although most of the provisions in this subsection provide legal certainty, the EFSA may have a discretion – as in subsection 256(2) of the IFA. Hence, the restrictive provisions are not justified under Article 65(1)(b) of the TFEU.

It is unlikely that the investment of the assets of investment funds in third countries could be justified under those derogations that apply specifically to capital movements to and from third countries.[430] This is

---

[426] s.265(1), IFA.

[427] s.266(2), IFA.

[428] s.266(3), IFA.

[429] See the subsection '*The requirements for a successful public policy/security derogation*', in section 2.1.3.

[430] See the subsection '*Derogations that apply only to capital movements to/from third countries*', in section 2.3.2.

because, in the absence of restrictions on the investment of assets, the applicant could freely choose whether to invest within the EEA or outside it. Consequently, for the restrictions imposed by the IFA in this subsection that discriminate against investments in the financial instruments of third countries, such as those relating to money market instruments in section 257 of the IFA, the derogation in Article 64(2) of the TFEU may not be available. In other words, the restrictions may not be justified, even if they are no more stringent than the equivalent provisions in Directive 2009/65/EC or Directive 2011/65/EU (as appropriate). Thus, the provisions of Division 3 of Chapter 7 of the IFA restrict the free movement of capital, in contravention of Article 63 of the TFEU.

Sections 296 to 300: Supervision

If a management company whose branch is established in a foreign country, or which provides cross-border services to a foreign state, contravenes the requirements of legislation of a Contracting State or a third country, then the EFSA is to promptly apply measures for termination of the breach, on the proposal of the financial supervision authority of Contracting State or third country.[431] The EFSA is to inform the financial supervision authority of the Contracting State or third country of the measures that it applies.[432]

If a management company manages an UCITS established in another Contracting State, the EFSA is to exercise supervision over the requirements stated in subsections 25(6) and 25(7) of the IFA, and the procedures and proceedings that the management company establishes for implementation thereof, and immediately apply measures for termination of contraventions of the requirements imposed on the activities of the management company.[433] A branch of a management company, or a

[431] s.296(1), IFA.

[432] s.296(1), IFA.

[433] s.296(1^1), IFA. If a management company manages an UCITS that is founded in another Contracting State through the establishment of a branch for this purpose, or for providing cross-border services, the management company is to comply with the requirements of sections 51-56^1, 57-58^2, 69-75, 85-88, 144^1, 144^2, 237-245, and 248 of the IFA with respect to the activities, management, organisational structure, and prudential requirements of the management company (s.25(6), IFA). In the cases that subsection 25(6) of the IFA provides for, the obligations of the management company stated in the fund rules and the prospectus of an UCITS established in another Contracting State are to comply with the requirements of section 25(6) of the IFA. The management company is to found an organisational administration, which is required according to the legislation of a Contracting State for pursuance of activities of an UCITS established in the Contracting State,

management company that provides cross-border services, is, at the request of the financial supervision authority of a Contracting State or a third country, to submit information that is necessary for the exercise of supervision over the activities of the management company in that country.[434] The EFSA is to co-operate with the financial supervision authority of the Contracting State or the third country, in order to ensure performance of the management company's obligations.[435]

The EFSA may require a management company of a Contracting State or a third country that provides its services in Estonia to submit additional documents and information that are necessary for the exercise of supervision over the management company.[436] A management company that supplies services in Estonia, and whose activity licence is suspended or revoked by the financial supervision authority of a Contracting State or a third country, is not to provide services in Estonia.[437] If a management company of a third country that provides services in Estonia contravenes Estonian legislative requirements, then the EFSA may apply measures that are necessary for the termination of this breach or revoke the authorisation for the establishment of a branch or the supply of cross-border services.[438] The EFSA may require a management company of a Contracting State that has established a branch in Estonia or provides cross-border services in Estonia to terminate contravention of the requirements provided for in the IFA or its secondary legislation.[439] If a management company of a Contracting State manages an UCITS that is established in Estonia, the EFSA is to exercise supervision over compliance with the requirements of subsections 34(6) and 34(7) of the IFA, and immediately implement measures for the termination of any breaches of the requirements established for the management of the UCITS.[440] If the management company of a

---

investment of the UCITS' assets, and performance of the obligations (on the basis of the IFA) that the fund rules and the prospectus specify (s.25(7), IFA).

[434] s.296(3), IFA.

[435] s.296(3), IFA.

[436] s.297(1), IFA.

[437] s.297(2), IFA.

[438] s.297(3), IFA.

[439] s.297(4), IFA.

[440] s.297(4^1), IFA. If a management company of another Contracting State manages an UCITS established in Estonia by the foundation of a branch for this purpose, or by the provision of cross-border services in Estonia, then the management company is to comply with the provisions of sections 111-154, 162-187, 217-226, and 237-245 of the IFA with respect to establishment of UCITS and management of the fund (s.34(6), IFA). In the cases that subsection 34(6) of the IFA provides for, the management company's obligations that the UCITS' fund

Contracting State has founded a branch in Estonia, the EFSA is to immediately take measures for the termination of the contraventions of the requirements established for the activities of the management company of the Contracting State to the extent that subsection 34(8) of the IFA specifies.[441] The EFSA is to immediately notify the financial supervision authority of the Contracting State of any contravention of the requirements specified in this subsection of the IFA, and of the measures that the EFSA applies.[442]

The EFSA is to exercise supervision over the compliance of the public offer of the shares or units of a foreign fund in Estonia, with the conditions that legislation provides.[443] If, upon the public offer or marketing of the shares or units of a foreign fund, legislative requirements are contravened, then the EFSA may prohibit the public offer of the shares or units of the foreign fund in Estonia or apply measures for the termination of the breach.[444] If, upon the public offer or marketing of the shares or units of an UCITS of another Contracting State, legislative requirements are contravened, then the EFSA is to inform the financial supervision authority of the other Contracting State; the EFSA may apply measures for the termination of contraventions, if the measures that the financial supervision authority of the other Contracting State applies are insufficient, or if the breach of legislative requirements is continued.[445]

The EFSA may, by its precept, suspend the public offer of the shares or units of a foreign fund in Estonia if: the offer does not comply with the legislative requirements,[446] incorrect, misleading, or contradictory information

---

rules and prospectus contains, and the performance of the management company's obligations, are to comply with the requirements of that subsection (s.34(7), IFA).

[441] s.297(4¹), IFA. The establishment by a management company of another Contracting State of a branch in Estonia, is to comply with the provisions of sections 58¹, 58², 70¹, 144¹, and 144² of the IFA, and legislation passed on the basis of subsection 70(5) of the IFA on the management company's general organisational structure, the settlement of client complaints, management and prevention of conflicts of interests, and operation in the best interests of the UCITS and its unit-holders (s.34(8), IFA).

[442] s.297(4¹), IFA. Section 297 of the IFA contains further requirements that relate to continued breach of legislative provisions.

[443] s.298(1), IFA.

[444] s.298(2), !FA.

[445] s.298(3), IFA. The EFSA is to immediately inform the financial supervision authority of the home state, the European Commission, and (if necessary) the European Securities and Markets Authority, of the measures taken (s.298(4), IFA).

[446] s.299(1)(1), IFA.

has been submitted or the information is not provided in time,[447] the re-purchase or redemption of the shares or units in the home state is suspended,[448] the fund, foreign management company, or the distributor of the shares or units of the fund submits or publishes incorrect, misleading, or contradictory information, advertising, or reports, that concern the fund,[449] the terms and conditions that are prescribed in the prospectus are not respected,[450] the requirements of the IFA have been contravened upon the re-purchase or redemption of the shares or units,[451] or information contained in prospectuses that are in Estonian, and the offer the units of an UCITS of a Contracting State, is different from information that is contained in the prospectus published in the Contracting State.[452] On the suspension of an offer, the EFSA is to issue a precept to require the offeror to terminate the circumstances that have caused the suspension of the offer.[453] After elimination of these circumstances, the offeror may resume the offer, once the EFSA has given its permission.[454]

The EFSA has the right to exercise supervision over the compliance of an offer of a pension fund scheme with the requirements of subsection 235(3)[455] or 236(1)[456] of the IFA, and to require that reports on the pension fund scheme are submitted an *ad hoc* or a regular basis.[457] If the

---

[447] s.299(1)(2), IFA.
[448] s.299(1)(3), IFA.
[449] s.299(1)(4), IFA.
[450] s.299(1)(5), IFA.
[451] s.299(1)(6), IFA.
[452] s.299(1)(7), IFA.
[453] s.299(2), IFA.
[454] s.299(2), IFA.
[455] The provisions of subsections 257(4) and 272(1) of the IFA apply to the part of the assets of the pension fund scheme that corresponds to that of the employees, servants, and members of the managing and controlling organisations of the Estonian employer (s.235(3), IFA). For subsection 257(4) of the IFA, see the subsection '*Chapter 7 Division 3 – Specifications for Investment of Assets of Open-ended Public Fund and of Risk-spreading*' above in this section. The value of securities that are issued by one person and specified in clauses 2(1)(1)-(3), 2(1)(5), and 2(1)(7) of the SMA are not to add to more than 5 per cent of the market value of the assets of a mandatory pension fund, unless provided for in Division 4 of Chapter 7 of the IFA (s.272(1), IFA).
[456] Within two months of the financial supervision authority of a Contracting State communicating the information specified in subsection 235(2) of the IFA to the EFSA, the EFSA may determine the conditions that an offer of a pension fund scheme is to satisfy in Estonia according to relevant Acts and legislation that is issued on the basis of these Acts (s.236(1), IFA).
[457] s.300(1), IFA.

requirements of subsection 235(3) or 236(1) of the IFA have been contravened upon an offer of a pension fund scheme, then the EFSA is to inform the financial supervision authority of the Contracting State thereof.[458] If the measures that a financial supervision authority of a Contracting State are insufficient, and if the offeror of a pension fund scheme continues to breach the requirements of subsection 235(3) or 236(1) of the IFA, then the EFSA may apply measures for the termination of the contravention, or prohibit the pension fund scheme in Estonia.[459] Exceptionally, the EFSA may, in order to protect the public interest or investors, apply measures with regard to an offeror of a pension scheme who contravenes the requirements of subsection 235(3) or 236(1) of the IFA, without giving prior notice of these measures to the financial supervision authority of the Contracting State of the offeror.[460]

Breach of legislation concerning the provision of investments in investment funds or pension schemes is not a 'capital movement' in the nomenclature in Annex I. Therefore, the rules described in this section do not contravene the free movement of capital under Article 63 of the TFEU. Nevertheless, the effect of these Estonian rules is to reduce cross-border capital movements, as the measures applied by the EFSA are likely to include the suspension or termination of some or all of the investments provided by the investment fund or pension scheme.

3.2 Securities Market Act 2001 (SMA)

This Act concerns securities' regulation and investment services. 'Securities' include shares, bonds, derivatives, investment fund units and money market instruments, but exclude cheques and bills of exchange.[461] Professional securities market participants include investment firms, credit institutions, management companies, and operators of the regulated securities market and of securities settlement systems.[462] An 'investment firm' is a financial institution other than a credit institution, the principal, permanent activity of which is to acquire holdings, or conduct at least one

---

[458] s.300(2), IFA.

[459] s.300(3), IFA. The EFSA must inform the financial supervision authority of the Contracting State of the measures to be applied (s.300(4), IFA).

[460] s.300(5), IFA. The EFSA is to promptly inform the European Commission, the European Securities and Markets Authority, and the financial supervision authority of the relevant Contracting State, of the application of the measures stated in subsection 300(5) of the IFA (s.300(6), IFA).

[461] s.2, SMA.

[462] s.7(1), SMA.

of the transactions stated in clauses 6(1)(2)-(12) of the CIA.[463] Only an investment firm, a credit institution, or a management company, or a branch of a foreign investment firm, credit institution or management company, or a foreign investment firm, credit institution or management company across a border, or an operator of a regulated market pursuant to the SMA, may offer investment services.[464] 'Investment services' comprise the reception and transmission of orders that relate to securities,[465] the execution of orders relating to securities in the name of, or for the account of, the client,[466] dealing in securities on own account,[467] securities' portfolio management,[468] the provision of investment advice,[469] the guarantee of securities,[470] the guarantee of the offer, issue, or sale of securities,[471] the organisation of an offer or issue of securities,[472] and the operation of a multilateral trading facility in which the interests of different persons for the acquisition and transfer of securities are brought together under uniform conditions whose result is the entry into a contract.[473] The EFSA issues an activity licence for the provision of individual or all investment services.[474]

---

[463] s.40(1), SMA and s.5, CIA. These activities comprise deposit transactions for the receipt of repayable funds from the public, borrowing and lending operations, leasing transactions, payment services for the purposes of the PIA, issue and administration of non-cash payment methods, transactions that form binding obligations to persons in the future, transactions for their own account or for the account of clients in traded securities provided in section 2 of the SMA and in money market instruments, acts and transactions that are related to the issue and sale of securities, provision of advice to clients on issues that concern economic activities, acts and transactions that concern the merger or division of companies or participation therein, money broking, portfolio investment, consultation on investment issues, and administration and safekeeping of securities (ss.6(1)(2)-6(1)(12), CIA).

[464] s.45, SMA.

[465] s.43(1)(1), SMA.

[466] s.43(1)(2), SMA.

[467] s.43(1)(3), SMA.

[468] s.43(1)(4), SMA.

[469] s.43(1)(5), SMA.

[470] s.43(1)(6), SMA.

[471] s.43(1)(6), SMA.

[472] s.43(1)(7), SMA.

[473] s.43(1)(8), SMA.

[474] s.49(1), SMA.

Chapter 8 Division 2: Activities Abroad

The EFSA must grant permission to an Estonian investment firm to establish a branch or subsidiary in a third country.[475] To apply for permission, a written application and the following information is to be supplied to the EFSA: the name of the country in which the subsidiary or branch is to be established,[476] the name and address of the subsidiary or the subsidiary or branch,[477] the annual reports for the most recent two financial years of the investment firm of a third country in which a holding is to be acquired,[478] a business plan of the subsidiary or branch,[479] a description of the relationship between the subsidiary or branch and the investment firm,[480] the information specified in clause 54(1)(5) of the SMA on the members of the subsidiary's directing bodies or the branch's director,[481] and the information in subsection 73(2) of the SMA on persons who have a qualifying holding in the subsidiary.[482] The EFSA may refuse to grant permission if the documents or information submitted upon application for permission do not satisfy the requirements provided for in the SMA or legislation established on the basis thereof, or are inaccurate, misleading, or incomplete,[483] the applicant fails, within the prescribed term, or refuses to submit, the documents or information to the EFSA,[484] the members of the subsidiary's directing bodies, or the branch's director, do not satisfy the SMA's requirements for the members of an investment firm's management board, persons with a qualifying holding in the

---

[475] s.59(1), SMA.
[476] s.59(2)(1), SMA.
[477] s.59(2)(2), SMA.
[478] s.59(2)(3), SMA.
[479] s.59(2)(4), SMA.
[480] s.59(2)(4), SMA.
[481] s.59(2)(5), SMA. Upon application for an activity licence, the applicant is to submit information on its managers, including, for each person, the name, personal identification code (or date and place of birth), the educational background, a list of places of employment and positions held during the most recent five years, and for members of the board of directors, a description of their areas of responsibility and other documents that certify the mangers' trustworthiness and conformity to the requirements of the SMA that the applicant considers to be necessary to submit (s.54(5), SMA).
[482] s.59(2)(6), SMA. The person with a qualifying holding must provide notification to the EFSA, after becoming aware of the control gained over the investment firm, or the acquisition or rise of qualifying holding in that company (s.73(2), SMA).
[483] s.61(1), SMA.
[484] s.61(2), SMA.

subsidiary in which a qualifying holding is being acquired do not satisfy the requirements of section 72 of the SMA,[485] The EFSA may revoke an authorisation granted to an investment firm in a third country if the investment firm or its branch does not satisfy the requirements in force with regard to the issue of permissions for the establishment of a branch,[486] the investment firm does not submit reports on its branch, as required,[487] upon application for a permission for the establishment of a branch, the investment firm has submitted misleading or inaccurate information, or misleading or falsified documents,[488] the investment firm, its managers, or the branch's director, has been punished for a specified offence (such as official misconduct),[489] the risks that arise from the activities of the branch are significantly larger than risks that arise from the investment firm's activities,[490] the investment firm's activity licence has been revoked,[491] the circumstances in section 61 of the SMA arise,[492] or the investment firm has not implemented a precept of the EFSA within the period, or to the extent, prescribed.[493]

Establishment of a branch is a 'capital movement' in Title I of the nomenclature in Annex I. The limitations in the previous paragraph restrict the free movement of capital. For these limitations to be justified under Article 65(1)(b) of the TFEU, they must be necessary for the protection of interests that they are intended to guarantee, be proportionate, provide legal certainty, and the persons affected by the measures must have access

---

[485] s.61(3), SMA. Qualifying holdings in an investment firm may be acquired by a person 1) who has an impeccable business reputation and whose activities in connection with the acquisition comply with the principles of sound, prudent management of the investment firm, 2) who is to elect, appoint, or designate only those persons as managers of the investment firm who comply with the requirements of section 79 of the SMA, 3) whose financial circumstances are sufficiently secure to ensure regular, reliable operation of the investment firm, 4) who is able to ensure that the investment firm is able to satisfy the prudential requirements of the SMA, and 5) with regard to whom there is no justified reason to believe that the acquisition of, holding in, increase of a holding in, or control over, an investment firm is related to terrorist financing or money laundering, or an attempt thereof, or increasing the risks of these activities (s.72, SMA).

[486] s.62(1)(1), SMA.

[487] s.62(1)(2), SMA.

[488] s.62(1)(3), SMA.

[489] s.62(1)(4), SMA.

[490] s.62(1)(5), SMA.

[491] s.62(1)(6), SMA.

[492] s.62(1)(7), SMA. See above in this subsection.

[493] s.62(1)(8), SMA.

to legal redress.[494] The SMA does not provide the applicant investment firm with access to legal redress because, although this Act requires the EFSA to accompany a decision to refuse to grant the applicant permission to establish a branch in a third country with reasons,[495] it does not permit the applicant to appeal against the decision in the Estonian courts. Furthermore, some of the national provisions in the previous paragraph do not provide the applicant with legal certainty. For example, the EFSA is empowered to revoke an authorisation if the branch's risks are, in the EFSA's view, significantly greater than those of the firm; the applicant requires specific guidance on what 'significantly greater' means in this context.

For these restrictions to be justified under Article 64(2) of the TFEU, the EU institutions must carefully take into account of the objective of the free movement of capital whilst enacting the relevant Directive (Directive 2004/39/EC), and the national legislation is not to limit the free movement of capital more than the Directive does.[496] The recitals to Directive 2004/39/EC do not mention the free movement of capital. In addition, Directive 2004/39/EC does not provide detailed authorisation requirements that relate to the establishment of a branch of an investment firm in a third country.[497] Hence, the restrictions to the free movement of capital in Articles 61 and 62 of the SMA are not justified under Article 64(2) of the TFEU.

An investment firm that wishes to establish a branch to provide investment services in another Contracting State is to notify the EFSA of its intention to do this,[498] and to submit to the EFSA the name of the

---

[494] See the subsection '*The requirements for a successful public policy/security derogation*, in section 2.1.3.

[495] Unless otherwise provided in this Division, applications for permission are to be subject to the provisions of subsections 51, 52, 53, 55, and 55¹ of the SMA (s.60(1), SMA). A decision refusing to grant, or revoking, an activity licence, is to contain the justification on which it is based (s.51(3), SMA).

[496] See the subsection '*Derogations that apply only to capital movements to/from third countries*', in section 2.3.2.

[497] Article 15 of Directive 2004/39/EC considers the provision of investment services to third countries. It empowers the Commission to take measures in cases in which the relevant third country does not provide sufficient access to investment firms from the EEA.

[498] s.64(1), SMA. If an investment firm wishes to use an investment agent established in another Contracting State, then the use of this agent is considered to be equal to the foundation of a branch, and the provisions that regulate the establishment and activities of branches provided by the SMA are to apply (s.64(12), SMA).

Contracting State in which the investment firm wishes to found the branch,[499] the branch's business plan, which is to contain information on the investment and ancillary services that it intends to provide in the Contracting State, describe the branch's organisational structure and whether it intends to use investment agents,[500] the branch's address,[501] and the names of the branch's managers.[502] The EFSA may refuse to review this information if it does not comply with the requirements of the EFSA or its secondary legislation,[503] or has not been submitted within the prescribed period.[504] The EFSA is to decide whether to forward, or to refuse to forward, this information to the securities market supervisory agency of the corresponding Contracting State within two months after the receipt of all the required information, but not later than within three months after receiving the corresponding application.[505] The EFSA is to immediately inform the investment firm of this decision.[506] The EFSA may decide to refuse to forward the information if the investment firm's resources are insufficient to provide the services specified in the business plan in the Contracting State,[507] the establishment of the branch or the implementation of the business plan may damage the interests of the firm's clients, or the financial situation or business of the firm,[508] the documents or information submitted for forwarding are incorrect, misleading, or incomplete,[509] or the investment firm wishes to supply only ancillary services.[510] The EFSA may prohibit an investment firm from providing services through a branch established in another Contracting State if there are grounds in subsection 64(5) of the SMA to refuse to

[499] s.64(1)(1), SMA.
[500] s.64(1)(2), SMA.
[501] s.64(1)(3), SMA.
[502] s.64(1)(4), SMA.
[503] s.64(4)(1), SMA.
[504] s.64(4)(2), SMA.
[505] s.64(3), SMA.
[506] s.64(3), SMA. If the EFSA forwards the information specified in subsection 64(1) of the SMA, then it is also to submit information about the investor protection scheme applicable in Estonia to the (other) Contracting State's securities market supervisory agency (s.64(6), SMA).
[507] s.64(5)(1), SMA.
[508] s.64(5)(2), SMA.
[509] s.64(5)(3), SMA.
[510] s.64(5)(4), SMA. Although authorisation may cover at least one of the ancillary services in Section B of Annex I to Directive 2004/39/EC, it is not to be granted solely for the provision of these services (Article 6(1), Directive 2004/39/EC).

forward information,[511] or the securities market supervisory agency of the Contracting State has notified the EFSA of a breach by the investment firm of that Contracting State's legislation.[512] The EFSA must immediately convey the precept specified in subsection 64(10) of the SMA to the investment firm.[513]

The establishment of a branch is a 'capital movement' in Title I of the nomenclature in Annex I. If the EFSA refuses to forward the information and documents to the securities market supervisory agency of the host EEA state, then the free movement of capital is restricted. To be justified under Article 65(1)(b) of the TFEU, the restrictive measures must be necessary for the protection of the interests that they are intended to guarantee, be proportionate, observe the requirements of legal certainty, and the persons affected by the measures must have access to legal redress.[514] The applicant investment firm does not have access to legal redress; although the SMA requires the EFSA to provide reasons for a decision to refuse to forward the information,[515] it does not give the applicant the right to appeal against the decision in the Estonian courts. Furthermore, not all of the grounds on which the EFSA may decide to forward the information provide the applicant with legal certainty; for example, the power that the SMA provides to the EFSA to refuse to forward the information if the investment firm's resources are insufficient to provide the services specified in the business plan in the Contracting State, gives the EFSA a discretion to decide what 'sufficient resources' are in the specific case, and, therefore, is not adequately specific or objective. Thus, the restrictive measures cannot be justified under Article 65(1)(b) of the TFEU. Consequently, they are contrary to the free movement of capital under Article 63 of the TFEU.

An investment firm that wishes to supply cross-border investment and ancillary services to a foreign country within the bounds of its authorisation is to notify the EFSA of its intention to provide these services,[516] and to submit the following documents and information to the

---

[511] s.64(10)(1), SMA.

[512] s.64(10)(2), SMA. Clause 64(10)(2) of the SMA refers to "legislation of a Contracting State". Since the supervisory agency of an EEA state is responsible for the oversight of firms which are authorised to provide services in that country, this reference is likely to be to the same country as that in which the agency operates.

[513] s.64(11), SMA.

[514] See the subsection '*The requirements for a successful public policy/security derogation*', in section 2.1.3.

[515] See note 495.

[516] s.65(1), SMA.

EFSA: the name of the state to which it intends to provide the investment and ancillary services,[517] and a business plan together with a description of the planned services.[518] If the investment firm intends to supply cross-border services to another Contracting State, then the EFSA is to decide to forward, or to refuse to forward, the specified information to the securities market supervisory agency of that State.[519] The EFSA is to immediately inform the investment firm of its decision to forward or refuse to forward the information.[520] If the EFSA decides to forward the information, then it is to be forwarded to the securities market supervisory agency of the corresponding Contracting State within one month of its receipt from the investment firm.[521] The EFSA is to take a decision to refuse to forward the information specified in subsection 65(1) of the SMA, if the documents and information submitted do not satisfy the requirements provided for in the SMA,[522] or are inaccurate, misleading, or incomplete,[523] or the investment firm wishes to supply only ancillary services.[524] The EFSA may issue a precept to prohibit an investment firm from providing cross-border services, if grounds to refuse to forward the information under subsection 65(4) of the SMA exist,[525] or the Contracting State's securities market supervisory agency has notified the EFSA of a breach by the investment firm of a Contracting State's legislation.[526] The investment firm is to terminate the provision of cross-border services in the Contracting State by the due date specified in the precept.[527]

Cross-border investment services are 'capital movements' under Titles III, IV and V of the nomenclature in Annex I.[528] If the EFSA refuses to forward the documents and information to the securities market supervisory agency of the other Contracting State, then it limits the free movement of capital. To be justified under Article 65(1)(b) of the TFEU, the restrictive measures must be necessary for the protection of the interests that they are intended to guarantee, be proportionate, meet the

---

[517] s.65(1)(1), SMA.
[518] s.65(1)(2), SMA.
[519] s.65(3), SMA.
[520] s.65(3), SMA.
[521] s.65(3), SMA.
[522] s.65(4)(1), SMA.
[523] s.65(4)(1), SMA.
[524] s.65(4)(2), SMA. See note 509.
[525] s.65(7)(1), SMA.
[526] s.65(7)(2), SMA.
[527] s.65(8), SMA.
[528] See chapter 2, note 37 for a description of investment services.

requirements of legal certainty, and the persons affected by the measures must have access to legal redress.[529] As the SMA does not provide the applicant investment firm with the right to appeal in the Estonian courts against a decision to refuse to forward the documents and information, the firm does not have access to legal redress. Thus, the restrictive measures cannot be justified under Article 65(1)(b) of the TFEU. Consequently, they are contrary to the free movement of capital under Article 63 of the TFEU.

Restrictions on the free movement of capital to third countries may be justified under Article 64(2) of the TFEU, provided that the national rules do not restrict the free movement of capital more than the equivalent provisions of the relevant Directive do, and that the EU institutions carefully take account of the objective of the free movement of capital whilst enacting the Directive.[530] Directive 2004/39/EC does not contain a provision similar to subsection 65(1) of the SMA.[531] Furthermore, the recitals to this Directive do not mention the free movement of capital, which is indicative that the EU institutions did not carefully take account of the objective of the free movement of capital whilst enacting Directive 2004/39/EC. Hence, the restrictions on the free movement of capital to foreign states are not justified by Article 64(2) of the TFEU, and are, therefore, contrary to Article 63 of the TFEU.

An investment firm that intends to provide cross-border multilateral trading facility operation services[532] to another country is to notify the EFSA of the name of this state.[533] The EFSA is to submit this information to the securities market supervisory agency of the corresponding Contracting State, within one month of its receipt, and is to immediately notify the investment firm thereof.[534] An investment firm is also to forward to the EFSA (if applicable) information on the participants of a

---

[529] See the subsection '*The requirements for a successful public policy/security derogation*', in section 2.1.3.

[530] See the subsection '*Derogations that apply only to capital movements to/from third countries*', in section 2.3.2.

[531] See note 496.

[532] The SMA does not define multilateral trading facility operation services. Directive 2004/39/EC defines a 'multilateral trading facility (MTF)' as a multilateral system, operated by a market operator or an investment firm, which brings together multiple third party buying and selling interests in financial instruments in a manner that results in a contract (Article 4(1)(15), Directive 2004/39/EC).

[533] s.65^1(1), SMA.

[534] s.65^1(2), SMA.

multilateral trading facility that is established in Estonia.[535] The EFSA is to submit this information to the securities market agency of the corresponding Contracting State within a reasonable time.[536]

Multilateral trading facility operation services are not explicitly included as 'capital movements' in the nomenclature in Annex I. Nevertheless, as the list of capital movements therein is not exhaustive,[537] and as Title XIII of the nomenclature includes "Miscellaneous" capital movements, these may be 'capital movements'. The provisions of section 65^1 of the SMA do not restrict the free movement of capital, as they only require the applicant market operator or investment firm to supply a small amount of information to the EFSA, and do not specify circumstances under which the provision of cross-border multilateral trading facility operation services are to be limited.

Chapter 8 Division 3: Activities of Foreign Investment Firms in Estonia

In order to establish a branch in Estonia, an investment firm that is registered in a third country is to apply for an authorisation from the EFSA.[538] Upon application for this permission, an investment firm must submit a written application, and the following documents and information, to the EFSA:[539] the name and address of the branch,[540] the names and personal identification codes of the branch's directors,[541] the names of persons with qualifying holdings in the investment firm,[542] an official certificate that concerns the existence of the company in its home country,[543] an authorisation document that certifies the authority of the branch's director or a copy of the resolution appointing this director,[544] a copy of the investment firm's articles of association or partnership

[535] s.65^1(3), SMA.
[536] s.65^1(3), SMA.
[537] See section 2.1.1.
[538] s.66(1), SMA.
[539] s.66(3), SMA.
[540] s.66(3)(1), SMA.
[541] ss.66(3)(2), SMA, and 387(10), Commercial Code.
[542] ss.66(3)(3) and 73(2), SMA. For the purposes of the SMA, a 'qualifying holding' is any holding in the share capital of a company that represents at least 10 per cent of the company's share capital, of all the rights related to this holding, or of the voting rights in the company, or of any holding that makes it possible to exercise a significant influence over the management of the company (s.9(1), SMA).
[543] ss.66(3)(4), SMA, and 386(2)(1), Commercial Code.
[544] ss.66(3)(4), SMA, and 386(2)(3), Commercial Code.

agreement,[545] the telecommunications data of the investment firm and of the branch,[546] the investment firm's annual reports for the most recent two financial years,[547] the branch's three-year business plan – which is to include a description of the planned activities, organisational structure, place(s) of business, technical facilities, and economic indicators of the branch,[548] and a description of the branch's relationship with the founding investment firm.[549] In addition to the documents and information specified in subsection 66(3) of the SMA, an investment firm registered in a third country is to submit the following items to the EFSA via the securities market supervisory authority of its home state: permission to found a branch in Estonia,[550] confirmation that the investment firm holds a valid activity licence in its home state and that it pursues its activities in a correct fashion and in accordance with good business practice,[551] and information on the investment firm's financial circumstances, including the size of its own funds, capital adequacy and solvency, and the investor protection scheme in its home state.[552]

Unless otherwise stated in this Division, applications for permission, and for the review, grant and revocation of permission, are to be subject to the provisions of subsections 51, 52, 53, 55(1)-(4^1), 55^1, 56 and 58 of the SMA.[553] A decision concerning an activity licence is to state the name and registry code of the person with regard to whom the decision is made,[554] the type of investment and ancillary services with regard to which the decision is made,[555] the date on which the decision is made,[556] and the date on which this decision enters into force.[557] The EFSA is to refuse to issue an activity licence if the documents or information submitted upon application for the activity licence do not satisfy the requirements provided for in the SMA or legislation established on the basis of this Act,[558] the documents or information are inaccurate, misleading or

[545] ss.66(3)(4), SMA, and 386(2)(4), Commercial Code.
[546] ss.66(3)(4), SMA, and 386(2)(5), Commercial Code.
[547] s.66(3)(5), SMA.
[548] ss.66(3)(6) and 54(1)(11), SMA.
[549] s.66(3)(6), SMA.
[550] s.66(4)(1), SMA.
[551] s.66(4)(2), SMA.
[552] s.66(4)(3), SMA.
[553] s.67(1), SMA.
[554] s.51(2)(1), SMA.
[555] s.51(2)(2), SMA.
[556] s.51(2)(3), SMA.
[557] s.51(2)(3), SMA.
[558] s.56(1), SMA.

incomplete,[559] the applicant does not submit the documents and information to the EFSA within the prescribed period,[560] the applicant does not satisfy the requirements of the SMA or its secondary legislation,[561] in the opinion of the EFSA, the person conducting the internal audit function of the applicant (or a person who has a qualifying holding in the applicant)[562] does not fulfil the requirements of the SMA,[563] the applicant has materially or repeatedly contravened requirements provided for in legislation,[564] the applicant's omission or activities are contrary to good business practice,[565] close links between the applicant and another person prevent adequate supervision of the investment firm,[566] or the requirements arising from legislation or the implementation of legislation of the country in which legal provisions are applied to the applicant or to the person with whom the applicant has close links prevent adequate supervision over the investment firm.[567] Furthermore, the EFSA may refuse to grant permission if the securities market supervisory agency, or the legislation, of the home country of the applicant investment firm do not guarantee sufficient supervision of the applicant, or if no agreement between the EFSA and the home state's securities market supervisory agency (concerning the exercise of supervision over the investment firm's subsidiary or branch) has been entered into and co-operation between the EFSA and the securities market supervisory agency of the home country is inadequate.[568]

The EFSA may revoke permission for an investment firm from a third country to found a branch or subsidiary in Estonia, if the circumstances in section 58 of the SMA, or in subsection 67(2) of the SMA, become evident.[569] The EFSA may revoke an activity licence if the investment firm does not commence activities within one year of the issue of this licence,[570] the investment firm's founders indicate that the firm will be unable to commence activities within one year of the issue of the

---

[559] s.56(1), SMA.
[560] s.56(2), SMA.
[561] s.56(3), SMA.
[562] See note 542, for the definition of 'qualifying holding'.
[563] s.56(4), SMA.
[564] s.56(5), SMA.
[565] s.56(5), SMA.
[566] s.56(6), SMA.
[567] s.56(6), SMA.
[568] s.67(2), SMA.
[569] s.67(4), SMA. Section 58 of the SMA is below in this paragraph. Subsection 67(2) of the SMA is the last sentence of the previous paragraph.
[570] s.58(2)(1), SMA.

licence,[571] the investment firm has not supplied investment services for more than half a year,[572] the investment firm has submitted misleading or inaccurate information, or misleading or falsified documents,[573] the investment firm has contravened repeatedly, or to a material extent, the provisions of legislation that regulates the activities thereof,[574] the investment firm or its manager has been punished for a specified offence (such as official misconduct),[575] the investment firm does not satisfy the current requirements with regard to the issue of activity licences,[576] the person conducting the investment firm's internal audit function (or a person who has a qualifying holding in the investment firm)[577] does not satisfy the requirements of the SMA,[578] close links between the investment firm and another person prevent adequate supervision of the investment firm,[579] the requirements that arise from legislation or the implementation of legislation of the country in which legal provisions are applied to the investment firm or to the person with whom the firm has close links prevent sufficient supervision over the firm.[580] the investment firm has not implemented a precept issued by the EFSA within the requirement period or to the extent prescribed,[581] the amount of the investment firm's own funds does not comply with the requirements of the SMA or its secondary legislation,[582] the activities of the investment firm significantly damage the interests of its clients or adversely affect the normal functioning of the securities market,[583] the investment firm has been involved in money laundering or contravenes the legislative procedure for preventing money laundering and terrorist financing,[584] the structure of the investment firm's group prevents the receipt of information necessary for the group's consolidated supervision,[585] a company that belongs to the same group as the investment firm operates on the basis of a foreign country's legislation

---

[571] s.58(2)(1), SMA.
[572] s.58(2)(1), SMA.
[573] s.58(2)(2), SMA.
[574] s.58(2)(3), SMA.
[575] s.58(2)(3), SMA.
[576] s.58(2)(4), SMA.
[577] See note 542, for the definition of 'qualifying holding'.
[578] ss.58(2)(5) and 56(4), SMA.
[579] ss.58(2)(5) and 56(6), SMA.
[580] ss.58(2)(5) and 56(6), SMA.
[581] s.58(2)(6), SMA.
[582] s.58(2)(7), SMA.
[583] s.58(2)(8), SMA.
[584] s.58(2)(9), SMA.
[585] s.58(2)(10), SMA.

– which prevents the exercise of adequate supervision,[586] the investment firm does not pay its contributions to the Investor Protection Sectoral Fund in full or within the specified period,[587] the investment firm has published materially incorrect or misleading information or advertising about its activities or managers,[588] the investment firm has contravened the requirements that are provided for in legislation of the Contracting State,[589] the internal rules specified in section 82 of the IFA are not sufficiently accurate or unambiguous to regulate the investment firm's activities,[590] or it becomes clear that the investment firm has chosen Estonia as the country for application of the activity licence and registration in order to evade stricter standards in force in another Contracting State within whose territory the firm conducts the majority of its activities.[591]

The establishment of a branch or a fully-owned subsidiary is a 'capital movement' under Title I of the nomenclature in Annex I. The above grounds for refusing to issue, or revoking, permission to found a branch or subsidiary of a third country investment firm in Estonia, limit the free movement of capital. To be justified under Article 65(1)(b) of the TFEU, the restrictive measures must be necessary for the protection of interests that they are intended to guarantee, be proportionate, and observe the requirements of legal certainty, and the persons whom the measures affect must have access to legal redress.[592] Not all of the restrictive measures observe the requirements of legal certainty; for instance, the ground in subsection 67(2) of the SMA for the EFSA to refuse to grant permission for the foundation of a branch or subsidiary in Estonia, gives the EFSA a discretion as to whether to grant or refuse permission, and, therefore, is not specific and objective so as to provide the applicant investment firm with legal certainty. Furthermore, the investment firm does not have sufficient access to legal redress, because the SMA does not provide it with the right

[586] s.58(2)(10), SMA.
[587] s.58(2)(11), SMA.
[588] s.58(2)(12), SMA.
[589] s.58(2)(13), SMA.
[590] s.58(2)(14), SMA. An investment firm is to establish and apply procedural rules that regulate the activities of the investment firm, its managers, and its employees, which ensure that legislation regulating the firm's activities is complied with, and that decisions taken by the directing bodies thereof are duly observed (s.82(1), SMA).
[591] s.58(2)(15), SMA.
[592] See the subsection '*The requirements for a successful public policy/security derogation*', in section 2.1.3.

to appeal in the Estonian courts against a decision to refuse or revoke permission.

To be justified under Article 64(2) of the TFEU, the EU institutions must carefully take account of the free movement of capital whilst legislating over the relevant area, and the national rules are not to restrict the free movement of capital more than the relevant Directive does.[593] The recitals of Directive 2004/39/EC do not mention the free movement of capital. Furthermore, although Article 15 of this Directive considers the access of EU investment firms to third countries, and Article 63 of the Directive empowers Member States and the European Securities and Markets Authority to conclude co-operation agreements for the exchange of information with the financial supervision authorities of third countries, the Directive does not explicitly provide for investment firms registered in third countries to establish a branch or subsidiary in an EEA state.[594] Thus, the restrictive measures of Division 3 of Chapter 8 of the ESMA are not justified under Article 64(2) of the TFEU, and limit the free movement of capital as required by Article 63 of the TFEU.

If an investment firm that is registered in a foreign state intends to open a representative office in Estonia, it is to submit a notice to the EFSA, together with the following documents and information: confirmation from the securities market supervisory authority of its home country that the investment firm possesses a valid activity licence,[595] an action plan for the representative office,[596] a document that certifies the authorisation of the representative,[597] a document that concerns the registration of the investment firm in its home state (such as an excerpt from the commercial register or a copy of the registration certificate),[598]

---

[593] See the subsection '*Derogations that apply only to capital movements to/from third countries*', in section 2.3.2.

[594] Recital 28 of Directive 2004/39/EC states: "The procedures for the authorisation, within the Community, of branches of investment firms authorised in third countries should continue to apply to such firms. Those branches should not enjoy the freedom to provide services … or the right of establishment in Member States other than those in which they are established. … ." The Directive's Articles do not consider this issue. As the internal market is within the area of shared competence between the EU and its Member States (Article 4(2)(a), TFEU), the Member States are able to exercise their competence to the extent that the EU has not exercised its competence (Article 2(2), TFEU).

[595] s.68(1)(1), SMA.

[596] s.68(1)(2), SMA.

[597] s.68(1)(3), SMA.

[598] s.68(1)(4), SMA.

the investment firm's articles of association,[599] and the seat, address, and telecommunications numbers of the representative office.[600] As the opening of a representative office does not involve the pursuit of an economic activity from that office, it is associated with the free movement of services, and is therefore not a 'capital movement' under Title I of the nomenclature in Annex I.[601]

An investment firm of a Contracting State that wishes to establish a branch in Estonia is to inform the securities market supervisory agency of that State thereof, and submit the following documents and information thereto: the branch's business plan, which is to contain information on all of the investment services or ancillary services to be provided, the branch's organisational structure, the fact as to whether the branch intends to use investment agents, and, if so, the agents' personal data,[602] the branch's address,[603] the names of the branch's managers,[604] and a description of the Contracting State's investor protection scheme.[605] The EFSA is to promptly inform the securities market supervisory agency of the Contracting State of the receipt of these documents and information.[606] An investment firm of a Contracting State may establish a branch and commence activities after receipt of a notice specified in subsection 69(3) of the SMA or two months after the date on which the documents and information specified in subsection 69(1) were received by the EFSA.[607] The EFSA is to confirm its receipt of the information specified in

[599] s.68(1)(5), SMA.
[600] s.68(1)(6), SMA.
[601] "[T]he concept of establishment within the meaning of Article 52 et seq. of the [Treaty Establishing the European Economic Community, now Article49 et seq. of the TFEU] involves the actual pursuit of an economic activity through a fixed establishment in another Member State for an indefinite period. Consequently the registration of a vessel does not necessarily mean establishment within the meaning of the Treaty [Establishing the European Economic Community, now the TFEU], in particular where the vessel is not used to pursue an economic activity or where the application for registration is made by or on behalf of a person who is not established, and has no intention of becoming established, in the State concerned." (*R. v Secretary of State for Transport, ex parte Factortame Ltd. and Others* [1991] ECR I-3905, at paragraphs 20-21).
[602] s.69(1)(1), SMA.
[603] s.69(1)(2), SMA.
[604] s.69(1)(3), SMA.
[605] s.69(1)(4), SMA.
[606] s.69(3), SMA.
[607] s.69(4), SMA.

subsection 69(1) upon the entry of a branch in the commercial register.[608] An Estonian branch of an investment firm of a Contracting State is to perform the obligations in clauses 85(1)(1)-85(1)(12) of the SMA,[609] and in sections 86-87^6, 88^1-88^12, 89^1, 90, and 91 of the SMA.[610]

The foundation of a branch is a 'capital movement' in Title I of the nomenclature in Annex I. The requirements stated in the above paragraph are informational. However, sections 56 and 58 of the SMA, which consider circumstances in which the EFSA may refuse to grant, or revoke, an activity licence, apply to applications for permission and the review, grant and revocation thereof.[611] Together, these requirements restrict the free movement of capital. To be justified under Article 65(1)(b) of the TFEU, the restrictive measures must be necessary for the protection of the interests that they are intended to guarantee, be proportionate, and observe the requirements of legal certainty, i.e. be specific, objective, and known to the parties beforehand; furthermore, the persons affected by the

---

[608] s.69(5), SMA.

[609] The SMA translation erroneously states "clauses 85 1) – 12)" rather than "clauses 85(1) 1) – 12)". Subsection 85(1) of the SMA contains general obligations of investment firms, such as to provide investment and ancillary services lawfully, with due professionalism and care, and in the client's best interests (s.85(1)(1), SMA).

[610] s.69(6), SMA. Sections 86-87^6 and 88^1-88^12 of the SMA contain provisions that relate to how the investment firm must conduct the process of providing investment services to clients. For example, an investment firm is to establish and implement legal, technical and organisational measures for the best execution of client orders, and to decide the procedure and rules for this best execution by its internal policies (s.87^3, SMA). Section 89^1 of the SMA considers reports on investment services provided to clients. An investment firm is to submit to its client a clear and appropriate report on the services that it provides to the client, including the costs associated with the services and transactions that are undertaken on behalf of the client (s.89^1, SMA). Section 90 of the SMA concerns the investment firm's record-keeping and retention obligation. An investment firm or a branch of a foreign investment firm, which is entered in the Estonian commercial register, is to keep records of the services provided and the transactions concluded and the communication between the investment firm and the client, and retain these records (s.90(1), SMA). Section 91 of the SMA considers the reporting of investment transactions. An investment firm or a branch of an investment firm of a Contracting State or a third country, which is entered in the Estonian commercial register, is to notify the EFSA of each transaction with securities that are admitted for trading on the regulated market of a Contracting State (s.91(1), SMA).

[611] s.67(1), SMA. Sections 56 and 58 of the SMA are discussed above in this subsection.

measures must have access to legal redress, i.e. intervention is to be accompanied by a formal statement of reasons and subject to review by the courts.[612] The applicant investment firm is not empowered to apply to the Estonian courts for the review of an adverse decision by the EFSA. Consequently, the restrictive measures cannot be justified by Article 65(1)(b) of the TFEU. Therefore, Article 69 of the TFEU, together with Articles 56 and 58 of the TFEU, limit the free movement of capital in contravention of Article 63 of the TFEU.

An investment firm that is registered in a Contracting State may start to provide cross-border investment services in Estonia, once the EFSA has received the information specified in subsection 65(1) of the SMA from the securities market supervisory agency of that Contracting State.[613] This information comprises a notification from the investment firm to that agency of the firm's intention to start providing cross-border services,[614] the name of the state to which the firm intends to supply investment and ancillary services,[615] and a business plan, which includes a description of the planned services.[616] Furthermore, the provision of cross-border multilateral trading facility operation services may be commenced in Estonia, after the EFSA has received the relevant notice from the securities market supervisory agency of the (other) Contracting State.[617]

Cross-border investment services are 'capital movements' under Titles III, IV and V of the nomenclature in Annex I.[618] The requirement for the investment firm to provide the small amount of information stated in the above paragraph does not (significantly) restrict the free movement of capital. Consequently, section 70 of the SMA does not contravene Article 63 of the TFEU.

To provide cross-border services in Estonia, an investment firm from a third country is required to apply for permission from the EFSA.[619] This firm must submit an application to which the following documents and

---

[612] See the subsection '*The requirements for a successful public policy/security derogation*', in subsection 2.1.3.
[613] s.70(1), SMA.
[614] s.65(1), SMA.
[615] s.65(1)(1), SMA.
[616] s.65(1)(2), SMA.
[617] s.65(1)(3), SMA. The EFSA may submit an application to the securities market supervisory authority of the Contracting State, in order to acquire the personal data of the firm's investment agents in Estonia, and to obtain information about the members and participants of the investment firm's multilateral trading facility (s.70(4), SMA).
[618] See chapter 2, note 37 for a description of investment services.
[619] s.70^1(1), SMA.

information are appended: the firm's name and address,[620] the scope of the firm's activity licence,[621] information concerning the agency that issued the activity licence,[622] the documents and information provided for in clauses 366(2)(1)-(3) and 366(2)(5) of the Commercial Code,[623] the information in clause 54(1)(5) of the SMA concerning the investment firm's managers,[624] the documents and information that subsection 74(1) of the SMA provides for – relating to shareholders who have qualifying holdings in the investment firm,[625] the investment firm's audited annual

---

620 s.70¹(1)(1), SMA.

621 s.70¹(1)(2), SMA.

622 s.70¹(1)(2), SMA.

623 s.70¹(1)(3), SMA. These documents and information are an official certificate that confirms the company's existence in its home country, such as an excerpt from a commercial register or a copy of a registration certificate (s.386(2)(1), Commercial Code), the permission to establish the branch (s.386(2)(2), Commercial Code), a document that certifies the authority of the branch's director or a copy of the resolution that appoints this director (s.386(2)(3), Commercial Code), and telecommunications data of the company and of the branch (s.386(2)(5), Commercial Code). Three of these four items refer to a branch, even though section 70¹ of the SMA concerns the provision of cross-border services (rather than the establishment of a branch).

624 s.70¹(1)(4), SMA. This information comprises, for each manager, the name, personal identification code (or date and place of birth), education and employment history, and for the board of directors, a description of each director's areas of responsibility, and documents that certify the trustworthiness of these managers and conformity to the requirements of the SMA (s.54(1)(5), SMA).

625 s.70¹(1)(5), SMA. These documents and information comprise a description of the company acquired (including an excerpt of the share register, and information on the type of shares and number of votes acquired or owned by the acquirer), the curriculum vitae of the acquirer (if a natural person), the name, registered office, registry code, authenticated copy of a registration certificate, and a copy of the acquirer's articles of association (if the acquirer is a legal person, or of the legal person that administers the asset pool), a list of the owners or members of the acquirer and the number of shares held by each owner/member or the size of the shareholding and the number of votes of each owner/member (if the acquirer is a legal person), information on the members of the supervisory board and the management board of the acquirer (if a legal person), confirmation that the persons who become managers of the investment firm as a result of acquiring a holding have not been punished for a specified offence (such as official misconduct), a description of the acquirer's business activities, a description of the financial and non-financial interests of persons connected with the acquirer, the acquirer's three most recent annual reports (including an auditor's report for each annual report), an audited interim report for the first six months of the financial year (if more than nine months have elapsed since the end of the previous financial year), the ratings

reports for the last two financial years,[626] and the firm's business plan – which is to satisfy the requirements provided for in clause 54(1)(11) of the SMA and to specify all the services that the investment firm is to provide in Estonia.[627] An investment firm of a third country is also to submit the following items to the EFSA: the permission of its home state's financial supervision authority to provide cross-border services in Estonia,[628] a confirmation by the home country's financial supervision authority that the applicant investment firm holds a valid activity licence in its home state and that it pursues its activities in a correct fashion and in accordance with good practice,[629] information that the financial supervision authority of the home state provides on the applicant's financial circumstances,[630] and a description of the prudential requirements that apply to the investment firm in its home state.[631]

---

for assessment of the acquirer's financial situation (if a natural person) and companies connected with the acquirer and their public reports, the credit ratings issued to the acquirer (if a legal person) and to its group, a description of the structure of the acquirer's group, data concerning the sizes of the shareholdings of the companies that belong to the acquirer's group, and the group's three most recent annual reports (including an auditor's report for each annual report), documents that certify the acquirer's financial status (if a natural person) during the last three years, documents and information that concern the sources of financial and non-financial resources that the acquirer intends to use in order to obtain or increase a qualifying holding in the investment firm or to gain control of this firm, the size of the qualifying holding, the business plan and other circumstances concerning the acquisition and exercise of control of the investment firm, and a review of the strategy that is applied in the investment firm (s.74(1), SMA).

[626] s.70¹(6), SMA.

[627] s.70¹(7), SMA. Upon application for an activity licence, the applicant is to submit its three year business plan, which includes a description of its planned activities, organisation structure, places of business, technical facilities, and a description of its economic indicators (s.54(1)(11), SMA).

[628] s.70¹(2)(1), SMA.

[629] s.70¹(2)(2), SMA.

[630] s.70¹(2)(3), SMA. This information is to include the amount the investment firm's own funds, and a description of the investor protection scheme that applies to the firm's clients in the home state (s.70¹(2)(3), SMA).

[631] s.70¹(2)(4), SMA. This description includes information about capital and liquidity requirements and the investment guarantee system of the home country, and a confirmation that these requirements are equivalent to those established by EU legislation (s.70¹(2)(4), SMA).

Unless otherwise provided for in this section,[632] applications for authorisations, review of these applications, and the grant and revocation of authorisations are to be subject to sections 55, 55^1, 56, and 58 of the SMA.[633] Section 56 states several grounds on which the EFSA is to refuse to issue an activity licence to the applicant.[634] Section 58 contains many grounds on which the EFSA may revoke an activity licence.[635] In addition to refusal to issue an activity licence on the bases in section 56 of the SMA, the EFSA may refuse to grant an authorisation for the supply of cross-border services to Estonia if the financial supervision authority of the relevant third country does not guarantee sufficient oversight of the applicant investment firm, or has no legal basis, possibilities or readiness for adequate, efficient co-operation with the EFSA.[636] The EFSA may revoke an authorisation for the provision of cross-border services to Estonia, if circumstances provided for in section 58 of the SMA[637] or in subsection 70^1(5) of the SMA[638] become evident.[639]

An investment firm from a third country that wishes to provide cross-border services to Estonia that are not specified in the business plan that it submitted upon its application for an authorisation for the provision of these services, is to submit an application for amendment of the authorisation for the provision of cross-border services to the EFSA.[640] In order to amend an authorisation for the supply of cross-border services, the investment firm is to submit the documents and information specified in clauses 70^1(2)(1), 70^1(2)(2), and 70^1(2)(5) of the SMA to the EFSA.[641] The provisions of sections 55, 55^1 and 56 of the SMA apply to the processing of applications for the amendment of authorisations for the supply of cross-border services, verification of information, and decisions on the amendment of the authorisations.[642]

---

[632] Section 70^1 of the SMA.

[633] s.70^1(4), SMA.

[634] See above in this subsection.

[635] See above in this subsection.

[636] s.70^1(5), SMA.

[637] See above in this subsection.

[638] See above in this paragraph.

[639] s.70^1(6), SMA.

[640] s.70^1(7), SMA.

[641] s.70^1(8), SMA. See above in this subsection. The English translation of the SMA erroneously refers to clause 70^1(5), which is not present in this document.

[642] s.70^1(9), SMA. Section 55 of the SMA considers the review of an application for an activity licence. Section 55^1 of the SMA concerns the issue of an activity

Cross-border investment services are 'capital movements' under Titles III, IV and V of the nomenclature in Annex I.[643] The extensive informational requirements in subsection $70^{1}(1)$ of the SMA, and the grounds contained in sections 56 and 58 of the SMA for the EFSA to refuse to issue, or revoke, an activity licence, limit the free movement of capital. To be justified under Article 65(1)(b) of the TFEU, the restrictive measures must be necessary for the protection of interests that they are intended to guarantee, be proportionate, and observe the requirements of legal certainty, and the persons affected by the measures are to have access to legal redress.[644] The applicant investment firm does not have sufficient access to legal redress, because the SMA does not provide it with the right to appeal against a decision to refuse to issue an authorisation to provide cross-border investment services in Estonia, or to revoke an authorisation to supply these services. Furthermore, the restrictive measures do not all observe the requirements of legal certainty; for example, section $70^{1}(5)$ of the SMA gives the EFSA a discretion to refuse to issue an authorisation to the third country investment firm on the ground that the financial supervision authority in that state has no legal basis, possibilities or readiness for adequate, efficient co-operation with the EFSA. In addition, the extensive informational requirements in subsection 70^{1} of the SMA may be disproportionate to the request for permission to provide cross-border investment services to Estonia. Hence, the restrictive measures are not justified under Article 65(1)(b) of the TFEU.

For these measures to be justified under Article 64(2) of the TFEU, the EU institutions must carefully take account of the objective of the free movement of capital whilst enacting the legislation, and the national rules should not restrict the free movement of capital more than the equivalent provisions of the Directive do. The recitals of Directive 2004/39/EC do not refer to the free movement of capital. Directive 2004/39/EC does not contain any specific rules on the provision of cross-border services from third countries to Estonia, and, as the internal market is an area of shared competence between the EU and its Member States, the Estonian legislature is free to legislate on this specific topic.[645] As derogations from

---

licence by the EFSA. Section 56 of the SMA contains grounds for the EFSA to refuse to issue an activity licence; see above in this subsection.

643 See chapter 2, note 37 for a description of investment services.

644 See the subsection '*The requirements for a successful public policy/security derogation*', above in section 2.1.3.

645 See note 594.

the free movement of capital are to be interpreted strictly,[646] these circumstances are outside the scope of the Article 64(2) of the TFEU. Consequently, the Estonian legal provisions in respect of the supply of cross-border services from third countries to Estonia restrict the free movement of capital, in contravention of Article 63 of the TFEU.

Section 82^6: outsourcing of operations related to investment services

For the better performance of its duties, an investment firm has the right to outsource operations that relate to investment services to third parties.[647] The outsourcing is to satisfy the following conditions.[648] It is to damage the interests of neither the investment firm, nor the firm's clients.[649] It is to preclude neither the investment firm's activities, nor adequate supervision over the firm.[650] The outsourcing must not result in the delegation by the investment firm's managers of its responsibilities.[651] The outsourcing is not to change the investment firm's relationship with, and obligations to, its clients.[652] The third party to whom operations are outsourced has the required qualifications and the ability to perform the functions assumed thereby.[653] The investment firm has the right to supervise those operations of the third person that are related to the supply of investment services.[654] The outsourcing is not to undermine the conditions with which the investment firm must comply, in order to be authorised (and remain authorised) in accordance with the SMA.[655] The outsourcing is not to modify or remove any other conditions subject to which the EFSA granted the authorisation to the investment firm,[656] and other requirements arising from, and established on the basis of, the SMA, are satisfied.[657]

---

[646] See *Eglise de Scientologie and Scientology International*, [2000] ECR I-1335, in the subsection '*Public policy, public security, general interest, and prior authorisation*', in section 2.1.3.
[647] s.82^6(1), SMA.
[648] s.82^6(2), SMA.
[649] s.82^6(2)(1), SMA.
[650] s.82^6(2)(2), SMA.
[651] s.82^6(2)(3), SMA.
[652] s.82^6(2)(4), SMA.
[653] s.82^6(2)(5), SMA.
[654] s.82^6(2)(5), SMA.
[655] s.82^6(2)(6), SMA.
[656] s.82^6(2)(7), SMA.
[657] s.82^6(2)(8), SMA.

An investment firm is to take measures for outsourcing, to ensure that the following conditions are fulfilled.[658] The provider or the outsourced service (the service provider) must have the ability, capacity, and any authorisation that legislation requires, to perform the functions, supply the services, or carry out the activities reliably and professionally.[659] The service provider is to conduct the services effectively.[660] The investment firm is to establish methods to evaluate and measure the service provider's standard of performance.[661] The service provider must supervise adequately the provision of the outsourced services, and sufficiently manage the risks associated with the activities.[662] The investment firm is to take suitable measures for proper performance of the outsourced operations (as necessary).[663] The investment firm is to retain the necessary expertise to supervise, the outsourced services effectively, and to manage the risks associated with the service provider, and is to oversee these services and manage these risks.[664] The service provider is to inform the investment firm of any circumstances that may have a material impact on its ability to conduct the outsourced functions effectively and in compliance with the requirements.[665] The investment firm has the right to terminate the contract for outsourcing as necessary, giving reasonable advance notice, without detriment to the quality and continuity of its provision of services to clients.[666] The service provider is to co-operate with the EFSA or a securities market supervisory agency of another country in connection with the provision of services, as necessary.[667] The investment firm, its auditors, and the EFSA or another state's securities market supervisory agency, is to have access to data relating to the outsourced operations and to the service provider's business premises.[668] The service provider is to protect any confidential information concerning the investment firm and its clients.[669] The investment firm and the service provider are to implement legal, organisational, and technical measures, in

---

658 s.82^6(7), SMA.
659 s.82^6(7)(1), SMA.
660 s.82^6(7)(2), SMA.
661 s.82^6(7)(2), SMA.
662 s.82^6(7)(3), SMA.
663 s.82^6(7)(4), SMA.
664 s.82^6(7)(5), SMA.
665 s.82^6(7)(6), SMA.
666 s.82^6(7)(7), SMA.
667 s.82^6(7)(8), SMA.
668 s.82^6(7)(9), SMA.
669 s.82^6(7)(10), SMA.

order to ensure regularity and continuity in the provision of investment services, by taking into consideration the nature of the outsourced activities.[670] The investment firm and the service provider shall establish, implement, and maintain a business continuity plan that prescribes periodic testing of backup systems and processes.[671] If an investment firm wishes to outsource the supply of securities portfolio management services that it provides to retail clients, to a service provider in a third country, the investment firm is to ensure that, in addition to the requirements of section 82^6 of the SMA, the following conditions are satisfied upon outsourcing: the service provider is authorised or registered in its home state to provide the outsourced service and is subject to adequate prudential supervision,[672] and a co-operation agreement is entered into between the EFSA and the third country supervisory authority of the service provider.[673] If these conditions are not satisfied, then an investment firm may only outsource the provision of investment services to a service provider situated in a third country only if the investment firm gives prior notification to the EFSA about the outsourcing arrangement and contract, and the EFSA does not object to this arrangement within 30 days of receipt of that notification.[674]

The EFSA has the right to issue a precept, in order to require termination of the outsourcing of operations that relate to investment services to a particular person, or of all contracts entered into between the investment firm and third parties for the outsourcing of the investment firm's operations.[675] The EFSA may issue this precept if the third party does not have the required qualifications for the conduct of the operations that are related to the investment firm's activities,[676] the legitimate interests of the investment firm's clients are contravened or there is a risk of contravention of these interests,[677] the securities market supervisory agency of a third country that exercises supervision over a person in that state has no legal basis or possibilities for co-operation with the EFSA,[678] a third party to whom the investment firm's operations are outsourced does not comply with the requirements necessary for the performance of

[670] s.82^6(7)(11), SMA.
[671] s.82^6(7)(11), SMA.
[672] s.82^6(9)(1), SMA.
[673] s.82^6(9)(2), SMA.
[674] s.82^6(10), SMA.
[675] s.82^6(12), SMA.
[676] s.82^6(13)(1), SMA.
[677] s.82^6(13)(2), SMA.
[678] s.82^6(13)(3), SMA.

these operations,[679] or other conditions specified in section 82^6 of the SMA are breached.[680]

Investment services are 'capital movements' in under Titles III, IV and V of the nomenclature in Annex I.[681] The free movement of capital rules apply if the investment firm and the service provider are situated in different countries, provided that the former is located in an EEA state. The provisions of section 82^6 of the SMA restrict the free movement of capital. To be justified under Article 65(1)(b) of the TFEU, these measures must be necessary for the protection of interests that they are intended to guarantee, be proportionate, and observe the requirements of legal certainty; furthermore, the persons affected by the measures are to have access to legal redress.[682] These persons do not have access to legal redress, because the SMA does not require the EFSA to provide reasons for issuing a precept in order to require termination of the outsourcing of operations that relate to investment services to a specific person, and because the Act does not provide this person with a right to appeal against the decision in the Estonian courts. Furthermore, not all of the grounds on which the EFSA may terminate the outsourcing arrangement are sufficiently specific and objective to provide the applicants with legal certainty. For instance, clause 82^6(2)(8), SMA states that other requirements arising from, and established on the basis of, the SMA, must be satisfied. This clause gives the EFSA discretion as to whether to permit or revoke the arrangement. Hence, the restrictive measures cannot be justified under Article 65(1)(b) of the TFEU.

To be justified under Article 64(2) of the TFEU, the EU institutions must carefully take into account the objective of the free movement capital whilst enacting the relevant legislation, and the national rules must not restrict the free movement of capital more than the equivalent provisions of the relevant Directive do. The recitals of Directive 2004/39/EC do not mention the free movement of capital. In addition, outsourcing is only mentioned once in this Directive.[683] Hence, the provisions of section 82^6

---

[679] s.82^6(13)(4), SMA.

[680] s.82^6(13)(5), SMA.

[681] See chapter 2, note 37 for a description of investment services.

[682] See the subsection '*The requirements for a successful public policy/security derogation*', in section 2.1.3.

[683] An investment firm may not outsource important operational functions in such a way as to materially impair the quality of its internal control and the ability of the supervisor to monitor the firm's compliance with all its obligations (Article 13(5), Directive 2004/39/EC). This paragraph is transposed as subsections 82^6(3) and 82^6(4) of the SMA, although these Estonian provisions do not refer to 'internal

of the SMA limit capital movement in contravention of Article 63 of the TFEU.

Sections 134^2 and 134^3: access to regulated markets[684] *in Contracting States*

A market operator that plans to permit access to the Estonian market to persons resident in another Contracting State is to submit the name of the State in which access is planned, and the names of market participants and remote members (if this information exists), to the EFSA.[685] If an operator plans to permit access to the Estonian market in another Contracting State, then the EFSA is to take a decision concerning the forwarding of this information to the securities market agency of the relevant Contracting State, and is to inform that agency thereof within one month of receiving the information.[686] A market operator may start its activities in another Contracting State, in compliance with the provisions of that State's legislation.[687] The EFSA is to submit, within a reasonable period of time, the data of the market participants and remote members established in Estonia to the securities market supervisory agency of the relevant Contracting State.[688]

A market operator that is registered in a Contracting State may permit access to a regulated market that it operates in that State, to persons resident in Estonia, after giving due notice thereof to the securities market supervisory agency of the Contracting State.[689] The EFSA may request from the securities market supervisory agency of that Contracting State information concerning the market participants and members of the market

control' and are broader than Article 13(5) of Directive 2004/39/EC in that reference is made to "operational functions or any other operations related to investment services" (s.82^6(3), IFA).

[684] For the purposes of the SMA, a 'regulated securities market' (or 'regulated market') is a multilateral system of organisational, legal, and technical measures that is managed or organised a Contracting State, which is established for the purpose of enabling continuous, regular trade for securities admitted for trading there, and under conditions in which the interests of different persons for the acquisition and transfer of securities are brought together under uniform conditions that result in the formation of a contract (s.3, SMA).

[685] s.134^2(1), SMA.

[686] s.134^2(2), SMA. The EFSA is to immediately inform the market operator of its decision to forward the information to the securities market agency of the other Contracting State (s.134^2(2), SMA).

[687] s.134^2(3), SMA.

[688] s.134^2(4), SMA.

[689] s.134^3(1), SMA.

regulated by this market operator.[690] The EFSA has the right to inform the agency that exercises supervision over a market operator of a Contracting State, of the contraventions that this operator commits in Estonia.[691]

The allowance of access to a regulated market is not a 'capital movement' in the nomenclature in Annex I. Nonetheless, this access makes way for the 'capital movements' of cross-border investment in the securities that are traded on this regulated market. The informational requirements in sections 134^2 and 134^3 of the SMA are light, and are, therefore, not restrictions on the free movement of capital.

Section 136: Suspension and termination of trading on a regulated market

A market operator has the right to cease or suspend trading with a security on the market if the security's issuer has contravened, with respect to the operator, an obligation that arises from legislation or the rules and regulations,[692] if the security "does not comply with the rules and regulations",[693] in order to protect investors' interests,[694] in order to prevent danger to the lawful or regular functioning of the market,[695] or on another basis that the rules and regulations provide.[696] An operator has the right to stop trading in a security on the market on the basis of an application from the issuer of this security, or from the person who requested admission of the securities for trading on the market, if the issuer has duly performed its obligations with respect to the operator, and arising from legislation, rules and regulations.[697] Suspension or cessation of trading with the securities specified in subsections 136(1) or 136(2) of the SMA must neither cause significant damage to investors, nor materially damage the regular functioning of the market.[698] A market operator is immediately to inform the EFSA of the suspension or cessation specified in subsections 136(1) or 136(2) of the SMA, and is to publish a notice to this effect on its website.[699]

---

[690] s.134^3(2), SMA.
[691] s.134^3(3), SMA.
[692] s.136(1)(1), SMA.
[693] s.136(1)(2), SMA. The SMA translation does not specify which rules and regulations the security should comply with.
[694] s.136(1)(3), SMA.
[695] s.136(1)(4), SMA.
[696] s.136(1)(4), SMA.
[697] s.136(2), SMA.
[698] s.136(3), SMA.
[699] s.136(4), SMA.

In order to protect investors' interests, avoid danger to the lawful, regular operation of the market, protect any other significant interest, or avoid any other threat, the EFSA has the right to issue a precept to a market operator,[700] or, in urgent cases, order a market operator to suspend trading with the securities for up to ten consecutive days every time that the requirements for trading or for forwarding or disclosure of regulated information provided by the SMA have been contravened, or there is reason to believe that this contravention is taking place,[701] stop trading with securities on the market,[702] or amend the suspension or cessation order provided for in subsection 136(1) of the SMA.[703] The EFSA has the right to demand from the securities market supervisory agency of another Contracting State the suspension of trading with securities on a market operating in that country, if this is necessary to protect the interests of Estonian investors, prevent danger to the lawful or regular operation of the market, protect another significant right or preclude another danger, unless circumstances in subsection 136(5) of the SMA exist.[704] The EFSA is to inform the securities market supervisory agency of other Contracting State, and the European Securities and Markets Authority, of the suspension or cessation of trading by the market operator in subsections 136(1) or 136(2) of the SMA, the precept or order to suspend or cease trading in subsection 136(5) of the SMA, or the EFSA's demand specified in subsection 136(6) of the SMA, and is to publish the relevant information on its website.[705]

Operations in securities on a regulated market are 'capital movements' under Title III, IV, or V of the nomenclature in Annex I.[706] The suspension or cessation of trading in these securities limits the free movement of capital. To be justified under Article 65(1)(b) of the TFEU, the restrictive measures must be necessary for the protection of interests that they are required to guarantee, be proportionate, observe the requirements of legal certainty, and the persons affected by the measures must have access to

[700] s.136(5), SMA.
[701] s.136(5)(1), SMA.
[702] s.136(5)(2), SMA.
[703] s.136(5)(3), SMA.
[704] s.136(6), SMA.
[705] s.136(7), SMA.
[706] Title III of the nomenclature comprises operations in securities that are normally dealt in on the capital market. Title IV of the nomenclature consists of operations in units of collective investment undertakings. Title V of the nomenclature comprises operations in securities and other instruments normally dealt with on the money market.

legal redress. [707] Not all of the above provisions provide legal certainty to the securities' issuer. For example, the EFSA's right to demand from the securities market agency of another Contracting State the suspension of trading with securities in that country on the ground of protecting another significant right or precluding another danger[708] is neither specific nor certain. Furthermore, the SMA does not provide persons affected by the measures with access to legal redress, as it neither requires the EFSA to give reasons for its decision, nor enables the securities' issuer to appeal against the adverse decision in the Estonian courts. Hence section 136 of the SMA restricts the free movement of capital in contravention of Article 63 of the TFEU.

Chapter 19 – Takeover Bids

The provisions of Chapter 19 of the SMA apply to takeover bids that are made to acquire voting rights in public limited companies that are registered in Estonia (Estonian target issuer), and of which all, or a certain type of, their shares, are traded on an Estonian market.[709] The provisions of the SMA, legislation established on the basis of the SMA, and other relevant legislation, are to apply to takeover bids that are made to acquire voting rights in Estonian target issuers, none of whose shares are traded on an Estonian market.[710]

The provisions of the SMA and legislation established on the basis thereof concerning takeover bids, are to apply to takeover bids that are made to acquire voting rights in public limited companies that are registered in another Contracting State (target issuer of Contracting State), provided that either of the following conditions have been satisfied:[711] the takeover bid for acquiring voting rights is made only with respect to voting shares that are being traded on an Estonian market,[712] or the takeover bid for acquiring voting rights is made simultaneously with respect to voting shares that are being traded on an Estonian market and a market of another Contracting State, provided that the shares were admitted for trading on an Estonian market for the first time, or that they were admitted for trading simultaneously on an Estonian market and a

---

[707] See the subsection '*The requirements for a successful public policy/security derogation*' in section 2.1.3.

[708] This is one of the grounds for demanding suspension in subsection 136(6) of the SMA.

[709] s.164(1), SMA.

[710] s.164(2), SMA.

[711] s.164(3), SMA.

[712] s.164(3)(1), SMA.

market of another Contracting State and the target issuer has decided to select the EFSA as the authority to supervise the takeover bid.[713] Only the provisions of the SMA, and legislation issued on the basis thereof that concerns the approval and processing of takeover bids, determination of fair purchase prices, and the disclosure of the contents of the prospectus for a takeover bid, shall apply to target issuers of Contracting States.[714] Other than this, the law of the country of the target issuer's seat is to apply to target issuers of Contracting States.[715]

For the purposes of the SMA, a 'takeover bid' is a public tender for the acquisition of shares for money, or securities traded on the market, to shareholders (target persons) of the target issuer.[716] The EFSA is to monitor the takeover bid's compliance "with legislation".[717] The EFSA is to execute supervision over the takeover bid.[718]

The acquirer is to obtain the EFSA's approval for the takeover bid.[719] The EFSA is not to approve a takeover bid that contravenes legislation.[720] The EFSA is to take a decision on the approval of a takeover bid, or of the exception stated in section 173 of the SMA,[721] within fifteen days of receiving a written application from the offeror.[722] If a share that serves as the object of a takeover bid registered in another Contracting State has been admitted for trading on the Estonian market, then a takeover bid may be made in Estonia, based on the prospectus of a takeover bid that is

---

713 s.164(3)(2), SMA.

714 s.164(4), SMA.

715 s.164(4), SMA. The provisions of Chapter 19 of the SMA neither apply to a public company that is established as an investment fund within the meaning of section 1 of the IFA, nor to an investment fund that is registered in another Contracting State (s.164(5), SMA). An 'investment fund' is a pool of assets that are established for collective investment, or a public limited company that is established for collective investment on the basis of the SMA, which is, or the assets of which are, managed by a management company on the principle of risk-spreading (s.1, IFA).

716 s.165(1), SMA. For the purposes of Chapter 19 of the SMA, a 'share' is a tradeable right, a tradeable depositary receipt, or any other transferable right for voting at a shareholders' general meeting (ss. 164(6), 2(1)(1), and 2(1)(7), SMA).

717 s.169(1), SMA; 'with legislation' probably means 'with Estonian legislation'.

718 s.169(3), SMA. This subsection states "together with the relevant operator of an exchange or the relevant operator", a phrase with an opaque meaning.

719 s.175(1), SMA.

720 s.175(2), SMA.

721 Section 173 of the SMA provides nine circumstances under which the EFSA has the right to grant an exception to the requirement for a mandatory takeover bid.

722 s.175(3), SMA.

approved by the competent supervision authorities of other Contracting States.[723]

If a person contravenes the obligations that are prescribe in section 166 of the SMA[724] but is not granted the right to withdraw from making a mandatory takeover bid in accordance with section 173 of the SMA, or if a person breaches the obligation in subsection 175(1) of the SMA,[725] then the person may not exercise voting rights in the target issuer, and these votes are not included in the quorum of the general meeting of the target issuer, until the time that the contravention is eliminated.[726] The EFSA has the right to issue a mandatory precept to the registrar of the Estonian Central Register of Securities for immediate execution to prohibit, for up to twenty days, the use and disposal of securities in a securities account that is held by an offeror, or a person acting in concert therewith, in the event that an illegal takeover bid is made, or that the offeror, and a person acting in concert therewith, performs other acts that are in contravention of the SMA or legislation that is established on the basis thereof.[727]

The acquisition in full of existing undertakings is a 'capital movement' in Title I of the nomenclature in Annex I. If the EFSA refuses to approve a takeover bid, it limits the free movement of capital. To be justified under Article 65(1)(b) of the TFEU, the restrictive measures are to be necessary for the protection of interests that they are intended to guarantee, be proportionate, observe the requirements of legal certainty, and the persons

---

[723] s.175(4), SMA.

[724] A person who has gained dominant influence over the target issuer is required to make a takeover bid for all the target issuer's shares, within twenty days as of gaining this influence (s.166(1), SMA). 'Dominant influence' is a situation in which the target company is a controlled company within the meaning of subsection 10(1) of the SMA (s.167(1), SMA). For the purposes of the SMA, a company controlled by a person is one that satisfies at least one of the following conditions: the person holds the majority of the votes that are represented by shares in the company, or holds the majority of the votes as a general partner or a limited partner, the person who is a general partner or a limited partner of the company has the right to appoint or remove the majority of members of the company's supervisory board or management board, the person who is a general partner, a limited partner, a partner, or a shareholder of the company controls alone the majority of votes pursuant to the agreement entered into with other general partners, limited partners, partners, or shareholders, or a person exercises, or has the power to exercise, control or dominant influence over a company (s.10(1), SMA).

[725] See above in this subsection.

[726] s.182(1), SMA.

[727] s.182(2), SMA.

affected by the measures must have access to legal redress. Section 175 of the SMA states that the EFSA must approve the takeover bid, but that it may refuse to approve a takeover bid that breaches legislation.[728] However, the Act does not provide any further specific grounds upon which the EFSA may not approve a bid. Hence, the EFSA has a discretion in taking the decision as to whether to approve or disapprove a takeover bid, which does not provide legal certainty to the offeror. In addition, the offeror does not have access to legal redress – the SMA neither requires the EFSA to provide reasons for its decision, nor gives the offeror a right to appeal against a refusal in the Estonian courts. Hence, the restrictive measures cannot be justified under Article 65(1)(b) of the TFEU. Consequently, they contravene Article 63 of the TFEU.

Sections 236^1 to 236^5: Supervision

The EFSA may require a foreign investment firm whose branch is registered in Estonia, or which provides its cross-border services in Estonia, to submit additional information and documents that are necessary for the exercise of supervision over that firm to the extent provided by the SMA, and, in addition, data necessary for the collection of statistical information – although not to a larger extent that that required from Estonian investment firms.[729] The EFSA has the right to demand, by issuing a precept, 1) performance of the duties provided by clauses 85(1)(1) to 85(1)(12) of the SMA, and sections 86 to 87^6, 88^1 to 88^8, and 89^1 to 91 of the SMA,[730] and by the legislation established for the specification of these duties, or 2) elimination of the circumstances that hinder the performance of these duties, with respect to an investment service that a foreign investment firm or its Estonian branch, supplies to persons located or resident in Estonia.[731] An investment firm whose branch is registered in Estonia or which provides cross-border investment services in Estonia, and whose activity licence has been suspended or

[728] See above in this subsection.

[729] s.236^1(1), SMA.

[730] Section 85 of the SMA considers general obligations of investment firms upon providing investment services and ancillary services to their clients. Sections 86 to 87^6, and 88^1 to 88^8, of the SMA, concern more specific obligations of investment firms towards their clients, such as the legal measures required for the impartial and expeditious execution of client orders (s.87^5, SMA). Sections 89^1 to 91 of the SMA concern the record-keeping and reporting obligations of investment firms.

[731] s.236^1(1), SMA.

revoked by a foreign securities market agency, is not to operate or provide services in Estonia.[732]

The EFSA may require a foreign investment firm or an operator of a regulated market of a Contracting State, which has a registered branch in Estonia, or which provides cross-border services in Estonia, to end contravention of the requirements provided for in the Acts (or in legislation established on the basis of these Acts) that apply to this investment firm or operator of a regulated market.[733] If a foreign investment firm or its branch breaches a requirement provided for in Estonian legislation, then the EFSA may apply the measures provided for in the SMA to terminate the contravention, or revoke the authorisation for establishment of the branch of provision of the cross-border services.[734] If a foreign investment firm, or market operator of a Contracting State, continues to breach the requirements provided for in legislation that is applicable to this investment firm or operator of a regulated market, then the EFSA is to inform the securities market supervisory agency of the Contracting State of the continuing contravention.[735] If the measures that the latter agency takes are insufficient, then the EFSA may apply, by issuing a precept, the measures specified in the EFSA for the termination of the contravention, or prohibit, by a precept, the foreign investment firm or market operator of a Contracting State from providing investment services to persons located or resident in Estonia or from operating in Estonia, and give prior notice thereof to the securities market supervisory agency of the foreign state.[736] The EFSA is to inform the foreign investment firm of the measures taken.[737] This firm may file a complaint against the applied measures with the Tallinn Administrative Court, either directly, or through a branch.[738]

In exceptional circumstances, the EFSA may, in order to safeguard investors and the public interest, apply measures provided for in (Estonian) legislation with regard to a foreign investment firm or market operator of a Contracting State, without informing the securities market agency of that foreign country in advance.[739] The EFSA is to promptly inform the European Commission, the European Securities and Markets

[732] s.236^1(2), SMA.
[733] s.236^1(3), SMA.
[734] s.236^1(4), SMA.
[735] s.236^1(5), SMA.
[736] s.236^1(6), SMA.
[737] s.236^1(7), SMA.
[738] s.236^1(7), SMA.
[739] s.236^1(8), SMA.

Authority, and the foreign state's securities market supervisory agency, of the measures taken on the basis of subsection 236^1(6) or subsection 236^1(8) of the SMA.[740] The EFSA is to co-operate with the securities market supervisory agency of a Contracting State, if the operations of a market operator of this State are significantly important from the viewpoint of the protection of investors and the functioning of the Estonian securities market,[741] and/or if the operations of the operator of the Estonian market are significantly important from the viewpoint of the functioning of the securities market of this State and the protection of local investors.[742]

The establishment of a branch and the provision of cross-border investment services are 'capital movements' in the nomenclature in Annex I. The issuance of a precept, or the taking of measures, in order to terminate a contravention of Estonian legislation with respect to these capital movements, limits the free movement of capital. To be justified under Article 65(1)(b) of the TFEU, the restrictive measures must be required for the protection of interests that they are intended to guarantee, be proportionate, and observe the requirements of legal certainty; furthermore, the persons who are affected by the measures are to have access to legal redress.[743] The foreign investment firm (or market operator) has insufficient access to legal redress because, whilst it may make a complaint against the restrictions to the national court, the SMA does not oblige the EFSA to provide the firm with reasons for placing these restrictions on it. In addition, the measures that the EFSA may take are neither specific nor objective, and, therefore, do not observe the requirements of legal certainty. For example, subsection 236^1(4) of the SMA empowers the EFSA to "apply the measures provided for in this Act or other legislation" in order to end the contravention, which is a vague phrase. Hence, the provisions of section 236^1 of the SMA cannot be justified under Article 65(1)(b) of the TFEU, and, therefore, restrict the free movement of capital in contravention of Article 63 of the TFEU.

If an Estonian investment firm that has established a branch in a foreign country, or which provides cross-border services to a foreign state, contravenes legislative requirements of that country, then the EFSA is to promptly apply measures for the termination of the breach on the proposal of the foreign securities market supervisory agency.[744] The EFSA is to

[740] s.236^1(9), SMA.

[741] s.236^1(10)(1), SMA.

[742] s.236^1(10)(2), SMA.

[743] See the subsection '*The requirements for a successful public policy/security derogation*', in section 2.1.3.

[744] s.236^2(1), SMA.

inform the foreign securities market supervisory agency of the measures that it is applying.[745] The EFSA is to immediately inform the securities market supervisory agency of the foreign country in which the branch of the Estonian investment firm is founded or to which the cross-border services are supplied, of revocation of the firm's activity licence or of permission for it to establish a branch in a foreign country, and of the precepts specified in subsections 64(8) and 65(7) of the SMA.[746] A branch of an investment firm, or an investment firm that provides cross-border services shall, at the request of a foreign securities market supervisory agency, submit information that is required for the exercise of supervision over the activities of the branch or investment firm in that foreign country.[747]

The foundation of a branch and the provision of cross-border investment services are 'capital movements' in the nomenclature in Annex I. If the EFSA revokes the investment firm's activity licence and/or permission to establish a branch in another Contracting State, or issues a precept to prohibit the supply of investment services through a branch or of cross-border investment services, then it limits the free movement of capital. To be justified under Article 65(1)(b) of the TFEU, the restrictive measures are to be necessary for the protection of the interests that they are intended to guarantee, be proportionate, and observe the requirements of legal certainty, and the persons who are affected by the measures must have access to legal redress.[748] As the SMA neither requires the EFSA to provide reasons for taking one (or more) of the above actions, nor gives the investment firm a right to appeal against these measures in the

---

[745] s.236^2(1), SMA.

[746] s.236^2(2), SMA. It is subsection 64(8) of the SMA, rather than subsection 64(10) of this Act, which contains the precept. The EFSA may prohibit the supply of services by an investment firm through the branch established in another Contracting State if grounds provided for in subsection 64(5) of the SMA for refusal to forward information and documents exist, or the securities market supervisory agency of the Contracting State has informed the EFSA of a breach by the investment firm of legislation of a Contracting State (s.64(10), SMA). The EFSA may issue a precept to prohibit the supply of cross-border services by an investment firm in a Contracting State, if grounds provided for in subsection 65(4) of the SMA for refusal to forward the information exists, or the securities market supervisory agency of the Contracting State has informed the EFSA of a contravention by the investment firm of a Contracting State's legislation (s.65(7), SMA).

[747] s.236^2(3), SMA.

[748] See the subsection '*The requirements for a successful public policy/security derogation*', in section 2.1.3.

Estonian courts, the firm does not have access to legal redress. Furthermore, the measures may be disproportionate, because they amount to (at least) the inability for the investment firm to continue to provide services in the relevant Contracting State. Thus, the restrictive measures are not scaled according to the severity of the breach of the Contracting State's legislation. Hence, these measures are not justified under Article 65(1)(b) of the TFEU, and are contrary to Article 63 of this Treaty.

If a third country issuer whose securities are offered to the public in Estonia, or are traded on a regulated market and whose home Contracting State is Estonia, contravenes Estonian legislative requirements concerning issuers, then the EFSA may apply measures for the termination of the breach provided for in the SMA, or issue a precept to prohibit the public offer of the issuer's securities or to trade the securities on a regulated market.[749] If an issuer whose securities are offered to the public in Estonia, or are traded on a regulated market and whose host Contracting State is Estonia, contravenes the requirements of Estonian legislation concerning issuers, then the EFSA is to inform the securities market supervisory agency of the issuer's home Contracting State and the European Securities and Markets Authority of the contravention.[750] If an issuer whose securities are traded on the regulated market of Estonia as the host Contracting State, a shareholder, an owner of other securities, or a person who pursuant to subsection 10(3) of the SMA is deemed to be the owner of the voting rights that arise from the shares of an issuer,[751] contravenes the requirements established by Estonian legislation, then the EFSA is to inform the securities market supervisory agency of this breach.[752]

If the measures that the securities market supervisory agency of the home Contracting State of an issuer are insufficient, then, in order to protect investors, the EFSA may issue a precept to apply measures provided for in the SMA for the termination of the breach, or to prohibit the public offer of the issuer's securities or trade its securities on a regulated market, and is to inform the securities market supervisory agency of the home Contracting State of the issuer and the European Securities and Markets Authority thereof in advance.[753] The EFSA is to inform the issuer of the measures that it has applied,[754] and is to promptly

[749] s.236^4(1), SMA.
[750] s.236^4(2), SMA.
[751] Subsection 10(3) of the SMA lists 12 categories of voting rights that a person may hold.
[752] s.236^4(2^{1}), SMA.
[753] s.236^4(3), SMA.
[754] s.236^4(4), SMA.

notify the European Commission and the European Securities Market Agency of the measures that it has taken on the basis of subsection 236^4(3) of the SMA.[755]

The offer of securities to the public, and the trading of securities on a regulated market, are ‘capital movements’ in Title III, IV or V of the nomenclature in Annex I. The issue of a precept to terminate these activities hinders the free movement of capital. To be justified under Article 65(1)(b) of the TFEU, the restrictive measures must be necessary for the protection of interests that they are intended to guarantee, be proportionate, and observe the requirements of legal certainty; furthermore, the persons affected by these measures must have access to legal redress.[756] The restrictive measures do not provide legal certainty to the securities' issuer, because they comprise any measures provided for in the SMA for the termination of the breach, or the prohibition of the offer of its securities to the public or the trade of these securities on a regulated market. Furthermore, this prohibition may be disproportionate, because it may be severe in relation to the magnitude of the particular contravention. In addition, the applicant securities' issuer is not entitled to legal redress, as the SMA neither requires the EFSA to provide reasons for issuing a precept, nor give the applicant the right to appeal against the restrictive measures in the Estonian courts. Hence, these measures are not justified under Article 65(1)(b) of the TFEU.

In the case of a third country, as specified in subsection 236^4(1) of the SMA, the restrictive measures may be justified under Article 64(2) of the TFEU if the EU institutions carefully take account of the free movement of capital whilst enacting the relevant legislation, and if the national provisions do not restrict the free movement of capital more than the equivalent provisions of the relevant Directive do.[757] The recitals of Directive 2004/39/EC do not mention the free movement of capital. Furthermore, this Directive makes no reference to the offer of securities to the public in an EEA state or the trading of securities on a regulated market in an EEA country, by a securities' issuer that is registered in a third country. As the internal market is an area of shared competence between the EU and its Member States, Estonia is free to legislate on this matter.[758] Since derogations from the free movement of capital are to be

---

[755] s.236^4(5), SMA.

[756] See the subsection ‘*The requirements for a successful public policy/security derogation*’, in section 2.1.3.

[757] See the subsection ‘*Derogations that apply only to capital movements to/from third countries*’, in section 2.3.2.

[758] See note 594.

interpreted strictly,[759] these circumstances are beyond the scope of the Article 64(2) of the TFEU. Consequently, Article 236^4(1) of the SMA is in breach of Article 63 of the TFEU.

If an issuer whose securities are offered to the public in a foreign country, or which are traded on a regulated market, and whose home Contracting State is Estonia, contravenes the legislative requirements of a foreign state regarding issuers, then the EFSA is to promptly apply measures for the termination of this breach, on the proposal of the foreign securities market supervisory agency.[760] The EFSA is to inform the foreign securities market supervisory agency of these measures.[761]

The offer of securities to the public, and the trading of securities on a regulated market, are 'capital movements' in Title III, IV or V of the nomenclature in Annex I. The application of measures to stop contravention of a foreign country's legislative requirements, limits the free movement of capital. To be justified under Article 65(1)(b) of the TFEU, the restrictive measures must be required for the protection of interests that they are intended to guarantee, be proportionate, and satisfy the requirements of legal certainty; furthermore, the persons affected by these measures must have access to legal redress.[762] The restrictive measures do not provide legal certainty to the securities' issuer, because section 236^5 of the SMA does not indicate what these measures might be. In addition, the applicant securities' issuer is not entitled to legal redress, because the SMA neither requires the EFSA to provide reasons for taking the restrictive measures, nor give the applicant the right to appeal against these actions in the Estonian courts. Hence, the measures are not justified under Article 65(1)(b) of the TFEU.

For the restrictive measures to be justified under Article 64(2) of the TFEU, the EU institutions must have carefully considered the free movement of capital whilst enacting the relevant legislation, and the national provisions are not to hinder the free movement of capital more than the equivalent provisions of the relevant Directive do.[763] The recitals of Directive 2004/39/EC do not mention the free movement of capital. In

[759] See *Eglise de Scientologie and Scientology International*, [2000] ECR I-1335, in the subsection '*Public policy, public security, general interest, and prior authorisation*', in section 2.1.3.

[760] s.236^5, SMA.

[761] s.236^5, SMA

[762] See the subsection '*The requirements for a successful public policy/security derogation*', in section 2.1.3.

[763] See the subsection '*Derogations that apply only to capital movements to/from third countries*', in section 2.3.2.

addition, Article 15 of the Directive provides for the EU institutions to take measures, if investment firms from the EEA do not have sufficient access to the markets of a third country; these actions are likely to limit the free movement of capital less than the measures that the EFSA would take pursuant to Article 236^5 of the SMA. Thus, the latter measures cannot be justified under Article 64(2) of the TFEU. Consequently, Article 236^5 of the SMA is in breach of Article 63 of the TFEU.

3.3 Credit Institutions

3.3.1 Credit Institutions Act 1999 (CIA)

A 'credit institution' is a company that receives repayable funds from the public and grants loans.[764] Cross-border credits are 'capital movements' within the nomenclature in Annex I.[765] Companies receiving repayable funds from the public must hold an authorisation from the EFSA.[766]

Chapter 2: Authorisation of credit institution (including passporting)

A credit institution that is established in Estonia, and which holds an activity licence issued by the EFSA, may supply the services specified in subsection 6(1) of the CIA in a foreign state by the establishment of a branch or the provision of cross-border services.[767] In the English translation, section 6 of the CIA is entitled "Financial services". For the purposes of the CIA, financial services are services to third parties, rendered by a person in the course of economic or professional activities, which comprise the conclusion of the following acts and transactions: deposit transactions – for the receipt of repayable funds from the public,[768] lending and borrowing operations,[769] leasing transactions,[770] payment services for the purposes of the PIA,[771] issue and administration of non-cash methods of payment,[772] transactions that create binding obligations to

[764] s.3(1), CIA.

[765] Current and deposit accounts, commercial credits and financial credits are in Titles VI, VII and VIII respectively.

[766] s.13, CIA.

[767] s.19¹, CIA. The CIA does not define "foreign" state.

[768] s.6(1)(1), CIA.

[769] s.6(1)(2), CIA.

[770] s.6(1)(3), CIA.

[771] s.6(1)(4), CIA. For the PIA, see section 3.5.

[772] s.6(1)(5), CIA.

persons in the future (including guarantees and commitments),[773] transactions for own account or the account of clients in traded securities provided in section 2 of the SMA[774] and in money market instruments,[775] acts and transactions that are related to the issue and sale of securities,[776] the provision of advice to clients on issues that concern economic activities,[777] acts and transactions that are related to the merger or division of companies,[778] money broking,[779] portfolio management,[780] investment advice,[781] the safeguarding and administration of securities,[782] the collection, processing, and transmission of credit information,[783] safe custody services,[784] and other acts and transactions that are similar in their essence to the financial transactions listed above.[785]

If a credit institution wishes to establish a subsidiary credit institution or branch in a foreign state, or acquire a shareholding in a foreign credit institution such that the latter would become a subsidiary, the credit institution is to submit an application for "the corresponding authorisation" to the EFSA,[786] which sets out the following data: the name of the foreign country,[787] the business name and address of the subsidiary or the address of the branch,[788] the foreign credit institution's most recent three annual reports in which the credit institution wishes to acquire a qualifying shareholding,[789] the action plan of the subsidiary or branch – together with a detailed description of its intended activities, a description of its

---

[773] s.6(1)(6), CIA.

[774] A 'security' comprises the following: a share or other similar tradeable right, a bond, convertible security or other tradeable debt obligation that is not a money market instrument, a subscription or other tradeable right to acquire the above securities, an investment fund unit, a money market instrument, a derivative security or a derivative contract, and a tradeable depositary receipt (s.2(1), SMA).

[775] s.6(1)(7), CIA.

[776] s.6(1)(8), CIA.

[777] s.6(1)(9), CIA.

[778] s.6(1)(9), CIA.

[779] s.6(1)(10), CIA.

[780] s.6(1)(11), CIA.

[781] s.6(1)(11), CIA.

[782] s.6(1)(12), CIA.

[783] s.6(1)(13), CIA.

[784] s.6(1)(14), CIA.

[785] s.6(1)(15), CIA.

[786] s.20(1), CIA.

[787] s.20(1)(1), CIA.

[788] s.20(1)(2), CIA.

[789] s.20(1)(3), CIA.

organisational structure, and "the relationship with the credit institution being founded",[790] data that relates to the subsidiary's managers or the branch's director – pursuant to subsection 48(7) of the CIA,[791] and data that relates to shareholders who have qualifying holdings in the subsidiary (pursuant to the requirements of section 30 of the CIA).[792] The EFSA is to inform the financial supervision authority of the foreign country of a submitted application within three months of the receipt of this application.[793]

The EFSA may refuse to provide an authorisation if the financial circumstances of the credit institution being acquired or founded or of the acquiring credit institution is insufficiently sound,[794] the organisational structure of the new branch or subsidiary credit institution is unsuitable for

---

[790] s.20(1)(4), CIA. This last phrase (in quotes) is opaque. It may mean the relationship between the subsidiary or branch and the credit institution that establishes the subsidiary or branch.

[791] s.20(1)(5), CIA. In order to appoint or elect a manager of a credit institution, the written consent of the person to be appointed or elected is required. A person is to submit his/her written consent, together with an overview of his/her education, work experience, engagement in enterprise, punishments in the punishment register, and confirmation that concern the absence of facts provided for in the CIA that prevent the right to be a manager of a credit institution. Eesti Pank (the Bank of Estonia) is to establish the procedure for the submission of documents and data to confirm that a person is suitable and trustworthy, and that he/she satisfies the requirements (s.48(7), CIA).

[792] s.20(1)(6), CIA. Upon assessment of an acquisition, increase of a qualifying holding, or converting a bank into a company that is controlled by an acquirer, the EFSA is to co-operate with the financial supervision authority of the relevant Contracting State if the acquirer is an insurer, credit institution, management company, investment fund, investment firm, or other person under financial supervision (provided that the relevant legal person has been authorised by the Contracting State's financial supervision authority), a parent company of one of the above institutions, or a person who controls one of the above institutions (s.30(6), CIA). For the purposes of the CIA, a 'qualifying holding' is a direct or indirect holding in the share capital of a company that represents at least 10 per cent of the share capital, or of all the rights or votes that are represented by the shares of the company, or which grants a dominant influence over the management of the company in another way (s.29(1), CIA).

[793] s.20(3), CIA. The EFSA may request additional documents and information, in order to verify the data specified in subsection 20(1) of the CIA (s.20(2), CIA). If the EFSA requests these additional items, then it is to inform the foreign financial supervision authority of a submitted application within three months of receiving these items (s.20(3), CIA).

[794] s.20(4)(1), CIA.

the proposed activities,[795] the branch's director or the managers of the subsidiary credit institution do not satisfy the requirements of sections 48, 53, 56 and 57 of the CIA,[796] or the foreign country's legislation precludes the exercise of sufficient supervision or the receipt of information that is required for this.[797] The EFSA shall send a written, reasoned decision on the grant, or refusal to grant, authorisation, to the credit institution within three months of the receipt of the application specified in subsection 20(1) of the CIA or of additional data specified in subsection 20(2) of the CIA.[798] The EFSA is to inform the foreign financial supervision authority of the grant of an authorisation, and is to co-ordinate the principles of supervision and liability.[799]

The EFSA may revoke the authorisation granted to a credit institution to found a branch in the foreign country, if the credit institution or its branch in the foreign state does not satisfy the requirements provided by legislation with which compliance was necessary in order to obtain the authorisation,[800] the credit institution does not submit reports on its branch as required,[801] the credit institution has submitted misleading documents or information, or incorrect information or falsified documents concerning its branch to the EFSA,[802] the credit institution has materially or repeatedly contravened requirements of the foreign country's legislation that may damage the interests of its clients,[803] the credit institution has not implemented one of the EFSA's precepts within the term or to the extent

---

795 s.20(4)(2), CIA.

796 s.20(4)(3), CIA. Section 48 of the CIA states the requirements that persons must satisfy in order to be managers of a credit institution. Section 53 of the CIA requires there to be at least 5 members on the supervisory board of a credit institution, and provides for persons with specified offices within the bank to be ineligible for appointment to this board. Section 56 of the CIA contains the requirements that persons need to satisfy in order to be members of a credit institution's management board, requires there to be at least three persons on this board, and provides for persons with specified offices to be ineligible for appointment to the board. Section 57 of the CIA requires the management board's chairman to have at least five years of practical experience as a manager in the financial field.

797 s.20(4)(4), CIA.

798 s.20(5), CIA.

799 s.20(5^1), CIA.

800 s.20(6^1)(1), CIA.

801 s.20(6^1)(2), CIA.

802 s.20(6^1)(3), CIA.

803 s.20(6^1)(4), CIA.

prescribed,[804] the risks arising from the branch's activities are substantially greater than those arising from the credit institution's activities,[805] or the credit institution, one of its managers, or the director of one of its branches has been punished for a specified offence – such as official misconduct.[806] The EFSA is to immediately inform the financial supervision authority of the host country of the branch about the revocation of the authorisation specified in subsection $20(6^1)$ of the CIA.[807] Once the credit institution is aware of the revocation of an authorisation for the establishment of one of its branches in a foreign country, it shall terminate the supply of its services through the branch no later than by the date that the EFSA has specified.[808]

The establishment of a branch or a wholly-owned subsidiary, and the acquisition in full of an existing organisation, is a 'capital movement' in Title I of the nomenclature in Annex I. The requirement for prior authorisation to found a branch or subsidiary credit institution in a foreign state,[809] and also the grounds for the revocation of this authorisation, limit the free movement of capital.

To be justified under Article 65(1)(b) of the TFEU, the restrictive measures must be necessary for the protection of interests that they are intended to guarantee, be proportionate (i.e. not be attainable for less restrictive measures), and observe the requirements of legal certainty (i.e. be specific, objective, and known to the parties beforehand); in addition, the persons whom the measures affect must have access to legal redress (i.e. the decision is to be supported by a formal statement of reasons, and subject to review in the national courts).[810] Some of the restrictions do not provide the applicant credit institution with legal certainty; for instance, neither a credit institution's financial circumstances being "not sufficiently sound"[811] nor the organisational structure of the foreign branch or subsidiary being "not suitable for the intended activities"[812] are specific,

---

[804] s.$20(6^1)(5)$, CIA.

[805] s.$20(6^1)(6)$, CIA.

[806] s.$20(6^1)(8)$, CIA.

[807] s.$20(6^2)$, CIA.

[808] s.$20(6^3)$, CIA.

[809] See *Eglise de Scientologie and Scientology International* [2000] ECR I-1335, in the subsection '*Public policy, public security, general interest, and prior authorisation*' in section 2.1.3.

[810] See the subsection '*The requirements for a successful public policy/public security derogation*', in section 2.1.3.

[811] s.20(4)(1), CIA.

[812] s.20(4)(2), CIA.

objective grounds for the EFSA to refuse authorisation of the branch or subsidiary. Furthermore, the applicant does not have sufficient access to legal redress; even though the EFSA must provide a written, reasoned decision on the grant, or refusal to grant, authorisation to the credit institution,[813] the CIA does not provide the latter with the right to challenge the decision in the national courts.

For a restrictive measure in the law of a Member State to be justified under Article 64(2) of the TFEU, it must not limit the free movement of capital more that the corresponding provision in the relevant Directive does, and the EU institutions must carefully take account of the objective of the free movement of capital whilst enacting this legislation. Directive 2013/36/EU contains the requirements for the authorisation of, and the passporting of services by, credit institutions.[814] Whilst the Directive contains equivalence provisions for the supply of services in the EEA by credit institutions that are established in third countries,[815] it is silent on the provision of services to third countries by credit institutions that are authorised in the EU.[816] In addition, Recital 13 of Directive 2013/36/EU states that supervisory decisions and practices should not impede the functioning of the internal market in respect of "the free flow of capital". This recital illustrates that the EU institutions were aware of the effect of this Directive on the free movement of capital. However, as there are no further references to capital movement in Directive 2013/36/EU, these institutions may not have carefully considered the objective of the free movement of capital whilst enacting the Directive. As derogations from

[813] s.20(5), CIA.

[814] See section 2.2.2.

[815] The EU may, through agreements made with one or more third countries, agree to apply provisions that accord to branches of a credit institution with its head office in a third country, identical treatment through the EU's territory (Article 47(1), Directive 2013/36/EU). However, Member States are not to apply to branches of credit institutions that have their head office in a third country, provisions that result in more favourable treatment than that accorded to branches of credit institutions that have their head office within the EU (Article 47(1), Directive 2013/36/EU).

[816] As the internal market is within the area of shared competence between the EU and its Member States (Article 4(2)(a), TFEU), the Member States may exercise their competence to the extent that the EU has not exercised its competence (Article 2(2), TFEU). Thus, the Estonian legislature is permitted to enact section 20 of the CIA – even though some of its provisions restrict the free movement of capital.

the free movement of capital are to be interpreted strictly,[817] Article 64(2) of the TFEU does not justify the restrictive measures in section 20 of the CIA. Hence, these measures contravene Article 63 of the TFEU.

A credit institution that wishes to establish a branch in another Contracting State must inform the EFSA of its intention to do so,[818] and submit the following documents and information to the EFSA: the name of the Contracting State in which the credit institution wishes to found the branch,[819] the branch's action plan, which is to contain data on the financial services that the branch proposes to offer in the Contracting State and a description of the branch's organisational structure,[820] the branch's address in that Contracting State,[821] and an overview of the education, work experience, business enterprises, and punishments of the branch's managers.[822] The EFSA is to take a decision to forward, or refuse to forward, these documents and this information to the financial supervision authority of the (other) Contracting State, within three months of their receipt.[823] The EFSA may take a decision to refuse to forward the documents and information, if they do not satisfy the requirements of the EFSA or its secondary legislation,[824] or are inaccurate, misleading or incomplete,[825] the credit institution's resources are insufficient for the provision of the services specified in the branch's action plan,[826] foundation of the branch or implementation of the action plan may damage the interests of the credit institution's clients, or its financial situation or activities,[827] or the financial supervision authority of the Contracting State has "no legal basis or possibilities for cooperation with" the EFSA, as a result of which the EFSA is unable to exercise adequate supervision over the branch.[828]

The EFSA may refuse to review the documents and information specified in subsection 20^1(1) of the CIA if they do not satisfy the

[817] See *Eglise de Scientologie and Scientology International* [2000] ECR I-1335, in the subsection '*Public policy, public security, general interest, and prior authorisation*' in section 2.1.3.
[818] s.20^1(1), CIA.
[819] s.20^1(1)(1), CIA.
[820] s.20^1(1)(2), CIA.
[821] s.20^1(1)(3), CIA.
[822] ss.20^1(1)(4), CIA and 48(7), CIA.
[823] s.20^1(3), CIA.
[824] s.20^3(1), CIA.
[825] s.20^3(1), CIA.
[826] s.20^3(2), CIA.
[827] s.20^3(3), CIA.
[828] s.20^3(4), CIA.

requirements of the CIA or legislation that is passed on the basis of this Act,[829] are incomplete,[830] or have not been submitted within the prescribed time period.[831] Upon forwarding these documents and information, the EFSA is to inform the financial supervision authority of the Contracting State of the amount of the credit institution's own funds and of its capital adequacy.[832]

The credit institution may establish the branch in the Contracting State, after it has received the conditions that this Contracting State's financial supervision authority has set for the foundation of the branch there.[833] If, within two months of receipt of the documents and information specified in section 20^1(1) of the CIA,[834] the Contracting State's financial supervision authority has not established any conditions, then the credit institution may establish a branch in that Contracting State.[835]

The EFSA may issue a precept to prevent a credit institution from supplying services through a branch established in (another) Contracting State if (at least one) basis for refusal to forward documents and information in section 20^3 of the CIA exists,[836] or the Contracting State's financial supervision authority has informed the EFSA that a credit institution has breached conditions contained in that State's legislation or established by its financial supervision authority.[837] The EFSA requires the credit institution to discontinue the provision of its services through this branch, by no later than the deadline that the former gives to the latter.[838]

The establishment of a branch is a 'capital movement' in Title I of the nomenclature in Annex I. If the EFSA decides to refuse to forward the information (that the law requires the credit institution to supply in order to found the branch) to the financial supervision authority of the host EEA state, refuses to review this information, or issues a precept to preclude the credit institution from providing services through the branch, then it is restricting the free movement of capital.

To be justified under Article 65(1)(b) of the TFEU, the restrictive measures must be necessary for the protection of interests that they are

---

[829] s.20^1(4)(1), CIA.
[830] s.20^1(4)(2), CIA.
[831] s.20^1(4)(3), CIA.
[832] s.20^1(5), CIA.
[833] s.20^1(6), CIA.
[834] See above in this subsection.
[835] s.20^1(6), CIA. For section 20^3 of the CIA, see above in this subsection.
[836] s.20^1(8)(1), CIA.
[837] s.20^1(8)(2), CIA.
[838] s.20^1(9), CIA.

intended to guarantee, be proportionate, and observe the requirements of legal certainty; furthermore, the persons whom the measures affect must have access to legal redress.[839] Some of these measures do not provide legal certainty to the applicant credit institution. For example, the EFSA may refuse to forward the information to the financial supervision authority of the host EEA state, if that authority has "no legal basis or possibilities for cooperation with" the EFSA, as a result of which the EFSA cannot exercise sufficient supervision over the branch;[840] this provision confers a discretion on the EFSA, which makes that rule neither sufficiently specific nor adequately objective to provide the applicant with legal certainty. Furthermore, the CIA does not furnish the applicant credit institution with access to legal redress – it does not require the EFSA to support its decision to refuse to review or to forward the information, or to issue a precept in order to prevent the applicant from supplying services through its branch, with a formal statement of reasons; furthermore, the CIA does not provide for the applicant to appeal against the decision in the Estonian courts. Hence, sections 20^1 and 20^3 of the CIA limit the free movement of capital in contravention of Article 63 of the TFEU.

A credit institution that intends to provide cross-border services in a foreign country is to inform the EFSA of this wish,[841] and shall submit the following information and documents to the EFSA: the name of the country in which the credit institution proposes to supply cross-border services,[842] and a description of the proposed cross-border services[843] – setting out the activities and transactions that the credit institution would like to undertake in the foreign state.[844] If a credit institution wishes to provide cross-border services in a Contracting State, then the EFSA is to take a decision to forward, or refuse to forward, this information and these documents to the financial supervision authority of that State within one month of receiving them.[845]

---

[839] See the subsection '*The requirements for a successful public policy/public security derogation*', in section 2.1.3.

[840] s.20^3(4), CIA.

[841] s.20^4(1), CIA.

[842] s.20^4(1)(1), CIA.

[843] Subsection 6(1) of the CIA lists these services. See above in this subsection, i.e. '*Chapter 2: Authorisation of credit institution (including passporting)*'.

[844] s.20^4(1)(2), CIA.

[845] s.20^4(3), CIA. The EFSA is to promptly inform the credit institution of a decision to forward, or refuse to forward, the information and documents to the financial supervision authority of Contracting State in which the institution intends to provide cross-border services.

The EFSA may refuse to review this information and these documents if they do not satisfy the requirements of the CIA,[846] are incomplete,[847] or have either of these deficiencies and the additional documents or information that the EFSA requires[848] are not submitted within the prescribed time period.[849] The EFSA may take a decision to refuse to forward the information and documents if they do not satisfy the requirements of the CIA or are incorrect, misleading or incomplete,[850] the credit institution's resources are inadequate for the provision of cross-border services,[851] the supply of cross-border services is likely to adversely affect the financial circumstances or economic soundness of the credit institution or the interests of the credit institution's clients,[852] or the financial supervision authority of the (other) Contracting State "has no legal basis or possibilities for cooperation with" the EFSA, due to which the latter is unable to exercise sufficient supervision over the supply of cross-border services to the Contracting State.[853]

After the information and documents have been forwarded to the Contracting State's financial supervision authority, the credit institution may start to provide cross-border services in that State – having regard to the conditions that the Contracting State's legislation lays down and its financial supervision authority administers.[854] The EFSA may issue a precept to prohibit a credit institution from supplying cross-border services if the one or more of the grounds for refusal to forward the information and documents that subsection 20^4(5) exists,[855] or the financial supervision authority of the (other) Contracting State has notified the EFSA that the credit institution has breached the conditions that that State's legislation formulates or its financial supervision authority establishes.[856]

Cross-border financial services[857] are 'capital movements' in Titles V, VI, VIII and XIII of the nomenclature in Annex I. If the EFSA refuses to

---

846 s.20^4(4)(1), CIA.
847 s.20^4(4)(1), CIA.
848 Section 20^4 of the CIA does not explicitly empower the EFSA to require additional documents from the applicant credit institution.
849 s.20^4(4)(2), CIA.
850 s.20^4(5)(1), CIA.
851 s.20^4(5)(2), CIA.
852 s.20^4(5)(3), CIA.
853 s.20^4(5)(4), CIA.
854 s.20^4(6), CIA.
855 s.20^4(8)(1), CIA.
856 s.20^4(8)(2), CIA.
857 Financial services for the purposes of the CIA are listed above in this subsection.

review the information and documents that the applicant credit institution submits to it, refuses to forward this information and these documents to the financial supervision authority of the EEA state in which the credit institution intends to provide cross-border services, or issues a precept in order to forbid the credit institution from supplying these cross-border services in that country, then it hinders the free movement of capital.

The restrictive measures must be necessary for the protection of the interests that they are intended to guarantee, be proportionate, observe the requirements of legal certainty, and be accompanied by provisions that provide the persons affected with access to legal redress, in order to be justified under Article 65(1)(b) of the TFEU.[858] Some of these measures are neither sufficiently specific nor adequately objective to provide the applicant with legal certainty; for instance, the EFSA may refuse to review, or take a decision to refuse to forward, the information and documents that the applicant submits to it if they do not satisfy the requirements of the CIA[859] – a judgment that the EFSA makes. Furthermore, section 20^4 of the CIA does not require the EFSA to provide reasons for refusing to forward the information and documents to the financial supervision authority of the (other) Contracting State, or for issuing a precept, and does not provide the applicant credit institution with the right to appeal against this decision in the Estonian courts; hence, this section does not provide the applicant with legal certainty. Thus, the restrictive measures breach Article 63 of the TFEU, and are not justified under Article 65 of the TFEU.

The provisions of sections 20¹ to 20^4 of the CIA apply to a financial institution[860] of Estonia that is a subsidiary of a credit institution (or jointly controlled by at least two credit institutions) and the articles of association of which allow the conclusion of transactions and the performance of acts specified in clauses 6(1)(2) to 6(1)(12) of the CIA,[861] and which would

---

[858] See the subsection '*The requirements for a successful public policy/public security derogation*', in section 2.1.3.

[859] ss.20^4(4)(1) and 20^4(5)(1), CIA.

[860] A 'financial institution' is a company other than a credit institution, the main, permanent activity of which is to "acquire holdings" or to conclude one or more of the transactions that are contained in clauses 6(1)(2) to 6(1)(12) of the CIA.

[861] Subsection 6(1) of the CIA describes 'financial services' for the purposes of this Act. See above in this subsection ('*Chapter 2: Authorisation of credit institution (including passporting)*') of the book.

like to establish a branch and(/or)[862] supply cross-border services in a Contracting State, unless section 20^5 of the CIA states otherwise.[863]

A parent credit institution of a financial institution that subsection 20^5(1) specifies, which would like to establish a branch in a Contracting State, or to offer cross-border services, is to apply to the EFSA for a written confirmation, which is to indicate that the financial institution satisfies the following requirements: the parent company (or companies) hold(s) an activity licence for acting as a credit institution that the EFSA has issued,[864] the financial institution undertakes the transactions and performs the acts stated in clauses 6(1)(2) to 6(1)(12) of the CIA in a Contracting State,[865] the parent company (or companies) hold(s) at least 90 per cent of the votes that are represented by the financial institution's shares or units,[866] the parent company (or companies) ensure that the financial institution is prudently managed,[867]the parent company (or companies) are prepared to guarantee the performance of the obligations that the financial institution assumes,[868] and, the financial institution's group is subject to consolidated supervision – in particular regarding the transactions and acts that are contained in clauses 6(1)(2) to 6(1)(12) of the CIA[869] and concerning capital adequacy and restrictions on investments and on the concentration of exposures.[870] The EFSA is to forward this confirmation, the name of the Contracting State in which the credit institution would like to establish a branch, the branch's action plan, the branch's address, data on the branch's managers, information about the financial institution's own funds, and the capital adequacy requirement of the credit institution (or institutions) that are the parent companies of the financial supervision authority.[871]

---

862 The English translation of the CIA states "and"; I have added "or" in brackets, as it is likely that the legislators intend section 20^5 of the CIA to apply to subsidiaries of credit institutions that provide services to other Contracting States, whether or not a branch is founded there.

863 s.20^5(1), CIA.

864 s.20^5(2)(1), CIA.

865 s.20^5(2)(2), CIA. See note 861.

866 s.20^5(2)(3), CIA.

867 s.20^5(2)(4), CIA.

868 s.20^5(2)(5), CIA.

869 See note 861.

870 s.20^5(2)(6), CIA.

871 s.20^5(3), CIA.

The establishment of a branch is a 'capital movement' in Title I(1) of the nomenclature in Annex I. Cross-border financial services[872] are 'capital movements' in Titles V, VI, VIII and XIII of this nomenclature. If the EFSA refuses to forward the information to the financial supervision authority of the (other) Contracting State, then it limits the free movement of capital. To be justified under Article 65(1)(b) of the TFEU, the restrictive measures must be necessary for the protection of the interests that they are intended to guarantee, be proportionate (i.e. not attainable by less restrictive measures), ;and observe the requirements of legal certainty (i.e. be specific, objective, and known to the parties beforehand). Furthermore, the persons that the restrictive measures affect must have access to legal redress – there should be a formal statement of reasons in support of intervention, and the decision must be open to review by the national courts.[873]

The requirement that the parent company must "ensure the prudent management of the financial institution"[874] does not provide legal certainty to the applicant, because this phrase is imprecise, and is not accompanied by criteria for this careful management. In addition, section 20^5 of the CIA does not provide the applicant with access to legal redress, because the CIA neither requires the EFSA to support its decision to refuse to forward the information by a formal statement of reasons, nor provides the applicant with the right to appeal against the decision to refuse to forward the information in the Estonian courts. Hence, section 20^5 of the CIA contravenes Article 63 of the TFEU, and this breach is not justified by Article 65(2) of this Treaty.

A person who, pursuant to the legislation of its home Member State, has the right to receive money from the public in order to acquire repayable funds, may, on the basis of the activity licence issued in that country, enter into similar transactions and perform the same acts in Estonia by establishing branches or providing cross-border services in Estonia.[875] The establishment of a branch is a 'capital movement' in Title I(1) of the nomenclature in Annex I. Furthermore, cross-border operations in current and deposit accounts with foreign financial institutions is a

---

872 Financial services for the purposes of the CIA are listed above in this subsection.

873 See the subsection '*The requirements for a successful public policy/public security derogation*', in section 2.1.3.

874 s.20^5(2)(4), CIA.

875 s.20^6(1), CIA. For the purposes of section 20^6 of the CIA, 'cross-border services' are services that a person who is not, or whose branch is not, registered in Estonia, provides (s.20^6(2), CIA).

'capital movement' in Title VIB of this nomenclature. As sections 21^1 to 21^3 (or sections 21^4 to 21^6), 22 and 97^2 apply to a person specified in subsection 20^6 of the CIA,[876] the restrictions to the free movement of capital and their possible justifications are considered as those sections are discussed.

A foreign credit institution that wishes to establish a subsidiary credit institution in Estonia is to apply for an authorisation from the EFSA, as specified in section 13 of the CIA.[877] A foreign credit institution that would like to open a branch in Estonia is required to apply for an authorisation from the EFSA,[878] and to submit an application to this authority to which the following documents and information are attached: the action plan of the branch being established, together with a detailed description of the planned activities, a description of the organisational structure, and the relationship between the credit institution and the branch,[879] the branch's address,[880] data concerning the branch's director pursuant to subsection 48(7) of the CIA,[881] the documents and data that subsection 30(3) of the CIA requires (in relation to shareholders who have qualifying holdings in the credit institution),[882] the official certificate

---

[876] ss.20^6(2) and 20^6(3), CIA. The Estonian legislature has repealed section 21^1 of the CIA. Subsection 20^6(3) of (the English translation of) the CIA should be updated to show this.

[877] s.21(1), CIA. A company that wishes to receive repayable funds from the public must hold an authorisation to do this. An authorisation also grants this company the right to provide investment services contained in subsection 43(1) of the SMA, and ancillary investment services stated in section 44 of the SMA, to the extent specified in the authorisation (s.13(1), CIA). See the first paragraph of section 3.2 for a list of these investment services.

[878] Subsection 21(2) of the CIA is confusing. This is because it requires the applicant foreign credit institution to provide a list of documents and information that are consistent with the passporting requirements of Article 35 of Directive 2013/36/EU, whilst also requiring the applicant to obtain an authorisation from the EFSA.

[879] s.21(2)(1), CIA. The subsection's wording is "and the relationship with the credit institution being founded", which cannot be correct, as it is the branch that is being established. Thus, in the text, I have rephrased this phrase to express a meaning that the Estonian legislators may have intended.

[880] s.21(2)(2), CIA.

[881] s.21(2)(3), CIA. See note 791.

[882] s.21(2)(4), CIA. This information is extensive, and includes, for instance, a description of the credit institution that comprises an excerpt of its share register and the type and number of votes of the shares that belong to the person with the qualifying holding (s.30(3)(1), CIA).

concerning the presence of the company in its home country,[883] an authorisation document that certifies the authority of the branch's director or a copy of the resolution that appoints the director,[884] a certified copy of the company's articles of association or partnership agreement,[885] and the telecommunications data of the company and of its branch.[886] In addition, the following information is also to be submitted to the EFSA:[887] the consent of the financial supervision authority of the credit institution's home country to the establishment of an Estonian subsidiary or branch, confirmation that the credit institution possesses a valid activity licence, data concerning the amount of the credit institution's own funds, and its capital adequacy, and data relating to the home state's deposit guarantee system.[888]

The EFSA may refuse to grant an authorisation if the applicant credit institution, its managers, its shareholders, or its auditors, do not satisfy the requirements for credit institutions provided by the CIA or its secondary legislation,[889] the resources for full payment of the applicant's share capital are not demonstrated,[890] the applicant has neither the requisite funds nor the necessary experience to continuously operate as a credit institution,[891] close links between the applicant and another person preclude adequate supervision over the applicant,[892] the requirements that arise from legislation or the implementation of legislation of the country in which the person with whom the applicant has close links is established, prevent sufficient supervision of the applicant,[893] the information that the applicant submits shows that the applicant plans to primarily operate in

[883] ss.21(2)(5), CIA, and 386(2)(1), Commercial Code.
[884] ss.21(2)(5), CIA, and 386(2)(3), Commercial Code.
[885] ss.21(2)(5), CIA, and 386(2)(4), Commercial Code. This document is only required if the company's home country requires that item to be registered there (s.386(2)(4), Commercial Code).
[886] ss.21(2)(5), CIA, and 386(2)(5), Commercial Code.
[887] Subsection 21(3) of the CIA does not state who is to submit this information to the EFSA. For instance, is the financial supervision authority of the credit institution's home country to forward the information to the EFSA? Or is the credit institution to supply the information directly to the EFSA?
[888] s.21(3), CIA.
[889] ss.21(5), 15(1)(1) and 15(1)(4), CIA.
[890] ss.21(5) and 15(1)(2), CIA.
[891] ss.21(5) and 15(1)(3), CIA.
[892] ss.21(5) and 15(1)(5), CIA.
[893] ss.21(5) and 15(1)(5), CIA.

another Contracting State,[894] a credit institution's internal rules (as specified in section 63 of the CIA) are insufficiently accurate or unambiguous to regulate its activities,[895] the applicant or its managers have been punished for a specified offence (such as official misconduct),[896] the foreign credit institution's financial situation (in the EFSA's opinion) is "not sufficiently sound",[897] the organisational structure of the subsidiary credit institution in Estonia, or the Estonian branch of the foreign credit institution, is unsuitable for the proposed activities,[898] the legislation of the credit institution's home country does not require adequate supervision,[899] the financial supervision authority of the home state does not exercise sufficient supervision,[900] or the financial supervision authority of the foreign country "has no legal basis, possibilities or readiness for cooperation with the" EFSA.[901] The EFSA shall give a reasoned decision on the grant, or refusal to grant, an authorisation, within two months of the date of the receipt of an application and the information specified in

---

[894] ss.21(5) and 15(1)(6), CIA. The CJEU has been reluctant to permit Member States from attempting to limit the benefits of the internal market, which provides an area of free movement of goods, persons, services, and capital (see section 1.2.3). For instance, in *Centros Ltd. v. Erhvervs-og Selskabsstyrelsen* [1999] ECR I-1459, the Court held that it was contrary to Articles 52 and 58 of the Treaty Establishing the European Communities for the Danish Authority to refuse to register a branch of Centros Ltd. in Denmark; Centros Ltd. was registered in the United Kingdom – allegedly to evade minimum capital requirements that Danish law imposed for the company's authorisation in Denmark. On this ground, clause 15(1)(6) of the CIA contravenes EU law.

[895] ss.21(5) and 15(1)(7), CIA. Subsection 63(1) of the CIA requires credit institutions to establish internal rules and rules of procedure to regulate the activities of its staff, which are to comply with legislation and with the resolutions made by their directing bodies. Subsection 63(2) of the CIA sets out issues that each credit institution's internal rules and rules of procedure are to include.

[896] ss.21(5) and 15(1)(8), CIA.

[897] ss.21(5)(1), CIA.

[898] s.21(5)(2), CIA.

[899] s.21(5)(3), CIA.

[900] s.21(5)(3), CIA.

[901] s.21(5)(4), CIA. Subsection 21(5) of the CIA rolls authorisation and passporting requirements into one, over the issue of refusal to grant an authorisation. As section 21^4 of the CIA considers specifications for the establishment of a branch of a credit institution from (another) Contracting State in Estonia, the references in section 21 of the CIA to a 'foreign' credit institution must be to one from outside the EEA – in which case an authorisation will be required in order to establish a branch (or subsidiary) in Estonia.

subsection 21(2) of the CIA,[902] and shall notify the applicant credit institution of this decision.[903]

Sections 13-15, 17 and 18 of the CIA apply to the processing of applications for an authorisation for the establishment of a branch, verification of information, and the grant and revocation of authorisations, unless section 21^2 of the CIA otherwise provides.[904] The EFSA may revoke an authorisation for the establishment of a branch, if circumstances stated in section 17, or subsection 21(5), of the CIA become evident.[905] Under section 17 of the CIA, the EFSA may revoke authorisation if the credit institution does not start its activities within one year of the issue of authorisation,[906] it has become clear that the credit institution has submitted misleading documents or information, incorrect information, or

---

902 s.21(6), CIA.

903 s.21(7), CIA.

904 s.21^2(1), CIA. For section 13 of the CIA, see the first paragraph of section 3.3.1. For section 15 of the CIA, see above in this subsection ('*Chapter 2: Authorisation of credit institution (including passporting)*'). Section 14 of the CIA requires the EFSA to take a decision to grant, or to refuse to grant, authorisation within six months of receipt of all the necessary information and documents, but not later than within one year of receipt of the application for authorisation (s.14(1), CIA), but requires the EFSA to take this decision without undue delay (s.14(3), CIA). Section 17 of the CIA lays down grounds on which the EFSA may revoke authorisation; these are stated above in the text. Section 18 of the CIA requires the EFSA to publish a decision on the grant, the amendment or the revocation of authorisation on its website by the next working day (s.18(1), CIA), and to publish a notice about revocation of authority in at least one daily national newspaper (s.18(2), CIA).

905 s.21^2(3), CIA. The previous paragraph of this subsection (('*Chapter 2: Authorisation of credit institution (including passporting)*') contains the requirements of subsection 21(5) of the CIA.

906 s.17(1)(1), CIA. The credit institution may also revoke authorisation, if an act or omission of the credit institution's founders shows that it will be unable to start its activities within one year of the issue of the authorisation (s.17(1)(1), CIA). This provision goes beyond the grounds on which Article 18(a) of Directive 2013/36/EU empowers competent authorities to withdraw authorisation, and also provides a discretion to the EFSA to decide whether or not the credit institution's founders have acted (or omitted to act) in a way that has this effect. Article 18(e) of Directive 2013/36/EU empowers competent authorities to withdraw authorisation, if the credit institution is within one of the other cases in which national law provides for withdrawal of authorisation. Therefore, subsection 17(1)(1) of the CIA does not contravene Article 18 of Directive 2013/36/EU.

falsified documents to the EFSA,[907] the credit institution does not satisfy the requirements in force with regard to the grant of authorisation,[908] the credit institution's managers, shareholders or auditors do not satisfy the requirements of the CIA or of legislation established on the basis of this Act,[909] close links between the applicant and another person preclude sufficient supervision over the credit institution,[910] the requirements that arise from legislation or from the implementation of legislation of the country in which the person with whom the credit institution has close links is established, prevent adequate supervision of the credit institution,[911] the credit institution has repeatedly or materially contravened provisions of legislation that regulate its activities,[912] the credit institution or its manager has been punished for a specified offence (such as official misconduct),[913] the credit institution's activities or omissions are not in accordance with good practice,[914] the credit institution does not satisfy secondary conditions that the EFSA sets in accordance with subsection 15(1) of the CIA,[915] the credit institution belongs to a group whose structure precludes the receipt of information that is required for consolidated supervision,[916] a company in the credit institution's group operates on the basis of a foreign country's legislation – which prevents the exercise of adequate supervision,[917] the credit institution has published materially inaccurate or misleading information or advertising about its activities or its directors,[918] the credit institution's activities significantly damage the interests of its clients or currency circulation, or adversely

---

907 s.17(1)(2), CIA. This includes information and documents submitted upon application for authorisation, as well as after the EFSA has granted authorisation (s.17(1)(2), CIA).
908 s.17(1)(3), CIA.
909 ss.17(1)(4) and 15(1)(4), CIA.
910 ss.17(1)(4) and 15(1)(5), CIA.
911 ss.17(1)(4) and 15(1)(5), CIA.
912 s.17(1)(5), CIA.
913 s.17(1)(5), CIA.
914 s.17(1)(5), CIA.
915 ss.17(1)(6) and 14(2), CIA. The previous paragraph of this subsection ('*Chapter 2: Authorisation of credit institution (including passporting)*') describes the content of subsection 15(1) of the CIA as grounds under subsection 21(5) of the CIA for the EFSA to refuse to grant authorisation for the establishment of a subsidiary credit institution, or a branch, in Estonia.
916 s.17(1)(7), CIA.
917 s.17(1)(7), CIA.
918 s.17(1)(8), CIA.

affect the regular functioning of the capital or money markets,[919] the credit institution's amount of own funds does not comply with the requirements of the CIA or legislation issued on the basis of this Act,[920] it becomes clear that the credit institution has selected Estonia as the place for application for authorisation and registration in order to evade compliance with stricter requirements for credit institutions in another Contracting State in which the credit institution primarily operates,[921] the credit institution engages in money laundering, or breaches the legislative procedure for the prevention of money laundering or terrorist financing,[922] the credit institution does not pay its contributions to the Deposit Guarantee Sectoral Fund and the Investor Protection Sectoral Fund prescribed in the Guarantee Fund Act and has not implemented a corresponding precept of the Financial Inspectorate within the period, or to the extent, prescribed,[923] the credit institution has not implemented a precept of the EFSA within the period, or to the extent, prescribed,[924] or the credit institution has contravened conditions provided by the (other) Contracting State's legislation or set by that State's financial supervision authority in conformity with the requirements of subsection $20^1(6)$ or subsection 20^4(6) of the CIA.[925] The EFSA may refuse to revoke an authorisation for the establishment of a branch, if the branch's clients have claims against it, or against the foreign credit institution.[926]

The establishment of a branch or a wholly-owned subsidiary is a 'capital movement' in Title I(1) of the nomenclature in Annex I. A refusal to grant authorisation, or the revocation of authorisation, hinders the free movement of capital.

To be justified under Article 65(1)(b) of the TFEU, the restrictive measures must be necessary for the protection of interests that they are intended to guarantee, be proportionate – i.e. not attainable by less restrictive measures, and observe the requirements of legal certainty – i.e. they must be specific, objective and known to the parties beforehand; in

---

919 s.17(1)(9), CIA.

920 s.17(1)(10), CIA.

921 s.17(1)(11), CIA. This clause is incompatible with EU law because it attempts to restrict the benefits of the internal market; see note 894.

922 s.17(1)(12), CIA.

923 s.17(1)(13), CIA.

924 s.17(1)(14), CIA.

925 s.17(1)(15), CIA. Information submitted by the (other) Contracting State's financial supervision authority to the EFSA must disclose this contravention (s.17(1)(15), CIA).

926 s.$21^2(4)$, CIA.

addition, the persons affected by the restrictive measures must have access to legal redress – intervention must be supported by a formal statement of reasons and be subject to review by the national courts.[927] Although the CIA does not state the interests that the measures are intended to guarantee, it is difficult to accept that they would cover the large number of limitations to the free movement of capital that sections 21 and 21^2 of the CIA provide for. Furthermore, some of these restrictions do not fulfil the requirements of legal certainty; for instance, in clause 17(1)(9) of the CIA, the EFSA has a discretion to decide whether or not the credit institution's activities damage the interests of its clients – unless it makes this decision on specific, clearly-listed grounds.[928] Whilst subsection 21(6) of the CIA requires the EFSA to make a reasoned decision on the grant of, or refusal to grant, an authorisation to a foreign credit institution to found a branch or subsidiary in Estonia, the CIA does not require the EFSA to make a reasoned decision for its revocation of an authorisation for the establishment of a branch of a foreign credit institution.[929] In addition, neither section 21 nor section 21^2 of the CIA provide for the applicant credit institution to appeal against a refusal to grant authorisation for the foundation for a branch (or subsidiary) of a foreign credit institution, or against a decision to revoke this authorisation, in the Estonian courts. Thus, neither of these sections of the CIA provides the credit institution with legal redress. Hence, Article 65(1)(b) of the TFEU does not justify the restrictive measures.

Under Article 64(1) of the TFEU, the EU may limit the free movement of capital between its Member States and third countries over the area of the supply of financial services (amongst others), as long as the EU institutions carefully consider the objective of the free movement of capital whilst enacting this legislation., and provided that the national laws do not restrict the free movement of capital more than the corresponding

---

[927] See the subsection '*The requirements for a successful public policy/public security derogation*', in section 2.1.3.

[928] Estonian secondary legislation, or the rules of the EFSA in its handbook, may be used to provide for, and publish, these grounds.

[929] Whilst subsection $21^2(3)$ of the CIA permits the EFSA to revoke an authorisation for the foundation of a branch of a foreign credit institution in Estonia, neither section 21 nor section 21^2 of the CIA explicitly provides for the EFSA to revoke an authorisation for the establishment of a subsidiary credit institution in Estonia of a foreign credit institution. However, section 17 of the CIA (revocation of authorisation) may (and should) apply to the latter case.

provisions of the relevant Directive do.[930] The 'relevant Directive' is Directive 2013/36/EU. Article 47(1) of this Directive requires Member States not to apply to branches of credit institutions with their head office in a third country, provisions that result in more favourable treatment than that given to branches of credit institutions with their head office in the EU. It contains no specific measures on the establishment of branches in Estonia of credit institutions that are resident in third countries. However, Article 48(1) of Directive 2013/36/EU empowers the Commission to submit proposals to the Council for the negotiation of agreements with third countries, which concern the means of exercising consolidated supervision over institutions the parent company of which has its head office in a third country, and institutions that are located in third countries the parent company of which has its office in the EU. Thus, the national provisions limit the free movement of capital more than the equivalent rules of the Directive do, because the Directive does not, in specific terms, address the requirements for the establishment of branches in the EEA of credit institutions that are authorised in third countries. Furthermore, the absence of specific provisions in Article 48 of Directive 2013/36/EU for the foundation of Estonian subsidiaries of foreign credit institutions, means that these companies are subject to the normal authorisation process under this Directive and the CIA. Recital 13 of Directive 2013/36/EU states that supervisory practices should not inhibit the functioning of the internal market in respect of "the free flow of capital". Hence, the EU institutions were aware of the free movement of capital whilst enacting this Directive. However, the Directive's Articles do not consider the free movement of capital.[931] Therefore, the EU institutions may not have taken the objective of the free movement of capital into account whilst enacting the Directive. Pursuant to these arguments, the restrictive measures in sections 21 and 21^2 of the CIA are not justified by Article 64(2) of the TFEU. Thus, these provisions breach Article 63 of the TFEU.

A credit institution of a Contracting State that would like to establish a branch in Estonia, must inform the financial supervision authority of that

[930] See the subsection '*Derogations that apply only to capital movements to/from third countries*', in section 2.3.2.

[931] The Directive's sister Regulation, No 575/2013 on prudential requirements for credit institutions and investment firms, mentions the free movement of capital once, in the context of national structural measures that Member States may impose to require credit institutions authorised there to lower their exposures to different legal entities, with a view to the preservation of financial stability and the protection of depositors (Article 395, Regulation (EU) No 575/2013).

State, which shall notify the EFSA.[932] The following information and documents are to be submitted to the EFSA: the branch's action plan, which is to include data on all of the financial services that the branch proposes to offer in Estonia and a description of the branch's organisational structure,[933] the branch's address,[934] and data concerning the branch's managers, pursuant to the requirements of subsection 48(7) of the CIA.[935] The EFSA is to promptly inform the financial supervision authority of the (other) Contracting State of receipt of this information and these documents.[936] Within two months of its receipt of these items, the EFSA may take a decision that determines the requirements with which the credit institution must comply in Estonia.[937] The EFSA is to immediately inform the Contracting State's financial supervision authority of its decision.[938] The credit institution may establish a branch, and commence activities, after receiving (through the financial supervision authority of its home state) this decision, or (in the absence of a decision)[939] two months after the date on which the EFSA receives the information and documents specified in subsection 21^4(1) of the CIA.[940] The EFSA shall confirm its receipt of these items, and its decision determining the requirements with which the credit institution must comply in Estonia (if it takes a decision), as soon as the branch's details are recorded in the commercial register.[941]

The establishment of a branch is a 'capital movement' in Title I(1) of the nomenclature in Annex I. The informational requirements that a credit institution registered in a (non-Estonian) Contracting State must provide,

---

932 s.21^4(1), CIA.

933 s.21^4(1)(1), CIA.

934 s.21^4(1)(2), CIA.

935 s.21^4(1)(3), CIA. To be elected or appointed as a manager of a credit institution, the person to be elected or appointed must provide his/her written consent, and shall submit an overview of his/her education, work experience, enterprise activity, punishments entered in the punishment register, and confirmation of the absence of facts provided for in the CIA that prevent the right of this candidate to be a manager of a credit institution (s.48(7), CIA). Thus, this data is also required for a person to be appointed as a manager of an Estonian branch of a credit institution that is established in (another) Contracting State.

936 s.21^4(2), CIA.

937 s.21^4(2), CIA.

938 s.21^4(2), CIA.

939 Subsection 21^4 of the CIA does not include this bracketed phrase. It is added for clarity.

940 s.21^4(3), CIA.

941 s.21^4(5), CIA.

in order found an Estonian branch, are not onerous. Hence, these do not restrict the free movement of capital.

The requirements that the EFSA lays down under subsection 21^4(2) of the CIA for the credit institution to be permitted to establish, and commence business through, an Estonian branch, may be sufficiently onerous to restrict the free movement of capital. Unless justified by a derogation that applies to Member States (as well as to third countries)[942] these requirements (if burdensome) would contravene Article 63 of the TFEU.

A credit institution registered in a (non-Estonian) Contracting State that wishes to supply cross-border services in Estonia must inform the financial supervision authority of that State thereof, and must list which transactions and acts in subsection 6(1) of the CIA it would like to provide.[943] That authority is to provide the EFSA with this information.[944] The credit institution may commence its provision of cross-border services in Estonia, as soon as the information has been forwarded to the EFSA.[945] After the EFSA receives this information, it may take a decision in which it determines the conditions under which the credit institution is to supply its services.[946] The EFSA must promptly inform the credit institution of this decision.[947]

---

942 Section 2.1.3 discusses derogations from the free movement of capital that apply to capital movements between Member States. The justifications that this section discusses also apply to capital movements between Member States and third countries.

943 s.21^5(1), CIA. The first paragraph of this subsection ('*Chapter 2: Authorisation of credit institution (including passporting)*') lists the financial services in subsection 6(1) of the CIA.

944 s.21^5, CIA.

945 s.21^5(2), CIA.

946 s.21^5(3), CIA.

947 s.21^5(3), CIA. Article 39 of Directive 2013/36/EU does not empower the national financial supervision authorities to determine the conditions under which credit institutions that are authorised in other EEA states are to provide cross-border services to the host state (see section 2.2.2). Nonetheless, the European Banking Authority is to develop draft regulatory technical standards to specify the information to be communicated in accordance with Article 39 of the Directive, and the Commission has the power to adopt these standards. (Article 39(4), Directive 2013/36/EU).

Cross-border financial services[948] are 'capital movements' in Titles V, VI, VIII and XIII of the nomenclature in Annex I. The informational requirements that a credit institution registered in another Contracting State must provide, in order to supply cross-border services in Estonia, are very light, and, therefore, do not limit the free movement of capital.

However, if the Estonian legislature retains subsection 21^5(3) of the CIA,[949] then the EFSA may impose requirements on credit institutions from other EEA states that are sufficiently burdensome to restrict the free movement of capital. Unless justified by a derogation that applies to Member States (and to third countries),[950] these requirements would breach Article 63 of the TFEU.

The provisions of sections 21^4, 21^5, 22 and 97² of the CIA apply to a financial institution of a Contracting State, which is a subsidiary of a credit institution, or jointly controlled by at least two credit institutions, and the articles of association of which allow the conclusion of transactions and the performance of acts specified in clauses 6(1)(2) to 6(1)(12) of the CIA, and which would like to establish a branch and supply cross-border services in Estonia, unless this section (21^6) of the CIA provides otherwise.[951] The parent credit institution of a financial institution that is registered in a Contracting State that would like to establish an Estonian branch, or provided cross-border services in Estonia, is to inform the financial supervision authority of that State, and shall submit the documents and information that subsection 21^4 of the CIA specifies regarding the financial institution,[952] information concerning the

---

[948] The first paragraph of this subsection ('*Chapter 2: Authorisation of credit institution (including passporting)*') lists these services for the purposes of the CIA.

[949] In the light of note 947, the legislature is obliged to repeal this subsection of the CIA.

[950] See note 942.

[951] s.21^6(1), CIA. Sections 21^4 and 21^5 of the CIA are discussed above, and section 22 of the CIA, below, in this subsection ('*Chapter 2: Authorisation of credit institution (including passporting)*'). Section 97² of the CIA is considered later in this section (3.3.1) of the book. A 'financial institution' is a company other than a credit institution, the main, permanent activity of which is to "acquire holdings" or to conclude one or more of the transactions that are contained in clauses 6(1)(2) to 6(1)(12) of the CIA. Subsection 6(1) of the CIA describes 'financial services' for the purposes of this Act – see above in this subsection ('*Chapter 2: Authorisation of credit institution (including passporting)*').

[952] Subsection 21^4(1) of the CIA is considered above in this subsection ('*Chapter 2: Authorisation of credit institution (including passporting)*'). The information that subsection 21^4(1) requires the applicant credit institution to submit concerns

financial institution's own funds, the capital adequacy indicator of the parent credit institution(s), and a confirmation of the Contracting State's financial supervision authority that the financial institution satisfies the following requirements:[953] the parent undertaking(s) are authorised as credit institutions in the Contracting State whose law governs the activities of the financial institution,[954] the financial institution concludes the transactions and performs the acts, in Estonia, that clauses 6(1)(2) to 6(1)(12) specify,[955] the parent undertaking(s) hold(s) more than 90% of the votes that are represented by units or shares of the financial institution,[956] the parent undertaking(s) ensure(s) that the financial institution is prudentially managed,[957] the parent undertaking(s) guarantee(s) performance of the obligations that the financial institution assumes,[958] and the financial institution is subject to consolidated supervision, in particular concerning the transactions and acts that clauses 6(1)(2) to 6(1)(12) specify,[959] and regarding capital adequacy and restrictions on investment and on the concentration of risk exposures.[960] The financial supervision authority of the (non-Estonian) Contracting State is to forward this information and these documents to the EFSA.[961]

The establishment of a branch is a 'capital movement' in Title I(1) of the nomenclature in Annex I. Furthermore, the services described in clauses 6(1)(2) to 6(1)(12) of the CIA are 'capital movements' in Titles III, IV, V, VIII and XIII of the nomenclature in Annex I. As sections 21^4 to 21^6, 22 and 97² of the CIA apply to a person specified in section 21^6 of the CIA,[962] limitations to the free movement of capital contained in the former sections and their possible justifications are considered as those

---

that which is necessary to establish a branch in Estonia. This is greater than the amount of information than an applicant would be required to supply, in order to supply cross-border services in Estonia (see subsection 21^5(1) of the CIA, which is discussed above in this subsection ('*Chapter 2: Authorisation of credit institution (including passporting)*').

953 s.21^6(2), CIA.

954 s.21^6(2)(1), CIA.

955 s.21^6(2)(2), CIA. The first paragraph of this subsection ('*Chapter 2: Authorisation of credit institution (including passporting)*') describes the financial services in subsection 6(1) of the CIA.

956 s.21^6(2)(3), CIA.

957 s.21^6(2)(4), CIA.

958 s.21^6(2)(5), CIA.

959 See note 955.

960 s.21^6(2)(6), CIA.

961 s.21^6(2), CIA.

962 s.21^6(1), CIA.

sections are discussed. In addition, the provisions in subsection 21^6(2) of the CIA hinder the free movement of capital.

For the restrictive measures to be justified by Article 65(1)(b) of the TFEU, they must be necessary for the protection of interests that they are intended to guarantee, be proportionate, and observe the requirements of legal certainty; furthermore, the persons affected by the measures are to have access to legal redress.[963] Subsection 21^6(2)(4) of the CIA does not satisfy the requirements of legal certainty, because the EFSA has a discretion to decide whether or not the financial institution's parent undertaking(s) are prudently managing the financial institution. Furthermore, section 21^6 of the CIA does not give the applicants[964] access to legal redress, because the EFSA is not required to provide reasons for taking a decision to prevent the financial institution from establishing a branch in Estonia, and because the CIA does not grant the applicants a right to appeal against this decision in the Estonian courts. Hence, the restrictive measures in subsection 21^6(2) of the CIA are not justified by Article 65(1)(b) of the TFEU, and therefore breach Article 63 of the TFEU.

A foreign credit institution that would like to open a representative office in Estonia is Estonia is to submit the following information to the EFSA: confirmation from the home country's financial supervision authority that the credit institution is authorised,[965] the representative office's programme of activities,[966] the authorisation document that certifies the authorisation of the representative,[967] a document concerning the registration of the credit institution in the home country,[968] the credit institution's articles of association,[969] and the representative office's seat, address, and telecommunications numbers.[970] The opening of a representative office is not a 'capital movement' in the nomenclature in Annex I. If the credit institution subsequently provides cross-border services through the representative office, then this will be a 'capital movement' in the nomenclature.

---

[963] See the subsection '*The requirements for a successful public policy/security derogation*', in section 2.1.3.

[964] In the context of section 21^6 of the CIA, 'the applicants' are the financial institution and its parent undertaking(s).

[965] s.22(1)(1), CIA.

[966] s.22(1)(2), CIA.

[967] s.22(1)(3), CIA.

[968] s.22(1)(4), CIA.

[969] s.22(1)(5), CIA.

[970] s.22(1)(6), CIA.

Chapter 9: Supervision

If an Estonian credit institution whose branch is established in a foreign country, or which provides cross-border services in a foreign state, contravenes the requirements of that country's legislation, the EFSA is promptly to apply measures for the termination of the breach, on the proposal of the foreign country's financial supervision authority.[971] The EFSA is to inform the foreign state's financial supervision authority of the measures that it applies.[972]

The EFSA is to promptly inform the foreign country's financial supervision authority, of revocation of the credit institution's activity licence, or revocation of an authorisation for the establishment of a branch in a foreign country, or the issue of a precept that either subsection $20^{1}(8)$ or subsection 20^4(8) of the CIA specifies.[973] A foreign branch of a credit institution, or a foreign credit institution that provides cross-border services, is to submit information that is required for the exercise of supervision over the activities of the branch or the credit institution in the foreign country.[974]

The revocation of the authorisation of a credit institution or foreign branch are not 'capital movements' in the nomenclature in Annex I. However, the establishment of a branch and the provision of cross-border services are 'capital movements' in the nomenclature. Thus, the revocation restricts the free movement of capital, because it reduces or removes the supply of the Estonian credit institution's financial services in the foreign country.

For this restriction to be justified under Article 65(1)(b) of the TFEU, the restrictive measures must be necessary for the protection of the interests that they are intended to guarantee, be proportionate, and observe the requirements of legal certainty; furthermore, the persons affected by the measures must have access to legal redress – i.e. intervention must be accompanied by a formal statement of reasons and be subject to review by

---

[971] s.$97^{1}(1)$, CIA.

[972] s.$97^{1}(1)$, CIA.

[973] s.$97^{1}(2)$, CIA. Subsection $20^{1}(8)$ of the CIA contains grounds under which the EFSA may issue a precept to preclude an Estonian credit institution from supplying services through a branch that is founded in a (non-Estonian) Contracting State. Subsection 20^4(8) of the CIA considers grounds under which the ESFA may issue a precept to prohibit an Estonian credit institution from supplying cross-border services. Both of these provisions are discussed in the subsection '*Chapter 2: Authorisation of credit institution (including passporting)*', above in this section.

[974] s.$97^{1}(3)$, CIA.

the national courts.[975] The credit institution is provided with legal certainty, provided that the foreign state's financial supervision authority is required to establish that that country's legislation is contravened – before the EFSA can take action. However, the CIA neither requires a decision to revoke the credit institution's activity licence or the branch's authorisation to be accompanied by reasons, nor provides the applicant credit institution with the right to appeal against the restrictive measures in the national courts; thus, the persons affected by the measures do not have access to legal redress, which is required in order for Article 65(1)(b) of the TFEU to justify the restrictive measures.

For the EFSA's revocation of the credit institution's activity licence or the branch's authorisation to be justified under Article 64(2) of the TFEU, the EU institutions must carefully consider the objective of the free movement of capital whilst they enact the legislation, and the domestic rules must not limit the free movement of capital more than the equivalent provisions of the relevant Directive do.[976] Recital 13 of Directive 2013/36/EU (the relevant Directive) states that supervisory decisions and processes should not impede the functioning of the internal market in respect of "the free flow of capital". However, the Directive's Articles do not address the free movement of capital. Thus, even though the EU institutions were aware of the free movement of capital whilst enacting Directive 2013/36/EU, they may not have considered the objective of the free movement of capital during this process.

Article 64(1) of Directive 2013/36/EU empowers competent authorities of EEA states to intervene in the activities of credit institutions that are "necessary for the exercise of their function", including the right to withdraw an authorisation in accordance with Article 18 of this Directive. Paragraph (e) of Article 18 of Directive 2013/36/EU permits these authorities to withdraw an authorisation in instances in which a credit institution is within a case "where national law provides for authorisation". Thus, the EFSA's supervisory power in section 97^1 of the CIA to revoke an Estonian credit institution's activity licence, or withdraw the authorisation of a branch of that credit institution in a third country, does not go beyond Articles 64(1) and 18(e) of Directive 2013/36/EU.

Hence, although the second part of the test for the restrictive measures in section 97^1 of the CIA to be justified by Article 64(2) of the TFEU is

---

[975] See the subsection '*The requirements for a successful public policy/public security derogation*', in section 2.1.3.

[976] See the subsection '*Derogations that apply only to capital movements to/from third countries*', in section 2.3.2.

satisfied, the first part of this test is not fulfilled. Consequently this section contravenes Article 63 of the TFEU.

The EFSA may demand that a foreign credit institution whose branch is established in Estonia submit additional information, documentation and reports that are required for the credit institution to be supervised.[977] A credit institution whose branch or representative office is established in Estonia, or which supplies cross-border services in Estonia, and whose activity licence has been revoked or suspended by a foreign financial supervision authority, must stop providing services in Estonia.[978] If a credit institution of a third country, or its Estonian branch, breaches Estonian legislation, the EFSA may apply the measures in sections 96 to 110 of the CIA,[979] and the sanctions that the CIA provides for, in order to terminate the contravention or revoke the authorisation for the establishment of the branch.[980]

The EFSA may insist that a credit institution of a Contracting State that has opened an Estonian branch, or provides cross-border services in Estonia, stops its contravention of the requirements that Estonian legislation provides for.[981] If this credit institution continues to breach these requirements, then the EFSA must inform the financial supervision authority of the Contracting State of this.[982] If the measures applied by the Contracting State's financial supervision authority are insufficient, and if the credit institution continues to contravene the requirements of Estonian legislation, then the EFSA may issue a precept to apply measures provided for in the CIA for the termination of the breach, or to prohibit the Estonian activities of, or the supply of cross-border services in Estonia by, the credit institution, and shall notify the Contracting State's financial supervision authority beforehand.[983] The EFSA is to promptly notify the European Commission, the European Banking Authority, and the financial supervision authority of the Contracting State, of the application of these measures.[984]

---

[977] s.97^{2}(1), CIA.
[978] s.97^{2}(2), CIA.
[979] These measures include on-site inspections (s.101, CIA), assessment and special audit (s.102, CIA), the issuance of a precept (s.103, CIA), and the imposition of a penalty payment for inadequate compliance with a precept (s.104^{1}, CIA).
[980] s.97^{2}(3), CIA.
[981] s.97^{2}(4), CIA.
[982] s.97^{2}(5), CIA.
[983] s.97^{2}(6), CIA.
[984] s.97^{2}(9), CIA.

The EFSA is to inform a foreign credit institution of the measures that it has taken.[985] A complaint against measures that the EFSA applies may be filed via a subsidiary of a foreign credit institution, with a court in the country in which that subsidiary is located.[986]

In exceptional cases, the EFSA may apply measures that Estonian legislation provides for – in order to protect the interests of depositors, investors, and the public, in respect of a credit institution that is registered in a (non-Estonian) Contracting State, without informing the financial supervision authority of that State beforehand.[987] The EFSA is to promptly inform the European Commission, the European Banking Authority, and the financial supervision authority of the Contracting State, of the application of these measures.[988]

The revocation of the authorisation of a credit institution or foreign branch, and other measures that the EFSA provides, such as on-site inspections, are not 'capital movements' in the nomenclature in Annex I. However, the foundation of a branch and the provision of cross-border services are 'capital movements' in the nomenclature. If the measure that the EFSA applies causes a reduction of the supply of financial services by the foreign credit institution in Estonia, or the closure of its branch, then that measure limits the free movement of capital.

For this restriction to be justified under Article 65(1)(b) of the TFEU, the restrictive measures must be necessary for the protection of the interests that they are intended to guarantee, be proportionate, and satisfy the requirements of legal certainty – i.e. be specific, objective, and known to the parties beforehand; furthermore, the persons whom the measures affect must have access to legal redress – i.e. intervention must be accompanied by a formal statement of reasons and be subject to review by the national courts.[989] As the EFSA (or the financial supervision authority of the other Contracting State) may apply restrictive measures from a selection that the national legislation provides, the measure that it takes in practice in may not be specific or objective, and will not be known to the parties beforehand; hence section 97^2 of the CIA does not provide the applicant with legal certainty. Furthermore, although subsection $97^2(7)$ of the CIA permits the foreign credit institution to file a complaint with a court in the relevant jurisdiction – a provision that is dubious because it

---

[985] s.$97^2(7)$, CIA.

[986] s.$97^2(7)$, CIA.

[987] s.$97^2(8)$, CIA.

[988] s.$97^2(9)$, CIA.

[989] See the subsection '*The requirements for a successful public policy/public security derogation*', in section 2.1.3.

concerns a right that a foreign legislature should provide to applicant credit institutions within its jurisdiction – it does not require the EFSA to provide reasons for its decision to impose the restrictive measures; thus, section 97^2 of the CIA does not give the applicant sufficient access to legal redress. Consequently, these measures are not justified by Article 65(1)(b) of the TFEU.

If the credit institution is registered in a third country, then the derogation provided in Article 64(2) of the TFEU may be pleaded. For the reasons provided in the analysis for section 97^1 of the CIA,[990] restrictive measures applied under section 97^2 of the CIA are not justified under Article 64(2). Hence, if these measures causes a reduction of the supply of financial services by the foreign credit institution in Estonia, or the closure of its branch, they will hinder the free movement of capital and, consequently, contravene Article 63 of the TFEU.

Chapter 10^1: Reorganisation of credit institutions in several states

For the purposes of the CIA, 'reorganisation measures' are acts that are performed in the course of reorganisation proceedings of an administrative authority of a court of another Contracting State, in order to preserve or restore the solvency of the credit institution of the corresponding Contracting State, or a branch thereof, or a branch that a third country credit institution establishes in that Contracting State, and which may affect the earlier rights of third parties or result in the suspension of payments or execution proceedings, or a reduction of claims.[991] The provisions of section 115^1 of the CIA also apply to a moratorium established in respect of an Estonian credit institution, its branch founded in a Contracting State, or a branch that a third country credit institution establishes in Estonia, and also to bankruptcy proceedings, before making a bankruptcy regulation in respect of an Estonian credit institution or third country credit institution with an Estonian branch.[992] Reorganisation measures in respect of a credit institution of a Contracting State or its branches have to be conducted according to the law of the home country of this Contracting State, unless section 115^1 of the CIA provides otherwise.[993]

[990] See above in this subsection ('*Chapter 9: Supervision*').
[991] s.115^1(1), CIA.
[992] s.115^1(2), CIA.
[993] s.115^1(3), CIA. Subsections 115^1(4) to 115^1(8) of the CIA apply various connecting factors according to private international law, in order to determine which Contracting State's law applies.

Only a court or administrative authority of the home country of the relevant credit institution has the right to decide upon the application of reorganisation measures with respect to a credit institution of a Contracting State, or a branch established thereby in another Contracting State (including Estonia).[994] A decision to apply reorganisation measures to a credit institution of a Contracting State, or a branch established thereby in Estonia, comes into force in Estonia simultaneously with the entry into force of the corresponding decision in the credit institution's home country.[995] The reorganisation measures that are applied to a credit institution of a Contracting State, or its Estonian branch, are valid under the same conditions, and to the same extent, in Estonia as in the credit institution's home country.[996]

The EFSA is to promptly notify the financial supervision authorities of the Contracting States in which the relevant credit institution has branches, of its decision to establish a moratorium in respect of, or of a court decision to start bankruptcy proceedings against, that institution.[997] If the establishment of a moratorium, or commencement of bankruptcy proceedings, in respect of a credit institution, is likely to affect the interests of third parties in a Contracting State in which there is a branch of the credit institution, and this decision can be contested, the EFSA is to promptly publish an extract of the decision in the Official Journal, and in at least two national newspapers in each Contracting State in which a branch of the credit institution is established.[998] This excerpt is to include the legal basis and objective of the decision, the time in which complaints may be submitted, and the full address of the court that is competent to review these complaints.[999]

The EFSA is to notify the financial supervision authority of the home country of the relevant credit institution of the requirement to apply reorganisation measure(s) with respect to the branch established in Estonia by the credit institution of the (other) Contracting State.[1000] The EFSA is to give immediate notice of its decision to establish a moratorium in respect of a branch of a third country credit institution, to the financial

---

[994] s.115^{2}(1), CIA.

[995] s.115^{2}(2), CIA.

[996] s.115^{2}(3), CIA.

[997] s.115^{3}(1), CIA. Information on materially significant practical consequences that arise from establishment of the moratorium or start of bankruptcy proceedings are to be added to this notification (s.115^{3}(1), CIA).

[998] s.115^{3}(2), CIA.

[999] s.115^{3}(3), CIA.

[1000] s.115^(4)(1), CIA.

supervision authorities of the Contracting States in which the credit institution's other branches are situated.[1001] For application of measures that are necessary to conduct a moratorium with respect to a branch of a third country credit institution, the EFSA shall co-operate with the financial supervision authorities in which the credit institution has branches.[1002]

The application of reorganisation measures is not a 'capital movement' in the nomenclature in Annex I. As the establishment of a branch is a 'capital movement' in Title I(1) of the nomenclature in Annex I, reorganisation measures may affect a 'capital movement', if any of the credit institution's branches are closed or relocated. Reorganisation measures may restrict the free movement of capital, although more information is required about the reorganisation in question, in order to specify whether, and the extent to which, they do.

Chapter 10^3: Expropriation of a holding in a credit institution

Expropriation of a holding in a credit institution is the expropriation by the Estonian State of a holding in common interests for fair compensation, without shareholders' approval[1003] Expropriation may only be conducted in order to ensure the stability of Estonia's financial system, and with the purpose of managing the risks that relate to this stability.[1004] This is mainly for the preservation of the financial resources of, and the protection of the interests of, a credit institution's depositors, and in case the measures taken to achieve financial stability are insufficient or inappropriate.[1005] A holding in a credit institution can be expropriated, if a credit institution's acts or omissions may endanger the stability of Estonia's financial system or cause significant disturbances in their payment and accounting systems,[1006] and at least one of the following conditions exists: the credit institution does not satisfy the required prudential ratios,[1007] the credit

[1001] s.115^(4)(2), CIA. Information on materially significant practical consequences that arise from establishment of the moratorium are to be added to this notice (s.115^(4)(2), CIA).

[1002] s.115^(4)(3), CIA.

[1003] ss.115^5(1) and 115^5(3), CIA. For the purposes of Chapter 10^3 of the CIA, a 'credit institution' is a company that is registered in Estonia, and to which the EFSA has granted an activity licence (s.115^5(2), CIA).

[1004] s.115^6(1), CIA.

[1005] s.115^6(1), CIA.

[1006] s.115^6(2), CIA.

[1007] s.115^6(2)(1), CIA.

institution does not fulfil the obligations stated in subsections 80(1),[1008] 80(2),[1009] or 80(4)[1010] of the CIA and is not able to meet the reasonable claims of its creditors,[1011] and the credit institution is not managed reliably or securely (with the competence and prudence that is expected from its managers), and the management does not pursue the interests or the credit institution or its clients, thereby creating material risks to the continuity of the credit institution's economic activity or operational continuity.[1012]

If the conditions specified in the previous paragraph exist, then the Ministry of Finances may start the expropriation proceeding and prepare the draft expropriation decision, after hearing the Bank of Estonia's opinion.[1013] Upon commencement of the expropriation proceeding, the Ministry of Finances informs the management board of the credit institution to be expropriated, and the shareholders of that organisation whose holding is to be expropriated, sending a notice specified in subsection 115^9(1) of the CIA to them.[1014] The Ministry of Finances is immediately to notify the registrar of the Estonian Central Register of Securities about the start of the expropriation proceeding.[1015] On the basis of this notice, the registrar shall enter a temporarily restrictive entry on the shares, or on the accounts that are related to the shares, of a credit

---

[1008] A credit institution is to invest its assets to the satisfaction of creditors' justified claims, i.e. liquidity must be guaranteed at all times. Thus, it must maintain the required ratio of current assets to current liabilities (s.80(1), CIA).

[1009] A credit institution's managers are required to structure its assets so that its financing includes long-term, sufficient funds. These managers are also required to regularly monitor the terms of the institution's claims and commitments (s.80(2), CIA).

[1010] Unless the Bank of Estonia states otherwise, credit institutions must deposits some of their liquid assets in this Bank (s.80(4), CIA).

[1011] s.115^6(2)(2), CIA.

[1012] s.115^6(2)(3), CIA.

[1013] s.115^8(1), CIA.

[1014] s.115^8(3), CIA. The notice of commencement of expropriation proceedings must contain the credit institution's business name, seat, and registry code, the names and registry (or personal identification) codes of the persons who have a qualifying holding in the credit institution and with respect to whose shareholding the expropriate proceeding has been started, the number of shares in the credit institution, the number of shares to be expropriated, the expected date of taking a decision on expropriation of shares, the term during which a shareholder has the right to submit an opinion on the expropriation, an objection to the expropriation, or an acceptance of the offer for his/her shares, and other circumstances that are relevant to the expropriation (s.115^9, CIA). See note 792 for the meaning of 'qualifying holding' within the CIA.

[1015] s.115^8(4), CIA.

institution whose shareholding is being expropriated.[1016] The EFSA shall inform the financial supervision authority of a foreign country that conducts consolidated supervision over the credit institution, or over the credit institution's subsidiary, about the start of expropriation proceedings.[1017]

[1018]The Estonian government shall decide partial expropriation of a shareholding in a credit institution according to the circumstances that subsections 115^6(1) and 115^6(2) of the CIA state.[1019] The Estonian government's order of expropriation is to set out the credit institution's business name, seat and registry code,[1020] the names and registry or personal identification codes of the persons who have a qualifying holding in a credit institution, and with respect to whose shareholding the expropriation proceeding has been started,[1021] the names of the other shareholders,[1022] the number of the credit institution's issued shares and the number of shares to be expropriated,[1023] the justifications for expropriation, together with the legal basis and the considerations upon which the decision is based,[1024] the amount of compensation (if the assessment of the credit institution's financial circumstances has been conducted by the time that the decision on expropriation is taken),[1025] and other information that relates to expropriation – unless the law provides otherwise.[1026] The expropriation order shall be published in *Riigi Teataja*,[1027] and is thereby deemed to have been delivered to the shareholders of the credit institution that is to be expropriated.[1028]

1016 s.115^8(4), CIA.

1017 s.115^8(5), CIA.

1018 s.115^8(5), CIA.

1019 s.115^11(1), CIA. See above in this subsection ('*Chapter 10³: Expropriation of a holding in a credit institution*').

1020 ss.115^11(2)(1) and 115^9(1)(1), CIA.

1021 ss.115^11(2)(1) and 115^9(1)(2), CIA. See note 792 for the meaning of 'qualifying holding' within the CIA.

1022 ss.115^11(2)(1) and 115^9(1)(2), CIA.

1023 s.115^11(2)(2), CIA.

1024 s.115^11(2)(3), CIA. These considerations include the position of the Bank of Estonia and the EFSA at the start of the expropriation, and the opinions and objections of the shareholders whose holdings are to be expropriated that were submitted before the decision was taken (s.115^11(2)(3), CIA).

1025 s.115^11(2)(4), CIA.

1026 s.115^11(2)5), CIA.

1027 *Riigi Teataja* is the Estonian State Gazette.

1028 s.115^11(3), CIA.

Upon the entry into force of the decision on expropriation, and the transfer of shares to the Ministry of Finances,[1029] the ownership of the expropriated shares is deemed to have transferred to the expropriating authority.[1030] Upon entry into force of the expropriation order, all rights that relate to the expropriated shares will terminate.[1031]

Unless the Estonian government has already fixed the compensation, it shall be determined by an assessment report within one month of the entry into effect of the decision on expropriation.[1032] Uniform treatment is to be extended to the subjects of expropriation, upon the determination and payment of compensation.[1033] The compensation must be paid to the subject of the expropriation within a reasonable period of time, and within three months from the grant of compensation.[1034] Compensation must be paid in cash or securities.[1035] The subject of appropriation may not demand compensation for a loss of profit from shares that was due to an act or omission of the credit institution that was impossible to forecast during expropriation.[1036] Whilst a third party has the right to demand damages caused to it,[1037] this person has no right to demand compensation for a loss of profit that arose due to an act or omission of the credit institution, and which could not be forecast during the expropriation.[1038]

Expropriation of the shares of a credit institution is not a 'capital movement' in the nomenclature in Annex I. However, the establishment of a branch and the provision of cross-border services are 'capital movements' in this nomenclature. The effect of expropriation on the provision of services by the (Estonian) credit institution to other states of the EEA or to third countries depends on the circumstances of the particular case. If expropriation reduces the supply of financial services to other countries, then it restricts the free movement of capital.

For any limitation on the free movement of capital to be justified under Article 65(1)(b) of the TFEU, then the restrictive measures must be necessary for the protection of the interests that they are intended to

---

[1029] s.115^12(3), CIA.

[1030] s.115^11(4), CIA. The Estonian State is the expropriating authority (s.115^5(3), CIA).

[1031] s.115^11(5), CIA.

[1032] ss.115^13(1)-(2) and 115^15(3), CIA.

[1033] s.115^13(4), CIA.

[1034] s.115^13(5), CIA.

[1035] s.115^13(6), CIA.

[1036] s.115^13(7), CIA.

[1037] s.115^16(1), CIA.

[1038] s.115^16(2), CIA.

guarantee, be proportionate, and satisfy the requirements of legal certainty; furthermore, the persons affected by the measures must have access to legal redress, i.e. intervention must be supported by a formal statement of reasons and be subject to review by the courts.[1039] Expropriation may only be conducted in order to ensure the stability of Estonia's financial system, together with a specified secondary objective.[1040] The measures must be proportionate – so the threat to the country's financial system should be substantial, in order for the Estonian government to be permitted expropriate the credit institution's assets. The restrictive measures do not provide the applicant with access to legal redress, because the CIA does not furnish the credit institutions whose shares are to be expropriated with a right to appeal in the Estonian courts against the decision to expropriate these assets. Thus, if measures taken under Chapter 10^3 of the CIA hinder the free movement of capital, then they are not justified under Article 65(1)(b) of the TFEU. Hence, the provisions of this chapter contravene Article 63 of the TFEU.

3.3.2 Regulation No. 19 of the President of the Bank of Estonia of 6 July 1999

Regulation No. 19 considers the procedure for the grant of authorisation to Estonian credit institutions and to the branches of foreign credit institutions.[1041] As the free movement of capital concerns the Regulation's cross-border provisions, the focus in this work is the authorisation of the branches of foreign credit institutions, rather than of Estonian credit institutions.

Authorisation of a credit institution shall be applied for by a company, or a branch of a foreign credit institution, the principal, permanent activity of which is to receive repayable funds from the public, and to grant loans for its own account and supply other financing.[1042] The Board of the Bank

---

[1039] See the subsection '*The requirements for a successful public policy/public security derogation*', in section 2.1.3.

[1040] See above in this subsection ('*Chapter 10^3: Expropriation of a holding in a credit institution*').

[1041] Title, Regulation No. 19 of the President of the Bank of Estonia of 6 July 1999.

[1042] Clause 3, Regulation No. 19. The Regulation does not define 'foreign credit institution'. As an authorisation is not required for the foundation of a branch of a credit institution in another EEA state (see the requirements of section 20^1 of the CIA, in the subsection '*Chapter 2: Authorisation of credit institution (including passporting)*', in section 3.3.1), then 'foreign credit institution' in this context means a credit institution that is authorised to provide services in a third country.

of Estonia is to adopt a resolution that concerns the grant, or refusal to grant, authorisation to a credit institution, as proposed by the Banking Supervision of the Bank of Estonia.[1043]

An application for the authorisation of a credit institution is to be submitted to the Banking Supervision.[1044] Persons who would like to establish a credit institution, and foreign credit institutions that wish to found an Estonian branch, shall apply for authorisation before the submission of a petition to the commercial register.[1045]

An application for authorisation shall be submitted by the director of the foreign credit institution's branch, or a representative who acts in the name of the foreign credit institution, on the basis of a notarised authorisation document.[1046] If a branch has several directors who are entitled to represent the branch only jointly, then they must all sign the application for authorisation.[1047]

An applicant for authorisation is to submit the documents specified in Annex 2 to Regulation No. 19.[1048] These documents include a written application for authorisation of the branch of the foreign credit institution, which sets out the foreign credit institution's, and its branch's, business name, seat, address, and telecommunications numbers, and the personal data and details of the branch's director(s).[1049] The director(s), or a representative who acts in the name of the foreign credit institution or of the branch's director, must sign the application for authorisation.[1050] A document that certifies the authorisation of the director or representative is to be attached to the application.[1051]

The documents also include the branch's business plan,[1052] which sets out general information on the branch being established,[1053] an overview

---

[1043] Clause 4, Regulation No. 19. Subsection 13(2) of the CIA states that the EFSA is to grant authorisation to companies that are established in Estonia (see the first paragraph of section 3.3.1). Hence, the CIA and Regulation No. 19 specify different supervisory authorities for credit institutions. Regulation No. 19 should be updated to state that the EFSA is the competent authority.

[1044] Clause 5, Regulation No. 19. See note 1043. This article does not mention the authorisation of a branch of a foreign credit institution.

[1045] Clause 6, Regulation No. 19.

[1046] Clause 7, Regulation No. 19.

[1047] Clause 7, Regulation No. 19.

[1048] Clause 8, Regulation No. 19.

[1049] Clause 3.1, Annex 2, Regulation No. 19.

[1050] Clause 3.1, Annex 2, Regulation No. 19.

[1051] Clause 3.1, Annex 2, Regulation No. 19.

[1052] Clause 3.2, Annex 2, Regulation No. 19.

[1053] Clauses 3.2 and 1.4.1, Annex 2, Regulation No. 19.

of the branch's strategy and the market segment in which it plans to operate,[1054] a detailed description of the planned activities, which sets out the services and products that the branch intends to provide,[1055] a forecast of the number of clients,[1056] a description of the conditions for competition in the branch's market,[1057] the estimated financial indicators of the first three years of the branch's activity and a description of the assumptions on the basis of which these calculations are made,[1058] an overview of the credit and investment policies,[1059] and an overview of the general principles of risk management and the risk management strategies.[1060] A description of the organisation of the Estonian branch, and of the relationship between the credit institution and this branch, are also to be included.[1061] The organisational description should include a list of positions at the branch,[1062] a description of the branch's management scheme,[1063] the rules for the activities of the branch's management board,[1064] the general principles of the activities and competence of the branch's credit committee,[1065] and of other committees and structural units that are formed for the purposes of its management.[1066]

The application for authorisation of an Estonian branch of a foreign credit institution must also include documents that certify the trustworthiness, suitability, and conformity to the requirements of the CIA, of the branch's director(s), pursuant to the requirements that the Bank of Estonia has established,[1067] documents and information that concern

[1054] Clauses 3.2 and 1.4.2, Annex 2, Regulation No. 19.
[1055] Clauses 3.2 and 1.4.3, Annex 2, Regulation No. 19.
[1056] Clauses 3.2 and 1.4.3, Annex 2, Regulation No. 19.
[1057] Clauses 3.2 and 1.4.3, Annex 2, Regulation No. 19.
[1058] Clauses 3.2 and 1.4.4, Annex 2, Regulation No. 19.
[1059] Clauses 3.2 and 1.4.5, Annex 2, Regulation No. 19. These are likely to be the credit and investment policies of the foreign credit institution, rather than those of its Estonian branch.
[1060] Clauses 3.2 and 1.4.6, Annex 2, Regulation No. 19. The foreign credit institution, rather than its Estonian branch, is likely to set the risk management principles and strategies.
[1061] Clause 3.3, Annex 2, Regulation No. 19.
[1062] Clauses 3.3 and 1.5.1, Annex 2, Regulation No. 19.
[1063] Clauses 3.3 and 1.5.2, Annex 2, Regulation No. 19.
[1064] Clauses 3.3 and 1.5.3, Annex 2, Regulation No. 19.
[1065] Clauses 3.3 and 1.5.4, Annex 2, Regulation No. 19.
[1066] Clauses 3.3 and 1.5.5, Annex 2, Regulation No. 19.
[1067] Clause 3.4, Annex 2, Regulation No. 19.

shareholders with qualifying holdings[1068] in the founding credit institution – pursuant to subsection 30(2) of the CIA and clause 1.19 of Annex 2 to Regulation No. 19,[1069] and the founding credit institution's most recent annual report.[1070] The applicant foreign credit institution must furnish an official certificate that attests to its existence in its home country (such as an excerpt from a commercial register, or of a copy of its registration certificate),[1071] an authorisation document that certifies the authority of the branch's director – or a copy of a resolution that appoints this director,[1072] a copy of the credit institution's articles of association or partnership agreement,[1073] and the telecommunications data of the credit institution and of its Estonian branch.[1074] The application for authorisation of the Estonian branch must also include the following information, as issued by the banking supervision authority of the founding credit institution's home country:[1075] this authority's consent to the establishment of a branch of the credit institution in Estonia,[1076] confirmation that the credit institution holds a valid activity licence,[1077] information about the amount of the credit institution's own funds and its capital adequacy,[1078] and information concerning the deposit guarantee system of the credit institution's home state.[1079]

A person, whom the head of the Banking Supervision appoints, is to prepare a report in the presence of the applicant foreign credit institution,[1080] which sets out the date that the report is prepared,[1081] the names and official titles of the person(s) who prepare the report and of the

---

[1068] Regulation No. 19 does not define 'qualifying holding'. See note 792 for the meaning of 'qualifying holding' within the CIA.

[1069] Clause 3.5, Annex 2, Regulation No. 19. The person with the qualifying holding in the foreign credit institution is required to notify the EFSA (s.30(2), CIA). The applicant for authorisation must submit documents that concern acquirers of qualifying holdings, pursuant to the requirements that the Bank of Estonia establishes (clause 1.19, Annex 2, Regulation No. 19).

[1070] Clause 3.6, Annex 2, Regulation No. 19.

[1071] Clause 3.7, Annex 2, Regulation No. 19, and s.386(2)(1), Commercial Code.

[1072] Clause 3.7, Annex 2, Regulation No. 19, and s.386(2)(3), Commercial Code.

[1073] Clause 3.7, Annex 2, Regulation No. 19, and s.386(2)(4), Commercial Code.

[1074] Clause 3.7, Annex 2, Regulation No. 19, and s.386(2)(5), Commercial Code.

[1075] Clause 3.8, Annex 2, Regulation No. 19.

[1076] Clause 3.8.1, Annex 2, Regulation No. 19.

[1077] Clause 3.8.2, Annex 2, Regulation No. 19.

[1078] Clause 3.8.3, Annex 2, Regulation No. 19.

[1079] Clause 3.8.4, Annex 2, Regulation No. 19.

[1080] Clause 9, Regulation No. 19.

[1081] Clause 9.1, Regulation No. 19.

persons in the presence of whom the report is prepared,[1082] the title, date of preparation and number of pages, of each of the documents received,[1083] the numbers of original copies of the report and the names of the persons who possess these items,[1084] and the signatures of the persons who prepare the report and those in whose presence the report is prepared.[1085] If an applicant for authorisation does not submit all of the documents specified in Annex 2 to Regulation No. 19, or if the submitted documents have deficiencies in form, then the Banking Supervision authority shall, within one month of the date following that of the preparation of the report (as specified in clause 9.1 of Regulation No. 19)[1086] ask the applicant in writing to submit additional documents.[1087] The Banking Supervision may request further documents and information, in order to specify and verify the submitted certificates and documents, and the technical equipment that it is to inspect.[1088]

The applicant for authorisation submits the basis for the grant, or the refusal to grant, authorisation, together with the documents and information, and reports that the Banking Supervision prepares concerning on-the-spot verification in the new Estonian branch of the foreign credit institution.[1089] The Banking Supervision is to conduct this on-the-spot procedure in order to verify the compliance of the rooms, technical equipment, and systems of the branch being founded with the requirements for the supply of financial services to clients and for security.[1090] An applicant for authorisation shall be informed of the conduct of an on-the-spot verification at least seven days in advance.[1091] The verification is to be carried out in the presence of a competent representative appointed by the applicant, who shall provide the person conducting the verification with explanations that are necessary for the performance of his/her duties.[1092] The person who conducts the verification shall prepare a report that concerns the results of the verification, which is to set out the time of the

[1082] Clause 9.2, Regulation No. 19.
[1083] Clause 9.3, Regulation No. 19.
[1084] Clause 9.4, Regulation No. 19.
[1085] Clause 9.5, Regulation No. 19.
[1086] See above in this paragraph.
[1087] Clause 10, Regulation No. 19.
[1088] Clause 12, Regulation No. 19. This inspection is part of the Banking Supervision's on-the-spot verification in the new branch, which is considered in the next paragraph.
[1089] Clause 13, Regulation No. 19.
[1090] Clause 14, Regulation No. 19.
[1091] Clause 15, Regulation No. 19.
[1092] Clause 16, Regulation No.19.

verification, the identity of the verified rooms, technical equipment and systems, and the verification results. One original copy of the report is to be submitted to the applicant against the signature of the applicant.[1093]

The Banking Supervision is to analyse the business plan, and the description of the organisational structure, of the applicant for authorisation[1094] from all perspectives, and substantively, in order to assess the plan's conformity to the requirements of the CIA and Regulation No. 19, and evaluate its feasibility.[1095] In order to assess the feasibility of a business plan, the following are to be analysed: the strategy of the branch being established,[1096] the suitability of the organisational structure for the proposed activities and the nature of the services to be provided,[1097] the assumptions upon which the financial estimate is based,[1098] and other aspects of the business plan that may significantly affect the plan's practicability.[1099]

The Banking Supervision is to review all information, documents, and certificates that an applicant for authorisation submits, and the reports that the Banking Supervision prepares pursuant to this Procedure, and evaluate them together.[1100] As a result of an assessment of these items, the Banking Supervision is to prepare a reasoned opinion, and make a proposal to the Board of the Bank of Estonia to grant, or to refuse to grant, authorisation.[1101] The Board is not obliged to follow this proposal.[1102]

The Board of the Bank of Estonia shall inform the applicant for authorisation of the resolution concerning the grant, or refusal to grant, authorisation in writing, within the period specified in subsections 14(2)[1103] or 21(8)[1104] of the CIA.[1105] On the basis of a resolution of the

---

[1093] Clause 17, Regulation No. 19.

[1094] Clause 21 of the Regulation refers to "a credit institution being founded". However, this clause should also apply to a newly established branch of a foreign credit institution – hence the use of 'the applicant for authorisation' in the text.

[1095] Clause 21, Regulation No. 19.

[1096] Clause 22.1, Regulation No. 19. This clause refers to "the credit institution being founded". However, our concern is with the establishment of an Estonian branch of a foreign credit institution, which Regulation No. 19 also covers.

[1097] Clause 22.2, Regulation No. 19.

[1098] Clause 22.3, Regulation No. 19.

[1099] Clause 22.4, Regulation No. 19.

[1100] Clause 25, Regulation No. 19.

[1101] Clause 26, Regulation No. 19.

[1102] Clause 26, Regulation No. 19.

[1103] Subsection 14(2) of the CIA empowers the ESMA to introduce secondary conditions to the applicant, based on the circumstances that subsection 15(1) of the CIA provides. Subsection 15(1) of the CIA considers grounds on which the EFSA

Board of the Bank of Estonia, the Banking Supervision is to issue authorisation,[1106] which contains the registration number, and date of issue, of authorisation,[1107] the business name and address of the branch to which authorisation is granted,[1108] the transactions and acts that clauses 6(1)(1) to 6(1)(15) of the CIA specify, which the branch is permitted to conclude and perform,[1109] the number and date of the Board of the Bank of Estonia's resolution, on the basis of which authorisation is issued,[1110] and the signature of the head of the Banking Supervision.[1111]

The establishment of a branch is a 'capital movement' in the nomenclature in Annex I. The need for a foreign credit institution to obtain prior authorisation in order to establish an Estonian branch, together with the extensive information requirements and the on-the-spot verification, limits the free movement of capital.

To be justified under Article 65(1)(b) of the TFEU, the restrictive measures must be necessary for the protection of interests that they are intended to guarantee, be proportionate, and satisfy the requirements of legal certainty – i.e. they must be specific, objective and known to the

---

may refuse to grant authorisation to an applicant credit institution. It is noteworthy that subsection 14(1) of the CIA states that the EFSA is to take a decision to grant, or to refuse to grant, authorisation within six months of receipt of all the necessary information and documents, and within twelve months of the application for authorisation. This may be the time period to which clause 26 of Regulation No. 19 refers – for the authorisation of a credit institution in Estonia.

[1104] The CIA does not contain subsection 21(8) – section 21 of the CIA contains seven subsections. Section 21 of the CIA concerns the establishment of subsidiary credit institutions, or branches of foreign credit institutions, in Estonia, and is, thus, relevant to Regulation No. 19. Subsection 21(6) of the CIA states that the EFSA shall make a reasoned decision on the grant, or the refusal to grant, an authorisation, within two months of the receipt of an application and all the required data and documents. This may be the time period to which clause 26 of Regulation 19 refers – for the authorisation of the establishment of an Estonian branch of a foreign credit institution. For section 21 of the CIA, see the subsection '*Chapter 2: Authorisation of credit institution (including passporting)*', in section 3.3.1.

[1105] Clause 27, Regulation No. 19.

[1106] Clause 29, Regulation No. 19.

[1107] Clause 29.1, Regulation No. 19.

[1108] Clause 29.2, Regulation No. 19.

[1109] Clause 29.3, Regulation No. 19. For these clauses, see the first paragraph of the subsection '*Chapter 2: Authorisation of credit institution (including passporting)*', in section 3.3.1.

[1110] Clause 29.4, Regulation No. 19.

[1111] Clause 29.5, Regulation No. 19.

parties beforehand; furthermore, the persons who are affected by the measures must be granted access to legal redress – intervention must be supported by a formal statement of reasons and be subject to review by the domestic courts.[1112] Whilst the measures may be proportionate, they lack legal certainty in that the Board of the Bank of Estonia has a discretion to refuse to grant an authorisation, even if the Banking Supervision recommends it. To show adequate legal certainty to the applicant, Regulation No. 19 should provide guidelines that the Board is required to follow, in deciding to reject an application for authorisation that the Banking Supervision has recommended, or in deciding to grant an authorisation that the Banking Supervision has advised against. With respect to the issue of legal redress, clause 26 of Regulation No. 19 requires the Banking Supervision to prepare a reasoned opinion; however, the Regulation does not require the Board of the Banking Supervision to give reasons for a decision to refuse to grant an authorisation, and does not provide the applicant credit institution with the right to appeal against the decision in the national courts. Thus, Article 65(1)(b) of the TFEU does not justify the restrictive measures.

For the restrictive measures to be justified under Article 64(2) of the TFEU, the EU institutions should carefully consider the objective of the free movement of capital whilst enacting the legislation, and the national rules must not limit the free movement of capital more than the equivalent provisions of the relevant Directive do.[1113] The 'relevant Directive' is Directive 2013/36/EU. Article 47(1) of the Directive requires Member States to refrain from applying to branches of credit institutions that have their head office in a third country, provisions that result in more favourable treatment than that accorded to branches of credit institutions that have their head office in the EU. It contains no precise rules on the establishment of branches in Estonia of credit institutions that are resident in third countries. Hence, Estonian Regulation No. 19 limits the free movement of capital more than the equivalent rules of Directive 2013/36/EU do, because the Directive does not specifically address the requirements for the establishment of branches in the EEA of credit institutions that are authorised in third countries. Furthermore, whilst Recital 13 of Directive 2013/36/EU states that supervisory decisions and processes should not obstruct the functioning of the internal market in respect of "the free flow of capital", the free movement of capital is not

---

[1112] See the subsection '*The requirements for a successful public policy/public security derogation*', in section 2.1.3.

[1113] See the subsection '*Derogations that apply only to capital movements to/from third countries*', in section 2.3.2.

mentioned in the Directive's Articles. Thus, the EU institutions were aware of the objective of the free movement of capital whilst enacting Directive 2013/36/EU, but did not carefully take it into account during this process. Therefore, Article 64(2) of the TFEU does not justify the restrictive measures. Consequently, Regulation No. 19 contravenes Article 63 of the TFEU.

3.4 Insurance Activities Act 2004 (IAA)

The IAA includes rules for the provision of insurance and reinsurance services, and of insurance mediation. 'Insurance activities' are an insurance undertaking's acceptance of the policyholder's risks under an insurance contract, which pays indemnities when an insured event occurs.[1114] An 'insurance undertaking' is a company whose "main permanent activity" is to compensate for damage resulting from insured events or payment of agreed sums.[1115] The IAA does not define 'insured events'.

The main classes of insurance are non-life insurance,[1116] life insurance,[1117] and reinsurance.[1118] The classes of non-life insurance are accidents insurance,[1119] sickness insurance,[1120] land vehicles insurance,[1121] railway rolling stock insurance,[1122] aircraft insurance,[1123] ships insurance,[1124] goods in transit insurance,[1125] fire and natural forces insurance,[1126] other damage to property,[1127] motor vehicle liability insurance,[1128] aircraft liability insurance,[1129] liability for ships,[1130] general

[1114] s.2(1), IAA.
[1115] s.3(1), IAA.
[1116] s.11(1)(1), IAA.
[1117] s.11(1)(2), IAA.
[1118] s.11(1)(3), IAA.
[1119] s.12(1), IAA.
[1120] s.12(2), IAA.
[1121] s.12(3), IAA.
[1122] s.12(4), IAA.
[1123] s.12(5), IAA.
[1124] s.12(6), IAA.
[1125] s.12(7), IAA.
[1126] s.12(8), IAA.
[1127] s.12(9), IAA.
[1128] s.12(10), IAA.
[1129] s.12(11), IAA.

liability insurance,[1131] credit insurance,[1132] suretyship insurance,[1133] insurance for miscellaneous financial losses,[1134] insurance for legal expenses,[1135] and assistance insurance.[1136] The classes of life insurance are term and whole life insurance,[1137] endowment assurance,[1138] birth insurance and marriage insurance,[1139] annuities,[1140] unit-linked life insurance,[1141] tontines,[1142] and the administration of pension schemes.[1143]

An insurance undertaking must hold an authorised issued by the EFSA in order to practise insurance activities.[1144] An authorisation is granted for an unspecified period.[1145] An authorisation is given for engaging in at least one class of insurance, or, at the request of the applicant for authorisation, for engaging in at least one subclass of insurance.[1146] An insurance undertaking may provide only those classes or subclasses of insurance for which an authorisation has been granted.[1147] Nonetheless, an insurance undertaking that supplies non-life insurance may operate in classes or subclasses of insurance without a further authorisation, if the risk additionally insured by the insurance undertaking is related to the object insured on the basis of the class or subclass of insurance that the authorisation expressly covers, and the "specified risk and object or person" are insured by the same contract.[1148] An insurance undertaking

---

1130 s.12(12), IAA. The IAA does not distinguish between ships insurance and liability for ships. The former may refer to the insurance of the goods on board a ship, whilst the latter may indicate the insurance of a ship.

1131 s.12(13), IAA.

1132 s.12(14), IAA.

1133 s.12(15), IAA.

1134 s.12(16), IAA.

1135 s.12(17), IAA.

1136 s.12(18), IAA.

1137 s.13(1), IAA.

1138 s.13(2), IAA.

1139 s.13(3), IAA.

1140 s.13(4), IAA.

1141 s.13(5), IAA.

1142 s.13(6), IAA. A 'tontine' is annuity that is shared by subscribers to a common fund.

1143 s.13(7), IAA. The management of pension funds that section 3 of the Funded Pensions Act provides for, is excluded from this category (s.13(7), IAA).

1144 s.16(1), IAA.

1145 s.16(3), IAA.

1146 s.17(1), IAA.

1147 s.17(2), IAA.

1148 s.17(3), IAA. The quoted phrase of the English translation of the IAA is difficult to understand. Perhaps the relevant subclasses of insurance need to be

that is engaged in life insurance may simultaneously provide life insurance, accidents insurance, and sickness insurance.[1149]

'Reinsurance activities' are the acceptance of the insured risks of an insurance undertaking, based on a reinsurance contract, with the objective of paying the insurance undertaking an agreed amount of indemnities in connection with the insured event, which is specified in an insurance contract entered into between the insurance undertaking and the policyholder.[1150] A 'reinsurance undertaking' is an insurance undertaking that may only engage in reinsurance activities and insurance mediation, and conduct transactions and acts that are directly ancillary and/or supplementary to its main activity.[1151] The classes of reinsurance are reinsurance of non-life insurance,[1152] and reinsurance of life insurance.[1153]

An insurance undertaking may simultaneously provide life insurance and the reinsurance of life insurance, or non-life assurance and its reinsurance.[1154] A reinsurance undertaking may simultaneously supply non-life insurance and the reinsurance of life insurance.[1155]

'Insurance mediation' (hereafter 'mediation')[1156] includes the conduct of work that is preparatory to the conclusion of insurance and reinsurance contracts, including the preparation of risk analyses,[1157] the conclusion of insurance and reinsurance contracts,[1158] and assistance in the administration and performance of insurance and reinsurance contracts.[1159] For the purposes of the IAA, the following activities are not included within insurance mediation: the engaging of insurance undertakings in mediation

---

ancillary to the life assurance, but with all of these services provided under the same insurance contract. The provisions of subsection 17(3) of the IAA do not apply to credit insurance, suretyship insurance, or insurance for legal expenses, unless the last of these is an additional class of ships insurance, liability for ships insurance, or assistance insurance (s.17(4), IAA).

[1149] ss.17(6), 12(1) and 12(2), IAA.

[1150] s.3¹(1), IAA.

[1151] s.3¹(2), IAA.

[1152] s.14(1), IAA.

[1153] s.14(2), IAA.

[1154] s.17(7), IAA.

[1155] s.17(8), IAA. The IAA does not (expressly) provide for a reinsurance undertaking to simultaneously supply life insurance and the reinsurance of non-life insurance.

[1156] The IAA uses this abbreviation for 'insurance mediation'. Section 3.4 follows this practice.

[1157] s.2(2)(1), IAA.

[1158] s.2(2)(2), IAA.

[1159] s.2(2)(3), IAA.

(except for mediation of insurance contracts of other insurance undertakings),[1160] the engaging of employees of insurance undertakings in mediation under an employment contract (except for mediation of insurance contracts of other insurance undertakings),[1161] and the supply of insurance-related information in the context of another professional activity – if the purpose of this activity is not to help the client to conclude or perform an insurance or reinsurance contract, to adjust for losses, to manage the appraisal of claims that are filed with an insurance undertaking on a professional basis, and the provision of this information is not usually part of the professional activity.[1162]

Mediation is split into insurance brokerage and the activities of insurance agents.[1163] 'Insurance brokerage' is engagement in mediation by a person in the policyholder's interests, or (in the case of reinsurance) in the interests of an insurance undertaking, with the purpose of offering an insurance contract that corresponds to the demands of the policyholder or the undertaking.[1164] The activities of an insurance agent comprise a person's engagement in mediation, in the case in which this person (the agent) represents at least one insurance undertaking.[1165]

For the purposes of the IAA, an 'insurance intermediary' (hereafter 'intermediary')[1166] is a person who engages in mediation for a fee.[1167] Only insurance brokers and insurance agents are intermediaries.[1168] Only an insurance broker may practice insurance brokerage.[1169] Only an insurance agent may pursue the activities of insurance agents.[1170] Chapter 10 of the IAA states requirements that intermediaries must satisfy, in order for the EFSA to enter them into the list of authorised intermediaries.[1171]

[1160] s.2(3)(1), IAA.
[1161] s.2(3)(2), IAA.
[1162] s.2(3)(3), IAA.
[1163] s.2(4), IAA.
[1164] s.129(1), IAA.
[1165] s.129(2), IAA. An insurance agent can only represent more than one insurance undertaking, if these entities are authorised to provide different classes or subclasses of insurance (s.129(2), IAA). These classes and subclasses are listed above in this section (i.e. section 3.4).
[1166] The IAA uses this abbreviation for 'insurance intermediary'. Section 3.4 follows this practice.
[1167] s.130(1), IAA.
[1168] s.130(2), IAA.
[1169] s.130(3), IAA.
[1170] s.130(3), IAA.
[1171] Divisions 2 and 3 of Chapter 10 (Insurance Mediation) of the IAA contain the requirements and procedure for the authorisation of an Estonian insurance broker.

Chapter 2 Division 2: Activities of Estonian Insurance Undertakings in Foreign States[1172]

Estonian insurance undertakings may pursue authorised insurance activities in a foreign state, by establishing a branch or supplying cross-border services.[1173] Upon engaging in insurance activities in a foreign country, an insurance undertaking is to comply with the requirements of the IAA, its secondary legislation, and the foreign state's legislation.[1174] Sections 30, 35, 36, 37, 38, 39 and 40 of the IAA apply to the provision of insurance services by an Estonian insurance company in a (non-Estonian) Contracting State.[1175] Sections 31, 32, 33, 34 and 37¹ of the IAA apply to the supply of insurance services by an Estonian insurance firm in a third country.[1176]

An Estonian reinsurance undertaking may provide reinsurance activities in third countries.[1177] Subsection 30(4) and sections 38, 39 and 40 of the IAA apply to these services.[1178] For the purposes of Chapter 2 Division 2 of the IAA, 'cross-border reinsurance activities' are reinsurance activities that an Estonian reinsurance company provides to an insurance undertaking established in a foreign state.[1179] As sections 38, 39 and 40 of the IAA regulate the provision of cross-border insurance services to (non-Estonian) Contracting States, the application of these sections to reinsurance activities means that they also regulate the supply of the latter to those States.

Divisions 4 and 5 of Chapter 10 of the IAA contain the requirements and procedure for the authorisation of an Estonian insurance agent.

1172 The IAA does not define the term 'foreign state'. The language of s.29(5) of the IAA (see note 1176) suggests that this term includes both Contracting States and third countries, both of which are defined at the start of this chapter (Chapter Three – Estonia: Legal Issues).

1173 s.29(1), IAA. If a person who is authorised to represent an Estonian insurance undertaking is permanently engaged in the activities of an insurance agent, or in insurance activities, in a foreign state, then the authorised person's activities are deemed to be the activities of a foreign branch of the Estonian insurance undertaking, and this company is to establish a branch in accordance with sections 31-37 of the IAA in order to continue to provide insurance activities (s.29(2), IAA).

1174 s.29(3), IAA.

1175 s.29(4), IAA.

1176 s.29(5), IAA. Subsection 29(5) of the IAA refers to "a state not specified in subsection (4) of this section (hereinafter *third country*)."

1177 s.29(6), IAA.

1178 s.29(6), IAA.

1179 s.30(4), IAA.

The next paragraphs consider the provision insurance (and reinsurance) services to Contracting States. Following this, the supply of insurance (and reinsurance) services to third countries is covered.

For the purposes of Chapter 2 Division 2 of the IAA, 'cross-border insurance activities' are those of an Estonian insurance undertaking that relate to insured risks that are located in a foreign state.[1180] A foreign state in which the insured risk is located means one where the object of insurance is situated – if the insurance relates to immovable property,[1181] the object of insurance has a licence plate, is in the register,[1182] and concerns vehicles of any type,[1183] an insurance contract has been agreed that covers risks which are related to travel services of four months or less,[1184] or the policyholder has his/her habitual residence (natural person)[1185] or place of business related to insurance contracts thereof (legal person).[1186]

An Estonian insurance company that wishes to establish a branch in a (non-Estonian) Contracting State is to notify the EFSA of its intention,[1187] and submit to this authority the following documents and information: the name of the Contracting State in which the insurance undertaking wishes to open the branch,[1188] and a scheme of operations that concerns the branch's insurance activities[1189] and sets out a list of the planned classes and subclasses of insurance,[1190] the planned amounts of reinsurance and the principles of reinsurance for each of these classes and subclasses,[1191] the amount of the available solvency margin,[1192] the principles and methods of computation of the technical provisions in section 75 of the

[1180] s.30(1), IAA.

[1181] s.30(2)(1), IAA.

[1182] The IAA does not explain which register this is – different provisions of the Act mention the commercial register, the punishment register, the share register, the land register, and the ship register. Clause 30(2)(2) of the IAA may refer to a register of vehicles.

[1183] s.30(2)(2), IAA.

[1184] s.30(2)(3), IAA.

[1185] s.30(3)(1), IAA.

[1186] s.30(3)(2), IAA.

[1187] s.35(1), IAA.

[1188] s.35(1)(1), IAA.

[1189] s.35(1)(2), IAA.

[1190] ss.35(1)(2) and 20(1)(1), IAA. The second paragraph of this section (section 3.4) sets out these classes.

[1191] ss.35(1)(2) and 20(1)(2), IAA.

[1192] ss.35(1)(2) and 20(1)(3), IAA.

IAA[1193] and of the financial liabilities in section 75¹ of the IAA,[1194] a technical business plan for each of the planned classes and subclasses of insurance,[1195] the estimated volume of insurance premiums, claims and operating expenses (and the proportion of reinsurance therein) during the first three years of insurance activity,[1196] and the amount of the technical provisions and the financial liabilities that the branch holds for each class and subclass of insurance.[1197] The insurance firm must also supply to the EFSA a detailed description of the branch's organisational structure,[1198] the address of the branch's seat in the Contracting State,[1199] information that clause 18(1)(7) of the IAA contains concerning the branch's director – who must be adequately empowered to be able to represent the insurance company in relation to third parties,[1200] and, if the planned insurance activities permit entry into motor third party liability contracts, has become a member of both the national bureau of motor third party liability insurance and the guarantee fund of the country in which the branch is situated.[1201]

[1193] 'Technical provisions' for the purposes of the IAA are the calculated amounts of commitments that arise from the (insured) risk that is transferred to an insurance company on the basis of the insurance contracts (s.75(1), IAA). The classes of technical provisions are a provision for unearned premiums (a calculated amount of an insurance premium that represents the extent to which an insured risk has been transferred to the insurance firm and this firm has not covered the costs that relate to that risk), a provision for outstanding claims (a computed value of commitments that are likely to arise from insured events and known circumstances), life insurance provision (the amount of the insured risk that life insurance contracts contain and the commitments that arise from covering this risk), a provision for bonuses (a computed amount of supplementary profit arising from insurance contracts), and other technical provisions that legislation or the insurance company's articles of association prescribe (ss.75(2)-(3), IAA).

[1194] ss.35(1)(2) and 20(1)(4), IAA. 'Financial liabilities' for the purposes of the IAA are the commitments of an insurance firm that arise from carrying the financial risk which the insurance contracts contain (s.75¹, IAA).

[1195] ss.35(1)(2) and 20(1)(5), IAA.

[1196] ss.35(1)(2) and 20(1)(7), IAA.

[1197] ss.35(1)(2) and 20(1)(7), IAA.

[1198] s.35(1)(2), IAA.

[1199] s.35(1)(3), IAA.

[1200] s.35(1)(4), IAA. This information includes the director's name, personal identification code (or date of birth if there is no code), residence, educational background, employment history, and documents that demonstrate his/her trustworthiness and conformity to the requirements of the IAA (s.18(1)(7), IAA).

[1201] s.35(1)(5), IAA.

The EFSA shall take a decision to forward, or to refuse to forward, the documents and information described in the previous sentence, together with a list of the branch's planned insurance activities by class and subclass, to the Contracting State's financial supervision authority, within three months of submission of the documents and information, and within two months of receipt of these items and compliance with all requirements.[1202] The EFSA may refuse to review the documents and information for forwarding to the financial supervision authority of the (other) Contracting State, if they do not comply with the requirements of the IAA or its secondary legislation,[1203] are incomplete,[1204] or have not been submitted for forwarding within this period.[1205] Upon forwarding the documents and information, the EFSA must inform the financial supervision authority of the Contracting State of the location of the branch's certification that the insurance firm's available solvency margin complies with the requirements of the IAA.[1206]

The Estonian insurance company may establish a branch in (another) Contracting State, after receiving (via the EFSA) the conditions that the financial supervision authority of that Contracting State sets for providing insurance services there.[1207] If this authority has not provided these conditions within two months of receipt of all the documents and information from the EFSA, then the insurance company may open a branch in the Contracting State.[1208]

The EFSA may take a decision to refuse to forward the documents and information if these items do not satisfy the requirements of the IAA or are inaccurate, misleading or incomplete,[1209] the insurance undertaking's resources are inadequate for it to engage in the insurance activities that the

---

[1202] s.35(3), IAA. Subsections 35(2) and 35(3) of the IAA do not refer to the name of the Contracting State and the scheme of operations for the branch's insurance activities, which the insurance company must provide to the EFSA in accordance with clauses 35(1)(1) and 35(1)(2) of the IAA, respectively. Additional requirements include certification of the documents' authenticity by a notary or sworn translator (s.35(2), IAA).

[1203] s.35(4)(1), IAA.

[1204] s.35(4)(2), IAA.

[1205] s.35(4)(3), IAA.

[1206] s.35(5), IAA.

[1207] s.35(6), IAA.

[1208] s.35(6), IAA. Subsection 35(6) of the IAA does not apply to reinsurance firms, who may establish a branch in a Contracting State after receiving from the EFSA confirmation of the latter's decision to forward the documents and information to the financial supervision authority of that State (s.35(8), IAA).

[1209] s.36(1), IAA.

branch's scheme of operations describes,[1210] the branch's director does not satisfy the requirements of section 52 of the IAA,[1211] and/or the establishment of the branch, or the implementation of the scheme of operations that the insurance company submits, may harm the interests of the policyholders, insured persons or beneficiaries, the insurance firm's financial position, or the reliability of the company's activities in Estonia or in the Contracting State in which the branch is situated.[1212] The EFSA may issue a precept in order to preclude an Estonian insurance undertaking from engaging in insurance activities through a branch established in a (non-Estonian) Contracting State, if a ground provided for in section 36 of the IAA for refusal to forward the documents and information exists,[1213] or the Contracting State's financial supervision authority has informed the EFSA of a contravention of that State's legislation or of the conditions stated in subsection 35(6) of the IAA[1214] by the insurance company.[1215]

If an Estonian insurance company wishes to supply cross-border insurance services to a (non-Estonian) Contracting State, then it is to notify the EFSA of its intention to do this,[1216] and submit the following information and documents to the EFSA: the name of the Contracting State where the insurance firm wishes to provide these services,[1217] and a description of the planned insurance activities.[1218] The EFSA shall take a decision to forward, or to refuse to forward, this information and these documents to the financial supervision authority of the Contracting State, within one month of receipt of all the requisite items, and shall promptly inform the insurance company of its decision.[1219] The EFSA may refuse to review these items if they are incomplete or do not comply with the

[1210] s.36(2), IAA.
[1211] s.36(3), IAA.
[1212] s.36(4), IAA.
[1213] s.37(1)(1), IAA.
[1214] See the previous paragraph.
[1215] s.37(1)(2), IAA. The EFSA must promptly deliver the precept to the insurance firm (s.37(2), IAA).
[1216] s.38(1), IAA.
[1217] s.38(1)(1), IAA.
[1218] s.38(1)(2), IAA. If these planned cross-border insurance services may involve entry into motor third party liability insurance contracts, then the applicant insurance firm must also provide the EFSA with confirmation that it has become a member of both the national bureau of motor third party liability insurance and the Contracting State's guarantee fund, and with the name and address of a representative with a permanent residence or place of business in that State whom the insurance undertaking has designated to the State (ss.38(1)(3) and 38(6), IAA).
[1219] s.38(3), IAA.

requirements of the IAA,[1220] or have these shortcomings and the information or documents that the EFSA additionally requires are not submitted within the prescribed period.[1221]

The EFSA shall forward the following information and documents to the financial supervision authority of the (other) Contracting State: a list of the classes of insurance that the insurance firm has the right to provide,[1222] information that concerns the insurance company's available solvency margin and that this margin complies with the requirements of the IAA,[1223] and a description of the planned cross-border insurance services.[1224] The insurance undertaking may start cross-border insurance activities in a Contracting State, after the EFSA has informed it of the latter's decision to forward these items to the Contracting State's financial supervision authority.[1225]

The EFSA may refuse to forward the information and documents, if these items do not satisfy the requirements of the IAA or are inaccurate, misleading, or incomplete,[1226] the insurance firm's resources are inadequate for engaging in insurance activities that are described in the scheme of operations for the supply of insurance services to the Contracting State,[1227] or the cross-border insurance activities may damage the interests of the policyholders, insured persons or beneficiaries, the insurance company's financial position, or the reliability of its activities in Estonia or in the (other) Contracting State.[1228] The EFSA may issue a precept in order to prohibit an Estonian insurance undertaking from supplying cross-border insurance services, if one of the grounds in section 39 of the IAA for refusal to forward the information and documents exists,[1229] or the Contracting State's financial supervision authority has informed the EFSA of a breach of this State's legislation by the insurance firm.[1230]

[1220] s.38(4)(1), IAA.

[1221] s.38(4)(2), IAA.

[1222] s.38(5)(1), IAA.

[1223] s.38(5)(2), IAA.

[1224] s.38(5)(3), IAA.

[1225] s.38(8), IAA.

[1226] s.39(1), IAA.

[1227] s.39(2), IAA.

[1228] s.39(3), IAA. Subsection 39(3) of the IAA refers to "the reliability of its activities in Estonia or the Contracting State of the location of the branch", which, in the context of the provision of cross-border services, must be mistaken.

[1229] s.40(1)(1), IAA.

[1230] s.40(1)(2), IAA. The EFSA is to promptly deliver the precept to the insurance company (s.40(2), IAA).

The establishment of a branch and the provision of cross-border insurance services are 'capital movements' in Titles I(1) and X of the nomenclature in Annex I, respectively. If the EFSA refuses to review the information and documents for forwarding to the financial supervision authority of the host EEA state, refuses to forward these items to that authority, or issues a precept in order to preclude the Estonian insurance company from establishing a branch in another EEA state or supplying cross-border services to that state, then it limits the free movement of capital.

For the restrictive measures to be justified under Article 65(1)(b) of the TFEU, they must be necessary for the protection of interests that they are intended to guarantee, be proportionate (i.e. not attainable by less restrictive measures), and satisfy the requirements of legal certainty (i.e. be specific, objective and known to the parties beforehand); furthermore, the persons who are affected by the measures must have access to legal redress (i.e. intervention must be supported by a formal statement reasons, and subject to review in the national courts). Whilst most of the informational requirements that relate to the establishment of a branch or the provision of cross-border insurance services are proportionate, and the measures based on them satisfy the requirements of legal certainty (for instance, the ground for the EFSA to refuse to forward information and documents to the host EEA state's financial supervision authority because they do not satisfy the requirements of the IAA), there is scope for the EFSA's discretion to be exercised – such as its capacity to refuse to forward the information and documents under subsection 35(6) of the IAA because it may consider that the scheme of operations that the insurance firm submits for its proposed branch in the host state may damage this company's interests in Estonia or in the host country. In addition, the applicant insurance undertaking is not provided with access to legal redress, because the IAA does not require the EFSA to accompany a decision to refuse to review, or to forward, the information and documents, or to issue a precept, with reasons, and because the IAA does not provide the applicant with the right to appeal against such a decision in the Estonian courts. Thus, Article 65(1)(b) of the TFEU does not justify the restrictive measures. Consequently, they contravene Article 63 of the TFEU.

An insurance company who wishes to establish a branch in a third country shall apply for an authorisation from the EFSA.[1231] In order to apply for the foundation of a branch, an insurance firm is to submit a

---

[1231] s.31(1), IAA.

written application and the following documents and information to the EFSA:[1232] the name of the third country in which the insurance firm wishes to open a branch, "together with a reference to the legislation of the corresponding state, according to which foundation of the branch of the insurance undertaking is permitted in the third country",[1233] the address of the branch's seat (in the third country)[1234] a scheme of the branch's operations that concerns insurance activities in the third country, which complies with the requirements contained in section 20 of the IAA (with the exception of clause 20(1)(6) of the IAA),[1235] and information that clause 18(1)(7) of the IAA provides concerning the branch's director – who must be provided with sufficient authority to be able to act in the insurance company's name in relation to third parties.[1236]

The provisions of section 21 of the IAA apply to the processing of applications for an authorisation for the establishment of a branch, verification of the information submitted, and verification of the organisational structure, financial situation, and technical systems of the applicant and the existence of adequate resources for the foundation of a branch.[1237] These rules are as follows. If an applicant has not submitted all of the information and documents that are specified in section 18 of the IAA,[1238] or if this information or these documents are incomplete or have

---

[1232] s.31(2), IAA.

[1233] s.31(2)(1), IAA. The meaning of the quoted passage is unclear. It may require the applicant insurance company to make reference to an agreement between Estonia and the selected third country, which expressly permits Estonian insurance undertakings to establish a branch within the latter state.

[1234] s.31(2)(2), IAA.

[1235] These requirements are the same as those of subsection 35(1)(2) of the IAA, which concerns the establishment of a branch of an Estonian insurance undertaking in (another) Contracting State – see above in this subsection ('*Chapter 2 Division 2: Activities of Estonian Insurance Undertakings in Foreign States*').

[1236] See note 1200, for the information prescribed in clause 18(1)(7) of the IAA.

[1237] s.32(1), IAA.

[1238] These documents include a copy of the insurance company's articles of association, documents that certify the amount of available solvency margin, a sworn auditor's report, the opening balance of the firm, a review of its income and expenditure, its latest balance sheet, income statement and three most recent annual reports, a scheme of operations that conforms to section 20 of the IAA, the standard terms of insurance contracts, information on the insurance undertaking's management board, supervisory board, external auditor, responsible actuary and internal auditor, a list of the firm's shareholders, information on the financial contribution, number of shares, and votes acquired/owned by each shareholder, the data specified in subsection 61(3) of the IAA concerning persons who have a qualifying shareholding in the insurance firm, information on companies in which

not been prepared in accordance with the requirements,[1239] then the EFSA shall require the applicant insurance undertaking to remove the deficiencies.[1240] The EFSA may require the submission of additional information and documents, if it is not satisfied on the basis of those items specified in section 18 of the IAA[1241] that the applicant for authorisation has sufficient facilities for providing insurance services, that the applicant satisfies the requirements for insurance undertakings that the IAA or its secondary legislation prescribe, or that other circumstances concerning the applicant need to be verified.[1242] In order to verify the information that the applicant submits, the EFSA may make check national databases, perform on-site inspections, order a special audit or assessment, and/or obtain verbal explanations from members of the applicant's supervisory or management board, auditors, internal auditors, representatives of these, and (if required) third parties, about the content of documents, and facts that are relevant to taking a decision on the granting of an authorisation.[1243] The applicant insurance undertaking must submit all of these items within a reasonable time, whose length the EFSA determines.[1244] The EFSA may refuse to review an application, if the applicant has not submitted all the required information and documents in the prescribed form by the due date.[1245]

---

the firm or any member of its supervisory board or management board exceeds 20 per cent, the planned organisational structure of the insurance undertaking (or, in this instance the branch to be founded?), the firm's internal rules pursuant to section 84 of the IAA, the name and address of the person who handles motor third party liability insurance claims (if the branch may be providing motor third party liability insurance), and a document according to which the insurance company assumes the obligation to pay the single contribution to the Pension Contracts Sectoral Fund that the Guarantee Fund Act requires – if the planned insurance activities of the firm (or its new branch?) may include the entry into pension contracts (s.18(1), IAA).

[1239] Subsection 21(1) of the IAA does not state what these requirements are. This phrase may refer to the requirements of the IAA for authorisation of the Estonian insurance company – or (as appropriate) for authorisation of the third country branch of the Estonian insurance firm.

[1240] s.21(1), IAA.

[1241] See note 1238.

[1242] s.21(2), IAA.

[1243] s.21(3), IAA.

[1244] s.21(4), IAA.

[1245] ss.21(5) and 21(1), IAA. If the EFSA refuses to review an application for authorisation, it shall return the submitted documents to the applicant insurance firm (s.21(5). IAA).

The EFSA shall take a decision to grant, or refuse to grant, an authorisation for the establishment of a branch in a third country, within two months of receipt of all the necessary information and documents (and compliance with the requirements), but not later than within three months of receipt of the application.[1246] The EFSA must promptly inform the applicant insurance company of its decision to grant, or refuse to grant, the latter an authorisation to open the branch.[1247]

The EFSA may refuse to provide an authorisation to an Estonian insurance undertaking to found a branch in a third country, if the information or documents that the company submits with its application for authorisation for the establishment of a branch do not satisfy the requirements of the IAA or its secondary legislation, or are inaccurate, misleading or incomplete,[1248] the branch's director does not fulfil the requirements provided for in section 52 of the IAA,[1249] the insurance

---

[1246] s.32(2), IAA.

[1247] s.32(3), IAA.

[1248] s.33(1), IAA.

[1249] s.33(2), IAA. Sections 48 to 51 of the IAA apply to the directors of foreign branches of Estonian insurance companies, and to the directors of Estonian branches of insurance firms from third countries (s.52, IAA). Each director must have the education, expertise and experience that is necessary to manage an insurance company, and an impeccable business reputation (s.48(1), IAA). Subsection 48(2) of the IAA excludes four categories of persons from being managers; these include, for instance, persons who are subject to a prohibition on business (s.48(2)(3), IAA). The management board of an insurance company is to have at least two members (s.48(5), IAA). As section 52 of the IAA does not exclude the application of subsection 48(5) of the IAA to branches in third countries of Estonian undertakings, this subsection applies to these branches. The manager and employees of an insurance firm must act with the competence and prudence that is expected of them, in accordance with the requirements for their position, and in the interests of the insurance company, policyholders, insured persons and beneficiaries (s.48(6), IAA). By virtue of section 52 of the IAA, subsection 48(6) of the IAA applies to third country branches of Estonian undertakings. Sections 48^1, 49, 50 and 51 of the IAA apply concern the bases and principles of remuneration of members of the management boards and employees of insurance firms, the election or appointment of a manager of an insurance company, grounds for the removal of a manager of an insurance undertaking, and restrictions on the other professional activities of managers of insurance firms, respectively. All of these sections apply to branches in third countries of Estonian insurance firms (and to Estonian branches insurance undertakings) by virtue of section 52 of the IAA. Thus, the EFSA has the right to issue a precept to require the removal of a director of such a branch if the director does not satisfy the requirements of the IAA, if the director has contravened the requirements of the

firm's resources are insufficient for it to engage in insurance activities described in its scheme of operations in a third country,[1250] the establishment of a branch in a third country or the implementation of the scheme of operations that that the insurance undertaking submits may harm the interests of policyholders, insured persons or beneficiaries, the firm's financial position, or the reliability of the company's activities in Estonia, (another) Contracting State, or a third country,[1251] the third country's financial supervision authority has "no legal basis or possibilities for cooperation with the" EFSA, and, consequently, the EFSA is unable to exercise adequate supervision over the branch to be established there,[1252] and/or the insurance company has been punished for a specified offence (such as official misconduct) and the information concerning the punishment has not been removed from the punishment register pursuant to the Punishment Register Act.[1253] The EFSA may revoke an authorisation for the establishment of a branch in a third country of an Estonian insurance undertaking, if the company has submitted misleading information or documents, incorrect information, or false documents, to the EFSA on any occasion,[1254] the insurance firm has repeatedly or materially breached the requirements that the legislation of the corresponding third country provides and these contraventions may injure the interests of policyholders, insured persons or beneficiaries,[1255] the insurance company or its branch does not satisfy the requirements for the granting of an authorisation for the establishment of a branch,[1256] the insurance undertaking does not submit the required reports on its branch,[1257] the insurance firm has not implemented a precept that the EFSA has issued concerning the functioning of the branch, by the due date or to the extent prescribed,[1258] the risks that arise from the branch's

---

IAA or its secondary legislation that relate to his/her professional activities, if misleading, incomplete or inaccurate documents or information were submitted to the EFSA in connection with the appointment or election of the director, and/or if the director's activities have shown that he/she is incapable of organising the management of the branch in a way that adequately protects the interests of policyholders, insured persons and beneficiaries (ss.50(1) and 52, IAA).

[1250] s.33(3), IAA.

[1251] s.33(4), IAA.

[1252] s.33(5), IAA.

[1253] s.33(6), IAA.

[1254] s.34(1)(1), IAA.

[1255] s.34(1)(2), IAA.

[1256] s.34(1)(3), IAA.

[1257] s.34(1)(4), IAA.

[1258] s.34(1)(5), IAA.

activities are substantially greater than risks that arise from the insurance company's activities,[1259] or the circumstances for which section 33 of the IAA provides become evident.[1260] The EFSA is to promptly deliver a decision to revoke an authorisation for the establishment of a foreign branch to the insurance undertaking and to the financial supervision authority of the third country.[1261]

An Estonian insurance company that would like to provide cross-border insurance services in third countries is required to apply to the EFSA for an authorisation to do so.[1262] The insurance firm is to submit a written application to the EFSA for authorisation to supply these services.[1263] It is to accompany the application with the following information and documents: the name of the third country in which the insurance undertaking wishes to provide cross-border insurance services,[1264] references to the provisions of that state's legislation pursuant to which the company's cross-border insurance activities may be supplied there,[1265] and a description of the planned cross-border services.[1266]

The provisions of subsections 21(1) to 21(5), 22(1), and 22(4), and section 28, of the IAA apply to the processing of applications for the authorisation of cross-border insurance services.[1267] Subsections 21(1) to 21(5) also apply to the processing of applications for the authorisation of the foundation of a branch in a third country, and are, therefore, considered above in this subsection of section 3.4.[1268] The remaining provisions are as follows. An authorisation is to be granted if the documents and information that are submitted comply with "the requirements",[1269] and if it is possible to verify on the basis of these documents and this information that the applicant insurance undertaking has sufficient facilities and organisational capacity to conduct insurance activities, and that the interests of policyholders, insured persons and

---

1259 s.34(1)(6), IAA.

1260 s.34(1)(7), IAA. See above in this paragraph for the contents of section 33 of the IAA.

1261 s.34(2), IAA.

1262 s.37¹(1), IAA.

1263 s.37¹(1), IAA.

1264 s.37¹(1)(1), IAA.

1265 s.37¹(1)(1), IAA.

1266 s.37¹(1)(2), IAA.

1267 s.37¹(3), IAA.

1268 This subsection is entitled '*Chapter 2 Division 2: Activities of Estonian Insurance Undertakings in Foreign States*'.

1269 Subsection 22(1) of the IAA does not state what these requirements are. The phrase probably means the requirements of the IAA.

beneficiaries are adequately protected.[1270] The EFSA shall promptly inform the applicant insurance company of a decision to grant, or refuse to grant, an authorisation.[1271] The EFSA must publish a decision to grant, amend or revoke an authorisation on its website no later than the working day following the day on which the decision is made,[1272] and must publish a decision to revoke an authorisation in at least one daily national newspaper.[1273]

The EFSA shall take a decision to grant, or to refuse to grant, an authorisation for the provision of cross-border insurance services in a third country within two months of the receipt of all the necessary documents and information and "compliance with requirements",[1274] but not later than three months after the submission of an application for authorisation for the supply of these services there.[1275] The EFSA may refuse to grant an authorisation to an Estonian insurance undertaking to provide cross-border services in a third country, if the insurance firm has submitted misleading documents or information, inaccurate information or falsified documents to the EFSA,[1276] the insurance company's resources are inadequate for engaging in the cross-border activities that this undertaking describes in its application for the provision of these activities in the third country,[1277] the insurance firm's activities in the third country may harm the interests of the policyholders, insured persons or beneficiaries, the financial position of the insurance company or the reliability of its activities,[1278] the third country's financial supervision authority "has no legal basis, possibilities or readiness for sufficient and efficient cooperation with" the EFSA, and, consequently, the EFSA is unable to exercise adequate supervision over the insurance firm's activities,[1279] the insurance undertaking has been punished for a specified offence (such as an offence against public trust) and information concerning the punishment has not been removed from the punishment register pursuant to the Punishment Register Act,[1280]

[1270] s.22(1), IAA.
[1271] s.22(4), IAA.
[1272] s.28(1), IAA.
[1273] s.28(2), IAA.
[1274] Section 37^1(4) of the IAA does not state what these requirements are. The phrase is likely to mean compliance with the requirements of the IAA.
[1275] s.37^1(4), IAA.
[1276] s.37^1(5)(1), IAA.
[1277] s.37^1(5)(2), IAA.
[1278] s.37^1(5)(3), IAA.
[1279] s.37^1(5)(4), IAA.
[1280] s.37^1(5)(5), IAA.

and/or the insurance firm is involved in money laundering or contravenes the procedure that legislation establishes for money laundering and terrorist financing.[1281]

The EFSA may revoke an authorisation that it has granted to an Estonian insurance undertaking to engage in cross-border insurance activities in a third country, if the insurance company has submitted misleading documents or information, inaccurate information or falsified documents to the EFSA,[1282] the insurance company has not notified the EFSA of a change in its circumstances in relation to cross-border activities,[1283] the insurance firm has repeatedly or substantially breached the provision of legislation that regulates its activities,[1284] the insurance undertaking does not satisfy the requirements for the granting of authorisation for cross-border insurance services to third countries,[1285] the insurance company has not implemented a precept of the EFSA that concerns the cross-border activities by the due date or to the extent that the EFSA prescribes,[1286] and/or the risks that arise from the company's insurance activities are "significantly greater" than risks that arise from the insurance firm's other activities.[1287] The EFSA shall promptly inform the financial supervision authority of the third country, and the Estonian insurance undertaking, of its decision to revoke an authorisation for the latter to provide cross-border services in the third country.[1288]

The establishment of a branch and the provision of cross-border insurance services are 'capital movements' in Titles I(1) and X of the nomenclature in Annex I, respectively. If the EFSA refuses to grant, or revokes, an authorisation to an Estonian insurance company to establish a branch, or to provide cross-border services, in a third country, then it restricts the free movement of capital.

To be justified by Article 65(1)(b) of the TFEU, the restrictive measures must be necessary for the protection of interests that they are intended to guarantee, be proportionate (i.e. not attainable by less restrictive measures), and observe the requirements of legal certainty (i.e. be specific, objective, and known to the parties beforehand); in addition, the persons whom the measures affect must have access to legal redress

[1281] s.37^1(5)(6), IAA.
[1282] s.37^1(6)(1), IAA.
[1283] s.37^1(6)(2), IAA.
[1284] s.37^1(6)(3), IAA.
[1285] s.37^1(6)(4), IAA.
[1286] s.37^1(6)(5), IAA.
[1287] s.37^1(6)(6), IAA.
[1288] s.37^1(7), IAA.

(i.e. intervention must be supported by a formal statement of reasons and be subject to review in the national courts).[1289] Some of the grounds on which the EFSA may refuse to grant, or revoke, an authorisation do not provide legal certainty to the applicant insurance undertaking, because they are insufficiently specific and objective. For instance, the EFSA may refuse to grant an authorisation to an insurance company to establish a branch, or to provide cross-border services, because the third country's supervisory authority has, in the EFSA's opinion, no legal basis or possibility to co-operate with the EFSA; this provides the EFSA with a discretion to refuse authorisation. Furthermore, the applicant insurance undertaking does not have sufficient access to legal redress, because the IAA does not require the EFSA to accompany a refusal to grant authorisation, or a withdrawal of authorisation, with a formal statement of reasons, and because this Act does not provide the applicant with the right to appeal against a refusal or revocation of authorisation in the Estonian courts. Hence the restrictive measures are not justified by Article 65(1)(b) of the TFEU.

For the restrictive measures to be justified by Article 64(2) of the TFEU, the EU institutions must have carefully considered the objective of the free movement of capital whilst enacting the pertinent legislation, and the domestic rules must not limit the free movement of capital more than the equivalent provisions of the relevant Directive do. The 'relevant Directive' is Directive 2009/138/EC. Recital 72 of Directive 2009/138/EC states that Member States should not require insurance or reinsurance companies to invest their funds in particular categories of assets, as this requirement could be incompatible with the liberalisation of capital movements for which Article 63 of the TFEU provides. The Directive contains no further references to the free movement of capital.

The way in which the EU legislators have worded Recital 72 demonstrates that they were aware of the objective of the free movement of capital, whilst enacting Directive 2009/138/EC, and that Member States should respect this principle. It is arguable that one provision in a recital is insufficient to establish that the legislators have carefully taken account of the principle. However, it is also claimable that Recital 72 advises Member States to adhere to the principle of the free movement of capital as far as is possible, within the framework of the Directive.

Directive 2009/138/EC does not contain provisions that specifically address the establishment of a branch in a third country of, or the

---

[1289] See the subsection '*The requirements for a successful public policy/public security derogation*', in section 2.1.3.

provision of cross-border insurance services in a third country by, a company that is authorised in an EEA state to provide insurance services there. Article 175(1) of Directive 2009/138/EC empowers the Commission to submit proposals to the Council for the negotiation of agreements with third countries as regards the means of supervision of EEA reinsurance undertakings that conduct reinsurance business in third countries. These agreements are to seek to ensure effective market access for reinsurance companies in the territory of each Contracting Party, provide for the mutual recognition of supervisory rules and practices concerning reinsurance, and ensure that the supervisory authorities of EEA states are able to obtain the information that is necessary for them to supervise reinsurance undertakings that have their head offices in the EEA and that provide reinsurance services in the relevant third countries.[1290] The equivalent Article for insurance services is more general, and less relevant, than Article 175 of Directive 2009/138/EC – the EEA may, by means of agreements with third countries that are concluded pursuant to the Treaty, agree to the application of provisions that are different to those in Section 1 of Title I, Chapter IX of Directive 2009/138/EC (which cover the establishment of a branch in the EEA by an insurance company or a reinsurance firm that has its head office in a third country), for the purposes of ensuring on a reciprocal basis sufficient protection for policyholders and insured persons in EEA countries.[1291] Thus, Directive 2009/138/EC empowers the EU institutions to make agreements with third countries, in order to regulate the supervision of the provision of reinsurance services there by reinsurance firms that have their head office in the EEA, but not to make similar agreements for the supply of insurance services to third countries. Hence, over the area of the provision of insurance services to third countries, the IAA restricts the free movement of capital more than the relevant Directive (Directive 2009/138/EC) does.

It follows from the comments in the previous paragraph that the restrictive measures in sections 31-34 and 37[1] of the IAA are not justified by Article 64(2) of the TFEU. Consequently, these provisions breach Article 63 of the TFEU.

Chapter 2 Division 3: Activities of Foreign Insurance Undertakings in Estonia

An entity that has the right to provide insurance services according to the legislation of the country in which it was founded, and where an

[1290] Article 175(2), Directive 2009/138/EC.

[1291] Article 171, Directive 2009/138/EC. Directive 2009/138/EC does not define the term "the Treaty". The relevant legal instrument is probably the TFEU.

authorisation to engage in insurance activities was provided thereto, may also supply insurance services in Estonia on the basis of the authorisation granted in its home country, by opening a branch or engaging in cross-border insurance activities.[1292] A foreign insurance company is to comply with the requirements of Estonian law, upon providing insurance services in Estonia.[1293]

Sections 42, 46 and 47 of the IAA apply to companies that are authorised to supply insurance services in Contracting States, which would like to provide these services in Estonia.[1294] Sections 42, 43, 44, 45 and 46¹ apply to firms that are authorised to supply insurance services in third countries, which would like to engage in these activities in Estonia.[1295] However, the latter undertakings are not allowed to enter into pension contracts.[1296] Furthermore, all foreign companies are prohibited from agreeing pension contracts within the framework of cross-border insurance services.[1297]

In *Commission v Poland*,[1298] the CJEU held that investment transactions of Open Pension Funds are 'movements of capital' within the meaning of Article 63 of the TFEU.[1299] Given this, it is only a step for the CJEU to declare that the setting up of a pension fund is a 'capital movement', on the ground that it will, or may, involve cross-border investments. The Estonian prohibition on insurance firms entering into pensions contracts limits the free movement of capital.[1300]

For the purposes of Chapter 2 Division 3 of the IAA, 'cross-border insurance activities' are the insurance activities of a foreign insurance company that concern insured risks that are located in Estonia.[1301] The

---

[1292] s.41(1), IAA. If a person who is authorised to represent a foreign insurance undertaking is permanently engaged in the activities of an insurance agent, or in insurance activities, in Estonia, then the authorised person's activities are deemed to be the activities of an Estonian branch of the foreign insurance firm, and this company is to establish a branch in accordance with sections 43-46 of the IAA in order to continue to supply insurance services (s.41(2), IAA).

[1293] s.41(3), IAA.

[1294] s.41(4), IAA.

[1295] s.41(5), IAA.

[1296] s.41(5), IAA.

[1297] s.41(7), IAA.

[1298] [2011] ECR I-13613.

[1299] See section 2.1.1.

[1300] It is difficult to comment further on this issue, because it would necessitate a discussion of Estonian laws according to which entities may provide cross-border pensions, which is beyond the scope of this work.

[1301] s.42(1), IAA.

insured risk is located in Estonia, if the object of insurance is immovable property that is situated there,[1302] the insured asset is a registered vehicle that has an attached licence plate,[1303] an insured contract that covers risks related to travel services for a duration of no more than four months has been agreed in Estonia,[1304] the policyholder (if a natural person) has his/her residence in Estonia,[1305] or Estonia is the place of business that relates to the insurance contracts of the policyholder (if a legal person).[1306]

Companies that are authorised to provide reinsurance services in third countries may undertake cross-border reinsurance activities in Estonia[1307] For the purposes of Chapter 2 Division 3 of the IAA, 'cross-border reinsurance activities' are the reinsurance activities of a foreign reinsurance company, in the framework of which the foreign firm supplies reinsurance services to an Estonian insurance undertaking.[1308] Section 47 of the IAA, which concerns cross-border insurance activities in Estonia of companies authorised in (another) Contracting State, applies to cross-border reinsurance services.[1309] However, section 46¹ of the IAA, which considers cross-border insurance activities in Estonia of firms authorised in a third country, does not explicitly apply to cross-border reinsurance services.[1310] This implies that reinsurance undertakings that are authorised to provide their services in third countries are not permitted to provide cross-border reinsurance services in Estonia. As reinsurance services are a 'capital movement' in either category C of Title X (Other transfers of capital in respect of insurance contracts) or category F of Title XIII (Miscellaneous capital movements), the narrow scope of subsection 41(6) of the IAA restricts the free movement of capital.

The next paragraphs consider the supply of insurance services in Estonia by companies that are authorised in (other) Contracting States. After this, the provision of insurance services in Estonia by firms that are authorised in third countries is discussed.

A insurance firm authorised to provide insurance services in a (non-Estonian) Contracting State that would like to establish a branch in Estonia, is to notify the EFSA of this through the financial supervision

---

[1302] s.42(2)(1), IAA.
[1303] s.42(2)(2). IAA.
[1304] s.42(2)(3), IAA.
[1305] s.43(3)(1), IAA.
[1306] s.43(3)(2), IAA.
[1307] s.41(6), IAA.
[1308] s.42(4). IAA.
[1309] s.41(6), IAA.
[1310] Subsection 41(6) of the IAA does not refer to section 46¹ of the IAA.

authority of that Contracting State.[1311] The following information and documents are to be submitted to the EFSA: the business name and address of the branch's seat in Estonia,[1312] a detailed description of the branch's structure,[1313] a list of the classes and subclasses of the insurance services that company plans to provide via the branch,[1314] the name of the branch's director,[1315] confirmation that the branch has become a member of the guarantee fund that is set out in the Motor Third Party Liability Insurance Act – if its planned insurance activities may involve entry into motor third party liability insurance contracts,[1316] confirmation from the Contracting State's financial supervision authority that the insurance undertaking's available solvency margin complies with the requirements for computation of the required solvency margin that the Contracting State has established,[1317] and a document according to which the branch assumes the duty to pay the contribution to the Pension Contracts Sectoral Fund that the Guarantee Fund Act prescribes – if the branch's planned insurance activities may involve its entry into pension contracts.[1318]

The EFSA shall promptly inform the Contracting State's financial supervision authority of its receipt of the information and documents.[1319] Within two months of receipt of these items, the EFSA shall take a decision that determines the requirements that the insurance company must comply with, in order to provide insurance activities in Estonia.[1320] The EFSA must notify the Contracting State's financial supervision authority of this decision.[1321] The insurance undertaking may establish its Estonian branch and start to provide insurance services, after it receives the EFSA's decision, or (if there is no decision) two months after the EFSA has received the information and documents.[1322] Once the new

---

[1311] s.46(1), IAA.
[1312] s.46(1)(1), IAA.
[1313] s.46(1)(2), IAA.
[1314] s.46(1)(2), IAA.
[1315] s.46(1)(3), IAA. The director of the branch must be adequately empowered to be able to act in the insurance company's name in dealings with third parties (s.46(1)(3), IAA).
[1316] s.46(1)(4), IAA.
[1317] s.46(1)(5), IAA.
[1318] s.46(1)(6), IAA.
[1319] s.46(2)(1), IAA.
[1320] s.46(2)(2), IAA.
[1321] s.46(2)(2), IAA.
[1322] s.46(2)(3), IAA.

branch is recorded in the commercial register, the EFSA shall confirm its receipt of the information and documents.[1323]

An insurance company that is authorised to supply insurance services in a (non-Estonian) Contracting State that wishes to provide cross-border services in Estonia, shall notify the EFSA through that Contracting State's financial supervision authority.[1324] The following information and documents must be submitted to the EFSA: a list of the classes of insurance that the firm has the right to provide,[1325] information on the insurance undertaking's available solvency margin,[1326] confirmation from the Contracting State's financial supervision authority that the insurance company's available solvency margin complies with the rules in force in the Contracting State,[1327] and a description of the cross-border insurance services that the firm plans to provide in Estonia.[1328] Once the information and documents have been forwarded to the EFSA, the insurance undertaking may provide cross-border insurance services in Estonia.[1329]

The establishment of a branch and the supply of cross-border services are 'capital movements' in Titles I(1) and X of the nomenclature in Annex I, respectively. The informational requirements of sections 46 and 47 of the IAA are insufficiently onerous to restrict the free movement of capital. However, under clause 46(2)(2) of the IAA, the EFSA is empowered to specify the conditions under which a newly established Estonian branch may provide insurance services in Estonia.[1330] If these conditions are onerous, then they would limit the free movement of capital.

[1323] s.46(2)(5), IAA. The purpose of this confirmation may be to complete the records for the establishment of the branch.

[1324] s.47(1), IAA.

[1325] s.47(1)(1), IAA.

[1326] s.47(1)(2), IAA.

[1327] s.47(1)(2), IAA.

[1328] s.47(1)(3), IAA. If the insurance firm's planned cross-border insurance activities in Estonia may involve entry into motor third party liability insurance contracts, then, in addition to the information and documents specified in subsection 47(1) of the IAA, it shall submit the following items to the EFSA: confirmation that it has become a member of the guarantee fund that the Motor Third Party Liability Insurance Act prescribes, and the name and address of the representative who it has appointed to Estonia, who has a permanent residence or place of business there, and who is to have adequate rights of representation to act in the insurance undertaking's name for the adjustment of losses and compensation for traffic damage, under motor third party liability insurance contracts (s.47(2), IAA).

[1329] s.47(3), IAA.

[1330] See above in this subsection.

To be justified under Article 65(1)(b) of the TFEU, any restrictive measures would need to be necessary for the interests that they are intended to guarantee, be proportionate, and fulfil the requirements of legal certainty – i.e. be specific, objective and known to the parties beforehand; in addition, the persons affected by the measures would need to have access to legal redress.[1331] As clause 46(2)(2) of the IAA provides the EFSA with a discretion to decide what the local conditions are (under which an insurance firm authorised to provide services in another EEA state may establish an Estonian branch), any restrictive measures that it imposes are not specific, objective and known to the parties beforehand.[1332] Hence, these measures would not be justified under Article 65(1)(b) of the TFEU, and would contravene Article 63 of this Treaty.

In order to establish a branch in Estonia, an insurance undertaking that is authorised to provide investment services in a third country, is required to apply for an additional, corresponding authorisation from the EFSA.[1333] The insurance company shall submit a written application,[1334] and the following information and documents, to the EFSA: the insurance firm's business name and address,[1335] the scope of the authorisation that its home state's financial supervision authority provided to it,[1336] information concerning that financial supervision authority,[1337] the business name and address of the Estonian branch,[1338] the name, personal identification code (or, in its absence, date of birth), residence, educational background, employment history, scope of responsibilities, and documents of proof of trustworthiness and conformity to the requirements of the IAA, of the

[1331] See the subsection '*The requirements for a successful public policy/public security derogation*', in section 2.1.3.

[1332] The EFSA should provide clear guidelines as to what the conditions are under which Estonian insurance companies are to establish a branch for the provision of insurance services in Estonia, and apply these rules consistently to each applicant insurance undertaking. This would render the restrictive measures specific, objective, and known to the applicant insurance undertaking beforehand, and would minimise the discretion that clause 46(2)(2) of the IAA provides to the EFSA.

[1333] s.43(1), IAA.

[1334] s.43(2), IAA.

[1335] s.43(2)(1), IAA.

[1336] s.43(2)(2), IAA.

[1337] s.43(2)(2), IAA.

[1338] s.43(2)(3), IAA.

branch's director(s),[1339] an official certificate that confirms the insurance company's existence in its home country (such as an excerpt from a commercial register or a copy of its registration certificate),[1340] an authorisation document that certifies the authority of the branch's director(s) or a copy of a resolution that appoints the director(s),[1341] a copy of the insurance undertaking's articles of association or partnership agreement,[1342] information on the branch's planned principal activity (or activities),[1343] the insurance firm's and the branch's telecommunications data,[1344] the insurance undertaking's audited annual reports for the most recent three financial years,[1345] the branch's scheme of operations concerning its provision of insurance services in Estonia,[1346] a detailed description of the branch's structure and the planned insurance services,[1347] a confirmation by the guarantee fund provided in the Motor Third Party Liability Act that the branch established in Estonia will become (if the proposed insurance activities prescribe entry into motor third party liability insurance contracts), after obtaining the EFSA's authorisation, a member of the guarantee fund,[1348] and a certificate from an Estonian credit institution that certifies the fact that the person who applies for authorisation for establishing a branch has planned at least 25 per cent of the minimum solvency information that subsections 71(3) or 71(3^1) of

[1339] ss.43(2)(4) and 18(1)(7), IAA. The branch's director(s) must have adequate rights of representation to be able to act in the insurance firm's name in relation to third parties (s.43(2)(4), IAA).

[1340] ss.43(2)(5), IAA, and 386(2)(1), Commercial Code.

[1341] ss.43(2)(5), IAA, and 386(2)(3), Commercial Code.

[1342] ss.43(2)(5), IAA, and 386(2)(4), Commercial Code.

[1343] ss.43(2)(5), IAA, and 386(2)(4^1), Commercial Code.

[1344] ss.43(2)(5), IAA, and 386(2)(5), Commercial Code.

[1345] s.43(2)(6), IAA.

[1346] s.43(2)(7), IAA. The scheme of operations is to set out a list of the proposed classes and subclasses of insurance, the planned quantity of reinsurance and the principles of reinsurance for each class and subclass of insurance, a list and the amount of the available solvency margin, the principles and methods of calculation of the technical calculations in section 75 of the IAA and the financial liabilities in section 75^1 of the IAA (see note 1193), a business plan for each class and subclass of insurance, the estimated balance sheet and income statement of the insurance company's first three years of operation, the estimated volume of insurance premiums, claims and operating expenses and the part of reinsurance therein during the first three years of the insurance firm's operation, and the amount of technical provisions and financial liabilities by each class of and subclass of insurance (s.20(1), IAA).

[1347] s.43(2)(7), IAA.

[1348] s.43(2)(8), IAA.

the IAA provide for with the Estonian credit institution – and that the deposit agreement may only be paid with the EFSA's written permission.[1349] In addition to these documents, a third country insurance firm shall provide the EFSA with the following items from the home state's financial supervision authority: the latter authority's permission to establish a branch in Estonia,[1350] confirmation from this authority that the insurance company holds a valid authorisation in its home country and that it pursues its activities in a correct fashion and in accordance with the public interest,[1351] and information about the amount of the available solvency margin and solvency of the insurance firm, the principles and methods of calculation of the financial liabilities and technical provisions, and the requirements towards the assets that cover the technical provisions, that are applicable in the home country.[1352]

Sections 21, 22, 23, 26 and 27 of the IAA apply to the processing of applications for an authorisation for the establishment of a branch, verification of information, and to the grant and revocation of authorisations, unless otherwise provided for in section 43 of the IAA.[1353] These sections are as follows. If an applicant has not submitted all of the information and documents that section 18 of the IAA specifies,[1354] or if these items are incomplete or have not been prepared according to "the requirements"[1355] then the financial supervision authority shall require the applicant to remove these deficiencies.[1356] The EFSA may require the submission of further information and documents, if it is not satisfied, on the basis of the items that section 18 of the IAA specifies, that the applicant for an authorisation has adequate facilities to provide insurance

---

[1349] s.43(2)(9), IAA. An insurance company's minimum solvency margin shall be 3.7 million euros, if the firm has the right to provide reinsurance, life insurance, motor vehicle liability insurance, aircraft liability insurance, liability for ships, general liability insurance, credit insurance or suretyship insurance, and 2.5 million EUR if the insurance undertaking has the right to supply other classes of insurance (ss.71(3) and 12(10)-(15), IAA). The minimum solvency margin of a reinsurance firm that does not belong to the same group as an insurance firm, and which satisfies a further condition, is to be 1.2 million EUR (ss.71(3^1) and 56(2^1), IAA).

[1350] s.43(4)(1), IAA.

[1351] s.43(4)(2), IAA.

[1352] s.43(4)(3), IAA.

[1353] s.44(1), IAA.

[1354] See note 1238, for the information and documents that subsection 18(1) of the IAA specifies.

[1355] Subsection 21(1) of the IAA does not refer to what requirements these are. They are probably the requirements of the IAA.

[1356] s.21(1), IAA.

services, that the applicant fulfils the requirements for insurance companies that Estonian legislation and regulation prescribes, or that other circumstances which relate to the applicant need to be confirmed.[1357] The EFSA may refuse to review an application, if the applicant has not removed the deficiencies that subsection 21(1) of the IAA specifies within the prescribed period, or has not submitted by the due date the information or documents that the EFSA has requested.[1358] Upon the processing of an application for an authorisation, the EFSA must co-operate with the financial supervision authority of the relevant Contracting State, if the applicant is a parent or subsidiary undertaking of an insurance company, investment fund, credit institution, management company or another subject of financial supervision that is established in the Contracting State,[1359] a subsidiary of the applicant's parent company is a subject of financial supervision that is founded in the Contracting State,[1360] or the applicant and a subject of financial supervision that is established in the Contracting State are all companies who are being supervised by the same person.[1361]

The EFSA is to take a decision to grant, or refuse to grant, an authorisation within three months of receiving all of the necessary items and after "the requirements" are fulfilled, but no later than within six

[1357] s.21(2), IAA. In order to verify the information that the applicant submits, the EFSA may check national databases, perform on-site inspections, order a special audit or an assessment, and obtain verbal explanations from members of the applicant's management board or supervisory board, external auditors, internal auditors, representatives of the above, and (if necessary) third parties, about information that is relevant in taking a decision on the granting of an authorisation (s.21(3), IAA). The information and documents that subsections 21(1)-(3) specify are to be submitted within a reasonable time, which the EFSA is to determine (s.21(4), IAA).

[1358] s.21(5), IAA. If the EFSA refuses to review an insurance firm's application for an authorisation, it must return the documents that the applicant has submitted (s.21(5), IAA).

[1359] s.21(6)(1), IAA.

[1360] s.21(6)(2), IAA.

[1361] s.21(6)(3), IAA. In the course of the co-operation that subsection 21(6) of the IAA specifies, the EFSA and the financial supervision authority of the (other) Contracting State shall consult with each other, in order to evaluate the shareholders' suitability and the reputation and experience of the "head of the other division of the consolidation group", and forward to each other all information that is relevant to the grant of an authorisation (s.21(7), IAA). The quoted phrase is unclear, and may mean the chief executive of the consolidation group in the other Contracting State, or, if different, the chief executive of the supervised entity in the other Contracting State.

months of submission of the application for an authorisation.[1362] It shall grant an authorisation, if the submitted information and documents comply with "the requirements", and if it is possible to verify on the basis of these items that the applicant has adequate facilities and organisational capacity to provide insurance services, and that the interests of policyholders, insured persons and beneficiaries are adequately protected.[1363] Upon granting an authorisation, the EFSA may establish obligatory secondary conditions that are based on the circumstances in section 23 of the IAA.[1364] The EFSA is to promptly deliver a decision to grant, or to refuse to grant, an authorisation to the applicant.[1365]

The EFSA may refuse to provide an authorisation if the applicant does not satisfy the requirements for insurance undertakings that the IAA or its subordinate legislation contain,[1366] the applicant does not have adequate facilities or experience to operate as a going concern,[1367] a member of the applicant's management board or supervisory board, an auditor, responsible actuary, or shareholder of the applicant do not satisfy the requirements that the IAA or its secondary legislation provide for,[1368] close links between the applicant and another person preclude sufficient supervision over the applicant,[1369] or the implementation of legislation of the country in which the person with whom the applicant has close links is established prevents adequate supervision over the insurance firm.[1370] In addition to these grounds, the EFSA may refuse to grant an authorisation for the establishment of a branch in Estonia of an insurance firm that authorised to provide services in a third country, if the financial supervision authority of that state is not able to ensure the exercise adequate supervision over the applicant, if that authority "has no legal

[1362] s.22(2), IAA.

[1363] s.22(1), IAA.

[1364] s.22(3), IAA. Section 23 of the IAA is considered in the next paragraph.

[1365] s.22(4), IAA. The terms that subsections 250(4) and 271(2) of the Commercial Code specify are to be calculated as of the delivery date of a decision to grant an authorisation to the applicant (s.22(5), IAA). A public limited company is not to be entered in the commercial register, if the petition for entry in this register is submitted more than one year after the conclusion of the memorandum of association or the passing of the resolution establishing the company (s.250(4), IAA). Subsection 271(2) of the Commercial Code has been repealed.

[1366] s.23(1)(1), IAA.

[1367] s.23(1)(2), IAA.

[1368] s.23(1)(3), IAA.

[1369] s.23(1)(4), IAA.

[1370] s.23(1)(4), IAA.

basis or possibility for cooperation with" the EFSA, or if the branch does not conform to the requirements of section 82 of the IAA.[1371]

Revocation of an authorisation is the partial or total deprivation of a right that is acquired by the decision to grant an authorisation.[1372] An authorisation may be wholly withdrawn, or revoked by individual classes or subclasses of insurance.[1373] A decision on the revocation of an authorisation is to be promptly communicated to the insurance firm.[1374]

The EFSA is required to revoke an authorisation for the establishment of an Estonian branch of a third country insurance undertaking, if a (non-Estonian) Contracting State's financial supervision authority informs the EFSA that it has withdrawn an authorisation for the foundation of a branch of this company, on the ground that its solvency margin does not conform to the required solvency margin.[1375] Furthermore, the EFSA may revoke such an authorisation, either completely or by individual classes or subclasses of insurance, if the insurance firm has not started to provide a class or subclass of insurance services within one year of the grant of the authorisation,[1376] the insurance firm's activities are suspended for more

---

1371 s.44(3), IAA. An Estonian branch of a third country insurance company is required to possess assets in the EEA an amount at least equal to the required solvency margin, possess assets in Estonia of an amount at least equal of the minimum solvency margin in subsections 71(3) or 71(3¹) of the IAA (including the deposit that clause 49(2)(9) of the IAA provides for), calculate the required solvency margin pursuant to sections 72 or 73 of the IAA on the basis of insurance contracts agreed in Estonia and comply with the requirements in the IAA for the available solvency margin, keep in Estonia the assets that cover technical provisions that correspond to the technical provisions and financial liabilities that arise from insurance contracts agreed in Estonia (in accordance with sections 77 and 78 of the IAA for insurance firms, or sections 77 and 78¹ of the IAA for reinsurance undertakings), and "organise accounting" that concerns, and store in Estonia all documents that relate to, operations in Estonia (s.82(1), IAA). See note 1349, for subsections 71(3) and 71(3¹) of the IAA. Subsections 82(2)-(7) and 82(9) of the IAA concern the operation of preferential conditions for third country insurance firms that have branches in more than one Contracting State, including Estonia. Subsection 82(10) of the IAA is stated below in this subsection ('*Chapter 2 Division 3: Activities of Foreign Insurance Undertakings in Estonia*'). See, also, the subsection '*Section 82: Requirements for financial soundness and available solvency margin of Estonian branches of third country insurance undertakings*', below in this section (section 3.4).

1372 s.26(1), IAA.

1373 s.26(2), IAA.

1374 s.26(4), IAA.

1375 ss.44(3) and 82(10), IAA.

1376 ss.44(3) and 27(1), IAA.

than six months,[1377] the insurance company has submitted misleading information or documents, incorrect information or false documents,[1378] the insurance firm does not satisfy the requirements for the granting of an authorisation,[1379] the circumstances described in clauses 23(1)(3) or 23(1)(4) of the IAA become evident,[1380] the insurance company does not satisfy the secondary conditions that subsection 22(3) of the IAA specifies,[1381] the insurance undertaking has materially or repeatedly breached the provisions of the legislation that regulates its activities,[1382] the insurance firm has been punished for a specified offence (such as official misconduct) and information about the punishment has not been removed from the punishment register pursuant to the Punishment Register Act,[1383] the insurance firm's activities or omissions conflict with the public interest,[1384] the insurance company has published substantially incorrect or misleading information concerning its activities,[1385] the insurance firm has published materially inaccurate or misleading advertisements,[1386] the insurance undertaking is part of a group "the structure of which prevents the receipt of information necessary for supervision on a consolidated basis",[1387] a company that is a member of the same group as the insurance firm operates on the basis of legislation of a foreign country – which precludes the exercise of adequate supervision,[1388] the insurance undertaking is involved in money laundering or contravenes the procedure for preventing money laundering and terrorist financing that legislation has established,[1389] the insurance company has breached, pursuant to information submitted to the EFSA by a financial supervision authority of a Contracting State, the provisions of that State's legislation, or the conditions set by the latter authority for the

---

[1377] ss.44(3), and 27(1), IAA.
[1378] ss.44(3) and 27(2), IAA.
[1379] ss.44(3) and 27(3), IAA.
[1380] ss.44(3) and 27(4), IAA. See above in this subsection ('*Chapter 2 Division 3: Activities of Foreign Insurance Undertakings in Estonia*').
[1381] ss.44(3) and 27(5), IAA. See above in this subsection ('*Chapter 2 Division 3: Activities of Foreign Insurance Undertakings in Estonia*').
[1382] ss.44(3) and 27(6), IAA.
[1383] ss.44(3) and 27(6), IAA.
[1384] ss.44(3) and 27(6), IAA.
[1385] ss.44(3) and 27(7), IAA.
[1386] ss.44(3) and 27(7), IAA.
[1387] ss.44(3) and 27(8), IAA. The quoted phrase is difficult to understand.
[1388] ss.44(3) and 27(8), IAA.
[1389] ss.44(3) and 27(9), IAA.

supply of insurance services there,[1390] the insurance undertaking is unable to satisfy its commitments,[1391] the insurance firm's activities significantly harm the interests of its policyholders, insured persons or beneficiaries,[1392] the amount of the insurance company's available solvency margin does not comply with the requirements of the IAA,[1393] the technical provisions, and the financial liabilities or assets that cover the technical provisions, of the insurance undertaking, do not comply with the requirements of the IAA,[1394] the insurance firm supplying motor third party liability insurance does not perform the duties of a member of the guarantee fund,[1395] the insurance company that enters into pension contracts did not pay contributions (within the specified period or in full) to the Pension Contracts Sectoral Fund that the Guarantee Fund Act prescribed,[1396] or the insurance undertaking did not implement a precept of the EFSA to the full extent stated or within the prescribed period.[1397] The EFSA may refuse to revoke an authorisation for the establishment of a branch, if the branch's policyholders, insured persons or beneficiaries have claims against it (or against the third country insurance firm that established it), or if withdrawal of the authorisation damages the policyholders', insured persons' or beneficiaries' interests.[1398]

A company that is authorised to provide insurance services in a third country, which would like to supply cross-border insurance services in Estonia, is required to apply for an authorisation from the EFSA in order to do so.[1399] Upon its application for authorisation for the provision of these cross-border services, the insurance firm must submit a written application[1400] and the following documents to the EFSA: the company's business name and address,[1401] confirmation by the third country's financial supervision authority that the insurance undertaking is entitled to provide insurance services in that state and across its borders, together with a list of the classes of insurance activities in which the company is

---

[1390] ss.44(3), 27(10) and 35(6), IAA. See note 1207, for subsection 35(6) of the IAA.
[1391] ss.44(3) and 27(11), IAA.
[1392] ss.44(3) and 27(11), IAA.
[1393] ss.44(3) and 27(12), IAA. See note 1349.
[1394] ss.44(3) and 27(13), IAA.
[1395] ss.44(3) and 27(14), IAA.
[1396] ss.44(3) and 27(14^1), IAA.
[1397] ss.44(3) and 27(15), IAA.
[1398] s.44(6), IAA.
[1399] s.46^1(1), IAA.
[1400] s.46^1(1), IAA.
[1401] s.46^1(1)(1), IAA.

entitled to engage,[1402] a description of the planned cross-border insurance services,[1403] information that concerns the amount of the insurance undertaking's available solvency margin, the principles of computation of this margin, and confirmation by the third country's financial supervision authority that the margin satisfies the requirements that are applicable there,[1404] and the insurance firm's audited annual reports for the most recent three financial years.[1405] Subsections 21(1) to 21(5), 22(1), 22(3), 22(4), 26(1), 26(2) and 26(4),[1406] and section 28,[1407] of the IAA apply to the processing of applications for authorisation of third country insurance companies for the provision of cross-border services in Estonia, verification of information, and revocation of this authorisation.[1408]

The EFSA shall take a decision to grant, or to refuse to grant, an authorisation for cross-border services within two months of receipt of all the documents and information and "compliance with requirements", but not later that within three months of submission of an application for authorisation of cross-border insurance services.[1409] The EFSA has the right to refuse to grant an authorisation to provide cross-border insurance services, if the insurance firm has submitted misleading information or documents, incorrect information or falsified documents to the EFSA,[1410] the insurance undertaking is unable to respect the commitments that it has assumed,[1411] the insurance firm's activities substantially damage the policyholders', insured persons' or beneficiaries' interests,[1412] the requirements that are applicable with regard to the insurance company's

---

1402 s.46¹(1)(2), IAA.

1403 s.46¹(1)(3), IAA.

1404 s.46¹(1)(4), IAA.

1405 s.46¹(1)(5), IAA. If the cross-border insurance services that the third country insurance firm plans to supply in Estonia may involve its entry into motor third party liability insurance contracts, then the information and documents that section 47(2) of the IAA specifies (see note 1328) shall be submitted to the EFSA (s.46¹(2), IAA).

1406 For all of these subsections of the IAA, see above in this subsection (*Chapter 2 Division 3: Activities of Foreign Insurance Undertakings in Estonia*').

1407 For section 28 of the IAA, see the subsection '*Chapter 2 Division 2: Activities of Estonian Insurance Undertakings in Foreign States*', above in this section (i.e. section 3.4).

1408 s.46¹(4), IAA.

1409 s.46¹(5), IAA. The quoted phrase probably means compliance with the requirements provided by the IAA.

1410 s.46¹(6)(1), IAA.

1411 s.46¹(6)(2), IAA.

1412 s.46¹(6)(2), IAA.

available solvency margin, the amount of that margin, or the principles of calculation of the margin, are inadequate (taking into account the volume of the cross-border services in Estonia that the insurance firm plans and the risk related thereto),[1413] or the third country's financial supervision authority "has no legal basis, possibilities or readiness for sufficient and efficient cooperation with" the EFSA, and, therefore, the EFSA is unable to exercise adequate supervision over the insurance undertaking."[1414]

The EFSA has the right to revoke an authorisation for cross-border investment services, if the insurance firm has submitted misleading information or documents, incorrect information, or falsified documents to the EFSA,[1415] has not notified the EFSA of a change to its circumstances in relation to cross-border insurance activities,[1416] has not implemented a precept of the EFSA concerning the cross-border insurance services by the due date or to the extent prescribed,[1417] does not satisfy the valid requirements for the granting of authorisations for cross-border insurance services,[1418] does not fulfil the secondary conditions that are established on the basis of subsection 22(3) of the IAA,[1419] has repeatedly or substantially contravened the provisions of legislation that regulates its activities,[1420] or does not perform the obligations of a member of the Estonian Traffic Insurance Foundation – if it is engaged in motor third party liability insurance.[1421] The EFSA may revoke an authorisation for cross-border insurance activities, in full or in part.[1422] It shall not withdraw this authorisation, if the policyholders, insured persons or beneficiaries have claims against the insurance firm, or if the revocation of the authorisation would harm the interests of the policyholders, insured persons or beneficiaries.[1423]

The foundation of a branch, and the provision of cross-border services, are 'capital movements' in Titles I(1) and X of the nomenclature in Annex I, respectively. If the EFSA refuses to grant an authorisation for the

---

1413 s.46¹(6)(3), IAA.
1414 s.46¹(6)(4), IAA.
1415 s.46¹(7)(1), IAA.
1416 s.46¹(7)(2), IAA.
1417 s.46¹(7)(3), IAA.
1418 s.46¹(7)(4), IAA.
1419 s.46¹(7)(5), IAA. See above in this subsection (*Chapter 2 Division 3: Activities of Foreign Insurance Undertakings in Estonia*).
1420 s.46¹(7)(6), IAA.
1421 s.46¹(7)(7), IAA.
1422 s.46¹(8), IAA.
1423 s.46¹(8), IAA.

establishment of a branch, or the provision of cross-border services, in Estonia, then it contravenes the free movement of capital.

To be justified under Article 65(1)(b) of the TFEU, the restrictive measures must be necessary for the protection of the interests that they are intended to guarantee, be proportionate (i.e. not attainable by less restrictive measures), and observe the requirements of legal certainty (i.e. be specific, objective and known to the parties in advance); furthermore, the persons that the measures affect must have access to legal redress (i.e. intervention should be supported by a formal statement of reasons and be subject to review in the national courts).[1424] The plethora of grounds on which the EFSA may revoke an authorisation of a third country insurance firm to establish a branch in Estonia may be disproportionate. Furthermore, not all of the bases on which the EFSA may refuse to grant an authorisation, or revoke an authorisation, satisfy the requirements of legal certainty; for instance, clause 46^1(6)(4) of the IAA, under which the EFSA may refuse authorisation to the applicant to provide cross-border services to Estonia, if third country's financial supervision authority "has no legal basis, possibilities or readiness for sufficient and efficient cooperation with" the EFSA, provides the regulator with a discretion, and is, therefore, neither specific nor objective.[1425] In addition, the IAA does not require the EFSA to give reasons for a decision to refuse to grant an authorisation, or to revoke an authorisation; nor does it provide the applicant with the right to appeal against the decision in the national courts. Hence, the applicant is not entitled to legal redress. Consequently, Article 65(1)(b) of the TFEU does not justify the restrictive measures.

For the restrictive measures to be justified under Article 64(2) of the TFEU, the EU institutions should carefully consider the objective of the free movement of capital whilst enacting the legislation, and the national rules should not limit the free movement of capital more than the equivalent provisions of the relevant Directive do.[1426] Although the Articles of the relevant Directive, Directive 2009/138/EC, do not consider the free movement of capital, Recital 72 of Directive 2009/138/EC states that Member States should not require insurance or reinsurance companies to invest their assets in specific categories, as this could be incompatible with the liberalisation of capital movements for which Article 63 of the

---

[1424] See the subsection '*The requirements for a successful public policy/public security derogation*', in section 2.1.3.

[1425] See above in this subsection (*Chapter 2 Division 3: Activities of Foreign Insurance Undertakings in Estonia*).

[1426] See the subsection '*Derogations that apply only to capital movement to/from third countries*', in section 2.3.2.

TFEU provides. As stated above, the wording of Recital 72 shows that EU legislators were aware of the free movement of capital whilst enacting Directive 2009/138/EC, although it is arguable whether or not the statement in the recital is sufficient to establish that these legislators had carefully considered this objective.[1427]

Chapter IX of Title I of Directive 2009/138/EC provides detailed requirements for the establishment of a branch in an EEA state of an insurance or reinsurance company with its head office located in a third country. There are no equivalent rules for the supply of cross-border insurance services by a third country (re)insurance undertaking in an EEA state.[1428]

A Member State may grant an authorisation to an insurance[1429] undertaking that satisfies the following conditions: the firm's national law entitles it to pursue insurance business,[1430] it founds a branch in the territory of the Member State in which authorisation is sought,[1431] it undertakes to set up, at the place at which the branch is managed, accounts that are specific to the business that it conducts there, and to keep in that location all the records that concern the business transacted,[1432] it appoints a general representative, which the supervisory authorities are to

---

[1427] See the subsection '*Chapter 2 Division 2: Activities of Estonian Insurance Undertakings in Foreign States*', above in this section.

[1428] Article 175(1)(a) of Directive 2009/138/EC states that the Commission may prepare proposals for the Council for the negotiation of agreements with third countries for the methods of supervision over third-country reinsurance undertakings that carry out reinsurance business in the EEA. However, as this provision is within Title I Chapter IX of Directive 2009/138/EC, which is entitled "Branches established within the community and belonging to insurance or reinsurance undertakings with head offices situated outside the community", these agreements are likely to apply to the supervision of branches of third country insurance firms within the EEA, rather than the supervision of the supply by these companies of cross-border services in EEA states.

[1429] As Title I, Chapter IX of Directive 2009/138/EC applies to reinsurance firms, 'insurance' in Articles 162-167 of this Directive includes reinsurance. It is noteworthy, however, that Article 162(1) of Directive 2009/138/EC states that Member States should make access to "the business referred to in the first subparagraph of Article 2(1)" by any firm with a head office outside the EEA subject to an authorisation. This subparagraph states that Directive 2009/138/EC is to apply to "direct life and non-life insurance undertakings", i.e. this provision omits reinsurance. Article 2(1)(1) of Directive 2009/138/EC refers to reinsurance undertakings and activities.

[1430] Article 162(2)(a), Directive 2009/138/EC.

[1431] Article 162(2)(b), Directive 2009/138/EC.

[1432] Article 162(2)(c), Directive 2009/138/EC.

approve,[1433] it possesses, in the Member State in which authorisation is sought, assets equal to at least one half of the absolute floor that Article 129(1)(d) of Directive 2009/138/EC prescribes for the Minimum Capital Requirement, and deposits one quarter of this absolute floor as security,[1434] it agrees to cover the Solvency Capital Requirement and the Minimum Capital Requirement in accordance with Articles 100 and 128 of Directive 2009/138/EC,[1435] it publishes the name and address of the claims representative who is appointed in each Member State (other than that in which the authorisation is sought), if the risks to be covered are in class 10 of Part A of Annex I of Directive 2009/138/EC (except for carrier's liability),[1436] its submits a scheme of operations for the branch that is prepared in accordance with Article 163 of Directive 2009/138/EC,[1437] and it satisfies the governance requirements in Title I, Chapter IV of Directive

---

1433 Article 162(2)(d), Directive 2009/138/EC.

1434 Article 162(2)(e), Directive 2009/138/EC. The minimum floor is 2.2 million EUR for non-life insurance undertakings that do not provide any of the following insurances: motor vehicle liability, aircraft liability, liability for ships, general liability, credit, and suretyship (Article 129(1)(d)(i) and paragraphs 10-15, Part A Annex I, Directive 2009/138/EC), 3.2 million for other non-life insurance companies, insurance firms, and reinsurance undertakings (Article 129(1)(d), Directive 2009/138/EC), and 1 million for captive reinsurance undertakings (Article 129(1)(d)(iii), Directive 2009/138/EC). A 'captive reinsurance undertaking' is a reinsurance firm whose purpose is to provide reinsurance cover exclusively for the risks of the companies of the group of which it is a member (Article 13(2), Directive 2009/138/EC).

1435 Article 162(2)(f), Directive 2009/138/EC. The Solvency Capital Requirement shall be computed, either in accordance with the standard formula in subsection 2 (Articles 103-111 of Directive 2009/138/EC) or using an internal model – as subsection 3 (Articles 112-127 of Directive 2009/138/EC) sets out (Article 100, Directive 2009/138/EC). Member States are to require insurance and reinsurance companies to hold "eligible basic own funds", in order to cover the Minimum Capital Requirement (Article 128, Directive 2009/138/EC). Article 129 of Directive 2009/138/EC states how to calculate the Minimum Capital Requirement. 'Basic own funds' shall comprise the excess of assets over liabilities, less the amount of own shares that the (re)insurance firm holds, plus subordinated liabilities (Article 88, Directive 2009/138/EC).

1436 Article 162(2)(g), Directive 2009/138/EC. These risks are accident, sickness, motor vehicle liability, liability for ships, general liability, credit, suretyship, miscellaneous financial loss, legal expenses, travel difficulties, and damage to, or loss of, land vehicles, railway rolling stock, aircraft, ships, goods in transit and property (Part A, Annex I, Directive 2009/138/EC).

1437 Article 162(2)(h), Directive 2009/138/EC. See the next sentence.

2009/138/EC.[1438] The branch's scheme of operations is to set out the nature of the risks that the insurance company intends to cover,[1439] the guiding principles of reinsurance,[1440] estimates of the future Solvency Capital Requirement and of the future Minimum Capital Requirement, on the basis of a forecast balance sheet, and the calculation methods used to derive each of these estimates,[1441] the state of the eligible own funds, and the eligible basic own funds, of the insurance undertaking with respect to the Minimum Solvency Requirement and the Minimum Capital Requirement,[1442] estimates of the cost of establishment of "the administrative services and the organisation for securing business", the funds that are required to pay this cost, and the resources that are available for the provision of assistance with travel difficulties,[1443] and information about "the structure of the system of governance".[1444] In addition, the branch's scheme of operations is to include the following predictions for the first three years of its operations: a forecast balance sheet,[1445] estimates of the funds that are set aside to cover technical provisions, the Minimum Capital Requirement and the Solvency Capital Requirement,[1446] for non-life insurance – estimates of management expenses, insurance premiums or contributions, and claims,[1447] and for life insurance – a plan that states

[1438] Article 162(2)(i), Directive 2009/138/EC. Section 2 (Articles 41-50) of Title I, Chapter IV of Directive 2009/138/EC contains various corporate governance requirements, which include general governance requirements (for instance, Article 41(3) states that (re)insurance companies are to have written policies in relation to risk management, internal control and internal audit), requirements as to experience and repute for directors and key employees, specifications for an effective risk management system, specifications for an effective internal control system (including compliance), requirements for an effective, objective and independent internal audit function, requirements for an effective actuarial function, and rules on the outsourcing of operational activities.

[1439] Article 163(1)(a), Directive 2009/138/EC.

[1440] Article 163(1)(b), Directive 2009/138/EC.

[1441] Articles 163(1)(c)-(d), Directive 2009/138/EC.

[1442] Article 163(1)(e), Directive 2009/138/EC.

[1443] Article 163(1)(f) and paragraph 18, Part A Annex I, Directive 2009/138/EC.

[1444] Article 163(1)(g), Directive 2009/138/EC. As the scheme of operations is that of the branch, the governance structure referred to in this clause is likely to be that proposed for the branch, rather than for the insurance company as a whole.

[1445] Article 163(2)(a), Directive 2009/138/EC.

[1446] Article 163(2)(b), Directive 2009/138/EC.

[1447] Article 163(2)(c), Directive 2009/138/EC.

detailed estimates of income and expenditure in respect of direct acceptances, reinsurance acceptances, and reinsurance relinquishments.[1448]

Each Member State shall require branches established in its territory to hold an amount of eligible funds that comprises Tier 1 (more than one third of the total), Tier 2, and Tier 3 (less than one third of the total).[1449] The eligible amount of basic own funds that are required to cover the Minimum Capital Requirement and the absolute floor of this Requirement, are to be equal to the sum of the Tier 1 and Tier 2 basic own fund items.[1450] For the purposes of computing the Solvency Capital Requirement and the Minimum Capital Requirement,[1451] account is to be taken only of the branch's operations.[1452] However, if the third country insurance undertaking has requested or been granted authorisation from more than one Member State, it may calculate its Solvency Capital requirement in relation to the whole business that it pursues within the EEA.[1453]

These requirements demonstrate that Directive 2009/138/EC limits the free movement of capital for the establishment of a branch in Estonia of a third country insurance firm – although not as much as the restrictive provisions of the IAA do.[1454] Furthermore, as, unlike the IAA, Directive 2009/138/EC does not include detailed conditions for the provision by such a company of cross-border insurance services in Estonia, these rules

---

[1448] Article 163(2)(d), Directive 2009/138/EC.

[1449] Articles 166(1) and 98(1), Directive 2009/138/EC. Tier 1 own-fund items must be available at all times to fully absorb losses, and their repayment in a liquidation of the insurance company is to be subordinated to all other obligations (Articles 94(1) and 93(1), Directive 2009/138/EC). Tier 2 own-fund items must be available to fully absorb losses in a winding-up of the insurance firm, and their repayment in this event is to be subordinated to all other obligations (Articles 94(2) and 93(1)(b), Directive 2009/138/EC). Other own-fund items are classified in Tier 3 (Article 94(3), Directive 2009/138/EC).

[1450] Articles 166(2) and 98(4), Directive 2009/138/EC. See note 1435, for a definition of basic own funds.

[1451] See note 1435.

[1452] Article 166(1), Directive 2009/138/EC.

[1453] Article 167(1)(a), Directive 2009/138/EC. Third country insurance companies that are authorised in more than one Member State may also lodge the deposit required under Article 162(2)(e) of Directive 2009/138/EC (see above in this subsection) in only one of these Member States (Article 167(1)(b), Directive 2009/138/EC), and localise the assets that represent the Minimum Capital Requirement in any one of the Member States in which it provides insurance services (Article 167(1)(c), Directive 2009/138/EC).

[1454] See above in this subsection.

within the IAA hinder cross-border capital movement more than relevant rules in the Directive do.[1455] Hence, with respect to the supply of insurance services by third country insurance undertakings in Estonia, the IAA restricts the free movement of capital more than the relevant Directive does.

Thus, Article 64(2) of the TFEU does not justify the restrictive measures with respect to the provision of insurance services in Estonia, by an insurance company that is authorised to supply these services in a third country. Consequently, these measures breach Article 63 of the TFEU.

Section 81: Requirements for financial soundness of insurance companies engaged in EEA co-insurance

EEA co-insurance operations are to conform to the provisions of sections 484 and 485 of the Law of Obligations Act, with the following specifications:[1456] co-insurance companies conclude one of these contracts – reinsurance contracts,[1457] railway rolling stock, aircraft or ship insurance contracts,[1458] insurance contracts for the carriage of goods,[1459] aircraft liability or ship liability insurance contracts,[1460] credit or suretyship insurance contracts,[1461] or land vehicle, fire and natural forces, financial loss or general liability insurance contracts,[1462] the home state of at least one of the co-insurance firms (or the country of location of its branch – if this branch concludes the insurance contract) shall be other than that of the

---

[1455] Section 46^1 of the IAA contains these rules – see above in this subsection ('*Chapter 2 Division 3: Activities of Foreign Insurance Undertakings in Estonia*').

[1456] s.81(2), IAA. Whilst the IAA does not define 'co-insurance', section 484 of the Law of Obligations Act does so. If one insurance, or the insurance of insured risks that relate to the same assets, is divided in fixed parts between several insurers (co-insurance), each insurer is only required to pay indemnities in proportion to the part that it insures (s.484, Law of Obligations Act 2001). For co-insurance, the contract shall designate the leading insurer, which is considered to be the representative of the other insurers (s.485(1), Law of Obligations Act 2001). The leading insurer is to arrange the satisfaction of claims that arise from the insurance contract (s.485(2), Law of Obligations Act 2001). If the contract does not specify the leading insurer, then the policyholder may choose one of the co-insurers to be the leading insurer (s.485(3), Law of Obligations Act 2001).

[1457] ss.81(2)(1), IAA and 427(2)(1), Law of Obligations Act 2001.

[1458] ss.81(2)(1), IAA and 427(2)(2), Law of Obligations Act 2001.

[1459] ss.81(2)(1), IAA and 427(2)(3), Law of Obligations Act 2001.

[1460] ss.81(2)(1), IAA and 427(2)(4), Law of Obligations Act 2001.

[1461] ss.81(2)(1), IAA and 427(2)(5), Law of Obligations Act 2001.

[1462] ss.81(2)(1), IAA and 427(3), Law of Obligations Act 2001.

leading insurance company,[1463] the leading insurance undertaking has the right to determine the insurance premium and the terms and conditions of the insurance,[1464] and the risk with which the insurance contract is concerned is located in a Contracting State (which may include Estonia).[1465] An Estonian co-insurance company is to establish the technical provisions and financial liabilities for co-insurance practice on the basis of the IAA and its secondary legislation.[1466] An Estonian insurance undertaking is required to collect and store information about the co-insurance operations.[1467]

Transfers in the performance of insurance contracts are 'capital movements' in Title X of the nomenclature in Annex I. However, the provisions of section 81 of the IAA concern the setting up of co-insurance within the EEA. They are, therefore, not 'capital movements' within the nomenclature in Annex I.

Section 82: Requirements for financial soundness and available solvency margin of Estonian branches of third country insurance undertakings

An Estonian branch of a firm that is authorised to provide insurance services in a third country is required to possess assets within the EEA of a quantity that is at least equal to the required solvency margin,[1468] possess assets in Estonia of an amount that is at least equal to one half of the minimum solvency margin under subsections 71(3) or 71(3^1) of the IAA,[1469] compute the required solvency margin pursuant to sections 72 or 73 of the IAA on the basis of insurance contracts agreed in Estonia,[1470] comply with the requirements for the available solvency margin for which

[1463] s.81(2)(2), IAA.

[1464] s.81(2)(3), IAA.

[1465] s.81(2)(4), IAA.

[1466] s.81(3), IAA. The provision for outstanding claims shall be computed pursuant to the procedure for the establishment of the provision for outstanding claims that is in force in the leading insurance firm's home country (s.81(4), IAA). At the discretion of an Estonian co-insurance company, the assets that cover technical provisions corresponding to the technical provisions and financial liabilities that subsections 81(3) and 81(4) of the IAA specify, may be localised either in Estonia or in the leading insurance undertaking's home state (s.81(5), IAA).

[1467] s.81(6), IAA.

[1468] s.82(1)(1), IAA.

[1469] s.82(1)(2), IAA. See note 1349, for subsections 71(3) and 71(3^1) of the IAA.

[1470] s.82(1)(3), IAA. Sections 72 and 73 of the IAA contain the calculations for the required solvency margin of Estonian insurance companies (and branches of third country insurance undertakings) that provide non-life insurance services, and life insurance services, respectively, in Estonia.

the IAA provides,[1471] keep in Estonia the assets that cover technical provisions corresponding to the technical provisions and financial liabilities which arise from the insurance contracts entered into in Estonia that observe the provisions of sections 77 and 78 of the IAA (or of sections 77 and 78^1 of the IAA for reinsurance undertakings),[1472] organise accounting procedures for operations in Estonia,[1473] and store in Estonia all documents that relate to business there.[1474] A third country insurance undertaking that, in addition to Estonia, has a branch in any other Contracting State, is entitled to request approval of the following preferential conditions from the financial supervision authorities of the relevant Contracting States: the required solvency margin is computed pursuant to sections 72 or 73 of the IAA based on insurance contracts that are concluded in any Contracting State (including Estonia),[1475] possession of the deposit specified in clause 43(2)(9) of the IAA is required only if the EFSA exercises supervision over the required solvency margin of the Estonian and (other) Contracting State branches of the third country insurance company,[1476] and assets that correspond to the minimum solvency margin may be localised in Estonia or in the country in which the third country insurance firm has founded a branch.[1477]

A third country insurance company that wishes to function under the preferential conditions that subsection 82(2) specifies shall submit a request to this effect to the EFSA, together with documents that certify that a similar request has been submitted to the financial supervision authorities of all the Contracting States in which the third country

---

[1471] s.82(1)(3), IAA.

[1472] s.82(1)(4), IAA. The assets that cover an insurance firm's technical provisions are, at all times, to be equal to at least the quantity of the insurance company's technical provisions and financial liabilities (s.77(1), IAA). Sections 78 and 78^1 of the IAA contain restrictions on investments of assets that cover technical provisions of insurance firms, and reinsurance undertakings, respectively. For example, assets that cover technical provisions may be invested in the securities of one issuer, or the loans secured by one borrower, in an amount of up to 5% of the total amount of technical provisions and financial liabilities, including the reinsurance undertaking's portion (s.78(2), IAA).

[1473] s.82(1)(5), IAA.

[1474] s.82(1)(5), IAA.

[1475] s.82(2)(1), IAA. See note 1470, for sections 72 and 73 of the IAA.

[1476] s.82(2)(2), IAA. This deposit is at least 25% of the minimum solvency margin that subsections 71(3) or $71(3^1)$ of the IAA provide for, and is required as one of the conditions for the EFSA to provide a third country insurance firm with an authorisation to found a branch in Estonia (s.43(2)(9), IAA).

[1477] s.82(2)(3), IAA.

insurance undertaking has opened a branch.[1478] In this request, the third country insurance firm shall indicate the financial supervision authority that is selected to exercise supervision over the required solvency margin branches of the company in Estonia and in the (other) Contracting State(s), and shall give reasons for this choice.[1479] If the third country insurance firm has chosen a financial supervision authority that is not the EFSA as the body that is to conduct this supervision, then the EFSA is to forward information to the other authority concerning the Estonian branch of the third country insurance undertaking that is necessary for the exercise of supervision over the firm's required solvency margin.[1480]

These preferential conditions shall come into force at the time at which the selected financial supervision authority informs the other financial authorities that the former has assumed the duty to exercise supervision over the required solvency margin of the third country insurance company's branches in Estonia and the (other) Contracting State(s).[1481] If the EFSA or a financial supervision authority of a Contracting State in which the third country insurance undertaking has a branch decides to cease the application of the preferential conditions to the third country insurance firm, then the application of these conditions to all branches of the third country in Contracting States (including Estonia) are to stop simultaneously.[1482]

If, under the preferential conditions, the EFSA exercises supervision over the required solvency margin of Estonian and Contracting State branches of a third country insurance company, then the EFSA must notify the financial supervision authorities of the other relevant Contracting States if it revokes the authorisation that it has granted to the third country insurance firm for the establishment of a branch in Estonia.[1483] If a Contracting State's financial supervision authority informs the EFSA that it has withdrawn an authorisation granted to a third country undertaking for the foundation of a branch in that State, on the ground that the company's available solvency margin does not conform to the required solvency margin that has been computed on the basis of insurance contracts agreed in Estonia and (other) Contracting States, then the EFSA

[1478] s.82(3), IAA.

[1479] s.82(4), IAA. This financial supervision authority shall only be the EFSA or the financial supervision authority of the Contracting State in which the third country insurance company has founded a branch (s.82(4), IAA).

[1480] s.82(5), IAA.

[1481] s.82(6), IAA.

[1482] s.82(7), IAA.

[1483] s.82(9), IAA.

is also required to revoke the authorisation that it has granted to the firm for the establishment of its branch in Estonia.[1484]

Section 75^2 of the IAA applies to the technical provisions and financial liabilities of Estonian branches of third country insurance companies.[1485] Thus, the technical provisions and financial liabilities of a branch of a third country insurance undertaking shall, at all times, cover the commitments that arise from the insurance contracts that the branch enters into, which it can reasonably foresee.[1486] If these provisions and liabilities do not satisfy this requirement, then the EFSA may issue a precept to prohibit the carrying out of transactions or the performance of acts that involve the insurance company's assets, or restrict the volume of the transactions or acts that are related to the assets thereof.[1487]

The establishment of a branch is a 'capital movement' in Title I(1) of the nomenclature in Annex I. The requirements to hold a minimum solvency margin (including a deposit) and a specified level of assets to cover the technical provisions and financial liabilities that arise from contracts entered into in Estonia, the revocation of an authorisation for a third country insurance firm to establish an Estonian branch, and the issuance of a precept to prohibit or restrict the volume of transactions, limit the free movement of capital.

To be justified under Article 65(1)(b) of the TFEU, the restrictive measures must be necessary for the protection of the interests that they are intended to guarantee, be proportionate (i.e. not achievable by less restrictive measures), and fulfil the requirements of legal certainty (i.e. be specific, objective and known to the parties beforehand); in addition, the persons whom the measures affect must have access to legal redress (i.e. there must be a formal statement of reasons for the decision and the right to appeal against it in the domestic courts).[1488] The restrictive measures are necessary for the protection of the required interests – i.e. the solvency and financial soundness of the branch of a third country insurance undertaking for the protection of policyholders and claimants under the insurance policy, are proportionate, and satisfy the requirements of legal certainty. However, they do not provide the applicant insurance firm with access to legal redress – the IAA neither requires the EFSA to give a formal statement of reasons for a decision to refuse authorisation or to issue a

---

[1484] s.82(10), IAA.

[1485] s.82(8), IAA.

[1486] ss.82(8) and 75^2(1), IAA.

[1487] ss.82(8) and 75^2(2), IAA.

[1488] See the subsection '*The requirements for a successful public policy/public security derogation*', in section 2.1.3.

precept, nor provides the applicant insurance firm with the right to appeal against this decision in the Estonian courts. Hence, Article 65(1)(b) of the TFEU does not justify the restrictive measures in section 82 of the IAA.

For the restrictive measures to be justified under Article 64(2) of the TFEU, the EU institutions must carefully take account of the objective of the free movement of capital whilst enacting the relevant Directive, and the domestic rules must not limit the free movement of capital more than the equivalent provisions of this Directive do. Although the Articles of Directive 2009/138/EC (the relevant Directive) do not mention the free movement of capital, Recital 72 of Directive 2009/138/EC states that Member States should not require insurance or reinsurance firms to invest their assets in specific classes of assets, because this could be incompatible with the liberalisation of capital movements for which Article 63 of the TFEU provides. As stated above, the wording of this recital shows that EU legislators were aware of the objective of the free movement of capital whilst enacting Directive 2009/138/EC, although it is unclear whether or not the statement in the recital is sufficient to establish that these legislators had carefully taken account of this objective.[1489]

To ascertain whether or not the rules in section 82 limit the free movement of capital more than the equivalent provisions of Directive 2009/138/EC, the latter must be considered. Each Member State shall require branches set up in its territory of insurance undertakings with their head offices outside the EEA, to hold a quantity of eligible own funds that comprises Tier 1, Tier 2 and Tier 3 own-fund items.[1490] The Solvency Capital Requirement and the Minimum Capital requirement are to be computed in accordance with the provisions of Title I Chapter VI, Sections 4 and 5, of Directive 2009/138/EC.[1491] For the purpose of calculating the Solvency Capital Requirement, and the absolute floor of the Minimum Capital Requirement, account is taken only of the operations that the branch conducts.[1492] The eligible amount of basic own funds that are necessary to cover the Minimum Capital Requirement and the absolute floor of this Requirement, shall be equal to the sum of the Tier 1 and Tier

---

[1489] See the subsection '*Chapter 2 Division 2: Activities of Estonian Insurance Undertakings in Foreign States*', above in this section.

[1490] Articles 166(1) and 98(3), Directive 2009/138/EC. See note 1449, for Articles 93 and 94 of Directive 2009/138/EC, which describe these items.

[1491] Article 166(1), Directive 2009/138/EC. See note 1435.

[1492] Article 166(1), Directive 2009/138/EC. Clause 82(1)(3) of the IAA transposes this paragraph of Article 166(1) of Directive 2009/138/EC – see above in this subsection ('*Section 82: Requirements for financial soundness and available solvency margin of Estonian branches of third country insurance undertakings*').

2 basic own fund items.[1493] The eligible amount of basic own funds must not be less than half of the absolute floor that Article 129(1)(d) of Directive 2009/138/EC requires.[1494] The deposit that is lodged in accordance with Article 162(2)(e) of Directive 2009/138/EC is to contribute to the eligible basic own funds to cover the Minimum Capital Requirement.[1495] The assets that represent the Solvency Capital Requirement are to be kept in the Member State in which the activities are pursued – up to the amount of the Minimum Capital Requirement, and the excess within the EEA.[1496]

Any third country insurance undertaking that has requested or obtained authorisation from more than one Member State may apply to the financial supervision authority of one of these countries for the following advantages, which may only be granted jointly:[1497] the Solvency Capital Requirement is to be computed in relation to the entire business that the insurance firm pursues within the EEA,[1498] the deposit that is required under Article 162(2)(e) of Directive 2009/138/EC is to be lodged in only one of these Member States,[1499] and the assets that represent the Minimum

---

[1493] Articles 166(2) and 98(4), Directive 2009/138/EC. See note 1435, for a definition of basic own funds.

[1494] Article 166(3), Directive 2009/138/EC. See note 1434, for the description of the floor of the Minimum Capital Requirement in Article 129(1)(d) of Directive 2009/138/EC.

[1495] Article 166(3), Directive 2009/138/EC. For Article 162(2)(e) of Directive 2009/138/EC, see the subsection '*Chapter 2 Division 3: Activities of Foreign Insurance Undertakings in Estonia*', above in this section.

[1496] Article 166(4), Directive 2009/138/EC. Clause 82(1)(1) of the IAA transposes the last phrase of Article 166(4) of Directive 2009/138/EC – see above in this subsection ('*Section 82: Requirements for financial soundness and available solvency margin of Estonian branches of third country insurance undertakings*'). However, clause 82(1)(2) of the IAA requires the Estonian branch of a third country insurance undertaking to hold assets in Estonia of a quantity that is at least equal to one half of the minimum solvency margin – which is not an exact transposition of the first phrase of Article 166(4) of Directive 2009/138/EC. The absolute floor of the minimum capital requirement in subsections 71(3) and 71(3^1) of the IAA differs from that in Article 129(1)(d) of Directive 2009/138/EC; see notes 1349 and 1434.

[1497] Articles 167(1)-(2), Directive 2009/138/EC.

[1498] Article 167(1)(a), Directive 2009/138/EC. Clause 82(2)(1) of the IAA transposes Article 167(1)(a) of Directive 2009/138/EC – see above in this subsection ('*Section 82: Requirements for financial soundness and available solvency margin of Estonian branches of third country insurance undertakings*').

[1499] Article 167(1)(b), Directive 2009/138/EC. For Article 162(2)(e) of Directive 2009/138/EC, see the subsection '*Chapter 2 Division 3: Activities of Foreign*

Capital Requirement are to be localised, in accordance with Article 134 of Directive 2009/138/EC, in any one of the Member States in which it conducts its activities.[1500] The application must state the financial supervision authority of the Member State that is to supervise the solvency of the entire business of the branches that are founded within the EEA.[1501] The third country insurance company must provide reasons for its choice of financial supervision authority.[1502] The deposit that Article 162(2)(e) refers to must be lodged with the Member State whose financial supervision authority is to supervise the solvency of the business of the branches that are established in the EEA.[1503]

The advantages that the previous paragraph refers to may only be granted if the financial supervision authorities of all Member States in which an application has been made agree to them.[1504] These advantages shall take effect from the time at which the selected financial supervision authority informs the other financial supervision authorities that it will

---

Insurance Undertakings in Estonia', above in this section. Clause 82(2)(2) of the IAA is consistent with Article 167(1)(b) of Directive 2009/138/EC – see above in this subsection ('*Section 82: Requirements for financial soundness and available solvency margin of Estonian branches of third country insurance undertakings*').

1500 Article 167(1)(c), Directive 2009/138/EC. With respect to insurance risks that are located within the EEA, Member States must not require the assets that are held to cover the technical provisions related to these risks, to be localised within the EEA or in a particular Member State (Article 134(1), Directive 2009/138/EC). Thus, Article 167(1)(c) of Directive 2009/138/EC states that the assets are to be localised in one of the relevant Member States, whist Article 134(1) of Directive 2009/138/EC (to which Article 167(1)(c) of the Directive refers) states that Member States are not to require the assets to be localised. Clause 82(2)(3) of the IAA transposes Article 167(1)(c) of Directive 2009/138/EC – see above in this subsection ('*Section 82: Requirements for financial soundness and available solvency margin of Estonian branches of third country insurance undertakings*').

1501 Article 167(2), Directive 2009/138/EC. Subsection 82(4) of the IAA transposes the first paragraph of Article 167(2) of Directive 2009/138/EC – see above in this subsection ('*Section 82: Requirements for financial soundness and available solvency margin of Estonian branches of third country insurance undertakings*').

1502 Article 167(2), Directive 2009/138/EC. See note 1501.

1503 Article 167(2), Directive 2009/138/EC. For Article 162(2)(e) of Directive 2009/138/EC, see the subsection '*Chapter 2 Division 3: Activities of Foreign Insurance Undertakings in Estonia*', above in this section. Clause 82(2)(2) of the IAA transposes the second paragraph of Article 167(2) of Directive 2009/138/EC – see above in this subsection ('*Section 82: Requirements for financial soundness and available solvency margin of Estonian branches of third country insurance undertakings*').

1504 Article 167(3), Directive 2009/138/EC.

supervise the state of solvency of the whole business of the third country insurance firm's EEA branches.[1505] The selected financial supervision authority shall acquire from the other Member States, the information that is necessary for the supervision of the overall solvency of the branches that are opened in their territory.[1506] At the request of one or more of the relevant Member States, the advantages shall be withdrawn simultaneously by all of these countries.[1507]

If the financial supervision authority of the Member State that supervises the solvency of the total business of the third country insurance firm's branches that are established within the EEA, revokes the authorisation, then this authority must notify the financial supervision authorities of the other Member States in which the company operates, and those authorities are to "take the appropriate measures".[1508] If the reason for withdrawal of the authorisation is the inadequacy of the overall state of solvency as specified by the Member States that agreed to the request for advantages under Article 167 of Directive 2009/138/EC, then the Member States that provided their approval shall also rescind their authorisations.[1509]

From the above consideration of the relevant provisions of Directive 2009/138/EC, it is clear that the equivalent rules in Article 82 of the IAA are consistent with the former, and, therefore, restrict the free movement of capital to a similar extent. In addition, as it is unclear whether or not the statement in Recital 72 of Directive 2009/138/EC is sufficient to establish that EU legislators carefully took account of the objective of the free movement of capital whilst enacting this Directive,[1510] Article 64(2) of the

---

[1505] Article 167(3), Directive 2009/138/EC. Subsection 82(6) of the IAA transposes the second paragraph of Article 167(3), Directive 2009/138/EC – see above in this subsection ('*Section 82: Requirements for financial soundness and available solvency margin of Estonian branches of third country insurance undertakings*').

[1506] Article 167(3), Directive 2009/138/EC.

[1507] Article 167(4), Directive 2009/138/EC. Subsection 82(7) of the IAA transposes Article 167(4) of Directive 2009/138/EC – see above in this subsection ('*Section 82: Requirements for financial soundness and available solvency margin of Estonian branches of third country insurance undertakings*').

[1508] Article 170, Directive 2009/138/EC. Section 82(9) of the IAA transposes the first paragraph of Article 170 of Directive 2009/138/EC – see above in this subsection ('*Section 82: Requirements for financial soundness and available solvency margin of Estonian branches of third country insurance undertakings*').

[1509] Article 170, Directive 2009/138/EC. Section 82(10) of the IAA transposes the second paragraph of Article 170 of Directive 2009/138/EC – see above in this subsection ('*Section 82: Requirements for financial soundness and available solvency margin of Estonian branches of third country insurance undertakings*').

[1510] See above in this subsection.

TFEU may (or may not) justify the restrictive measures in section 82 of the IAA. If the statement in the recital is deemed to be sufficient, then Article 64(2) of the TFEU justifies these measures, and, consequently, there is no contravention of Article 63 of the TFEU.

Section 93: Obligation to co-operate with financial supervision authorities of Contracting States

If an insurance portfolio to be transferred includes insurance contracts that are concluded by a branch of an Estonian insurance company in a (non-Estonian) Contracting State, or contracts that are agreed in the course of an Estonian insurance firm's provision of cross-border insurance services, and the transferee is an insurance undertaking that is authorised to supply investment services in a (non-Estonian) Contracting State, then the EFSA shall grant the authorisation to transfer the insurance portfolio only after receiving confirmation from the financial supervision authority of the relevant Contracting State that, after acceptance of the insurance portfolio, the quantity of the assets included in the available solvency margin of the transferee continues to satisfy the required solvency margin.[1511] If an insurance portfolio to be transferred includes insurance contracts that are concluded by a branch of an Estonian insurance undertaking in a (non-Estonian) Contracting State, then the EFSA shall grant the authorisation to transfer the insurance portfolio only after the financial supervision authority of the Contracting State in which the branch is located agrees to the transfer of the insurance portfolio.[1512] The EFSA is to grant the authorisation to transfer an insurance portfolio, only if the financial supervision authorities if the Contracting States in which the insured risks that relate to the insurance contracts are situated, agree to the transfer of the insurance portfolio.[1513]

If the financial supervision authority of a Contracting State that is specified in section 93 of the IAA, has not informed the EFSA of its agreement or disagreement to the transfer within three months after it receives a corresponding request, then this financial supervision authority is deemed to agree to the transfer of the insurance portfolio.[1514] If the transferor is an Estonian branch of an insurance firm that is authorised to provide insurance services in a (non-Estonian) Contracting State, or if the insured risk of the insurance contracts to be transferred is located in Estonia, then the EFSA is to grant this consent within three months of its

[1511] s.93(1), IAA.
[1512] s.93(2), IAA.
[1513] s.93(3), IAA.
[1514] s.93(4), IAA.

receipt of a request to this effect from the financial supervision authority of that Contracting State.[1515]

Transfers of insurance portfolios are 'capital movements' in Title X of the nomenclature in Annex I. However, if the insurance portfolio is not moved across a border, i.e. if it remains in Estonia or in another EEA state, then there is no cross-border movement of capital. If, in the particular case, there is a cross-border transfer of an insurance portfolio, and, therefore a cross-border capital movement, then section 93(3) of the IAA[1516] restricts the free movement of capital.

For the restrictive measures to be justified under Article 65(1)(b) of the TFEU, they must be necessary for the protection of interests that they are intended to guarantee, be proportionate (i.e. not be attainable by less restrictive measures), and satisfy the requirements of legal certainty (i.e. be specific, objective, and known to the parties beforehand); furthermore, the persons whom the measures affect must have access to legal redress (i.e. intervention must be accompanied by a formal statement of reasons, and be subject to review by the domestic courts).[1517] With respect to section 93(3) of the IAA, the 'interests' are that the relevant financial supervision authorities consider that the risks that relate to the insurance contracts will not increase in consequence of the transfer of the insurance portfolio. Given this, allowing these authorities to refuse to agree to the transfer may be disproportionate – it may be sufficient protection for this interest if the relevant financial supervision authorities monitor the risks, and report to the financial supervision authority of the EEA state to which the insurance portfolio is transferred, if there is a reason for concern.[1518] Furthermore, the persons who are affected by the measures do not have access to legal redress – Article 93 of the IAA does not require the EFSA to give reasons for a refusal to transfer an insurance portfolio, nor gives a right to appeal against this decision. Hence, the restrictive measure in

[1515] s.93(5), IAA. Subsections 93(1), 93(3) and 93(4) of the IAA also apply, if the insurance portfolio transferred contains insurance contracts that are agreed in Estonia, and the transferee is an insurance company that is authorised to provide insurance services in a (non-Estonian) Contracting State (s.93(6), IAA). Subsection 93(5) of the IAA also applies, if the insured risk of the insurance contracts of a firm that is authorised to provide insurance services in a (non-Estonian) Contracting State, is not situated in Estonia, and the transferee is an Estonian insurance company (s.93(7), IAA).

[1516] See above in this section.

[1517] See the subsection '*The requirements for a successful public policy/public security derogation*', in section 2.1.3.

[1518] See section 2.1.3 for similar arguments relating to prior authorisation.

subsection 93(3) of the IAA is not justified under Article 65(1)(b) of the TFEU. Consequently, this subsection breaches Article 63 of the TFEU.

Section 94: Specifications for transfer of insurance portfolios of third country insurance undertakings

The EFSA provides authorisation for the transfer of an insurance portfolio of an Estonian branch of a company that is authorised to provide insurance services in a third country, to one that is authorised to supply insurance services in Estonia, only if the EFSA is convinced, based on the information that it possesses, that after acceptance of the insurance portfolio, the transferee will continue to satisfy the required solvency margin.[1519] The EFSA gives permission for the transfer of an insurance portfolio to an insurance firm that is authorised to provide insurance services in a (non-Estonian) Contracting State, only after the financial supervision authority of that State confirms that, after acceptance of the insurance portfolio, the transferee will still fulfil the required solvency margin.[1520] The EFSA grants permission for the transfer of an insurance portfolio to a Contracting State branch of a third country insurance firm, only after the financial supervision authority of this State confirms that the transfer of the insurance portfolio is allowed pursuant to the legislation of the State, and the State's financial supervision authority has agreed to the transfer of the portfolio,[1521] and, after acceptance of the insurance portfolio, the transferee will continue to satisfy the required solvency margin.[1522]

The EFSA is to give an authorisation to transfer an insurance portfolio, only if the financial supervision authority of the Contracting States of the location of the insured risks that relate to the insurance contracts agrees to this transfer.[1523] If a financial supervision authority of a (non-Estonian) Contracting State has not informed the EFSA of its agreement or disagreement to the transfer within three months of the receipt of a

---

[1519] s.94(1), IAA. If subsection 82(2) of the IAA applies, then the EFSA also bases its decision in subsection 94(1) of the IAA on the information that is available to the financial supervision authority that the applicant selects under subsection 82(3) off the IAA (s.94(1), IAA). For section 82 of the IAA, see the subsection '*Section 82: Requirements for financial soundness and available solvency margin of Estonian branches of third country insurance undertakings*', above in this section.

[1520] s.94(2), IAA.

[1521] s.94(3)(1), IAA.

[1522] s.94(3)(2), IAA.

[1523] s.94(4), IAA.

corresponding request, then the former is deemed to agree to the transfer of the insurance portfolio.[1524]

Transfers in performance of insurance contracts are 'capital movements' in Title X of the nomenclature in Annex I. However, the transfer of an insurance portfolio that subsection 94(1) of the IAA envisages is from an Estonian branch of a third country insurance firm to an Estonian insurance company.[1525] As the portfolio remains in Estonia, there is no cross-border movement of capital.

By contrast, in subsections 94(2) and 94(3) of the IAA,[1526] the insurance portfolio is transferred from Estonia to another EEA state. There is a cross-border capital movement, in accordance with Annex I. The conditions that these subsections lay down are not onerous, and, therefore, do not restrict the free movement of capital. However, if the insurance portfolio is transferred pursuant to subsections 94(2) or 94(3) of the IAA (rather than to subsection 94(1) of the IAA), then subsection 94(4) of the IAA[1527] limits the free movement of capital.

To be justified under Article 65(1)(b) of the TFEU, the restrictive measures must be necessary for the protection of interests that they are intended to guarantee, be proportionate (i.e. not be attainable by less restrictive measures), and satisfy the requirements of legal certainty (i.e. be specific, objective, and known to the parties beforehand); furthermore, the persons who are affected by the measures must have access to legal redress (i.e. intervention must be accompanied by a formal statement of reasons, and be subject to review by the national courts).[1528] The 'interests' in this instance are that the relevant financial supervision authority considers that the risks which relate to the insurance contracts will not rise as a result of the transfer of the insurance portfolio. Given this, the option for this authority to refuse to agree to the transfer may be disproportionate – it may be sufficient protection with respect to this interest for the relevant financial supervision authorities to monitor the risks, and to report to the financial supervision authority of the EEA state to whom the insurance portfolio is transferred, if there is specific reason for concern.[1529] In addition, the persons who are affected by the measures do not have access to legal redress – Article 94 of the IAA neither requires the EFSA

[1524] s.94(5), IAA.

[1525] See above in this subsection.

[1526] See above in this subsection.

[1527] See above in this subsection.

[1528] See the subsection '*The requirements for a successful public policy/public security derogation*', in section 2.1.3.

[1529] See section 2.1.3 for similar arguments relating to prior authorisation.

to give reasons for a refusal to transfer an insurance portfolio, nor provides a right to appeal against this decision. Hence, Article 65(1)(b) of the TFEU does not justify the restrictive measure in subsection 94(4) of the IAA. Consequently, this subsection breaches Article 63 of the TFEU.

Chapter 10 Division 6: Activities of Estonian Intermediaries in Foreign States[1530]

An intermediary that is entered in the list in Estonia may practice mediation in a foreign state, by opening a branch or engaging in cross-border mediation.[1531] For the purposes of Division 6 of Chapter 10 of the IAA, 'cross-border mediation' is mediation business by an insurance intermediary in a foreign state, without the establishment of a branch for this purpose.[1532] Upon pursuing insurance mediation in a foreign state, an intermediary is to comply with the requirements of the IAA and its secondary legislation, and of the foreign state's legislation.[1533]

Sections 156, 157, 158 and 159 of the IAA apply to the mediation business of Estonian intermediaries in a (non-Estonian) Contracting State.[1534] Sections 152, 153, 154, 155 and 157 of the IAA apply to the mediation business of Estonian intermediaries in a third country.[1535] Sections 156, 157, 158 and 159 of the IAA are considered first.

An Estonian intermediary, which is a company, and would like to establish a branch in a (non-Estonian) Contracting State, must notify the EFSA of this intention,[1536] and provide it with the following documents and information: the name of the Contracting State in which the intermediary wishes to open the branch,[1537] the address of the branch's registered office,[1538] information contained in clause 143(1)(5) of the IAA concerning the branch's director, who must have adequate right of representation to act in the intermediary's name in relation to third parties,[1539] and a list of the types of insurance contract that the

---

1530 See above in this section, for the definitional aspects of insurance mediation. See note 1172, for a comment on the term 'foreign state'.

1531 s.151(1), IAA.

1532 s.151(2), IAA.

1533 s.151(3), IAA.

1534 s.151(4), IAA.

1535 s.151(5), IAA.

1536 s.156(1), IAA.

1537 s.156(1)(1), IAA.

1538 s.156(1)(2), IAA.

1539 s.156(1)(3), IAA. This information comprises the director's name, personal identification code (or date of birth in the absence of this code), address,

intermediary plans to mediate in the Contracting State.[1540] The EFSA is to inform the financial supervision authority of the Contracting State in which the intermediary wishes to establish a branch of its intention to do so, within one month of receiving the documents and information, and is to forward these items to that authority – including information on the intermediary that is entered in the list of authorised intermediaries.[1541]

The EFSA must inform the intermediary that it has forwarded the documents and information to the Contracting State's financial supervision authority.[1542] The intermediary may establish a branch in the Contracting State, one month after the date of receipt of that notice from the EFSA.[1543] The EFSA shall add the name of the Contracting State in which an intermediary has opened a branch, to the information that concerns the intermediary in the list of authorised intermediaries.[1544]

The EFSA may issue a precept, in order to prohibit an intermediary's operations through a branch that it has founded in a Contracting State, if this Contracting State's financial supervision authority has informed the EFSA that the intermediary has breached the legislation of that State.[1545] The EFSA is to promptly deliver this precept to the intermediary.[1546]

An Estonian insurance intermediary which, for the first time, wishes to provide cross-border insurance mediation in at least one (non-Estonian) Contracting State, is to notify the EFSA of its intention to do this,[1547] and submit the following documents and information: the name of the Contracting State in which the intermediary plans to engage in cross-border mediation,[1548] and a list of the types of insurance contracts that the

---

educational background, and employment history for the past five years (s.143(1)(5), IAA).

[1540] s.156(1)(4), IAA.

[1541] s.156(3), IAA.

[1542] s.156(4), IAA.

[1543] s.156(5), IAA. Subsection 156(6) of the IAA provides an exception to the rule in subsection 156(5) of the IAA, but is difficult to interpret in the light of subsections 156(4) and 156(5) of the IAA. An Estonian intermediary may establish a branch in a Contracting State immediately after it sends the documents and information to the EFSA, unless that State would like the EFSA to notify it of the foundation of branches (s.156(6), IAA).

[1544] s.156(9), IAA.

[1545] s.157(1), IAA. The branch is prohibited from operating, if the insurance broker, or insurance agent, is deleted from the list of authorised intermediaries, under sections 146 and 150 of the IAA, respectively (s.157(1), IAA).

[1546] s.157(2), IAA.

[1547] s.158(1), IAA.

[1548] s.158(1)(1), IAA.

intermediary wishes to mediate in the Contracting State.[1549] The EFSA is to inform the Contracting State's financial supervision authority of the intermediary's intention to engage in cross-border mediation there within one month, and is to forward to the EFSA the documents and information, including information on the intermediary that is entered in the list of authorised intermediaries.[1550]

The EFSA is to inform the intermediary that it has forwarded the information and documents to the Contracting State's financial supervision authority.[1551] An intermediary may engage in cross-border mediation in that Contracting State, one month after it has received this notice from the EFSA.[1552] The EFSA must add the name of the Contracting State in which an intermediary engages in cross-border mediation, to the information about the intermediary in the list of authorised intermediaries.[1553]

The EFSA may issue a precept, in order to prohibit an Estonian intermediary from engaging in cross-border mediation in a (non-Estonian) Contracting State, if the financial supervision authority of that State has informed the EFSA of a breach of the State's legislation by the intermediary.[1554] The EFSA shall promptly deliver the precept to the intermediary.[1555]

Insurance mediation comprises operations that are "necessary for the purposes of capital movements",[1556] and is, therefore, a 'capital movement' in Title X (Transfers in Performance of Insurance Contracts) of the nomenclature in Annex I.[1557] Furthermore, the establishment of a branch is a 'capital movement' in Title I(1) of the nomenclature in Annex I. The issuance of a precept to an Estonian insurance intermediary, in order to

---

[1549] s.158(1)(2), IAA.
[1550] s.158(3), IAA.
[1551] s.158(4), IAA.
[1552] s.158(5), IAA. Subsection 158(6) of the IAA provides an exception to the rule in subsection 158(5) of the IAA. An Estonian intermediary may engage in cross-border mediation in the Contracting State immediately after it sends the documents and information to the EFSA, unless that State would like the EFSA to notify it of the supply of cross-border mediation (s.158(6), IAA). This provision is analogous to subsection 156(6) of the IAA for the establishment of branches – see note 1543.
[1553] s.158(9), IAA.
[1554] s.159(1), IAA. The insurance broker, or insurance agent, is prohibited from engaging in cross-border meditation, if it is removed from the list of authorised intermediaries, under sections 146 and 150 of the IAA, respectively (s.159(1), IAA).
[1555] s.159(2), IAA.
[1556] Annex I.
[1557] See the first paragraph of section 2.1.1.

prohibit it from establishing a branch in a (non-Estonian) EEA state or from engaging in cross-border mediation there, limits the free movement of capital.

To be justified under Article 65(1)(b) of the TFEU, the restrictive measures must be necessary for the protection of interests that they are intended to guarantee, be proportionate (i.e. not be attainable by less restrictive measures), and observe the requirements of legal certainty (i.e. be specific, objective and known to the parties beforehand); in addition, the persons whom the measures affect must have access to legal redress – the decision should be accompanied by reasons, and subject to review in the domestic courts.[1558] Whilst prohibition on the ground of transgressing the legislation of a (non-Estonian) EEA state is proportionate and provides legal certainty, the insurance intermediary that is prohibited from opening a branch in that country, or from engaging in cross-border mediation there, is not provided with access to legal redress – the IAA does not require the EFSA to provide reasons for issuing a precept under subsection 157(1) or subsection 159(1) of the IAA, and does not grant the intermediary the right to appeal against the decision in the national courts. Hence, Article 65(1)(b) of the TFEU does not justify these provisions, which, consequently, contravene Article 63 of the TFEU.

An Estonian intermediary that would like to establish a branch in a third country shall apply for an authorisation to do so from the EFSA.[1559] In order to apply for an authorisation for the establishment of a branch in a third country, the intermediary shall submit a written application and the following documents and information to the EFSA:[1560] the name of the country in which the intermediary wishes to open a branch, together with a reference to the legislation of the third country, according to which the foundation of the intermediary's branch is allowed,[1561] the address of the branch's registered office,[1562] the information contained in clause 143(1)(5) of the IAA concerning the branch's director, who must have a sufficient right of representation to operate in the intermediary's name in relation to third parties,[1563] a list of the types of insurance contracts that the

[1558] See the subsection '*The requirements for a successful public policy/public security derogation*', in section 2.1.3.
[1559] s.152(1), IAA.
[1560] s.152(2), IAA.
[1561] s.152(2)(1), IAA.
[1562] s.152(2)(2), IAA.
[1563] s.152(2)(3), IAA. See note 1539, for the information required by clause 143(1)(5) of the IAA.

intermediary would like to mediate in the third country,[1564] and a copy of the intermediary's valid liability insurance contract that section 134 of the IAA provides for,[1565] or of a guarantee contract of an insurance company or a credit or financial institution,[1566] or a confirmation from the insurance firm that it takes full responsibility for the intermediary's engagement in mediation.[1567] Sections 134,[1568] 138,[1569] and 147[1570] of the IAA apply to

---

[1564] s.152(2)(4), IAA.

[1565] In order to ensure compensation for harm caused by professional negligence, an intermediary shall agree an obligatory liability insurance contract on the following conditions: the insured event involves direct pecuniary loss that is caused by the professional negligence of the policyholder, insured person, or beneficiary, that is set out in the insurance contract that the intermediary or its representative mediates, the sum insured is at least 1.2 million EUR for one insured event and 1.7 million EUR per year for all submitted claims, the insurance cover is valid within the EEA, and the insurance cover applies to damage that is caused by an event or act that took place during the insurance period (s.134(1), IAA).

[1566] In order to ensure compensation for harm caused by professional negligence, an intermediary may, in place of a liability insurance contract, enter into a guarantee contract with an insurance company or a credit or financial institution; the guarantee contract shall be equivalent to the provisions of subsection 134(1) of the IAA (s.134(2), IAA). See note 1565, for subsection 134(1) of the IAA.

[1567] s.152(2)(5), IAA. The requirements contained in subsections 134(1) and 134(2) of the IAA do not apply to an insurance agent in respect of whom an insurance firm has provided a confirmation that it is responsible for the agent's mediation activities (s.134(3), IAA). See notes 1565 and 1566, for subsections 134(1) and 134(2) of the IAA, respectively. The insurance cover or guarantee must be valid in the third country in which the insurance company wishes to establish a branch, and the confirmation is to include a condition that the insurance undertaking is responsible for the intermediary's mediation business in that state (s.152(2)(5), IAA).

[1568] See notes 1565, 1566 and 1567, for section 134 of the IAA.

[1569] Section 138 of the IAA contains requirements for an insurance broker. The insurance broker (if a natural person) is to have an impeccable professional and business reputation (s.138(1), IAA). Specified persons, such as those who have caused a company to be bankrupt or been punished for official misconduct, are not to act as insurance brokers (s.138(2), IAA). An insurance broker (if a natural person), and his/her representative, must have experience of working in financial services, and have received the training in the field of insurance that section 133 of the IAA lays out (ss.138(3)-(4), IAA). A person who has received this training must know the general principles of insurance, the nature of the class or subclass of insurance being mediated, the conditions and the procedures for the agreement of insurance contracts, the principles for the determination of the sum insured, the processing of applications, and adequacy of resources, for the establishment of a branch, and to verification of the submitted information and of the financial circumstances, organisational structure and technical systems of the applicant intermediary.[1571]

If the intermediary, upon application for authorisation for the establishment of a branch in a third country, has not submitted all of the documents and information specified in clauses 143(2)(1)-(5) of the IAA,[1572] or if these items are not complete or "have not been prepared in accordance with the requirements",[1573] then the EFSA shall require that the applicant removes the deficiencies within a specified period.[1574] The EFSA shall take a decision to grant, or to refuse to grant, an authorisation for the establishment of a branch in a third country, within two months of submission of all of the necessary, conforming documents and information,

---

determinants of the insurance premiums, the principles of compensation (if the insured event occurs), and Acts that regulate insurance contracts (s.133(2), IAA).

1570 Section 147 contains the requirements for an insurance agent. The insurance agent (if a natural person) must satisfy the requirements of subsection 138(2) of the IAA (see note 1569), and have an impeccable professional and business reputation (s.147(1), IAA). An insurance agent (if an natural person), and his/her representative, must have experience of working in financial services, and must have received the training in the insurance field for which section 133 of the IAA provides (ss.147(3)-(4), IAA). The insurance firm whom the agent represents is to provide training in the field of insurance to the agent (s.147(6), IAA).

1571 s.153(1), IAA.

1572 In this English translation of the IAA, subsection 143(2) of this Act does not contain any clauses. As subsection 143(1) of the IAA identifies the documents and information that an applicant must provide to the EFSA, in order to be entered as an insurance broker in the list of authorised intermediaries, subsection 153(1^1) of the IAA may mean the documents and information that are specified in clauses 143(1)(1)-(5) of the IAA. These items include the applicant's articles of association (if the applicant is a company), a list of the applicant's shareholders or unit-holders and information on the amount contributed, the number of shares or units, and number of votes, of each shareholder or unit-holder (if the applicant is a company), the business name of the insurance firm in which the applicant has a qualifying holding and the size of this holding, and information on each member of the applicant's management board (if the applicant is a company) that comprises the name, personal identification code (or date of birth in the absence of this code), address, educational background, and employment history for the most recent five years (ss.143(1)(1) and 143(1)(3)-(5), IAA).

1573 Subsection 153(1^1) of the IAA does not state what these requirements are. The quoted phrase probably refers to the requirements in the IAA for the establishment of a branch in a third country of an Estonian insurance intermediary.

1574 s.153(1^1), IAA.

but not later than within three months of receipt of the application.[1575] The EFSA shall promptly communicate this decision to the intermediary.[1576] If the decision is to grant an authorisation to the applicant to found a branch in the third country, then the EFSA shall add the name of the third country to the information that concerns the applicant in the list of authorised intermediaries.[1577]

The EFSA may refuse to grant an authorisation for the foundation of a branch of an Estonian intermediary in a third country, if the documents or information submitted upon application for the authorisation do not satisfy the requirements of the IAA or its secondary legislation, or are incorrect, misleading or incomplete,[1578] the branch's director does not comply with the requirements of section 138 of the IAA concerning a member of an insurance broker's management board,[1579] the intermediary's resources (if the intermediary is a company) are insufficient for the provision of insurance mediation in the third country,[1580] the establishment of the branch may harm the interests of policyholders, insured persons or beneficiaries, the intermediary's financial position (if the intermediary is a company) or the reliability of its operations,[1581] the intermediary does not have a valid liability insurance contract, a guarantee contract, or a confirmation from the insurance undertaking that the latter takes complete responsibility for the intermediary's engagement in mediation,[1582] the third country's financial supervision authority "has no legal basis or possibilities for cooperation with" the EFSA, and, therefore, the EFSA is unable to exercise adequate supervision over the branch,[1583] or the intermediary has been punished for a specified offence (such as official misconduct) that has not been removed from the punishment register pursuant to the Punishment Register Act.[1584] The EFSA may revoke an authorisation for the establishment of a branch in a third country, and remove the relevant intermediary from the list of authorised

---

[1575] s.153(2), IAA.
[1576] s.153(3), IAA.
[1577] s.153(4), IAA.
[1578] s.154(1), IAA.
[1579] s.154(2), IAA. See note 1569, for the requirements of section 138 of the IAA.
[1580] s.154(3), IAA.
[1581] s.154(4), IAA.
[1582] ss.154(5) and 152(2)(5), IAA. See above in this subsection ('*Chapter 10 Division 6 Activities of Estonian Intermediaries in Foreign States*'), for clause 152(2)(5) of the IAA.
[1583] s.154(6), IAA.
[1584] s.154(7), IAA.

intermediaries, if the intermediary[1585] has submitted false information to the EFSA,[1586] has repeatedly or substantially contravened the requirements contained in the third country's legislation, which may harm the interests of policyholders, insured persons or beneficiaries,[1587] does not submit reports on its branch in the third country as required,[1588] has not implemented a precept from the EFSA that relates to the branch's activities within the period or to the extent prescribed,[1589] or has been removed from the list of authorised intermediaries,[1590] or if the branch does not satisfy the requirements for the granting of an authorisation for its establishment in the third country.[1591]

The EFSA is to promptly communicate a decision to revoke an authorisation for the establishment of a branch of an Estonian intermediary in a third country, and to remove the intermediary from the list of authorised intermediaries, to the intermediary and the third country's financial supervision authority.[1592] After becoming aware of this decision, the intermediary is to cease all mediation business by the date that the EFSA specifies.[1593] The EFSA must inform the third country's financial supervision authority of the sanctions and coercive measures that it imposes on the intermediary.[1594]

An Estonian intermediary that wishes to pursue cross-border mediation in a third country, is required to apply to the EFSA for an authorisation to do so.[1595] Upon application for this authorisation, the intermediary must submit a written application, and the following documents and information, to the EFSA:[1596] the name of the third country in which the intermediary

---

[1585] Subsection 155(1) of the IAA refers to "the intermediary which is a company". Insurance intermediaries comprise insurance brokers and insurance agents (s.130(2), IAA). An insurance broker may be a natural person (s.138(1), IAA), as may an insurance agent (s.147(1), IAA). Thus, the IAA does not contain provisions for the revocation of an authorisation that the EFSA has granted to an Estonian insurance intermediary who is a natural person, to establish a branch in a third country.

[1586] s.155(1)(1), IAA.

[1587] s.155(1)(2), IAA.

[1588] s.155(1)(4), IAA.

[1589] s.155(1)(5), IAA.

[1590] s.155(1)(6), IAA.

[1591] s.155(1)(3), IAA.

[1592] s.155(2), IAA.

[1593] s.155(3), IAA.

[1594] s.155(4), IAA.

[1595] s.157¹(1), IAA.

[1596] s.157¹(1), IAA.

wishes to engage in cross-border mediation,[1597] reference to the provisions of this third country's legislation pursuant to which the intermediary is permitted to engage in cross-border mediation in that state,[1598] a list of the types of insurance contracts that the intermediary intends to mediate in the third country,[1599] and a copy of the liability insurance contract that section 134 of the IAA provides for, or of a guarantee contract of an insurance firm or a credit or financial institution, which states that such a contract is effective in the third country.[1600] If the intermediary has not submitted all of these items, or if they do not conform to the requirements of the IAA or its secondary legislation, then the EFSA shall require the applicant to remove the deficiencies within a period that it specifies.[1601]

The EFSA shall take the decision to grant, or to refuse to grant, an authorisation for cross-border mediation in a third country, within two months of receipt of all the necessary, conforming documents and information and the "compliance with requirements",[1602] and within three months of the receipt of the application for authorisation.[1603] The EFSA must promptly notify the intermediary of a decision to grant, or to refuse to grant, this authorisation.[1604] If the EFSA's decision is to grant the authorisation, then it shall add the name of the third country in which the intermediary has the right to pursue cross-border mediation to the information concerning the intermediary that is presented in the list of authorised intermediaries.[1605]

The EFSA may refuse to grant an authorisation to an Estonian intermediary that wishes to engage in cross-border mediation in a third country, if the documents and information submitted upon application for this authorisation do not satisfy the requirements of the IAA or its secondary legislation,[1606] or are inaccurate, misleading or incomplete,[1607]

[1597] s.157^1(1)(1), IAA.
[1598] s.157^1(1)(1), IAA.
[1599] s.157^1(1)(2), IAA.
[1600] s.157^1(1)(3), IAA. See notes 1565, 1566 and 1567, for the requirements of section 134 of the IAA.
[1601] s.157^1(2), IAA.
[1602] Subsection 157^1(3) of the IAA does not state what requirements these are. As subsection 157^1(2) of the IAA refers to the requirements of the EFSA and its secondary legislation (see the previous paragraph), the quoted phrase refers to this description of requirements.
[1603] s.157^1(3), IAA.
[1604] s.157^1(4), IAA.
[1605] s.157^1(5), IAA.
[1606] s.157^1(6)(1), IAA.
[1607] s.157^1(6)(2), IAA.

the intermediary's activities in the third country may substantially harm the interests of the policyholders, insured persons or beneficiaries, or damage the intermediary's reliability,[1608] the intermediary's liability insurance contract or guarantee contract with an insurance undertaking, credit institution, or financial institution, does not comply with the requirements of subsection 134(1) of the IAA[1609] or is ineffective in the third country,[1610] the third country's financial supervision authority "has no legal basis, possibilities or readiness for sufficient and efficient cooperation with" the EFSA, and, therefore, the EFSA is unable to exercise adequate supervision over the intermediary,[1611] or the intermediary has been punished for a specified offence (such as an offence against property) and information about the punishment for this offence has not been erased from the punishment register in conformance with the Punishment Register Act.[1612] The EFSA may revoke an authorisation that it has granted to an Estonian intermediary to pursue cross-border mediation in a third country, if the intermediary has submitted inaccurate information that was of material significance in the EFSA's decision to grant this authorisation,[1613] has failed to inform the EFSA of a change to its circumstances that relates to cross-border mediation,[1614] has significantly or repeatedly breached the provisions of legislation that regulates its activities,[1615] does not fulfil the conditions for the granting of an authorisation for cross-border mediation,[1616] has not implemented a precept of the EFSA that relates to the cross-border mediation by the due date or to the extent laid down,[1617] or has been removed from the list of authorised intermediaries.[1618] The EFSA shall promptly notify the intermediary, and the third country's financial supervision authority, of a decision that it has taken to revoke an authorisation for cross-border mediation.[1619]

[1608] s.157^{1}(6)(3), IAA.
[1609] See note 1565, for the requirements of subsection 134(1) of the IAA.
[1610] s.157^{1}(6)(4), IAA.
[1611] s.157^{1}(6)(5), IAA.
[1612] s.157^{1}(6)(6), IAA.
[1613] s.157^{1}(8)(1), IAA.
[1614] s.157^{1}(8)(2), IAA.
[1615] s.157^{1}(8)(3), IAA.
[1616] s.157^{1}(8)(4), IAA.
[1617] s.157^{1}(8)(5), IAA.
[1618] s.157^{1}(8)(6), IAA.
[1619] s.157^{1}(9), IAA.

The establishment of a branch is a 'capital movement' in Title I(1) of the nomenclature in Annex I. As insurance mediation consists of operations that are "necessary for the purposes of capital movements",[1620] it is a 'capital movement' in Title X of the nomenclature in Annex I.[1621] If the EFSA refuses to grant an authorisation to an Estonian insurance intermediary to establish a branch, or to provide cross-border mediation, in a third country, or if the EFSA revokes such an authorisation, then it limits the free movement of capital.

For Article 65(1)(b) of the TFEU to justify the restrictive measures, they must be necessary for the protection of interests that they are intended to guarantee, be proportionate (i.e. not be achievable by less restrictive measures), and satisfy the requirements of legal certainty (i.e. be specific, objective and known to the parties beforehand); furthermore, the persons whom the measures affect must have access to legal redress – intervention must be accompanied by reasons, and be subject to review in the national courts.[1622] Some of the grounds on which the EFSA may refuse to grant, or withdraw, an authorisation for engagement in insurance mediation (directly or via a branch) are neither specific nor objective; thus, they do not fulfil the requirements of legal certainty. For example, subsections 154(4) and 154(6) of the IAA provide the EFSA with a discretion to decide whether the applicant Estonian intermediary should be granted an authorisation to establish a branch in a third country, as does clause $157^1(6)(5)$ of the IAA in respect of an authorisation to provide cross-border mediation in that state.[1623] Furthermore, the IAA does not require the EFSA to give reasons for a decision to refuse to grant an authorisation for engagement in insurance mediation in a third country, nor to withdraw this authorisation, and does not provide the insurance intermediary with a right to appeal against either of these decisions in the Estonian courts. Therefore, the persons whom the measures affect do not have access to legal redress. Hence, the restrictive measures are not justified under Article 65(1)(b) of the TFEU.

For Article 64(2) of the TFEU to justify the restrictive measures, the EU institutions must carefully consider the objective of the free movement of capital whilst enacting the relevant legislation, and the national rules should not restrict the free movement of capital more than the equivalent

[1620] Annex I.

[1621] See the first paragraph of section 2.1.1.

[1622] See the subsection '*The requirements for a successful public policy/public security derogation*', in section 2.1.3.

[1623] See above in this subsection ('*Chapter 10 Division 6 Activities of Estonian Intermediaries in Foreign States*'), for these provisions of the IAA.

provisions of the relevant Directive do.[1624] The relevant Directive is 2002/92/EC.[1625] Neither the recitals nor the Articles of Directive 2002/92/EC mention the movement of capital. Thus, the EU institutions did not carefully take account of the objective of the free movement of capital whilst enacting this Directive. Furthermore, Directive 2002/92/EC does not regulate insurance mediation activities that are conducted in third countries.[1626] Hence, sections 152, 153, 154, 155 and 157¹ of the IAA limit the free movement of capital more than do the equivalent provisions of the relevant Directive (of which there are none). Thus, the restrictive measures are not justified by Article 64(2) of the TFEU. Accordingly, the rules of Chapter 10 Division 6 of the IAA that regulate the engagement by Estonian insurance intermediaries in insurance mediation in third countries contravene Article 63 of the TFEU.

Chapter 10 Division 7: Activities of Foreign Intermediaries in Estonia[1627]

A person who, pursuant to the legislation of its home country, has the right to engage in mediation there, may also provide mediation in Estonia by establishing a branch or engaging in cross-border mediation.[1628] For the purposes of Division 7 of Chapter 10 of the IAA, 'cross-border mediation' is mediation business in Estonia by a foreign intermediary without establishing a branch.[1629] Upon its pursual of mediation in Estonia, a foreign intermediary is to comply with the requirements of the IAA and its secondary legislation, and with foreign country's legislation.[1630]

Section 165 of the IAA applies to the mediation business in Estonia of intermediaries that are authorised to engage in mediation in other Contracting States.[1631] Sections 161, 162, 163, 164 and 165¹ of the IAA apply to the mediation activities of intermediaries that are authorised to provide mediation in third countries.[1632] Section 165 of the IAA is discussed first.

[1624] See the subsection '*Derogations that apply only to capital movements to/from third countries*', in section 2.3.2.
[1625] See section 2.2.4.
[1626] Article 1(3), Directive 2002/92/EC.
[1627] See above in this section, for the definitional aspects of insurance mediation. See note 1172, for a comment on the term 'foreign state'.
[1628] s.160(1), IAA.
[1629] s.160(2), IAA.
[1630] s.160(3), IAA.
[1631] s.160(4), IAA.
[1632] s.160(5), IAA.

If an intermediary, which is a company registered in a (non-Estonian) Contracting State,[1633] wishes to establish a branch in Estonia, then it shall notify the EFSA of this intention through the financial supervision authority of its home country. The following documents and information shall be submitted to the EFSA: the business name and address of the branch's seat in Estonia,[1634] the name of the branch's director,[1635] and a list of the types of insurance contracts the mediation of which the branch is expected to conduct.[1636] The EFSA shall inform the intermediary through its home country's financial supervision authority of the conditions pursuant to which it must "provide its services in Estonia",[1637] within one month after the home country's financial supervision authority has forwarded the documents and information to the EFSA.[1638] The intermediary may establish a branch in Estonia as soon as the conditions in subsection 165(3) of the IAA have been fulfilled, or one month after the documents and information are forwarded to the EFSA.[1639] The EFSA shall enter the business name, the commercial registry code, the address of the Estonian seat, and the name of the director, of the branch in the list of authorised intermediaries.[1640]

The establishment of a branch is a 'capital movement' in Title I(1) of the nomenclature in Annex I. The informational requirements contained in subsection 165(1) of the IAA are not onerous, and do not restrict the free movement of capital. Consequently, the section 165 of the IAA does not contravene Article 63 of the TFEU.

The IAA does not contain provisions that regulate the engagement in cross-border mediation in Estonia by an intermediary from a (non-Estonian) Contracting State – although subsection 165(3) of the IAA refers to the provision of services in Estonia after the documents in subsection 165(1) of the IAA, which relate to the opening of a branch in Estonia, have been forwarded to the EFSA. This is likely to be the result of an

---

[1633] Section 165 of the IAA requires the intermediary to be a company. The text that considers section 165 of the IAA makes no further reference to this fact.

[1634] s.165(1)(1), IAA.

[1635] s.165(1)(2), IAA. The director of the branch must be able to operate in the intermediary's name in transactions with third parties (s.165(1)(2), IAA).

[1636] s.165(1)(3), IAA.

[1637] Subsection 165(3) of the IAA does not mention the establishment of a branch in Estonia – although subsection 165(4) of the IAA covers the timing issues for the foundation of a branch.

[1638] s.165(3), IAA.

[1639] s.165(4), IAA.

[1640] s.165(6), IAA.

oversight by the Estonian legislature, which should be corrected with immediate effect. Consequently, this omission should not be interpreted as a contravention of the rules on the free movement of capital.

In order to open a branch in Estonia, a third country intermediary, which is a company,[1641] is required to apply for an authorisation from the EFSA.[1642] Upon application for an authorisation for the establishment of a branch, the third country intermediary shall submit a written application and the following documents and information, to the EFSA:[1643] the business name and address of the intermediary[1644] and of its branch in Estonia,[1645] the information that clause 143(1)(5) contains concerning the branch's director – who must be empowered to transact business with third parties in the name of the intermediary,[1646] an official certificate that confirms the intermediary's presence in its home country (such an excerpt from a commercial register or a copy of the firm's registration certificate),[1647] a document that certifies the authority of the branch's director or a copy of the resolution appointing this director,[1648] a copy of the intermediary's articles of association (if a company) or partnership agreement (if a partnership),[1649] the telecommunications data of the company and of the branch,[1650] the intermediary's audited annual accounts for the most recent two financial years,[1651] a list of the types of insurance

[1641] Sections 161, 163 and 164 of the IAA require the intermediary to be a company. These sections concern the establishment of an Estonian branch of a third country intermediary. By contrast, section 165^1 of the IAA does not require the third country intermediary to be a company, in order to engage in cross-border insurance mediation in Estonia. The text makes no further reference to this issue.

[1642] s.161(1), IAA.

[1643] s.161(2), IAA.

[1644] s.161(2)(1), IAA.

[1645] s.161(2)(2), IAA.

[1646] s.161(2)(3), IAA. See note 1539, for the information that clause 143(1)(5) of the IAA requires.

[1647] ss.162(2)(4), IAA, and 386(2)(1), Commercial Code.

[1648] ss.162(2)(4), IAA, and 386(2)(3), Commercial Code.

[1649] ss.162(2)(4), IAA, and 386(2)(4), Commercial Code. The wording of the clause 386(2)(4) of the Commercial Code (in the English translation of the Code) is "a copy of the articles of association or partnership agreement of the company". Thus, it appears that partnerships which are authorised to engage in insurance mediation in third countries may be authorised by the EFSA to open a branch in Estonia, in order to provide insurance mediation there.

[1650] ss.162(2)(4), IAA and 386(2)(5), Commercial Code.

[1651] s.162(2)(5), IAA.

contracts that the intermediary wishes to mediate in Estonia,[1652] and a copy of the valid liability insurance contract that section 134 of the IAA provides for, or of the intermediary's guarantee contract with an insurance company or a credit or financial institution.[1653] The third country intermediary also must submit to the EFSA the permission of its home state's financial supervision authority for it to establish a branch in Estonia,[1654] and confirmation from the latter authority that the intermediary has the right to provide mediation in its home country and that it conducts its activities in a correct way and in accordance with the public interest.[1655]

Sections 134,[1656] 138[1657] and 147[1658] of the IAA apply to the processing of applications for the authorisation, and adequacy of resources, for the establishment by a third country intermediary of a branch in Estonia, and to verification of the submitted information and of the intermediary's financial circumstances, organisational structure and technical systems.[1659] If the third country intermediary, upon application for authorisation for the foundation of a branch in Estonia, has not submitted all the necessary documents and information to the EFSA, or if these items are not complete or "have not been prepared in accordance with the requirements",[1660] then the EFSA shall require the applicant to remove these deficiencies within an additional period that it has set for this purpose.[1661]

The EFSA shall take a decision to grant, or to refuse to grant, an authorisation for a third country intermediary to found a branch, within two months of receipt of all the required documents and information, and within three months of submission of the application,[1662] and shall promptly inform the intermediary of this decision.[1663] The EFSA shall

---

[1652] s.161(2)(6), IAA.

[1653] s.161(2)(7), IAA. See notes 1565, 1566 and 1567, for the requirements of section 134 of the IAA.

[1654] s.161(3)(1), IAA.

[1655] s.161(3)(2), IAA.

[1656] See notes 1565, 1566 and 1567, for the requirements of section 134 of the IAA.

[1657] See note 1569, for the requirements of section 138 of the IAA.

[1658] See note 1570, for the requirements of section 147 of the IAA.

[1659] s.162(1), IAA.

[1660] Subsection 162(1^1) of the IAA does not state what these requirements are. The quoted phrase probably refers to the requirements in the IAA for the establishment of a branch in Estonia of a third country insurance intermediary.

[1661] s.162(1^1), IAA.

[1662] s.162(2), IAA.

[1663] s.162(3), IAA.

enter the business name and commercial registry code of the branch in the list of authorised intermediaries, together with the address of its seat in Estonia and the name of its director.[1664]

The EFSA may refuse to grant an authorisation for the establishment of a branch in Estonia of a third country intermediary, if the documents or information submitted upon application for the authorisation do not satisfy the requirements of the IAA or its secondary legislation, or are incorrect, misleading, or incomplete,[1665] the branch's director does not comply with the requirements of section 138 of the IAA that concern a member of the management board of an insurance broker,[1666] the intermediary's resources are inadequate to engage in mediation in Estonia,[1667] the foundation of the branch may harm the interests of policyholders, insured persons or beneficiaries,[1668] the intermediary does not have a valid liability insurance contract or a guarantee contract with an insurance company or a credit or financial institution,[1669] the intermediary does not satisfy the requirements of the IAA,[1670] or the third country's financial supervision authority "has no legal basis or possibilities for cooperation with" the EFSA, and, therefore, the EFSA is unable to exercise adequate supervision over the branch.[1671] The EFSA may revoke an authorisation for the establishment of a branch in Estonia of a third country intermediary, and delete an intermediary from the list of authorised intermediaries, if the intermediary has submitted incorrect information to the EFSA,[1672] has repeatedly or substantially contravened the requirements of Estonian legislation, which may damage policyholders', insured persons' or beneficiaries' interests,[1673] does not submit reports on its branch (as necessary),[1674] or has not implemented a precept of the EFSA that relates to the branch's activities, within the period or the extent prescribed,[1675] or if the branch does not fulfil the requirements for the provision of an authorisation for the establishment of a branch.[1676]

1664 s.162(4), IAA.
1665 s.163(1), IAA.
1666 s.163(2), IAA. See note 1569, for the requirements of section 138 of the IAA.
1667 s.163(3), IAA.
1668 s.163(4), IAA.
1669 ss.163(5) and 161(2)(7), IAA.
1670 s.163(5), IAA.
1671 s.163(6), IAA.
1672 s.164(1)(1), IAA.
1673 s.164(1)(2), IAA.
1674 s.164(1)(4), IAA.
1675 s.164(1)(5), IAA.
1676 s.164(1)(3), IAA.

The EFSA shall promptly notify the intermediary, and the third country's financial supervision authority, of a decision to revoke an authorisation for the establishment of a branch and to delete an intermediary from the list of authorised intermediaries[1677] As soon as the intermediary becomes aware of these events, it shall cease mediation business in Estonia by the due date that the EFSA specifies.[1678] The EFSA is required to inform the third country's financial supervision authority of the coercive measures and sanctions that it imposes on the branch.[1679] The EFSA may refuse to revoke an authorisation for the establishment of a branch, if the branch's policyholders, insured persons or beneficiaries have claims against it, or against the intermediary that has founded it.[1680]

An intermediary that is authorised to engage in mediation in a third country, is required to apply for an authorisation from the EFSA in order to provide cross-border mediation in Estonia.[1681] Upon application for authorisation for cross-border mediation, the intermediary must submit a written application, and the following documents and information, to the EFSA:[1682] the intermediary's business name and address,[1683] its audited annual reports for the most recent two financial years,[1684] a list of the types of insurance contract that the intermediary wishes to mediate in Estonia,[1685] and a liability insurance contract that satisfies the requirements of section 134 of the IAA and which is effective in Estonia, or a guarantee contract with an insurance company, credit institution or financial institution.[1686] In addition to these items, a third country intermediary is to submit to the EFSA the consent of its home country's financial supervision authority to its engagement in cross-border mediation in Estonia, and a confirmation that it has the right to provide mediation in its home state.[1687] If the intermediary has not submitted all of the documents and information, or if these items do not fulfil the requirements of the IAA

[1677] s.164(2), IAA.
[1678] s.164(3), IAA.
[1679] s.164(4), IAA.
[1680] s.164(5), IAA.
[1681] s.165^{1}(1), IAA.
[1682] s.165^{1}(1), IAA.
[1683] s.165^{1}(1)(1), IAA.
[1684] s.165^{1}(1)(2), IAA.
[1685] s.165^{1}(1)(3), IAA.
[1686] s.165^{1}(1)(4), IAA. See notes 1565, 1566 and 1567, for the requirements of section 134 of the IAA
[1687] s.165^{1}(2), IAA.

or its secondary legislation, then the EFSA shall require the applicant to remove the deficiencies within a term that it provides.[1688]

The EFSA may refuse to grant an authorisation to a third country intermediary to engage in cross-border mediation in Estonia, if the documents and information submitted upon application for the authorisation do not satisfy the requirements of the EFSA or its delegated legislation and the applicant has not eliminated the deficiencies within an additional period that the EFSA specifies,[1689] the documents or information submitted upon application for the authorisation are inaccurate, misleading or incomplete,[1690] the intermediary's resources are not adequate to attain the requirements that apply in Estonia with regard to mediation,[1691] the intermediary's activities in Estonia may harm the interests of policyholders, insured persons or beneficiaries,[1692] the intermediary's guarantee contract with an insurance undertaking, credit institution or financial institution, or its liability insurance contract, does not comply with the requirements of section 134 of the IAA or is ineffective in Estonia,[1693] or the third country's financial supervision authority "has no legal basis, possibilities or readiness for sufficient and efficient cooperation with" the EFSA, and, therefore, the EFSA is unable to exert adequate supervision over the intermediary.[1694] The EFSA shall take a decision to grant, or to refuse to grant, an authorisation for cross-border mediation within two months of its receipt of all necessary, conforming documents and information and "compliance with requirements",[1695] and within three months of the submission of an application for authorisation for cross-border mediation.[1696] The EFSA shall promptly notify the intermediary of its decision to grant, or refuse to grant, the latter an authorisation for cross-border mediation,[1697] and, if

---

[1688] s.165^{1}(3), IAA.
[1689] s.165^{1}(4)(1), IAA.
[1690] s.165^{1}(4)(2), IAA.
[1691] s.165^{1}(4)(3), IAA.
[1692] s.165^{1}(4)(4), IAA.
[1693] s.165^{1}(4)(5), IAA.
[1694] s.165^{1}(4)(6), IAA.
[1695] Subsection 165^{1}(5) of the IAA does not state what these requirements are. They are, most likely, the requirements for the EFSA to grant an authorisation to a third country intermediary to engage in cross-border mediation in Estonia, which are described in the previous paragraph
[1696] s.165^{1}(5), IAA.
[1697] s.165^{1}(6), IAA.

granted, shall enter the intermediary's business name and address (in its home state) in the list of authorised intermediaries.[1698]

The EFSA may revoke an authorisation granted to a third country intermediary to provide cross-border mediation in Estonia, and delete an intermediary from the list of authorised intermediaries, if the intermediary has submitted incorrect information upon its application for authorisation for cross-border mediation, which was of material significance in the decision to grant the authorisation,[1699] has failed to inform the EFSA of the change to the information,[1700] has not implemented a precept of the EFSA concerning the cross-border mediation by the due date or to the extent prescribed,[1701] has repeatedly or substantially breached the provisions of legislation that regulates its activities,[1702] or does not fulfil the requirements for the EFSA to grant an authorisation for cross-border mediation.[1703] The EFSA shall promptly communicate a decision to revoke an authorisation for cross-border mediation, and to remove an intermediary from the list of authorised intermediaries, to the intermediary and to the third country's financial supervision authority.[1704] After an intermediary becomes aware that the EFSA has revoked its authorisation for cross-border mediation, and that it has been deleted from the list of authorised intermediaries, it shall stop conducting mediation business in Estonia by the date that the EFSA specifies for this cessation.[1705] The EFSA may refuse to revoke the authorisation for cross-border mediation at the intermediary's request, if its policyholders, insured persons or beneficiaries have claims against it, or if the revocation would harm the interests of these policyholders, insured persons or beneficiaries.[1706]

The foundation of a branch is a 'capital movement' in Title I(1) of the nomenclature in Annex I. Furthermore, insurance mediation comprises operations that are "necessary for the purposes of capital movements",[1707] and is, therefore, a 'capital movement' in Title X of the nomenclature in Annex I. If the EFSA refuses to grant an authorisation for a third country insurance intermediary to establish an Estonian branch or to engage in

[1698] s.165^{1}(7), IAA.
[1699] s.165^{1}(9)(1), IAA.
[1700] s.165^{1}(9)(2), IAA.
[1701] s.165^{1}(9)(3), IAA.
[1702] s.165^{1}(9)(4), IAA.
[1703] s.165^{1}(9)(5), IAA.
[1704] s.165^{1}(10), IAA.
[1705] s.165^{1}(11), IAA.
[1706] s.165^{1}(12), IAA.
[1707] Annex I.

cross-border insurance mediation in Estonia, or revokes such an authorisation, then it limits the free movement of capital.

For the restrictive measures to be justified under Article 65(1)(b) of the TFEU, they must be necessary for the protection of the interests that they are intended to guarantee, be proportionate, and observe the requirements of legal certainty (i.e. be specific, objective and known to the parties beforehand); furthermore, the persons affected by the measures must have access to legal redress (i.e. intervention should be accompanied by reasons and subject to review by the national courts).[1708] Some of the restrictive measures do not observe the requirements of legal certainty. For instance, subsection 163(4) and clause 165^{1}(4)(4) of the IAA enable the EFSA to refuse to grant an authorisation to the third country intermediary to establish a branch and to engage in cross-border insurance mediation, respectively, if the foundation of the branch, or the intermediary's activities in Estonia, may harm the interests of policyholders, insured persons or beneficiaries.[1709] As the IAA does not define the activities that damage the interests of these parties, nor state a threshold for this harm, these provisions of the IAA are neither specific nor objective. In addition, the IAA does not require the EFSA to give reasons for a decision to refuse to grant an authorisation for the foundation of a branch or the engagement in cross-border mediation, or to withdraw this authorisation. Furthermore, the IAA does not provide a right of appeal against a decision to refuse to grant, or to revoke, an authorisation, in the domestic courts. Hence, the insurance intermediary is not provided with legal certainty. Thus, Article 65(1)(b) does not justify the restrictive measures.

For Article 64(2) of the TFEU to justify the restrictive measures, the EU institutions must carefully take account of the objective of the free movement of capital whilst enacting the applicable legislation, and the domestic rules should not restrict the free movement of capital more than the equivalent provisions of the relevant Directive do.[1710] The relevant Directive is 2002/92/EC,[1711] which does not mention the movement of capital. Thus, the EU institutions did not carefully consider the objective of the free movement of capital whilst enacting the applicable legislation. In addition, Directive 2002/92/EC does not affect the law of a Member

---

[1708] See the subsection '*The requirements for a successful public policy/public security derogation*', in section 2.1.3.

[1709] See above in this subsection ('*Chapter 10 Division 7 Activities of Foreign Intermediaries in Estonia*').

[1710] See the subsection '*Derogations that apply only to capital movements to/from third countries*', in section 2.3.2.

[1711] See section 2.2.4.

State in respect of insurance mediation activities which are pursued by insurance and reinsurance companies that are founded in a third country, and which operate on that Member State's territory by virtue of the freedom to provide services, provided that all persons who are authorised to conduct insurance mediation on this market are treated equally.[1712] Thus, sections 161, 162, 163, 164 and 165¹ of the IAA hinder the free movement of capital more than do the equivalent provisions of the relevant Directive. Consequently, the restrictive measures are not justified under Article 64(2) of the TFEU. Hence, the rules of Chapter 10 Division 7 of the IAA that regulate the provision of insurance mediation in Estonia by intermediaries which are authorised to engage in insurance mediation in a third country, contravene Article 63 of the TFEU.

Chapter 11 Division 1: General Supervision over Insurance Activities and Mediation

The EFSA exercises supervision over the compliance of the activities of persons who provide insurance services and mediation in Estonia, with the IAA and other legislation that regulates their activities.[1713] The purpose of supervision is to ensure that the establishment, activities, and dissolution of insurance companies and intermediaries comply with Estonian legislation, whilst giving particular attention to protection of the rights and interests of the policyholders, insured persons and beneficiaries.[1714]

The EFSA exerts supervision over branches of Estonian insurance undertakings and of Estonian intermediaries that are established in a (non-Estonian) Contracting State, and over cross-border insurance services or mediation in (non-Estonian) Contracting States by these undertakings or

---

[1712] Article 1(3), Directive 2002/92/EC.

[1713] s.167(1), IAA. The EFSA also exerts supervision over persons who have a qualifying holding in an insurance firm, and third parties from whom operations that relate to insurance activities are outsourced pursuant to section 65 of the IAA (s.167(1), IAA). The IAA does not define 'qualifying holding'. Section 65 of the IAA contains the conditions under which an insurance firm is permitted to outsource its operations to third parties. The insurance company may outsource the following operations, provided that they are related to insurance activities: the assessment of the value of insured items, the conclusion of insurance contracts, the adjustment of the losses that arise from insurance contracts, the management of assets or investments, accounting, the management of information systems, internal audit functions, and other activities that the EFSA has provided the insurance undertaking with permission to outsource (s.3(6), IAA).

[1714] s.167(2), IAA.

intermediaries.[1715] By contrast, the financial supervision authority of a (non-Estonian) Contracting State exercises supervision over Estonian branches of insurance firms or intermediaries that are authorised in that State, and over cross-border insurance activities or mediation in Estonia by those firms and intermediaries.[1716]

The EFSA exercises supervision over a branch of an Estonian insurance company or intermediary that is established in a third country, or cross-border insurance activities or mediation in that state, unless the third country's financial supervision authority and the EFSA have agreed otherwise.[1717] The EFSA exerts supervision over an Estonian branch of a third country insurance undertaking or intermediary, and over cross-border insurance services or mediation in Estonia that such a company or intermediary provides, unless the third country's financial supervision authority and the EFSA have agreed otherwise.[1718]

Thus, within the EEA, the identity of the home country of the insurance firm or intermediary determines the financial supervision authority that is to supervise insurance activities and insurance mediation. By contrast, if the insurance activities or mediation are provided between Estonia and a third country, then the EFSA supervises these services – unless the two authorities have agreed that the third country's financial supervision authority will oversee them.

In its exercise of supervision, the EFSA shall determine the grant, amendment and withdrawal of the authorisations for which the IAA provides,[1719] verify all items that relate to the acquisition, increase or reduction of shareholdings,[1720] perform the registration and approvals for which the IAA provides,[1721] monitor whether the activities of the insurance firm or intermediary comply with the law,[1722] monitor an insurance undertaking's compliance with the scheme of operations,[1723] monitor the insurance company's or intermediary's organisation of its accounting,[1724] monitor the adequacy and efficiency the insurance firm's or intermediary's

[1715] s.167(3), IAA.
[1716] s.167(5), IAA.
[1717] s.167(4), IAA.
[1718] s.167(5), IAA.
[1719] s.168(1), IAA.
[1720] s.168(2), IAA.
[1721] s.168(3), IAA.
[1722] s.168(4), IAA.
[1723] s.168(5), IAA.
[1724] s.168(6), IAA.

internal control system,[1725] verify the compliance of an insurance undertaking's required solvency margin, technical provisions, financial liabilities, and the assets covering these technical provisions, with the provisions of the IAA,[1726] verify the presence and sufficiency of the means that are necessary for the supply of assistance, which are at the disposal of an insurance company that holds an authorisation for assistance insurance,[1727] verify the adequacy of the rules of procedure for the assessment of insured risks and the adjustment of losses,[1728] verify the compliance of the insurance firm's reinsurance programme with the requirements that the IAA has established and "their correspondence to the nature of the insured risks",[1729] issue (as required) mandatory precepts to insurance companies and intermediaries,[1730] and perform other duties that arise from Acts or delegated legislation issued on the basis thereof, and duties that arise from the protection of interests of policyholders, insured persons and beneficiaries.[1731] In order to exercise supervision, the EFSA has the right to demand documents, information, and oral or written explanations, which concern facts that are relevant in the exercise of supervision, from the following persons: insurance undertakings, their managers, and their employees,[1732] intermediaries, their managers, and their employees,[1733] managers and employees of companies that belong to the same consolidation group as insurance firms or intermediaries,[1734] shareholders of insurance undertakings,[1735] shareholders or unit-holders of intermediaries,[1736] liquidators, trustees in bankruptcy, or special regime trustees of insurance firms or intermediaries,[1737] state and local government agencies,[1738] and authorised data processors of state

---

[1725] s.168(6), IAA.
[1726] ss.168(7)-(9), IAA.
[1727] s.168(10), IAA.
[1728] s.168(11), IAA.
[1729] s.168(12), IAA. It is unclear from the wording of the English translation of the IAA whether the insurance company's reinsurance programme, or the requirements that the IAA has established, are to correspond to the insured risks.
[1730] s.168(13), IAA.
[1731] s.168(14), IAA.
[1732] s.170(1)(1), IAA.
[1733] s.170(1)(2), IAA.
[1734] s.170(1)(3), IAA.
[1735] s.170(1)(4), IAA.
[1736] s.170(1)(4), IAA.
[1737] s.170(1)(5), IAA.
[1738] s.170(1)(6), IAA.

databases.[1739] The EFSA has the right to require this information from third parties (in order to exercise supervision), only if there is a justified need for it.[1740]

The EFSA has a right to issue a precept, if upon its exercise of supervision, it has discovered contraventions of the IAA, the IFA, the SMA, the CIA, the PIA, the Funded Pensions Act, the Motor Third Party Liability Insurance Act, the Estonian Central Register of Securities Act, the Guarantee Fund Act, the Money Laundering and Terrorist Financing Prevention Act, the International Sanctions Act, or the secondary legislation of any of these Acts,[1741] for the prevention of breaches of any of these laws,[1742] or if circumstances that endanger, or may endanger, the activities of an insurance company or an intermediary, the interests of policyholders, insured persons or beneficiaries, or the insurance market's reliability or transparability.[1743] Furthermore, by issuing a precept, the EFSA "has the right" to forbid a Contracting State insurance undertaking or intermediary from engaging in insurance activities in Estonia and to prohibit an Estonian insurance firm or intermediary from practising such activities in a Contracting State.[1744]

Transfers that relate to insurance contracts that cross a national boundary are 'capital movements' in Title X of the nomenclature in Annex I. If the EFSA issues a precept, then it limits the free movement of capital.

Article 65(1)(b) of the TFEU permits Member States "to take all requisite measures to prevent infringements of national law and regulations, in particular in the field of taxation and the prudential supervision of financial institutions", even if this is contrary to Article 63 of the TFEU.[1745] To be justified under Article 65(1)(b) of the TFEU, the restrictive measures must be necessary for the protection of interests that they are intended to guarantee, be proportionate, and observe the requirements of legal certainty (i.e. be specific, objective, and known to the parties beforehand); furthermore, the persons whom the measures affect must have access to legal redress (i.e. intervention should be

---

[1739] s.170(1)(6), IAA.

[1740] s.170(2), IAA.

[1741] ss.172(1), IAA, and 2(1) and 6(1)(7), Financial Supervision Authority Act 2001.

[1742] s.172(2), IAA.

[1743] s.172(3), IAA.

[1744] ss.173(4)-(5), IAA. Section 173 of the IAA grants 11 further rights to the EFSA, upon its issue of a precept.

[1745] The TFEU does not define 'financial institution'. However, in this context, insurance firms and insurance intermediaries qualify.

accompanied by a formal statement of reasons and subject to review in the national courts).[1746] The reason for the issue of a precept that subsection 172(3) of the IAA contains is neither specific nor objective, and, therefore, does not fulfil the requirements of legal certainty. Furthermore, Division 1 of Chapter 11 of the IAA neither requires the EFSA to provide reasons for it to issue a precept, nor gives the insurance company or intermediary a right to appeal against the issue of the precept in the Estonian courts. Thus, sections 172 and 173 of the IAA are not justified by Article 65(1)(b) of the TFEU. Therefore, these provisions contravene Article 63 of the TFEU.

If an Estonian insurance firm or intermediary that engages in cross-border insurance activities or mediation in a foreign state,[1747] or whose branch is established in a foreign state, breaches the requirements of that country's legislation, then, on a proposal from the foreign state's financial supervision authority, the EFSA shall promptly apply measures for the cessation of the contravention.[1748] In the course of the exercise of its supervision, the EFSA may perform the on-site inspection for which section 175 of the IAA provides,[1749] on a branch of an insurance firm or intermediary that is situated in a foreign country.[1750] The EFSA is to promptly inform the financial supervision of a Contracting State in which an insurance company has established a branch, or provides cross-border services, of revocation of the authorisation and of precepts that sections 37

[1746] See the subsection '*The requirements for a successful public policy/public security derogation*', in section 2.1.3.

[1747] See note 1172, for a comment on the term 'foreign state'.

[1748] s.179(1), IAA. The EFSA shall inform the financial supervision authority of the foreign state of the measures taken (s.179(1), IAA).

[1749] In order to exert supervision, the EFSA has the right to perform the on-site inspection of insurance firms, and of companies that belong to the same group as those firms; the EFSA may also inspect intermediaries, companies that are members of the same group as these intermediaries, and third parties to whom operations relating to insurance activities are outsourced pursuant to section 65 of the IAA (s.175(1), IAA). See note 1713, for a description of outsourcing as determined by the IAA. During on-site inspection, the person who conducts the inspection has the right to enter all premises, request the presence of working conditions that enable the inspection to be made, study documents that are required for the exercise of supervision, make copies, excerpts and transcripts thereof, and monitor the work processes without restrictions, and acquire oral and written explanations from the managers and employees of the person who is being inspected (s.175(3), IAA).

[1750] s.179(2), IAA. If this branch is situated in a Contracting State, then the financial supervision authority of this State has the right to take part in this on-site inspection (s.179(2), IAA).

and 40 of the IAA specify,[1751] and shall, at this time, apply all measures to protect policyholders', insured persons', and beneficiaries' interests.[1752]

A non-Estonian insurance undertaking whose authorisation has been suspended or revoked by the financial supervision authority of its home country, is not to provide insurance services in Estonia.[1753] A foreign intermediary that has been removed from the register of intermediaries, is not to engage in mediation in Estonia.[1754] If a third country insurance firm or intermediary that supplies cross-border insurance services or mediation in Estonia contravenes the requirements of Estonian legislation, then the EFSA may implement measures that are necessary in order to terminate the contravention or revoke an authorisation for the establishment of a branch, the provision of cross-border insurance services, or engagement in cross-border mediation.[1755]

The EFSA may require an insurance company or intermediary from a (non-Estonian) Contracting State to stop its contravention of the requirements of Estonian legislation.[1756] If the insurance undertaking or intermediary continues to breach these requirements, then the EFSA shall inform the Contracting State's financial supervision authority.[1757] If the measures that the latter authority takes are inadequate and the insurance firm or intermediary continues to contravene the requirements of Estonian legislation, then the EFSA may issue a precept to introduce measures that the IAA provides for cessation of the breach, or prohibit the insurance company or intermediary from supplying insurance services or mediation (respectively) in Estonia, and shall inform the Contracting State's financial supervision authority beforehand.[1758] The EFSA shall inform the insurance undertaking or intermediary, and promptly notify the European Commission, of the measures that it has taken.[1759]

[1751] Section 37 of the IAA lays down circumstances under which the EFSA may issue a precept to forbid an Estonian insurance undertaking from providing insurance services through a branch located in a (non-Estonian) EEA state (see notes 1213, 1214 and 1215, and accompanying text). Section 40 of the IAA states conditions under which the EFSA may issue a precept to prohibit an Estonian insurance firm from engaging in cross-border insurance activities in a (non-Estonian) EEA country (see notes 1229 and 1230, and accompanying text).

[1752] s.179(3), IAA.

[1753] s.180(1), IAA.

[1754] s.180(1), IAA.

[1755] s.180(3), IAA.

[1756] s.180(4), IAA.

[1757] s.180(5), IAA.

[1758] s.180(6), IAA.

[1759] ss.180(7)-(8), IAA.

The establishment of a branch is a 'capital movement' in Title I(1) of the nomenclature in Annex I. The provision of cross-border insurance services and mediation are 'capital movements' in Title X of the nomenclature in Annex I.[1760] If the EFSA applies measures or issues a precept in order to terminate the contravention of Estonian or foreign legislation by an insurance undertaking or intermediary, or to prohibit the provision of insurance services or mediation by these respective entities (in Estonia or in a foreign country), then it breaches the free movement of capital.

Article 65(1)(b) of the TFEU gives Member States the right "to take all requisite measures to prevent infringements of national law and regulations, in particular in the field of taxation and the prudential supervision of financial institutions", even if these measures contravene Article 63 of the TFEU. However, for Article 65(1)(b) of the TFEU to apply, the restrictive measures must be necessary for the protection of interests that they are intended to guarantee, be proportionate, and observe the requirements of legal certainty (i.e. be specific, objective, and known to the parties beforehand); furthermore, the persons who are affected by the measures must have access to legal redress (i.e. intervention should be supported by a formal statement of reasons and be open to review by the courts).[1761]

Sections 179 and 180 of the IAA do not require the EFSA to provide reasons for applying measures or issuing a precept to terminate the breach of legislation or to prohibit the supply of insurance services or mediation. Furthermore, the IAA does not furnish the insurance firm or intermediary with the right to appeal in the Estonian courts against the decision to apply the measures or to issue a precept. Thus, Article 65(1)(b) of the TFEU does not justify the restrictive measures.

Subsection 179(1) of the IAA applies to insurance services and mediation to third countries. Subsections 180(1) and 180(3) of the IAA regulate insurance services and mediation from these territories. Article 64(2) of the TFEU states that, whilst attempting to achieve the objective of the free movement of capital between Member States and third countries as far as possible and without prejudice to the EU Treaties,[1762] the European Parliament and the Council, under the ordinary legislative

---

[1760] Insurance mediation comprises operations that are "necessary for the purposes of capital movements" (Annex I).

[1761] See the subsection '*The requirements for a successful public policy/public security derogation*', in section 2.1.3.

[1762] The EU Treaties are the Treaty on European Union and the TFEU.

procedure,[1763] shall adopt measures on the movement of capital to or from third countries that involve direct investment, establishment, the provision of financial services, or the admission of securities to capital markets. Thus, the EU may limit the free movement of capital between Member States and third countries, if it legislates over these areas, provided that the EU institutions carefully consider the free movement of capital, whilst enacting this legislation.[1764] Furthermore, for Article 64(2) of the TFEU to apply, the national provisions must not restrict the free movement of capital more than the equivalent rules in the relevant Directive do.[1765]

The relevant Directives are 2009/138/EC for insurance services and 2002/92/EC for insurance mediation. Directive 2002/92/EC does not mention the free movement of capital. Thus, Article 64(2) of the TFEU does not justify subsections 179(1), 180(1) and 180(3) of the IAA with respect to engagement in insurance mediation.

Directive 2009/138/EC refers to the free movement of capital in Recital 72 only. Recital 72 of this Directive states that Member States should not require insurance or reinsurance firms to invest their funds in particular classes of assets, because this requirement could be incompatible with the liberalisation of capital movements for which Article 63 of the TFEU provides. It is debatable whether or not this reference to the free movement of capital is sufficient to demonstrate that the EU institutions have taken account of the objective of the free movement of capital, whilst enacting Directive 2009/138/EC.[1766]

It is argued above that the IAA restricts the free movement capital more than the Directive 2009/138/EC with respect to the provision of insurance services in third countries by an Estonian insurance company,[1767] and also with respect to the supply of insurance services in Estonia by a third country insurance firm – even though the Chapter IX of Title I of Directive 2009/138/EC contains extensive provisions that regulate the establishment of branches within the EU by insurance (or reinsurance) undertakings that (each) have a head office that is located in a

[1763] Article 294 of the TFEU contains the ordinary legislative procedure.

[1764] See the subsection '*Derogations that apply only to capital movements to/from third countries*', in section 2.3.2.

[1765] See the subsection '*Derogations that apply only to capital movements to/from third countries*', in section 2.3.2.

[1766] See the subsection '*Chapter 2 Division 2: Activities of Estonian Insurance Undertakings in Foreign States*', above in this section.

[1767] See the subsection '*Chapter 2 Division 2: Activities of Estonian Insurance Undertakings in Foreign States*', above in this section.

third country.[1768] In the latter case, subsection 180(3) of the IAA states that the EFSA may take restrictive measures "[i]f a third country insurance undertaking … which engages in insurance activities … in Estonia violates the requirements provided for in this Act or in other legislation". Thus, the restrictive measures in the IAA are incorporated by reference into subsection 180(3) of the IAA. By contrast, subsection 179(1) of the IAA states that the EFSA may apply the restrictive measures on the proposal of the foreign state's financial supervision authority "[i]f an Estonian insurance undertaking who engages in … insurance activities … in a foreign state … violates the requirements of legislation established in the foreign state". Furthermore, subsection 180(1) of the IAA forbids a foreign insurance firm "whose authorisation has been suspended or revoked by the foreign financial supervision authority" from providing insurance services in Estonia. As it is the contravention of the insurance legislation of the foreign state, rather than the breach of the IAA, that is of concern in the application of subsections 179(1) and 180(1) of the IAA, the relevant issue is whether the laws of the foreign country restrict the free movement of capital more than do the equivalent provisions of Directive 2009/138/EC – which is beyond the scope of this book. Thus, in so far as the restrictive measures are based on the breach of the relevant provisions of the IAA (rather than of the insurance laws of a third country), they limit the free movement of capital more than the equivalent provisions in Directive 2009/138/EC do, and, therefore, Article 64(2) of the TFEU does not justify them. This is true for subsection 180(3) of the IAA.

In summary, sections 179 and 180 of the IAA are not justified by either Article 64(2) or Article 65(1)(b) of the TFEU, and, therefore, are contrary to Article 63 of the TFEU. This is subject to the qualification that the insurance services aspect of subsections 179(1) and 180(1) of the IAA may remain intact, because the relevant assessment involves the legislation of third countries rather than that of Estonia. However, if Recital 72 of Directive 2009/138/EC is considered to be insufficient to establish that the EU institutions carefully took account of the objective of the free movement of capital whilst enacting this Directive, then this qualification does not apply.

[1768] See the subsection '*Chapter 2 Division 3: Activities of Foreign Insurance Undertakings in Estonia*', above in this section.

Section 186: Supervision over Consolidation Group – co-operation with financial supervision authority of Contracting State

If two insurance firms that are authorised to provide insurance services in Estonia and another Contracting State, respectively, have a common parent undertaking[1769] that is an insurance holding company,[1770] third country insurance firm, or mixed-activity insurance company,[1771] then the EFSA shall agree with the financial supervision authority of the other Contracting State as to who is to exercise supplementary supervision over the insurance firm.[1772] If an Estonian insurance company is related to an insurance firm from (another) Contracting State, then the EFSA is to communicate the necessary information that allows or facilitates the exercise of supplementary supervision to the financial supervision authority of that Contracting State, at the latter authority's request.[1773] The EFSA shall transmit, on its own initiative, to the financial supervision authority of the (non-Estonian) Contracting State, all other information which that authority needs for the exercise of supplementary supervision (in the EFSA's opinion).[1774]

[1769] A 'parent undertaking' is a person who controls at least one legal person pursuant to subsections 10(1) and 10(2) of the SMA (s.5(1), IAA). See note 724, for subsection 10(1) of the SMA. Voting rights that are held by a company that is controlled by a person, are deemed to be held by the person who is a general partner or limited partner of the company who has the right to appoint or remove the majority of the members of the company's management board or supervisory board (ss.10(2) and 10(1)(2), SMA)).

[1770] An 'insurance holding company' is a parent undertaking that is not a mixed financial holding company, but the majority or all of whose subsidiaries are insurance firms (s.5(3), IAA). A 'mixed financial holding company' is a parent undertaking that is not an insurance firm, credit institution or investment firm, which has at least one subsidiary that is an insurance company, credit institution or investment firm of any Contracting State and which, together with its subsidiaries, forms a financial conglomerate (s.5(5), IAA).

[1771] A 'mixed-activity insurance holding company' is a parent undertaking that is not an insurance firm, insurance holding company or mixed financial holding company, and which has at least one subsidiary that is an insurance firm (s.5(4), IAA).

[1772] s.186(1), IAA. Although the English translation of the IAA does not specify whether the insurance firm over which supplementary provision is to be exercised is the Estonian insurance undertaking or that of the other Contracting State, it is likely to refer to the Estonian insurance firm.

[1773] s.186(2), IAA.

[1774] s.186(2), IAA.

The transmission of information is not a 'capital movement' in the nomenclature in Annex I. Consequently, section 186 of the IAA does not contravene Article 63 of the TFEU.

Section 197: Supervision over subsidiary of entity located in third country

If no supervision is exercised at the level of the financial conglomerate,[1775] on the basis of section 191 of the IAA,[1776] over an insurance undertaking, credit institution or investment firm whose parent undertaking is a third country mixed financial holding company, insurance undertaking, credit institution or investment firm, then the EFSA (if a 'co-ordinator' pursuant to section 189 of the IAA)[1777] shall assess the

[1775] A 'financial conglomerate' (for the purposes of the IAA) is a group that contains at least one insurance undertaking, credit institution, or investment firm, one or more of the entities in the group is within the insurance sector, at least one of the group companies is within the banking sector, the consolidated activities of the entities in each of these sectors are 'significant' in the consolidation group (i.e. the ratio of the balance sheet total of the group's entities within that sector to those in the whole group, and the ratio of the required solvency margin of the group's entities with the sector to those in the whole group, are both more than 0.1, or the assets of the group's entities within that sector exceed 6 billion euros), and either the parent undertaking is an entity that is an insurance company, credit institution or investment firm which is also a parent company of an organisation within, with "a participation" in an entity within, or which has a dominant influence in an entity within, the financial sector, or the group is not headed by an insurance firm, credit institution or insurance undertaking but the balance sheet total of the financial sector entities within the group exceeds 40% of the group 's balance sheet total (ss.187(1)-(2) and 188(2)-(4), IAA). See note 1769, for the definition of 'parent undertaking'.

[1776] In order to exercise supervision over the financial conglomerate, the EFSA and the financial supervision authority of the (non-Estonian) Contracting State that granted an authorisation to an insurance undertaking, credit institution or investment firm, which is a member of a financial conglomerate, and the financial supervision authority of the country in which a mixed financial holding company is situated, shall appoint from among themselves a co-ordinator who is responsible for the exercise of supervision over the financial conglomerate (s.189(1), IAA). The co-ordinator is to exert supervision at financial conglomerate level over an insurance undertaking, credit institution or investment firm 1) which heads the financial conglomerate, 2) the parent undertaking of which is a mixed financial holding company of a Contracting State (including Estonia), or 3) which has a dominant influence in another company within the financial sector, or in which a firm in the financial sector has dominant influence (s.191(1), IAA). See note 1770, for the definition of a 'mixed financial holding company'.

[1777] See note 1776, for subsection 189(1) of the IAA. Subsections 189(2) and 189(3) of the IAA contain rules that determine the circumstances under which the equivalence of the supervision that the third country's financial supervision authority exerts to the requirements for supervision at the level of the financial conglomerate that this Division of the IAA establishes.[1778] In this assessment of equivalence, the EFSA shall follow the guidelines of the Joint Committee of European Supervisory Authorities,[1779] and pass a resolution that concerns equivalence, after consulting the financial supervision authorities of the relevant Contracting States.[1780]

If, pursuant to this resolution, the supervision that third country's financial supervision authority exercises is not equivalent to the supervision at financial conglomerate level that corresponds to the requirements that this Division of the IAA establishes,[1781] then the supervision over the activities of the insurance undertaking, credit institution or investment firm is to be exercised at financial conglomerate level by the EFSA.[1782] If the financial supervision authority is not a co-ordinator, then supervision at financial conglomerate level shall be exercised by the co-ordinator that is appointed pursuant to section 189 of the IAA.[1783]

If the provisions of subsection 197(4) of the IAA are not applicable,[1784] then the EFSA as the co-ordinator has the right, upon agreement with other relevant financial supervision authorities, to apply other means of supervision that ensure supervision at financial conglomerate level over

---

EFSA is to be appointed the co-ordinator. Section 190(1) of the IAA states the EFSA's tasks as co-ordinator in the exercise of supervision over a financial conglomerate.

1778 s.197(1), IAA. This Division is Division 3 (Supervision over Financial Conglomerates) of Chapter 11 (Supervision over Insurance Activities and Mediation) of the IAA.

1779 The Joint Committee of European Supervisory Authorities comprises the Chairpersons of the European Supervisory Authorities (i.e. the European Banking Authority, the European Insurance and Occupational Pensions Authority, and the European Securities and Markets Authority), and as far as is applicable, the Chairperson of the Sub-Committee on Financial Conglomerates, and of any other sub-committees that the Joint Committee of European Supervisory Authorities establishes (Articles 55(1) and 57, Regulation (EU) No 1093/2010, Articles 55(1) and 57, Regulation (EU) No 1094/2010, and Articles 55(1) and 57, Regulation (EU) No 1095/2010).

1780 s.197(2), IAA.

1781 See note 1778.

1782 s.197(4), IAA.

1783 s.197(4), IAA. See note 1776, for subsection 189(1) of the IAA. See note 1777, for subsections 189(2)-(3) of the IAA.

1784 See the previous paragraph, for subsection 197(4) of the IAA.

the activities of an insurance undertaking, credit institution or investment firm within a financial conglomerate that complies with the objectives of this supervision, and shall (specifically) require that a mixed financial holding company be established in a Contracting State.[1785] The EFSA shall inform the European Commission and the other relevant financial supervision authorities of the forms of supervision that it applies.[1786]

The decision as to whether a financial supervision authority is appointed the co-ordinator for supervision of a financial conglomerate, the application of equivalence of supervision rules, and the empowerment of a financial supervision authority to apply other means of supervision if it is not the co-ordinator, are not 'capital movements' in the nomenclature in Annex I. Furthermore, although the establishment of new undertakings that are fully owned by the person who provides the capital is a 'capital movement' in the nomenclature in Annex I, a mixed financial holding company is to be founded as a parent company, and is, therefore, not owned by the Estonian insurance undertaking, credit institution or investment firm.[1787] Thus, section 197 of the IAA does not breach Article 63 of the TFEU.

Section 198: Information necessary for exercise of supervision at financial conglomerate level and co-operation between the EFSA and other financial supervision authorities

Upon the exercise of supervision at the level of the financial conglomerate, the EFSA shall co-operate with the financial supervision authority of the Contracting State that granted an authorisation to an insurance undertaking, credit institution, or investment firm within a financial conglomerate and the co-ordinator, unless the EFSA has been appointed as the co-ordinator pursuant to section 189 of the IAA.[1788] These financial supervision authorities shall submit to each other information that is necessary for the exercise of supervision over the activities of an insurance undertaking, credit institution or investment firm, for the exercise of supervision at the level of the financial conglomerate, or is otherwise significant for the particular financial supervision authority.[1789] The EFSA shall collect and forward information on the following: the

[1785] s.197(5), IAA. See note 1770, for the definition of a 'mixed financial holding company'.
[1786] s.197(6), IAA.
[1787] See the definition of 'mixed financial holding company', in note 1770.
[1788] s.198(1), IAA. See note 1776, for subsection 189(1) of the IAA. See note 1777, for subsections 189(2)-(3) of the IAA.
[1789] s.198(2), IAA.

financial conglomerate's entities and structure,[1790] strategy,[1791] financial circumstances,[1792] management scheme,[1793] internal control system,[1794] and risk management principles,[1795] persons who have a 10% or greater holding in all of the financial conglomerate's constituent companies,[1796] the financial supervision authorities that exert supervision over the activities of insurance undertakings, credit institutions and investment firms within the financial conglomerate,[1797] procedures for the collection, and the verification, of information from a financial conglomerate's constituent entities,[1798] events from a company within the financial conglomerate that may have a significant effect on an insurance undertaking, credit institution or investment firm within this group,[1799] and exceptional measures that the EFSA takes concerning an insurance undertaking, credit institution or investment firm.[1800]

The EFSA may exchange information that is necessary for the performance of duties that relate to an Estonian insurance undertaking, credit institution or investment firm that is within a financial conglomerate, with the Bank of Estonia, the Estonian Ministry of Finance, the European Systemic Risk Board, the Joint Committee of European Supervisory Authorities, the European Central Bank, and the central banks that are part of the European System of Central Banks.[1801] The EFSA has the right to ask any company that is established in Estonia and has received its authorisation there (if authorisation is required) or which is part of a financial conglomerate, for information that is necessary for the exercise of supervision and the performance of co-ordination tasks for which this Division of the IAA provides.[1802]

[1790] s.198(3)(1), IAA.
[1791] s.198(3)(2), IAA.
[1792] s.198(3)(3), IAA.
[1793] s.198(3)(4), IAA.
[1794] s.198(3)(5), IAA.
[1795] s.198(3)(5), IAA.
[1796] s.198(3)(4), IAA.
[1797] s.198(3)(6), IAA.
[1798] s.198(3)(7), IAA.
[1799] s.198(3)(8), IAA.
[1800] s.198(3)(9), IAA.
[1801] s.198(4), IAA. The European System of Central Banks comprises the central bank of each Member State and the European Central Bank (Article 282(1), TFEU). Its primary objective is to maintain price stability, although it is also to support the EU's general economic policies, in order to contribute to the EU's objectives (Article 282(2), TFEU).
[1802] s.198(6), IAA. See note 1778, for a description of the Division.

If the EFSA wishes to specify, or to verify, the information, documents or explanations that concern a company within a financial conglomerate, then it shall apply to the financial supervision authority of the corresponding Contracting State for this purpose.[1803] The EFSA shall take the required measures to perform this specification or verification, or to permit the financial supervision authority to which it applies to conduct the specification or verification or to authorise an auditor or expert to carry it out.[1804]

If a decision that the EFSA takes affects supervision that is exercised by the financial supervision authority of a (non-Estonian) Contracting State, then the EFSA shall, before taking this decision, consult that authority on changes in the shareholder, management or organisational structure of an Estonian insurance undertaking, credit institution or investment firm within a financial conglomerate that require the EFSA's authorisation or approval, or major sanctions or exceptional measures that are taken in regard to an Estonian insurance undertaking, credit institution or investment firm within a financial conglomerate.[1805] The EFSA may decide not to consult that Contracting State's financial supervision authority on these issues, in urgent cases or in instances in which this consultation may endanger the effectiveness of a decision.[1806] In these cases, the EFSA shall inform the other authority immediately after the decision comes into force.[1807]

A request for, the provision of, the exchange of, the specification of, and the verification of, information for the purpose of supervision is not a 'capital movement' in the nomenclature in Annex I. Therefore, section 198 of the IAA does not contravene Article 63 of the TFEU.

3.5 Payment Institutions and E-money Institutions Act 2009 (PIA)

The PIA regulates the supply of payment services and e-money services, the activities and liability of payment institutions and e-money institutions, and supervision over these entities.[1808] It applies to payment institutions that are established and operating in Estonia, Estonian

---

[1803] s.198(9), IAA.
[1804] s.198(10), IAA.
[1805] s.198(12), IAA.
[1806] s.198(13), IAA.
[1807] s.198(13), IAA.
[1808] s.1(1), PIA.

branches of foreign payment institutions, and all other persons who provide payment services or e-money services in Estonia.[1809] The PIA also applies to the activities of Estonian payment institutions and e-money institutions and their branches outside Estonia, unless the relevant foreign legislation provides otherwise.[1810]

For the purposes of the PIA, the following are payment services – if provided for professional or economic activities: services that enable cash to be paid into, and cash to be withdrawn from, payment accounts,[1811] the execution of payment transactions,[1812] the acquisition and issue of payment instruments,[1813] and the remittance of money.[1814] 'Payment transactions' comprise direct debit orders,[1815] transactions that are executed via a payment card,[1816] and credit transfers (including standing orders).[1817] Payment services may be provided by payment institutions,[1818] e-money institutions,[1819] credit institutions,[1820] postal service providers that supply financial services,[1821] the European Central Bank,[1822] and the central banks and governments of Contracting States.[1823]

A 'payment institution' is a company whose permanent activity is the provision of payment services.[1824] In addition to the payment services that the previous paragraph lists, a payment institution may supply ancillary services that are closely related to payment services – including safekeeping activities, foreign exchange services, and data storage and processing,[1825] operate payment systems,[1826] and engage in activities that

[1809] s.2(1), PIA.
[1810] s.2(2), PIA.
[1811] ss.3(1)(1) and 3(1)(2), PIA.
[1812] ss.3(1)(3), 3(1)(4) and 3(1)(7), PIA.
[1813] s.3(1)(5), PIA.
[1814] s.3(1)(6), PIA.
[1815] s.3(2)(1), PIA.
[1816] s.3(2)(2), PIA.
[1817] s.3(2)(3), PIA.
[1818] s.3(6)(1), PIA. See the next paragraph, for a definition of 'payment institution'.
[1819] s.3(6)(2), PIA. See the next paragraph, for a definition of 'e-money institution'.
[1820] s.3(6)(3), PIA. See the first paragraph of section 3.3.1, for a definition of 'credit institution'.
[1821] s.3(6)(4), PIA.
[1822] s.3(6)(5), PIA.
[1823] ss.3(6)(5) and 3(6)(6), PIA.
[1824] s.5(1), PIA.
[1825] s.5(2)(1), PIA.

are unrelated to the provision of payment services (unless Estonian law states otherwise).[1827] An 'e-money institution' is private or public limited company, the permanent activity of which is the issue of e-money in its name.[1828]

In addition to the issue of e-money, an e-money institution may also provide payment services,[1829] grant loans that relate to the supply of payment services,[1830] provide ancillary services that are closely related to the issue or administration of payment services or e-money,[1831] operate payment systems,[1832] and engage in activities that are unrelated to the issue of e-money (unless Estonian law provides otherwise).[1833] Other than e-money institutions,[1834] the following persons may issue e-money: credit institutions,[1835] the European Central Bank,[1836] and the central banks and governments of Contracting States.[1837]

For a company that is established in Estonia to be able to be a payment institution or e-money institution, the EFSA must issue it with a relevant activity licence.[1838] The other entities that may provide payment services

---

[1826] s.5(2)(2), PIA. A 'payment system' is a system for the transfer of funds that operates on the basis of agreed, standardised rules, and which enables payment transactions to be processed and settled (s.3(4), PIA).
[1827] s.5(2)(3), PIA.
[1828] s.7(1), PIA. 'E-money' is monetary value that is stored on an electronic medium, which expresses a monetary claim against the issuer, and satisfies all of the following conditions: it is issued at the par value of the amount of the monetary payment received, used as a payment instrument to execute payment transactions, and accepted as a payment instrument by at least one person who is not its issuer (s.6(1), PIA).
[1829] s.7(2)(1), PIA.
[1830] s.7(2)(2), PIA. Payment institutions and e-money institutions may provide loans under the following conditions: loans are only granted for the execution of a payment transaction, these loans shall be repaid within one year, loans shall not be granted from the funds held or received in order to execute a payment transaction, and the payment institution's own funds shall be adequate to cover the risks that are related to the granted loans (ss.5(4) and 7(2)(2), PIA).
[1831] s.7(2)(3), PIA.
[1832] s.7(2)(4), PIA.
[1833] s.7(2)(5), PIA.
[1834] s.6(7)(1), PIA.
[1835] s.6(7)(3), PIA. See the first paragraph of section 3.3.1, for a definition of 'credit institution'.
[1836] s.6(7)(4), PIA.
[1837] ss.6(7)(4) and 6(7)(5), PIA.
[1838] ss.14(1) and 14(3), PIA.

or issue e-money are not required to apply to the EFSA for an activity licence specifically for this purpose.[1839]

Sections 29 and 30: The supply of services by Estonian payment institutions and e-money institutions in another Contracting State

A payment institution or e-money institution established in Estonia that wishes to open a branch in another Contracting State, shall inform the EFSA of its intention to do so,[1840] and shall submit the following documents and information to the EFSA: the name of the Contracting State in which the branch is to be established,[1841] the names of the branch's managers,[1842] the address of the branch's seat in the Contracting State,[1843] and the business plan of the branch.[1844] This plan shall include information about all of the services that the institution intends to provide through its branch in the Contracting State, describe the branch's organisational structure, and state whether the branch is to use agents.[1845] The EFSA may refuse to review the documents and information, if these items do not satisfy the requirements of the PIA,[1846] are incomplete,[1847] or have not been submitted within the prescribed period.[1848]

The EFSA may take a decision to forward, or to refuse to forward, the documents and information to the financial supervision authority of the (non-Estonian) Contracting State, if the resources of the payment institution or the e-money institution are inadequate for the provision of services specified in the branch's business plan,[1849] the establishment of the branch or the implementation of the business plan may harm the institution's financial situation or the interests of its clients, or may damage the reliability of its activities,[1850] or the items submitted for

---

[1839] ss.14(5)-(6), PIA.
[1840] s.29(1), PIA.
[1841] s.29(1)(1), PIA.
[1842] s.29(1)(2), PIA.
[1843] s.29(1)(3), PIA.
[1844] s.29(1)(4), PIA.
[1845] s.29(1)(4), PIA. If a payment institution or e-money institution wishes to use an agent who is founded in a (non-Estonian) Contracting State, then the use of the agent is deemed to be equivalent to the establishment of a branch, and the provisions of section 29 of the PIA apply (s.29(11), PIA).
[1846] s.29(4)(1), PIA.
[1847] s.29(4)(1), PIA.
[1848] s.29(4)(2), PIA.
[1849] s.29(6)(1), PIA.
[1850] s.29(6)(2), PIA.

forwarding are inaccurate, misleading or incomplete.[1851] Upon forwarding of the documents and information, the EFSA shall also submit information about the amount of the institution's own funds to the (other) Contracting State's financial supervision authority.[1852] The EFSA shall take the decision to forward, or to refuse to forward, the documents and information to the Contracting State's financial supervision authority within one month of the receipt of all of the required items, and shall immediately inform the institution of this decision.[1853]

The EFSA may issue a precept, in order to prohibit the provision of services by an Estonian payment institution or e-money institution through a branch established in a (non-Estonian) Contracting State, if at least one of the grounds provided by subsection 29(6) of the PIA for refusal to forward the documents and information exists,[1854] or if the financial supervision authority of the (non-Estonian) Contracting State has informed the EFSA that the payment institution or e-money institution has breached the conditions for which the legislation of that State provides or which that State's financial supervision authority has established.[1855] The EFSA shall immediately deliver this precept to the payment institution or e-money institution.[1856] On its receipt of the precept, this institution is required to cease the provision of its services through the branch by the date that the EFSA specifies therein.[1857]

A payment institution or e-money institution that is founded in Estonia may establish a branch in a (non-Estonian) Contracting State "pursuant to the provisions of legislation of the Contracting State".[1858] This phrase may mean that the host state is invited to enact the terms under which the Estonian branch may provide services there.[1859]

[1851] s.29(6)(3), PIA.
[1852] s.29(5), PIA.
[1853] s.29(3), PIA.
[1854] s.29(9)(1), PIA. See the previous paragraph, for subsection 29(6) of the PIA.
[1855] s.29(9)(2), PIA.
[1856] s.29(10), PIA.
[1857] s.29(10), PIA.
[1858] s.29(7), PIA.
[1859] Article 36(1) of Directive 2013/36/EU contains a phrase of this type – the competent authority of the host state is empowered to "indicate the conditions under which, in the interests of the general good, [the activities of the credit institution's branch] shall be carried out in the host Member State". However, Article 25 of Directive 2007/64/EC lacks an equivalent phrase (see section 2.2.8).

A payment institution or e-money institution that intends to provide cross-border services in a Contracting State[1860] shall inform the EFSA of this aim,[1861] and shall submit the following documents and information to the EFSA: the name of the country in which it intends to provide cross-border services,[1862] and a description of these planned services.[1863] This description must contain information about the provision of the cross-border services, and whether the institution intends to use agents. [1864] The EFSA may refuse to review the documents and information if they do not fulfil the requirements of the PIA or are incomplete,[1865] or have these deficiencies and the additional documents or information that the EFSA requisitions have not been submitted within the prescribed period.[1866]

The EFSA may take a decision to forward, or to refuse to forward, the documents and information if the items submitted do not satisfy the requirements of the PIA,[1867] are incorrect, misleading or incomplete,[1868] the resources of the payment institution or e-money institution are not adequate for the provision of cross-border services,[1869] or the supply of cross-border services may damage the institution's financial situation or the interests of its clients, or unfavourably affect the reliability of its activities.[1870] The EFSA shall take this decision within one month of its receipt of all the necessary documents and information, and shall immediately inform the institution of the decision.[1871]

The EFSA may issue a precept, in order to forbid the payment institution or e-money institution from providing cross-border services in a (non-Estonian) Contracting State, if one or more of the grounds in

[1860] The English translation of subsections 30(1), 30(6), 30(8) and 30(9) of the PIA refer to a 'foreign state', which the PIA does not define. As these subsections apply to the supply of services by Estonian payment institutions and e-money institutions in both (non-Estonian) Contracting States and third countries, a foreign state may be any country outside Estonia. When reporting on section 30 of the PIA, the text refers to either 'Contracting State' or 'third country' in place of 'foreign state', as appropriate.

[1861] s.30(1), PIA.

[1862] s.30(1)(1), PIA.

[1863] s.30(1)(2), PIA.

[1864] s.30(1)(2), PIA.

[1865] s.30(4)(1), PIA.

[1866] s.30(4)(2), PIA.

[1867] s.30(5)(1), PIA.

[1868] s.30(5)(1), PIA.

[1869] s.30(5)(2), PIA.

[1870] s.30(5)(3), PIA.

[1871] s.30(5)(3), PIA.

subsection 30(5) of the PIA for the refusal to forward documents and information exists,[1872] or the Contracting State's financial supervision authority has informed the EFSA that the institution has contravened the conditions for which that State's legislation provides or which that country's financial supervision authority has established.[1873] The EFSA shall immediately convey this precept to the institution.[1874] On its receipt of the precept, the institution is required to stop supplying its services in the Contracting State by the date that the EFSA specifies therein.[1875]

An Estonian payment institution or e-money institution may start to provide cross-border services in a (non-Estonian) Contracting State "pursuant to the provision of legislation of the [Contracting] State".[1876] This phrase may mean that it is the host State's enactment of Directive 2007/64/EC which regulates the conduct of the payment services in that country.[1877]

The nomenclature in Annex I does not refer to payment services. However, heading F of Title XIII refers to 'Miscellaneous' capital movements, and the CJEU has held that the list of capital movements in the nomenclature in Annex I is "not exhaustive".[1878] As a cross-border payment involves the movement of funds between countries, it is a 'capital movement' in Title XIII(F) of the nomenclature in Annex I. Furthermore, the foundation of a branch (in this instance, in order to provide payment services) is a 'capital movement' in Title I(1) of the nomenclature in Annex I. If the EFSA refuses to review the documents and information that it has received from the Estonian payment service provider (or e-money institution) wishing to found a branch in a (non-Estonian) EEA state or to provide services there, or refuses to forward these items to the

---

[1872] s.30(8)(1), PIA.

[1873] s.30(8)(2), PIA.

[1874] s.30(9), PIA.

[1875] s.30(9), PIA.

[1876] s.30(6), PIA.

[1877] The meaning of section 30(6) of the PIA is uncertain. Note 1859 does not apply, because Article 39 of Directive 2013/36/EU (on a credit institution's freedom to provide services) does not contain an 'interests of the general good' phrase. Provisions of Title III (Transparency of Conditions and Information Requirements for Payment Services) of Directive 2007/64/EC require the enactment of national legislation, in order to govern payment service providers in host EEA states; these requirements are consistent with the interpretation of subsection 30(6) of the PIA that the text gives.

[1878] See, for instance, *Trummer and Mayer* [1999] ECR I-1661, at paragraph 21. Section 2.1.1 considers how capital movements are defined.

financial services authority of that country, then it contravenes the free movement of capital.

For the restrictive measures to be justified under Article 65(1)(b) of the TFEU, they must be necessary for the protection of interests that they are intended to guarantee, be proportionate, and satisfy the requirements of legal certainty (i.e. be specific, objective and known to the parties beforehand); furthermore, the persons whom the measures affect must have access to legal redress (i.e. the decision to impose the restrictive measures should be accompanied by reasons, and be subject to review in the national courts).[1879] The EFSA has a discretion to refuse to forward the documents and information to the financial supervision authority of the (non-Estonian) Contracting State, and to issue a precept to prevent the provision of services, if the establishment of the institution's branch in the Contracting State, implementation of the branch's action plan, or the supply of cross-border of services, may (in the EFSA's opinion) damage the institution's financial situation, the interests of its clients or the reliability of its activities.[1880] These provisions do not give legal certainty to the applicant, as they are insufficiently specific and objective. In addition, the PIA neither requires the EFSA to provide reasons for refusing to review the documents and information or to forward these items, or for issuing a precept, nor grants the institution with a right to appeal against this refusal or issue in the Estonian courts. Hence, the restrictive measures in sections 29 and 30 of the PIA are not justified under Article 65(1)(b) of the TFEU, and, consequently, breach Article 63 of the TFEU.

Sections 25 to 28 and subsections 30(1), (2), (4) and (6)-(9): The supply of services by Estonian payment institutions and e-money institutions in a third country

In order to apply for an authorisation to establish a branch in a third country, an Estonian payment institution or e-money institution must submit a written application and the following documents and information to the EFSA:[1881] the name of the third country in which the branch is to be opened,[1882] the address of the branch's seat in that territory,[1883] a business

[1879] See the subsection '*The requirements for a successful public policy/public security derogation*', in section 2.1.3.
[1880] See above in this subsection.
[1881] s.25(2), PIA.
[1882] s.25(2)(1), PIA.
[1883] s.25(2)(2), PIA.

plan for the branch's activities in the third country,[1884] and specified information about the branch's managers.[1885] If the applicant institution has not submitted all the required documents and information, or if these items are incorrect, misleading or incomplete or "have not been prepared in accordance with the requirements",[1886] then the EFSA has the right to require the applicant to eliminate the deficiencies.[1887]

The EFSA may require the applicant payment institution or e-money institution to submit additional documents and information, if it is not convinced on the basis of the items already submitted that the applicant has sufficient facilities to supply payment services or e-money services through its branch, or that the applicant fulfils the requirements for payment institutions or e-money institutions that the EFSA and its delegated legislation provide, or if it considers that other circumstances that relate to the applicant need to be verified.[1888] In order to verify the information that the applicant submits, the EFSA may perform on-site inspections, order a special audit or an assessment, acquire information from local government authorities and state agencies, consult state

---

[1884] s.25(2)(3), PIA. The business plan is to include a description of the planned business activities, the branch's organisational structure, a description of the rights, obligations and liability that relate to the supply of the planned services, and a description, prediction and analysis of the following factors: the quantity of revenue and expenditure by area of activity, obligations that relate to the provision of payments services or e-money services, the amount of the applicant payment institution's or e-money institution's share capital and assets, "the level of the technical administration of" the applicant's activities, the applicant's strategy and target market share in the market in which it proposes to provide services, the branch's planned activities, services and products to be offered, the potential agents, distributors, clients and competitors, financial forecasts of revenue, expenditure, profit and cash flows and the assumptions on which these are based, the applicant's risk management principles and strategy, and its investment policy (s.16(1), PIA). The business plan shall cover at least three years (s.16(2), PIA).

[1885] s.25(2)(4), PIA. This information includes the name, personal identification code (or, in its absence, the date of birth), address, educational background, employment history and areas of responsibility, of each manager, and documents that the applicant payment institution or e-money institution considers to be necessary to submit to the EFSA in order to certify the managers' trustworthiness and conformity to the requirements of the PIA (s.15(1)(14), PIA).

[1886] Subsection 17(1) of the PIA does not state what these requirements are. This phrase probably refers to the requirements that the applicant's documents and information must satisfy under the PIA, in order to be eligible for the EFSA to consider the application for the relevant authorisation.

[1887] ss.26(1) and 17(1), PIA.

[1888] ss.26(1) and 17(2), PIA.

databases, and obtain oral explanations about the content of documents and facts that are relevant to the authorisation decision from the applicant's auditors, managers and their representatives, and (if necessary) from third parties.[1889]

The applicant institution must submit the additional (and the corrected) documents and information to the EFSA within a reasonable period, which the EFSA determines.[1890] The EFSA may refuse to review an application for authorisation, if the applicant has not corrected the deficiencies within the prescribed period, or has not submitted the additional documents or information that the EFSA has requested by the expiry of this term.[1891]

The EFSA shall take a decision to grant, or to refuse to grant, an authorisation for the establishment of a branch of an Estonian payment institution or e-money institution, within two months of receipt of all the required documents and information – and within three months of receipt of the application.[1892] The EFSA must immediately notify the applicant institution of its decision to grant, or to refuse to grant, an authorisation for the branch's foundation.[1893]

The EFSA may refuse to provide an authorisation to an Estonian payment institution or e-money institution to establish a branch in a third country, if the branch's managers do not fulfil the requirements for managers of these institutions for which the PIA provides,[1894] the documents and information that are submitted upon application for the establishment of a branch do not satisfy the requirements of the PIA or its delegated legislation, or are incorrect, misleading or incomplete,[1895] the institution's resources are not sufficient for the provision of services that the business plan specifies,[1896] the foundation of the branch or the implementation of the business plan may damage the institution, its financial situation or the interests of its shareholders, or may adversely affect the reliability of the institution's activities in any country, [1897] or the third country's financial supervision authority "has no legal basis or possibilities for cooperation with" the EFSA, as a consequence of which

[1889] ss.26(1) and 17(3), PIA.
[1890] ss.26(1) and 17(4), PIA.
[1891] ss.26(1) and 17(5), PIA. If the EFSA refuses to review an application, it shall return the submitted documents to the applicant (s.17(5), PIA).
[1892] s.26(2), PIA.
[1893] s.26(3), PIA.
[1894] s.27(1), PIA.
[1895] s.27(2), PIA.
[1896] s.27(3), PIA.
[1897] s.27(4), PIA.

the EFSA is unable to exercise adequate supervision over the branch.[1898] The EFSA may revoke an authorisation that it has granted to a payment institution or an e-money institution to establish a branch in a third country, if the institution has submitted incorrect information to the EFSA,[1899] the institution has significantly contravened the requirements of the third country's legislation and this breach may damage the institution's clients,[1900] the institution or its branch does not comply with the requirements in force with regard to the issue of authorisations for the establishment of a branch,[1901] the institution does not submit reports on its branch as required,[1902] the manager of the institution or its branch has been punished for a specified offence (such as official misconduct) and the information about the punishment has not been removed from the punishment register pursuant to the Punishment Register Act,[1903] the institution has not implemented a precept of the EFSA within the period or to the extent prescribed,[1904] the risks that arise from the branch's activities are "significantly greater" than those that arise from the institution's operations,[1905] the institution's activity licence has been revoked,[1906] or one or more grounds become evident on which the EFSA may refuse to provide an authorisation to the institution to found the branch.[1907]

The EFSA shall immediately notify the institution, and the third country's financial supervision authority, of a decision to revoke an authorisation for the establishment of a branch in that territory.[1908] After it becomes aware of this revocation, the institution shall cease provision of its services through the branch by the due date that the EFSA specifies.[1909]

A payment institution or e-money institution founded in Estonia that intends to provide cross-border services in a third country[1910] shall inform the EFSA of this wish,[1911] and shall submit the following documents and information to the EFSA: the name of the country in which it intends to

---

[1898] s.27(5), PIA.
[1899] s.28(1)(1), PIA.
[1900] s.28(1)(2), PIA.
[1901] s.28(1)(3), PIA.
[1902] s.28(1)(4), PIA.
[1903] s.28(1)(5), PIA.
[1904] s.28(1)(6), PIA.
[1905] s.28(1)(7), PIA.
[1906] s.28(1)(8), PIA.
[1907] s.28(1)(9), PIA. For these grounds, see the first sentence of this paragraph.
[1908] s.28(2), PIA.
[1909] s.28(3), PIA.
[1910] See note 1860.
[1911] s.30(1), PIA.

supply cross-border services,[1912] and a description of these planned services.[1913] This description must include information on the provision of the cross-border services, and whether the institution intends to use agents. [1914] The EFSA may refuse to review the documents and information, if these items do not satisfy the requirements of the PIA or are incomplete,[1915] or show such deficiencies and the additional documents or information that the EFSA requires have not been submitted within the prescribed period.[1916]

The EFSA may issue a precept, in order to prohibit the payment institution or e-money institution from providing cross-border services in a third country, if the third country's financial supervision authority has informed the EFSA that the institution has breached the conditions for which that state's legislation provides or which that country's financial supervision authority has settled.[1917] The EFSA shall immediately deliver this precept to the institution.[1918] The institution is required to terminate the supply of its services in the third country by the date that the EFSA specifies in the precept.[1919]

The establishment of a branch and the provision of cross-border payment services are 'capital movements' in Titles I(1) and XIII(F) of the nomenclature in Annex I, respectively.[1920] If the EFSA refuses to review the documents and information that it has received from the Estonian payment service provider or e-money institution wishing to found a branch

---

[1912] s.30(1)(1), PIA.
[1913] s.30(1)(2), PIA.
[1914] s.30(1)(2), PIA.
[1915] s.30(4)(1), PIA.
[1916] s.30(4)(2), PIA.
[1917] s.30(8)(2), PIA. Clause 30(8)(1) of the PIA does not apply to an Estonian payment institution or e-money institution that wishes to provide cross-border services in a third country, because this clause relies upon subsection 30(5) of the PIA, which subsection 24(3) of the PIA excludes from applying to these circumstances. Nevertheless, clause 30(8)(1) of the PIA applies to an Estonian payment institution or e-money institution that intends to supply cross-border services in a (non-Estonian) Contracting State (see the subsection '*Sections 29 and 30: The supply of services by Estonian payment institutions and e-money institutions in another Contracting State*', above in this section).
[1918] s.30(9), PIA.
[1919] s.30(9), PIA.
[1920] See the subsection '*Sections 29 and 30: The supply of services by Estonian payment institutions and e-money institutions in another Contracting State*', above in this section, for an explanation as to why the provision of cross-border payment services is included in Title XIII(F) of the nomenclature in Annex I.

in a third country or to supply cross-border payment services there, then it breaches the free movement of capital. The EFSA also contravenes the free movement of capital if it refuses to grant, or revokes, an authorisation to an Estonian payment service provider or e-money institution to establish a branch in a third country, and/or if it issues a precept to forbid the payment service provider or e-money institution from providing cross-border services there.[1921]

For Article 65(1)(b) of the TFEU to justify the restrictive measures, they must be necessary for the protection of interests that they are intended to guarantee, be proportionate, and observe the requirements of legal certainty (i.e. be specific, objective and known to the parties beforehand); furthermore, the persons who are affected by the measures must have access to legal redress (i.e. the decision to impose the restrictive measures is to be supported by reasons, and be open to review in the national courts).[1922] Some of the restrictive measures are neither specific nor objective, and, therefore, do not provide the application payment service provider (or e-money institution) with legal certainty. For instance, the EFSA may refuse to grant an authorisation to an institution to establish branch in a third country, and may revoke such an authorisation, if (it becomes evident that (in the case of revocation of the authorisation)) the third country's financial supervision authority (in the EFSA's opinion) "has no legal basis or possibilities for cooperation with" the EFSA,[1923] due to which the EFSA is not able to exercise adequate supervision over the branch. Furthermore, the PIA does not require the EFSA to give reasons for refusing to review an application for the authorisation of an Estonian payment service provider or e-money institution to found a branch in a third country, for refusing to grant this authorisation, for revoking the authorisation, or for issuing a precept in order to forbid an Estonian payment service provider or e-money institution from supplying cross-

---

[1921] The PIA requires a payment service provider or e-money institution that is established in Estonia to obtain an authorisation from the EFSA in order to found a branch in a third country, but not to provide cross-border services there; see above in this subsection ('*Sections 25 to 28 and subsections 30(1), (2), (4) and (6)-(9): The supply of services by Estonian payment institutions and e-money institutions in a third country*'). This treatment of cross-border services results from the fact that section 30 of the PIA applies to services by Estonian institutions in Contracting States and in third countries – and services between Contracting States are covered by the passport regime of Article 25 of Directive 2007/64/EC (see section 2.2.8).

[1922] See the subsection '*The requirements for a successful public policy/public security derogation*', in section 2.1.3.

[1923] ss.27(5) and 28(1)(9), PIA.

border services in a third country; nor does the PIA grants the payment service provider or e-money institution with a right to appeal against the EFSA's decision in the Estonian courts. Hence, Article 65(1)(b) of the TFEU does not justify the restrictive measures in sections 25 to 28 (and 30) of the PIA.

The restrictive measures (on the free movement of capital from Estonia to a third country) may be justified under Article 64(2) of the TFEU, if the EU institutions carefully take account of the free movement of capital whilst enacting legislation, and if the national rules do not limit the free movement of capital more than do the equivalent provisions of the relevant Directive.[1924] The relevant legal instrument is Directive 2007/64/EC. Recital 1 of Directive 2007/64/EC states that it is crucial for the internal market for all internal frontiers within the EU to be removed, in order to make possible the free movement of goods, persons, services and capital, and that the lack of harmonisation in the area of payment services impedes the operation of the single market in payment services. The co-existence of an incomplete EU framework and domestic laws causes confusion and legal uncertainty.[1925] Therefore, it is vital to establish a modern, coherent EU legal framework for payment services.[1926] Whilst these recitals stress the importance of the internal market, they do not specifically address the free movement of capital. Furthermore, the Articles of Directive 2007/64/EC do not mention the free movement of capital. Thus, the EU institutions do not carefully consider the free movement of capital whilst enacting this Directive. In addition, the Estonian rules restrict the free movement of capital more than the equivalent provisions in Directive 2007/64/EC do, because the Directive contains no Articles that specifically address third countries. Hence, the restrictive measures in sections 25 to 28 (and 30) of the PIA are not justified under Article 64(2) of the TFEU. Consequently, these measures contravene Article 63 of the TFEU.

Sections 35 and 36: The supply of services in Estonia by payment institutions and e-money institutions that are established in another Contracting State

A payment institution or e-money institution that is authorised to provide services in a (non-Estonian) Contracting State, which would like to establish a branch in Estonia, shall inform the financial supervision

---

[1924] See the subsection '*Derogations that apply only to capital movement to/from third countries*', in section 2.3.2.

[1925] Recital 2, Directive 2007/64/EC.

[1926] Recital 3, Directive 2007/64/EC.

authority of that Contracting State of its intention to supply these services,[1927] and shall submit the following documents and information to this authority: the branch's business name and address,[1928] the names of the branch's managers,[1929] and the branch's action plan – which shall contain information on all of the services to be supplied in Estonia, and describe the branch's organisational structure and whether it intends to use agents.[1930] The EFSA shall immediately notify the (non-Estonian) Contracting State's financial supervision authority of receipt of these items.[1931] Within one month of this receipt, the EFSA may take a decision that determines the requirements with which the institution must comply in Estonia, and according to which the institution shall supply its services there.[1932] The institution may found the branch and begin the provision of services after this decision is taken, or (in the absence of a decision) one month after the date on which the EFSA received the documents and information.[1933] The EFSA shall submit confirmation concerning receipt of these items, and about its decision on the requirements for the provision of services through the new branch, upon entry of the branch in the commercial register.[1934]

A payment institution or e-money institution that is authorised to provide services in a (non-Estonian) Contracting State, which wishes supply cross-border services in Estonia, shall inform the EFSA of this intention through that Contracting State's financial supervision authority.[1935] An action plan is to be submitted to the EFSA, which shall describe the services to be provided in Estonia.[1936] After the EFSA has received this action plan, the institution may start to supply cross-border services in Estonia.[1937]

The EFSA shall immediately notify the (non-Estonian) Contracting State's financial supervision authority of receipt of the action plan.[1938] Within one month of its receipt of the action plan, the EFSA may take a

---

[1927] s.35(1), PIA.
[1928] s.35(1)(2), PIA.
[1929] s.35(1)(3), PIA.
[1930] s.35(1)(1), PIA.
[1931] s.35(3), PIA.
[1932] s.35(3), PIA. The EFSA shall immediately inform the financial supervision authority of the (non-Estonian) Contracting State of its decision (s.35(3), PIA).
[1933] s.35(4), PIA.
[1934] s.35(6), PIA.
[1935] s.36(1), PIA.
[1936] s.36(1), PIA.
[1937] s.36(3), PIA.
[1938] s.36(4), PIA.

decision in which it determines the requirements according to which the institution shall provide its services in Estonia.[1939] The EFSA shall immediately inform the institution of this decision.[1940]

The foundation of a branch and the provision of cross-border payment services are 'capital movements' in Titles I(1) and XIII(F) of the nomenclature in Annex I, respectively.[1941] If the EFSA decides that the payment service provider or e-money institution must satisfy onerous conditions in order to open a branch in Estonia, or to provide cross-border payment services there, then it restricts the free movement of capital.

To be justified under Article 65(1)(b) of the TFEU, the restrictive measures must be necessary for the protection of the interests that they are intended to guarantee, be proportionate, and observe the requirements of legal certainty – i.e. be specific, objective and known to the parties beforehand; in addition, the persons whom the measures affect must have access to legal redress – i.e. intervention must be accompanied by a statement of reasons and be subject to review in the national courts.[1942] Subsections 35(3) and 36(4) of the PIA are neither specific nor objective, and, therefore, do not provide the payment service provider or e-money institution with legal certainty. To do so, the legislation (or a statutory instrument) should state detailed guidelines that the EFSA is to follow in its determination of the requirements that institutions from non-Estonian EEA states need to satisfy, in order to establish an Estonian branch or to provide cross-border payments services in Estonia. Furthermore, the PIA neither requires a decision under subsection 35(3) or 36(4) of this Act to be supported by reasons, nor to be subject to review in the Estonian courts; therefore, the institution that seeks to provide payment services in Estonia does not have access to legal redress. Thus, the restrictive measures in subsections 35(3) and 36(4) of the PIA are not justified under Article 65(1)(b) of the TFEU, and, consequently, breach Article 63 of the TFEU.

[1939] s.36(4), PIA.

[1940] s.36(4), PIA.

[1941] See the subsection '*Sections 29 and 30: The supply of services by Estonian payment institutions and e-money institutions in another Contracting State*', above in this section, for an explanation as to why the supply of cross-border payment services is included in Title XIII(F) of the nomenclature in Annex I.

[1942] See the subsection '*The requirements for a successful public policy/public security derogation*', in section 2.1.3.

Sections 32 to 34: The supply of services in Estonia by payment institutions and e-money institutions that are established in a third country

A payment institution or e-money institution that is authorised to provide services in a third country is required to apply to the EFSA for a further authorisation, in order to establish a branch or supply cross-border services in Estonia.[1943] Upon application for this (further) authorisation, a written application, and the following documents and information, must be submitted to the EFSA:[1944] the institution's name and address,[1945] information about the institution's and (if a branch is to be founded) the branch's managers in accordance with clause 15(1)(14) of the PIA,[1946] documents and information concerning shareholders who have qualifying holdings in the institution as provided in section 40 of the PIA,[1947] the

---

[1943] s.32(1), PIA.

[1944] s.32(2), PIA.

[1945] s.32(2)(1), PIA.

[1946] s.32(2)(2), PIA. See note 1884, for clause 15(1)(4) of the PIA.

[1947] s.32(2)(3), PIA. These documents include a description of the institution that contains a list of the shares and information on the type of shares and the number of votes that the shareholder owns, the shareholder's curriculum vitae (if a natural person) which contains his/her name, addresses, education, work experience, and personal identification code (or, in the absence of this code, the shareholder's date of birth), a list of the shareholders or members of the qualifying shareholder (if a legal person) and information on the number of shares and votes that each of these shareholders or members holds, the name, seat, registry code, registration certificate and articles of association of the qualifying shareholder (if a legal person), information on the members of the supervisory board and the management board of the qualifying shareholder (if a legal person), a confirmation that persons who become the institution's managers in consequence of acquiring a shareholding have not been punished for a specified offence (such as an offence against public trust) or that information concerning the punishment has been erased from the punishment register pursuant to the Punishment Register Act (or foreign equivalent), a confirmation for each of these managers that no circumstances have existed or currently exist that legally preclude the right of this person to be a manager of a payment institution or e-money institution, a description of the shareholder's business activities, a description of the interests of persons who are connected with the shareholder, the most recent three annual reports and auditor's reports of the shareholder (if a legal person), ratings that are required for the assessment of the acquirer's financial circumstances (if a natural person), credit ratings issued to the acquirer and its group (if a legal person), a description of the structure of the shareholder's group (if a legal person), data concerning the sizes of the shareholdings of the companies that belong to the shareholder's group (if a legal person) and the group's most recent three annual and auditor's reports, documents that certify the shareholder's financial status during the past three years

ambit of the activity licence that the third country has issued to the institution,[1948] information about the agency that has issued this activity licence,[1949] the branch's business name and address (if a branch is to be established),[1950] an official certificate concerning the company's existence in its home country (such as an excerpt from a commercial register or a copy of the institution's registration certificate),[1951] an authorisation document that certifies the authority of the branch's director or a copy of the resolution appointing this director (if a branch is to be established),[1952] a copy of the company's articles of association (or partnership agreement, if the institution is a partnership),[1953] the telecommunications data of the company and of the branch (if a branch is to be founded),[1954] the institution's two most recent annual reports,[1955] a business plan which satisfies the requirements of section 16 of the PIA and sets out all of the

---

(if a natural person), documents and information that concern the sources of resources for which the shareholder intends to acquire or increase a qualifying holding or gain control of the institution, the circumstances that relate to the acquisition of a shareholding pursuant to sections 9, 10 and 72¹ of the SMA, the size of the shareholder's qualifying holding, a business plan that relates to the gaining and exercising of control (if the institution becomes a controlled company), and a review of the strategy that is applied in the institution in connection with the acquisition of shareholdings (s.40(1), PIA). See note 542, for subsection 9(1) of the SMA. See note 724, for subsection 10(1) of the SMA. For the purposes of the PIA, a 'qualifying holding' is a direct or indirect holding in the share capital of a payment institution or an e-money institution that represents at least 10% of the institution's share capital, of all rights that are related to this share capital, or of voting rights in the company, or which make it possible to exert a significant influence over the institution's management bodies (s.37(1), PIA). A 'direct' qualifying holding is one that a person holds or exercises personally (s.37(2), PIA). An 'indirect' qualifying holding one that a person holds or exercises together with at least one controlled company, is held or exercised by one or more companies that a person controls, is held or exercised by a person (or a company controlled by this person) on agreement with a third party, or the voting rights arising from this holding are deemed to belong to a person (s.37(3), PIA).

[1948] s.32(2)(4), PIA.

[1949] s.32(2)(4), PIA.

[1950] s.32(2)(5), PIA.

[1951] s.32(2)(6), PIA, and s.386(2)(1), Commercial Code.

[1952] s.32(2)(6), PIA, and s.386(2)(3), Commercial Code.

[1953] s.32(2)(6), PIA, and s.386(2)(4), Commercial Code.

[1954] s.32(2)(6), PIA, and s.386(2)(5), Commercial Code.

[1955] s.32(2)(7), PIA.

services that the institution provides in Estonia,[1956] and the personal data of the agent (if there is one).[1957] The institution shall also submit the following documents and information to the EFSA: the permission of the financial supervision authority of the institution's home state for it to establish a branch in Estonia or to provide cross-border services there,[1958] a confirmation from the home country's financial supervision authority to the effect that the institution holds a valid activity licence in that territory and that it pursues its activities in a correct way and in accordance with good practice,[1959] and information about the institution's financial circumstances – including the amount of own funds and the description of the consumer protection scheme that applies to the institution's clients in its home country.[1960]

Sections 17, 18, 19, 22 and 23 of the PIA apply to the processing of applications for an authorisation for a third country payment institution or e-money institution to found an Estonian branch or provide cross-border services in Estonia, to the verification of information in respect of these applications, and to the grant and revocation of such authorisations, unless section 33 of the PIA provides otherwise.[1961] Sections 18, 19, 22 and 23 of the PIA are considered next.[1962]

The EFSA shall take a decision to issue, or to refuse to issue, an authorisation within three months of all the required documents and information that "comply with the requirements",[1963] and within six

---

[1956] s.32(2)(8), PIA. See note 1884, for subsections 16(1) and 16(2) of the PIA. The EFSA has the right to require a business plan to be amended if, in its opinion, the information presented there is unreliable, and the minimum amount of own funds that is computed whilst taking the obligations in the business plan into consideration does not comply with the legislative requirements concerning payment institutions and e-money institutions (s.16(3), PIA).

[1957] s.32(2)(9), PIA.

[1958] s.33(3)(1), PIA.

[1959] s.33(3)(2), PIA.

[1960] s.33(3)(3), PIA.

[1961] s.33(1), PIA.

[1962] See the subsection '*Sections 25 to 28 and subsections 30(1), (2), (4) and (6)-(9): The supply of services by Estonian payment institutions and e-money institutions in a third country*', above in this section (i.e. section 3.5), for subsections 17(1)-17(5) of the PIA. Subsection 17(6) of the PIA concerns co-operation between the EFSA and financial supervision authorities of (non-Estonian) Contracting States, and is, therefore, not relevant in the current context.

[1963] Subsection 18(1) of the PIA does not state what these requirements are. It is likely that the quoted phrase refers to the requirements of the PIA for an Estonian applicant to be issued with an activity licence to provide services as a payment

months of the receipt of the application.[1964] If it is clear from the items that the applicant has submitted to the EFSA that the risks relating to the its planned services are insufficiently covered, the applicant's structure is inadequate for it to operate as a payment institution or e-money institution on an ongoing basis, and the applicant's internal control and processes do not ensure adequate risk management, then the EFSA may establish secondary conditions upon the issue of the authorisation in order to protect the interests of the institution's clients,[1965] which limit the supply of payment services or e-money services (or ancillary services that relate to payment or e-money services),[1966] or require the establishment of a separate subsidiary in order to provide accompanying non-payment services.[1967] The EFSA's decision concerning an authorisation shall state the applicant's name and registry code,[1968] the type(s) of services in respect of which the decision is taken,[1969] the date on which the decision is taken,[1970] and the date that the decision comes into effect.[1971] The EFSA shall immediately convey a decision to issue, or to refuse to issue, an authorisation to the applicant.[1972]

The EFSA may refuse to grant an authorisation for a third country payment institution to establish an Estonian branch or provide cross-border services in Estonia, if the third country's financial supervision authority "does not guarantee adequate supervision of the applicant or … has no legal basis or possibilities for cooperation with" the EFSA,[1973] the

---

institution or e-money institution in Estonia. In the present context, 'the requirements' mean the requirements that a third country payment institution or e-money institution must fulfil, in order to provide services in Estonia.

[1964] s.18(1), PIA. Before the EFSA takes the decision to issue, or to refuse to issue, an authorisation, it shall (if necessary) consult the Bank of Estonia (s.18(2), PIA). After issuing an authorisation, the EFSA may provide more favourable conditions to the applicant that permit the applicant to derogate (as appropriate) from the circumstances on the basis of which the authorisation is granted, and/or extend the term that subsection 18(1) of the PIA specifies during the course of which the applicant shall conform with the requirements on the basis of which the authorisation is issued (s.18(3), PIA).

[1965] s.18(4), PIA.

[1966] s.18(4)(1), PIA.

[1967] s.18(4)(2), PIA.

[1968] s.18(5)(1), PIA.

[1969] s.18(5)(2), PIA.

[1970] s.18(5)(3), PIA.

[1971] s.18(5)(3), PIA.

[1972] s.18(6), PIA.

[1973] s.33(2), PIA.

applicant does not fulfil the requirements for payment institutions or e-money institutions that the PIA and its secondary legislation contain,[1974] the applicant does not have the required experience or funds to continuously function as a payment institution or e-money institution,[1975] the applicant's minimum amount of own funds does not satisfy the legislative requirements for payment institutions and e-money institutions,[1976] the applicant's managers, auditor, or shareholders do not meet the requirements of the PIA and its delegated legislation,[1977] close links between the applicant and another person prevent adequate supervision over the applicant,[1978] the requirements that arise from legislation or the implementation of legislation of the other state in which the person with whom the applicant has close links is established prevent adequate supervision over the applicant,[1979] the information that the applicant submits indicates that the applicant mainly plans to provide its services in another Contracting State (i.e. other than Estonia),[1980] the internal rules for which section 50 of the PIA provides are not sufficiently clear or accurate to regulate the institution's activities,[1981] or the applicant

---

[1974] s.19(1)(1), PIA. Clause 19(1)(2) of the PIA accords the EFSA the right to refuse to issue an activity licence to the applicant, if the applicant is unable to demonstrate the necessary resources for full payment of the share capital for a company being established. This ground for refusal is not relevant to the present context, i.e. the foundation of an Estonian branch of, or the provision of cross-border services in Estonia by, a payment institution or e-money institution that is authorised to provide services in a third country.

[1975] s.19(1)(3), PIA. The EFSA shall consider the following issues (amongst other matters) in its assessment of the applicant's experience and funds as sufficient to continuously function as a payment institution or e-money institution: the level of the technical and organisational administration of the applicant's activities, the education, work experience, business connections, reputation and trustworthiness of "the persons connected with the management of the applicant", the adequacy of the applicant's business plan, and the activities, financial circumstances, reputation and experience of the applicant and its group (s.19(2), PIA).

[1976] s.19(1)(4), PIA.

[1977] s.19(1)(5), PIA.

[1978] s.19(1)(6), PIA.

[1979] s.19(1)(6), PIA.

[1980] s.19(1)(7), PIA.

[1981] s.19(1)(8), PIA. A payment institution or e-money institution must establish and apply rules of procedure that regulate the activities of the institution, its managers, and its employees, which ensure that legislation which regulates the institution's activities and decisions that its management bodies take are complied with (s.50(1), PIA). The institution's internal rules shall ensure that it legally and regularly provides services (s.50(2), PIA). The rules shall set out the following

or one of its managers has been punished for an offence against public trust, or for support and financing of an act of terrorism, and the information about the punishment has not been deleted from the punishment register pursuant to the Punishment Register Act.[1982]

The EFSA may revoke an authorisation,[1983] if circumstances that subsection 33(2) or section 19 of the PIA provide for become evident,[1984] the institution does not start its activities within one year from the issue of the authorisation,[1985] an act of the institution's founders shows that the institution will be unable to begin its activities within the specified period,[1986] the institution's operations are suspended for more than six consecutive months,[1987] the institution has submitted inaccurate information to the EFSA,[1988] the institution does not fulfil the requirements that are in force in respect of the issue of activity licences,[1989] it becomes evident that the applicant's managers, auditor, or shareholders do not fulfil the requirements of the PIA and its secondary legislation,[1990] the institution

---

(amongst other things): the procedure for the distribution of internal information and documents, the procedure for the provision of payment services or e-money services, the procedure for conclusion of transactions and performance of acts, functions and duties of employees, reporting chains, the procedure for reporting and the delegation of rights, the recording of services, risk assessment, the procedure for processing data and maintaining databases, rules for the safety and monitoring of information technology systems, systems used for the safekeeping of clients' assets, the procedure for the operation of the internal control system, and internal rules of procedure for imposing international sanctions that are established on the basis of the International Sanctions Act and for application of the Money Laundering and Terrorist Financing Prevention Act and the code of conduct for verification of compliance with this legislation (s.50(3),PIA).

[1982] s.19(1)(9), PIA. The English in clause 19(1)(9) of the English translation of the PIA provides a literal meaning that is different from that stated in the text. I have interpreted this clause in the light of other references to punishments and the punishment register in the Estonian legislation, some of which are recorded in this chapter.

[1983] Revocation of an activity licence means the loss of a right that this licence grants (s.22(1), PIA). The EFSA shall immediately convey its decision on the revocation of an activity licence to the addressee of the decision (s.22(7), PIA).

[1984] s.33(3), PIA. See the previous paragraph, for subsection 33(2) and section 19 of the PIA.

[1985] s.22(2)(1), PIA.

[1986] s.22(2)(1), PIA.

[1987] s.22(2)(1), PIA.

[1988] s.22(2)(2), PIA.

[1989] s.22(2)(3), PIA.

[1990] ss.22(2)(4) and 19(1)(5), PIA.

has repeatedly or materially contravened legislative provisions that regulate its activities,[1991] the institution or its manager has been punished for a specified offence (such as official misconduct) and information concerning the punishment has not been removed from the punishment register pursuant to the Punishment Register Act,[1992] the institution is not compliant with the secondary conditions that subsection 18(4) of the PIA specifies,[1993] the institution has published significantly inaccurate or misleading information or advertising about its activities or managers,[1994] the institution's activities materially damage the interests of its clients, currency circulation, the functioning of the money markets or the payment system's stability,[1995] the amount of the institution's own funds does not satisfy the requirements of the PIA and/or its secondary legislation,[1996] the institution belongs to a group the structure of which precludes the receipt of information that is necessary for consolidated supervision,[1997] a company that is a member of the same group as the institution operates on the basis of foreign legislation that prevents the exercise of adequate supervision,[1998] close links between the institution and other persons preclude the exercise of sufficient supervision,[1999] the institution has committed money laundering, supported or financed a terrorist act, or breaches the procedure for preventing the legislative procedure for money laundering and terrorist financing,[2000] it becomes clear that the institution has selected Estonia as the place for application of its activity licence and registration in order to evade compliance with more stringent requirements that apply to payment institutions or e-money institutions in another Contracting State in which the institution mainly operates,[2001] the payment institution has contravened the conditions that are provided for in the legislation of another Contracting State or a third country or are established by the financial supervision authority in that jurisdiction,[2002] or

---

[1991] s.22(2)(5), PIA.

[1992] s.22(2)(6), PIA. See note 1982, which applies to clause 22(2)(6) of the PIA.

[1993] s.22(2)(7), PIA. See above in this subsection ('*Sections 32 to 34: The supply of services in Estonia by payment institutions and e-money institutions that are established in a third country*'), for subsection 18(4) of the PIA.

[1994] s.22(2)(8), PIA.

[1995] s.22(2)(9), PIA.

[1996] s.22(2)(10), PIA.

[1997] s.22(2)(11), PIA.

[1998] s.22(2)(11), PIA.

[1999] s.22(2)(12), PIA.

[2000] s.22(2)(13), PIA.

[2001] s.22(2)(14), PIA.

[2002] s.22(2)(15), PIA.

the institution has not implemented a precept that the EFSA has issued within the period or the extent prescribed.[2003] However, the EFSA may refuse to revoke an authorisation if the third country institution's clients have claims against it, or against its Estonian branch,[2004] or if the withdrawal of the authorisation damages the institution or the interests of its clients or shareholders.[2005]

Prior to taking a decision on the revocation of an activity licence, the EFSA may issue a precept to the institution, and set a term for the removal of the deficiencies that are the reasons for the revocation.[2006] The EFSA shall take a decision to revoke, or to refuse to revoke, a payment institution's or e-money institution's activity licence, if this organisation no longer wishes to provide payment services[2007] or e-money services.[2008] However, it shall not withdraw an activity licence on this basis, if "there is good reason to believe" that revocation of the activity licence may harm the legitimate interests of clients or other creditors of the institution.[2009]

The EFSA must publish a decision to issue, amend or revoke an authorisation on its website no later than on the working day following the day on which this decision enters into effect.[2010] In addition, if the EFSA revokes an authorisation, it shall publish its decision to do so in at least one national daily newspaper.[2011]

A third country payment institution or e-money institution that wishes to provide services in Estonia that are not specified in the business plan that it sent to the EFSA with its application for authorisation, shall submit an application for the amendment of its authorisation to the EFSA.[2012] In

---

[2003] s.22(2)(16), PIA.
[2004] s.33(4), PIA.
[2005] s.33(4), PIA.
[2006] s.22(3), PIA.
[2007] Subsection 3(1) of the PIA states the payment services. See above in this section (i.e. section 3.5).
[2008] ss.22(4) and 22(6), PIA. In this English translation, subsection 22(4) of the PIA refers to "clause 6(3)(1) of this Act". This is an error, as the PIA has no clause 6(3)(1). The correct reference may be to subsection 6(4) of the PIA, which states that (for the purposes of the PIA) e-money services include the issue of e-money and ancillary services that are closely related to the administration or issue of e-money (s.6(4), PIA). The EFSA shall take the decision to revoke, or to refuse to revoke, the payment institution's activity licence, within two months of receiving an application from the institution (s.3(6), PIA).
[2009] s.6(5), PIA.
[2010] s.23(1), PIA.
[2011] s.23(2), PIA.
[2012] s.34(1), PIA.

order to amend an authorisation, the institution shall submit to the EFSA the documents and information that are specified in clauses 32(2)(1) to (5) and 32(8) of the PIA.[2013] Sections 17, 18 and 19 of the PIA apply to the processing of applications for the amendment of authorisations for the establishment of a branch, verification of information, and decisions that relate to the amendment of authorisations.[2014]

The establishment of a branch and the supply of cross-border payment services are 'capital movements' in Titles I(1) and XIII(F) of the nomenclature in Annex I, respectively.[2015] The requirement for the EFSA to issue an authorisation, a decision to refuse to issue an authorisation, and a decision to revoke of an authorisation, for the provision of services in Estonia by a third country payment service provider or electronic money institution, limits the free movement of capital.

For Article 65(1)(b) of the TFEU to justify the restrictive measures, they must be necessary for the protection of interests that they are intended to guarantee, be proportionate (i.e. be unattainable by less restrictive measures), and fulfil the requirements of legal certainty (i.e. be specific, objective and known to the parties beforehand); furthermore, the persons who are affected by the measures must be provided with legal redress (i.e. intervention must be supported by a formal statement of reasons and be subject to review in the national courts).[2016] The PIA provides many grounds upon which an authorisation under section 32 of the PIA may be revoked, which may be disproportionate. In addition, not all of the restrictive measures satisfy the requirements of legal certainty. For example, subsection 33(2) of the PIA empowers the EFSA to refuse to grant an authorisation if the third country's financial supervision authority does not (in the EFSA's opinion) guarantee satisfactory supervision of the applicant or (in the EFSA's view) "has no legal basis or possibilities for

---

[2013] s.34(2), PIA. See above in this subsection ('*Sections 32 to 34: The supply of services in Estonia by payment institutions and e-money institutions that are established in a third country*')', for subsection 32(2) of the PIA.

[2014] s.34(3), PIA. See note 1962, for section 17 of the PIA. See above in this subsection ('*Sections 32 to 34: The supply of services in Estonia by payment institutions and e-money institutions that are established in a third country*'), for sections 18 and 19 of the PIA.

[2015] See the subsection '*Sections 29 and 30: The supply of services by Estonian payment institutions and e-money institutions in another Contracting State*', above in this section, for an explanation as to why the provision of cross-border payment services is included in Title XIII(F) of the nomenclature in Annex I.

[2016] See the subsection '*The requirements for a successful public policy/public security derogation*', in section 2.1.3.

cooperation with" the EFSA.[2017] This provision is neither specific nor objective. Furthermore, the Act neither requires the EFSA to support a decision not to grant, or to revoke, an authorisation with a formal statement of reasons, nor provides the applicant payment service provider or e-money institution with the right to question a decision in the national courts. Thus, the Act does not provide the institution with legal certainty. Hence, the restrictive measures are not justified under Article 65(1)(b) of the TFEU.

Article 64(2) of the TFEU may justify the restrictive measures, if the EU institutions carefully take account of the objective of the free movement of capital whilst they enact the pertinent legislation, and if the relevant domestic rules do not limit the free movement of capital more than do the equivalent provisions of the relevant Directive.[2018] Directive 2007/64/EC is the relevant Directive. The Articles of this Directive do not refer to the free movement of capital. Furthermore, whilst Recitals 1, 2 and 3 of Directive 2007/64/EC emphasise the internal market's importance, they do not specifically consider the free movement of capital.[2019] Hence, the EU institutions do not carefully consider the objective of the free movement of capital, whilst enacting the Directive. In addition, the rules in the PIA restrict the free movement of capital more than do the equivalent provisions in Directive 2007/64/EC, because the none of the Directive's Articles specifically address third countries. Thus, Article 64(2) of the PIA does not justify the restrictive measures. Consequently, these Estonian provisions breach Article 63 of the TFEU.

Section 83: Accounting and reporting – disclosure of reports

A branch of a foreign payment institution or e-money institution is to disclose the institution's annual report.[2020] This document must be prepared in accordance with the legislation of the country of the institution's seat and translated into Estonian.[2021]

[2017] s.33(2), PIA. See above in this subsection ('*Sections 32 to 34: The supply of services in Estonia by payment institutions and e-money institutions that are established in a third country*')'.

[2018] See the subsection '*Derogations that apply only to capital movement to/from third countries*', in section 2.3.2.

[2019] See the subsection '*Sections 25 to 28 and subsections 30(1), (2), (4) and (6)-(9): The supply of services by Estonian payment institutions and e-money institutions in a third country*', above in this section.

[2020] s.83(2), PIA.

[2021] s.83(2), PIA.

Disclosure of information is not a 'capital movement' in the nomenclature in Annex 1. Hence, section 83 of the PIA does not contravene Article 63 of the TFEU.

Section 92: Supervision of Estonian payment institutions and e-money institutions that have branches in foreign states and/or provide cross-border services

If an Estonian payment institution or e-money institution that has established a branch in a foreign country, or that provides cross-border services there, breaches the requirements of that state's legislation, then the EFSA shall immediately apply measures in order to stop the contravention – on the proposal of the foreign financial supervision authority.[2022] The EFSA shall immediately inform the financial supervision authority of the foreign state in which the branch of the payment institution or e-money institution is established or in which the institution provides cross-border services, of revocation of the institution's activity licence, withdrawal of its authorisation for the establishment of a branch in a foreign state, or the issuance of the precepts specified in subsections 29(9) or 30(8) of the PIA.[2023] A branch of a payment institution or e-money institution, or a payment institution or e-money institution that provides cross-border services, shall, at the request of the financial supervision authority of a foreign state, provide information that is necessary for the exercise of supervision over the branch's or institution's activities in the foreign country.[2024]

The foundation of a branch and the provision of cross-border payment services are 'capital movements' in Titles I(1) and XIII(F) of the

[2022] s.92(1), PIA. The EFSA shall inform the foreign financial supervision authority of the measures that it has taken (s.92(1), PIA).

[2023] s.92(2), PIA. See subsection '*Sections 29 and 30: The supply of services by Estonian payment institutions and e-money institutions in another Contracting State*', above in this section (i.e. section 3.5), for subsections 29(9) and 30(8) of the PIA.

[2024] s.92(3), PIA. This English translation of the PIA does not state whether the institution or its branch should submit this information to the EFSA or to the financial supervision authority of the foreign state. It makes more sense if the latter is the recipient of the information, rather than the former. However, it is arguably an issue for the legislature of the foreign country, rather than the Estonian legislature, to provide for branches of payment service providers or e-money institutions in that state to supply its financial supervision authority with the necessary information for branch supervision.

nomenclature in Annex I, respectively.[2025] The application of measures in order to terminate the breach of foreign legislative provisions limits the free movement of capital.[2026] The provision of information for supervision also restricts the free movement of capital, if the informational requirements are onerous.

Article 65(1)(b) of the TFEU grants Member States the right "to take all requisite measures to prevent infringements of national law and regulations, in particular in the field of taxation and the prudential supervision of financial institutions", even if these measures breach Article 63 of the TFEU. To be justified under Article 65(1)(b) of the TFEU, the restrictive measures be necessary for the interests that they are intended to guarantee, be proportionate, and satisfy the requirements of legal certainty (i.e. be specific, objective, and known to the parties beforehand); furthermore, the persons whom the measures affect must have access to legal redress, i.e. intervention must be supported by a formal statement of reasons and be subject to review in the national courts.[2027] Subsection 92(1) of the PIA is neither specific nor objective and, therefore, does not provide legal certainty to the payment service provider or e-money institution. In order to give legal certainty, the Estonian legislation should provide detailed guidance on the precise measures that the EFSA will apply, on receipt of particular pieces of advice from the financial supervision authority of the foreign state. In addition, the PIA neither grants the applicant payment service provider or e-money institution the right to appeal in the Estonian courts against the decision imposing the restrictive measures, nor requires the EFSA to give reasons for laying down these measures. Thus, the PIA does not provide the persons whom the measures affect with access to legal redress. Hence, Article 65(1)(b) of the TFEU does not justify subsection 92(1) of the PIA.

If the Estonian payment service provider or e-money institution has established a branch in a third country, or is providing cross-border services in that state, then Article 64(2) of the TFEU applies. For the

---

[2025] See the subsection '*Sections 29 and 30: The supply of services by Estonian payment institutions and e-money institutions in another Contracting State*', above in this section, for an explanation as to why the provision of cross-border payment services is included in Title XIII(F) of the nomenclature in Annex I.

[2026] The extent to which the measures restrict the free movement of capital depends upon their severity. For example, a two-week suspension of the provision of payment services limits the free movement of capital less than does a suspension that lasts for one month.

[2027] See the subsection '*The requirements for a successful public policy/public security derogation*', in section 2.1.3.

restrictive measures to be justified under Article 64(2), the EU institutions must carefully consider the objective of the free movement of capital whilst enacting the pertinent legislation, and the national rules must not restrict the free movement of capital more do than the equivalent provisions of the relevant Directive.[2028] The relevant Directive is Directive 2007/64/EC. The Articles of this Directive do not mention the free movement of capital. Furthermore, whilst Recitals 1, 2 and 3 of the Directive stress the significance of the internal market, they do not specifically consider the free movement of capital.[2029] Thus, the EU institutions do not carefully take account of the objective of the free movement of capital, whilst enacting Directive 2007/64/EC. In addition, the Estonian rules limit the free movement of capital more than do the equivalent provisions in the Directive, because none of the latter's Articles specifically concern third countries. Hence, Article 64(2) of the TFEU does not justify the restrictive measures. Consequently, subsection 92(1) of the PIA contravenes Article 63 of the TFEU.

Section 93: Supervision of Estonian branches of foreign payment institutions and e-money institutions, and of foreign payment institutions and e-money institutions that provide cross-border services in Estonia

The EFSA may require a foreign payment institution that provides services in Estonia to submit reports and additional items that are necessary for the exercise of supervision over the foreign payment institution or e-money institution, and also data that are necessary for the collection of statistical information.[2030] A payment institution or e-money institution that provides services in Estonia and whose activity licence has been revoked or suspended by the financial supervision authority of a foreign country, shall cease to supply these services in Estonia.[2031]

If a third country payment institution or e-money institution that provides services in Estonia breaches the requirements of Estonian legislation, then the EFSA may apply sanctions and measures that are necessary for the cessation of the contravention, or revoke the authorisation for the establishment of a branch or for the supply of cross-

---

[2028] See the subsection '*Derogations that apply only to capital movement to/from third countries*', in section 2.3.2.

[2029] See the subsection '*Sections 25 to 28 and subsections 30(1), (2), (4) and (6)-(9): The supply of services by Estonian payment institutions and e-money institutions in a third country*', above in this section.

[2030] s.93(1), PIA.

[2031] s.93(2), PIA.

border services.[2032] Furthermore, the EFSA may require a payment institution or e-money institution of a (non-Estonian) Contracting State that has established an Estonian branch or supplies cross-border services in Estonia, to terminate its breach of the requirements for which Estonian legislation provides.[2033] If this institution of a Contracting State continues to transgress these requirements, then the EFSA shall inform that State's financial supervision authority thereof.[2034]

If the measures that the (non-Estonian) Contracting State applies are inadequate, and the payment institution or e-money institution of that State continues to contravene the requirements of Estonian legislation, then the EFSA may issue a precept in order to apply measures for which the PIA provides for the cessation of the transgression, or in order to prohibit the suppliance of services by this institution in Estonia.[2035] The EFSA shall immediately notify the European Commission and the Contracting State's financial supervision authority of the measures that it has taken.[2036]

In exceptional cases, the EFSA may, in order to protect the public interest and a payment institution's or e-money institution's creditors and clients, apply measures for which the law provides with regard to a payment institution or an e-money institution of a Contracting State, without informing that State's financial supervision authority beforehand.[2037] The EFSA shall immediately inform that financial supervision authority and the European Commission of the measures that it has taken.[2038]

The EFSA shall inform the foreign payment institution or e-money institution of the measures that it has applied, pursuant to section 93 of the PIA.[2039] The institution may file a complaint through its branch against measures that the EFSA is applying, with a court in the location of the branch.[2040]

The establishment of a branch and the provision of cross-border services are 'capital movements' in Titles I(1) and XIII(F) in the

---

[2032] s.93(3), PIA.

[2033] s.93(4), PIA.

[2034] s.93(5), PIA.

[2035] s.93(6), PIA. The EFSA shall inform the (non-Estonian) Contracting State's financial supervision authority, before it issues the precept to the institution (s.93(6), PIA).

[2036] s.93(9), PIA.

[2037] s.93(8), PIA.

[2038] s.93(9), PIA.

[2039] s.93(7), PIA.

[2040] s.93(7), PIA.

nomenclature in Annex I, respectively.[2041] The revocation of an authorisation for the foundation of a branch or the suppliance of cross-border services, the application of sanctions and measures in order to terminate a breach of Estonian legislation, and the issuance of a precept in order to apply measures for which the PIA provides for the cessation of a transgression of Estonian legislation or in order to prohibit the provision of services by a payment service provider or e-money institution, contravene the free movement of capital.

Article 65(1)(b) of the TFEU provides Member States with the right "to take all requisite measures to prevent infringements of national law and regulations, in particular in the field of taxation and the prudential supervision of financial institutions", even if these measures contravene Article 63 of the TFEU. For Article 65(1)(b) TFEU to justify the restrictive measures, they must be necessary for the protection of interests that they are intended to guarantee, be proportionate, and observe the requirements of legal certainty (i.e. the measures must be specific, objective and known to the parties beforehand); furthermore, the persons whom the measures affect must have access to legal redress (i.e. intervention must be supported by reasons and be liable to review by the national courts).[2042] The measures for which section 93 of the PIA provides are neither specific nor objective; therefore, they do not fulfil the requirements of legal certainty. In order to address this difficulty, the PIA or its subordinate legislation should precisely state the measures that the EFSA is to apply in specified combinations of circumstances, for instance, by classifying the possible transgressions of Estonian legislation into categories of seriousness, and assigning appropriate remedial measures for the EFSA to apply to payment service providers and e-money institutions in each class. In addition, the PIA neither requires the EFSA to give reasons for its decision to revoke an authorisation, apply measures or sanctions, or issue a precept, nor grants the applicant institution with the right to appeal against the EFSA's decision in the Estonian courts; therefore, the persons whom the measures affect do not have access to legal redress. Hence, Article 65(1)(b) of the TFEU does not justify the restrictive measures in section 93 of the PIA.

[2041] See the subsection '*Sections 29 and 30: The supply of services by Estonian payment institutions and e-money institutions in another Contracting State*', above in this section, for an explanation as to why the provision of cross-border payment services is included in Title XIII(F) of the nomenclature in Annex I.

[2042] See the subsection '*The requirements for a successful public policy/public security derogation*', in section 2.1.3.

Article 64(2) of the TFEU may apply to subsections 93(1)-(3) and 93(7) of the PIA, as they concern third country payment service providers and e-money institutions that supply services in Estonia. However, this Article does not apply to subsections 93(4)-(6) and 93(8)-(9) of the PIA, as they concern the provision of services within the EEA. For the restrictive measures in section 93 of the TFEU to be justified under Article 64(2) of the TFEU, the EU institutions must carefully take account of the objective of the free movement of capital whilst enacting the pertinent legislation, and the national rules must not limit the free movement of capital more than do the equivalent provisions of the relevant Directive. The Articles of the relevant Directive, Directive 2007/64/EC, do not refer to the free movement of capital. Furthermore, whilst Recitals 1, 2 and 3 of this Directive emphasise the internal market's significance, they do not specifically consider the free movement of capital. Hence, the EU institutions do not carefully take account of the free movement of capital, whilst enacting Directive 2007/64/EC. In addition, section 93 of the PIA restricts the free movement of capital more than corresponding provisions in the Directive do, because none of the Directive's Articles specifically concern third countries. Thus, the restrictive measures in section 93 of the PIA are not justified under Article 64(2) of the TFEU. Consequently, these measures breach Article 63 of the TFEU.

3.6 Comment

The Estonian financial services legislation is comprehensive in respect of passporting. Its provisions consider almost every perceivable variation of the supply of services across Estonia's borders. Many of these rules contravene Article 63 of the TFEU.

In most cases of breach of Article 63, the restrictive measures that the EFSA may take are not justified under Article 65(1)(b) of the TFEU, because the financial institution that is affected by these measures is not provided with legal certainty, and this organisation does not have access to legal redress. In addition, restrictive measures that the EFSA may apply to capital movements between Estonia and third countries are often not justified under Article 64(2) of the TFEU, because the EU institutions do not take account of the free movement of capital whilst enacting the relevant legislation. Furthermore, for many Estonian provisions discussed in this chapter that empower the EFSA to apply restrictive measures to capital movements to or from third countries, Article 64(2) of the TFEU does not provide a justification for these measures because the relevant Directive contains few or no equivalent provisions to the national legislation. Directives 2011/61/EU and 2009/138/EC are fairly concerned with the position of the movement of services to and/or from third countries. However, Directives 2002/92/EC and 2007/64/EC do not consider the issue of the suppliance of services between the EEA and third countries.

As the EU institutions have been less forthcoming in their consideration of the conditions under which financial services can be supplied to or from third countries than in their legislative treatment of the intra-EEA movement of these services, it is correspondingly more difficult for national legislatures to effectively address breaches in the free movement of capital to or from third countries than those within the EEA – at least from the point of view of justifications that apply only to limitations to the free movement of capital to and from third countries. Nevertheless, the restrictions that apply to capital movements to or from third countries may be justified by Article 65(1)(b) of the TFEU, if the conditions for this justification are satisfied. Therefore, the approach that the Estonian legislature should take to the contraventions of Article 63 of the TFEU discussed in this chapter, is to enact the provisions that are necessary in order to satisfy these conditions.

Therefore, the Estonian legislature should insert provisions into the IFA, the SMA, the CIA, the IAA and the PIA, which require the EFSA to provide a formal statement of reasons for its decisions – especially those that impose measures which restrict the free movement of capital on financial institutions. In addition, this legislature should add provisions into these Acts that grant financial institutions which are recipients of decisions that impose restrictive measures, the right to appeal in the Estonian courts against such measures. If these rules are added to the Estonian legislation, then the persons whom the measures affect have access to legal redress – as Article 65(1)(b) of the TFEU requires.[2043]

Furthermore, the Estonian legislature should ensure that the measures that the EFSA applies to financial institutions that restrict the free movement of capital observe the requirements of legal certainty – i.e. are specific, objective and known to the parties beforehand (as Article 65(1)(b) of the TFEU requires).[2044] This is a challenge, for it requires the government and its advisers to understand what measures the EFSA is likely to take in response to specific factual situations concerning insufficiencies and misdemeanours that financial institutions display. For example, if, as proposed by some of the Estonian legislative provisions

[2043] See the subsection '*Public policy, public security, general interest, and prior authorisation*', in section 2.1.3.
[2044] See note 2043.

considered in this chapter, the EFSA refuses to forward documents to the financial supervision authority of a Contracting State in which it intends to establish a branch or provide cross-border services, or refuses to grant an authorisation for the foundation of a branch in a third country, or revokes this authorisation, because the financial institution or the carrying out of its business plan may damage the interests of its clients, then the Estonian legislature or the EFSA must state in advance what is meant by 'damage', 'interests' and 'clients'. The legislature or the EFSA should then classify, as appropriate, the 'damage' into types and/or grades of severity, and assign a 'punishment' to each of these classes – such as (in the case of revocation of an authorisation), revocation for the particular financial services affected, revocation of financial services 'a', 'b' and 'c' (to be specified), and withdrawal of the authorisation for all financial services. As a result of these classifications, it must be possible for financial institutions whose interests are adversely affected by a decision of the EFSA that limits the free movement of capital to know what the measures will be beforehand, and that these measures are sufficiently specific and objective to be able to provide the relevant financial institution with legal certainty. It may be appropriate for this degree of detail to be placed in delegated legislation, which can be passed by the Estonian Ministry of Finance or other suitable Estonian public organisation. Alternatively, and if appropriate, the EFSA could publish detailed guidelines on the precise measures to be applied in the different situations that the Estonian legislation envisages. If the detailed rules are reserved for secondary legislation or for guidelines that the EFSA publishes, then the Estonian legislature should ensure that they include provisions in the relevant Act(s) that authorise the delegated legislation to be produced and published.

Article 65(1)(b) of the TFEU requires (amongst other things) the measures that the EFSA imposes on financial institutions to be necessary for the protection of the interests that they are intended to guarantee.[2045] Most of the Estonian legislative provisions that this chapter considers do not state what these interests are. For each rule that restricts the free movement of capital to be justified by Article 65(1)(b) of the TFEU, it is necessary for the Estonian legislature to state what these interests are – even if they are provided in the guidance notes that accompany the legislation (rather than in the Acts). For example, if, as in some of the Estonian provisions considered in this chapter, the EFSA refuses to review the documents submitted by a financial institution, or refuses to forward them to the financial supervision authority of a (non-Estonian) EEA state,

[2045] See note 2043.

because it considers that the institution does not possess sufficient resources to establish a branch in that country, then the Estonian legislature may state (in the relevant Act or its guidance notes) that this restriction is necessary in order to protect potential customers of this branch from providing funds for its provision of financial services to them without receiving these services from the branch.

Article 65(1)(b) of the TFEA also requires measures that the EFSA imposes on financial institutions that restrict the free movement of capital to be proportionate – i.e. not to be attainable by less restrictive measures. As the analysis in this chapter shows, proportionality is an issue if the national legislation requires an Estonian financial institution to obtain an authorisation from the EFSA in order to establish a branch, or provide cross-border services, in a third country, and if it requires a third country financial institution to obtain an authorisation in order to found a branch, or supply cross-border services, in Estonia. The requirement to obtain prior authorisation from a public office-holder institution has been held to be disproportionate in the case of (for instance) foreign investment[2046] and the supply of petroleum.[2047] In some of the Estonian provisions discussed in this chapter, the legislature imposes many grounds for the EFSA to refuse to grant an authorisation, or to revoke an authorisation, for the establishment of a branch by a third country financial institution in Estonia or by an Estonian institution in a third country and, in fewer instances, for the provision of cross-border services to or from a third country. The Estonian legislature should check all of these provisions carefully, in order to ensure that they are not disproportionate. Furthermore, if it concludes that they are disproportionate, then it should either reduce the severity of the measures, or reduce the number (or severity) of the conditions that are required in order for the EFSA to grant an authorisation, or to refrain from withdrawing it.

Thus, there is plenty that the Estonian legislature is able to do, in order to bring the rules of its national legislation considered in this chapter within the ambit of the derogation in Article 65(1)(b) of the TFEU. If it is successful in these changes, then this would ensure that provisions of the IFA, the SMA, the CIA, the IAA and the PIA that restrict the free movement of capital are justified under this Article, and, therefore, do not breach Article 63 of the TFEU.

A few years ago, I made the following conclusions.

[2046] *Eglise de Scientologie and Scientology International*, [2000] ECR I-1335.
[2047] *Commission v France*, [2002] ECR I-4781.

> "The EFSA has wide discretion in granting and revoking authorisations, refusing to forward information, issuing precepts and prohibiting cross-border services, which the European Commission and CJEU will not accept in derogation from the free movement of capital. This is a consequence of Estonia's recent accession to the European Union. Estonia has not yet had time to set in place a comprehensive legal and regulatory framework for its cross-border capital flows."[2048]

Today, the situation is thus. The EFSA has wide discretion in some instances in granting and revoking authorisations, refusing to forward information, and issuing precepts, which the European Commission and CJEU are unlikely to accept in derogation from the free movement of capital. Whilst the Estonian legislature has set in place a comprehensive legal and regulatory framework for capital flows to and from Estonia, many of the provisions within this framework restrict the free movement of capital. This section suggests measures that the legislature might take in order to make a reasonable attempt to ensure that they do not breach Article 63 of the TFEU.

This chapter contains a comprehensive review of Estonian financial legislation for compliance with the EU's rules on the free movement of capital. Owing to the length of the chapter, and the consequential shortage of both time and space for the consideration of legislation and regulations of other Member States, the subsequent chapters will take a more concise approach than this chapter does to the compliance of national provisions with EU law. As the legislative framework of Estonia is comprehensive,[2049] this structure will be used as a benchmark with which to compare the rules of the other countries that this book examines.

Chapter 4 analyses the compliance of Polish financial regulatory law with the EU's free movement of capital rules that Chapter 2 considers.

[2048] Baber (2010), *The Impact of Legislation and Regulation on the Freedom of Movement of Capital in Estonia, Poland and Latvia*, 86.

[2049] See the previous paragraph.

CHAPTER FOUR

POLAND: LEGAL ISSUES

> "The history of Polish Parliamentarism dates back to the 15th century. In contrast, the history of Poland's constitutionalism is a little over 200 years old. It was only in 1791 that the so-called 'Constitution of the 3d of May' was adopted, an endeavor that would lead to a modern system of government. Unfortunately, the Constitution was never implemented due to the subsequent collapse of the Polish state in 1795. … It was the rebirth of a fully independent Poland in the wake of World War One that paved the way for the development of a truly indigenous constitution, which was adopted in March of 1921".[1]

The fall of communism in 1989 led to substantial constitutional and legal changes as Poland prepared for its membership of the European Union in 2004. Poland implemented a new constitution in 1997, which replaced the largely redundant Soviet-imposed version of 1952. The codified legal system survived, with modifications. Many of the Acts are recent, but there is older legislation, such as the Act of 24 March 1920 on the Acquisition of Immovable Properties by Foreign Persons. This chapter reviews Polish financial services legislation, which is available from the Polish Financial Supervision Authority (PFSA).

Section 4.1 considers the Investment Funds Act. Section 4.2 discusses legal instruments that regulate providers of financial instruments. Sections 4.3 and 4.4 consider laws that regulate credit institutions and insurance entities, respectively. Section 4.5 reviews the Act on Payment Services.

4.1 Act of 27 May 2004 on Investment Funds (IFA)

An investment fund is a legal person that raises cash by issuing participation units or investment certificates in securities, money market

[1] S. Frankowski *(ed.)* (2005), *Introduction to Polish Law*, 1.

instruments and other property rights in the IFA.[2] An investment fund may only be created by a management company,[3] subject to the authorisation of the PFSA.[4]

An investment fund may be an open-end investment fund,[5] a specialised open-end investment fund,[6] or a closed-end investment fund.[7] Open-end investment funds transfer and repurchase participation units.[8] Closed-end investment funds issue public or non-public investment certificates in bearer form, and the latter as registered securities.[9]

A Polish management company shall attach the following items to its application for an authorisation to found an investment fund in Poland: the investment fund's articles of association,[10] the agreement with the depositary on the maintenance of the investment fund's assets,[11] personal details of the depositary's management board members (including a

---

[2] Article 3(1), IFA.

[3] The management company's activities comprise founding and managing investment funds – which includes intermediation in the sale and redemption of units, representation of investment funds in dealings with third parties, and management of a unit investment trust (Article 45(1), IFA), and may include intermediation in the sale and redemption of units of investment funds that other management companies establish or units of foreign funds, and acting as a representative of foreign funds (Article 45(2a), IFA). See note 22, for the definition of a 'foreign fund'. With the approval of the PFSA, a management company may manage portfolios of securities and/or provide advisory services with respect to the trading of securities (Article 45(2), IFA).

[4] Article 14(1), IFA. A management company may bring more than one investment fund into existence (Article 14(2), IFA).

[5] Article 14(3)(1), IFA.

[6] Article 14(3)(2), IFA. The IFA does not define the term 'specialised open-end investment fund'. Only the entities that the articles of association of a specialised open-end investment fund specify, or which satisfy the conditions that these articles of association specify, may be unit-holders of the fund; the fund's articles of association must make this fact clear (Article 113(1), IFA). Unless Chapter 2 (Specialised Open-End Investment Funds) of Part V (Types of Investment Funds) of the IFA states otherwise, the rule on open-end investment funds are to govern specialised open-end investment funds (Article 112, IFA).

[7] Article 14(3)(3), IFA.

[8] Article 82, IFA. These funds may also buy participation titles in foreign funds and joint investment institutions with a non-Polish seat (Article 101(1)-(2), IFA). See note 22, for the definition of a 'foreign fund'.

[9] Articles 117(1) and 121(1), IFA.

[10] Article 22(1), IFA.

[11] Article 22(2), IFA. The depositary's main function is to maintain a register of the investment fund's assets (Article 9, IFA).

description of their qualifications and professional experience),[12] personal details of those employees of a management company (or its delegate brokerage firm) who have a material influence on the activities of the investment fund (including a description of their qualifications and professional experience),[13] personal details of the persons to whom the depositary designates the responsibilities defined in the agreement (including a description of their qualifications and experience),[14] extracts from the relevant register that concern the entities which the management company commissions to conduct its activities,[15] the investment fund's prospectus and simplified prospectus,[16] specification of the originator and of the main terms and conditions of the agreements that the management company concludes in connection with the securitisation process,[17] and a statement by a qualified auditor that the rules and methods applied in the valuation of the fund's assets (that are described in its articles of association) comply with the regulations on the accountancy of investment funds – and (for a closed-end investment fund) that the rules are complete and consistent with the fund's investment policy.[18] The PFSA shall issue the authorisation for the establishment of an investment fund within two months of its receipt of the application for authorisation.[19]

In Poland, an investment fund shall sell and redeem its units directly, or through its management company or an entity that conducts brokerage activities, subject to the following exception.[20] Units in investment funds, foreign investment funds,[21] open-end investment funds registered in an EEA state, and open-end investment funds registered in an OECD member state (other than an EEA state), may be sold and redeemed through the intermediation of an entity other than one that conducts brokerage activities, provided that the PFSA grants it an authorisation to do so.[22] The PFSA shall grant this entity an authorisation if the latter submits an

---

[12] Article 22(5), IFA.
[13] Articles 22(6), 22(8) and 46(1), IFA.
[14] Articles 22(7) and 22(8), IFA.
[15] Article 22(9), IFA.
[16] Article 22(10), IFA.
[17] Article 22(11), IFA.
[18] Article 22(12), IFA.
[19] Article 23(1), IFA.
[20] Article 32(1), IFA.
[21] The IFA does not define 'foreign investment fund'. A 'foreign fund' is an open-end investment fund or an investment firm that is registered in a (non-Polish) Member State, that conducts its operations in accordance with EU law that governs collective investments in securities (Article 2(9), IFA).
[22] Article 32(2), IFA.

application to which the following items are appended:[23] documents that define the applicant's legal form,[24] a description and chart of "capital links",[25] the entity's latest financial statements together with an auditor's report on these,[26] specification of the investment funds whose units the applicant (as intermediary) plans to sell and redeem,[27] a detailed description for the procedure for the sale and redemption of units,[28] documents that specify in detail the manner of making the payments that are connected with the sale and redemption of units,[29] a list of the places where units are to be sold or redeemed,[30] the resources that the applicant proposes to use in the sale and redemption of units,[31] a specification of the persons who are responsible for the performance of the activities that are connected with the sale and redemption of units,[32] affirmation that the applicant's employees have undertaken training with regard to the procedures that are involved in the sale and redemption of units,[33] procedures to prevent the abuse or disclosure of inside information,[34] internal audit procedures,[35] rules for storing and archiving documents that are connected with the sale and redemption of units,[36] the personal details of the applicant's supervisory or management board members (including a description of their qualifications and experience),[37] and a certificate that confirms the absence of arrears of tax (or stating the amount of these arrears) pursuant to the (Polish) Tax Legislation Act.[38] The PFSA shall refuse to grant this authorisation in the event that the documents attached to the application fall short of those that the IFA requires,[39] the application or the items attached to it do not comply with "the law" or are "contrary to

[23] Articles 32(3) and 32(4), IFA.
[24] Article 32(4)(1), IFA.
[25] Article 32(4)(2), IFA. The IFA does not define what 'capital links' are.
[26] Article 32(4)(3), IFA.
[27] Article 32(4)(4), IFA.
[28] Article 32(4)(5), IFA.
[29] Article 32(4)(6), IFA.
[30] Article 32(4)(7), IFA.
[31] Article 32(4)(8), IFA.
[32] Article 32(4)(9), IFA.
[33] Article 32(4)(10), IFA.
[34] Article 32(4)(11), IFA.
[35] Article 32(4)(11), IFA.
[36] Article 32(4)(12), IFA.
[37] Article 32(4)(13), IFA.
[38] Article 32(4)(14), IFA.
[39] Article 32(6)(1), IFA.

the facts",[40] and/or an analysis of the application and its attached documents shows that the applicant may perform its activities in contravention of the principles of fair trading or in a way that does not duly protect the interests of unit-holders or persons subscribing for the investment units.[41]

Subject to Articles 92(2),[42] 94,[43] and 101,[44] an open-ended investment fund may invest its assets exclusively in securities that the Polish State Treasury or the National Bank of Poland guarantee,[45] securities and money market instruments that have been admitted to trading on a regulated market within the EU or on an organised market in an OECD member state (other than an EU Member State),[46] securities and money market

---

[40] Article 32(6)(2), IFA. 'The law' probably means the IFA's requirements. 'Contrary to the facts' may mean that the items that the applicant submits suggest different circumstances to those that the IFA would like it to demonstrate. For instance, the applicant may submit evidence that its employees have undergone some training with respect to the procedures that are involved in the sale and redemption of investment units (as required by Article 32(4)(10) of the IFA) but that this training is insufficient (in the PFSA's view).

[41] Article 32(6)(3), IFA.

[42] The net asset value of an open-end investment fund must be at least 2 million Polish zloty (Article 92(1), IFA). The fund is to announce each decline in its net asset value to a level below 2.5 million zloty in the manner that its articles of association specify (Article 92(2), IFA). In this announcement, the fund is to state the reasons for the decline, and actions that the fund will take to raise its net asset value (Article 92(3), IFA).

[43] Subject to the conditions that this Article lays down, an open-end investment fund may conclude agreements that concern derivatives (Article 94, IFA).

[44] Article 101 of the IFA concerns an open-end investment fund's acquisition of units in other investment funds and undertakings, and limitations to the money that it may place in these vehicles, and is considered below in this section.

[45] Article 93(1)(1), IFA.

[46] Article 93(1)(1), IFA. For the open-end investment fund to invest its assets in these financial instruments, its articles of association must permit it to do so (Article 93(1)(1), IFA). A 'regulated market' is a system for trading in financial instruments, which functions on a continuous basis and provides investors with universal, equal, concurrent access to market information when they match the offers to acquire and to sell financial instruments, ensures equal terms for the acquisition and the disposal of financial instruments, and which is organised and supervised by a competent authority pursuant to the provisions of the Act on Trading in Financial Instruments, as well as being recognised by a relevant Member State as compliant with these requirements, and notified to the European Commission as a regulated market (Articles 2(22a), IFA and 14(1), Act of 29 July 2005 on Trading in Financial Instruments). An 'organised market' is a distinct trading system, which operates regularly and ensures uniform conditions for the

instruments that have been admitted to public trading or which are acquired in an initial public offering or in primary trading,[47] deposits with Polish banks or credit institutions that have a maturity of one year or less that are payable on demand or before the agreed maturity date,[48] money market instruments (other than those specified above) if these instruments or their issuers are subject to regulations the purpose of which is to protect investors and their savings,[49] and are issued or guaranteed by the Polish State Treasury, the National Bank of Poland, a local government institution, the central bank or a public authority of a (non-Polish) Member State, the European Central Bank, the EU, the European Investment Bank, a country outside the EU (or one of its members – if it is a federation), or by an international organisation to which at least one Member State belongs,[50] issued or guaranteed by an entity that is subject to supervision that is in accordance with the criteria of EU law,[51] issued or guaranteed by an entity that is subject to, and applies, rules that are at least strict as those of EU law,[52] issued by an entity whose securities are traded on a regulated market within the EU,[53] or issued by other entities that the investment

---

execution of transactions, and universal, equal access to information on transactions, in accordance with the applicable laws of the country in which trading takes place (Article 2(22), IFA).

[47] Article 93(1)(2), IFA. For the open-end investment fund to invest its assets in these securities and money-market instruments, the terms and conditions of the initial public offering or public issue must provide for admission to trading on a regulated market within the EU or on an organised market in an OECD member state, the admission to trading must take place within one year from the day on which the securities or money-market instruments are first offered, and the investment fund's articles of association must allow it to invest in these financial instruments (Article 93(1)(2), IFA).

[48] Article 93(1)(3), IFA. The PFSA may consent to investment of the fund's assets in deposits with a foreign bank, provided that this bank is subject to supervision by the relevant (foreign) financial supervision authority to an extent that is at least equal to that specified in EU law (Article 93(3), IFA). A 'foreign bank' is one with a registered office outside the territory of Poland, except for a foreign credit institution (Article 2(15), IFA). The IFA does not define the term 'foreign credit institution'. A 'credit institution' is a company that has its registered office in an EEA state (other than Poland), which conducts the business of receiving repayable funds, and of providing loans, or of issuing electronic money (Article 2(17), IFA; Articles 4(1)(17) and 4(3), Act of 29 August 1997: Banking Law).

[49] Article 93(1)(4), IFA.

[50] Article 93(1)(4)(a), IFA.

[51] Article 93(1)(4)(b), IFA.

[52] Article 93(1)(4)(b), IFA.

[53] Article 93(1)(4)(c), IFA. See note 46, for the definition of 'regulated market'.

fund's articles of association specifies, on condition that investments in these securities provide protection to investors that is at least equivalent to the protection referred to in Article 93(1)(4)(a)-(c) of the IFA[54] and that the issuer fulfils all of the following requirements: it is a company whose equity adds to at least 10 million EUR, publishes its annual financial statements in accordance with EU law, is a member of a group that includes at least one company whose securities are traded on a regulated market, and is engaged in the financing of such a group or of structures that are designed to convert debt into securities that use credit facilities,[55] or securities and money market instruments other than those specified above – provided that the total value of these investments does not exceed 10% of the value of the investment fund's assets.[56]

Subject to Articles 97, 98, 99 and 100,[57] an open-end investment fund must not invest more than 5% of the value of its assets in securities or money market instruments of a single issuer.[58] This limit may be raised to 10%, if the total value of investments in securities and money market instruments of this issuer adds to no more than 40% of the value of the fund's assets, and if the fund's articles of association so provide.[59]

An open-end investment fund is not to invest more than 20% of the value of its assets in deposits with a single Polish bank or a single credit institution.[60] The total value of investments in securities or money market instruments that a single entity issues, deposits with this entity, and the value of counterparty risk associated with transactions in non-standard derivatives concluded with this entity, must not exceed 20% of the value of the investment fund's assets.[61]

---

[54] See above in this sentence.

[55] Article 93(1)(4)(d), IFA.

[56] Article 93(1)(5), IFA.

[57] See below in this section.

[58] Article 96(1), IFA.

[59] Article 96(3), IFA. These limits do not apply to deposits and transactions in non-standard derivatives that are made with entities that are subject to supervision by the relevant financial supervision authority (Article 96(4), IFA). A 'non-standard derivative' is a derivative instrument that is traded outside an organised market, whose terms are (or may be) subject to negotiation between parties (Article 2(19), IFA). See note 46, for the definition of 'organised market'. Investments in mortgage bonds shall not be counted, when determining the limit to which Article 96(3) refers (Article 97(4), IFA). See below in this section, for the investment limits in mortgage bonds.

[60] Article 96(2), IFA. See note 48, for the definition of 'credit institution'.

[61] Article 96(5), IFA. See note 59, for the definition of 'non-standard derivative'.

An open-end investment fund shall not invest more than 25% of its assets in mortgage bonds that a single mortgage bank issues.[62] The total value of investment in mortgage bonds is not to exceed 80% of the value of the fund's assets.[63] The aggregate value of investments in securities or money market instruments that a single mortgage bank issues, deposits with this mortgage bank, and the value of counterparty risk associated with transactions in non-standard derivatives that are made with the mortgage bank, must be less than or equal to 35% of the fund's assets.[64]

An open-end investment fund may invest up to 20% of the value of its assets in securities or money market instruments issued by members of the same group,[65] if the fund's articles of association provide for this.[66] The fund shall not invest more than 5% of the value of its assets in securities or money market instruments that any member of the group issues;[67] this investment limit may be raised to 10%, if the fund's articles of association so provide.[68] However, the total value of the fund's investments in securities and money market instruments in which the fund has invested between 5% and 10% of the value of its assets, is not to exceed 40% of the value of these assets.[69]

An open-end investment fund may invest up to 20% of the value of its assets in shares or debt securities of a single issuer, provided that, in accordance with the investment policy contained in the fund's articles of association, its investments will mirror the composition of a recognised equity or debt securities index.[70] A fund may raise this limit to 35% of the value of its assets if the percentage share of an issuer's shares (or debt securities) in the index rises, and if permitted under the fund's articles of association.[71]

An open-end investment fund may invest up to 35% of the value of its assets in securities issued by the Polish State Treasury, the National Bank

---

[62] Article 97(1), IFA. The Act of 29 August 1997 on Mortgage Bonds and Mortgage Banks provides further information on mortgage bonds and mortgage banks.

[63] Article 97(2), IFA.

[64] Article 97(3), IFA.

[65] Members of one group preparing consolidated financial statements shall be treated as a single entity, for the purposes of investment limits (Article 98(1), IFA).

[66] Article 98(2), IFA.

[67] Article 98(3), IFA.

[68] Article 98(4), IFA.

[69] Article 98(5), IFA.

[70] Article 99(1), IFA.

[71] Article 99(2), IFA. This limit may only apply to shares or debt securities of only one issuer (Article 99(2), IFA).

of Poland, a Member State, a local government institution of a Member State (including Poland), an OECD member state, or an international financial institution of which at least one (EU) Member State is a member.[72] An open-end investment may invest up to 35% of the value of its securities that are guaranteed by these entities.[73]

An open-end investment fund may acquire units in other open-end investment funds that are registered in Poland,[74] and/or units in foreign investment funds.[75] It may also acquire units in collective investment undertakings[76] that are registered outside Poland, if the units in these entities are offered to the public and are redeemable at the unit-holder's request,[77] the collective investment undertakings are supervised by the competent financial supervision authority of a Member State or of an OECD member state and it is ensured that this authority's co-operation with the PFSA is reciprocal,[78] holders of units that collective investment undertakings issue enjoy the same protection of units of open-end investment funds,[79] and these undertakings are required to prepare annual and semi-annual financial statements.[80] The acquisitions that the previous sentence specifies are subject to the condition that not more than 10% of the value of the assets of the "open-end investment funds, foreign funds or undertakings" may, in accordance with their articles of association or

[72] Article 100(1), IFA.

[73] Article 100(2), IFA. The total value of investments in securities or money market instruments issued by an entity whose securities are guaranteed, deposits with this entity, and the value of counterparty risk associated with transactions in non-standard derivatives that are made with such an entity, are not to exceed 35% of the value of the investment fund's assets (Article 100(2), IFA). An open-end investment fund is not obliged to apply the limits to which Article 100(2) of the IFA refers, if its articles of association provide as such and indicate the identity of the issuer or guarantor (Article 100(3), IFA). In this case, the investment fund must invest in securities of at least six different securities' issues of one issuer, as long as no investment in securities of a single issue exceeds 30% of the value of the fund's assets (Article 100(4), IFA).

[74] Article 101(1)(1), IFA.

[75] Article 101(1)(2), IFA.

[76] The IFA does not define the term 'collective investment undertaking'.

[77] Article 101(1)(3)(a), IFA.

[78] Article 101(1)(3)(b), IFA.

[79] Article 101(1)(3)(c), IFA. In particular, these undertakings must apply investment limits that are at least as strict as those defined in this chapter of the IFA (Article 101(1)(3)(c), IFA). 'This chapter' is Chapter 1 (Open-End Investment Funds) of Part V (Types of Investment Funds) of the IFA.

[80] Article 101(1)(3)(c), IFA.

rules, be invested in units of "other open-end investment funds, foreign funds, and collective investment undertakings".[81]

An open-end investment fund may not invest more than 20% of the value of its assets in units of a "single open-end investment fund, foreign fund or collective investment undertaking referred to in Art. 101.1".[82] The total value of investments in units in collective investment undertakings (except for units of open-end investment funds or foreign funds) are not to be greater than 30% of the investment fund's assets.[83]

An open-end investment fund may lend dematerialised securities up to an aggregate value of 30% of the fund's asset value.[84] The total value of the securities lent and the securities of the same issuer that the investment fund holds in its portfolio, are not to exceed the limits specified in Articles 96 to 100 of the IFA.[85]

An open-end investment fund is not to acquire securities that confer the right to more than 10% of the total vote in one of their issuer's governing bodies,[86] more than 10% of the non-voting shares in a single issuer,[87] more than 25% of the total number of units of a single open-end investment fund, foreign fund, or collective investment undertaking registered outside Poland, which are offered to the public and redeemed at the unit-holder's request,[88] or more than 10% of the par value of money

---

[81] Article 101(1)(3)(d), IFA. It is unclear how this statement fits in with the investment limits that the next paragraph describes. The limits in Article 101(2) and 101(3) of the IFA are broader than those of Article 101(1)(3) of the IFA. Consequently, for the former investment limits to be consistent with the latter, the former needs to refer to 'non-Polish collective investment undertakings' and the latter to 'all collective investment undertakings'. This interpretation is unlikely, because Article 101(2) of the IFA describes the investment vehicles as "referred to in Art. 101.1".

[82] Article 101(2), IFA.

[83] Article 101(3), IFA.

[84] Article 102(2), IFA. 'Dematerialised securities' are securities that exist without certificates of ownership – as of the date of their registration under the agreement on the registration of the securities in the depositary; these include securities that are part of a public offering, those that are admitted to trading on a regulated market, those introduced to a multilateral trading facility, and those that the Polish State Treasury or the National Bank of Poland issues (Articles 2(35), IFA and 5(1), Act of 29 July 2005 on Trading in Financial Instruments).

[85] Article 102(3), IFA. See above in this section.

[86] Article 104(1), IFA.

[87] Article 104(2), IFA.

[88] Article 104(3), IFA.

market instruments[89] or debt securities[90] that a single entity issues.[91] If securities acquired by open-end investment funds that are managed by one management company confer the right to more than 10% of the total vote in the issuer's governing bodies, then the funds may only exercise voting rights attached to securities that represent 10% of the total vote.[92]

An open-end investment fund may acquire loans with a maturity of up to one year exclusively from credit institutions[93] and Polish banks, provided that the aggregate value of these loans is not more than 10% of the fund's net asset value at the time that the loan agreement is made.[94] An open-end investment fund may only keep its assets in bank accounts to the extent necessary to satisfy the fund's current liabilities.[95]

A specialised open-end investment fund[96] may invest in units of other open-end investment funds, of foreign funds, or of collective investment undertakings registered outside Poland, which (further to their articles of association or rules) invest more than 10% of their assets in units of other open-end investment funds, foreign funds, or collective undertakings.[97] The fund may only do this if its articles of association state that its unit-holders may not be open-end investment funds, foreign funds, or collective investment undertakings resident outside Poland, that are managed by the fund's management company or an entity from that company's group.[98]

A specialised open-end investment fund may invest between 20% and 50% of its assets in units of a single open-end investment fund, foreign fund or collective investment undertaking, to which Article 101(1) of the IFA refers,[99] provided that the fund's articles of association state this and specify the identity of the investee.[100] If the articles of association of a specialised open-end investment fund so provide, this fund may invest up

---

[89] Article 104(4), IFA.

[90] Article 104(5), IFA.

[91] An open-end investment fund is not required to apply the limits that Articles 104(3), 104(4) and 104(5) specify, if the gross value of the money market instruments or debt securities, or the net value of the securities in issue, cannot be determined (Article 104(6), IFA).

[92] Article 104(7), IFA.

[93] See note 48, for the definition of 'credit institution'.

[94] Article 108, IFA.

[95] Article 109, IFA.

[96] See note 8, for fundamental provisions on open-end investment funds.

[97] Article 113(4), IFA.

[98] Article 113(4), IFA.

[99] See above in this section, for Article 101(1) of the IFA.

[100] Article 113(5), IFA.

to 100% of its assets in units of a single open-end investment fund, foreign fund, or collective investment undertaking, to which Article 101(1) of the IFA refers,[101] as long as the articles of association specify the identity of the investee,[102] define the principles that underlie the investee's investment policy,[103] and state the rates of management fees that the investee charges.[104]

Subject to Articles 145(2) to 145(8), 146 and 147,[105] a closed-end investment fund may invest its assets in securities,[106] debt issued by legal persons,[107] shares in limited liability companies,[108] currencies,[109] derivatives,[110] property rights,[111] or money market instruments,[112] provided that these items are transferable.[113] A closed-end investment fund that is created as securitisation fund[114] or a private equity fund[115] may invest its asset in transferable debt issued by natural persons.[116] The total of securities, money market instruments or debt of a single entity, or shares

---

[101] Article 113(6), IFA. See above in this section, for Article 101(1) of the IFA.
[102] Article 113(6)(1), IFA.
[103] Article 113(6)(2), IFA. An investment fund's investment policies shall define the methods of reaching the investment goal, in particular the types of property rights in which the fund will invest, the criteria for investments to be selected, rules that govern the diversification of investments and other investment limits, and the permissible level of the fund's indebtedness (Article 20(1), IFA).
[104] Article 113(6)(3), IFA.
[105] These Articles are considered below in this section.
[106] Article 145(1)(1), IFA.
[107] Article 145(1)(2), IFA.
[108] Article 145(1)(3), IFA.
[109] Article 145(1)(4), IFA.
[110] Article 145(1)(5), IFA.
[111] Article 145(1)(6), IFA. For property rights to be eligible, their price must depend "on the value of items of specified type, specified types of energy, measurements and allowances of production or pollution emissions" (Article 145(1)(6), IFA).
[112] Article 145(1)(7), IFA.
[113] Article 145(1), IFA.
[114] A closed-end investment fund may be established as a securitisation fund, which issues investment certificates in order to accumulate funds for the acquisition of debt (Article 183, IFA). See below in this section, for a description of a securitisation fund's investment limits.
[115] A closed-end investment fund, or a specialised open-end investment fund that applies the principles and investment limits of a closed-end investment fund, may be established as a private equity fund (Article 196, IFA). See below in this section, for a private equity fund's investment limits.
[116] Article 145(2), IFA.

in this corporation, shall not represent more than 20% of the value of closed-end investment fund's assets[117] – subject to the exception that mortgage bonds that a single mortgage bank issues are not to comprise more than 25% of the value of the fund's assets.[118] These investment limits do not apply to securities that are issued or guaranteed by the Polish State Treasury, the National Bank of Poland, an OECD member state, or an international financial institution in which at least one OECD member state is a member.[119]

A closed-end investment fund may invest its assets in deposits held with Polish banks, credit institutions[120] or foreign banks.[121] However, deposits held with a single bank or credit institution are not to account for more than 20% of the fund's assets.[122] A single currency shall not comprise more than 20% of the value of the closed-end investment fund's assets.[123]

A closed-end investment fund must not invest more than 50% of the value of its assets in units or investment certificates of a single investment fund, or in units in a single collective investment undertaking that is registered outside Poland.[124] If the closed-end investment fund's articles of association provide, it may invest up to 100% of the value of its assets in the units or investment certificates of a single investment fund, or in units in a single collective investment undertaking registered outside Poland,[125] as long as these articles of association specify this investment fund or collective investment undertaking,[126] define the principles that underlie the investment policy of the investment fund or collective investment undertaking,[127] and specify the rates of management fee that the investment fund or collective investment undertaking charges.[128] Investment certificates

---

[117] Article 145(3), IFA.

[118] Article 145(4), IFA. The Act of 29 August 1997 on Mortgage Bonds and Mortgage Banks gives information about mortgage bonds and mortgage banks.

[119] Article 145(8), IFA.

[120] See note 48, for the definition of 'credit institution'.

[121] Article 145(5), IFA. A 'foreign bank' is a bank that has its registered office in a country that is outside the EEA (Article 2(16), IFA; Articles 4(1)(17) and 4(3), Act of 29 August 1997: Banking Law).

[122] Article 145(6), IFA.

[123] Article 145(7), IFA.

[124] Article 146(1), IFA.

[125] Article 146(2), IFA.

[126] Article 146(2)(1), IFA.

[127] Article 146(2)(2), IFA. See note 103, for the information that an investment fund must include in its investment policies.

[128] Article 146(2)(3), IFA.

of another closed-end investment fund that is managed by the same management company shall constitute no more than 20% of the value of the fund's assets.[129]

A closed-end investment fund may invest in the ownership or co-ownership of land,[130] buildings and premises that represent separate real estate,[131] sea vessels,[132] and "perpetual usufruct rights".[133] The fund's assets may also include plant and equipment that are necessary to use the resources specified in the first sentence in accordance with their social and commercial purpose, and that are essential for ensuring that the condition of these items does not deteriorate or that their value rises.[134]

A closed-end investment fund may only acquire rights to real estate that are of a clear legal status, which are not collateral and are not subject to enforcement.[135] The fund may only acquire real estate that is encumbered with third party rights, if the exercise of these rights does not create the risk of the loss of ownership of the real estate.[136] The closed-end investment fund must hold at least four items of real estate.[137] A fund must not apportion in total more than 25% of the value of its assets to acquire one of the assets that Article 147(1) of the IFA refers to, or to invest in these assets.[138] A closed-end investment fund may encumber the assets to which Articles 147(1) and 147(2) refer, provided that their total value does not exceed 50% of the fund's net assets at the time of the encumbrance, subject to the consent of the depositary and in accordance with the fund's articles of association.[139]

---

129 Article 146(6), IFA.

130 Article 147(1)(1)(a), IFA.

131 Article 147(1)(1)(b), IFA.

132 Article 147(1)(1)(c), IFA.

133 Article 147(1)(2), IFA. 'Usufruct' is "a right to benefit from the yields of something owned by another person, without impairing the thing itself" (MacFarlane (1984), *The Layman's Dictionary of English Law*, 303).

134 Article 147(2), IFA.

135 Article 148(1), IFA.

136 Article 148(1), IFA.

137 Article 148(2), IFA. Article 148(2) of the IFA states "The number of items of real estate owned by the fund and held under perpetual usufruct shall not be less than four." On the basis of the definition of 'usufruct' in note 133, Article 148(2) of the IFA is a contradiction, because it states that the real estate is owned by the fund, whilst usufruct involves ownership of the asset by another person.

138 Article 148(4), IFA. See the previous paragraph, for Article 147(1) of the IFA.

139 Article 149, IFA.

A closed-end investment fund is permitted to lend securities.[140] The total value of securities lent and the securities of the same issuer that are held in the fund's investment portfolio must not exceed 20% of the value of the fund's assets.[141]

A closed-end investment fund may take out loans "exclusively from domestic banks and credit institutions or foreign banks", as long as the total value of these loans does not exceed 75% of the fund's net asset value at the time that the loan agreement is made.[142] Subject to the provisions of Article 188(4) of the IFA,[143] and as long as the fund's articles of association so provide, a closed-end investment fund that has an investors' meeting in place may issue bonds that are worth up to 15% of the value of the fund's net assets, as at the day preceding the date of adoption of a resolution on the bond issue by the meeting.[144] If the fund issues bonds, then the total value of loans and bonds in issue must not exceed 75% of the fund's net assets.[145]

Provided that a closed-investment fund gives due regard to its investment goal, the fund may advance cash loans of up to 50% of the value of the fund's assets, as long as any cash loan granted to a single entity does not exceed 20% of the value of the fund's assets,[146] and sureties and guarantees of up to 50% of the value of the fund's assets, as long as guarantees for the liabilities of a single entity are not more than 20% of the value of the fund's assets.[147] The borrower must enable the fund to evaluate the borrower's financial and economic standing, and to monitor drawdowns and repayments under the loan.[148]

---

[140] Article 151(1), IFA.

[141] Articles 151(2) and 145(3), IFA. Article 151(2) of the IFA states that the value of the securities "shall not exceed the limits specified in Art. 145.3-4". As Article 145(4) of the IFA refers specifically to mortgage bonds, the text refers to the investment limit that Article 145(3) of the IFA states. See above in this section, for Articles 145(3) and 145(4) of the IFA.

[142] Article 152(1), IFA. The quoted phrase is difficult to interpret, because the translation of the IFA does not make clear the priority between the 'and' and the 'or'. See note 48, for the definition of 'credit institution'. See note 121, for the definition of 'foreign bank'.

[143] See below in this section, for Article 188(4) of the IFA.

[144] Article 152(2), IFA.

[145] Article 152(3), IFA.

[146] Article 153(1)(1), IFA.

[147] Article 153(1)(2), IFA.

[148] Article 153(2), IFA.

A closed-end investment fund may be established as a securitisation fund.[149] A securitisation fund may be founded as a standard securitisation fund,[150] or a non-standard securitisation fund.[151]

A standard securitisation fund is to be established as an umbrella fund.[152] It must invest at least 75% of the asset value of each sub-fund in one debt pool, or in the rights to all income that the originator receives from one debt pool, subject to the following proviso.[153] If the fund's assets so provide, the fund may invest at least 75% of the asset value of a given sub-fund in more than one debt pool, or in the rights to all income received from more than one debt pool,[154] as long as the originators are Polish banks or credit institutions,[155] the debts in the debt pools are all of the same type,[156] and the agreements to which Article 183(5) of the IFA refers are to be concluded (for each of the debt pools) within three months of the fund's registration.[157]

A non-standard securitisation fund shall not be established as an umbrella fund.[158] The fund is required to invest at least 75% of the value of its assets in specific debts,[159] securities that incorporate monetary claims,[160] and/or rights to income from specific claims.[161]

Subject to Articles 185(4), 185(5) and 187(2),[162] a securitisation fund shall invest its all of its assets in debt securities,[163] units in money market

[149] Article 183(1), IFA. See note 114, for the definition of 'securitisation fund'.
[150] Article 183(2)(1), IFA.
[151] Article 183(2)(2), IFA.
[152] Article 185(1), IFA.
[153] Article 185(4), IFA.
[154] Article 185(5), IFA.
[155] Article 185(5)(1), IFA. See note 48, for the definition of 'credit institution'.
[156] Article 185(5)(2), IFA.
[157] Article 183(5)(3), IFA. An agreement that provides for an obligation to acquire a debt pool, and a sub-participation agreement, shall be concluded in writing; if they are not, they shall be void (Article 183(5), IFA).
[158] Article 187(1), IFA.
[159] Article 187(2)(1), IFA.
[160] Article 187(2)(2), IFA.
[161] Article 187(2)(3), IFA. Article 187(3) of the IFA states: "The investments referred to in Art. 187(2) shall not account for more than 25% of the fund's net asset value.". This statement is difficult to reconcile with that of Article 187(2) of the IFA, which requires the fund to invest at least 75% of its asset value in the items specified in that Article.
[162] See above in this section, for Articles 185(4), 185(5) and 187(2) of the IFA.
[163] Article 188(1)(1), IFA.

funds,[164] deposits at Polish banks or credit institutions,[165] money market instruments,[166] and/or derivatives.[167] It is neither to grant loans, nor to issue guarantees or sureties.[168] A securitisation fund that has an investors' meeting in place may issue bonds whose value shall not exceed 25% of the net assets value – for a standard securitisation fund, and 75% of the net asset value – for a non-standard securitisation fund, as at the day preceding the date of adoption of a resolution on a bond issue by the meeting, on condition that the securitisation fund's articles of association provide for the issue of bonds.[169]

A closed-end investment fund, or a specialised open-end investment fund that applies the principles and investment limits of a closed-end investment fund, may be founded as a private equity fund.[170] This fund invests at least 80% of its assets other than in securities that are offered in a public offering or are admitted to trading on a regulated market (unless the offering or admission occurs after the fund has acquired the securities) or money market instruments (unless a private company whose shares are held in the fund's investment portfolio has issued these items).[171]

If a foreign investment fund[172] intends to sell all of its units in Poland, then the fund or the foreign management company[173] shall inform the PFSA in writing.[174] The fund or management company must attach the following items to this notification: a document that the financial supervision authority of the foreign fund's home state draws up which states that the foreign fund complies with the EU law that pertains to collective investments in securities,[175] the foreign fund's rules,[176] the

---

[164] Article 188(1)(2), IFA.

[165] Article 188(1)(3), IFA. See note 48, for the definition of 'credit institution'.

[166] Article 188(1)(4), IFA.

[167] Article 188(1)(5), IFA. Investments in derivatives may only be made in order to limit investment risk (Article 188(2), IFA).

[168] Article 188(3), IFA.

[169] Article 188(4), IFA.

[170] Article 196, IFA.

[171] Article 196, IFA.

[172] The IFA does not define 'foreign investment fund'. A 'foreign fund' is an open-end investment fund, or an investment firm, registered in a Member State, which carries out its operations in accordance with EU laws pertaining to collective investments in securities (Article 2(9), IFA).

[173] A 'foreign management company' is an entity that is registered in a Member State, whose core business is the management of foreign funds (Article 2(10), IFA).

[174] Article 253(1), IFA.

[175] Article 253(2)(1), IFA.

foreign fund's prospectus and simplified prospectus,[177] the foreign fund's latest annual and semi-annual statements,[178] a detailed description of the procedures for the sale of the foreign fund's units in Poland,[179] the name, registered office or place of residence, and address in Poland, of the foreign fund's representative in Poland,[180] and the company name, registered office, and address of the foreign fund's paying agent in Poland.[181] Within two months of its receipt of all of these items,[182] the PFSA may take a decision to prohibit the sale of the fund's units in Poland, if the proposed sale procedures do not satisfy the conditions that the Polish regulations specify,[183] the fund does not guarantee that payments connected with the purchase and redemption of units will be efficient,[184] and/or the fund does not provide its unit-holders with sufficiently ready access to information about the fund.[185] In the absence of this decision, and after two months of the PFSA's receipt of the documents, the fund may start to sell its units in Poland.[186]

The PFSA shall ensure that a foreign fund's units are sold in Poland in compliance with "the law and the principles of fair trading".[187] Apart from this, each foreign fund is to be supervised by the financial regulation authority of its home Member State.[188] Only that authority is permitted to take supervisory measures, if the foreign fund is in contravention of its own rules, the law, or the principles of fair trading.[189] The PFSA shall inform that authority of any breach of the rules, the law, or the principles of fair trading, that the fund commits in Poland.[190] If there is a transgression of the rules, the law, or the principles of fair trading during

---

176 Article 253(2)(2), IFA. These rules include the foreign fund's articles of association (Article 253(3), IFA).

177 Article 253(2)(3), IFA.

178 Article 253(2)(4), IFA.

179 Article 253(2)(5), IFA.

180 Article 253(2)(6), IFA.

181 Article 253(2)(7), IFA.

182 Articles 253(6) and 253(5), IFA.

183 Article 253(6)(1), IFA.

184 Article 253(6)(2), IFA.

185 Article 253(6)(3), IFA.

186 Article 253(5), IFA.

187 Article 259(4), IFA. In this context, 'the law' probably means the laws of Poland. Even though the IFA frequently refers to 'the principles of fair trading', it does not define what these principles are.

188 Article 259(1), IFA.

189 Articles 259(2) and 253(2)(2), IFA. See note 187.

190 Article 259(3), IFA.

the sale of a foreign fund's units in Poland, then the PFSA may issue a decision to prohibit further sale of the fund's units,[191] and/or impose a penalty of 500,000 zloty on the foreign fund.[192]

If an open-end investment fund that is registered in Poland intends to sell and redeem units in a (non-Polish) Member State, then it must notify the financial supervision authority of that Member State in writing.[193] It shall attach the following documents to this notification: a certificate that the PFSA issues to the effect that the fund complies with EU law that governs collective investments in securities,[194] the fund's articles of association,[195] the fund's prospectus and simplified prospectus,[196] the fund's latest annual and semi-annual financial statements,[197] and a detailed description of the procedures in the host Member State for the sale of units in an open-end investment fund.[198]

Articles 253 to 261 of the IFA apply to the sale in Poland of units in open-end investment funds that are registered in an EEA state, provided that these funds comply with EU laws that pertain to collective investments in securities.[199] These Articles also apply to the sale in EEA states of units in open-end investment funds that a Polish management company manages.[200]

A Polish management company that manages one or more open-end investment funds may conduct its activities in a (non-Polish) Member State through a branch.[201] If this management company intends to establish a branch in a Member State, then it shall notify the PFSA of this intention in writing.[202] This notification is to include the name of the Member State in which the management company wishes to found a

---

[191] Article 259(5)(1), IFA.

[192] Articles 259(5)(2) and 259(5)(3), IFA. Articles 259(2) and 259(5) of the IFA are contradictory – if only the financial supervision authority of the foreign fund's home state is authorised to take supervisory measures (Article 259(2), IFA), then the PFSA would not be able to issue the decisions that Article 259(5) of the IFA contains, unless the other financial supervisory authority ordered the PFSA to do so.

[193] Article 261(1), IFA.

[194] Article 261(2)(1), IFA.

[195] Article 261(2)(2), IFA.

[196] Article 261(2)(3), IFA.

[197] Article 261(2)(4), IFA.

[198] Article 261(2)(5), IFA.

[199] Article 262, IFA.

[200] Article 262, IFA.

[201] Article 264(1), IFA.

[202] Article 264(2), IFA.

branch,[203] and the branch's address and registered office.[204] The management company shall attach the following documents to the notification: the branch's organisational structure,[205] a business plan which specifies the services that the branch is to provide,[206] the personal details of the persons who are responsible for managing the branch,[207] and the documents to which Article 261(2) of the IFA refers[208] – if the branch is to sell units in open-end investment funds that the management company manages.[209]

Within three months of receiving all of the information that the previous paragraph specifies, the PFSA shall forward it to the host State's financial supervision authority, together with information concerning Poland's compensation scheme, and shall notify the management company that it has done this.[210] Within two months of receiving all of this information, the PFSA may decide to refuse to forward the information to the host Member State's financial supervision authority, if it determines that the management company's standing does not permit it to carry out its activities within the scope of the business plan,[211] the manner in which the branch is organised indicates that it may carry out its activities in contravention of the principles of fair trading,[212] and/or the persons who manage the branch do not guarantee that the management company will conduct its operations in a proper way.[213]

The branch may be established, after the management company receives information that concerns the terms and conditions of carrying out activities in the host Member State from its financial supervision authority, or (if this information is not forthcoming) after two months of the receipt by the host Member State's competent supervision authority of all of the documents concerning the foundation of the branch.[214] At the moment at which the branch is established, the management company may start to sell units in the open-end investment fund that it manages, unless

---

[203] Article 264(3)(1), IFA.
[204] Article 264(3)(2), IFA.
[205] Article 264(4)(1), IFA.
[206] Article 264(4)(2), IFA.
[207] Article 264(4)(3), IFA.
[208] See above in this section, for Article 261(2) of the IFA.
[209] Article 264(4)(4), IFA.
[210] Article 264(5), IFA.
[211] Article 264(6)(1), IFA. The 'business plan' is that to which the previous paragraph refers.
[212] Article 264(6)(2), IFA. See note 187.
[213] Article 264(6)(3), IFA.
[214] Article 264(7), IFA.

the host Member State's financial supervision authority does not authorise these sales.[215]

A Polish management company that manages at least one open-end investment fund, which intends to carry out activities in the territory of a (non-Polish) Member State other than through a branch, must notify the PFSA of this intention in writing.[216] This notification shall include the name of the host Member State,[217] and the business plan – which must specify the scope of the services to be provided.[218]

Within one month of receiving this information, the PFSA shall forward it to the host Member State's financial supervision authority, together with information about Poland's compensation scheme.[219] The PFSA shall notify the management company of the date on which it forwards this information to the host Member State's financial supervision authority.[220] The management company may start operations in the host Member State, after it has received this notification.[221]

Management companies that have established a branch, or provide cross-border services, in the territory of (another) Member State shall furnish the financial supervision authority in that Member State with the information that the regulations in force in the Member State require.[222] If the financial supervision authority of the host Member State informs the PFSA that the management company which carries out activities in the that Member State's territory (via a branch or otherwise), is in contravention of the regulations in force in that country and has not remedied the breach within the time period that the financial supervision authority has determined, then the PFSA may require the management company to discontinue the transgression of those regulations,[223] impose a penalty of up to 500,000 zloty on the management company,[224] prohibit the management company from carrying out its activities in the host

---

[215] Article 264(8), IFA.

[216] Article 265(1), IFA.

[217] Article 265(2)(1), IFA.

[218] Article 265(2)(2), IFA.

[219] Article 265(3), IFA. The PFSA shall inform the management company of the date on which it forwards this information to the host Member State's financial supervision authority.

[220] Article 265(4), IFA.

[221] Article 265(5), IFA. The sale of units in open-end investment funds in the host Member State requires prior fulfilment of the conditions in Article 261 of the IFA (see above in this section).

[222] Article 266, IFA.

[223] Article 267(1), IFA.

[224] Article 267(2), IFA.

Member State,[225] introduce both the penalty and the prohibition,[226] or[227] prohibit the sale of units in open-end investment funds that are managed by the management company in the host Member State.[228]

If the PFSA revokes an authorisation to carry out management company business, then (with respect to non-Polish operations) this is equivalent to cancellation of an authorisation to conduct this business in another host Member State.[229] If the PFSA withdraws an authorisation to conduct management company business, then it must notify the financial supervision authority of the host Member State of this fact.[230]

A foreign management company[231] may establish a branch in Poland, provided that the PFSA receives the information stated in Articles 264(3), 264(4)(1), 264(4)(2), 264(4)(3) and 264(5) of the IFA from the financial supervision authority of the foreign management company's home Member State, and if pursuant to the branch's business plan the branch is to sell units in foreign funds[232] that the foreign management company manages, the documents specified in Article 523(2) of the IFA.[233] The

---

[225] Article 267(3), IFA.

[226] Article 267(4), IFA.

[227] Article 267 of the IFA states neither 'and' or 'or'. It would be reasonable to assume that the PFSA could take any combination of the four measures. However, since Article 267(4) of the IFA empowers the PFSA to take both the measure in Article 267(2) of the IFA and that in Article 267(3) of the IFA, it is rational to assume that the legislators do not intend to include other combinations of the four measures amongst the options available to the PFSA. Similar reasoning applies to Article 273(2) of the IFA (see note 258).

[228] Article 267(5), IFA.

[229] Article 269(1), IFA. If Poland is a host Member State of the management company, rather than its home Member State, then Article 269(1) of the IFA is controversial, because this provision is granting the PFSA authority over issues that are within the jurisdiction of the financial supervision authorities of other host Member States. If Poland is the management company's home state, then this provision is valid – because no authorisation from the financial supervision authority of the host Member State is required in order to set up a branch or provide cross-border services in that Member State (see sections 2.2.6 and 2.2.7).

[230] Article 269(2), IFA.

[231] See note 173, for the definition of 'foreign management company'.

[232] See note 172, for the definition of 'foreign fund'.

[233] Article 270(1), IFA. For Articles 264(3)-(5) of the IFA, see above in this section. As the IFA does not contain Article 523, the reference to Article 523(2) of the IFA may mean Article 253(2) of the IFA, which is considered above in this section. If the foreign management company sells units in foreign funds through its Polish branch that were not covered by the notification to which Article 270(1) of

PFSA must notify the foreign management company of the date on which it receives this information.[234]

Within two months of the date that it received the information, the PFSA may state terms and conditions that a branch must follow in its operations in Poland.[235] These terms and conditions are to include the rules that govern the sale of units,[236] the rules that control advertising activities,[237] and the rules of conduct that must be followed in the provision of services that comprise the discretionary management of securities' portfolios, advisory services on securities' trading, and administrative services in respect of investment units.[238] The foreign management company may open the Polish branch two months after the PFSA has received the information.[239]

Subject to the following sentence, the foreign management company may begin to sell units in the foreign funds that it manages, as soon as it has established its Polish branch.[240] By way of a decision that is issued before the period referred to in the previous paragraph has elapsed, the PFSA may prohibit the sale of units in foreign funds in Poland, if the proposed sale procedures do not fulfil the conditions that the regulations of Poland specify,[241] the foreign fund that the foreign investment company manages does not guarantee the efficiency of payments that are associated with the purchase and redemption of units,[242] and/or the fund does not provide unit-holders with sufficiently ready access to information about it.[243] The PFSA shall notify the financial supervision authority of the foreign management company's home Member State of this decision.[244]

A foreign management company[245] may provide cross-border services in Poland, provided that the PFSA receives the name of the host Member State (which should be Poland) and the business plan that specifies the scope of the services that the company intends to supply in Poland, from

---

the IFA refers, then Article 253 applies to the sale of these units. See above in this section, for Article 253 of the IFA.

234 Article 270(2), IFA.

235 Article 270(3), IFA.

236 Article 270(3)(1), IFA.

237 Article 270(3)(2), IFA.

238 Article 270(3)(3), IFA.

239 Article 270(4), IFA.

240 Article 270(5), IFA.

241 Article 270(6)(1), IFA.

242 Article 270(6)(2), IFA.

243 Article 270(6)(3), IFA.

244 Article 270(7), IFA.

245 See note 173, for the definition of 'foreign management company'.

the financial supervision authority of the company's home Member State, together with information about the compensation scheme that is operative in that country.[246] The PFSA must notify the foreign management company of the date on which it receives these items.[247]

Within one month of receiving this information, the PFSA may specify the terms and conditions that the foreign management company is to follow.[248] These conditions may include the rules of conduct that must be respected in the provision of services, which comprise the discretionary management of securities portfolios, advisory services with respect to securities' trading, and depository and administrative services for investment units in Poland.[249] A foreign management company may start to provide cross-border services in Poland one month after the PFSA receives the information, provided that the conditions that Article 253 of the IFA specifies for the sale of units of foreign funds in Poland is satisfied.[250]

A foreign management company that has founded a branch in Poland must furnish the PFSA, for statistical purposes, with periodic reports on its operations in Poland, and must supply other information concerning its activities to the same extent as is required from a Polish management company.[251] Similar information is also required from a foreign management company that provides cross-border services in Poland, in order to enable the PFSA to ensure that regulations which are in force in Poland are observed.[252]

If the PFSA ascertains that a foreign management company is in contravention of the laws that regulate the conduct of its activities in Poland, then the PFSA shall notify the company of the breach, and specify a time frame for the transgression to be corrected.[253] If the company does not remedy the contravention within the specified time period, then the PFSA shall send a relevant notification to the financial supervision authority of the company's home member state.[254] If, despite the measures that the home member state takes, or because these measures are

---

[246] Articles 271(1) and 265(2), IFA.
[247] Article 271(2), IFA.
[248] Article 271(3), IFA.
[249] Article 271(3), IFA.
[250] Article 271(4), IFA. See above in this section, for Article 253 of the IFA. See note 172, for the definition of 'foreign fund'.
[251] Article 272(1), IFA.
[252] Article 272(2), IFA.
[253] Article 273(1), IFA.
[254] Article 273(1), IFA.

inadequate or unenforceable in Poland, the company's transgression continues, then the PFSA may take a decision to prohibit the company or its branch from providing services in Poland,[255] impose a financial penalty of up to 500,000 zloty on the company,[256] introduce both of these sanctions,[257] or[258] preclude the company from executing any transactions in Poland.[259] "If the protection of the best interests of the investors or other entities to which a foreign management company provides services in the Republic of Poland so requires", then the PFSA may take such a decision without going through the previous steps.[260] The PFSA shall inform the financial supervision authority of the company's home Member State, and the European Commission, if it imposes a penalty on the company.[261]

Articles 253 to 263 of the IFA[262] shall apply to the sale of investment units in Poland, in accordance with the provisions of Articles 264 to 273 of the IFA.[263] Articles 264 to 269 of the IFA[264] shall apply to the foundation of branches and provision of cross-border services by

---

[255] Article 273(2)(1), IFA.

[256] Article 273(2)(2), IFA.

[257] Article 273(2)(3), IFA.

[258] Article 273(2) of the IFA states neither 'and' or 'or'. It would be reasonable to assume that the PFSA could take any combination of the three measures. However, as Article 273(2)(3) of the IFA empowers the PFSA to take both the measure in Article 273(2)(1) of the IFA and that in Article 273(2)(2) of the IFA, it is logical to assume that the legislators do not intend to include other combinations of the three measures amongst the options available to the PFSA. Similar reasoning applies to Article 267 of the IFA (see note 227).

[259] Article 273(2)(4), IFA.

[260] Article 273(3), IFA. The PFSA has a discretion to decide whether or not the protection of these interests requires it to take an immediate decision under Article 273(2) of the IFA.

[261] Article 273(3), IFA. The PFSA shall change or annul the decisions that Article 273(3) of the IFA specify, if the European Commission orders it to alter or annul the measures adopted (Article 273(4), IFA). "To the extent necessary to perform supervisory responsibilities," the PFSA shall inform the financial supervision authority of the Member State in which the foreign management company has its registered office, of the decision to which Article 273(3) refers (Article 286(3), IFA). Article 286(3) of the IFA is superfluous, because Article 273(3) of the IFA requires the PFSA to inform the financial supervision authority of the company's home Member State of the imposition by the PFSA of a sanction on the company (see the text).

[262] See above in this section, for Articles 253, 259, 261 and 262 of the IFA.

[263] Article 275, IFA.

[264] See above in this section, for Articles 264-267 and 269 of the IFA. Article 268 of the IFA concerns the inspection of a management company's premises.

management companies in EEA states.[265] They shall also apply to the establishment of branches and the suppliance of cross-border services by companies that manage investment funds that operate under "the Community laws pertaining to collective investments in securities" and that are registered in EEA states.[266]

Units that are issued by an open-end investment fund that is registered in an OECD member state outside the EEA[267] may be sold in Poland, as long as this investment fund offers these units to the public and redeems them at each unit-holder's request,[268] holders of units that such an investment fund issues benefit from the same protection as holder of units in Polish open-end investment funds,[269] the investment fund is required to prepare annual and semi-annual financial statements,[270] the investment fund is open to supervision by the financial supervision authority of the country in which it is registered and arrangements have been agreed in order to ensure reciprocal exchange of information that concerns the financial standing and operations of the investment fund between that authority and the PFSA,[271] and the country in which the investment fund is registered assures equal access to its market for open-end investment funds that Polish management companies manage.[272] Articles 253 to 263 of the IFA[273] shall apply to the sale of investment units of this OECD investment fund in Poland.[274]

The company that manages OECD investment funds that are registered in an OECD member state outside the EEA, may establish a branch in Poland,[275] provided that this company is subject to supervision by the financial supervision authority of the country in which it is registered and arrangements have been made in order to ensure reciprocal exchange of information about the financial standing and operations of the company

---

[265] Article 276(1), IFA

[266] Article 276(2), IFA. The quoted phrase refers to Directive 2009/65/EC, which section 2.2.6 considers. It does not refer to Directive 2011/61/EU, as this entered into force recently (in July 2011) – although I expect this to change. Section 2.2.7 discusses Directive 2011/61/EU.

[267] If this investment fund is a natural person, then his/her registered office shall be the registered office of the company that manages the fund (Article 277(2), IFA).

[268] Article 277(1)(1), IFA.

[269] Article 277(1)(2), IFA

[270] Article 277(1)(3), IFA

[271] Article 277(1)(4), IFA

[272] Article 277(1)(5), IFA

[273] See above in this section, for Articles 253, 259, 261 and 262 of the IFA.

[274] Article 277(3), IFA.

[275] Article 279(1), IFA.

between that authority and the PFSA,[276] and the country in which the company is registered permits Polish management companies to found branches on its territory.[277] Articles 270 to 276 (other than Article 270(9)[278]) of the IFA shall apply to Polish branches of this company.[279] Anyone who, without satisfying the conditions that Article 279 of the IFA contains,[280] establishes a branch in Poland of a company that manages investment funds in OECD member states that are outside the EEA, is liable to a fine of up to 5 million zlotys and/or a penalty of imprisonment of up to 5 years.[281]

The PFSA shall co-operate with the financial supervision authorities of host Member States in respect of the supervision of Polish and foreign management companies that have founded a branch, or provide cross-border services, in those countries.[282] The PFSA shall furnish the financial supervision authorities of host Member States with information about the management companies that have established a branch, or supply cross-border services, in these countries, and with information that concerns the structure of their groups.[283]

The establishment of a branch in another EEA state is a 'capital movement' in Title I(1) of the nomenclature in Annex I. The provision of cross-border services is a 'capital movement' under Title IV of the nomenclature in Annex I.[284] Furthermore, the investment transactions of

[276] Article 279(1)(1), IFA.

[277] Article 279(1)(2), IFA.

[278] Articles 38, 39, 40(3) and 41 of the Business Activity Act of 19 November 1999 shall not apply to a Polish branch of a foreign management company (Articles 270(9) and 270(1), IFA). The Polish Business Activity Act is beyond the scope of this chapter.

[279] Article 279(2), IFA. See above in this section, for Articles 270-273, 275 and 276 of the IFA. Article 274 of the IFA concerns the inspection of the premises of a foreign management company's Polish branch.

[280] See above in this paragraph, for Article 279 of the IFA.

[281] Article 294, IFA.

[282] Article 286(1), IFA. See note 173, for the definition of 'foreign management company'.

[283] Article 286(2), IFA.

[284] Title IV of the nomenclature in Annex I is entitled 'Operations in units of collective investment undertakings'. The explanatory notes in Annex I state that 'collective investment undertakings' are entities whose object is the collective investment in assets of the capital that they collect and which function according the principle of spreading risk, and the units of which are repurchased or redeemed at the request of their holders out the assets of these undertakings.

collective investment undertakings are movements of capital within the meaning of Article 63 of the TFEU.[285]

Several of the provisions discussed in this section restrict the free movement of capital. The investment limits that apply to open-end investment funds, specialised open-end investment funds and/or closed-end investment funds hinder capital movement. The sanctions that the IFA empowers the PFSA to take, if, for example, a branch of a Polish management company contravenes legislation of a non-Polish EEA state,[286] also restrict the free movement of capital.

These restrictive measures may be justified under Article 65(1)(b) of the TFEU, if they are necessary for the protection of interests that they are intended to guarantee, are proportionate, and observe the requirements of legal certainty, i.e. are specific, objective and known to the parties beforehand, and if the persons affected by the measures have access to legal redress – intervention must be supported by a formal statement of reasons and be subject to review by the national courts.[287] Whilst the investment limits of the funds satisfy the requirements of legal certainty, the sanction that the PFSA may impose under Articles 267 or 273 of the IFA is not specific.[288] The IFA neither requires the PFSA to include a formal statement of reasons for its imposition of restrictive measures, nor provides the applicant management company or investment fund with the right to appeal in the Polish courts against a decision that the PFSA has taken. Thus, Article 65(1)(b) of the TFEU does not justify the restrictive measures.

Measures that restrict capital movements between EEA states and third countries are justified under Article 64(2) of the TFEU, if the EU institutions carefully take account of the objective of the free movement capital whilst enacting the relevant legislation and if the national rules do not limit the free movement of capital more than do the equivalent provisions of the pertinent Directive.[289] The relevant legislation comprises

---

[285] See section 2.1.1, in particular the CJEU's judgment in *Commission v Poland* [2011] ECR I-13613.

[286] See Articles 259, 267 and 273 of the IFA, which this section considers above.

[287] See the subsection '*The requirements for a successful public policy/security derogation*' in section 2.1.3.

[288] The sanction that the PFSA may impose under Article 259 of the IFA is fairly specific, as the PFSA has four options – do nothing, prohibit further sale of the units, impose a penalty of 500,000 zloty, or introduce both of these remedies (see above in this section).

[289] See the subsection '*Derogations that apply only to capital movements to/from third countries*', in section 2.3.2.

Directives 2009/65/EC and 2011/61/EU. Other than an acknowledgement of the EU law on capital movements in Article 1(6) of Directive 2009/65/EC,[290] neither Directive mentions the free movement of capital. Thus, the EU institutions did not carefully consider the objective of the free movement of capital, whilst enacting the relevant legislation. Thus, Article 64(2) of the TFEU does not justify any of the restrictive measures. Hence, these measures breach Article 63 of the TFEU.

Whilst the EIFA[291] provides reasons for refusing to grant, or for revoking, an authorisation in relation to the provision of services (through the establishment of a branch or otherwise) across the boundary of the EEA, the Polish IFA does not consider third countries – other than those that are members of the OECD. Consequently, there is little law in the latter Act that concerns authorisation requirements in respect of capital movements between EEA states and third countries – its emphasis is on investment limits. The Polish authorities should address further the issue of the provision of services by investment funds to and from third countries. This is consistent with Article 63 of the TFEU, which requires Member States to prohibit all restrictions on the movement of capital between Member States and third countries, subject to the specified derogations.

4.2 Providers of Financial Instruments

4.2.1 Act of 29 July 2005 on Public Offers and the Conditions for Introducing Financial Instruments to the Organised Trading System, and on Public Companies (POA)

The POA defines rules and conditions for conducting a public offer of securities, effecting subscription or sales of these securities, and seeking admission and introduction of financial instruments to trading on a regulated market.[292] This Act also considers the obligations of entities that participate in trading of financial instruments,[293] and the consequences of

---

[290] "Subject to the provisions in Community law governing capital movements … no Member State shall apply any other provisions in the field covered by this Directive to UCITS established in another Member State or to the units issued by such UCITS, where those UCITS market their units within the territory of that Member State" (Article 1(6), Directive 2009/65/EC).

[291] The 'EIFA' is the Estonian Investment Funds Act 2004, which section 3.1 considers.

[292] Article 1(1), POA.

[293] Article 1(2), POA.

obtaining the status of a public company and the special rights and obligations that relate to the holding of, and trading in, the shares of public companies.[294] The POA does not apply to promissory notes and cheques,[295] bank deposits,[296] and money market instruments.[297]

Subject to two exceptions, the home Member State[298] is that in which the securities' issuer has its registered office.[299] The host Member State is the Member State (other than the home Member State) in which the public offering is being made, or in which the securities' issuer or the entity that is authorised to apply for admission of securities to trading on a regulated market (if not the issuer) is requesting admission of securities on a regulated market.[300]

In a situation in which the PFSA receives notification from the financial supervision authority of the host Member State that the issuer for whom Poland is the home Member State, or a financial institution that participates in a public offering on behalf, or on orders, of this issuer, contravenes legislation in force in that Member State in association with the public offering or admission or introduction to trading on a regulated market on the basis of the prospectus for the issue of its securities that the PFSA has approved, the PFSA may request the issuer to terminate its breach of legislation in force in the territory of the host Member State,[301]or apply measures that Article 16 or 17 of the POA define.[302] According to these Articles, the PFSA may order that the start of a public offering, subscription or sale be withheld, or that a public offering, subscription or sale that is already underway be discontinued for a period of up to 10 business days,[303] forbid the issuer from seeking the admission or introduction of its securities to trading on a regulated market,[304] publish (at the expense of the issuer or the securities' holder) the illegal activities in respect of the public offering, subscription or sale,[305] order that the

---

[294] Article 1(3), POA.
[295] Article 2(1), POA.
[296] Article 2(2), POA.
[297] Article 2(3), POA.
[298] For the purposes of the POA, a 'Member State' is an Contracting Party to the EEA Agreement (Article 4(21), POA).
[299] Article 11(1), POA. This rule and the exceptions (in Articles 11(2)-(4) of the POA) transpose Article 2(1)(m) of Directive 2003/71/EC.
[300] Article 11(5), POA.
[301] Article 18(2)(1), POA.
[302] Article 18(2)(2), POA.
[303] Article 16(1)(1), POA.
[304] Article 16(1)(2), POA.
[305] Article 16(1)(3), POA.

application for seeking admission or introduction of the securities to trading on a regulated market be withheld for up to 10 days,[306] disallow the application for admission or introduction of the securities to trading on a regulated market,[307] or publish (at the issuer's expense) information about the illegal activities with respect to the seeking of admission or introduction of securities to trading on a regulated market.[308]

If the issuer for whom Poland is a host Member State, or an entity that participates in the public offering, admission or introduction of securities to trading on a regulated market or promotional activities on behalf, or upon orders, of this issuer, contravenes legislation in force in association with the public offering or admission or introduction of securities to trading on a regulated market or carrying out promotional activities on Polish territory, then the PFSA shall inform the financial supervision authority of the issuer's home Member State of this fact.[309] If, despite notification by the PFSA, the competent authority of the issuer's home Member State does not take measures to prevent further contravention of the legislation in force, or if these measures are ineffective, then the PFSA may, with a view to the protection of the interests of investors and having first notified the PFSA, apply measures for which Articles 16, 17 or 53(5) of the POA provide.[310] According to Article 53(5) of the POA, the PFSA may order that the start of the promotional activities be suspended, or that the promotional activities already taking place be discontinued, in each case for a period that does not exceed 10 business days, for the purpose of correcting the identified irregularities,[311] forbid the promotional activities, in the event that the issuer or the securities' holder evades the rectification of the irregularities (which the PFSA has identified) within 10 business days,[312] or the contents of the advertising or promotional materials contravene the statutory provisions,[313] publish, at the expense of the issuer or of the securities' holder, information that concerns the illegality of the promotional activities, specifying the identified breaches.[314] The PFSA

[306] Article 17(1)(1), POA.
[307] Article 17(1)(2), POA.
[308] Article 17(1)(3), POA.
[309] Article 19(1), POA.
[310] Article 19(2), POA. For Articles 16 and 17, please see the previous paragraph.
[311] Article 53(1), POA.
[312] Articles 53(1) and 53(2)(a), POA.
[313] Article 53(2)(b), POA.
[314] Article 53(3), POA.

shall promptly inform the European Commission that it has applied these measures.[315]

For a public company[316] with its registered office in a Member State other than Poland, whose shares have been admitted to trading on a regulated market only in Polish territory,[317] have been admitted for the first time to trading on a regulated market on Polish territory and in another Member State other than the one in which the company's registered office is situated,[318] or have been simultaneously admitted to trading on a regulated market on Polish territory and in another Member State other than that in which the registered office of the company is situated (if the company has indicated the PFSA as the supervisory authority in respect of the acquisition of substantial shareholdings of this company),[319] then Article 74 of the POA does not apply.[320] According to that Article, a shareholder may exceed 66% of the total vote in a public company only pursuant to a tender offer to acquire or exchange the company's remaining shares.[321] Instead, the entity that acquires the shares is obliged to announce a tender offer for sale or exchange of all of the remaining shares in the company, in accordance with the legislation in force of the Member State in which the public company has its registered office.[322]

---

[315] Article 19(2), POA.

[316] A 'public company' is one in which one or more shares are dematerialised as defined in the Act on Trading in Financial Instruments, other than a company whose shares have been registered in accordance with Article 5a(2) of the Act on Trading in Financial Instruments (Article 4(20), POA). The English translation of the Act on Trading in Financial Instruments does not define 'dematerialised securities'. Securities that are issued by entities that have their registered offices outside Poland may be registered in a depositary for securities, if they are acquired by the participants of the National Depositary for Securities or their customers, or by the members of the entity to which the National Depositary for Securities has delegated the performance of activities for the operation of the depository for securities or their customers (Articles 5a(2) and 48(1)(1), Act of 29 July 2005 on Trading in Financial Instruments).

[317] Article 90a(1)(1), POA.

[318] Article 90a(1)(2), POA.

[319] Article 90a(1)(3), POA.

[320] Article 90a(1), POA.

[321] Article 74(1), POA. Articles 74(2)- 74(5) of the POA provide refinements to Article 74(1) of the POA.

[322] Article 90a(1), POA. This is subject to one exception, in Article 90a(2) of the POA.

The admission of securities to the capital market is a 'capital movement' in Title IIIB of the nomenclature in Annex I. If the PFSA forbids, suspends, or disallows the issuer's securities to be admitted to trading on a regulated market, then it restricts the free movement of capital. By contrast, the requirement of Article 90a(1) of the TFEU to announce a tender offer for the remaining shares in the circumstances described therein does not constitute a limitation on the free movement of capital.

For Article 65(1)(b) of the TFEU to justify the restrictive measures, they must be necessary for the protection of the interests that they are intended to guarantee, be proportionate (i.e. not be attainable by less restrictive measures), and satisfy the requirements of legal certainty (i.e. be specific, objective and known to the parties beforehand); furthermore, the persons whom the measures affect must have access to legal redress (i.e. intervention must be accompanied by a formal statement of reasons, and be subject to review in the national courts).[323] Whilst the measures may be proportionate (if the PFSA exercises them appropriately), they give a discretion to the PFSA, and are therefore are not specific – as a result of which they do not provide the securities' issuer with legal certainty. Furthermore, the POA neither requires the PFSA to accompany its decision to apply the restrictive measures with a formal statement of reasons, nor grants the issuer with a right to appeal against this decision in the Polish courts. Thus, the restrictive measures in Articles 18 and 19 of the POA breach Article 63 of the TFEU.

4.2.2 Regulation 916 of the Minister of Finance of July 6th 2007 on Detailed Conditions to be Met by the Information Memorandum Referred to in Articles 39(1) and 42(1) of the Act on Public Offers and the Conditions for Introducing Financial Instruments to the Organised Trading System, and on Public Companies (RIM)

Articles 39(1) and 42(1) of the POA specify circumstances in which a securities' issuer or holder is to construct an information memorandum. This memorandum is to contain true, correct and complete information about the issuer and other persons that Regulation 916 specifies, on their legal and financial standing, on securities that the memorandum covers and the rules that offer these instruments to the public and seek their

[323] See the subsection '*The requirements for a successful public policy/security derogation*' in section 2.1.3.

admission to trading on a regulated market, as at the day that the PFSA approves the memorandum (if its approval is required), or at the date of making the memorandum available to the public or to the relevant investors.[324] The information that the memorandum contains is to be presented to investors in a way in which enables them to assess its effect on the issuer's financial and economic standing and the issuer's assets.[325]

If non-equity securities that the European Central Bank, a Member State's[326] central bank, or a public international body (of which at least one Member State is a member) issues, or which the Polish State Treasury, a Member State, or a Member State's regional or local authority unconditionally and irrevocably guarantees, are to be offered to the public or admitted to trading on a regulated market, then the provisions of paragraphs 18 to 27 of the RIM are to apply.[327] These are as follows. The information memorandum is to comprise an introduction, and chapters on risk factors, persons responsible for the information that the memorandum contains, information on the issue, information on the issuer, documents to display, and appendices.[328] Paragraphs 19, and 20-25, respectively list the information that the introduction and each chapter of the memorandum are to contain – for example, the chapter entitled 'Risk Factors' is to comprise a clear description of the risk factors that may affect the issuer's ability to discharge its obligations that relate to the securities towards investors.[329] Paragraph 26 requires the memorandum to contain information on the guarantor (if security has been provided).[330] If the securities are issued continuously or repeatedly, then the information for the subsequent issues of the securities is to be made available to the public in a supplementary memorandum, no later than prior to the start of the subscription for the securities of each subsequent issue.[331]

If the equity securities of a regional or local authority of a Member State are to be offered to the public or admitted to trading on a regulated market, then the information memorandum is to contain an introduction,

---

[324] Paragraph 3.1, RIM.

[325] Paragraph 3.1, RIM.

[326] The RIM does not define 'Member State'. As the Regulation is pursuant to the POA, the definition of 'Member State' in that Act applies – see note 298.

[327] Paragraph 8, RIM.

[328] Paragraph 18, RIM.

[329] Paragraph 20, RIM.

[330] Paragraph 26(1), RIM. This requirement is waived under three circumstances that are specified in paragraphs 26(2), 26(3) and 26(6) of the RIM, respectively.

[331] Paragraph 27, RIM. Paragraph 27 of the RIM proceeds to state the information that the supplementary memorandum must contain.

and chapters on risk factors, persons responsible for the information that the memorandum contains, information on the issue, information on the issuer, documents to display, and appendices.[332] Paragraphs 10 to 16 of the RIM list the information that must be present under each of these titles – for example, the chapter that is headed 'Appendices' must contain (at least) the explanation of abbreviations used, and definitions.[333] Paragraph 17 requires the memorandum to include information on the guarantor (if security has been provided).[334]

The supply of information is not a 'capital movement' in the nomenclature in Annex I. Hence, the RIM's requirements for non-Polish securities' issuers to provide the information specified above for the benefit of investors in Poland, do not restrict the free movement of capital.

4.2.3 Act of 29 July 2005 on Trading in Financial Instruments (TFIA)

The TFIA defines the manner of, and the rules and conditions for starting and conducting business that involves, trading in financial instruments, and the rights and obligations of entities that are engaged in this trading and the supervision thereof.[335] Within the meaning of the TFIA, 'financial instruments' include securities,[336] UCITS,[337] money market instruments,[338] derivatives that are based on securities, currencies, interest rates, profitability ratios, other derivatives, financial indices, or financial measures that are settled in cash or by delivery,[339] derivatives that are based on commodities and which are cash-settled (or may be cash-settled if one of the parties so wishes),[340] derivatives that are based on commodities and which are settled by delivery – provided that they are

---

[332] Paragraph 9, RIM. Paragraph 9 of the RIM provides for the same structure for the information memorandum as does Paragraph 18 of the RIM (see above in this section).
[333] Paragraph 16, RIM.
[334] Paragraph 17(1), RIM. This requirement is waived under three circumstances that are specified in paragraphs 17(2), 17(3) and 17(6) of the RIM, respectively.
[335] Article 1(1), TFIA. The TFIA's provisions do not apply to cheques and promissory notes (Article 1(2), TFIA).
[336] Article 2(1), TFIA.
[337] Article 2(1)(2)(a), TFIA.
[338] Article 2(1)(2)(b), TFIA.
[339] Article 2(1)(2)(c), TFIA.
[340] Article 2(1)(2)(d), TFIA.

admitted to trading on a regulated market or multilateral trading facility,[341] derivatives that are not admitted to trading on a regulated market or multilateral trading facility and which are based on commodities and may be settled by delivery – which are not intended to be for the purposes of trading and have the features of other derivative instruments,[342] credit risk transfer derivatives,[343] contracts for difference,[344] and options, futures contracts, swaps, forward rate agreements, climate change, freight rate and emission allowance derivatives, and derivatives that are based on interest rates or other official statistics, which are cash-settled or may be cash-settled if one of the parties so wishes,[345] and other derivatives based on assets, rights, obligations, and indices that have the characteristics of other financial instruments.[346]

An entity that operates a foreign regulated market[347] may, without the PFSA's permission, establish in Polish territory systems of information technology and technical equipment that provide access to this market for investment firms that "conduct activities" in Poland.[348] Investment firms may only commence these activities after the competent supervisory authority that granted the authorisation to the entity that operates a foreign regulated market, informs the PFSA of that undertaking's intention to start

---

[341] Article 2(1)(2)(e), TFIA.
[342] Article 2(1)(2)(f), TFIA.
[343] Article 2(1)(2)(g), TFIA.
[344] Article 2(1)(2)(h), TFIA.
[345] Article 2(1)(2)(i), TFIA.
[346] Article 2(1)(2)(i), TFIA. Article 2(1) of the TFIA implements the list of financial instruments in Section C of Annex I of Directive 2004/39/EC.
[347] For the purposes of the TFIA, a 'regulated market' is a system for trading in financial instruments that are admitted to trading, which operates continuously and provides investors with universal, equal and simultaneous access to market information when matching the offers to purchase and to sell financial instruments, ensures equal terms for the acquisition and disposal of these instruments, and which is organised and supervised by a competent authority pursuant to the TFIA, as well as recognised by a particular Member State as compliant with these requirements, and notified to the European Commission as a regulated market (Article 14(1), TFIA)). A 'foreign regulated market' is a regulated market that functions in the territory of another Member State (Article 14(2), TFIA). A 'Member State' is a country that is a Contracting Party to the EEA Agreement (Article 3(22), TFIA). A regulated market in Poland may be a stock exchange or an "off-exchange regulated market" (Article 15(1), TFIA). The firm that operates a regulated market is called a 'market operator' (Article 4(1)(13), Directive 2004/39/EC).
[348] Article 14a(1), TFIA.

to operate the regulated market in Poland.[349] The PFSA may request that the (other) competent supervisory authority indicate the participants in the regulated market.[350] In cases in which the activities of the entity that operates the regulated market become important for the protection of investors and for the functioning of the securities market in Poland, the PFSA shall co-operate with the supervisory authority that granted authorisation to this entity.[351]

For a (Polish) firm to provide investment services in Poland, it must hold a licence to do so that the PFSA has granted.[352] 'Investment services' comprise the acceptance and transfer of orders to purchase or sell financial instruments,[353] the execution of orders for a customer's account,[354] the acquisition or disposal of financial instruments for the broker's own account,[355] portfolio management,[356] investment advice,[357] offering financial instruments for sale,[358] the provision of services under firm commitment and standby underwriting agreements,[359] and the organisation of a multilateral trading facility.[360] The following activities of an investment firm are also 'investment services': the registration or storage of financial instruments,[361] the grant of loans in respect of transactions in one or more financial instruments, if the transaction is effected through the intermediation of the firm that provides the loan,[362] the provision of advice to companies on capital structure, corporate strategy and matters that are related to these,[363] services that related to acquisitions, mergers and demergers of companies,[364] the provision of foreign exchange services – if

---

[349] Article 14a(2), TFIA. The English in this provision of the translated TFIA is unclear.
[350] Article 14a(3), TFIA.
[351] Article 14a(4), TFIA.
[352] Article 69(1), TFIA.
[353] Article 69(2)(1), TFIA.
[354] Article 69(2)(2), TFIA.
[355] Article 69(2)(3), TFIA.
[356] Article 69(2)(4), TFIA.
[357] Article 69(2)(5), TFIA.
[358] Article 69(2)(6), TFIA.
[359] Article 69(2)(7), TFIA.
[360] Article 69(2)(8), TFIA. Article 69(2) of the TFIA implements the list of investment services and activities in Section A of Annex I of Directive 2004/39/EC.
[361] Article 69(4)(1), TFIA.
[362] Article 69(4)(2), TFIA.
[363] Article 69(4)(3), TFIA.
[364] Article 69(4)(4), TFIA.

these are associated with investment services,[365] the supply of investment and financial analyses, and other general recommendations that relate to transactions in financial instruments,[366] additional services that concern underwriting,[367] and the provision of investment services in relation to the underlying instruments of derivatives that Articles 2(1)(2)(d) to 2(1)(2)(f) and 2(1)(2)(i) of the TFIA specify – if these activities are associated with investment services.[368]

The PFSA shall provide a brokerage licence[369] to a partnership or company that is a subsidiary of, or of a parent company of, a foreign investment firm,[370] a foreign bank,[371] or a legal person that provides

---

[365] Article 69(4)(5), TFIA.

[366] Article 69(4)(6), TFIA.

[367] Article 69(4)(7), TFIA.

[368] Article 69(4)(8), TFIA. For Articles 2(1)(2)(d)-2(1)(2)(f) and 2(1)(2)(i) of the TFIA, see above in this section. Article 69(4) of the TFIA implements the list of ancillary services in Section B of Annex I of Directive 2004/39/EC.

[369] The TFIA does not define 'brokerage licence'. This phrase is likely to mean a licence to provide investment services.

[370] A 'foreign investment firm' is (i) a legal person, or an organisational unit without legal personality, which has its registered office in the territory of another (i.e. non-Polish) Member State, and if the laws of the other Member State do not require offices to be registered – a head office in the territory of that country, (ii) a natural person who is resident in the territory of another Member State and who provides investment services in that State's territory on the basis of a licence that its financial supervision authority has granted, or (iii) a foreign credit institution (Article 3(32), TFIA). See note 371, for the definition of 'foreign credit institution'. An 'investment firm' is an "intermediary house", a bank that provides investment services, a foreign investment firm that supplies investment services in Poland, or a foreign legal person with a registered office in the territory of a WTO member state or an OECD country that provides investment services in Poland (Article 3(33), TFIA). In Article 3(32) of the TFIA, 'intermediary house' probably means 'financial intermediary', and is considered further in Article 95 of the TFIA (although the TFIA does not define this term).

[371] A 'foreign bank' is a bank that has a registered office outside Poland, excluding a foreign credit institution (Article 3(38), TFIA). A 'foreign credit institution' is a credit institution to which Article 4(1)(17) of the Banking Law refers, which conducts investment services, or maintains accounts in which securities that are admitted to trading on a foreign regulated market are registered (Article 3(31), TFIA). A 'credit institution' is an entity that has its registered office in one of the non-Polish Member States of the EEA, which, acting for its own account and on its own behalf, on the basis of an authorisation that its financial supervision authority provides, conducts the business of receiving repayable funds entrusted to it and of granting loans, or of issuing electronic money (Articles 4(1)(17) and 4(3), Banking Law of 29 August 1997). See note 347, for the definition of 'foreign regulated

investment services in the territory of a WTO member state or an OECD country,[372] or "is under a significant influence of" the same persons that exercise such an influence on a foreign investment firm, a foreign bank, or a legal person that supplies investment services in the territory of a WTO member state or an OECD country,[373] upon obtaining a written opinion from the financial supervision authority of another Member State, an WTO member state, or an OECD country, which has provided the partnership or company with the authorisation to provide investment services in that country.[374] The written opinion concerns the way in which the partnership or company carries out its activities, in particular its compliance with legal regulations in the relevant country.[375]

The PFSA is to grant a brokerage licence[376] to a partnership or company that is a subsidiary of, or of a parent company of, a credit institution[377] or a foreign insurance company that the financial supervision authority of another Member State authorises to conduct its activities there,[378] or "is under a significant influence of" the same persons that exert a such an influence over a credit institution or a foreign insurance firm that the financial supervision authority of another Member State authorises to carry out its activities there,[379] only upon the receipt of a written opinion from that financial supervision authority.[380] The written opinion is to assess the shareholders of the partnership's or company's group entities, and the experience and reliability of the members of the management board of these entities, or of other persons that may exercise influence over the management of the partnership or company.[381]

---

market'. Thus, a 'foreign bank' under the TFIA is one with registered offices outside the EEA.

[372] Article 96(1)(1)-(2), TFIA.

[373] Article 96(1)(3), TFIA. 'Significant influence' is the holding of between 20% and 50% of the total vote at the general shareholders meeting, or a power to take decisions that concern the financial policy or daily operations of the partnership or company (Article 96(3), TFIA).

[374] Article 96(1), TFIA. See note 347, for the definition of 'Member State'.

[375] Article 96(1), TFIA.

[376] See note 369.

[377] See note 371, for the definition of 'credit institution'.

[378] Article 96(2)(1)-(2), TFIA.

[379] Article 96(2)(3), TFIA. See note 272, for the definition of 'significant influence'.

[380] Article 96(2), TFIA. See note 347, for the definition of 'Member State'.

[381] Article 96(2), TFIA.

The brokerage licence shall permit an intermediary house[382] to provide investment services[383] via a branch, or without founding a branch, in the territory of all other (i.e. non-Polish) Member States.[384] An intermediary house must notify the PFSA of its intention to establish a branch or provide cross-border investment services.[385] This notification is to contain the name of the Member State in which the branch is to be opened or the cross-border services are to be supplied,[386] the planned scope of operations,[387] the organisational structure,[388] the address at which the documents that relate to the operations will be available,[389] personal details of the persons who manage these operations,[390] information as to whether the intermediary house intends to benefit from an investment firm's agents in another Member State in which territory it plans to provide investment services,[391] and personal details of these agents.[392] The PFSA shall forward this information to the financial supervision authority of the Member State in which the branch is to function within three months of its receipt, or in which the cross-border investment services are

---

[382] See note 370.

[383] Article 104(1) of the TFIA mentions "the licensed activities referred to in Art 69.1". See above in this section, for Article 69(1) of the TFIA.

[384] Article 104(1), TFIA. See note 347, for the definition of 'Member State'.

[385] Article 104(2), TFIA.

[386] Article 104(3)(1), TFIA.

[387] Article 104(3)(2), TFIA. The planned scope of operations may not consist only of the services that are contained in Article 69(4) of the TFIA (see above in this paragraph). This is consistent with Articles 31(1) and 32(1) of Directive 2004/39/EC, which requires ancillary services only to be provided with at least one investment services.

[388] Article 104(3)(2), TFIA.

[389] Article 104(3)(3), TFIA. This requirement does not apply to the provision of cross-border services (Article 104(4), TFIA). See note 590.

[390] Article 104(3)(4), TFIA. This requirement does not apply to the provision of cross-border services (Article 104(4), TFIA). Article 104(4a) of the TFIA states "The provisions of Art. 104-3-4 shall not apply if the investment services are conducted in the form of a branch.". This provision is contrary to Article 32(2)(c)-(d) of Directive 2004/39/EC, which states that Member States must require an investment firm that would like to found a branch in the territory of another Member State, to provide the home Member State's competent authority with the address in the host State from which documents may be obtained and the names of the branch's managers – see section 2.2.1.

[391] Article 104(3)(5), TFIA.

[392] Article 104(3)(6), TFIA.

to be provided within one month of its receipt.[393] The PFSA shall inform the intermediary house that it has provided the information to the financial supervision authority of the host Member State.[394] The PFSA may, within three months – if the investment services are to be supplied via a branch, or within one month – if cross-border investment services are to be provided, raise an objection to the intermediary house's intention to found a branch or to provide cross-border services, if these actions might "pose a threat to the operation of" the intermediary house in Poland.[395] The branch may commence the suppliance of investment services in the host Member State as soon as its financial supervision authority has specified the terms and conditions under which the investment house is to provide these services, or (in the absence of these terms and conditions) following the lapse of two months from the date that the host State's financial supervision authority receives the information from the PFSA.[396] Investment services that are to be provided without the establishment of a branch may be commended as soon as the PFSA has notified the intermediary house that it has supplied the information to the financial supervision authority of the host State.[397] An intermediary house may apply for an authorisation to establish a branch, or to provide cross-border services, in a country that is not a Member State,[398] provided that the PFSA has concluded the agreement to which Article 20(2) of the Act on Capital Market Supervision refers, with the financial supervision authority in the state in which the activities are to be carried out; the provisions of Articles 104(2)-(4) and 104(9) of the TFIA are to apply.[399]

---

[393] Article 104(5), TFIA. If the investment services are to be provided through a branch, then in addition to the above items, the PFSA shall supply information on the general rules of the investor compensation scheme that is effective in Poland (Article 104(5), TFIA).
[394] Article 104(6), TFIA.
[395] Article 104(9), TFIA.
[396] Article 104(10), TFIA.
[397] Article 104(10), TFIA. This is the notification that Article 104(6) of the TFIA requires – see above in this paragraph.
[398] See note 347, for the definition of 'Member State'.
[399] Article 104(14), TFIA. See the previous paragraph, for Articles 104(2)-(4) and 104(9) of the TFIA. The PFSA or its authorised representative may provide to, and receive from, a foreign financial supervision authority, information that is necessary (with respect to the securities or financial market) to duly undertake specific supervisory responsibilities, or ensure the proper conduct of administrative, audit, court, criminal and explanatory proceedings in cases that relate to the exercise of supervision (Article 20(1), Act of 29 July 2005 on Capital Market Supervision). The rules and procedures for the supply of information shall

An intermediary house is required to notify the PFSA of its intention to organise a multilateral trading facility, indicating the Member State in whose territory the facility is to be structured.[400] This authorisation entitles the intermediary house to install equipment and information systems in the territory of the host Member State, in order to ensure that entities operating there have access to the multilateral trading facility.[401] The PFSA shall forward the notification within one month of its receipt, to the financial supervision authority of the host Member State.[402]

A foreign legal person[403] that provides investment services and has its registered office in the territory of a WTO member state or an OECD country may supply these services in Poland through a branch.[404] This branch is to be an organisational unit without legal personality that is separated within the organisational structure of that legal person, and which supplies investment services in Poland.[405] All organisational units of the foreign legal person that are located in Poland and which provide investment services are to constitute a single branch.[406] The PFSA is to

---

be defined by the agreements referred to in Article 20(1) of the Act on Capital Market Supervision, concluded by the PFSA with other supervisory authorities. The PFSA may provide information on the basis of the agreement to which Article 20(2) of the Act on Capital Market Supervision refers, if (i) it will not adversely affect the security, sovereignty or public interest of Poland, (ii) the laws in force in the home country of the foreign financial supervision authority to which the information is provided ensure that the information will only be used for the purpose of exercising supervision, or carrying out administrative or court proceedings in cases that are related to the exercise of this supervision, or (iii) it is ensured that each further transfer of this information “outside the foreign [financial] supervision authority” for purposes other than those that Article 20(1) of the Act on Capital Market Supervision specifies, is only possible upon obtaining the PFSA’s prior approval (Article 20(3), Act of 29 July 2005 on Capital Market Supervision).

[400] Article 104a(2), TFIA.

[401] Article 104a(1), TFIA. See note 347, for the definition of ‘Member State’.

[402] Article 104a(3), TFIA.

[403] The TFIA does not define ‘foreign legal person’. However, the definition of ‘investment firm’ refers to “any foreign legal person with a registered office in the territory of an OECD state or WTO member state”, which indicates that ‘foreign’ in this context means non-Polish – in June 2014, the WTO had 160 member states (source: http://www.wto.org/english/thewto_e/whatis_e/tif_e/org6_e.htm [accessed 29 June 2014]).

[404] Article 115(1), TFIA.

[405] Article 115(2), TFIA.

[406] Article 115(2), TFIA. Articles 100(1) and 100(3) of the TFIA shall apply to the supervision over a foreign legal person that provides investment services in Poland

grant a brokerage licence to the foreign legal person, upon obtaining a written opinion from the financial supervision authority which has granted that person the authorisation to carry out activities in the country in which its registered office is situated.[407] This opinion is to concern the way in which the foreign legal person conducts its activities, including in particular its compliance with legal regulations that apply in that country.[408] The PFSA shall grant the brokerage licence to the foreign legal person, on condition that there are systems in place which enable the PFSA to acquire information that is necessary in the context of its supervision over investment services which are provided in Poland,[409] that in the country in which the foreign legal person has its registered office, this person is subject to capital requirements which are equivalent to those specified in the regulations issued under Article 94(1)(2) of the TFIA,[410] and that (if the business is to carried out through a branch) the foreign legal person has separate funds – in order to provide investment services in Poland – whose amount is at least that of the amount specified in the regulations which govern the initial capital of an intermediary house.[411] The branch's governing bodies shall include at least two persons who hold

---

through a branch, if the branches of this legal person are required (according to other regulations) to prepare financial statements (Article 115(6), TFIA). If there are doubts as to the reliability or accuracy of the financial statements or other financial information, or as to the proper maintenance of accounting books, then the PFSA may require a qualified auditor to audit the statements, information or accounting books; if any material irregularities are found during the audit, then the person whose finances are audited shall reimburse the costs of the audit to the PFSA (Article 100(1), TFIA). The qualified auditor(s) may be required to promptly submit to the PFSA any information of which they become aware in connection with their activities and which relates to any circumstances that results in reasonable suspicion of a transgression of the law or principles of fair trading or of a compromise of the interests of customers, any threat to the continuity of operations, a refusal to issue an opinion on the financial statements, or the issue of a negative or qualified opinion on these statements (Article 100(3), TFIA).

[407] Article 115(3), TFIA.

[408] Article 115(3), TFIA.

[409] Article 115(4)(1), TFIA.

[410] Article 115(4)(2), TFIA. The minister who is responsible for financial institutions shall define by way of regulation the scope and detailed rules for the determination of the total capital requirement and of the maximum amount of loans and issued debit securities to intermediary houses, taking into consideration the need to ensure sufficient capital cover in relation to each of the risks that are incurred in investment services, the quantity of fixed costs and liabilities, the initial capital and the scope of operation (Article 94(1)(2), TFIA).

[411] Article 115(4)(3), TFIA.

a university degree, have at least three years of experience in working for financial institutions, and have a good reputation with respect to the positions that they have occupied.[412]

Without the licence to which Article 69(1) of the TFIA refers,[413] a foreign investment firm[414] may provide any investment services within Article 69(2) or Article 69(4) of the TFIA,[415] as long as the financial supervision authority of the country in which the investment firm has its registered office has authorised it to supply investment services.[416] Investment services may be provided in Poland via a branch (as defined in Article 115(2) of the TFIA), or without founding a branch.[417] In order for the foreign investment firm to start to provide investment services in Poland, the PFSA must have received a notification of the firm's intended supply of these services from the financial supervision authority of its home Member State.[418] A foreign legal person[419] may start to supply cross-border investment services upon the PFSA's receipt of the relevant information from the financial supervision authority of its home state.[420] It may provide investment services through a Polish branch upon the PFSA specifying the conditions for its provision of investment services or (in the absence of this specification) upon the lapse of two months of the PFSA's receipt of the information from foreign financial supervision authority.[421] If the PFSA receives a notice of an intention to provide cross-border investment services, then it may ask the financial supervision authority of

[412] Article 115(5), TFIA.

[413] The provision of investment services shall require an activity licence, to be granted by the PFSA upon the application referred to in Article 82 of the TFIA and submitted by the applicant (Article 69(1), TFIA). Article 82 of the TFIA contains the information that must accompany an application for a brokerage licence.

[414] See note 370, for the definition of 'foreign investment firm'.

[415] See above in this section, for Articles 69(2) and 69(4) of the TFIA. Article 117(1) of the TFIA states "within the meaning of Art 69.2-4"; however, Article 69(3) of the TFIA has been repealed.

[416] Article 117(1), TFIA.

[417] Article 117(1), TFIA. See the previous paragraph, for Article 115(2) of the TFIA. Article 117(1) of the TFIA shall not apply to activities that are provided under an agreement with the National Bank of Poland, the Polish State Treasury, or a governmental authority that performs activities concerning the exchange rate, monetary, or public debt management policies, or a policy of managing the Polish State Treasury's free cash (Article 117(2), TFIA).

[418] Article 117(3), TFIA.

[419] See note 403.

[420] Article 117(3), TFIA.

[421] Article 117(3), TFIA.

the foreign investment firm's home Member State to furnish it with information about the agents that the firm intends to use in order to supply investment services in Poland.[422] Within two months of its receipt of the notification from the other financial supervision authority, the PFSA shall prepare for supervision of the foreign investment firm's activities, and shall advise the firm of the conditions under which it is to provide its specified investment services in Poland.[423] These conditions shall include, in particular, the rules that are stated in Article 83 of the TFIA and in the regulations that are issued under Article 94(1)(1) of the TFIA – if the firm is to provide its investment services through a Polish branch,[424] and the rules that are specified in the regulations that are issued under Article 94(1)(1) of the TFIA – if the firm is to supply cross-border investment services in Poland.[425]

A foreign investment firm[426] that operates a regulated market in a Member State[427] other than Poland may, without the PFSA's permission,

---

[422] Article 117(3)(a), TFIA.

[423] Article 117(4), TFIA.

[424] Article 117(5)(1), TFIA. An investment firm shall employ at least one securities broker to provide each of the investment services that Articles 69(2)(1)-(3), 69(2)(6), 69(2)(8) and 69(4)(1) specify, two investment advisers to supply the investment services that Article 69(2)(4) states, and one securities broker or one investment adviser to provide the investment services that Article 69(2)(5) specifies (Article 83(1), TFIA). See above in this section, for Articles 69(2) and 69(4) of the TFIA. Article 83(1) of the TFIA does not apply to foreign investment firms providing investment services in Poland that are not required to establish a branch for this purpose (Article 83(3), TFIA). The minister who is responsible for financial institutions is to define, by way of regulation, the conditions and procedures that investment firms and custodian banks are to follow in the course of their activities related to the promotion of their brokerage services, the maintenance of relations with potential customers, the execution and clearing of transactions, the assignment of customers to different categories, the supply of brokerage services, the recording of the transactions executed, the archiving of documents that are prepared in connection with activities, the creation and realisation of collateral for loans that are advanced in order to finance the purchase of financial instruments, and the creation of security interests in financial instruments in order to secure claims, in relation to the performance of these activities with due diligence, customer protection, the swift and safe execution and clearance of transactions, and the safety and transparency of trading (Article 94(1)(1), TFIA).

[425] Article 117(5)(2), TFIA. See note 424, for Article 94(1)(1) of the TFIA.

[426] See note 370, for the definition of 'foreign investment firm'.

establish technical equipment and information technology systems that provide access to this market for entities that carry out activities in Poland.[428] In order to undertake these activities, the foreign investment firm must inform the PFSA via the financial supervision authority that granted the authorisation to organise a multilateral trading facility to that firm.[429] The PFSA may request the other financial supervision authority to state the participants of the regulated market.[430]

A foreign investment firm[431] that provides investment services in Poland shall be subject to supervision in another Member State[432] by the financial supervision authority that has granted it a brokerage licence.[433] However, the PFSA shall supervise compliance with the rules for investment services for which Polish law provides.[434]

If the PFSA ascertains that an entity which operates a foreign regulated market,[435] sets up technical equipment and information technology systems for providing access to a foreign regulated market for firms that conduct activities in Poland, or organises a multilateral trading facility in accordance with Article 117a of the TFIA,[436] breaches legal provisions of the law in force in the country of the regulated market's registered office in the scope of the regulated market or the organisation of a multilateral trading facility, then the PFSA shall notify (about the contraventions) the financial supervision authority that granted this entity a licence to operate.[437] If, despite measures that that financial supervision authority takes, the activity of the entity is a threat to investors' interests or to the proper functioning of the trading of financial instruments in another Member State, then the PFSA may prohibit that entity from establishing technical equipment and information technology systems in order to

---

[427] See note 347, for the definition of 'Member State', 'regulated market', and 'foreign regulated market'. As stated there, the firm that operates a regulated market is a 'market operator' (Article 4(1)(13), Directive 2004/39/EC).
[428] Article 117a(1), TFIA.
[429] Article 117a(2), TFIA.
[430] Article 117a(3), TFIA.
[431] See note 370, for the definition of 'foreign investment firm'.
[432] See note 347, for the definition of 'Member State'.
[433] Article 118, TFIA.
[434] Article 118, TFIA.
[435] See note 347, for the definition of 'foreign regulated market'. As stated there, the firm that operates a regulated market is a 'market operator' (Article 4(1)(13), Directive 2004/39/EC).
[436] See above in this section, for Article 117a of the TFIA.
[437] Article 166a(1), TFIA.

provide access to the foreign regulated market for Polish firms.[438] The PFSA shall issue this decision after a hearing,[439] convey it to the European Commission and the financial supervision authority that granted the entity a licence to operate the regulated market,[440] and publish it in the Official Journal of the PFSA.[441] The PFSA may order that the decision be published in two national newspapers at the expense of a foreign firm which is engaged in the regulated market.[442] If a foreign investment firm[443] is prohibited from carrying out activities in Poland, it shall not resume these activities for five years from the date on which the decision prohibiting these activities becomes final, unless the PFSA agrees to shorten this time.[444] If justified by the requirement to protect the public interest, and before taking the steps in Article 166a(1)-(2) of the TFIA,[445] the PFSA may suspend for up to one month the authorisation of a foreign investment firm to operate a regulated market in Poland, and shall notify the European Commission and the financial supervision authority of the foreign investment firm's home Member State.[446]

Subject to Article 167(2) of the TFIA, the PFSA may revoke the brokerage licence, or limit the scope of an investment firm's activities, if this firm seriously contravenes "the provisions of the law" – especially the regulations issued under Articles 94(1)(1), 94(1)(2) and 94(1)(5) of the TFIA,[447] does not "comply with the principles of fair trading",[448]

---

[438] Article 166a(2), TFIA.
[439] Article 166a(3), TFIA.
[440] Article 166a(2), TFIA.
[441] Article 166a(4), TFIA.
[442] Article 166a(4), TFIA. This would not be popular, especially if the entity concerned is not the market operator that had breached the law.
[443] See note 370, for the definition of 'foreign investment firm'.
[444] Article 166a(5), TFIA.
[445] For Article 166a(1)-(2) of the TFIA, see above in this paragraph.
[446] Article 166a(6), TFIA.
[447] Article 167(1)(1), TFIA. The quoted phrase probably means the rules of Polish law. See notes 424 and 410, for Articles 94(1)(1) and 94(1)(2), respectively. The minister who is responsible for financial institutions shall define by regulation detailed organisational and technical requirements for the provision of investment services by an investment firm, a bank with its registered office in Poland, and a custodian bank, for detailed conditions for internal control system functions and risk management in an intermediary house, and for "the intermediary house estimation of the internal capital and a review of estimating and maintaining the capital" (Articles 94(1)(5), TFIA and 70(2), TFIA).

"compromises" the interests of the customer,[449] has been awarded the licence on the basis of false documents or misrepresentations,[450] has discontinued the activities for which the licence provides for at least six months,[451] or no longer satisfies the conditions on the basis of which the licence was granted (subject to Article 95(10) of the TFIA).[452] In the first four of these situations, the PFSA may decide to impose a penalty of up to 500,000 zloty on the investment firm, instead of, or in addition to, revoking the firm's brokerage licence or restricting the scope of its activities – if this is justified by the nature of the firm's misconduct.[453] The PFSA may also apply these sanctions to an investment firm that has commissioned an agent to perform the activities to which Article 79(2) of the TFIA refers if, in connection with its services for the investment firm, the agent "compromises" the interests of customers or breaches "the provisions of the law or the principles of fair trading".[454] The entity whose brokerage licence has been withdrawn is not to reapply for this licence for five years from the date on which the decision revoking the licence became final, unless the PFSA agrees to reduce this period.[455] If justified by the need to protect the public interest, the PFSA may suspend, in whole or in part, the firm's authorisation to provide investment services, for up to

---

[448] Article 167(1)(2), TFIA. Even though the TFIA refers to 'the principles of fair trading' on several occasions, it does not define what these principles are. See note 187, which describes similar circumstances for the IFA.

[449] Article 167(1)(3), TFIA.

[450] Article 167(1)(6), TFIA.

[451] Article 167(1)(4), TFIA,

[452] Article 167(1)(5), TFIA. If the number of partners in a limited joint-stock partnership, limited partnership, limited-liability partnership or general partnership that satisfy the conditions that Article 95(1) of the TFIA states for these partners, falls below two, then (subject to Article 83 of the TFIA), the intermediary house is required to promptly restore compliance with the provisions of Article 95(1) of the TFIA, no later than six months from the day on which the intermediary house ceased to satisfy the conditions that Article 95(1) of the TFIA specifies; until compliance with Article 95(1) of the TFIA is restored, the intermediary house shall only act under agreement upon execution of orders that are then in force to acquire or dispose of financial instruments, but shall not make new agreements (Article 95(10), TFIA). See note 424, for Articles 83(1) and 83(3) of the TFIA.

[453] Article 167(2), TFIA.

[454] Article 167(3), TFIA. See notes 447 and 448. On the basis of the agreement between the investment firm and its agent, the agent may conduct activities that are related to the execution of agreements for the supply of services by the investment firm or which facilitate the performance of these agreements (Article 79(1)-(2), TFIA).

[455] Article 167(4), TFIA.

one month of the initiation of the proceedings concerning the revocation of its brokerage licence.[456] If it is necessary for the protection of the public interest, the PFSA may (in the decision to revoke the licence) specify the date on which investment services are to be discontinued.[457] The PFSA's decision (as to whether or not to revoke the investment firm's activity licence) shall be published in the Official Journal of the PFSA, as soon as it has been taken.[458] The PFSA may order that the decision is to be published in two daily national newspapers, at the investment firm's cost.[459] Articles 167(1), 167(2), 167(3), 167(7) and 167(8) of the TFIA shall apply, if the PFSA becomes aware of a transgression of the regulations that govern investment services in another Member State, by a Polish intermediary house that provides investment services there.[460]

If the PFSA ascertains that a foreign investment firm,[461] or an agent that represents the foreign investment firm, breaches the provisions that regulate brokerage or custodial activities that apply in Poland, then it shall order this firm to discontinue the contravention, and shall determine the deadline for its remedy.[462] The PFSA shall notify the financial supervision authority of the foreign investment firm's home country, of the contravention and of the failure to remedy this transgression by the deadline.[463] If the foreign investment firm does not discontinue or remedy the transgression within the set timeframe, then following one month from the notification, the PFSA, upon informing the home Member State's financial supervision authority, may prohibit (in whole or in part) the carrying out of brokerage or custodial services in Poland,[464] suspend (in whole or in part) the right to conduct brokerage or custodial services in Poland for up to six months,[465] impose a penalty of up to 500,000 zloty,[466] or introduce the pecuniary sanction together with either the prohibition or

---

[456] Articles 167(5) and 167(1), TFIA.
[457] Article 167(5a), TFIA.
[458] Article 167(8), TFIA.
[459] Article 167(8), TFIA.
[460] Article 167(9), TFIA. For Articles 167(1)-(3), 167(7) and 167(8) of the TFIA, see above in this paragraph. See note 347, for the definition of 'Member State'.
[461] See note 370, for the definition of 'foreign investment firm'.
[462] Article 169(1), TFIA.
[463] Article 169(2), TFIA.
[464] Article 169(3)(1), TFIA.
[465] Article 169(3)(2), TFIA.
[466] Article 169(3)(3), TFIA.

the suspension.[467] The PFSA shall take this decision following a hearing,[468] and publish it in the Official Journal of the PFSA.[469] It may order that the decision be published in two daily national newspapers, at the foreign investment firm's cost.[470] If a foreign investment firm is prohibited from carrying out brokerage or custodial activities in Poland, then it shall not resume these activities for five years from the date on which the decision prohibiting these activities became final, unless the PFSA agrees to reduce this time.[471] If justified by the need for the public interest to be protected, then, before taking the above steps, the PFSA may suspend, in whole or in part, the foreign investment firm's right to carry out brokerage or custodial activities in Poland for up to one month, and shall notify (of this suspension) the European Commission and the financial supervision authority of the investment firm's home state.[472]

If the PFSA ascertains that a foreign investment firm[473] contravenes provisions that remain under the supervision of another Member State's[474] financial supervision authority (in accordance with Article 118 of the TFIA),[475] then the PFSA shall inform this financial supervision authority of these transgressions.[476] If, in spite of the measures that the foreign financial supervision authority has taken, the foreign investment firm's activity is "a threat to the proper functioning of trading in financial instruments or the interests of investors", then the PFSA may, upon informing the foreign financial supervision authority, prohibit (in whole or in part) the foreign investment firm's provision of investment services in Poland,[477] suspend (in whole or in part) the firm's right to carry out investment services in Poland for up to six months,[478] or forbid the foreign investment firm from setting up technical equipment and information

[467] Article 169(3)(4), TFIA. The PFSA shall notify the European Commission of the sanctions that it has imposed in accordance with Article 169(3) of the TFIA (Article 169(8), TFIA).
[468] Article 169(4), TFIA.
[469] Article 169(5), TFIA.
[470] Article 169(5), TFIA.
[471] Article 169(6), TFIA.
[472] Article 169(7), TFIA.
[473] Article 169(10), TFIA. See note 370, for the definition of 'foreign investment firm'.
[474] See note 347, for the definition of 'Member State'.
[475] See above in this section, for Article 118 of the TFIA.
[476] Article 169(10), TFIA.
[477] Article 169(11)(1), TFIA.
[478] Article 169(11)(2), TFIA.

technology systems in Poland, which enable Polish firms to access the regulated market that it operates in another Member State.[479]

If a company that operates a regulated market, an intermediary house, a bank which provides investment services, or a foreign legal person[480] that supplies investment services in Poland, contravenes the provisions of the law that governs the operation of a regulated market or the provision of investment services, then the PFSA may take a decision to impose a pecuniary penalty of up to 100,000 zloty on the persons who are responsible for the transgression.[481] This decision is to be issued following a hearing.[482]

The establishment of a branch and the provision of cross-border investment services are 'capital movements' in Title I(1), and in Titles III, IV and V, of the nomenclature in Annex I, respectively. The revocation of, or the suspension of, a licence to provide investment services, or to extend the operation of a regulated market to another EEA state, restrict the free movement of capital.

To be justified under Article 65(1)(b) of the TFEU, the restrictive measures must be necessary for the protection of the interests that they are intended to guarantee, be proportionate (i.e. not attainable by less restrictive measures), and observe the requirements of legal certainty (i.e. be specific, objective and known to the parties beforehand); furthermore, the persons whom the measures affect must have access to legal redress (i.e. intervention must be supported by reasons and be subject to review by the national courts).[483] Some provisions furnish the PFSA with a discretion to act – for instance Article 104(9) of the TFIA, which allows the PFSA to raise an objection to an intermediary house's intention to establish a branch or to provide cross-border investment services, if these actions may "pose a threat to the operation of" the intermediary house in Poland,[484] and Article 166a(6) of the TFIA, according to which the PFSA may suspend for up to one month the authorisation of a foreign investment firm to operate a regulated market in Poland – if this action is justified by the

---

479 Articles 169(11)(3) and 117a(1), TFIA. In the case that Article 169(11) of the TFIA refers to, the provisions of Articles 169(4)-(8) of the TFIA shall apply (Article 169(12), TFIA). See the previous paragraph, for Articles 169(4)-(7) of the TFIA. See note 467, for Article 169(8) of the TFIA.

480 See note 403.

481 Article 169a, TFIA.

482 Article 169a, TFIA.

483 See the subsection '*The requirements for a successful public policy/security derogation*' in section 2.1.3.

484 See above in this section.

requirement to protect the public interest.[485] These Articles do not provide legal certainty to the intermediary house or investment firm, and may be disproportionate. In addition, the TFIA neither requires the PFSA to give reasons for its decisions, nor provides the person(s) who are adversely affected by a decision of the PFSA with the right to appeal against this decision in the Polish courts. Hence, Article 65(1)(b) of the TFEU does not justify the restrictive measures in the TFIA.

Restrictive measures that affect capital movements between an EEA state and a third country may be justified under Article 64(2) of the TFEU, if the EU institutions carefully take account of the objective of the free movement of capital whilst enacting the relevant legislation, and if the national rules do not limit the free movement of capital more than do the equivalent provisions of the pertinent Directive.[486] As the relevant Directive, Directive 2004/39/EC, does not mention the free movement of capital, the EU institutions did not carefully consider the free movement of capital whilst enacting the Directive. Therefore, Article 64(2) of the TFEU may not justify restrictive measures in the TFEU. Thus, these measures contravene Article 63 of the TFEU.

4.3 Credit Institutions

4.3.1 Act of 29 August 1997: Banking Law (BL)

Polish banks may be founded as state banks, co-operative banks, or banks that are incorporated as joint-stock companies.[487] A state bank is established by a regulation of the Council of Ministers at the request of the minister for State Treasury matters, after the minister has obtained the PFSA's opinion.[488] A 'cooperative bank' is a bank that is a co-operative; its articles of association are drawn up as a notarial deed.[489]

A bank that is incorporated as a joint-stock company, and a co-operative bank, require authorisation from the PFSA.[490] The application for authorisation must include the bank's proposed name and registered office,[491] the operations for which the bank is to be authorised,[492]

---

[485] See above in this section.

[486] See the subsection '*Derogations that apply only to capital movements to/from third countries*', in section 2.3.2.

[487] Article 12, BL.

[488] Article 14(1), BL.

[489] Article 20(1), BL.

[490] Article 30a, BL.

[491] Article 31(1)(1), BL.

information concerning the bank's objectives and the ambit of its intended activity,[493] and information on its founders, persons proposed for its management board and its initial capital[494] – which must be the zloty equivalent of at least 5 million EUR if the bank is a joint-stock company,[495] and the zloty equivalent of at least 1 million EUR if it is a co-operative bank.[496] The following items must be appended to the bank's application for authorisation: a draft of its articles of association,[497] its programme of operations and financial plan for the next three years,[498] the documents that the PFSA requires concerning the bank's founders and their financial circumstances,[499] its organisational and internal audit rules,[500] its rules for the supervision of the applicant's "compliance with the operations of the law",[501] its rules to protect the flow of inside information,[502] information that is protected by professional secrecy,[503] the internal procedures to counteract insider dealing,[504] and its rules for managing conflicts of interest,[505] and for investing in financial instruments by persons who are connected with the bank.[506]

Banking operations are to comprise the acceptance of deposits that are payable on demand or at a stated maturity,[507] the operation of accounts that contain these deposits,[508] the operation of other bank accounts,[509] the provision of loans,[510] the issue and confirmation of bank guarantees,[511] the

---

[492] Article 31(1)(2), BL.
[493] Article 31(1)(2), BL.
[494] Article 31(1)(3), BL.
[495] Article 32(1), BL.
[496] Article 32(2), BL.
[497] Article 31(2)(1), BL.
[498] Article 31(2)(2), BL.
[499] Article 31(2)(3), BL.
[500] Articles 31(2)(3a), BL, and 82(2)(3), TFIA.
[501] Articles 31(2)(3a), BL, and 82(2)(3), TFIA. The quoted phase from Article 82(2)(3) of the TFIA does not refer to which law. It probably means all the relevant provisions of the law of Poland.
[502] Articles 31(2)(3a), BL, and 82(2)(4), TFIA.
[503] Articles 31(2)(3a), BL, and 82(2)(4), TFIA.
[504] Articles 31(2)(3a), BL, and 82(2)(4), TFIA.
[505] Articles 31(2)(3a), BL, and 82(2)(4a), TFIA.
[506] Articles 31(2)(3a), BL, and 82(2)(5), TFIA.
[507] Article 5(1)(1), BL.
[508] Article 5(1)(1), BL.
[509] Article 5(1)(2), BL.
[510] Article 5(1)(3), BL.
[511] Article 5(1)(4), BL.

issue and confirmation of letters of credit,[512] the issue of bank securities,[513] the execution of bank monetary settlements,[514] the issue of electronic money,[515] and the performance of other operations that are reserved for banks under other legislation.[516] If the following operations are performed by banks, they shall be deemed to be banking operations: the extension of cash advances,[517] operations that concern bills of exchange and cheques,[518] operations that relate to warrants,[519] the issue of payment cards,[520] the performance of operations that involve payments cards,[521] transactions in financial forwards,[522] the purchase and sale of monetary claims,[523] the safekeeping of securities and valuables,[524] the provision of facilities for safe deposit,[525] the purchase and sale of foreign exchange,[526] the grant and confirmation of sureties,[527] the execution of actions on customers' instructions that relate to the issue of securities,[528] and acting as an intermediary in the performance of foreign exchange settlements and in the execution of monetary transfers.[529] In addition to the performance of any of these banking operations, banks may also purchase shares (and rights on such shares) in other legal persons,[530] acquire units in investment funds,[531] incur liabilities in relation to the issue of securities,[532] trade in securities,[533] exchange claims for assets that belong to the debtor (on terms agreed with the debtor),[534] acquire and dispose of real estate,[535]supply

[512] Article 5(1)(4), BL.
[513] Article 5(1)(5), BL.
[514] Article 5(1)(6), BL.
[515] Article 5(1)(6a), BL.
[516] Article 5(1)(7), BL.
[517] Article 5(2)(1), BL.
[518] Article 5(2)(2), BL.
[519] Article 5(2)(2), BL.
[520] Article 5(2)(3), BL.
[521] Article 5(2)(3), BL.
[522] Article 5(2)(4), BL.
[523] Article 5(2)(5), BL.
[524] Article 5(2)(6), BL.
[525] Article 5(2)(6), BL.
[526] Article 5(2)(7), BL.
[527] Article 5(2)(8), BL.
[528] Article 5(2)(9), BL.
[529] Article 5(2)(10), BL.
[530] Article 6(1)(1), BL.
[531] Article 6(1)(1), BL.
[532] Article 6(1)(2), BL.
[533] Article 6(1)(3), BL.
[534] Article 6(1)(4), BL.

financial consulting and advisory services,[536] provide certification services (as the regulations on electronic signatures define).[537] supply "other financial services",[538] and perform other operations – if the provisions of separate legislation so authorise.[539]

Subject to Articles 48a to 48g of the BL,[540] the foundation of a bank abroad by a Polish bank, and the establishment of a branch of a Polish bank outside Poland, shall require the PFSA to provide authorisation.[541] The application for the establishment of a Polish bank or branch abroad is to include the bank's name, registered office, and organisational structure,[542] and information about the bank's founders and its initial capital.[543] The applicant shall append the following documents: a draft of its articles of association and reasons for the foundation of a bank abroad,[544] the bank's financial plan and programme of operations for at least the next 3 years,[545] information on the legal regulations that are in force in the country of the bank's establishment with respect to authorisations for the bank to conduct its activities,[546] tax regulations that apply to these operations,[547] and regulations on the transfer of foreign exchange and on the supervision of banks.[548] An application for the establishment of a branch of a Polish bank abroad should include reasons

---

[535] Article 6(1)(5), BL.
[536] Article 6(1)(6), BL.
[537] Article 6(1)(6a), BL.
[538] Article 6(1)(7), BL. The BL does not define 'financial services'. Consequently, the expression 'other financial services' is imprecise.
[539] Article 6(1)(8), BL.
[540] Articles 48a to 48g of the BL concern the taking up and pursuit of business by Polish banks in host Member States, and are considered in the next paragraph. A 'Member State' is a Member State of the EU (Article 4(1)(17), BL). The provisions of the BL that refer to Member States shall also apply to the countries that are not Member States but are within the EEA (Article 4(3), BL). The 'home Member State' is a Member State in which a particular credit institution has been authorised to conduct its business, and in which its registered office is situated (Article 4(1)(22), BL). A 'host Member State' a Member State in which a domestic bank carries out, or intends to pursue, its business (Article 4(1)(23), BL).
[541] Article 39(1), BL.
[542] Article 39(2)(1), BL.
[543] Article 39(2)(2), BL.
[544] Article 39(3)(1), BL.
[545] Article 39(3)(2), BL.
[546] Article 39(3)(3)(a), BL.
[547] Article 39(3)(3)(b), BL.
[548] Article 39(3)(3)(c), BL.

for this foundation and the last three pieces of information in the previous paragraph, as applicable to bank branches.[549]

A Polish bank may enact business in a host Member State through a branch or by cross-border activity.[550] In the host Member State, a Polish bank may conduct the activities that derive from the authorisation to which Article 34(1) of the BL refers.[551] A Polish bank that intends to found a branch in a host Member State is to provide a written notification of this fact to the PFSA.[552] This notification shall include the name of the host Member State in which the bank intends to establish the branch,[553] the branch's name,[554] the address of the branch at which documentation that concerns its activity shall be available,[555] a programme of operations for the branch, which specifies the branch's organisational structure and the activities that the bank intends to perform through the branch,[556] and the names of the persons who are nominated for the posts of branch manager and deputy branch manager.[557] Within three months of receiving the notification or supplementary information thereto, the PFSA shall send a (further) notification to the financial supervision authority of the host Member State, together with information on the level of the applicant's

---

549 Article 39(4), BL.

550 Article 48a, BL. 'Cross-border activity' is the performance by a Polish credit institution, or by a host Member State's domestic bank, of some or all of the operations that derive from the authorisation granted to it, without involving a branch of that organisation (Article 4(1)(21), BL). This definition refers to a host Member State's domestic bank, rather than to a bank from a Member State or a country outside the EEA. Hence the BL does not provide for the supply of cross-border services between Poland and third countries.

551 In the authorisation to establish the bank, the PFSA shall state the bank's name, its registered office, the name of its founders and the shares that they subscribe for, the amount of initial capital, the activity for which authorisation is to be granted, and the conditions that the bank is to satisfy for the PFSA to authorise the bank to start business (Article 34(1), TFIA).

552 Article 48(c)(1), BL.

553 Article 48(c)(2)(1), BL.

554 Article 48(c)(2)(2), BL.

555 Article 48(c)(2)(3), BL.

556 Article 48(c)(2)(4), BL.

557 Article 48(c)(2)(5), BL. The PFSA may require the applicant bank to supplement the notification with regard to the information that Article 48(c)(2)(2)-(5) specifies (Article 48(c)(3), BL). This provision may mean that the specified information must be supplied along with the notification. Alternatively, and more probably, Article 48(c)(3) of the BL empowers the PFSA to provide additional information that is not specified in Article 48(c)(2) of the BL.

own funds and capital solvency ratio.[558] The PFSA shall advise the applicant that it has sent this notification to the host Member State's financial supervision authority.[559]

The PFSA shall refuse to send this notification, if the requirements that Article 48(c)(2) of the BL contains have not been met,[560] the financial circumstances or organisational structure of the applicant are insufficient to support the planned business,[561] the proposed activities "would contravene provisions of law",[562] and/or the business envisaged "could prove detrimental to the sound and prudent management of the bank".[563] The PFSA shall deliver its refusal to the applicant, within three months of receiving the (initial) notification or supplementary information thereto.[564]

A Polish bank that intends to provide cross-border services shall notify the PFSA of this fact.[565] This notification should state the operations that derive from the authorisation that the PFSA granted to the bank, which it intends to conduct.[566] The PFSA shall communicate the notification to the financial supervision authority of the host Member State within one month of its receipt, and shall inform the applicant that it has done so.[567]

A foreign bank that intends to establish a branch in Poland requires an authorisation from the PFSA to do so.[568] The authorisation is issued after the PFSA has consulted the minister who is responsible for financial

---

558 Article 48(c)(4), BL.
559 Article 48(c)(4), BL.
560 Article 48(d)(1)(1), BL.
561 Article 48(d)(1)(2), BL.
562 Article 48(d)(1)(3), BL. The quoted phrase does not specify the scope of the law that might be contravened and, therefore, bring Article 48(d)(1) of the BL into operation. The legislators are likely to mean the whole system of laws in Poland.
563 Article 48(d)(1)(4), BL.
564 Article 48(d)(2), BL.
565 Article 48(f)(1), BL.
566 Article 48(f)(1), BL.
567 Article 48(f)(2), BL. The PFSA must immediately inform the financial supervision authority of the host Member State, if the Polish bank loses its authorisation to provide services in Poland (whether or not the supply of services to the host Member State is via a branch of the bank located there (Article 48g, BL)).
568 Article 40(1), BL. A 'foreign bank' is one that has its registered office in a country that is not a Member State of the EU (Article 4(1)(2), BL). In the BL, 'Member State' means a Contracting Party to the EEA Agreement – see note 540. Hence, the term 'foreign bank' means a bank that has its registered office outside the EEA.

institutions, following an application from the foreign bank.[569] This application shall include the business name and registered office of the foreign bank,[570] a description of the applicant bank's activities,[571] a specification of the types of banking activities for the execution of which the bank's branch is to be authorised,[572] the branch's registered office,[573] the amount of funds with which the branch has been endowed,[574] and information about at least 2 persons who are nominated for the posts of branch manager and deputy branch manager.[575] The foreign bank must append to the application the branch's draft by-laws, and a commitment from the bank that it will fulfil all claims on the branch that may arise from its relations with third parties.[576] In the authorisation to establish a branch of a foreign bank in Poland, the PFSA shall specify, in particular, the branch's registered office, the banking operations for which the branch has been granted authorisation, and the minimum amount of funds that are required for the branch to be able to pursue its activities.[577] In addition, the PFSA must approve the branch's draft by-laws.[578] Branches of foreign banks must be recorded in the business register.[579] Articles 32 to 38 of the BL apply, as necessary, to procedures for the foundation of a branch of a foreign bank in Poland.[580] A branch of a foreign bank shall provide

---

[569] Article 40(1), BL.
[570] Article 40(2)(1), BL.
[571] Article 40(2)(1), BL.
[572] Article 40(2)(2), BL.
[573] Article 40(2)(2), BL.
[574] Article 40(2)(3), BL.
[575] Article 40(2)(4), BL.
[576] Article 40(3), BL. Article 31(2) of the BL applies, as necessary (Article 40(3), BL). See above in this section, for Article 31(2) of the BL.
[577] Article 40(4), BL. A 'branch of a foreign bank' in an organisational unit of a foreign bank, which performs on the foreign bank's behalf, and for its benefit, some or all of the operations that derive from the authorisation that has been granted to this bank; all organisational units of the foreign bank that are founded in Poland, and which have the above characteristics, are considered to be a single branch (Article 4(1)(20), BL). See note 568, for the definition of 'foreign bank'.
[578] Article 40(4), BL.
[579] Article 40(5), BL.
[580] Article 40(6), BL. Article 32 of the BL concerns the capital requirements of banks that are joint-stock companies and co-operative banks; see above in this section, for Article 32(1)-(2) of the BL. Article 33 of the BL provides the PFSA with the power to require applicants to furnish it with additional information, in cases in which this information is essential for it to take a decision on the authorisation to found a bank in Poland. Article 34 of the BL states the information that the PFSA must place on an authorisation to establish a bank in Poland. Article

services pursuant to the by-laws that the foreign bank issues.[581] Branches of foreign banks that supply services in Poland are to be governed by Polish law.[582]

Whilst the BL contains no reference to the provision of cross-border services by a foreign bank or credit institution[583] in Poland,[584] it permits these to open a representative office there, on the basis of an authorisation that the PFSA grants.[585] The scope of the activities of a representative office is limited to those that comprise advertising and promoting the foreign bank or credit institution.[586] Thus, a representative office may not be set up in order to facilitate the provision of cross-border banking services.

A financial institution[587] that has its registered office in Poland may perform the operations that Articles 5(2), 6(1)(1) to 6(1)(4), and 6(1)(6) to

---

35 of the BL empowers the PFSA to participate in registration proceedings in respect of banks. Article 36 of the BL states that a bank may start its business (in Poland) after it receives an appropriate authorisation from the PFSA, and that the PFSA may issue an authorisation for the bank to commence its business after it has determined that the bank is properly organised to start business, possesses the full amount of the initial capital, has appropriate facilities for the safekeeping of valuables (including monetary funds), and satisfies other conditions that the decision on granting the authorisation to establish the bank specifies. Article 37 of the BL empowers the PFSA to refuse authorisation to found a bank in Poland (or to approve amendment of its articles of association) in instances in which the requirements in force for the establishment of banks have not been satisfied, the activity that the bank intends would breach Polish law, "prejudice the interests of its customers" or not guarantee the safety of the bank's funds, or provisions of the law in force in the place where the founder's registered office or residence is situated – or the founder's relations with other persons, could stop effective supervision of the bank. Article 38 of the BL states that the authorisations to establish a bank in Poland, and to commence its business there, will expire, if the bank has not started its business within one year from the date on which the PFSA granted the authorisation to found the bank.

[581] Article 40(7), BL.

[582] Article 41, BL.

[583] See notes 48 and 371, for the definition of 'credit institution'.

[584] See note 550.

[585] Article 42(1), BL. Following an application from the foreign bank or credit institution concerned, the PFSA will consult with the minister who is responsible for financial institutions, before granting the authorisation (Article 42(1), BL).

[586] Article 42(4), BL.

[587] A 'financial institution' is an entity other than a bank or a credit institution, whose main income-generating activity comprises business operations that involve: acquiring, and disposing of, equity instruments, providing "externally

6(1)(8) specify, in a host Member State (via a branch or as cross-border services), provided that it is the subsidiary undertaking of at least one Polish bank which is subject to consolidated supervision,[588] it itself is subject to consolidated supervision,[589] it conducts business in Poland,[590] the controlling Polish bank(s) are entitled to exercise at least 90% of the voting rights in the financial institution's governing body,[591] the controlling Polish bank(s) satisfy the requirements that the BL lays down concerning their own funds, capital solvency ratio, risk exposure concentration, market risk and liquidity risk,[592] and the controlling Polish bank(s) have submitted a guarantee of their joint and several liability for the commitments that the financial institution enters into – having first obtained approval from the PFSA for this.[593] The PFSA shall verify the financial institution's compliance with these conditions,[594] and shall issue a certificate to the financial institution that attests to this compliance.[595] The financial institution shall supply a written notification to the PFSA of its intention to found a branch or conduct cross-border activity in the host Member State.[596] Articles 48c(2) to 48c(4), and 48d to 48f, of the BL shall apply as necessary,[597] provided that the PFSA notifies the financial supervision authority of the host Member State of the amount of own funds of the subsidiary financial institution and of the consolidated capital solvency ratio of the parent Polish bank(s),[598] attaches the certificate to the notification,[599] and refuses to send the notification to the host Member State's financial supervision authority – if the financial institution does not

---

funded loans", making assets available under leasing contracts, providing services that relate to the acquisition and disposal of claims, providing payment services, issuing and administering payment instruments, providing guarantees or sureties, trading, participating in issues of securities, providing services that relate to issues of securities, providing asset management services, giving financial advice, and/or supplying brokerage services on the money market (Article 4(1)(7), BL). See notes 48 and 371, for the definition of 'credit institution'.

588 Article 48h(1)(1), BL.

589 Article 48h(1)(2), BL.

590 Article 48h(1)(3), BL.

591 Article 48h(1)(4), BL.

592 Article 48h(1)(5), BL.

593 Article 48h(1)(2), BL.

594 Article 48h(2), BL.

595 Article 48h(2a), BL.

596 Article 48h(3), BL.

597 See above in this paragraph, for Articles 48c-48f of the BL.

598 Article 48h(3)(1), BL.

599 Article 48h(3)(1a), BL.

comply with the conditions contained in Article 48h(1) of the BL.[600] If the financial institution ceases to comply with the conditions that Article 48h(1) of the BL states, then the PFSA shall notify the host State's financial supervisory authority of this.[601] From the moment of this notification, the business that the financial institution pursues in the host Member State shall be governed by that State's legislation.[602] At the request of the host Member State's financial supervision authority, the PFSA may apply to the financial institution the measures that Articles 138(3)(1),[603] 138(3)(2),[604] 138(3)(3a)[605] and/or 141[606] of the BL contain, or

---

[600] Article 48h(3)(2), BL. For Article 48h(1) of the BL, see above in this paragraph.

[601] Article 48h(4), BL.

[602] Article 48h(4), BL.

[603] Article 138(3)(1) of the BL (under the circumstances specified in Article 138(3) of the BL)) empowers the PFSA to apply to the bank's management body for the discharge of a member of the management board who is directly responsible for the noted irregularities.

[604] Article 138(3)(2) of the BL (under circumstances that Article 138(3) of the BL specifies) empowers the PFSA to suspend from office a member of the management board who is directly responsible for the noted irregularities, pending the adoption of a resolution on the application for his/her discharge at the supervisory board's next meeting.

[605] Article 138(3)(3a) of the BL (under circumstances that Article 138(3) of the BL specifies) empowers the PFSA to impose a financial penalty on the bank of no more than 10% of its income as stated in the most recent audited financial statements (and, in the absence of these statements, a financial penalty of up to 10% of the forecast income determined on the basis of the bank's financial and economic standing), but not more than 10 million zloty.

[606] If a bank does not comply with the recommendation issued in response to its conduct of business activity in breach of legislation or the bank's articles of association, or of a refusal to provide the information and explanations to which Article 139 of the BL refers (accounting ledgers, balance sheets, records, plans, reports and other documents, and the provision of explanations that authorised persons require), or in the event of a bank failing to satisfy the requirements that Articles 141f-141l of the BL (supervision on a consolidated basis) specify, then the PFSA may impose financial penalties on members of the management board of up to the equivalent of three months gross remuneration of the person penalised (Article 141(1), BL). These sanctions are not to be imposed, if six months or more have passed since the PFSA or other financial supervision authority became aware of the irregularity, or more than two years have elapsed since the breach took place (Article 141(2), BL). The imposition of a financial penalty shall not inhibit implementation of other measures that Articles 131-141 of the BL may impose (Article 141(3), BL). The PFSA shall forward these amounts to the Bank Guarantee Fund (Article 141(4), BL). The penalties to which Article 141(l) of the

forbid that institution from carrying out business in the host Member State.[607]

A credit institution[608] may pursue business in Poland through a branch or "within the framework of its cross-border activity".[609] A credit institution may perform any of the operations that are specified in Articles 5(1), 5(2), 6(1)(1) to 6(1)(4), and 6(1)(6) to 6(1)(8) of the BL, within the scope that derives from the authorisation that the financial supervision authority of its home Member State grants to it.[610] Polish law is to govern the activity of credit institutions within Poland.[611] A credit institution may start cross-border activity in Poland, as soon as it has received from the PFSA a notification from the financial supervision authority of its home Member State, which specifies the banking operations that it is allowed to perform.[612] Subject to Article 48l(2) of the BL,[613] a branch of a credit institution may start its business in Poland as soon as 2 months has passed from the time that the PFSA receives the following information from the financial supervision authority of the credit institution's home Member State: the name of the branch,[614] the branch's address in Poland at which documentation that concerns its activity shall be obtainable,[615] a programme of operations that specifies, in particular, the activities that the credit institution intends to perform and the branch's organisational structure,[616] the names of the persons who are nominated for the posts of

BL refers shall be subject to enforced collection, pursuant to the procedures considered "in the regulations on enforcement proceedings in the administration" (Article 141(5), BL).

607 Article 48h(5), BL

608 See notes 48 and 371, for the definition of 'credit institution'.

609 Article 48i, BL. See note 550, for the definition of 'cross-border activity'. A 'branch of a credit institution' is an organisational unit of a credit institution, which performs on the credit institution's behalf, and for its benefit, some or all of the operations that derive from the authorisation granted to this institution; all of the credit institution's units in a particular country (other than Poland) with the above characteristics are considered to be a single branch (Article 4(1)(18), BL). See notes 48 and 371, for the definition of 'credit institution'.

610 Article 48j, BL.

611 Article 48k(1), BL. Articles 48k(2) and 48k(3) of the BL provide two refinements of this principle.

612 Article 48ł, BL.

613 See below in this paragraph.

614 Article 48l(1)(1), BL.

615 Article 48l(1)(1), BL.

616 Article 48l(1)(2), BL.

branch manager and branch deputy manager,[617] the level of the credit institution's own funds,[618] and the credit institution's solvency ratio.[619] Within 2 months of receiving this information, the PFSA may specify the conditions that, in the interests of the general good, the branch must satisfy whilst conducting business in Poland.[620] In stating these conditions, the PFSA must consider, in particular, the protection of consumers, ensuring the safety of trading, and the prevention of "contraventions of law".[621] A branch of a credit institution that pursues business in Poland is required to file periodic reports on its activity to the National Bank of Poland.[622]

A credit institution[623] that carries out banking activities in Poland through a branch may found a domestic bank as a joint-stock company, by providing the new bank with all the assets of the branch that are intended for conducting banking activities.[624] Only this credit institution may hold shares in the new bank.[625] Subject to Articles 42b to 42e of the BL,[626] the provisions for establishing a bank as a joint-stock company in Poland shall apply to the foundation of a domestic bank by a credit institution.[627] In addition to the documents to which Article 31(2) of the BL refers,[628] the application for authorisation to establish a Polish bank by a credit

---

[617] Article 48l(1)(3), BL.
[618] Article 48l(1)(4), BL.
[619] Article 48l(1)(4), BL.
[620] Article 48l(2), BL.
[621] Article 48l(2), BL. Although the quoted phrase does not specify the ambit of these contraventions, it probably means all transgressions of Polish law.
[622] Article 48m, BL. The filing of these reports must be in accordance with the procedure, and scope of information, that is established pursuant to Article 23(3)-(4) of the Act of August 29 1997 on the National Bank of Poland (Article 48m, BL).
[623] See notes 48 and 371, for the definition of 'credit institution'.
[624] Article 42a(1), BL.
[625] Article 42a(1), BL.
[626] See below in this paragraph.
[627] Article 42a(2), BL. Articles 30(2), 30(4) and 36 of the BL do not apply, however (Article 42a(2), BL). Article 30(2) of the BL states that part of the initial capital for the establishment of a bank may be provided as non-cash contributions (in the form of equipment or real estate), where these will be of direct value in conducting banking activity – subject to the initial capital being at least the amount that Article 32(1) of the BL specifies (i.e. 5 million EUR), and to the value of the non-cash contributions being no more than 15% of the initial capital. Article 30(4) of the BL states that, in "particularly justified cases", the PFSA may consent to the limit (for non-cash contributions) in Article 30(2) of the BL to be exceeded. See note 580, for Article 36 of the BL.
[628] See above in this section, for Article 31(2) of the BL.

institution shall be appended with a verification (by an entity that is entitled to audit financial statements) of a determination of the branch's asset value at a specified date of the month that precedes the submission of the application for founding a Polish bank (in accordance with the accounting principles that this branch currently adopts),[629] and of a statement that comprises information on the accounts of the branch that are drawn up for the purpose of establishing a Polish bank at this date (in accordance with the accounting principles that the branch presently adopts),[630] a certified copy of the notice concerning the intention to cease the activities of the branch in Poland,[631] and information about authorisations, concessions and reliefs that have been granted to the credit institution in association with the establishment of a branch or the provision of its services, together with a certified copy of the notice from an entity that has issued the authorisation or granted the concession (other than the PFSA) – notifying of the intention to found a Polish bank and the possibility of submitting an objection under Article 42(2)(3) of the BL.[632] Before issuing a decision concerning the authorisation to establish a Polish bank, an examination shall be conducted at the credit institution's Polish branch.[633] The PFSA shall refuse to issue the authorisation to found the

---

[629] Article 42b(1)(a), BL.

[630] Article 42b(1)(b), BL.

[631] Article 42b(2), BL.

[632] Article 42b(3), BL. See below in this paragraph, for Article 42(2)(3) of the BL.

[633] Article 42c(1), BL. Articles 133(2)-(4), 135 and 136 shall apply as necessary to this examination (Article 42c(1), BL). Article 133(2) of the BL states the measures that may be taken in the exercise of banking supervision. Inspection activities shall be conducted by employees of the Office of the PFSA (Article 133(3), BL). The PFSA, the National Bank of Poland, and persons conducting banking supervision activities, are not liable for damage that results from legitimate actions (or omission of action) that are connected with the supervision exercised by the PFSA over the activities of banks, branches and representative offices of foreign banks, branches of credit institutions, and supervision exercised over electronic money institutions and branches of foreign electronic money institutions pursuant to the Act of 12 September 2002 on Electronic Payment Institutions (Article 133(4), BL). Article 135 of the BL concerns financial irregularities and an audit review of the bank. The certified auditor that performs an audit of the financial statements of the bank, or of undertakings that have close links to the bank, or the audit reviews to which Articles 134 and 135 of the BL refer, is required to notify the PFSA immediately of any facts disclosed during the audit that indicate the commission of a criminal offence, a breach of provisions that regulate banking activity, a transgression of sound banking practices (and other risks that jeopardise the interests of the bank's customers), and the possibility that the auditor will give a

Polish bank, if this may cause a substantial loss to the national economy or for an important interest of the State.[634] The authorisation to establish a Polish bank shall cease to have effect, if the new bank has not been registered in the business register within one year of the grant of the authorisation.[635] The bank shall commence its activities upon its entry in the business register.[636] The Polish branch of the credit institution shall be expunged from the business register on the day on which the new bank is entered in the register.[637] On its entry in the business register, the new Polish bank shall assume all of the rights and obligations of the credit institution that relate to the operations of the branch.[638] The authorisations, concessions and reliefs that were granted to the credit institution in relation to the foundation of the branch or its activity under provisions of Polish law shall be transferred to the new bank, as long as information to which Article 42b(3) of the PL refers has been disclosed,[639] a separate decision or other provisions on the grant of the authorisation, concession or relief do not state otherwise,[640] and any authority that issued the authorisation or granted the concession (other than PFSA) has not submitted an objection – before the authorisation to establish the new Polish bank is issued.[641] A company that is to become the new bank may apply to the PFSA for authorisations referred to in Articles 6a(1)(1)(k)[642] and 6d(1)[643] of the BL, if these permissions are required at time of the

negative opinion or a disclaimer on the bank's financial statements (Articles 136(1) and 136(3), BL).

[634] Article 42c(2), BL.

[635] Article 42d, BL. The PFSA may shorten this time limit by up to 6 months, provided that this is justified by the requirement of sound and prudent performance of the new bank's activities (Article 42d, BL).

[636] Article 42e(1), BL.

[637] Article 42e(1), BL.

[638] Article 42e(2), BL.

[639] Article 42e(2)(1), BL. See above in this paragraph, for Article 42b(3) of the BL.

[640] Article 42e(2)(2), BL.

[641] Article 42e(2)(3), BL.

[642] A bank may, by written agreement, entrust an entrepreneur or a foreign entrepreneur with the performance of operations that relate to the issuance and safekeeping of securities, and of other commissioned operations that concern the issuance and servicing of securities (Article 6a(1)(1)(k), BL). 'Entrepreneur' and 'foreign entrepreneur' are defined in Articles 4 and 5(3), respectively, of the Act of 2 July 2004 on the Freedom of Business Activity (Articles 4(1)(16a) and 4(1)(16b), BL).

[643] The conclusion of the agreement between a bank and a foreign entrepreneur with no registered office or permanent residence in any EEA state, or an agreement

bank's entry in the business register.[644] The bank is required to maintain its solvency ratio at no less than 12%, for the first 18 months of its operation.[645]

The PFSA shall revoke authorisation to found a branch of a foreign bank,[646] if the financial supervision authority of the country in which the foreign bank has its registered office or place of management has withdrawn authorisation for that bank from carrying out banking activities.[647] Prior to revoking the authorisation to establish a branch of a foreign bank, the PFSA shall seek the opinion of the financial supervision authority of the country in which the foreign bank has its registered office or place of management, if the agreement to which Article 131(2) of the BL refers provides that this opinion may be sought.[648] If it is necessary to withdraw the authorisation immediately, then the PFSA may refrain from seeking the opinion.[649] The PFSA shall notify the financial supervision authority of the home country of the foreign bank, of the former's revocation of the authorisation to conduct banking activities in Poland.[650] The PFSA shall immediately notify the financial supervision authority of the state in which a branch of a Polish bank operates, of the revocation of an authorisation to "create the domestic bank".[651]

---

that specifies that the entrusted operations are to performed outside the EEA, shall require the PFSA to authorise it, upon an application by the bank (Articles 6d(1) and 4(3), BL). 'Foreign entrepreneur' is defined in Article 5(3) of the Act of 2 July 2004 on the Freedom of Business Activity (Article 4(1)(16b), BL).

[644] Article 42e(2)(6), BL.

[645] Article 42f(1), BL. No limit on the amount of the non-cash contributions in the new bank's principal funds shall apply to its own funds (Article 42f(2), BL). Thus, the statement in Article 128(1)(1) of the BL that the bank's non-cash contributions is not to exceed 15% of the bank's principal funds, is disapplied. 'Principal funds' in a bank that is incorporated as joint-stock company, comprise registered and paid-up share capital, reserve capital and capital surplus, but exclude liabilities that are due to preference shares (Article 127(2)(1)(b), BL).

[646] See notes 121 and 568, for the definition of 'foreign bank'.

[647] Article 138(6a), BL.

[648] Article 138(6b), BL. Supervision of the activity of a branch or a representative office of a foreign bank in Poland, and of a branch or a representative office of a Polish bank abroad, may be performed on terms that are stated in an agreement between the PFSA and the financial supervision authority of the foreign country (Article 131(2), BL).

[649] Article 138(6b), BL.

[650] Article 138(6c), BL.

[651] Article 138(6d), BL. The quoted phrase refers to an authorisation by the PFSA to permit a Polish joint-stock company or co-operative bank to provide banking services in Poland.

If a credit institution[652] that pursues its business in Poland (through a branch or by engaging in cross-border activity) does not adhere to the provisions of Polish law, then the PFSA shall ask the credit institution (in writing) to comply with these provisions, and shall set a suitable time limit for the removal of the noted irregularities.[653] If this time limit expires with no remedy having been effected, then the PFSA shall notify the financial supervision authority of the credit institution's home Member State of these irregularities.[654] If, despite the measures which that financial supervision authority takes, a branch of the credit institution persists in failing to comply with the provisions of Polish law, or if the measures that are taken prove to be insufficient to remedy the breach or it is impossible to apply them in Poland, then the PFSA may implement the measures that Articles 138(1),[655] 138(3)[656] and 141[657] of the BL specify, and with respect to liquidity, the measures that are stated Articles 138(1)(1)[658] and 138(2)[659]

---

[652] See notes 48 and 371, for the definition of 'credit institution'.

[653] Article 141a(1)(1), BL.

[654] Article 141a(1)(2), BL.

[655] In performance of its supervisory responsibilities, the PFSA may issue recommendations to banks that involve, in particular, taking the measures that are required to restore payment liquidity or to achieve and observe the standards to which Article 137 of the BL refers (i.e. standards that regulate permissible risks in banking activity, such as mandatory standards of bank liquidity), increasing the amount of own funds, abandoning specified forms of advertising, developing and implementing procedures that shall ensure maintenance, updated assessment and review of the operation and internal capital of the bank management system, implementing special rules for the creation of provisions for banking risk, charges to provisions for the depreciation of assets or special treatment of assets while capital requirements are computed, and limiting banking activity risk (Article 138(1), BL).

[656] These measures include the discharge, or suspension, of the member of the management board who is directly responsible for the noted irregularities, restriction of the scope of banking activity or the activity of the bank's organisational units, the imposition of a financial penalty on the bank of up to 10% of its income – as stated in the most recent audited financial statements (and, if these statements are absent, a financial penalty of up to 10% of the projected income determined on the basis of the bank's financial and economic standing) – but not higher than 10 million zloty, and the withdrawal of authorisation to found a bank and decide upon the bank's liquidation (Article 138(3), BL).

[657] See note 606, for Article 141 of the BL.

[658] In performance of its supervisory responsibilities, the PFSA may issue recommendations to banks that involve, in particular, taking the measures that are required to restore payment liquidity or to achieve and observe the standards that to which Article 137 of the BL refers (Article 138(1)(1), BL). These standards are

of the BL.[660] If a credit institution that pursues its business in Poland through a branch does not comply with the provisions of Chapters II and III of the Act of 19 August 2011 on Payment Services, then the PFSA shall require the credit institution (in writing) to stick to these regulations, and shall set a suitable time limit for the credit institution to remove the noted irregularities.[661] If this time limit expires with no remedy having been put into effect, then the PFSA may apply the measures to which Articles 138(3)(1),[662] 138(3)(3)[663] and 138(3)(3a)[664] of the BL refer, and notify the financial supervision authority of the credit institution's home Member State of the measures that it has taken.[665] In emergencies, the PFSA may, before applying the procedures to which Articles 141a(1) and 141a(2) of the BL refer,[666] and with no need to give prior written notice to the credit institution, apply as necessary the measures to which Articles 138(3)(1),[667] 138(3)(3)[668] and 138(3)(3a)[669] of the BL refer, "with a view to the protection of depositors".[670] Within 7 days of the receipt of a decision of the PFSA under Articles 141a(2), 141a(2a) or 141a(3) of the BL,[671] the credit institution may file a complaint against this decision with a Polish administrative court.[672]

On receipt from the financial supervision authority of a host Member State of information that a Polish bank that performs operations within that

---

those that regulate permissible risks in banking activity, such as mandatory standards of bank liquidity (Article 137(3), BL).

[659] The PFSA may order a bank to stop payments from net earnings, or refrain from founding organisational units, until payment liquidity is restored or the bank achieves the standards to which Article 137 of the BL refers (Article 138(2), BL). See note 655, for these standards.

[660] Article 141a(2), BL.

[661] Article 141a(2a)(1), BL.

[662] See note 603, for Article 138(3)(1) of the BL.

[663] Article 138(3)(3) of the BL (under circumstances that Article 138(3) of the BL specifies) empowers the PFSA to restrict the scope of banking activity, or the activity of the bank's organisational units.

[664] See note 605, for Article 138(3)(3a) of the BL.

[665] Article 141a(2a)(2), BL.

[666] See above in this paragraph, for Articles 141a(1) and 141a(2) of the BL.

[667] See note 603, for Article 138(3)(1) of the BL.

[668] See note 663, for Article 138(3)(1) of the BL.

[669] See note 605, for Article 138(3)(3a) of the BL.

[670] Article 141a(3), BL.

[671] See above in this paragraph, for Articles 141a(2), 141a(2a) and 141a(3) of the BL.

[672] Article 141a(5), BL.

Member State (through a branch or by engaging in cross-border activity) is in breach of "the provisions of law in force in that host Member State", the PFSA may take measures for which Article 138(3) of the BL provides, in respect of the Polish bank.[673] Within 7 days of the receipt of a decision of the PFSA pursuant to Article 141b(1) of the BL, the Polish bank may appeal against the decision in the local administrative court.[674]

The establishment of a branch is a 'capital movement' in Title I(1) of the nomenclature in Annex I. Cross-border banking services are 'capital movements' in Titles V, VI and VIII of the nomenclature in Annex I.[675] The refusal to forward information to the host EEA state's financial supervision authority or to grant an authorisation, to revoke an authorisation, to prohibit or suspend banking operations, or to impose a (substantial) financial penalty, restrict the free movement of capital.[676]

For the restrictive measures to be justified under Article 65(1)(b) of the TFEU, they must be necessary for the protection of the interests that they are intended to guarantee, be proportionate (i.e. not attainable by less restrictive measures), and observe the requirements of legal certainty (i.e. be specific, objective and known to the parties beforehand; in addition, the persons whom the measures affect must have access to legal redress (i.e. intervention must be supported by reasons, and be subject to appeal in the national courts).[677] In a minority of instances, an interest is stated – such as the protection of depositors.[678] Some of the measures do not satisfy the requirement of legal certainty, because the BL gives a discretion to the

[673] Article 141b(1), BL. See note 656, for Article 138(3) of the BL.

[674] Article 141b(2), BL. See the previous sentence, for Article 141b(1) of the BL.

[675] Title V of the nomenclature in Annex I concerns operations in financial instruments that are normally dealt with on the money market. Title VI of this nomenclature considers operations in current and deposit accounts with financial institutions. Title VIII concerns financial loans and credits.

[676] When I considered Articles 141a and 141b of the BL previously, I concluded that the sanctions contained therein "do not hinder the free movement of capital because the [PFSA] may apply them to Polish banks for breaking Polish law – provided that violations with a cross-border element are not treated more harshly than those without". (Baber (2010), *The Impact of Legislation and Regulation on the Freedom of Movement of Capital*, 109). Although this is true taking these Articles individually, it is not so if they are taken holistically, i.e. in the context of the other provisions of the BL that affect cross-border capital movements (discussed above in this section).

[677] See the subsection '*The requirements for a successful public policy/security derogation*' in section 2.1.3.

[678] Article 141a(3) BL requires the protection of depositors – see above in this section.

PFSA as to whether to impose a restriction and/or the severity of the restrictive measure to introduce. The existence of this discretion may also render the measure that the PFSA takes disproportionate. For example, Article 48l(2) of the BL provides a discretion to the PFSA to lay down local business conditions for branches of credit institutions authorised to provide services in (non-Polish) EEA states "in the interest of the general good", without providing specific guidance on what these conditions are. Although the Polish legislature is unable to remove 'interests of the general good' clause – as this phrase is contained in Directive 2013/36/EU,[679] it should pass legislation to require the PFSA to prescribe specific guidelines that make these conditions specific, objective and known beforehand to credit institutions, thereby providing them with legal certainty. The BL provides for the right to appeal in the national court against a decision of the PFSA for taking measures against a credit institution for breach of Polish law,[680] the protection of depositors in emergencies,[681] or contravention of the law of a (non-Polish) EEA country.[682] However, the BL does not require the PFSA to give reasons for its decisions, and, therefore, does not provide the applicant credit institution with a sufficient degree of legal redress to fulfil the condition in the derogation. Thus, the restrictive measures in the BL cannot be justified by Article 65(1)(b) of the TFEU.

Articles 39 and 40 of the BL limit the movement of capital between Poland and third countries.[683] For these restrictions to be justified under Article 64(2) of the TFEU, the EU institutions must carefully take account of the objective of the free movement of capital whilst enacting the relevant legislation, and the national rules must not restrict the free movement of capital more than do the equivalent provisions of the

---

[679] Before the branch of a credit institution may begin its activities, the financial supervision authority of the host Member State shall (within two months of receiving the information about the applicant from the financial supervision authority of its home Member State) prepare for the supervision of the credit institution in accordance with Chapter 4 of Directive 2013/36/EU, and, if required, "indicate the conditions under which, in the interests of the general good", the credit institution may conduct these activities in the host Member State (Article 36(1), Directive 2013/36/EU). See section 2.2.2, for Directive 2013/36/EU.

[680] Article 141a(5), BL. See above in this paragraph.

[681] Article 141a(5), BL. See above in this paragraph.

[682] Article 141b(3), BL. See above in this paragraph.

[683] See above in this paragraph, for Articles 39 and 40 of the BL. Article 42 of the BL does not limit the movement of capital between Poland and third countries, because the opening of a representative office is not a 'capital movement' in the nomenclature to Annex I. See above in this paragraph, for Article 42 of the BL.

pertinent Directive.[684] The relevant Directive is Directive 2013/36/EU. Recital 13 of Directive 2013/36/EU states that supervisory decisions and processes should not impede the functioning of the internal market in respect of "the free flow of capital". However, the Directive's Articles do not mention the free movement of capital.[685] Thus, although the EU institutions were aware of the free movement of capital whilst enacting Directive 2013/36/EU, they may not have considered the objective of the free movement of capital whilst enacting the Directive. Hence, the restrictive measures in Articles 39 and 40 of the BL are not justified by Article 64(2), TFEU.

Pursuant to the reasoning in the above two paragraphs, the provisions in the BL that limit the free movement of capital are not justified under Articles 64(2) and 65(1)(b) of the TFEU. Hence, these laws contravene Article 63 of the TFEU.

4.3.2 Resolution No. 359/2012 of the Polish Financial Supervision Authority of 20 December 2012 on the list of documents relating to business activity of enterpreneurs or foreign entrepreneurs enclosed with requests for authorisation referred to in Articles 6a(1)(1)(m) and 6d(1) of the Banking Law (RLDEFE)

The RLDEFE defines a list of documents that a bank is to enclose with the request for authorisation referred to in Articles 6a(1)(1)(m) and 6d(1) of the BL.[686] Subject to Article 6d of the BL, a bank may, by a written agreement, charge an entrepreneur or foreign entrepreneur with the performance of operations other than those stated in paragraphs (a) to (l) of Article 6a(1)(1) of the BL, if the PFSA grants an authorisation for it to do so.[687] The conclusion of an agreement to which paragraphs (1) and (7) of Article 6a of the BL refer between a bank and a foreign entrepreneur with no permanent residence or registered office in any EEA country, or

[684] See the subsection '*Derogations that apply only to capital movements to/from third countries*', in section 2.3.2.

[685] Regulation No 575/2013 on prudential requirement for credit institutions and investment firms refers to the free movement of capital once. See Chapter 3, note 685.

[686] s.(1)(1), RLDEFE. If the RLDEFE refers to a Member State, this means a country that belongs to the EEA (s.1(2), RLDEFE).

[687] Article 6a(1)(1)(m), BL. 'Entrepreneur' and 'foreign entrepreneur' are defined in Articles 4 and 5(3), respectively, of the Act of 2 July 2004 on the Freedom of Business Activity (Articles 4(1)(16a) and 4(1)(16b), BL).

an agreement that states that the charged operations are to be undertaken outside the EEA, shall require authorisation from the PFSA, upon an application by the bank.[688]

Section 2 of the RLDEFE contains the core documentation requirement, which includes, for instance, a written statement by the entrepreneur or foreign entrepreneur that contains information on the name, place of residence and address, or company name, registered office and address, of the entrepreneur or foreign entrepreneur,[689] the (foreign) entrepreneur's legal and organisational form for conducting business activity,[690] the place at which the activities entrusted to the (foreign) entrepreneur will be carried out,[691] and the (foreign) entrepreneur's "object of business activity".[692] Sections 3 to 9 of the RLDEFE contain additional documentation requirements, based upon the particular classification of the entrepreneur or foreign entrepreneur. For example, if the (foreign) entrepreneur is to supply services that relate to information technology under its contract with the bank, then the bank shall include the result of a specialised information system security audit of the (foreign) entrepreneur or a certificate of information system security (that covers the scope of these services), which the (foreign) entrepreneur holds.[693] Some of these informational requirements are waived, if the foreign entrepreneur is a credit institution,[694] an entity that operates within the same foreign banking group, domestic banking group, or hybrid group as the bank,[695] or a firm that is regulated by the financial supervision authority of a Member State.[696]

---

688 Articles 6d(1) and 4(3), BL. See note 643. 'Foreign entrepreneur' is defined in Article 5(3) of the Act of 2 July 2004 on the Freedom of Business Activity (Article 4(1)(16b), BL).

688 Article 42e(2)(6), BL.

689 s.2(1)(a), RLDEFE.

690 s.2(1)(b), RLDEFE.

691 s.2(1)(c), RLDEFE.

692 s.2(1)(d), RLDEFE. The quoted phrase may mean the foreign entrepreneur's objects clause – if it is a company, or, more broadly, the aim that the foreign entrepreneur has in respect of its business operations.

693 s.8, RLDEFE.

694 s.13(1), RLDEFE.

695 s.13(2), RLDEFE. 'Foreign banking group', 'domestic banking group' and 'hybrid holding company' are defined in Articles 4(1)(11a), 4(1)(11b) and 4(1)(11c) of the BL, respectively.

696 s.13(3), RLDEFE, and Article 4(1)(13), BL.

The supply of information is not a 'capital movement' within the nomenclature in Annex I. Hence, the provisions of the RLDEFE do not breach Article 63 of the TFEU.

4.3.3 Resolution No. 389/2008 of the Polish Financial Supervision Authority of 17 December 2008 concerning the list of documents attached to the application to the Polish Financial Supervision Authority on issuing a permit to establish a bank, consent to appoint the members of the bank's Management Board and information about the composition of the board presented to the Polish Financial Supervision Authority by the Supervisory Board of the Bank (RLDAIP)

The RLDAIP sets out a list of documents to be attached to an application to the PFSA on issuing an authorisation to found a bank, and to agree on appointments of members of the bank's management board.[697] These documents are required pursuant to paragraphs 1 and 2 of Article 137 of the BL. The PFSA shall specify, by resolution, the scope of information to which Article 22a(2) of the BL refers,[698] a list of documents and information to which Article 22b(2) of the BL refers,[699] a list of documents to which Article 6a(5) of the BL refers,[700] and a list of documents to which Article 31(2)(3) of the BL refers.[701]

---

[697] s.1, RLDAIP.

[698] Article 137(1), BL. The bank's supervisory board shall advise the PFSA of the composition of the bank's management board immediately after its appointment, of any alterations in the composition thereof immediately after these changes, and of the members of the management board who, consequential to the division of responsibilities, shall in particular manage the internal audit unit and credit risk (Article 22a(2), BL).

[699] Article 137(1), BL. The appointment of two members of the bank's management board, including its president, shall require the approval of the PFSA; the bank's supervisory board shall submit the application for approval (Article 22b(1), BL). The PFSA may require the submission of information and documents concerning these two persons that may be necessary for it to give approval (Article 22b(2), BL).

[700] Article 137(1a), BL. The bank shall append to the application for authorisation to which Article 6a(1)(1)(m) of the BL refers, documents that concern the business activity of the entrepreneur or foreign entrepreneur who will undertake the entrusted operations, a draft of the agreement to which Article 6a(1) of the BL refers (to be concluded between the bank and an entrepreneur or foreign entrepreneur), action plans that ensure continuous and uninterrupted operation

Section 3 of the RLDAIP prescribes the documents that the bank's supervisory board should append to its application, pursuant to Article 22b(2) of the BL.[702] For example, these documents must include a candidate's statement that provides the candidate's name, maiden name, parents' names, mother's maiden name, nationality, permanent address, temporary address, and address of residence as of the date the application is filed and in the most recent 5 years.[703] The three candidate's statements that paragraphs 2, 5 and 6 of section 3 of the RLDAIP three require from each of the two persons to be appointed to the bank's management board, must be signed by the candidate and attested by a notary.[704] The bank's supervisory board must append the documents in subsections 3(1) to 3(8) of the RLDAIP to its advice to the PFSA under Article 22a(2) of the BL.[705]

Section 6 of the RLDAIP specifies the documents on each founder of the bank that the bank should append to its application for authorisation, pursuant to Article 31(2)(3) of the BL.[706] These documents differ, depending upon whether the founder is a legal person or a natural person. For instance, if the founder is a legal person, the bank should provide the founder's articles of association, contract or other equivalent item, which specifies the legal form, company, headquarters, business activity, paid-up

---

within the ambit of the agreement, a description of organisational and technical solutions that ensure safe and proper performance of the operations that are entrusted to the (foreign) entrepreneur, and a description of the risk management principles in association with entrusting the performance of the operations to which Article 6a(1) of the BL refers to the (foreign) entrepreneur (Article 6a(5), BL). See section 4.3.2, for Article 6(1)(1)(m) of the BL. 'Entrepreneur' and 'foreign entrepreneur' are defined in Articles 4 and 5(3), respectively, of the Act of 2 July 2004 on the Freedom of Business Activity (Articles 4(1)(16a) and 4(1)(16b), BL).

701 Article 137(2), BL. An application to the PFSA for authorisation to establish a bank shall have appended to it the documents that the PFSA requires on the bank's founders and the financial circumstances of each of these persons (Article 31(2)(3), BL).

702 See note 699, for Article 22b(2) of the BL.

703 s.3(2), RLDAIP.

704 s.4, RLDAIP.

705 s.5, RLDAIP. See note 698, for Article 22a(2) of the BL. The documents required under Articles 22a(2) and 22b(2) of the BL in relation to each person to whom they relate, are identical – except for the fact that the latter provision additionally requires documents which certify that the candidate has a knowledge of Polish, if he/she is a citizen of another country (s.3(9), RLDAIP).

706 See note 701, for Article 31(2)(3) of the BL.

capital, "the manner of representation" and organisational structure of the founder.[707] If the founder is a natural person, then its documentation requirements include (for instance) items that relate to its business (such as its certificate of registration in the register of economic activities) or, if the founder pursues its business in a country other than Poland, any other equivalent documents that the competent authority of that state issues.[708]

The provision of information is not a 'capital movement' in the nomenclature to Annex I. Therefore, the laws in the RLDAIP do not contravene Article 63 of the TFEU.

4.3.4 Resolution No. 312/2012 of the Polish Financial Supervision Authority of 27 November 2012 on the Mode of Exercising Supervision over Banking Activity (RMESBA)

The RMESBA provides for the manner of exercising supervision over banking activity.[709] This supervision shall cover the consideration of motions that relate to incorporation, organisation and operation of banks, branches, representative offices of foreign banks, and representative offices of credit institutions,[710] regulatory activities,[711] analytical supervision,[712] the performance of supervisory actions,[713] the acceptance of notifications about the intention of credit institutions to carry out activity on Polish territory,[714] and the delivery of notifications about the intention of Polish banks to conduct activity on the territory of another Member State and of a financial institution with its registered office on Polish territory to provide services on the territory of a host Member State.[715]

The Polish Financial Supervision Authority Office (PFSA Office) checks and verifies much of the information for authorisation. For example, the PFSA Office verifies whether the motions for granting an authorisation, and the notifications about the intention of credit institutions

---

[707] s.6(1)(b), RLDAIP.

[708] s.6(2)(e), RLDAIP.

[709] s.1(1), RMESBA.

[710] s.1(2)(1), RMESBA. The RMESBA define neither 'foreign bank' nor 'credit institution'. The BL defines both of these terms. See notes 48 and 371, for the definition of 'credit institution'. See note 568, for the definition of 'foreign bank'.

[711] s.1(1)(2), RMESBA.

[712] s.1(1)(3), RMESBA.

[713] s.1(1)(4), RMESBA.

[714] s.1(1)(5), RMESBA.

[715] s.1(1)(5), RMESBA. Article 4(1)(23) of the BL defines the term 'host member State (s.1(1)(5), RMESBA); see note 540.

to carry out their activities on Polish territory, of Polish banks to conduct their activities on the territory of a host Member State, or of a financial institution with its registered office in Poland to conduct its activities on the territory of a host Member State, contain the information that is necessary for accepting and considering these motions/notifications, and, in particular, whether they satisfy the requirements of the BL and "other provisions".[716]

The PFSA Office may conduct supervisory actions at branches of Polish banks abroad.[717] 'Supervisory actions' include controls of preparation to start operate activities,[718] inspections,[719] explanatory proceedings,[720] and validation proceedings.[721] Supervisory actions are performed by approved employees of the PFSA Office.[722]

The inspection of documents and performance of supervisory actions are not 'capital movements' in the nomenclature to Annex I. Consequently, these activities do not restrict the free movement of capital. Hence, there is no breach of Article 63 of the TFEU.

4.4 Insurance and Pension Funds

4.4.1 Act of 22 May 2003 on Insurance and Pension Funds Supervision and on Insurance Ombudsman (IPFSA)

The PFSA is the supervisory authority for insurance, reinsurance, insurance mediation, the organisation and operation of pension funds and the supply of occupational pension fund programs.[723] The supervised entities comprise insurance undertakings, reinsurance undertakings, insurance intermediaries, pension funds and pension fund companies.[724] The purpose of the supervision is the protection of the interest of insurance firms, insured persons, beneficiaries of insurance contracts, members of

---

716 s.2, RMESBA. 'Other provisions' probably means provisions of Polish legislation and regulation, other than those of the BL. The RMESBA does not define 'financial institution'. See note 587, for the definition of this term in the BL.

717 s.38(3), RMESBA.

718 s.38(1)(1), RMESBA.

719 s.38(1)(2), RMESBA.

720 s.38(1)(3), RMESBA.

721 s.38(1)(4), RMESBA.

722 s.39(1), RMESBA.

723 Articles 2(1) and 2(3), IPFSA.

724 Article 2(2), IPFSA.

pension funds, members of occupational pension schemes and persons receiving a pension.[725]

4.4.2 Act of 22 May 2003 on Insurance Activity (IAA)

'Insurance activity' consists of insurance acts plus insurance cover for the risk of events.[726] Firms that intend to pursue insurance activity must possess a permit issued by the PFSA.[727] 'Insurance acts' include agreeing insurance and reinsurance contracts,[728] determining premiums and commissions,[729] risk evaluation,[730] payment of indemnity and other dues from the contracts,[731] and investing the insurance firm's funds.[732] Capital transfers in respect of insurance contracts are 'capital movements' under Title X of the nomenclature in Annex I.

Should the circumstances that Article 92(3)(23) of the IAA take place,[733] before authorising the insurance company, reinsurance firm, credit institution or investment firm the PFSA shall submit a written request to the financial supervision authority of the relevant Member

---

725 Article 3, IPFSA.
726 Article 3(1), IAA.
727 Article 6(1), IAA.
728 Article 3(3)(1), IAA.
729 Article 3(3)(3), IAA.
730 Article 3(4)(1), IAA.
731 Article 3(4)(2), IAA.
732 Article 3(4)(6), IAA.
733 The following documents (amongst others) must be included with an application by a Polish insurance undertaking to provide insurance services in Poland: a declaration of the founders on whether a Polish insurance undertaking will be a subsidiary of, or in which "participation will be held by" (i) the insurance firm, reinsurance company, credit institution or investment firm that received sufficient authorisation to provide services in a Member State, (ii) the parent entity of an insurance undertaking, reinsurance company, credit institution or investment firm that received adequate authorisation to provide services in a Member State, or (iii) a (natural or legal) person who "holds a significant participation in" an insurance company, reinsurance undertaking, credit institution or investment firm that has received sufficient authorisation to provide services in a Member State; the declaration should show the names and addresses of the entities to which (i) and (iii) refer (Article 92(3)(23), IAA). Whenever the IAA refers to a Member State of the EU, this also means member states of the European Free Trade Association – all of whom (except Switzerland) are Contracting Parties to the EEA Agreement (Article 2(2), IAA).

State[734] regarding the supply of information about the insurance company, reinsurance firm, credit institution or investment firm that the latter authority supervises,[735] the founders, shareholders and parent companies of these entities,[736] and natural or legal persons who hold "a substantial participation in" those entities,[737] which may be useful for evaluating whether the founders, shareholders, or persons assigned as members of the supervisory board or management board of a Polish insurance company provide a warranty to carry out that firm's affairs in an appropriate manner.[738]

A foreign insurance undertaking may engage in insurance activity on Polish territory under the principle of reciprocity.[739] This principle shall not apply to countries that are members of the WTO.[740] The taking up of insurance activity by a foreign insurance company – other than the freedom to provide insurance services to EEA states – requires authorisation from the PFSA.[741] A foreign insurance company can pursue insurance activity on Polish territory by establishing a branch there.[742] The branch shall be regulated by its articles of association and by Polish law; the foreign insurance undertaking is to draw up the branch's articles of association in the form of a notarial deed.[743] The branch's articles of association are subject to authorisation by the PFSA.[744] They shall specify, in particular, the branch's organisational structure,[745] rules for establishing regional units of the branch and the principles of their representation,[746] the types of technical provisions for the main branch and the methods of creating them,[747] and the rules for settlement with the foreign insurance firm's headquarters.[748] The main branch must be registered in the Polish

[734] 'Member State' in the IAA means a Contracting Party to the EEA Agreement – see note 733.

[735] Article 93a(1), IAA.

[736] Article 93a(2)-(3), IAA.

[737] Article 93a(4), IAA.

[738] Article 93a, IAA.

[739] Article 104(1), IAA.

[740] Article 104(2), IAA. As many countries are members of the WTO (see note 403), the principal of reciprocity is not a significant issue for the PFSA.

[741] Article 104(3), IAA.

[742] Article 105(1), IAA.

[743] Article 105(2), IAA.

[744] Article 105(3), IAA.

[745] Article 105(4)(1), IAA.

[746] Article 105(4)(2), IAA.

[747] Article 105(4)(3), IAA.

[748] Article 105(4)(4), IAA.

National Court Register.[749] It may start to engage in insurance activity from the time of its registration.[750] Registration may (only) take place after the PFSA has authorised the foreign insurance undertaking to provide insurance services in Poland.[751] On application[752] by the foreign insurance undertaking, the PFSA shall take a decision to issue an authorisation for the insurance firm to engage in insurance activity through a Polish branch.[753] This application shall include the foreign insurance company's name and registered office,[754] the name of the country in which this registered office is situated,[755] "the subjective scope of activity" and the registered office of the Polish branch,[756] and the names of the persons who are nominated as the director of the main branch, the deputy branch's deputy directors, the actuary, the persons responsible for maintaining the accounts, and the investment adviser (in cases in which the IAA requires one to be appointed).[757] The following items shall be included with the application: the foreign insurance company's articles of association,[758] drafts of general terms and conditions of insurance that relate to the insurance activities for which authorisation is to be issued,[759] a computation of the foreign insurance firm's required solvency margin and of the value of its available solvency margin,[760] a scheme of operations that satisfies the conditions in Article 93 of the IAA, concerns the branch's activity within Poland and covers the first three years of the branch's operations,[761] the draft articles of association of the branch,[762] a certificate

[749] Article 105(5), IAA.
[750] Article 105(5), IAA.
[751] Article 105(6), IAA.
[752] The English translation of the IAA refers to the foreign insurance company's application a 'motion'.
[753] Article 107(1), IAA.
[754] Article 107(2)(1), IAA.
[755] Article 107(2)(1), IAA.
[756] Article 107(2)(2), IAA. The quoted term probably means the specific types of insurance services that the foreign insurance firm intends to provide in Poland through its Polish branch.
[757] Article 107(2)(3), IAA.
[758] Article 107(3)(1), IAA.
[759] Article 107(3)(2), IAA.
[760] Article 107(3)(3), IAA.
[761] Article 107(3)(4), IAA. The branch's scheme of operations shall specify the data and conditions which, with respect to the type and volume of insurance carried on, are required to ensure the capacity of the Polish insurance company to satisfy its obligations (Articles 107(3)(4) and 93(1), IAA). The branch's scheme of operation shall (in particular) contain a statement of the types of risks against

that the financial supervision authority of the country of the registered office of the foreign insurance company has issued which provides information about the foreign insurance company's financial standing and which confirms that this authority has authorised the foreign insurance firm to provide insurance services in its home state and that the firm possesses the required solvency margin,[763] financial statements for the foreign insurance undertaking's last 3 years of activity together with a chartered accountant's opinion,[764] "evidence that domestic insurance undertakings may take up insurance activity in the territory of the country in which the insurance undertaking have their registered office",[765] information on the amount of the initial fund for the establishment of the branch's administration and the organisation of its regional units,[766] an indication of the financial resources that are required to pay insurance benefits and meet the necessary solvency margin,[767] consent of the person nominated for the position of director of the branch, of the persons proposed as his/her deputies, and of the actuary, for performance of the

---

which the foreign insurance undertaking and its Polish branch intend to insure, a reinsurance programme, which specifies the scope and form of reinsurance and reinsurers, specification of the size of a minimum guarantee fund and the required solvency margin, an assessment of the expenses of founding the administration of the branch and the organisation of its activity – including a specification of the sources of financial resources for these costs, a specification of the funds that the branch possesses that are required to provide services of assistance – if the branch intends to insure against the risks in class 18 of Section II of the Annex to the IAA (i.e. the insurance of assistance for persons who get into difficulties while travelling or when away from their place of residence), and a specification of the organisation of insurance services – including the branch's organisational structure, the manner of conclusion of insurance contracts, rules for the acceptance of risks, the manner of determination of insurance premiums, the manner of determination of technical provisions, accepted accounting standards, the system of determination of the value of benefits or claims, the system of internal control and the system of asset management (Articles 107(3)(4) and 93(1), IAA).

[762] Article 107(3)(5), IAA.

[763] Article 107(3)(6), IAA.

[764] Article 107(3)(7), IAA. The 'chartered accountant's opinion' to which the IAA refers is probably the external auditor's report.

[765] Article 107(3)(8), IAA. It is difficult to understand the place of this quoted phrase in the context of a foreign insurance company applying to the PFSA for it to authorise the establishment of a Polish branch of that company. This requirement is not to apply to countries with which Poland has signed "relevant international agreements" (Article 107(3)(8), IAA).

[766] Article 107(3)(9), IAA.

[767] Article 107(3)(10), IAA.

main branch's duties,[768] the curricula vitae of the persons nominated for the positions of director of the main branch and his/her deputies and of the actuary,[769] documents that confirm that the persons nominated as director of the branch and his/her deputies have suitable education and business experience for the management of an insurance undertaking,[770] data concerning the education and business experience of the person proposed for the position of actuary,[771] a declaration or certificate that the persons suggested for the post of director of the branch, his/her deputies and actuary have no criminal record,[772] a declaration of the person nominated as director of the branch and his/her deputies and the actuary concerning pending court proceedings against them and reporting their participation in supervisory and management bodies of commercial partnerships or companies,[773] a declaration from the investment adviser about providing approval for employment – if the application for authorisation covers unit-linked insurance,[774] and a list of claims representatives for every Member State – if the application for authorisation includes third party liability insurance of any kind that arises out of "the possession and use of self-propelled land vehicles".[775] The authorisation is issued for the pursuit of insurance activity with respect to at least one of the insurance classes to which the Annex to the IAA refers.[776] It may be issued if, in the country of the foreign insurance undertaking's registered office, that firm holds appropriate authorisations to provide insurance services within the scope applied for (in its application to open a branch in Poland) and functions in the legal form of a mutual insurance undertaking or joint-stock company.[777] A foreign insurance firm is obliged to commence insurance activity within one year following the day on which the authorisation is provided.[778] A change in the scope of the insurance services supplied by

---

[768] Article 107(3)(11), IAA.

[769] Article 107(3)(12), IAA.

[770] Article 107(3)(13), IAA.

[771] Article 107(3)(14), IAA.

[772] Article 107(3)(15), IAA.

[773] Article 107(3)(16), IAA.

[774] Article 107(3)(17), IAA, and Section I class 3, Annex, IAA. The Annex to the IAA contains a classification of the risks according to 5 categories of life insurance, and 18 categories of non-life insurance.

[775] Article 107(3)(18), IAA, and Section II class 10, Annex, IAA.

[776] Article 108(1), IAA.

[777] Article 108(2), IAA. The requirement in Article 108(2) of the IAA concerning the foreign insurance company's legal form, does not apply if the firm's registered office is located in a state that is a member of the WTO (Article 108(3), IAA).

[778] Article 111, IAA.

the branch requires the authorisation of the PFSA.[779] The PFSA shall refuse to grant an authorisation to a foreign insurance undertaking to provide insurance services in Poland, if the firm's application does not satisfy the requirements that the IAA specifies,[780] the persons nominated for the positions of director of the branch and his/her deputies do not fulfil the requirements that the IAA contains,[781] the foreign insurance company does not provide a warranty that it will engage in insurance activity on Polish territory in a satisfactory manner,[782] the foreign insurance firm does not possess financial resources that amount to the branch's initial fund and available solvency margin as stated in business plan for the branch,[783] the foreign insurance company does not possess the financial resources that are necessary to ensure the coverage of the branch's technical provisions,[784] the foreign insurance company makes use of assets that come from illegal or undisclosed sources,[785] the business plan for the branch does not ensure that there is the capacity to satisfy the branch's commitments,[786] or the pursuit of the insurance service(s) "threatens the defence of security of the state" or public security and order.[787] The branch shall be obliged to establish the technical provisions to which paragraph 1(2) of Article 149 of the IAA refers, in order to cover the liability that may arise from insurance contracts that the branch concludes on Polish territory.[788] A foreign insurance undertaking shall be obliged to possess on Polish territory the available solvency margin – which must be equal to or

779 Article 112, IAA.
780 Article 114(1)(1), IAA.
781 Article 114(1)(2), IAA.
782 Article 114(1)(3), IAA.
783 Article 114(1)(4), IAA.
784 Article 114(1)(5), IAA.
785 Article 114(1)(6), IAA.
786 Article 114(1)(7), IAA.
787 Article 114(1)(8), IAA. The PFSA is not to issue an authorisation to engage in insurance activity within the scope of Section II class 10 of the Annex to the IAA (i.e. third party liability insurance that arises from the possession and use of self-propelled land vehicles) except for insurance of carrier's liability, unless the foreign insurance company presents it with the list of claims representatives (Article 114(2), IAA). See note 800, for the withdrawal of an authorisation in relation to these insurance services.
788 Article 115, IAA. Insurance companies may establish the following funds as cost items: a fund for "financing preventive activity" to an amount that does not exceed 1% of the premiums paid to the firm in the past financial year, and special funds and provisions as the articles of association specify (Article 149, IAA).

greater than the required solvency margin and the guarantee fund.[789] The PFSA may take a decision to revoke the foreign insurance undertaking's authorisation to provide insurance services in Poland, if this foreign insurance firm, in the country in which its office is situated, has lost the authorisation to provide insurance services,[790] has been declared bankrupt,[791] or has gone into liquidation.[792] Furthermore, the PFSA may take a decision to withdraw the foreign insurance company's authorisation to provide one or several classes of insurance services in Poland, if the foreign insurance company no longer fulfils the conditions that are necessary to obtain the authorisation,[793] the Polish branch of this company engages in insurance activity in contravention of "the provisions of the law" or its articles of association,[794] the branch "does not ensure the capacity of that foreign insurance undertaking to fulfil the obligations",[795] the foreign insurance firm has applied to the PFSA for the authorisation to be revoked – where the protection of the interests of the policyholders, insured persons and beneficiaries under the insurance contracts (in particular with regard to the payment of benefits and compensation) must be guaranteed,[796] the foreign insurance undertaking has not commenced the pursuit of insurance activity in Poland within one year following the day on which the PFSA issued the authorisation for it to do so,[797] the

---

789 Article 116, IAA. The basis for the computation of the required solvency margin shall be (i) the amount of the branch's technical provisions and the amount of the sums insured under insurance contracts that the branch concludes – in the case of a foreign insurance firm that provides services within Section I classes 1-4 of the Annex to the IAA (i.e. life insurance, dowry and birth insurances, unit-linked insurance and annuity insurance), (ii) the premium, or the benefit due from the branch, in the case of a foreign insurance company that provides services within Section I class 5 of the Annex to the IAA (i.e. accident and sickness insurance, if it supplements the insurances to which Section I classes 1-4 refer), and (iii) the premium, or the benefit due, in the case of a foreign insurance firm that provides insurance services within Section II of the Annex to the IAA (i.e. non-life insurance).

790 Article 119(1)(1), IAA.

791 Article 119(1)(2), IAA.

792 Article 119(1)(2), IAA.

793 Article 119(2)(1), IAA.

794 Article 119(2)(2), IAA. The quoted phrase probably means any relevant provisions of Polish law.

795 Article 119(2)(2), IAA.

796 Article 119(2)(3), IAA.

797 Articles 119(2)(4) and 111, IAA. In this case, the PFSA may revoke the authorisation for the classes of insurance (in the Annex to the IAA) in which the insurance activity has not been started (Article 119(3), IAA).

foreign insurance company has ceased to provide insurance services for a period of 6 months or more,[798] the foreign insurance undertaking is not fulfilling the schedule for the restoration of a sound financial position or short-term solvency,[799] and/or the circumstances that clauses (3) to (6) of paragraph 1 of Article 98 of the IAA occur in respect of the foreign insurance firm's shareholders.[800] A foreign insurance firm is obliged, within 7 days, to notify the PFSA of ceasing to provide insurance services (or conclude insurance contracts) in a particular class of insurance.[801] The PFSA may order the Polish branch of a foreign insurance company to be wound up, if the activity of this branch is pursued "in violation of the principles of law", its articles of association, or the business plan for the branch, or "does not ensure the capacity of the insurance undertaking to fulfil operations",[802] the branch does not pay insurance benefits in Poland, only partly pays them, or pays them but subject to delay,[803] or bankruptcy or winding-up proceedings have been initiated towards the foreign

---

[798] Article 119(2)(5), IAA.

[799] Article 119(2)(6), IAA.

[800] Article 119(2)(7), IAA. These circumstances are as follows: the insurance company's founders have been convicted of a purposeful offence (Article 98(1)(3), IAA), do not provide a warranty to carry out the insurance firm's business in a way that duly protects the interests of the policyholders, insured persons, or beneficiaries under the insurance contracts (Article 98(1)(4), IAA), are not able to show the possession of funds in an amount equal to at least the initial fund and the value of the shares issued by the insurance company and determined in the business plan (Article 98(1)(5), IAA), and use material assets that derive from illegal or undisclosed sources (Article 98(1)(6), IAA). Article 98(1) of the IAA refers to the 'domestic insurance undertaking'. As Article 119(2)(7) of the IAA refers to Article 98(1) of the IAA in the context of the provision of services in Poland by a foreign insurance undertaking, Article 98(1) of the IAA (in this context) should be read as mentioning a 'foreign insurance undertaking' rather than a 'domestic insurance undertaking'. The PFSA shall withdraw the authorisation to supply the insurance services for which Section II, class 10 of the Annex to the IAA provides (i.e. third party liability insurance that arises from the possession and use of self-propelled land vehicles) except for insurance of carrier's liability, if it finds that there is no claims representative in any Member State (Article 119(4), IAA). See note 787, for a reason for refusal to issue an authorisation in relation to these insurance services.

[801] Article 119(5), IAA.

[802] Article 122(1)(1), IAA. The 'principles of law' are probably the provisions of Polish law. The second quoted phrase in Article 122(1) of the IAA is difficult to understand.

[803] Article 122(1)(2), IAA.

insurance undertaking in the country of its registered office.[804] If the PFSA makes a winding-up order, it will also appoint a receiver.[805] In consequence of this order, the branch may not enter into new insurance contracts,[806] the previously concluded contracts are not to be prolonged,[807] the sums insured in respect of insurance contacts that have already been agreed may not be increased,[808] the branch may not conclude "accepted reinsurance contracts or accepted retrocession contracts",[809] previously concluded reinsurance and retrocession contracts are not to be prolonged,[810] the branch may not "accept new cessions" within reinsurance and retrocession contracts,[811] and the branch may not increase liability within reinsurance and retrocession contracts.[812] The foreign insurance company shall be accountable for the liabilities of its Polish branch "with its entire assets".[813]

A Polish insurance undertaking may, within the freedom to provide services, engage in insurance activity on the territory of another Member State.[814] This insurance activity is subject to the supervision of the PFSA.[815] A Polish insurance company that intends to provide insurance services on the territory of another Member State shall notify the PFSA thereof.[816] A Polish insurance company that engages in insurance activity within the freedom to provide services must inform the policyholder of its registered office, before the conclusion of any insurance contract.[817] A Polish insurance firm that provides insurance services outside Polish

---

[804] Article 122(1)(3), IAA.
[805] Article 122(2), IAA.
[806] Article 122(2)(1), IAA.
[807] Article 122(2), IAA.
[808] Article 122(3), IAA.
[809] Article 122(4), IAA. The difference is between concluding and accepting a contract is not clear.
[810] Article 122(5), IAA.
[811] Article 122(6), IAA. The meaning of the quoted phrase is unclear.
[812] Article 122(7), IAA.
[813] Article 126, IAA. This may mean that the foreign insurance firm must be prepared to pay, from the sale of its assets, the debts of its Polish branch, i.e. the branch's creditors have full recourse to the insurance undertaking for the satisfaction of their claims, in the event that the branch is unable to pay these debts.
[814] Article 127(1), IAA. 'Member State' in the IAA means a Contracting Party to the EEA Agreement. See note 733.
[815] Article 127(2), IAA.
[816] Article 134, IAA.
[817] Article 140, IAA.

territory must inform the PFSA (separately for transactions carried out through a foreign branch and for cross-border services) about the amount of premiums, commission and benefits – including reinsurance – classified into Member States and insurance classes.[818]

If the insurance firm intends to establish a branch in the host Member State in order to supply insurance services there, then this notification shall contain the name of the Member State in the territory of which the insurance company intends to engage in insurance activity,[819] the type of activity planned,[820] the branch's organisational structure,[821] the scheme of operations for the branch,[822] the branch's address in the host Member State,[823] the names of the persons who are authorised to represent the insurance company and to manage affairs in respect of the activity of its branch,[824] and a declaration that the insurance company is a member of a national bureau and a foreign insurance guarantee fund – if it intends to provide insurance services within Section II class 10 of the Annex to the IAA (i.e. third party liability insurance that arises from the possession and use of self-propelled land vehicles) other than carrier's liability insurance.[825] Within 3 months of receiving the notification, the PFSA shall forward the information, together with a declaration that the insurance undertaking has adequate available solvency margin to meet the required solvency margin, to the financial supervision authority of the host Member State.[826] The PFSA may take a decision to refuse to forward this information to the host Member State's financial supervision authority, if the insurance firm's financial circumstances do not permit a branch to be founded,[827] the branch's organisational structure does not ensure the

---

[818] Article 142, IAA. For insurance services within Section II class 10 of the Annex to the IAA (i.e. third party liability insurance that arises from the possession and use of self-propelled land vehicles) except for carrier's liability insurance, the Polish insurance firm shall also inform the PFSA about the average volume, and frequency, of damages (Article 142, IAA).
[819] Article 135(1)(1), IAA.
[820] Article 135(1)(2), IAA. The notification of the planned insurance services must also include the types of risk that the insurance firm intends to cover in the host Member State (Article 135(1)(2), IAA).
[821] Article 135(1)(3), IAA.
[822] Article 135(1)(4), IAA.
[823] Article 135(1)(5), IAA.
[824] Article 135(1)(6), IAA.
[825] Article 135(1)(7), IAA.
[826] Article 135(2), IAA.
[827] Article 135(3)(1), IAA.

proper provision of insurance services,[828] the persons appointed to manage the branch do not have a suitable education and appropriate professional experience for the management of an insurance undertaking, do not give a warranty to carry out the insurance firm's business in an appropriate manner, or have been convicted for a deliberate crime,[829] or the scheme of operations for the branch does not ensure that the branch has the capacity to meet its obligations.[830] The PFSA shall promptly inform the insurance company of the reasons for the refusal to forward the information.[831] The branch of the Polish insurance undertaking may be established in the host Member State if, after the PFSA forwards the information to the host Member State's financial supervision authority, the insurance firm receives from the latter authority information that states the conditions under which it may provide insurance services through its branch in the host Member State.[832]

---

828 Article 135(3)(2), IAA.

829 Article 135(3)(3), IAA.

830 Article 135(3)(4), IAA.

831 Article 135(5), IAA.

832 Article 135(4), IAA. "The branch may be established within 2 months following the day of receiving information by the undertaking." (Article 136(4), IAA). This statement in the English translation of the IAA is unclear, in the context of the first sentence of Article 135(4) of the IAA, which is stated in the text. Part of the difficulty is that Article 135(4) of the IAA does not strictly follow the corresponding provision in Directive 2009/138/EC, which is as follows. "Before the branch of an insurance undertaking starts business, the supervisory authorities of the host Member State shall … within two months of receiving the information [about the insurance undertaking from the supervisory authority of the home Member State], inform the supervisory authority of the home Member State of the conditions under which, in the interests of the general good, that business may be pursued in the host Member State. The supervisory authority of the home Member State shall communicate this information to the insurance undertaking concerned. The insurance undertaking may establish the branch and start business as from the date upon which the supervisory authority of the home Member State has received such a communication, or if no communication is received, on expiry of the [two month] period." (Article 146(3), Directive 2009/138/EC). Thus, under the Directive, the branch may start to provide insurance services in the host Member State at the earlier of the time at which the home Member State's financial supervision authority receives the communication from the host Member State's financial supervision authority about the local business conditions that the branch must follow, and the expiry of two months.

If the Polish insurance firm intends to provide insurance services in a (non-Polish) Member State[833] without establishing a branch there (i.e. the insurance company provides cross-border insurance services in the host Member State), then the notification to which Article 134 of the IAA refers[834] shall contain an indication of the types of risk that the insurance company intends to cover,[835] and, in the case in which it engages in insurance activity within the scope of Section II class 10 of the Annex to the IAA (i.e. third party liability insurance that arises from the possession and use of self-propelled land vehicles) except for carrier's liability insurance, it shall also contain a declaration that the insurance undertaking is a member of a foreign insurance guarantee fund and a national bureau,[836] and the personal data of that insurance undertaking's representatives who are empowered to represent the firm to the extent required for the acceptance and satisfaction of claims that authorised persons have lodged,[837] and for ensuring that the company is legally represented in the disputes before the courts.[838] Within 30 days following this notification, the PFSA shall forward the following information to the financial supervision authority of the host Member State: a certificate that confirms that the Polish insurance company possesses sufficient available solvency margin to cover the required solvency margin,[839] the information concerning the insurance classes for which the firm obtained authorisation,[840] information about the types of risk that the insurance firm intends to cover in the host Member State,[841] and, in a case in which the insurance firm engages in insurance activity within the scope of Section II class 10 of the Annex to the IAA[842] other than carrier's liability insurance, the personal data of the insurance company's personal representatives and a declaration that the insurance firm is a member of the foreign guarantee

---

833 'Member State' in the IAA means a Contracting Party to the EEA Agreement. See note 733.

834 See above in this section, for Article 134 of the IAA.

835 Article 137(1), IAA.

836 Article 137(1)(2), IAA.

837 Article 137(1)(1)(a), IAA.

838 Article 137(1)(1)(b), IAA.

839 Article 137(2)(1), IAA.

840 Article 137(2)(2), IAA. This must mean the services that the financial supervision authority of the insurance company's home Member State authorised it to provide, in accordance with Article 148(1)(b) of Directive 2009/138/EC (see section 2.2.3).

841 Article 137(2)(3), IAA.

842 See above in this paragraph.

fund and the national bureau.[843] The insurance company may start to provide insurance services in the host Member State, once it receives confirmation from the financial supervision authority of that Member State that this authority has received the information from the PFSA.[844] The PFSA may refuse to forward the information to the financial supervision authority of the host Member State, if the Polish insurance undertaking's financial situation does not enable it to provide the insurance services that it specifies in its notification to the PFSA[845] The PFSA shall promptly inform the insurance firm of the reasons for its decision, if it refuses to forward the information to the host Member State's financial supervision authority.[846]

A foreign insurance undertaking from a (non-Polish) Member State[847] may engage in insurance activity on Polish territory, provided that it has obtained suitable authorisation for the pursuit of this activity in the country in which its registered office is situated.[848] The foreign insurance firm's provision of insurance services in Poland is subject to supervision by the competent authority of the Member State in which the firm's registered office is located.[849] A foreign insurance company from a (non-Polish) Member State that provides insurance services in Poland is obliged to comply with Polish law, unless an international agreement to which Poland is party states otherwise.[850] This insurance firm shall be accountable "with its entire assets" for liabilities that arise from the insurance activity pursued.[851]

A foreign insurance firm from a (non-Polish) Member State[852] may provide insurance services on Polish territory via a branch, after the PFSA has received the information to which Articles 132(1)(1) and 135(1) of the IAA refer[853] concerning the foreign insurance company from the financial

---

[843] Article 137(2)(4), IAA.
[844] Article 137(4), IAA.
[845] Article 137(3), IAA.
[846] Article 137(5), IAA.
[847] See note 814.
[848] Article 128(1), IAA.
[849] Article 128(2), IAA.
[850] Article 129(1), IAA.
[851] Article 129(2), IAA. Thus, the freedom to provide insurance services in Poland is accompanied by full recourse to the foreign insurance undertaking's assets for the payment of its debts. See note 813.
[852] 'Member State' in the IAA means a Contracting Party to the EEA Agreement. See note 733.
[853] See the following paragraph, for Article 132(1)(1) of the IAA. See above in this section, for Article 135(1) of the IAA.

supervision authority of the country in which the registered office of that insurance undertaking is situated,[854] having received information from the PFSA about the conditions under which the foreign insurance firm may provide insurance services on Polish territory.[855] The PFSA shall forward the information to which Article 131(1)(2) of the IAA refers,[856] to the financial supervision authority of the Member State in which the insurance company's registered office is located, within two months of the day on which the PFSA receives the information to which Articles 132(1)(1) and 135(1) of the IAA refer.[857] If the PFSA does not provide this information to the financial supervision authority of the foreign insurance company's home Member State within the two month period, then the foreign insurance firm may commence insurance activity through the Polish branch once this time has passed, unless the PFSA specifies an earlier period from which the branch's operations may be started.[858]

A foreign insurance company from a (non-Polish) Member State[859] may provide insurance services on Polish territory other than via a branch (i.e. the firm provides cross-border insurance services in Poland), as soon as the PFSA has received the following items from the financial supervision authority of the Member State in which the registered office of the foreign insurance undertaking is situated: a certificate which confirms that the insurance firm possesses sufficient available solvency margin to cover the required solvency margin,[860] information on the classes of insurance services for the provision of which it has authorisation,[861] and information concerning the types of risks that the foreign insurance company intends to cover on Polish territory.[862] A foreign insurance undertaking from a (non-Polish) Member State that intends to provide cross-border insurance services in Poland within the scope of Section II class 10 of the Annex to the IAA (i.e. third party liability insurance that arises from the possession and use of self-propelled land vehicles) other than carrier's liability insurance, must provide – through the competent

[854] Article 131(1)(1), IAA.

[855] Article 131(1)(2), IAA.

[856] See the previous sentence.

[857] Article 131(2), IAA. See the following paragraph, for Article 132(1)(1) of the IAA. See above in this section, for Article 135(1) of the IAA.

[858] Article 131(3), IAA.

[859] 'Member State' in the IAA means a Contracting Party to the EEA Agreement. See note 733.

[860] Article 132(1)(1), IAA.

[861] Article 132(1)(2), IAA.

[862] Article 132(1)(3), IAA.

authority of the country in which the foreign insurance firm's registered office is located – the PFSA with the following items: a declaration on the wish to become a member of the Polish Motor Insurers' Bureau,[863] and personal data of the insurance firm's representatives that are empowered to represent it to the extent that is required for the acceptance and satisfaction of claims made by authorised persons,[864] and for ensuring legal representation of the foreign insurance undertaking in disputes before the Polish courts.[865]

If the PFSA finds that a foreign insurance company that supplies insurance services in Poland (either through a Polish branch or across the border) does not comply with the provisions of Polish law, then it shall require the foreign insurance firm to remedy the breach.[866] If the foreign insurance undertaking does not take the necessary measures to do so, then the PFSA shall inform the financial supervision authority of the Member State in which the foreign insurance firm's registered office is situated.[867] If the measures that that financial supervision authority takes are insufficient or are not applied, or in spite of these measures, the foreign insurance undertaking continues to contravene provisions of Polish law, then the PFSA may – having informed the other financial supervision authority – apply all powers to which it is entitled under the IAA to prevent further transgressions of this law.[868]

The policy (or other) document that confirms the conclusion of an insurance contract within the freedom to provide services (either through a branch or via the provision of cross-border services) must contain the following information: the insurance firm's address and registered office (or the address branch of the insurance company that provides the insurance cover),[869] the place that insurance contract is concluded,[870] the competence of the court in the event of a dispute between the parties to an insurance contract,[871] the date that the insurance contract is concluded,[872]

---

[863] Article 133(1)(2), IAA.
[864] Article 133(1)(1)(a), IAA.
[865] Article 133(1)(1)(b), IAA.
[866] Article 139(1), IAA.
[867] Article 139(2), IAA.
[868] Article 139(3), IAA. As one of these measures, the PFSA may prohibit the foreign insurance company from providing insurances services on Polish territory (Article 139(4), IAA).
[869] Article 141(1), IAA.
[870] Article 141(2), IAA.
[871] Article 141(3), IAA.
[872] Article 141(4), IAA.

the period of the insurance contract's validity,[873] the insurance contract's subject matter,[874] the conditions for the performance of the insurance contract,[875] the identities of the parties to the insurance contract,[876] the amount of the insurance premium,[877] and the general terms and conditions of the insurance agreement on the basis of which the insurance contract has been concluded – and the fact that these terms and conditions have been delivered to the policyholder.[878] A Polish insurance company may conclude a contract with an insurance firm that has its registered office in a (non-Polish) Member State,[879] for the transfer of an insurance portfolio from the former to the latter.[880] The PFSA shall approve this contract, provided that the conditions contained in Articles 181 to 186 of the IAA are satisfied,[881] having received confirmation from the financial supervision authority of the Member State in which the registered office of the insurance firm taking over the portfolio is situated that this company (having taken over the portfolio) will possess sufficient available solvency margin to cover the required solvency margin,[882] having consulted (for life insurance) the financial supervision authority of the Member State in which the policyholder has its habitual place of residence or the seat of its management board,[883] and (for non-life insurance) the financial supervision authority of the Member State in which the risk is located.[884]

The PFSA shall exercise supervision over insurance companies that provide insurance services on Polish territory.[885] The PFSA's tasks shall

---

[873] Article 141(4), IAA.
[874] Article 141(5), IAA.
[875] Article 141(5), IAA.
[876] Article 141(6), IAA.
[877] Article 141(7), IAA.
[878] Article 141(8), IAA.
[879] 'Member State' in the IAA means a Contracting Party to the EEA Agreement. See note 733.
[880] Article 143(1), IAA.
[881] Articles 181 to 186 of the IAA govern the transfer of insurance contracts from one (Polish) insurance undertaking to another.
[882] Article 143(2)(1), IAA.
[883] Article 143(2)(2)(a), IAA, and Section I, Annex, IAA.
[884] Article 143(2)(2)(b), IAA, and Section II, Annex, IAA.
[885] Article 202(1), IAA. This supervision is subject to Article 11 of the IAA (Article 202(1), IAA). The pursuit of insurance activity by a Polish insurance company, or by a foreign insurance firm that has its registered office in a country other than a Member State, that has obtained authorisation to supply insurance services on Polish territory, shall be subject to the PFSA's supervision (Article 11,

include, in particular, the protection of the interests of the policyholders, insured persons, and beneficiaries entitled under insurance contracts, by preventing situations in which insurance firms will not be able to pay benefits due to these persons,[886] the issuance of authorisations to engage in insurance activity,[887] and performing other activities that the IAA specifies.[888] If the members of an insurance group include a Polish insurance company and a foreign insurance firm with its registered office in a Member State,[889] the PFSA may conclude an agreement with the financial supervision authorities of other (i.e. non-Polish) Member States on co-operation in the supplementary supervision of the insurance undertakings that form part of this insurance group.[890] The PFSA may request information, data, or explanations that are necessary for supplementary supervision from a firm that is not an insurance undertaking, but which is founded in Poland and forms part of an insurance group.[891]

The PFSA may carry out an on-site inspection of the operation and financial state of an insurance firm.[892] Within the framework of this on-site inspection, the PFSA may (at any time) conduct an on-site inspection of the activity and financial state of companies that "perform insurance operations" on the insurance company's behalf.[893] Employees of the PFSA Office shall carry out the on-site inspection.[894] To the extent determined in the PFSA's mandate for inspection, these employees shall have the right of admission to all premises of the insurance undertaking,[895] of access to a separate office and means of communication,[896] of access to all of the insurance company's documents – and to request duplicates, copies and extracts of these documents,[897] of access to the data in the insurance firm's information system – and to request duplicates, copies and extracts of

---

PFSA). 'Member State' in the IAA means a Contracting Party to the EEA Agreement. See note 733.

[886] Article 202(2)(1), IAA.

[887] Article 202(2)(2), IAA.

[888] Article 202(2)(3), IAA.

[889] Member State' in the IAA means a Contracting Party to the EEA Agreement. See note 733.

[890] Article 204(1), IAA.

[891] Article 207a(1), IAA.

[892] Article 208(1), IAA.

[893] Article 208(2), IAA.

[894] Article 208(3), IAA.

[895] Article 208(4)(1), IAA.

[896] Article 208(4)(2), IAA.

[897] Article 208(4)(3), IAA.

these data,[898] of access to all documents of the insurance undertaking's insurance intermediary – and to request duplicates, copies and excerpts of these documents,[899] to request explanations (verbally or in writing) from persons engaged under an employment contract, commission contract, or similar legal relationship with the insurance company, and from insurance agents of the insurance firm,[900] to request the insurance company to prepare the required data (in electronic form, if necessary),[901] and to secure documents and other evidence.[902] The on-site inspection of an insurance firm involves an assessment of the compliance of its operations with "the law", the company's articles of association and business plan, and the interests of its policyholders, insured persons, and beneficiaries entitled under insurance contracts, as well as of the firm's financial circumstances.[903] The PFSA may (at any time) carry out an on-site inspection of the entities to which Article 207a of the IAA refers, as to the integrity of the information, data or explanations that are provided under this Article.[904]

The PFSA shall inform the European Commission and the financial supervision authorities of other Member States[905] about its grant of authorisation to provide insurance services to a Polish insurance firm that is a subsidiary of a parent company with its registered office in a country other than a Member State,[906] and the taking up or acquisition of shares or rights in shares of a Polish insurance undertaking by a company that is founded in a country other than a Member State – if, due to this taking up or acquisition, the Polish insurance firm becomes a subsidiary of the other entity.[907] The PFSA shall inform the European Commission about difficulties that Polish insurance firms encounter, in countries (other than

[898] Article 208(4)(4), IAA.
[899] Article 208(4)(5), IAA.
[900] Article 208(4)(6), IAA.
[901] Article 208(4)(7), IAA.
[902] Article 208(4)(8), IAA.
[903] Article 208b(1), IAA. The quoted phrase probably means relevant provisions of Polish law. On-site inspection activities should be completed within 60 days from the start of this inspection (Article 208b(2), IAA).
[904] See the previous paragraph, for Article 207a(1) of the IAA.
[905] Member State' in the IAA means a Contracting Party to the EEA Agreement. See note 733.
[906] Article 213(1)(1), IAA.
[907] Article 213(1)(2), IAA. The PFSA shall provide the European Commission and the financial supervision authorities of other Member States with information about the insurance group's capital structure (Article 213(2), IAA).

Member States) in which they intend to provide insurance services.[908] At the European Commission's request, the PFSA shall furnish it with information about applications for granting authorisation to provide insurance services to insurance firms that are subsidiaries of a parent company with its registered office in a country that is not a Member State,[909] and information about the taking up or acquisition of shares or rights in shares of an insurance company from a Member State (including Poland) by an entity whose registered office is in a country that is not a Member State – in an amount which results in that insurance undertaking becoming a subsidiary of that entity.[910] The PFSA shall, in accordance with any decision of the European Commission to this effect, suspend proceedings that are being conducted, limit the number of authorisations granted, or take other decisions pursuant to the European Commission's decision, on issues that concern the grant of authorisation to engage in insurance activity on Polish territory to a foreign insurance firm from a country other than a Member State,[911] and the taking up or acquisition of shares or rights in shares of companies to which Article 35 of the IAA refers[912] by an entity whose registered office is situated in a country other than a Member State – or by a subsidiary of such an entity.[913]

The PFSA may submit to the European Commission a proposal to negotiate with countries other than Member States[914] concerning the exercise of supplementary supervision over insurance firms from Member States whose registered offices are situated in a country other than a Member State,[915] and insurance companies from countries other than Member States that have "participating entities" whose registered offices are located in a Member State.[916] This proposal should be aimed at

[908] Article 214(1), IAA.

[909] Article 214(2)(1), IAA. See note 901.

[910] Article 214(2)(2), IAA. The provisions of Article 214(2) of the IAA are not to apply to foreign insurance companies that possess authorisation to provide insurance services on the territory of a Member State (Article 214(4), IAA).

[911] Article 214(3)(1), IAA.

[912] Article 35 of the IAA concerns the obligation of an entity that takes up substantial shareholdings (and/or the rights that accompany these shares) in a Polish insurance firm, to notify the PFSA of its intention to take up or acquire the shares (and/or rights in the shares).

[913] Article 214(3)(2), IAA.

[914] Member State' in the IAA means a Contracting Party to the EEA Agreement. See note 733.

[915] Article 214a(1)(1), IAA.

[916] Article 214a(1)(2), IAA. 'Participating entities' are parent entities, or other entities that possess a "substantial capital interest", or an organisation that is

providing information that is required for the supplementary supervision of insurance firms which are founded in the territory of the EU that have subsidiaries or participating entities in organisations whose registered offices are in the territory of countries other than Member States – to financial supervisory authorities that are from Member States,[917] and information that is required for the performance of supplementary supervision of insurance companies whose registered offices are in the territory of countries other than Member States that have subsidiaries or participating entities whose registered offices are in Member States – to financial supervision authorities from countries other than Member States.[918]

Articles 128, 129(1), 129(2) and 139 of the IAA apply to a foreign reinsurance company from a Member State that provides reinsurance services on Polish territory.[919] A Polish reinsurance undertaking that has been granted the authorisation to which Article 223y of the IAA refers, may engage in reinsurance activity on the territory of a Member State, through the provision of cross-border services or the establishment of a branch.[920] If the PFSA has doubts as to whether the activity of a foreign reinsurance firm within the freedom to provide services does not breach provisions on financial management in force in the Member State in which this company has its registered office, then it shall inform the financial supervision authority of that Member State of these doubts.[921] In a case in which the foreign reinsurance undertaking that provides reinsurance services through a branch, engages in insurance activity, the PFSA may (after notifying the financial supervision authority of the foreign

---

affiliated with that entity in such a manner that it may engage in other activities, referred to in clause 37 of paragraph 1 of Article 3 of the Act of 29 September 1994 on Accounting (Article 214a(3), IAA).

[917] Article 214a(2)(1), IAA.

[918] Article 214a(2)(1), IAA.

[919] Article 223zn, IAA. See above in this section, for Articles 128, 129(1), 129(2) and 139 of the IAA. 'Member State' in the IAA means a Contracting Party to the EEA Agreement. See note 733.

[920] Article 223zo, IAA. The authorisation to engage in reinsurance activity is to be issued in accordance with the application for authorisation to pursue reinsurance activity in the ambit of reinsurance of (i) life insurance to which Section I of the Annex to the IAA refers, (ii) other personal insurance and property insurance to which Section II of the Annex to the IAA refers, and (iii) insurance to which both Section I and Section II of the Annex to the IAA refer (Article 223y, IAA).

[921] Article 223zp, IAA.

reinsurance company's home Member State), conduct an on-site inspection of the branch – as referred to in Article 208 of the IAA.[922]

A Polish insurance company may conclude a contract with an insurance or reinsurance undertaking that has its registered office in a Member State, for transfer of the reinsurance portfolio to the latter firm.[923] The PFSA shall approve this contract, observing the conditions in Articles 223zzi to 223zzm of the IAA,[924] having received confirmation from the financial supervision authority of the Member State in which the recipient (re)insurance undertaking has its registered office, that this company (having taken over this portfolio) will possess adequate available solvency margin to cover the required solvency margin,[925] and assets that cover technical provisions.[926]

The establishment of a branch, and capital transfers in respect of insurance contracts, are 'capital movements' in the Titles I(1) and X, respectively, of the nomenclature in Annex I. If the PFSA refuses to grant an authorisation to provide insurance services in Poland (if the non-Polish insurance firm has its registered office outside the EEA), or to forward information to the host EEA state's financial supervision authority, or withdraws an authorisation, then it limits the free movement of capital. In the case of the provision of cross-border insurance services, these restrictions are potential (rather than actual), as the cross-border insurance contracts are to be concluded before capital is transferred in respect of them.[927]

For Article 65(1)(b) of the TFEU to justify the restrictive measures, they must be necessary for the protection of the interests that they are intended to guarantee, be proportionate (i.e. not attainable by less restrictive measures), and observe the requirements of legal certainty (i.e. be specific, objective and known to the parties beforehand); in addition, the persons whom the measures affect must have access to legal redress (i.e. intervention must be supported by reasons and be subject to review in the national courts.[928] Some of the IAA's measures provide discretion to

---

922 Article 223zq(1), IAA. See above in this section, for Article 208 of the IAA.

923 Article 223zr(1), IAA.

924 Articles 223zzi to 223zzm of the IAA regulate the transfer of reinsurance contracts from a (Polish) reinsurance firm to a (Polish) insurance or reinsurance undertaking.

925 Article 223zr(2)(1), IAA.

926 Article 223zr(2)(2), IAA.

927 This was noted in Baber, *The Impact of Legislation and Regulation*, at 113.

928 See the subsection '*The requirements for a successful public policy/security derogation*' in section 2.1.3.

the PFSA, and, therefore, do not provide the applicant insurance firm with legal certainty – and may be disproportionate. For example, Articles 114(1)(7) and 119(2)(2) of the IAA provide the PFSA with discretion.[929] To observe the requirements of legal certainty, these provisions should be accompanied by published guidelines – in the form of a statutory instrument or a document that the PFSA issues. Articles 135(5) and 137(5) of the IAA require the PFSA to give reasons to a company that is authorised to provide insurance services in Poland and intends to provide insurance services in another EEA country – through a branch in the case of Article 135 of the IAA and directly across the border in the case of Article 137 of the IAA – for refusing to forward the information required from the insurance firm to the financial supervision authority of the host EEA state.[930] However, neither Article 135 nor Article 137 of the IAA grant the applicant insurance firm the right to appeal in the Polish courts against a refusal to forward the information. Thus, the persons whom the restrictive measures affect do not have sufficient access to legal redress. Hence, Article 65(1)(b) of the TFEU does not justify these measures.

Some of the restrictive measures, such as those in Articles 114 and 119 of the IAA,[931] affect capital movements between Poland and third countries. To be justified under Article 64(1) of the TFEU, the EU institutions must carefully take account of the objective of the free movement of capital whilst enacting the pertinent legislation, and the national rules must not limit the free movement of capital more than do the equivalent provisions of the relevant Directive.[932] The relevant Directive is Directive 2009/138/EC.

Although the Articles of this Directive do not mention the free movement of capital, Recital 72 of Directive 2009/138/EC states that Member States should not require insurance or reinsurance firms to invest their assets in specific categories, because this could be incompatible with the liberalisation of capital movements for which Article 63 of the TFEU provides. The wording of Recital 72 shows that EU legislators were aware of the free movement of capital whilst enacting Directive 2009/138/EC, although it is arguable whether or not the statement in the Recital is

---

929 See above in this section, for Articles 114(1)(7) and 119(2)(2) of the IAA.

930 See above in this section, for Articles 135(5) and 137(5) of the IAA.

931 See above in this section, for Articles 114 and 119 of the IAA.

932 See the subsection '*Derogations that apply only to capital movements to/from third countries*', in section 2.3.2.

sufficient to establish that these legislators had carefully considered this objective.[933]

Directive 2009/138/EC does not contain provisions that specifically address the foundation of a branch, or the provision of cross-border services, in a third country by a company that is authorised in an EEA country to provide insurance services there.[934] In addition, Chapter IX of Title I of Directive 2009/138/EC provides detailed requirements for the foundation of a branch in an EEA state of an insurance or reinsurance company with its head office located in a third country.[935] There are no equivalent rules for the supply of cross-border insurance services in an EEA state by a third country (re)insurance undertaking.[936] Whilst the IAA does not provide for a third country insurance firm to provide cross-border services to an EEA state, Articles 105 and 107 of the IAA contain detailed requirements for such a firm to establish a branch there.[937] In addition, Articles 114 and 119 of the IAA provide several grounds on which the PFSA may refuse to issue, and withdraw, respectively, an authorisation for a third country insurance undertaking to found a branch in an EEA state.[938] Chapter IX of Title I of Directive 2009/138/EC does not contain provisions that correspond to Articles 114 and 119 of the IAA. Hence, the IAA restricts the free movement of capital from third countries more than do the equivalent provisions of Directive 2009/138/EC. As far as the free movement of capital to third countries is concerned, the IAA is as silent as Directive 2009/138/EC.

Further to the previous three paragraphs, the IAA's restrictive measures on the free movement of capital from third countries to Poland are not justified by Article 64(1) of the TFEU. As the IAA contains no provisions on the foundation of a branch, or the supply of cross-border services, in countries outside the EEA, there are no rules regarding the provision of insurance services by Polish firms to which Article 64(1) of the TFEU might be applied. Thus, as neither Article 65(1)(b) nor Article 64(1) of the TFEU justify the restrictive measures in the IAA, these provisions contravene Article 63 of the TFEU.

---

[933] See the subsection '*Chapter 2 Division 2: Activities of Estonian Insurance Undertakings in Foreign States*', in section 3.4.

[934] For further discussion on this point, see the subsection '*Chapter 2 Division 2: Activities of Estonian Insurance Undertakings in Foreign States*', in section 3.4.

[935] These requirements are stated in the subsection '*Chapter 2 Division 3: Activities of Foreign Insurance Undertakings in Estonia*', in section 3.4.

[936] See Chapter 3, note 1428.

[937] See above in this section, for Articles 105 and 107 of the IAA.

[938] See above in this section, for Articles 114 and 119 of the IAA.

4.4.3 Act of 22 May 2003 on Insurance Mediation (IMA)

'Insurance mediation' involves the performance, for payment, of "factual or legal acts" in the "conclusion and performance of" insurance contracts.[939] Insurance mediation must be performed by insurance agents or insurance brokers.[940] An 'insurance agent' is an entrepreneur, entered in the insurance agents' register, which performs "agency activities" under a contract with an insurance company.[941] 'Agency activities' include seeking clients, preparing and concluding insurance contracts, and assisting both in matters relating to insurance contracts and in organising and supervising such activities.[942]

An 'insurance broker' is a natural or legal person, entered in the insurance brokers' register, which is authorised to perform "brokerage activities".[943] 'Brokerage activities' are conducted on behalf of persons seeking insurance coverage, and include preparing, concluding and participating in issues concerning, insurance contracts.[944]

An insurance agent that has its seat or place of residence in another Member State of the EU[945] may engage in agency activities in Poland, provided that it is entered in the "appropriate register" in that home Member State.[946] The insurance agent may start to engage in agency activities on Polish territory, no less than 30 days after the PFSA has received information from the home Member State's financial supervision authority of the agent's intention to provide insurance mediation in Poland.[947]

An insurance agent, which is entered in the register of insurance agents in Poland, may engage in insurance activities on the territory of another

---

939 Article 2(1), IMA.

940 Article 2(2), IMA. Reinsurance mediation must be undertaken by insurance brokers with a reinsurance permit (Article 2(3), IMA).

941 Article 7, IMA.

942 Article 4(1), IMA.

943 Article 20, IMA.

944 Article 4(2), IMA.

945 A reference in the IMA to EU Member States also includes member states of the European Free Trade Association, who together (except Switzerland) make up the Contracting Parties to the EEA Agreement (Article 1a, IMA). Thus, 'Member State' in the IMA means 'EEA state'.

946 Article 16(1), IMA.

947 Article 16(2), IMA. If the PFSA becomes aware that the insurance agent's agency activities in Poland transgress the law, then it may inform the financial supervision authority of the insurance agent's home Member State of this breach (Article 16(3), IMA).

Member State,[948] provided that it notifies the PFSA of its intention to do so,[949] and states in this notification the name of the Member State in which the activities are to be carried out,[950] the address of the branch or representative office in the host Member State (if a branch or representative office is to be founded there),[951] the name and seat of the insurance firm on behalf of which the insurance agent may engage in insurance mediation in the territory of the host Member State,[952] and the liability insurance or equivalent guarantee of 1 million EUR for one event and 1.5 million EUR in respect of all events for any damage that arises in connection with the performance of agency acts that is caused to the entity that seeks insurance coverage, the insurer, the insured person, or the beneficiary under the insurance contract, if the insurance agent was not entitled to conclude this contract.[953] Within 30 days of the notification, the PFSA shall send to the financial supervision authority of the host Member State, the facts that the agent intends to engage in agency activities in the territory of the host Member State and that the agent is registered in the register of insurance intermediaries which the PFSA holds.[954] The PFSA shall not send this information, if the host Member State is not willing to receive information about the intention of insurance agents registered in other Member States to engage in agency activities.[955] The PFSA shall immediately notify the insurance agent about its transmission of the information to the financial supervision authority of the host Member State,[956] or the fact that the host Member State is not willing to receive pertinent information.[957]

An insurance broker that has its seat or place of residence in a Member State[958] may engage in brokerage activities in Poland, as long as its details

---

[948] Article 17(1), IMA. See note 945, for the definition of 'Member State'.

[949] Article 17(2), IMA.

[950] Article 17(3)(1), IMA.

[951] Article 17(3)(2), IMA.

[952] Article 17(3)(3), IMA.

[953] Article 17(3)(4), IMA. As regards liability for damage which is caused in association with the performance of agency activities, the insurance agent that acts on behalf of more than one insurance firm in same insurance field (in accordance with the Annex to the IAA), shall be subject to compulsory civil liability insurance (Article 11(3), IMA).

[954] Article 17(4), IMA.

[955] Article 17(5), IMA.

[956] Article 17(6)(1), IMA.

[957] Article 17(6)(2), IMA.

[958] See note 945, for the definition of 'Member State'.

are entered in the "appropriate register" in its home Member State.[959] The insurance broker may start to pursue brokerage activities on Polish territory, as soon as the PFSA receives confirmation from the financial supervision authority of the insurance broker's home Member State that the broker's details are entered in this register.[960]

An insurance broker, which holds a permit issued by the PFSA to pursue brokerage activities in Poland, may engage in brokerage activities in the territory of another Member State,[961] provided that it notifies the financial supervision authority of the host Member State thereof.[962] This notification shall state the name of the host Member State,[963] and the address of the branch or representative office in the host Member State (if the broker is to establish a branch or representative office there).[964] Within 30 days of the notification, the PFSA shall convey to the financial supervision authority of the host Member State, the facts that the broker holds a permit to engage in brokerage activities in the territory of the host Member State and that the broker is registered in the register of insurance intermediaries which the PFSA holds.[965] The PFSA shall not send this information, if the host Member State is not willing to receive information about the intention of insurance brokers registered in other Member States to engage in brokerage activity.[966] The PFSA shall immediately notify the insurance broker about its transmission of the information to the financial supervision authority of the host Member State,[967] or the fact that the host Member State is not willing to receive relevant information.[968]

Agency and brokerage activities are 'capital movements' in Title X of the nomenclature in Annex I, because they are "operations necessary for the purpose of capital movements",[969] which the Annex includes as 'capital movements'. However, none of the above provisions restrict the

---

959 Article 31(1), IMA.
960 Article 31(2), IMA.
960 Article 16(2), IMA. If the PFSA becomes aware that the insurance broker's brokerage activities in Poland contravene the law, then it may inform the financial supervision authority of the insurance broker's home Member State of this breach (Article 31(3), IMA).
961 Article 32(1), IMA.
962 Article 32(2), IMA.
963 Article 32(3)(1), IMA.
964 Article 32(3)(2), IMA.
965 Article 32(4), IMA.
966 Article 32(5), IMA.
967 Article 32(6)(1), IMA.
968 Article 32(6)(2), IMA.
969 Annex I.

free movement of capital, as they concern the transmission of information and are not onerous.

4.4.4 Act of 28 August 1997: Law on the Organisation and Operation of Pension Funds (LPF)

The LPF defines the terms of the formation and operation of pension funds (hereafter referred to as 'funds').[970] A fund is to be a legal person.[971] A fund shall accumulate and invest financial resources in order to make payments to fund members[972] of pensionable age and to pay periodic capital pensions.[973] A voluntary fund is to operate an individual retirement account (IRA) or an individual retirement savings account (IRSA).[974] An occupational fund[975] that is managed by an occupational society[976] whose shareholder or founder is a foreign employer,[977] may collect contributions[978] from foreign employees[979] for the implementation of the

---

[970] Article 1, LPF.

[971] Article 2(1), LPF.

[972] A 'fund member' is a natural person who has become a member of the fund in accordance with the LPF (Article 8(2), LPF).

[973] Article 2(2), LPF.

[974] Article 2(3), LPF. A 'voluntary fund' is a fund that operates an IRA or an IRSA, and which a general society manages (Article 8(3a), LPF). A 'general society' is a general pension society – which manages a voluntary fund or an open fund (Article 8(8), LPF).

[975] An 'occupational fund' is an occupational pension fund that an occupational society establishes and manages (Article 8(6), LPF).

[976] An 'occupational society' is an occupational pension society that is the governing body of an occupational fund (Article 8(9). LPF).

[977] A 'foreign employer' is an entity that has its registered office on the territory of an EEA state or the Swiss Confederation, which is a sole trader or an employer (Article 8(10), LPF).

[978] 'Contributions' are contributions to an open fund, shares transferred and contributions paid to an occupational fund, and contributions to a voluntary fund (Article 8(3b), LPF).

[979] A 'foreign employee' is a natural person whom a foreign employer engages (Article 8(14), LPF).

foreign employer's pension scheme,[980] under a contribution collection agreement between the occupational fund and a life insurance company.[981]

A pension society (hereafter referred to as a 'society')[982] is to be the governing body of a fund.[983] Only a society may establish a fund.[984] A society shall create the fund, manage it, and represent the fund as its governing body before third parties.[985] The society's registered office is to be the registered office of the fund.[986] For a fund to be founded, the society must adopt the fund's articles of association,[987] the society and the depositary must conclude an agreement for the custody of the assets of the fund,[988] the society must be granted a licence for the establishment of the fund,[989] and the fund must be entered in the register of funds.[990]

The assets of a fund are to be the contributions paid to it, the rights acquired for or in relation to these contributions, and benefits from those rights.[991] The value of the fund's net assets are to be determined by deducting the fund's commitments from its assets.[992] A fund may be founded as an open fund, a voluntary fund, or an occupational fund.[993]

The PFSA shall issue a licence for the establishment of a fund within three months of the submission of a "relevant application".[994] The PFSA shall refuse to issue a licence, if the application and the documents appended to it do not fulfil the requirements of the LPF,[995] the fund's

---

[980] A 'pension scheme of a foreign employer' is the set of rules of accumulating savings for the purpose of pensions that are mandatory for a foreign employer (Article 8(12), LPF).

[981] Article 2(4), LPF. A 'life insurance company' is an insurance firm that carries out activities to which Section I of the Annex to the IAA refers. See note 789, for a list of these activities.

[982] A 'society' is a joint-stock company that is the governing body of an open fund or a voluntary fund (Article 8(7), LPF).

[983] Article 3(1), LPF.

[984] Article 9(2), LPF.

[985] Article 3(2), LPF.

[986] Article 4, LPF.

[987] Article 12(1), LPF.

[988] Article 12(2), LPF.

[989] Article 12(3), LPF.

[990] Article 12(4), LPF.

[991] Article 6(1), LPF.

[992] Article 6(2), LPF.

[993] Article 9(1), LPF.

[994] Article 15(1), LPF. The issuance of a licence for the creation of a fund shall amount to approval of the fund's articles of association (Article 15(1), LPF).

[995] Article 15(2)(1), LPF.

articles of association do not protect the interests of the fund's members,[996] and the persons to which clauses 4 and 5 of Article 14(1) of the LPF refer "do not provide any guarantee of the proper performance of their duties".[997] A licence for the foundation of a fund shall expire, if the society does not submit an application to the registration court for the entry of the fund in the register of funds, within 2 months of the date of delivery of the licence.[998]

A society must be a joint-stock company,[999] and shall function as a general society or an occupational society.[1000] A general society shall found and manage only one open fund, and may establish and manage just one occupational fund.[1001] An occupational society may create and manage only one occupational fund, unless the management of more than one occupational fund, open fund or voluntary fund is consequent to its management being taken over by a society or a merger of societies.[1002]

Whilst a general society is a profit-making entity,[1003] an occupational society is a not-for-profit organisation.[1004] A general society must employ at least one investment adviser, to manage the open fund's assets.[1005] The minimum share capital of a general society shall be at least 5 million zloty.[1006]

An occupational fund may select a life insurance company to which it may it shall transfer (in whole or in part) foreign employee contributions, under a contribution collection agreement with that firm.[1007] The contribution collection agreement shall state the obligations of the life insurance company and the occupational fund, the way in which these duties shall be performed, and list persons that the life insurance

---

[996] Article 15(2)(2), LPF.

[997] Article 15(2)(3), LPF. These persons are the employees of the society, or persons that the society intends to employ, who have, or will have, significant influence on the management of the finances of the fund (Article 14(1)(4), LPF), and the persons who the depositary designates as directly responsible for the proper implementation of the duties that the agreement between the society and the depositary specifies (Article 14(1)(5), LPF).

[998] Articles 18 and 16(1), LPF.

[999] Article 27(1), LPF.

[1000] Article 27(2), LPF.

[1001] Article 29(2), LPF.

[1002] Article 29(2), LPF.

[1003] Article 29(3), LPF.

[1004] Article 29(4), LPF.

[1005] Article 29(5), LPF.

[1006] Article 31, LPF.

[1007] Article 106a, LPF.

undertaking designates to be directly responsible for the proper performance of the contribution collection agreement.[1008] If a foreign employer is a shareholder of an occupational society, and the national labour law and social insurance regulations require it, the contribution collection agreement shall include regulation concerning the provision of additional information by the occupational fund to that employer or its employees concerning the type of risks which relate to the implementation of the foreign employer's pension scheme,[1009] the distribution of these risks,[1010] the expected levels of benefits (if the foreign employer's pension scheme provides for the coverage of biometric risks or guarantees),[1011] the amount of the payments or benefits from the foreign employer's pension scheme that provide for the coverage of biometric risks or guarantees after the termination of employment,[1012] provisions that regulate the transfer of rights to payments under the foreign employer's pension scheme to another occupational pension scheme after the termination of employment,[1013] and (if participants in the foreign employer's pension scheme are exposed to investment risks) the extent of investment policy choices (if applicable), the investment portfolios, and information on costs and risks that relate to investments.[1014]

A fund that invests its assets shall proceed in accordance with the provisions of the LPF, seeking to optimise the rate of return on its investments.[1015] Assets of the fund may be invested, subject to the Articles 143(5) and 146 of the LPF,[1016] only in the following financial instruments:

[1008] Article 106c(1), LPF.

[1009] Article 106c(3)(1), LPF.

[1010] Article 106c(3)(2), LPF.

[1011] Article 106c(3)(3), LPF. 'Biometric risks' are risks that relate to death, longevity or disability (Article 8(15), LPF). 'Guarantees' are guarantees of investment results and a specified level of benefits (Article 8(16), LPF).

[1012] Article 106c(3)(4), LPF.

[1013] Article 106c(3)(6), LPF.

[1014] Article 106c(3)(5), LPF.

[1015] Article 139, LPF. This English translation of Article 139 of the LPF states "seeking to maximise the security and rate of return".

[1016] See the next paragraph, for Article 143(5) of the LPF. An occupational fund shall invest no more than 5% of its assets in securities of shareholders of the occupational society that is its manager (Article 146(1), LPF). An occupational fund shall investment no more than 10% of its assets in securities of affiliates of the occupational society that is its manager (Article 146(2), LPF). If the fund's articles of association so allow, an occupational fund may invest its assets in securities of shareholders of the occupational society that is its manager, or in securities of affiliates of these shareholders (Article 146(3), LPF).

securities issued by the Polish State Treasury or the National Bank of Poland (and in credits given pursuant to these securities),[1017] debt instruments which represent the issuer's pecuniary duties that are guaranteed or backed by the National Bank of Poland or the Polish State Treasury,[1018] credits and loans that are guaranteed or backed by the National Bank of Poland or the Polish State Treasury,[1019] bank securities and deposits in zloty,[1020] bank securities and deposits in currencies of countries that are members of the OECD – and other countries with which Poland has concluded memoranda of understanding on the support and mutual protection of investments – in cases in which these currencies may be bought only for the clearance of current liabilities of the fund,[1021] shares of companies that are listed on a regulated stock market (and pre-emption rights, rights to shares, and bonds that are convertible to the shares of these companies),[1022] shares of companies that are listed on a "regulated off-exchange market" or shares of companies that are not traded on a regulated market but are dematerialised in accordance with the TFIA (and pre-emption rights, rights to shares, and bonds convertible into the shares of these companies),[1023] investment certificates that closed-end investment funds issue,[1024] units that open-end or specialised open-end investment funds sell,[1025] debt securities that are issued by local government bodies, their unions, or "the capital city of Warsaw",[1026] revenue bonds (as referred to in the Act on Bonds of 29 June 1995),[1027] debt securities that are issued by organisations other than local government bodies, their unions, or Warsaw, secured to their par value and interest (if any),[1028] debt securities that are issued by public companies,[1029] debt securities that are dematerialised in accordance with the TFIA,[1030] mortgage bonds,[1031] depositary receipts within the meaning of the TFIA that are admitted to

---

[1017] Article 141(1)(1), LPF.
[1018] Article 141(1)(2), LPF.
[1019] Article 141(1)(2), LPF.
[1020] Article 141(1)(3), LPF.
[1021] Article 141(1)(3a), LPF.
[1022] Article 141(1)(4), LPF.
[1023] Article 141(1)(5), LPF.
[1024] Article 141(1)(7), LPF.
[1025] Article 141(1)(8), LPF.
[1026] Article 141(1)(9)-(10), LPF.
[1027] Article 141(1)(10a), LPF.
[1028] Article 141(1)(11)-(12), LPF.
[1029] Article 141(1)(13), LPF.
[1030] Article 141(1)(13a), LPF.
[1031] Article 141(1)(13b), LPF.

trading on a regulated market in Poland,[1032] and bonds issued by Bank Gospodarstwa Krajowego on the terms that the Act on Toll Motorways and the National Road Fund of 27 October 1994 has laid down.[1033] Article 142 of the LPF provides for percentage limitations in investment in the asset categories of Article 141 of the LPF. Of particular relevance to the free movement of capital is the cross-border investment limitation – the total value of a fund's investment in the investment categories to which Article 141(1)(3a) of the LPF refers shall not exceed 5% of the value of the fund's assets.[1034]

Under a general permit that the minister responsible for financial institutions may issue by ordinance, and on the terms stated therein, assets of an open fund may be invested outside Poland in securities of companies that are listed on the main stock markets of OECD member states, or in other countries that the permit specifies, as well as in treasury bonds and bills that are issued by the governments or central banks of these countries, and in units issued by mutual investment institutions with their registered offices in those countries, if these institutions offer units to the public and redeem them on demand.[1035] No more than 5% of an open fund's assets may be invested in these investment categories.[1036] Furthermore, no more than 30% of an occupational fund's assets may be invested in securities in currencies other than the zloty.[1037] An occupational fund's articles of association shall determine whether or not the fund may invest its assets outside Poland, and shall specify the securities, treasury bonds, and shares or units of mutual investment institutions in which the occupational fund may invest.[1038] The assets of a voluntary fund may be invested in an EEA or OECD state, in the following financial instruments: shares that are issued by companies that are listed on the stock markets of these countries and rights to these shares (including their pre-emption rights),[1039] debt securities that are issued by companies that are listed on the main stock

[1032] Article 141(1)(13c), LPF.
[1033] Article 141(1)(15), LPF.
[1034] Article 142(2)(6), LPF. See above in this paragraph, for Article 141(1)(3a) of the LPF.
[1035] Article 143(1), LPF.
[1036] Article 143(2), LPF.
[1037] Article 143(3), LPF.
[1038] Article 147, LPF.
[1039] Article 143(5)(1), LPF.

markets of those countries,[1040] securities that are issued by the governments or central banks of EEA\OECD states,[1041] unit trust certificates that are issued by "joint investment institutions" that have their registered office in these countries (if those institutions offer unit trust certificates to the public and redeem these certificates on demand),[1042] and depositary receipts that are listed on the main stock markets of those countries.[1043] In respect of a fund's foreign investment activity, the fund may entrust the management of its assets, to the extent that Article 143 of the LPF determines, to entities that are domiciled in the countries that are referred to therein, which, under the laws in effect in those states, may legitimately provide the services of a portfolio manager.[1044]

If a fund has unintentionally breached any provision of this Section of the LPF[1045] due to developments that are beyond its direct control, then it shall take suitable steps without delay to adjust its investment portfolio to the requirements of the LPF.[1046] The fund shall adapt its investment portfolio to the LPF's requirements within 6 months from the day on which an illegal situation develops, or from the day on which a valuation of the fund's assets reveals the fund's unlawful circumstances, whichever is the later.[1047]

The Council of Ministers may, by ordinance, place additional constraints on investments by funds, if these limitations are imposed in order to protect the interests of members of those funds.[1048] If a fund does not comply with the investment requirements and standards that the LPF contains, or does not fulfil its duties under Article 149 of the LPF, then the

[1040] Article 143(5)(2), LPF. These must be investment-grade securities, as rated by a reputable credit rating agency on the international capital market (Article 143(6), LPF).

[1041] Article 143(5)(3), LPF. See note 1035.

[1042] Article 143(5)(4), LPF.

[1043] Article 143(5)(5), LPF.

[1044] Article 153, LPF.

[1045] 'This Section of the LPF' is Section 15 – Pension fund: investment, which comprises Articles 139-156 of the LPF.

[1046] Article 149(1), LPF.

[1047] Article 149(2), LPF. At the fund's request, the PFSA may extend this time limit by up to one year, if this extension protects the interests of the fund's members (Article 149(3), LPF). The fund must file this request with the PFSA within one month of the day following that on which an illegal situation develops or is revealed (Article 149(3), LPF).

[1048] Article 155, LPF.

PFSA may impose a fine on the society that manages it, of up to 500,000 zloty.[1049]

A fund may appoint a depositary to have custody over its assets under an agreement.[1050] A depositary shall be a bank that has its registered office in Poland,[1051] has own funds of at least the zloty equivalent of 100 million EUR – if the agreement is for the custody of an open fund's assets, or of 30 million EUR – if the agreement is for the custody of an occupational fund's assets,[1052] does not hold shares in the society that manages the fund whose assets it keeps – or stocks or shares in an affiliate of this society,[1053] is not a lender of the fund whose assets it keeps, or of the society that manages this fund – unless the amount of the credit or loan does not exceed 1% of the value of the fund's net assets as of the date that the loan or credit is made,[1054] and does not employ or have on its governing bodies persons who sit on the supervisory board or management board or are employees of the society that manages the fund,[1055] or who sit on the supervisory board or management board or are employees of an affiliate of this society.[1056] The duties of a depositary in respect of the custody of a fund's assets include: maintaining a register of the fund's assets as entered in the appropriate accounts and as kept by the depositary and by other authorised persons,[1057] ensuring that the fund's net asset value is established in a way in which that the fund is able to carry out its duties in section 17 of the LPF,[1058] ensuring that agreements which concern acquisitions and disposals of fund assets are lawful and in accordance with the fund's articles of association,[1059] carrying out instructions that the fund gives (unless these directions are illegal or contrary to the fund's articles of association, or unless, in the depositary's opinion, they put the security of the fund's assets at risk),[1060] ensuring the assets of the fund are invested legally and in accordance with its articles of association,[1061] ensuring the

[1049] Article 156, LPF.
[1050] Article 157, LPF.
[1051] Articles 158(1)(1), LPF, and Article 4(1)(1), BL.
[1052] Article 158(1)(2), LPF.
[1053] Article 158(1)(3), LPF.
[1054] Article 158(1)(4), LPF.
[1055] Article 158(1)(5)(a), LPF.
[1056] Article 158(1)(5)(b), LPF.
[1057] Article 159(1)(1), LPF.
[1058] Article 159(1)(2), LPF. Section 17 of the LPF is entitled "Valuating pension funds' assets and rates of return". It comprises Articles 166-174 of the LPF.
[1059] Article 159(1)(3), LPF.
[1060] Article 159(1)(4), LPF.
[1061] Article 159(1)(5), LPF.

timely settlement of agreements that relate to the fund's assets,[1062] following the instructions of the liquidator (if the fund is wound up),[1063] and discharging other duties for which the LPF provides.[1064] If the depositary sanctions agreements for others to keep a register of the fund's assets, then the depositary may, if the fund instructs it to do so, enter into contracts to do this with financial institutions whose seat is outside Poland – provided that these entities possess "own capital" of at least 200 million EUR.[1065]

The PFSA shall superintend the performance of funds,[1066] analyse the pension market with regard to occupational pension schemes, open funds, voluntary funds, IRAs and IRSAs in Poland, the degree of security as concerns the interests of occupational pension scheme participants and pension fund members, competitive risks in the market of open pension funds, the development of funded and voluntary pension savings plans, maximisation of the level of pension savings, and proposals for amendments to legislation in respect of these issues,[1067] oversee the working of occupational pension schemes,[1068] increase public knowledge on the objectives and terms of operation of funds – in particular of the rights that relate to members of the fund,[1069] raise public awareness of the terms of operation and the objectives of occupational pension funds – especially the rights that belong to members of the fund,[1070] work with the government's administrative agencies, the National Bank of Poland, the Social Insurance Institution, funds' agents, societies, employers' unions, trade unions and other civic organisations towards shaping the policy of the state in order to ensure the secure development of occupational pension schemes and pension funds,[1071] provide the National Bank of Poland with the information that may be required for the exercise of supervision of depositary banks and banks that are shareholders of societies,[1072] co-operate with foreign financial supervision authorities within the framework of the cross-border activity of institutions that

[1062] Article 159(1)(6), LPF.
[1063] Article 159(1)(7), LPF.
[1064] Article 159(1)(8), LPF.
[1065] Article 159(2), LPF.
[1066] Article 200(2)(1), LPF.
[1067] Article 200(2)(1a), LPF.
[1068] Article 200(2)(3), LPF.
[1069] Article 200(2)(4), LPF.
[1070] Article 200(2)(5), LPF.
[1071] Article 200(2)(6), LPF.
[1072] Article 200(2)(7), LPF.

provide occupational pension schemes,[1073] and take other action as the LPF requires.[1074] In supervision funds' operations, the PFSA shall in particular be entitled to request that the relevant society make available copies of documents related to its or its fund's operations for officers of the PFSA to read,[1075] request information and explanations that relate to a society's or a fund's activities from members of the society's supervisory board, management board or employees, or other persons who are related to the society or the fund by a contract for services, contract for specific work, or other similar legal relationship,[1076] and request that a depositary or third party in which the society or the fund has vested the performance of certain tasks make all information, documents and explanations available in relation to the activities performed for the society or the fund.[1077] In cases in which, on the basis of information, documents and explanations provided pursuant to Article 204(1) of the LPF,[1078] the PFSA discovers a breach of "the law" or of "the interests of fund members", it shall notify the society, depositary, or third party in which the society or the fund has entrusted the performance of certain tasks, about the irregularities revealed, and shall specify a deadline by which these difficulties are to be rectified.[1079] The notified entity may, within 7 days from the delivery of the notification, file in writing justified objections to its content.[1080] If the notified entity does not meet this deadline, then the PFSA may, at the request of that entity, reinstate the time limit.[1081] The deadline may be restored, if the notified entity demonstrates that its transgression happened for reasons which were beyond its control.[1082] The PFSA shall inform the notified entity in writing as to whether it agrees, or refuses, to reinstate the deadline.[1083] If the notified entity files written objections to the content of the notification, then the PFSA, after its consideration of these points, shall inform the notified entity of the way in which it appraised them.[1084] In particular, the PFSA may take the

---

[1073] Article 200(2)(8a), LPF.
[1074] Article 200(2)(9), LPF.
[1075] Article 204(1)(1), LPF.
[1076] Article 204(1)(2), LPF.
[1077] Article 204(1)(3), LPF.
[1078] See the previous sentence, for Article 204(1)(3) of the LPF.
[1079] Article 204(3), LPF. "The law" probably means any provisions of Polish law.
[1080] Article 204(4), LPF.
[1081] Article 204(4a), LPF.
[1082] Article 204(4a), LPF.
[1083] Article 204(4a), LPF.
[1084] Article 204(5), LPF. If the notified entity files objections in accordance with Article 204(4) of the LPF, then the 7 day deadline for this entity to remove the

objections into full or part consideration and make sufficient modifications to the notification's content,[1085] or not take the objections into account (if they are irrelevant).[1086] Within three days from the day of lapse of the deadline for removing the irregularities, the notified entity shall inform the PFSA in writing about the way in which it eliminated these deficiencies.[1087] If the notified entity does not remove the irregularities by the specified deadline, then the PFSA may impose on it a fine of up to 500,000 zloty.[1088] In a case in which, on the basis of information, documents and explanations pursuant to Article 204(1) of the LPF, the PFSA finds a clear infringement of "the law" or of "the interests of fund members", the PFSA may charge a fine of up to 500,000 zloty on the society, depository or third party in which the society or the fund entrusted the performance of specified tasks, immediately after such infringements are disclosed.[1089] If a fund or society carries out its activities in contravention of "the law" or of its articles of association, or in severe breach of the interests of members of the fund, then the PFSA may impose a fine on the responsible member of the society's management board of up to three times the gross monthly remuneration of that person.[1090]

The PFSA may carry out an inspection of the operation of a society, fund, depositary or third party in which the society or the fund has entrusted the performance of specified tasks.[1091] The person whom the PFSA authorises to conduct an inspection may enter the premises of the following entities: a society – in order to check whether the society's or fund's activity complies with "the law", the society's or fund's articles of association or the interests of members of the fund,[1092] a depositary – in order to verify whether its operations that relate to the maintenance of the fund's assets complies with "the law", the agreement on the maintenance of these assets or the interests of members of the fund,[1093] or a third party in which the society has entrusted the performance of certain tasks – in

irregularities shall be computed from the day of delivery to it of the PFSA's notification concerning the latter's appraisal of these objections (Article 204(6), LPF).

1085 Article 204(5)(1), LPF.

1086 Article 204(5)(2), LPF.

1087 Article 204(7), LPF.

1088 Article 204(8), LPF.

1089 Article 204(9), LPF. See note 1079.

1090 Article 204c, LPF. See note 1079

1091 Article 204a(1), LPF.

1092 Article 204a(2)(1), LPF. See note 1079

1093 Article 204a(2)(2), LPF. See note 1079.

order to check whether this third party's activity in relation to the performance of these tasks complies with "the law" or the interests of members of the fund.[1094] Inspection activities shall be undertaken by at least two employees of the PFSA Office, each of whom shows a valid identity card and an authorisation (that the PFSA has issued) to conduct the inspection.[1095] The inspectors are entitled to inspect all books, documents and other items that contain data,[1096] require the preparation and provision of copies of these items,[1097] require the provision of information from members of statutory bodies, employees of the organisation inspected, or other persons who are connected with the entity inspected by a service agreement, agreement for specific work, or other similar legal relationship,[1098] or require that evidence is obtained.[1099] An inspector must prepare and sign an inspection report concerning the activities conducted, which the organisation inspected is also to sign.[1100] Within 14 days from the day of confirmation of delivery of an inspection report, the inspected entity may provide substantiated written objections and comments to the PFSA that relate to the contents of the report, and to its position in relation to the issues that the inspection has covered.[1101] The PFSA shall inform the organisation inspected on the way in which it is to consider the objections, within 14 days from the date on which it receives them.[1102] After an inspection report has been signed, the PFSA shall inform the entity inspected about any irregularities discovered, and shall set a time limit in which the organisation inspected is to rectify them.[1103] If "significant irregularities" are discovered during an inspection, then the PFSA may impose a fine on the organisation inspected of up to 500,000 zloty immediately after finding them.[1104]

Although the provision of information is not a 'capital movement' in the nomenclature in Annex I¸ the CJEU has held that investment transactions of Open Pension Funds are 'movements of capital' within the

---

[1094] Article 204a(2)(3), LPF. See note 1079.
[1095] Article 204a(4)-(5), LPF.
[1096] Article 204a(3)(1), LPF.
[1097] Article 204a(3)(2), LPF.
[1098] Article 204a(3)(3), LPF.
[1099] Article 204a(3)(4), LPF.
[1100] Article 204g(1), LPF.
[1101] Article 204i(1), LPF.
[1102] Article 204i(2), LPF.
[1103] Article 204j(1), LPF. Clauses 4-8 of Article 204 of the LPF shall apply accordingly (Article 204j(1), LPF). See above in this section, for Article 204(4)-(8) of the LPF.
[1104] Article 204j(2), LPF.

meaning of Article 63 of the TFEU.[1105] It is likely that the CJEU would hold that investment transactions of occupational funds and voluntary funds are 'movements of capital', too. Thus, cross-border restrictions on the investment transactions of pension funds limit the free movement of capital.[1106] The restrictive effect of these measures is augmented by enabling the PFSA to impose a fine for breach of Polish law and/or of the society's or the fund's articles of association.[1107] The empowerment of the Council of Ministers to impose additional limitations on investment by pension funds in order to protect the interests of their members, backed by a fine for breach of these provisions, also limits the free movement of capital.[1108] Furthermore, if an inspection of the relevant pension fund (or the society that manages it) reveals organisational procedures and/or practices that breach cross-border investment limitations that the LPF imposes, and if either the PFSA classifies these contraventions as "significant irregularities" or they are not rectified within the time scale that it lays down, then it will impose a fine on the organisation inspected.[1109] These processes (pursuant to the inspection) contravene the free movement of capital.

For these restrictive measures to be justified under Article 65(1) of the TFEU, they must be necessary for the protection of interests that they are intended to guarantee, be proportionate (i.e. not accomplishable by less restrictive measures), and observe the requirements of legal certainty (i.e. be specific, objective and known to the parties beforehand); furthermore, the persons whom the measures affect must have access to legal redress (i.e. intervention must be supported by a statement of reasons and be subject to review by the national courts).[1110] The protection of the interests of the members of the fund, and the rectification of breaches of Polish law and of the articles of association of the pension fund and of the society that manages it, are interests that (at least some) of the restrictive measures are intended to guarantee. The fines that the PFSA may impose under the LPF may be necessary for one or more of these purposes, and will probably be

---

[1105] *Commission v Poland* [2011] ECR I-13613. See section 2.1.1, and the subsection 'Chapter 2 Division 3: Activities of Foreign Insurance Undertakings in Estonia', in section 3.4.

[1106] See, in particular, Articles 142(2)(6), 143(2), 143(3) and 147 of the LPF, above in this section.

[1107] See Articles 149, 156 and 204 of the LPF, above in this section.

[1108] See Articles 155 and 204 of the LPF, above in this section.

[1109] See Article 204j of the LPF, above in this section.

[1110] See the subsection '*The requirements for a successful public policy/security derogation*', in section 2.1.3.

proportionate, as they are not excessive in amount. Nevertheless, the LPF grants discretion to the PFSA as to whether or not to impose a fine,[1111] and as to its size.[1112] Therefore, these measures are not specific and known to the parties beforehand, and, therefore, do not fulfil the requirements of legal certainty. Furthermore, the LPF does not require the PFSA to provide a formal statement of reasons for a decision that it addresses to a society, pension fund, or other entity, which instructs that entity to rectify irregularities or on which it imposes a fine; nor does the LPF provide the applicant entity with a right to appeal against this decision in the Polish courts. Hence, the persons affected by the restrictive measures do not have access to legal redress. Thus, Article 65(1) of the TFEU does not justify the restrictive measures.

A few of the restrictive measures affect countries outside the EEA,[1113] Furthermore, Articles 141(1)(3a) and 143 of the LPF exclude some third countries by virtue of their definitions.[1114] The CJEU may interpret this feature as discriminatory against those states. As Article 147 of the LPF empowers an occupational pension fund to exclude investments outside Poland by virtue of provisions in its articles of association,[1115] this Article enables the society which manages the occupational pension fund to forbid this fund from investing in financial instruments that entities resident in third countries have issued.

As these provisions limit the free movement of capital from Poland to third countries, Article 64(2) of the TFEU may apply. For Article 64(2) of the TFEU to justify the restrictive measures, the EU institutions must carefully take account of the objective of the free movement of capital whilst enacting the pertinent legislation, and the national rules must not restrict the free movement of capital more than do the provisions of the relevant Directive.[1116] The relevant Directive, Directive 2003/41/EC,

---

[1111] Under Articles 156, 204(8), 204(9) and 204j(2) of the LPF, the PFSA "may impose a fine" on the relevant entity.

[1112] Articles 156, 204(8), 204(9) and 204j(2) of the LPF permit the fine to be "up to PLN 500,000".

[1113] For instance, Article 142(2)(6) of the LPF affects members of the OECD, some of whom are not EEA states, and other third countries with which Poland has memoranda of understanding on the support and mutual protection of investments . See above in this section for Article 142(2)(6) of the LPF, and for Article 141(1)(3a) of the LPF, with which the investment limitation in Article 142(2)(6) of the LPF is concerned.

[1114] See above in this section, for Articles 141(1)(3a) and 143 of the LPF.

[1115] See above in this section, for Article 147 of the LPF.

[1116] See the subsection '*Derogations that apply only to capital movements to/from third countries*', in section 2.3.2.

contains no reference to the free movement of capital in its Articles. However, Recital 6 of Directive 2003/41/EC states that the Directive is a first step on the path to an internal market for occupational retirement provisions. Furthermore, Recital 32 of Directive 2003/41/EC acknowledges that, whilst Member States should be granted discretion to decide the particular investment rules which they wish to apply to the institutions that are situated on their territories, these rules must not limit the free movement of capital – unless this is "justified on prudential grounds". Thus, the EU institutions considered the free movement of capital whilst enacting Directive 2003/41/EC. Nonetheless, it is arguable that these institutions did not 'carefully took account of the objective of the free movement of capital', as this free movement is absent from the Directive's legal provisions. In addition, as Directive 2003/41/EC contains no provisions that mention countries outside the EEA, the Polish rules restrict the free movement of capital more than do the provisions of the relevant Directive (of which there are none). Hence, Article 64(2) of the TFEU does not justify the restrictive measures. Consequently, these measures breach Article 63 of the TFEU.

4.4.5 Act of 20 April 2004 on Occupational Pension Schemes (OPSA)

The OPSA defines the principles of the foundation and functioning of occupational pension schemes, the conditions that entities which introduce occupational pension schemes are to satisfy, and the terms of participation in occupational pension schemes.[1117] Persons who have been employed with an organisation for at least three months may participate in its occupational pension scheme, unless the relevant company pension scheme states otherwise.[1118] On the date of submission of an application for the registration of an occupational pension scheme, at least 50% of the applicant's employees must hold this right to take part in the scheme.[1119] A pension scheme may operate as a pension fund,[1120] "under an agreement on employer contributing employee's contributions to an investment

[1117] Article 1, OPSA.

[1118] Article 5(1), OPSA.

[1119] Article 5(2), OPSA. If the applicant has more than 500 employees, then at least one-third of these persons must have the right to take part in the occupational pension scheme (Articles 5(3) and 5(1), OPSA).

[1120] Article 6(1)(1), OPSA.

fund”,[1121] under a group life insurance contract – as group life insurance with an insurance capital fund,[1122] and as a scheme that a foreign manager operates.[1123]

A pension scheme may be founded by taking the following steps: 1) conclusion of a company or an inter-company pension scheme agreement,[1124] 2) conclusion of an agreement with a financial institution (subject to Article 17(3) of the OPSA),[1125] foundation of a pension fund company and a pension fund, or the employer’s acquisition of shares in an extant pension fund,[1126] and 3) registration of the pension scheme with the PFSA.[1127] The contractual terms and conditions that govern employees’ participation in a pension scheme must not contravene the provisions of the OPSA.[1128] If the pension scheme is to run as a scheme that a foreign manager operates, then the PFSA shall only register it if notified by the

---

[1121] Article 6(1)(2), OPSA. This description may refer to an investment fund that a company (or group of companies) sets up for the payment of pensions to its retired employees, into which both it as employer and its employees make regular contributions, as determined by the rules of the fund. An agreement to which Article 6(1)(2) of the OPSA refers may also be concluded by an employer with various investment funds that the same investment fund company manages – in which case an employee is permitted to change investment fund or apportion assets invested in these investment funds in accordance with the company’s pension scheme arrangement (Article 6(2), OPSA).

[1122] Article 6(1)(3), OPSA.

[1123] Article 6(1)(4), OPSA. A ‘foreign manager’ is a legal person whose registered office is situated in the territory of a Member State, which is supervised by that country’s financial supervision authority, and whose activity comprises the accumulation and investment of funds that are intended to be distributed to participants in pension schemes when they reach the age of retirement (Article 2(24), OPSA).

[1124] Article 10(1)(1), OPSA.

[1125] An employer is to enter into an agreement with a financial institution, which shall state the rules for the accumulation and management of assets (Article 17(1), OPSA). If an insurance undertaking is also an employer that sponsors and managers a pension scheme, then an agreement to which Article 17(1) of the OPSA refers is not to be concluded; the company pension scheme agreement shall contain the rules for the accumulation and the management of assets (Article 17(3), OPSA). An ‘insurance undertaking’ is a life insurance company that operates as a joint-stock company or a mutual insurance society (Article 2(3), OPSA).

[1126] Article 10(1)(2), OPSA. A ‘pension fund company’ is an occupational fund company within the meaning of the LPF (Article 2(5), OPSA). A ‘pension fund’ is an occupational pension fund within the meaning of the LPF (Article 2(6), OPSA).

[1127] Article 10(1)(3), OPSA.

[1128] Article 10(2), OPSA.

foreign supervisory authority of that manager's home Member State.[1129] Any disputes that arise from legal relationships between the parties to a company pension scheme agreement are to be resolved by the courts that have jurisdiction over the place in which the employer's registered office is located.[1130]

An employer shall register its pension scheme with the PFSA.[1131] Its application for registration of the pension scheme shall include the following details for both the employer and the scheme manager: the company or business name, the address of the registered office, the industry identification number, and the address for correspondence.[1132] The following documents shall be appended to the application: information concerning the authorisation of the employees' representatives to enter into the pension scheme agreement,[1133] a certificate which confirms that the employer is up to date with its obligatory social insurance contributions (that the Polish Social Insurance Institution (ZUS) issues),[1134] a certificate which confirms that the employer is up to date with the payment of its taxes,[1135] the pension scheme agreement,[1136] the pension fund's articles of association or an agreement with a financial institution,[1137] the form of the declaration that employees must complete on joining the pension scheme,[1138] a declaration by the employer that the terms and conditions that govern participation in the pension scheme comply with Articles 5(2) and 5(3) of the OPSA,[1139] and documents that

---

1129 Article 10(3), OPSA. This registration condition also applies, if a foreign manager takes over the management of an extant pension scheme (Article 10(3), OPSA). See note 1123, for the definition of 'foreign manager'. A 'foreign supervisory authority' is a national authority in a Member State, which this country has appointed to supervise the implementation of a pension scheme by an employer whose registered office is situated in the territory of another Member State (Article 2(24), OPSA).

1130 Article 12, OPSA.

1131 Article 29(1), OPSA. The PFSA shall maintain a register of pension schemes (Article 29(2), OPSA).

1132 Article 30(1), OPSA.

1133 Article 30(2)(1), OPSA.

1134 Article 30(2)(2), OPSA.

1135 Article 30(2)(3), OPSA.

1136 Article 30(2)(4), OPSA.

1137 Article 30(2)(5), OPSA. This information is required pursuant to Article 10(1)(2) of the OPSA. See above in this section, for Article 10(1)(2) of the OPSA.

1138 Article 30(2)(6), OPSA.

1139 Article 30(2)(7), OPSA. See note 1119 and accompanying text, for Articles 5(2) and 5(3) of the OPSA.

confirm the employer's details (to which Article 30(1) of the OPSA refers).[1140] If the PFSA receives notification from a foreign supervisory authority that the latter has approved a foreign manager's planned acquisition of the management of a Polish pension scheme, then it shall register the scheme in the register of pension schemes – as long as the application for registration of the scheme satisfies all of the criteria that the OPSA defines.[1141]

The PFSA shall exert supervision over pension schemes in respect of "their compliance with the law".[1142] A foreign manager is subject to supervision by the PFSA in respect of the compliance of its pension scheme management activities with Polish law.[1143] If the PFSA obtains information that provides grounds for suspicion that there have been irregularities in the operation of a pension scheme, then it has the right to require from the employer, or the scheme manager, any relevant documents, information and explanations.[1144] If the PFSA finds any irregularities in the operation of a pension scheme, then it shall notify the employer of this fact, and shall require the latter to rectify these difficulties by a specified deadline, which shall be at least 14 days hence.[1145] If the employer does not remove these deficiencies by this time limit, then the PFSA may impose on it a fine of up to 50,000 zloty.[1146] The PFSA shall take into account the type and significance of the irregularities that it has found.[1147]

If the PFSA finds irregularities in the implementation of a pension scheme by an insurance undertaking, an investment fund, or a pension fund, then it shall apply measures for which the applicable laws provide.[1148] If the PFSA discovers irregularities in the implementation of a

---

[1140] Article 30(2)(8), OPSA. See the previous sentence, for Article 30(1) of the OPSA.

[1141] Article 35a, OPSA. See notes 1123 and 1129, respectively, for the definitions of 'foreign manager' and 'foreign supervisory authority'.

[1142] Article 36(1), OPSA. "The law" probably means any provisions of Polish law.

[1143] Article 36(1a), OPSA. See note 1123, for the definition of 'foreign manager'.

[1144] Article 36(2), OPSA.

[1145] Article 36(3), OPSA.

[1146] Article 36(4), OPSA.

[1147] Article 36(5), OPSA.

[1148] Articles 36(6)(1), 2(3), 2(4) and 2(6), OPSA. See note 1125, for the definition of 'insurance undertaking'. An 'investment fund' is an open-end investment fund or a specialist open-end investment fund, as defined in the IFA (Article 2(4), OPSA). See section 4.1, for a description of an 'open-end investment fund'. The IFA does not define the term 'specialised open-end investment fund' (see note 6). See note 1126, for the definition of 'pension fund'. The 'applicable laws' are the IAA for insurance undertakings, the IFA for investment funds, and the LPF for

pension scheme by a foreign manager, then the PFSA shall immediately report these difficulties to the "relevant financial supervisory authority".[1149]

The PFSA shall prepare information on the requirements under the Polish social insurance and labour laws that apply to a foreign manager which takes over the management of the assets of an occupational pension scheme.[1150] The PFSA shall supply this information to the "relevant foreign supervisory authority", within 2 months of its receipt of the notification to which Article 35a of the OPSA refers.[1151] The registration of an occupational pension scheme, a refusal to register an occupational pension scheme, the imposition of a fine, and the removal of an occupational pension scheme from the register of pension schemes, amongst other things, shall be brought into effect by means of an administrative decision.[1152]

The nomenclature in Annex I does not explicitly include pensions as a 'capital movement'. Nevertheless, pensions might be included in Title XIIIF (Other Capital Movements – Miscellaneous) of the nomenclature, and the list of capital movements in the nomenclature is "not exhaustive".[1153]

Since the same standard is applied to the registration of a Polish occupational pension fund if the management of its assets is to be performed by a foreign manager, as to the registration of a Polish occupational fund if a manager that is registered in Poland is to undertake the management of the fund's assets,[1154] the registration requirements of

---

pension funds (Articles 2(3), 2(4) and 2(6), OPSA). For the IAA, the IFA and the LPF, see sections 4.4.1, 4.1 and 4.4.4, respectively.

[1149] Articles 36(6)(2) and 2(24), OPSA. See notes 1123 and 1129, respectively, for the definitions of 'foreign manager' and 'foreign supervisory authority'. The quoted phrase means the financial supervision authority of the foreign manager's home Member State.

[1150] Article 36(7), OPSA. See note 1123, for the definition of 'foreign manager'.

[1151] Article 36(8), OPSA. See note 1129, for the definition of 'foreign supervisory authority'. See note 1149, for an interpretation of the quoted phrase. See above in this section, for Article 35a of the OPSA.

[1152] Article 37(1), OPSA. These 'other things' are the entry of changes into the register of pension schemes, a refusal to enter changes into this register, and the approval of, and a refusal to approve, suspension of the calculation and allotment of basic contributions to occupational pension schemes (Article 37(1), OPSA).

[1153] *Trummer and Mayer* [1999] ECR I-1661. See section 2.1.1. See also the subsection '*Chapter 6 Division 3: Cross-border Offer of Occupational Pension Funds*', in section 3.1.

[1154] See above in this section, especially Article 35a of the OPSA.

the OPSA for occupational pension funds do not restrict the free movement of capital.[1155] However, a refusal to register an occupational pension scheme, the imposition of a fine, and the removal of an occupational pension scheme from the register of pension schemes are limitations on the free movement of capital – if the operation of a pension fund is held to be a 'capital movement'.[1156]

For Article 65(1)(b) of the TFEU to justify the restrictive measures, they must be necessary for the protection of the interests that they are intended to guarantee, be proportionate, and observe the requirements of legal certainty (i.e. be specific, objective and known to the parties beforehand); in addition, the persons whom the measures affect must have access to legal redress (i.e. intervention must be accompanied by a formal statement of reasons and be subject to review in the national courts).[1157] As the PFSA is to take into account the type and significance of the irregularities, in its assessment of the size of a fine (of up to 50,000 zloty) to impose on an employer for the non-removal of these breaches of Polish law,[1158] then this measure is, to an extent, specific and objective, thereby providing a degree of legal certainty to the employer. However, the PFSA gives no guidance in relation to the refusal to register an occupational pension scheme, and to the removal of an occupational pension scheme from the register of pensions. These measures lack legal certainty. Furthermore, the OPSA neither requires the PFSA to provide a formal statement of reasons for a decision to impose a fine, refuse to register an occupational pension scheme, or remove an occupational pension scheme from the register of pensions, nor grants the applicant the right to appeal against such a decision in the Polish courts. Hence, the persons whom the measures affect do not have access to legal redress.

Thus, if the CJEU classifies the provision of an occupational pension scheme as a 'capital movement', then the OPSA imposes measures that limit these capital movements. These restrictive measures are not justified by Article 65(1)(b) of the TFEU, and, therefore, contravene Article 63 of the TFEU. As the OPSA does not consider the provision of occupational pension schemes to or from third countries, the justification in Article 64(1) of the TFEU in respect of capital movements to and from third countries does not need to be considered in the context of the OPSA.

[1155] See section 2.1.2, especially the first paragraph of that section.

[1156] See the previous paragraph.

[1157] See the subsection '*The requirements for a successful public policy/security derogation*', in section 2.1.3.

[1158] See above in this section, in particular Articles 36(4) and 36(5) of the OPSA.

4.5 Act of 19 August 2011 on Payment Services (PSA)

The PSA contains the rules for the supply of payment services, which include the conditions for the provision of payment services,[1159] the rights and obligations of the parties that arise out of contracts for the supply of payment services and the extent of the responsibilities of providers in respect of payment services,[1160] the principles of conduct of the business of payment service offices and payment institutions,[1161] and the principles of supervision of these offices and institutions.[1162] 'Payment services' are the acceptance of cash deposits into, and the making of cash withdrawals from, a payment account, and all of the operations that are required for the maintenance of a payment account,[1163] execution of payment transactions[1164] – including direct debits,[1165] transactions by payment

---

[1159] Article 1(1), PSA.

[1160] Article 1(2), PSA.

[1161] Article 1(3), PSA. A 'payment institution' is a Polish payment institution or an EU payment institution (Article 2(8), PSA). An 'EU payment institution' is a legal person to which the competent supervisory authorities have issued an authorisation to supply payment services (Article 2(32), PSA). 'Competent supervisory authorities' are authorities of Member States other than Poland that are empowered by laws in force in those Member States to issue authorisations for the provision of payment services by EU payment institutions (Article 2(35), PSA). 'Member State' means a Member State of the EU or of the European Free Trade Association, or a Contracting Party to the EEA Agreement (Article 2(21), PSA). Iceland, Liechtenstein and Norway are Member States of the European Free Trade Association and Contracting Parties to the EEA Agreement. Switzerland is a Member State of the European Free Trade Association, but is not a Contracting Party to the EEA Agreement.

[1162] Article 1(3), PSA.

[1163] Article 3(1)(1), PSA. 'Payment account' means an account that is maintained for the execution of payment transactions (Article 2(26), PSA). A 'payment transaction' is an act that a payer or payee initiates for the placement, transferral or withdrawal of funds (Article 2(29), PSA). A 'payer' is a natural or legal person, or an organisational unit that is not a legal person on which the law confers legal capability, who places a payment order (Article 2(22), PSA). A 'payee' is a natural or legal person, or an organisational unit that is not a legal person on which the law confers legal capability, who is the recipient of funds that are subject to a payment transaction (Article 2(18), PSA).

[1164] Article 3(1)(2), PSA.

[1165] Article 3(1)(2)(a), PSA. 'Direct debit' means a payment service that consists of debiting by a specified amount a payer's payment account, so as to effect a payment transaction that a payee initiates, which is carried out on the basis of

card,[1166] and standing orders,[1167] execution of these payment transactions in cases in which the funds made available to the user come from credit,[1168] the issuance of payment instructions,[1169] the conclusion of contracts with businesses for the acceptance of payments – with the use of payment instructions,[1170] the supply of money remittance services,[1171] and the execution of payment transactions in cases in which the payer's consent to execute a payment transaction is provided by means of any telecommunication, digital or information technology device and the payment is transferred only to an intermediary between the user and the payee.[1172]

Only the following entities may be payment service providers and, therefore, supply payment services:[1173] a bank whose registered office is in Poland,[1174] a foreign bank's branch,[1175] a credit institution,[1176] a credit institution's branch,[1177] an electronic money institution,[1178] a branch of an entity that provides postal payment services in a Member State other than Poland and is authorised so to do (in accordance with that Member State's law)[1179] the Polish Post Office in so far as it is authorised to supply

---

consent that the payer extends to the payee, the payee's payment service provider, or the payer's payment service provider (Article 3(2), PSA).

[1166] Article 3(1)(2)(b), PSA.

[1167] Article 3(1)(2)(c), PSA.

[1168] Article 3(1)(3), PSA. A 'user' is a natural or legal person, or an organisational unit that is not a legal person on which the law confers legal capability, who uses payment services either as a payer or a payee (Article 2(34), PSA).

[1169] Article 3(1)(4), PSA.

[1170] Article 3(1)(5), PSA.

[1171] Article 3(1)(6), PSA. 'Money remittance' means a payment service which is provided without the intermediation of a payment account that is maintained for the payer, which comprises the transfer to the payee or to another payment service provider which accepts funds for the payee, of funds that are received from the payer or that comprise the acceptance of funds for the payee, and their release to the payee (Article 3(3), PSA).

[1172] Article 3(1)(7), PSA.

[1173] Article 4(1), PSA.

[1174] Articles 4(2)(1), PSA and 4(1)(1), BL.

[1175] Article 4(2)(2), PSA. See note 577, for the definition of 'branch of a foreign bank'.

[1176] Article 4(2)(3), PSA. See notes 48 and 371, for the definition of 'credit institution'.

[1177] Article 4(2)(3), PSA. See note 609, for the definition of 'branch of a credit institution'.

[1178] Article 4(2)(4), PSA.

[1179] Article 4(2)(5), PSA. See note 1161, for the definition of 'Member State'.

payment services,[1180] a payment institution,[1181] the European Central Bank, the National Bank of Poland, or a central bank of another Member State (if they are not acting in their roles of organ of public administration or monetary authority),[1182] a public administration body,[1183] a co-operative savings and credit union or the (Polish) National Co-operative Savings and Credit Union – in so far as it is authorised to provide payment services,[1184] and a payment service office.[1185] Polish payment institutions, payment service offices, and branches and agencies of these entities, as well as savings and credit unions and their affiliated persons, are subject to registration in the registry of Polish payment institutions and other providers (hereafter 'the register').[1186]

Payment institutions and payment service offices may not carry out the business of taking repayable funds within the meaning of the BL.[1187] Funds that are placed into a payment account in a payment institution may neither "bear interest" nor "bring any other benefits".[1188]

Regulations of contracts for payment services that are less favourable than the PSA for the user, are invalid.[1189] In their place, the relevant provisions of the PSA shall apply.[1190]

The supply of payment services by a Polish payment institution, must be authorised by the PFSA.[1191] Authorisation may be provided to a legal person whose registered office is in Poland, upon its application.[1192] An application for authorisation must contain current information about the

---

[1180] Article 4(2)(5), PSA.

[1181] Article 4(2)(6), PSA. See note 1161, for the definition of 'payment institution'.

[1182] Article 4(2)(7), PSA.

[1183] Article 4(2)(8), PSA.

[1184] Article 4(2)(9), PSA.

[1185] Article 4(2)(10), PSA.

[1186] Article 4(3), PSA. An 'agent' is a natural or legal person, or an organisational unit that is not a legal person on which the law confers legal capability, who acts for, or on behalf of, a payment service office or a payment institution in the provision of payment services (Article 2(1), PSA).

[1187] Article 7(2), PSA. Funds that payment institutions and payment services offices receive from users in association with the provision of payment services, shall not be 'repayable funds' within the meaning of Article 726 of the Polish Civil Code of 23 April 1964 (Article 7(1), PSA).

[1188] Article 7(3), PSA. See note 1163, for the definition of 'payment account'.

[1189] Article 8(1), PSA.

[1190] Article 8(1), PSA.

[1191] Article 60(1), PSA. See note 1161, for the definition of 'payment institution'.

[1192] Article 60(2), PSA.

number of the applicant's entry in the National Court Register,[1193] the applicant's statutes or memorandum and articles of incorporation,[1194] a schedule of the payment services that the applicant intends to provide,[1195] a financial plan and a programme of operations for a period of at least three years,[1196] documents that confirm that the applicant has funds which have been allocated to own funds,[1197] a description of the applicant's governance and internal control mechanisms that concern duties related to the prevention of money laundering and terrorist financing, in accordance with the Act on Countering Money Laundering and the Financing of Terrorism of 16 November 2000,[1198] a description of the applicant's organisational arrangements to which Articles 64(1)(3) and 64(1)(4) of the PSA refer,[1199] information that makes it possible to discover the identity of persons who have a substantial shareholding in the company or co-operative that intends to provide payments services – which must indicate (for each significant shareholding) the size of the holding – and documents that confirm that these shareholders ensure prudent and sound management

---

[1193] Article 61(1)(1), PSA.
[1194] Article 61(1)(2), PSA.
[1195] Article 61(1)(3), PSA.
[1196] Article 61(1)(4), PSA.
[1197] Article 61(1)(5), PSA.
[1198] Article 61(1)(6), PSA.
[1199] Article 61(1)(7), PSA. Article 64(1)(3) of the PSA refers to organisational arrangements that are "adequate", considering the type of payment services, their complexity, and their scale, including effective procedures for the identification, monitoring, reporting and management of risks to which the applicant is, or may be, exposed, an organisational structure that has consistent and transparent lines of responsibility, and sufficient internal control mechanisms (including those for countering money laundering and terrorist financing, and accounting and administrative procedures). Article 64(1)(4) of the PSA refers to organisational arrangements that are made to protect the funds of users, in accordance with Article 78 of the PSA. If a Polish payment institution accepts funds from users for the execution of payment transactions, then it must keep them safely in accordance with the following principles: 1) funds that are accepted for the carrying out of payment transactions may not, at any time during their safekeeping, be combined with funds that the payment institution holds for other purposes, and 2) funds that are accepted for the execution of payment transactions, which have not been transferred to the payee or another payment service provider by the end of the business day that follows the date of receipt of these funds, shall be placed in a separate bank account which is established for this purpose, or invested in safe, liquid assets of low risk that are deposited in a separate account which is opened for this purpose (Article 78(1), PSA).

of the payment institution,[1200] information that permits the identification of managers and documents which make it possible to evaluate whether these persons ensure prudent and sound management of the payment institution – including whether they possess the education and professional experience that is required for the management of operations which relate to the supply of payment services,[1201] and information that permits persons who are authorised to audit accounts to be identified.[1202]

A Polish payment institution may provide payment services under the authorisation in Article 60(1) of the PSA, on the territory of another (i.e. non-Polish) Member State, through a branch, "in the course of cross-border business", or via an agent.[1203] A Polish payment institution shall inform the PFSA of its intention to provide cross-border payment services.[1204] This notification must identify each payment service that the payment institution intends to supply, and the names of the Member States in which the institution intends to provide cross-border services.[1205] The PFSA shall forward the notification to the competent supervisory authorities of the host Member States within one month of its receipt, and shall inform the Polish payment institution that it has done so.[1206]

The institution shall inform the PFSA in writing of its intention to provide payment services in another Member State through a branch or an agent, and shall request that the branch or agent be entered in the register.[1207] This notification shall contain the name of the Member State on the territory of which the Polish payment institution intends to supply

---

1200 Article 61(1)(8), PSA.

1201 Article 61(1)(9), PSA.

1202 Article 61(1)(10), PSA.

1203 Article 91, PSA. See above in this section, for a description of 'payment services'. See note 1161, for the definition of 'Member State'. See the previous paragraph, for Article 60(1) of the PSA. See note 1186, for the definition of 'agent'.

1204 Article 95(1), PSA.

1205 Article 95(1), PSA.

1206 Article 95(2), PSA. See note 1161, for the definition of 'competent supervisory authorities'. 'Host Member State' means a Member State, apart from the home Member State, in which a payment service provider supplies payment services (Article 2(6), PSA). 'Home Member State' means the Member State in which a payment service provider's registered office is located, or (if the payment service provider has no registered office under its national law) the Member State in which its head office is situated (Article 2(17), PSA). See note 1161, for the definition of 'Member State'.

1207 Article 92(1), PSA. See note 1161, for the definition of 'Member State'. See note 1186, for the definition of 'agent'.

payment services,[1208] the payment institution's name, registered office, and address,[1209] the name and address of the branch or agent,[1210] a description of the branch's organisational structure,[1211] a description of the internal control mechanisms that are related to the prevention of money laundering and terrorist financing (in accordance with the Act on Countering Money Laundering and the Financing of Terrorism of 16 November 2000),[1212] the names of the persons who are responsible for the management of the branch or "the business of the agent",[1213] and a list of the payment services that the Polish payment institution intends to provide in the host Member State.[1214] If the notification does not fulfil these requirements, then the PFSA gives the applicant a specified time in which to supplement it accordingly.[1215] Within one month of the date of the receipt of the notification (or of the supplementary information), the PFSA shall forward this notification to the competent supervisory authorities of the host Member State or, shall take a decision to refuse to forward it.[1216] The PFSA shall refuse to forward the notification to these authorities, if the notification does not satisfy the requirements in Article 92(2) of the PSA and the supplementary information was not forthcoming within the designated time period,[1217] the branch's organisational structure is "inadequate" for the payment services that the applicant intends to provide through it in the host Member State,[1218] the branch's planned business or the provision of payment services via an agent would contravene "the

---

[1208] Article 92(2)(1), PSA.
[1209] Article 92(2)(2), PSA.
[1210] Article 92(2)(3), PSA. Article 92(2)(3) of the PSA reads "the name (or brand) and address of the branch or the forename and surname or the name (or brand) of the agent and the registered office and address or place of residence and address and the address of the principal place of business", which is difficult to clarify for readers. The legislators or translators should specify which requirements apply to a branch, which requirements apply to an agent that is a natural person, and which requirements apply to an agent that is a legal person.
[1211] Article 92(2)(4), PSA.
[1212] Article 92(2)(5), PSA.
[1213] Article 92(2)(6), PSA.
[1214] Article 92(2)(7), PSA. See note 1206, for the definition of 'host Member State'.
[1215] Article 92(3), PSA.
[1216] Article 92(4), PSA. See note 1161, for the definition of 'competent supervisory authorities'.
[1217] Article 92(5)(1), PSA.
[1218] Article 92(5)(2), PSA.

regulations of the law",[1219] or the PFSA possesses information which suggests that there are reasonable grounds on which to suspect that the applicant's provision of payment services in the host Member State is associated with the committing of an offence under Articles 165a or 299 of the Penal Code of 6 June 1997 – or that the supply of payment services through a branch or via an agent could increase the risk of money laundering or terrorist financing.[1220] If, within 30 days of the date on which the PFSA has forwarded the notification to the competent supervisory authorities of the host Member State, these authorities have not raised objections, then the PFSA shall enter the branch or the agent in the register.[1221] If objections are received, then the PFSA may refuse to enter the branch or the agent in the register.[1222] The PFSA shall inform the applicant Polish payment institution that it has entered the branch or the agent in the register.[1223]

An EU payment institution may provide payment services on Polish territory through a branch, via an agent, or as cross-border activity, over the area that the authorisation issued by the competent supervisory authorities covers.[1224] An EU payment institution may start to supply cross-border services in Poland, after the PFSA receives from the competent supervisory authorities of the home Member State a notification that contains the name, the registered office, and the address of the EU payment institution, and a schedule of the payment services that the payment institution intends to provide as cross-border services.[1225]

An EU payment institution may start to provide payment services in Poland through a branch or via an agent located there, one month after the date on which the PFSA receives from the competent supervisory authorities of the home Member State the following information: the name of the branch or the name and address in Poland of the agent at which it will be possible to obtain documents concerning the payment institution's

[1219] Article 92(5)(3), PSA. The quoted phrase probably means the relevant provisions of Polish law.

[1220] Article 92(5)(4), PSA.

[1221] Article 93(1), PSA.

[1222] Article 93(1), PSA.

[1223] Article 93(2), PSA. The PFSA may refuse to make an entry in the register for a branch or agent of a payment institution, if the conditions in Article 92(5)(4) of the PSA are present (Article 93(3), PSA). See above in this paragraph, for Article 92(5)(4) of the PSA.

[1224] Article 96, PSA. See note 1161, for the definitions of 'EU payment institution' and 'competent supervisory authorities'. See note 1186, for the definition of 'agent'. See above in this section, for a description of 'payment services'.

[1225] Article 98, PSA. See note 1206, for the definition of 'home Member State'.

activities,[1226] a description of the branch's organisational structure and the internal control mechanisms that concern obligations which relate to the branch's or the agent's prevention of money laundering and terrorist financing,[1227] the names of the persons who are responsible for the management of the branch or of the agent's business,[1228] and a schedule of the payment services that the EU payment institution wishes to provide in Poland (through the branch or the agent).[1229] The PFSA shall inform the competent supervisory authority of the home Member State, if the PFSA has reasonable grounds to suspect that the EU payment institution's intended provision of payment services through the branch or the agent is associated with the commission of an offence under Articles 165a or 299 of the Penal Code, or that the start of the suppliance of services by the branch or via the agent could increase the risk of money laundering or terrorist financing.[1230]

Activities in the field of payment services that Polish payment institutions carry out, including through their agencies, and entities that perform specified operational functions on the basis of an agreement in Article 86(1) of the PSA,[1231] are subject to supervision by the PFSA on the principles that the PSA and the Act of Financial Market Supervision contain.[1232] The purposes of the supervision are to make sure that Polish payment institutions are financially secure,[1233] to ensure that the activities of Polish payment institutions, their agents and their outsourcees, comply with the provisions of Regulation (EC) No 924/2009 of the European Parliament and of the Council of 16 September 2009 on cross-border payments in the Community and with the authorisation that Article 60(1) of the PSA introduces,[1234] and to protect the interests of users.[1235] Activities that the PFSA undertakes as part of supervision include an assessment of a Polish payment institution's financial situation,[1236] a study

---

[1226] Article 97(1)(1), PSA.

[1227] Article 97(1)(2), PSA.

[1228] Article 97(1)(3), PSA.

[1229] Article 97(1)(4), PSA.

[1230] Article 97(3), PSA.

[1231] A Polish payment institution may, on the basis of a contract made in writing with another entrepreneur, outsource to that person "the performance of specific operational functions" which relate to the provision of payment services (Article 86(1), PSA).

[1232] Article 99(1), PSA.

[1233] Article 99(2)(1), PSA.

[1234] Article 99(2)(2), PSA. See above in this section, for Article 60(1) of the PSA.

[1235] Article 99(2)(3), PSA. See note 1168, for the definition of 'user'.

[1236] Article 100(1), PSA.

of the quality of a Polish payment institution's management system (including the internal control system),[1237] and a study of the "correctness" of operations that are associated with the provision of payment services.[1238] As part of the exercise of its supervision, the PFSA shall request a Polish payment institution to forward within a prescribed time information that is necessary to achieve the objectives of supervision in Article 99(2) of the PSA,[1239] require a Polish payment institution to periodically report specified information that is needed for assessment of the payment institution's financial situation,[1240] make recommendations to a Polish payment institution that concern i) ensuring the conformity of the payment institution's activities with the provisions of Regulation (EC) No 924/2009 of the European Parliament and of the Council of 16 September 2009 on cross-border payments in the Community,[1241] ii) increasing own funds – if their quantity is less than would result from the PSA or from the decision to which Article 76(7) of the PSA refers,[1242] iii) the taking of measures that are required to achieve and maintain the standards that Articles 64(1)[1243] and 76 of the PSA contain,[1244] iv) the creation and

---

[1237] Article 100(2), PSA.

[1238] Article 100(3), PSA.

[1239] Article 102(1)(1), PSA. See above in this section, for Article 99(2) of the PSA.

[1240] Article 102(1)(2), PSA.

[1241] Article 102(1)(3)(a), PSA.

[1242] Article 102(1)(3)(b), PSA. The PFSA may issue a decision, on the basis of risk analysis and assessment of the internal control mechanisms and risk management processes of a Polish payment institution, that requires the payment institution to increase its own funds (but not to more than 120% of the amount to which Article 76(4)(2) of the PSA refers), or allows the payment institution to lower the quantity of its own funds (but not to less than 80% of the amount to which Article 76(4)(2) of the PSA refers) (Article 76(7), PSA). The amount of a Polish payment institution's own funds must be at least the higher of (1) the minimum value of initial capital that Article 64(1)(1) of the PSA requires, and (2) the quantity computed in accordance with regulations that are issued on the basis of Article 76(6) of the PSA (Article 76(4), PSA). The minister who is responsible for financial institutions shall, after consulting the PFSA, issue a regulation to determine the method to be used for calculating the amount to which Article 76(4)(2) of the PSA refers, taking into consideration the total value of payment transactions that the Polish payment institution has performed during the most recent financial year, and the type of payment services that this institution may supply on the basis of the authorisation that it possesses (Article 76(6), PSA).

[1243] The authorisation to which Article 60(1) of the PSA refers may be issued to entities that 1) have initial capital of the equivalent in zloty of a) 125,000 EUR – if the applicant intends to provide all or several of the payment services that Article 3 of the PSA lists, b) 50,000 EUR – if the applicant intends to supply only the

application of procedures in order to ensure the maintenance and on-going monitoring of the level of own funds,[1245] and v) the taking of measures in order to prevent contravention of the interests of users,[1246] order a Polish payment institution to stop the distribution of its own profits or to cease the establishment of new organisational units – pending achievement of the standards that Articles 64(1)(1) and 76 of the PSA contain,[1247] and instruct a Polish payment institution to create and implement a plan "for the restoration of correct financial relations".[1248] The PFSA may issue recommendations that concern good practice in the stable and prudent management of Polish payment institutions, taking in account the protection of users' interests.[1249]

---

payment services that Article 3(1)(7) of the PSA contains, and c) 20,000 EUR – if the applicant intends to supply only the payment service of money remittance, 2) possess funds that are dedicated to the required amount of own funds, 3) ensure sound and prudent management of operations in the field of the suppliance of payment services, by having organisational arrangements that are sufficient given the type of payment services, their scale and their complexity, including a) effective procedures for the identification, monitoring, management and reporting of risks to which the applicant is or may be exposed, b) an organisational structure with consistent and transparent lines of responsibility, and c) satisfactory control mechanisms, and 4) have organisational arrangements that are designed to protect users' funds in accordance with Article 78 of the PSA (Article 64(1), PSA). See above in this section, for Article 3 of the PSA. Article 78 of the PSA states the responsibilities of Polish payment institutions for the safekeeping of users' funds, and bank guarantees or equivalent in lieu of these duties.

[1244] Article 102(1)(3)(c), PSA. Article 76 of the PSA contains provisions that regulate the maintenance of own funds by a Polish payment institution. Such a payment institution must possess at all times own funds that are appropriate for the size of the firm's business, and the type of payment services that it may provide on the basis of the authorisation it holds (Article 76(1), PSA). A Polish payment institution's funds consist of initial capital, revaluation reserves, and retained profit (Article 76(2), PSA). Own funds are lowered by shares in the payment institution that are held by this institution, all liabilities that relate to preference shares, intangible assets, losses from earlier years, "losses during the course of approval" and net losses for the current financial period (Article 76(3), PSA).

[1245] Article 102(1)(3)(d), PSA.

[1246] Article 102(1)(3)(e), PSA.

[1247] Article 102(1)(4), PSA. See notes 1243 and 1244, respectively, for Articles 64(1) and 76 of the PSA.

[1248] Article 102(1)(5), PSA.

[1249] Article 102(2), PSA.

The PFSA may carry out an inspection of the activities and of the financial circumstances of a Polish payment institution.[1250] As part of this inspection, the PFSA may assess the activities and financial situation of an agent (through the intermediation of which the payment institution supplies payment services) or of an entity that conducts operational functions on the basis of an outsourcing contract (as contained in Article 86(1) of the PSA).[1251] Employees of the PFSA Office shall conduct this inspection, after they have each presented a PFSA identification card and evidence of an authorisation that the Chairman of the PFSA (or his authorised delegate) has issued.[1252] These authorised employees shall (in the area that the authorisation specifies) have the right to enter the premises of the entity that is being inspected,[1253] free access to communication facilities and to separate office accommodation,[1254] examine documents of the organisation being inspected and require copies to be made and excerpts to be taken from these documents,[1255] and examine data that are contained in the information technology system of the entity being inspected and require the making of copies and the taking of excerpts from these data.[1256]

If a branch or an agent of a Polish payment institution in another Member State is to be inspected, then the PFSA shall (before each inspection) inform the competent supervisory authorities of this host Member State of its intention to perform the inspection at the premises of the branch or agent.[1257] Article 103 of the PSA shall apply to branches of EU payment institutions and their agents that operate in Poland, if it is agreed with the competent supervisory authorities of the home Member State that the PFSA is to conduct an inspection.[1258]

If the PFSA determines that a Polish payment institution does not (adequately) satisfy its obligation to provide the information that Article

[1250] Article 103(1), PSA.

[1251] Article 103(2), PSA. See note 1231, for Article 86(1) of the PSA.

[1252] Article 103(3), PSA.

[1253] Article 103(4)(1), PSA.

[1254] Article 103(4)(2), PSA.

[1255] Article 103(4)(3), PSA.

[1256] Article 103(4)(4), PSA.

[1257] Articles 104(1) and 109, PSA. The PFSA may delegate to the competent supervisory authorities of the host Member State, the task of performing inspections at the premises of the branch or agent (Article 104(2), PSA). See note 1206, for the definition of 'host Member State'. See note 1161, for the definition of 'competent supervisory authorities'.

[1258] Article 104(3), PSA. See note 1161, for the definition of 'EU payment institution'.

102(1)(1) of the PSA specifies or the information that Article 102(1)(2) of the PSA requires, has not implemented within the prescribed time period the recommendations to which Article 102(1)(3) of the PSA refers, is making it difficult or impossible to conduct an inspection in accordance with Article 103 of the PSA, or has not carried out the orders of the PFSA that Articles 102(1)(4) and 102(1)(5) of the PSA specify,[1259] and/or if the business of a Polish payment institution is conducted in contravention of "the law"[1260] or pressurises the interests of users, then the PFSA may (subject to Article 106 of the PSA):[1261] request the Polish payment institution to dismiss the manager who is directly responsible for the irregularities detected,[1262] suspend the exercise of this manager's functions, pending the Polish payment institution's adoption of a resolution on the request for his/her dismissal,[1263] restrict the Polish payment institution's area of activities or its organisational units,[1264] impose on the manager who is directly responsible for the irregularities identified a monetary penalty of up to three time his/her gross monthly remuneration,[1265] impose a monetary penalty of up to 1 million zloty on the Polish payment institution,[1266] or[1267] withdraw the payment

[1259] For Articles 102(1) and 103 of the PSA, see the previous paragraph.
[1260] "The law" probably means relevant provisions of Polish law.
[1261] See the next paragraph, for Article 106 of the PSA.
[1262] Article 105(1)(1), PSA.
[1263] Article 105(1)(2), PSA.
[1264] Article 105(1)(3), PSA. A decision of the PFSA to restrict the Polish payment institution's activities may include conditions and time limits (Article 105(5), PSA).
[1265] Article 105(1)(4), PSA. See note 1265.
[1266] Article 105(1)(5), PSA. In setting the amount of this penalty, the PFSA shall take into account the nature and the seriousness of the transgression, the scale of the business carried out, and the Polish payment institution's financial circumstances (Article 105(2), PSA). "The regulation of Article 2 shall apply *mutatis mutandis* to the penalty spoken of in paragraph 1 point 4 [of Article 105 of the PSA]" (Article 105(3), PSA); as Article 2 of the PSA contains definitions that the PSA uses, Article 105(3) of the PSA may mean that Article 105(2) of the PSA applies to the monetary penalty that Article 105(1)(2) of the PSA imposes on the manager – but scaled according the maximum possible sum of this penalty in the particular case. A decision of the PFSA to impose a monetary penalty shall set a time limit before which the sum due must be paid (Article 105(5), PSA).
[1267] Whilst Article 105(1) in this English translation of the PSA states "or", the PFSA might be permitted to take more than one of the six actions that this paragraph recommends.

institution's authorisation (for which Article 60(1) of the PSA provides).[1268]

Information that concerns a payment institution and the payment services that it provides, must be presented for publication "in a fair and understandable manner".[1269] If the dissemination of this information is misleading, or may be misleading, then the PFSA may issue a recommendation to the payment institution to cease distribution of the information,[1270] and/or issue a decision to order the payment institution to publish a correction (the content of which the PFSA may specify), in a specified form and within a stipulated time period,[1271] If the payment institution does not comply with this decision, then the PFSA may issue a (further) decision, to impose on the manager who is directly responsible for non-compliance with the (first) decision a monetary penalty of up to three times his/her gross monthly remuneration,[1272] or impose on the payment institution a penalty of up to 1 million zloty.[1273]

If an EU payment institution or its agent in Poland contravenes Polish law, then the PFSA shall require the institution in writing to adhere to the provisions of this law, and shall set a time limit for the rectification of the irregularities that it has discovered,[1274] and, if this time limit expires without change, shall inform the competent supervisory authorities of the home Member State of the irregularities that it has detected.[1275] If the breach of Polish law concerns the provisions of Parts II and III of the

---

1268 Article 105(1)(6), PSA. If the PFSA revokes the payment institution's authorisation, then it shall immediately notify the competent supervisory authorities of the host Member State (Article 105(7), PSA). See above in this section, for Article 60(1) of the PSA.

1269 Article 73, PSA.

1270 Article 106(1)(1), PSA.

1271 Article 106(1)(2), PSA.

1272 Article 106(2)(1), PSA. See note 1273.

1273 Article 106(2)(2), PSA. Articles 105(2), 105(4) and 105(5) of the PSA shall apply *mutatis mutandis* to the imposition of these financial penalties (Article 106(3), PSA). See note 1266, for Articles 105(2) and 105(5) of the PSA. Article 105(4) of the PSA requires all the measures in Article 105(1) of the PSA to take effect by the issue of a decision (other than Article 105(1)(1)), and states that the decisions in Article 105(1) of the PSA which impose non-financial sanctions on the payment institution are to take immediate effect.

1274 Article 107(1)(1), PSA.

1275 Article 107(1)(2), PSA. See note 1161, for the definitions of 'EU payment institution' and 'competent supervisory authorities'. See note 1186, for the definition of 'agent'. See note 1206, for the definition of 'host Member State'.

PSA,[1276] then the PFSA may apply the measures in Articles 105(1) and 105(3) of the PSA, and notify the competent supervisory authorities of the home Member State of the irregularities that it has detected and the measures that it has taken.[1277] If, despite the application of supervisory measures that the competent supervisory authorities of the home Member State has taken, an EU payment institution or its agent carrying out business in Poland continues to transgress provisions of the PSA, then the PFSA may apply the measures in Articles 105(1), 105(3) and 105(4) of the PSA to the extent that is appropriate in the circumstances.[1278] The PFSA may also apply these measures in cases in which the actions that the competent supervisory authorities of the home Member State take prove to be insufficient to rectify the infringements or impossible to apply in Poland,[1279] or the home Member State's competent supervisory authorities (without justification) refuse to apply supervisory measures or unreasonably delay the application of these actions.[1280] If the application of the procedure in Article 107(1) of the PSA would cause "excessive delay" that might "directly endanger significant interests of users", then the PFSA may apply the measures in Articles 105(1), 105(3) and 105(4) of the PSA to the extent that is suitable in the circumstances.[1281] An EU payment institution may appeal to the Polish administrative court against a decision of the PFSA under paragraphs 2 to 5 of Article 107 of the PSA, within seven days of being informed of this decision.[1282]

[1276] Part II of the PSA is entitled "Informational Obligations Regarding the Provision of Payment Services", and contains Articles 16 to 33. Part III of the PSA is entitled "Rights and Responsibilities Regarding the Provision of Payment Services and Making Use of Them", and contains Articles 34 to 59.

[1277] Article 107(2), PSA. See above in this section, for Articles 105(1) and 105(3) of the PSA.

[1278] Article 107(3), PSA. The PFSA shall inform the home Member State's competent supervisory authorities of the supervisory measures that it has taken (Article 107(6), PSA). See above in this section, for Articles 105(1), 105(3) and 105(4) of the PSA.

[1279] Article 107(4)(1), PSA.

[1280] Article 107(4)(2), PSA.

[1281] Article 107(5), PSA. The PFSA shall notify the home Member State's competent supervisory authorities of the supervisory actions that it has taken (Article 107(6), PSA). See note 1168, for the definition of 'user'. See above in this section, for Articles 105(1), 105(3) and 105(4) of the PSA. See above in this paragraph, for Article 107(1) of the PSA.

[1282] Article 107(8), PSA. See above in this paragraph, for Articles 107(2), 107(3), 107(4) and 107(5) of the PSA.

In order to perform the tasks that the PSA imposes, the PFSA shall co-operate with competent supervisory authorities and other entities,[1283] especially the European Central Bank,[1284] the National Bank of Poland and the central banks of other Member States,[1285] and public authorities in those Member States that are responsible for the supervision of payment systems.[1286] The PFSA may make agreements with competent supervisory authorities, on co-operation in the area of supervision.[1287] In order to carry out the activities that Article 107 of the PSA specifies in relation to an EU payment institution, and also in Articles 102 to 105 of the PSA in relation to a Polish payment institution that provides payment services on the territory of a host Member State through a branch or an agent, or with the assistance of an outsourcee on the basis of the contract that Article 86(1) of the PSA stipulates, the PFSA shall co-operate with the competent supervisory authorities of the home Member State or the host Member State (as appropriate).[1288] The PFSA shall transfer to the competent supervisory authority of a host Member State (on request or on its own initiative) the information that is required for the purposes of the co-operation for which Article 109 of the PSA provides – especially in cases in which the PFSA has confirmed, or suspects, transgressions of "the law" by a branch, an agent, or an entity that performs operational functions on the basis of the contract that Article 86(1) of PSA specifies.[1289] The PFSA may provide information that it obtains in association with the exercise of its functions under the PSA, to competent supervisory authorities in the circumstances that Article 110 of the PSA describes,[1290] to central banks of other (i.e. non-Polish) Member States or other institutions of these countries that perform tasks in the area of monetary policy, and other public authorities of those Member States that carry out tasks in the field

---

[1283] Article 108(1), PSA. See note 1161, for the definition of 'competent supervisory authorities'.

[1284] Article 108(1)(1), PSA.

[1285] Article 108(1)(2), PSA. See note 1161, for the definition of 'Member State'.

[1286] Article 108(1)(3), PSA.

[1287] Article 108(2), PSA.

[1288] Article 109, PSA. See note 1161, for the definitions of 'payment institution' and 'EU payment institution'. See note 1186, for the definition of 'agent'. See note 1206, for the definitions of 'home Member State' and 'host Member State'. See note 1231, for Article 86(1) of the PSA. See the previous paragraph, for Article 107 of the PSA. See above in this section, for Articles 102 to 105 of the PSA.

[1289] Article 110, PSA. "The law" probably means any provisions of Polish law. See the previous sentence, for Article 109 of the PSA. See note 1231, for Article 86(1) of the PSA.

[1290] Article 111(1), PSA. See the previous sentence, for Article 110 of the PSA.

of the supervision of payment systems,[1291] and to EU authorities and institutions that are competent in the area of issues that relate to the supervision of payment institutions (or other providers of payment services), or of payment systems.[1292]

A natural or legal person, or an organisational unit (that is not a legal person) on which the law confers legal capacity, may provide money remittance services as a payment services office.[1293] These services may only be supplied in Poland.[1294] A payment service office may engage in business other than the supply of payment services.[1295] A payment service office may provide payment services, as soon as it has been entered in the register.[1296]

The PFSA shall maintain the register in electronic form.[1297] The register shall be public, and accessible via the PFSA's website.[1298] The register shall comprise sections that relate to Polish payment institutions, their branches and their agents,[1299] savings and credit institutions and their branches,[1300] and payment service offices, their branches and their agents.[1301] An entry in the register that concerns a Polish payment institution shall contain the following information: the number of the entry,[1302] the payment institution's name,[1303] the payment institution's number in the commercial register,[1304] the payment institution's registered office and address,[1305] the date of issue of the authorisation for which Article 60(1) of the PSA provides,[1306] the date(s) of amendments to this authorisation,[1307] a schedule of the payment services that are within the

---

1291 Article 111(2), PSA.
1292 Article 111(3), PSA.
1293 Articles 118(1) and 3(1)(6), PSA.
1294 Articles 118(2), PSA.
1295 Articles 118(5), PSA.
1296 Articles 119, PSA.
1297 Articles 133(1), PSA.
1298 Articles 133(2), PSA.
1299 Articles 133(3)(1), PSA. See notes 1161 and 1186, respectively, for the definitions of 'payment institution' and 'agent'.
1300 Articles 133(3)(2), PSA
1301 Articles 133(3)(3), PSA.
1302 Articles 134(1), PSA.
1303 Articles 134(2)(a), PSA.
1304 Articles 134(2)(b), PSA.
1305 Articles 134(2)(c), PSA.
1306 Articles 134(3)(a), PSA. See above in this section, for Article 60(1) of the PSA.
1307 Articles 134(3)(a), PSA.

ambit of the authorisation,[1308] the name of each of the payment institution's agents,[1309] the registered office and address (or the place of residence and address (including that of each principal place of business)) of each agent,[1310] the name and address of each of the payment institution's branches,[1311] and the following items of information on the payment services that the Polish payment institution provides in another Member State: a schedule of the countries in which the payment institution supplies payment services,[1312] the information that Articles 134(4) and 134(5) of the PSA specify – which concerns the agency or branch through which the payment institution provides payment services in another Member State,[1313] and a schedule of the payment services that the payment institutions supplies.[1314] Entry of a Polish payment institution in the register, and entry of an amendment to the services that a payment service provider supplies, shall be made on the PFSA's initiative, within 14 days of the receipt of the issue of its authorisation or of amendments to this authorisation.[1315] The PFSA may refuse to insert an entry into the register,[1316] if the application is incomplete, and if supplementary information has not been provided within the time limit that it has set or the information that the application contains is "inconsistent with the facts".[1317] It shall refuse to make an entry in the register for a natural person who has been legally forbidden from transacting business in the area that the entry covers.[1318] The PFSA shall cancel an entry in the register in the event of expiry or revocation of the authorisation to which Article 60(1) of the PSA refers,[1319] cessation of business by a savings and credit union on the basis of the notification to which Article 131(2) of the

---

[1308] Articles 134(3)(b), PSA.
[1309] Articles 134(4)(a), PSA.
[1310] Articles 134(4)(b), PSA.
[1311] Articles 134(5), PSA.
[1312] Articles 134(6)(a), PSA. See note 1161, for the definition of 'Member State'.
[1313] Articles 134(6)(b), PSA. See above in this sentence, for Articles 134(4) and 134(5) of the PSA.
[1314] Articles 134(6)(c), PSA.
[1315] Articles 138(1), PSA.
[1316] A refusal to make an entry in the register is an administrative decision of the PFSA (Article 140, PSA).
[1317] Articles 141(1), PSA.
[1318] Articles 141(2), PSA.
[1319] Articles 142(1)(1), PSA. See above in this section, for Article 60(1) of the PSA.

PSA refers,[1320] cessation of operations by a payment services office on the basis of the notification to which Article 123 of the PSA refers,[1321] and/or a final, binding judgment against a natural person in the register that forbids him from conducting business in the area that the entry covers.[1322] The PFSA may cancel an entry in the register that concerns a branch or an agent of a Polish payment institution, if it receives from the competent supervisory authorities of a host Member State in which this payment institution supplies payment services (through a particular branch or agent) information that indicates there are reasonable grounds to consider that, in connection with this activity, a criminal offence in Article 165a or Article 299 of the Criminal Code is being (or has been) committed, or the provision of services by the branch or the agent might increase the risk of money laundering or terrorist financing.[1323]

The nomenclature in Annex I does not refer to 'payment services'. Nevertheless, Title XIII(F) of this nomenclature concerns miscellaneous capital movements. Furthermore, the CJEU has held that the list of capital movements in the nomenclature in Annex I is "not exhaustive".[1324] In addition, Article 63(2) of the CJEU prohibits restrictions on payments between Member States, and between Member States and third countries.[1325] As the PSA concerns the provision of payment services, it is within the ambit of Article 63(2) of the TFEU – the free movement of capital includes the free movement of payments. Thus, the provision of cross-border payment services is a 'capital movement' by virtue of Article 63(2) of the TFEU, and also within Title XIII(F) of the nomenclature in Annex I. The foundation of a branch is a 'capital movement' in Title I(1) of the nomenclature in Annex I.

If the PFSA refuses to forward notification of the details of a Polish payment service provider to the financial supervision authority of the host

---

[1320] Articles 142(1)(2), PSA. A savings and credit institution must notify the PFSA of its commencement of activities in respect of the provision of payment services within 30 days of the date that it starts these activities, and include in this notice its name, registered office, address, and number in the commercial register, and the name and address of its branches (Article 131(2), PSA).

[1321] Articles 142(1)(3), PSA. A payment service office shall notify the PFSA of its intention to stop business or activities as a payment service office, giving the date on which it will be ceasing these activities (Article 123, PSA).

[1322] Articles 142(1)(4), PSA.

[1323] Articles 142(2), PSA.

[1324] See, for instance, *Trummer and Mayer* [1999], ECR I-1661, at paragraph 21. Section 2.1.1 considers how capital movements are defined. See also Chapter 3, note 1877, and the accompanying text.

[1325] See the opening paragraph of section 2.1

Member State (in which it wishes to supply payment services), refuses to enter this payment service provider's details in the register of payment service providers, restricts the payment service provider's portfolio of payment services, imposes a (substantial) fine on the payment service provider, or withdraws the payment service provider's authorisation, then it limits the free movement of capital. The PFSA also restricts the free movement of capital, if it limits the portfolio of payment services that a payment service provider from another EEA state can supply in Poland, imposes a (substantial) fine on this EEA payment service provider, or revokes the EEA payment service provider's authorisation.

For the restrictive measures to be justified under Article 65(1)(b) of the TFEU, they must be necessary for the protection of interests that they are intended to guarantee, be proportionate (i.e. not attainable by less restrictive measures), and observe the requirements of legal certainty (i.e. be specific, objective and known to the parties beforehand); in addition, the persons whom the measures affect must have access to legal redress, i.e. intervention must be accompanied by reasons, and be subject to review in the national courts.[1326] Most of the restrictive measures do not state the interests that they are intended to guarantee. Article 107(5) of the PSA is a notable exception – the PSA can apply restrictive measures to the extent that is appropriate in the circumstances, if the procedure that Article 107(1) of the PSA contains would cause excessive delay that may materially endanger the interests of the users of payment services.[1327] As the PFSA is provided with discretion as to what measures to apply and in the specific circumstances in which to apply them, these measures do not fulfil the requirements of legal certainty, and may be disproportionate. In the case of measures that the PFSA applies to an EU payment institution for its contravention of Polish law, Article 107(8) of the PSA provides this entity with a right of appeal to the Polish administrative court against the PFSA's decision.[1328] However, the PSA does not always provide a right of appeal in the national courts to a payment institution that is subject to a measure which limits the free movement of capital. In addition, this Act does not require the PFSA to provide reasons to a payment institution for a decision to impose a restrictive measure that affects it. Thus, the persons whom the measures affect do not have sufficient access to legal redress. Hence, Article 65(1)(b) of the TFEU cannot justify the restrictive measures.

[1326] See the subsection '*The requirements for a successful public policy/security derogation*' in section 2.1.3.

[1327] See above in this section, for Article 107(5) of the PSA.

[1328] See above in this section, for Article 107(8) of the PSA.

As none of the provisions in the PSA concern the movement of capital between Poland and third countries, the derogation in Article 64(2) of the TFEU does not apply to the Act's restrictive measures. Consequently, these measure contravene Article 63(2) of the TFEU.

4.6 Comment

When I previously compared the Estonian and Polish rules, I made the following statements.

> "The Polish legislation is less well organised than the Estonian legislation. In Estonia, the [E]FSA tends to have more discretion in granting and withdrawing authorisations than the [PFSA] does in Poland. The broad, prescriptive Estonian rules may provide a more rigid framework for capital movement than the detailed Polish laws. It is essential that the [E]FSA carefully considers the facts of each case in deciding whether or not to grant an authorisation, and that it gives reasons for its decision, thereby enabling the development of specific, objective criteria for authorisation known beforehand to applicant firms.".[1329]

The issue of the discretion that the Estonian laws provide to the EFSA remains a debatable point. Chapter 3 raises the EFSA's discretion 29 times, which is more than once every 10 sides. This compares unfavourably with the PFSA's discretion, which Chapter 4 raises 9 times. Given that a refusal to forward information, the imposition of substantive informational requirements, a refusal to grant an authorisation (if this is required) and a revocation of this authorisation restrict the free movement of capital, it is important that the legislatures in both countries take the derogations to the free movement of capital seriously.

In *Commission v Belgium*[1330] and *Commission v Spain*,[1331] the CJEU stated the requirements for the derogation for the free movement of capital in Article 65(1)(b) of the TFEU to operate.[1332] As, exceptionally, the CJEU accepted the derogation on the facts in *Commission v Belgium*, it may be helpful to re-visit this case in depth – in order to draw conclusions that might be applicable to the financial services legislation with which this work is concerned.

[1329] Baber, *The Impact of Legislation and Regulation*, 121.

[1330] [2002] ECR I-4809.

[1331] [2003] ECR I-4581.

[1332] See the subsections '*Derogations in the Commission's cases introduced in subsection 2.1.2*' and '*Reasons why the CJEU accepted the justification only in Commission v Belgium*', in section 2.1.3.

In *Commission v Belgium*, the European Commission applied to the CJEU for a declaration that, by keeping in force the provisions of the Royal Decree of 10 June 1994 that conferred on the Belgian government a 'golden share' in Société nationale de transport par canalisations (SNTC), and the provisions of the Royal Decree of 16 June 1994 that vested in the Belgian government a 'golden share' in Société de distribution du gaz SA (Distrigaz), and by failing to state precise, objective, stable criteria for approval of, or opposition to, the operations referred to therein, Belgium had not complied with its obligations under Articles 49 (now amended) and 63 of the TFEU.[1333] Each of these golden shares provides two rights, as follows: 1) advance notice of any transfer, change or use as security in the company's strategic assets must be provided to the responsible Minister, who is entitled to oppose these operations if "he considers that they adversely affect the national interest in the energy sector";[1334] 2) the Minister may appoint two government representatives to the company's board of directors, who "may propose to the Minister the annulment of any decision of the board of directors which they regard as contrary to the guidelines for the country's energy policy".[1335]

[1333] Article 49 of the TFEU contains the main rule for the freedom of establishment. At the time of the judgment (4 June 2002), this provision (before amendment) was Article 52 of the Treaty Establishing the European Community, and Article 63 of the TFEU was Article 73b of the Treaty Establishing the European Community.

[1334] *Commission v Belgium* [2002] ECR I-4809, at I-4813.

[1335] *Commission v Belgium* [2002] ECR I-4809, at I-4813. Articles 1, 3 and 4 of the Royal Decree of 10 June 1994 are as follows. Article 1: On the day on which the shares that the Belgian State currently holds in the capital of the Société nationale d'investissement are transferred to natural or legal person(s) in the private sector, the Société nationale d'investissement shall assign one share in the capital of SNTC (a public company) to the State. The special rights that Articles 2 to 5 of this Decree define shall attach to this share (in addition to the information rights that accompany ordinary shares in SNTC), only for as long as the State owns the share – which it may only assign or transfer pursuant to prior legislative authorisation. The Minister responsible for energy shall exercise these rights. Article 3: The 'golden share' shall confer on the Minister the right to oppose any transfer, change, or use as security in the intended destination of SNTC's system of lines and conduits that are used (or are capable of being used) as major infrastructures for the conveyance of energy products within Belgium, if he considers that the operation at issue adversely affects the national interest in the energy industry. The Minister must be given prior notice of this operation, and may lay down detailed rules that concern the contents and form of the notice to be provided. The Minister may exercise his right of opposition within 21 days of receipt of notice of the operation. Article 4: The 'golden share' shall provide the

The Commission argued that those Belgian rules, although non-discriminatory, cause obstacles to the freedom of establishment of nationals from other Member States and to the free movement of capital within the EU, because they impede the exercise of these freedoms. According to the Commission, the opacity of the domestic provisions is likely to indirectly introduce an element of legal uncertainty and discrimination.

Belgium (supported by the UK) claimed that any limitations on the freedom of establishment and the free movement of capital that may result from the Royal Decrees in issue are justified by the public security exception in Articles 52 and 65(1)(b) of the TFEU,[1336] and by "overriding requirements of the general interest".[1337] The safeguarding a country's energy supplies amounts to an overriding requirement of the general interest, as the CJEU has held in respect of petroleum products[1338] and electricity supplies.[1339]

Belgium also claimed that these restrictions "are proportionate and adequate in relation to the objective pursued by them".[1340] SNTC and Distrigaz hold a strategic position in respect of the country's energy supplies, especially given Belgium's dependence on resources of foreign energy. SNTC owns a system of lines and conduits that are important for the transmission of energy products within the country. Distrigaz possesses infrastructures for the domestic transport and storage of gas. The

---

Minister with the right to appoint two representatives of the federal government to SNTC's board of directors. These persons will sit on the board in a non-voting capacity. In addition, these representatives may apply to the Minister, within 4 working days, for annulment of any decision of SNTC's board of directors that they consider to be contrary to the guidelines for the country's energy policy – including the government's objectives in respect of Belgium's energy supply. The time limit of four days shall run from the date of the meeting at which the decision in question was taken – if the representatives of the government were invited to attend the meeting, or, if they were not so invited, from the date on which the representatives (or either one of them) became aware of the decision. The implementation of the decision shall be suspended, pending the Minister's confirmation or annulment of it. If the Minister does not annul the decision within 8 working days of representatives' application to him, then it shall become final. Articles 1, 3 and 4 of the Royal Decree of June 1994 contain fundamentally the same rules concerning Distrigaz.

[1336] At the time of the judgment (4 June 2002), these provisions were Articles 56 and 73d(1)(b), respectively, of the Treaty Establishing the European Community.

[1337] *Commission v Belgium* [2002] ECR I-4809, paragraph 26, at I-4827.

[1338] *Campus Oil and Others* [1984] ECR 2727.

[1339] *Almelo* [1994] ECR I-1477.

[1340] *Commission v Belgium* [2002] ECR I-4809, paragraph 26, at I-4827.

government requires some control of these strategic assets. The measures for which the Royal Decrees provide are proportionate. The prior notification (if not accompanied by a suspension) keeps the government informed. Similarly, the Minister's powers relate only to specific issues and are limited in time.[1341] Thus, it would be inadmissible to argue that the Belgium government had not established precise, objective and stable criteria.

A formal statement of reasons must accompany a decision of the Minister to exercise the rights that the Royal Decrees confer on him, which sets out the considerations of law and fact on which it is based. Furthermore, there is a right of appeal to the Belgian Conseil D'État for the suspension or annulment of this decision. The costs are low. There is a procedure for obtaining interim relief.

Belgium stated that there was no less restrictive way to attain the objectives that it was pursuing. It is for the Commission to produce evidence that shows the existence of alternative, less restrictive solutions. It is highly unlikely that the Commission's suggested licensing system (the outlines of which are vague) would provide investors with a level of legal certainty that was greater than that which results from the Royal Decrees.

The CJEU held that the free movement of capital may only be restricted by national rules which are justified by reasons to which Article 65(1) of the TFEU refers,[1342] or by "overriding requirements of the general interest", and which apply to all entities and persons that carry out an activity in the host Member State.[1343] In order to be justified in this way, the national law must be appropriate for securing the objective that it pursues, and must not go beyond what is required in order to attain this objective, so as to comply with the principle of proportionality. In the present case, the objective that the Royal Decrees pursue – the safeguarding of energy supplies in a crisis – is an acceptable public interest.

However, the public security derogation may only be relied upon if there is a "genuine and sufficiently serious threat to a fundamental interest

[1341] Article 3 of the Royal Decree of 10 June 1994 states that the Minister may exercise his right of opposition within 21 days of receipt of notice of the operation in question, and must decide whether or not to annul a decision of the board of directors within 8 working days of the application from the representatives of the government on this board. See note 1335.

[1342] At the time of the judgment (4 June 2002), Article 65(1) of the TFEU was Article 73d(1) of the Treaty Establishing the European Community.

[1343] *Commission v Belgium* [2002] ECR I-4809, paragraph 45, at I-4832.

of society".[1344] It is necessary, therefore, to determine whether the Royal Decrees enable Belgium to ensure an adequate level of energy supplies if there is a genuine and serious threat, and whether or not they go beyond what is required for this purpose.

First, the Belgian regime is one of opposition. It upholds the principle of respect for the autonomy of the entity concerned to take decisions. In each instance, the government authorities must take the initiative in order for the Minister to exercise control. There is no need for the Minister's prior approval. Furthermore, for the Belgian government to exercise its power of opposition, it is required to do this within strict time-limits.

Second, the regime is limited to specified decisions that concern the strategic assets of SNTC and Distrigaz, and to specific management decisions that relate to these assets. Third, the Minister may only intervene on an occasion on which there is a threat that the objectives of the Belgian government's energy policy may be compromised. Fourth, this intervention "must be supported by a formal statement of reasons and may be the subject of an effective review by the courts".[1345]

Therefore, the scheme "makes it possible to guarantee, on the basis of objective criteria which are subject to judicial review," the availability of the lines and conduits that provide the main infrastructures for the transportation of energy products within Belgium, in addition to other infrastructures for the transportation and storage of gas in that country.[1346] Thus, the regime enables the Belgian government to intervene in order to ensure that SNTC and Distrigaz comply with their obligations of public service, whilst "observing the requirements of legal certainty".[1347]

The Commission has not shown that the Belgium government could have taken less restrictive measures, in order to reach the objective pursued. It is not certain that planning for natural gas companies to agree long-term supply contracts, diversify their sources of energy supply, or operate a system of licences, would be sufficient to enable a swift reaction in any specific situation. Furthermore, the introduction of rules that precisely define the standards that entities are required to satisfy in the sector concerned, may be more restrictive than a right of opposition that is restricted to specific situations. Therefore, the Royal Decrees are "justified by the objective of guaranteeing energy supplies in a crisis".[1348]

[1344] *Commission v Belgium* [2002] ECR I-4809, paragraph 47, at I-4833.
[1345] *Commission v Belgium* [2002] ECR I-4809, paragraph 51, at I-4834.
[1346] *Commission v Belgium* [2002] ECR I-4809, paragraph 52, at I-4834.
[1347] *Commission v Belgium* [2002] ECR I-4809, paragraph 52, at I-4834.
[1348] *Commission v Belgium* [2002] ECR I-4809, paragraph 55, at I-4835.

This judgment raises several pertinent issues. First, there is the matter of scope of the derogation in Article 65(1)(b) of the TFEU. Member States may

> "take all requisite measures to prevent infringements of national law and regulations, in particular in the field of taxation and the prudential supervision of financial institutions, or to lay down procedures for the declaration of capital movements for the purposes of administrative or statistical information, or take measures which are justified on the grounds of public policy or public security"[1349]

although these measures

> "shall not constitute a means of arbitrary discrimination or a disguised restriction on the free movement of capital and payments as defined in Article 63 [of the TFEU]".[1350]

Most of the case law in which Article 65(1)(b) of the TFEU applies concerns the public policy/security derogation.[1351] However, the restrictions to the free movement of capital that this chapter and the previous chapter discuss are (in the main) not public policy or public security issues. Of much more relevance is that these restrictive provisions lay down national law in the field of prudential supervision of financial institutions, which, under this particular head of Article 65(1)(b) of the TFEU, the legislators may attempt to defend. The absence of case law concerning the head of the 'prudential supervision of financial institutions' in Article 65(1)(b) of the TFEU has necessitated (in the analysis applied in Chapters 3 and 4) the application of the rules for the public policy/security head – but without the need for a genuine and sufficiently serious threat to a fundamental interest of society.[1352] However, as these analyses show, most of the provisions in the Estonian and Polish financial services legislation that restrict the free movement of capital do not satisfy at least one of the remaining four requirements for the public policy/security head in Article 65(1)(b) of the TFEU.[1353]

[1349] Article 65(1)(b), TFEU.
[1350] Article 65(1)(b), TFEU.
[1351] See section 2.1.3.
[1352] See the subsection '*The requirements for a successful public policy/security derogation*' in section 2.1.3.
[1353] See the subsection '*The requirements for a successful public policy/security derogation*' in section 2.1.3.

Second, the CJEU in *Commission v Belgium*[1354] states that the Belgian system satisfies the requirements of legal certainty, even though it does not state specifically the circumstances under which the Minister will oppose the use of SNTC's or Distrigaz's strategic assets.[1355] Thus, the Minister, and the representatives of the Belgian government on the board of directors of the two companies, have a discretion to act. This discretion for the representatives is whether to report each decision of the board of directors to the Minister, bearing in mind the objectives of the Belgian government's energy policy – although they have only 4 working days in which they can exercise it. The Minister's discretion is as to whether to oppose the use of SNTC's or Distrigaz's strategic assets – although he/she has to consider the issue and to take the decision to oppose it (if he/she decides to do so) within 21 days of learning about it (whilst taking into account the objective of the government's energy policy), and as to whether to annul the decision of the board of directors that the representatives of the government refer to him/her within 8 working days of this referral.[1356] In the majority of the instances in which the EFSA or the PFSA is granted a discretion (as described in Chapters 3 and 4), the national legislation does not grant the relevant financial supervision authority a time limit in which to do so. Furthermore, in most cases, the financial supervision authority does not have to exercise its discretion whilst bearing in mind an overarching objective. The presence of such an objective is mandatory, if a system such as that in *Commission v Belgium* is to provide any reasonable degree of legal certainty to the persons whom decisions taken pursuant to the operation of this system affect.

In the context of authorisation and passporting, a system of post-hoc declaration without detailed guidelines, as in *Commission v Belgium*, may not work – due to the large volume of applications that the national financial supervision authorities are required to process on an on-going basis. In the case of the cross-border provision of financial services (with or without a branch or an agency in the host Member State), applicants may be provided with legal certainty by specific, detailed criteria that the legislators or the financial supervision authority publish, in relation either to services to be provided in other EEA states – or (in the case of the foundation of a branch only) to services to be supplied by firms from other countries of the EEA in the territory of the particular financial supervision authority. The EU legislators may be aware of this need for legal certainty, as indicated, for instance, by requiring the European Banking Authority to

---

[1354] [2002] ECR I-4809.

[1355] See above in this section.

[1356] See note 1335.

publish draft regulatory technical standards for the information that an applicant credit institution must provide to its home Member State's financial supervision authority, in order to establish a branch or provide cross-border services, and to empower the Commission to implement these standards.[1357]

Third, the CJEU holds that the regime in *Commission v Belgium* is proportionate, i.e. not attainable by less restrictive measures.[1358] It is the Commission's responsibility, as the party bringing the case, to prove to the CJEU that another system might work at least as well, whilst being more favourable to SNTC and/or Distrigaz and/or other parties that are involved. The objective on which government action under the Royal Decrees is based is the national interest in the energy sector. In situations in which the objective differs considerably from this, the least restrictive measure (as judged by the CJEU) is not necessarily a system of post-hoc declaration. Herein is a difficulty in recommending what the national legislatures should do, in order to protect their legislation from reasonable claims of imposing restrictions on the free movement of capital, by a justification under Article 65(1)(b) of the TFEU. As the judgment in *Commission v Belgium* is unusual in being a successful application of Article 65(1)(b) of the TFEU, as this derogation was not applied in *Commission v Belgium* in the context of the 'prudential supervision of financial institutions' head of this Article, and as the proportionality of the scheme applied was specific to the objective pursued in the case, there is little basis on which to provide general recommendations as to the form of the legislation that countries need to produce in cases in which they limit the free movement of capital.

Finally, the judgment in *Commission v Belgium* affirms that the measures that restrict the free movement of capital must be accompanied by reasons and be subject to review by the national courts.[1359] As the reportage and analysis in this chapter and the previous chapter show, the Polish and Estonian legislation that restricts the free movement of capital rarely provides either of these rights. Both legislatures should, as an urgent issue, introduce provisions into all of their financial services legislation that obliges the PFSA/EFSA to accompany each of its decisions (especially those with cross-border ramifications) with a statement of reasons, and provide the applicant financial institution with a right to appeal in the domestic courts against any decision of the PFSA/EFSA that

[1357] Articles 35(4) and 39(4), Directive 2013/36/EU.

[1358] See above in this section.

[1359] See above in this section, and the subsection '*The requirements for a successful public policy/security derogation*' in section 2.1.3.

adversely affects it. Whilst this may lead to more domestic legislation, it will ensure that applicants have access to legal redress, which is a requirement for the derogation in Article 65(1)(b) of the TFEU to apply.

Some pertinent comments should also be made that concern the movement of capital between Estonia or Poland and third countries. First, not all of the Acts provide for the explicit freedom of establishment, and, especially, the free movement of services between the EEA state and the third country. One such Act is the Polish IMA,[1360] which does not mention third countries. This is not surprising, given that the relevant Directive (Directive 2002/92/EC) does not refer to third countries either – although the Estonian IAA does consider the supply of insurance mediation between Estonia and third countries.[1361]

Second, the analyses in Chapters 3 and 4 have shown that the derogation in Article 64(2) of the TFEU is often unsuccessful, because the EU institutions have not carefully taken account of the objective of the free movement of capital whilst enacting the relevant single market Directive.[1362] In some of the Directives, the free movement of capital is mentioned in the recitals but in none of the Articles. The EU institutions should rework these Directives. They should go through each one Article by Article, with the free movement of capital in mind, introducing the concept in the form of safeguards, exceptions and directions at each place in the relevant Directive that they consider to be appropriate. In this context, it should be re-emphasised that the free movement of capital is a fundamental freedom, of equal standing to the free movement of services (and the freedom of establishment), and these freedoms should be integrated into the financial services Directives together.

Third, the analyses in this chapter and the previous chapter demonstrate that two countries, and especially Estonia, tend to impose measures that restrict the free movement of capital more than do the equivalent provisions in the Directive. This is a ground for the non-application of the derogation to Article 63 of the TFEU in Article 64(2) of the TFEU.[1363] The Polish and Estonian legislatures should revisit the provisions of their financial services laws that affect the free movement of

---

[1360] See section 4.4.3, for the IMA.

[1361] See the subsections '*Chapter 10 Division 6 Activities of Estonian Intermediaries in Foreign States*' and '*Chapter 10 Division 7 Activities of Foreign Intermediaries in Estonia*', in section 3.4.

[1362] See the subsection '*Derogations that apply only to capital movements to/from third countries*', in section 2.3.2.

[1363] See the subsection '*Derogations that apply only to capital movements to/from third countries*', in section 2.3.2.

capital between the home EEA state and third countries, in order to ensure that these rules are not providing excessive authorisation requirements for the establishment of a branch or the suppliance of cross-border services between the home state and third countries, and/or too many stringent reasons for refusing to grant and/or revoking this authorisation. This check should be done with knowledge of the provisions for the establishment of a branch and the supply of cross-border services by a home institution in a third country, and by a third country entity in the home EEA state, which the relevant single market Directive contains (if any).

In spite of the critical nature of some of the comments in this section, close scrutiny of the financial services legislation of Estonia and Poland has revealed that both of these countries, and Estonia in particular, have worked hard to provide a comprehensive system for the authorisation of domestic firms to supply financial services in the home country, and for the provision of these services across borders within the EEA and between the EEA and third countries. Whilst the continuing presence in this legislation of rules that contravene Article 63 of the TFEU remains a difficulty for the governments of these countries, both have the legal framework to be able to address this issue along the lines proposed above.

Chapter 5 will consider a sample of the financial services rules from Latvia, Germany and Croatia, in the light of the points made in this section. The discussions in the forthcoming chapter will attempt to corroborate or refute observations made in the detailed analyses performed in the work so far.

CHAPTER FIVE

LATVIA, GERMANY AND CROATIA

This Chapter samples the financial services laws of Latvia, Germany and Croatia for their compliance with the free movement of capital, on the basis of the findings and comments from previous Chapters. Although Estonia, Poland and Latvia joined the European Union simultaneously in May 2004, accession negotiations for Estonia and Poland commenced two years earlier than those for Latvia.[1] Consequently, Latvia had four years to implement the *acquis communautaire*,[2] compared with six years for Estonia and Poland. The Latvian Translation and Terminology Centre (LTTC) translates Latvian legislation and regulations into English, and is the main source of the materials used in this Chapter.[3] The LTTC is a state institution, which is "widely recognised nationally and internationally as Latvia's leading provider of high-quality translation and terminology services".[4]

West Germany was one of the six founder states of the European Economic Community. The Treaty Establishing the European Economic Community came into force on 1 January 1958. When East Germany joined with West Germany to form Germany in October 1990, the former East Germany 'joined' the EU as part of the continuing membership of the re-unified country. The English translations of the financial services laws come from the following two sources: the Centre for German Legal

---

[1] Accession talks began in March 1998 for Cyprus, the Czech Republic, Estonia, Hungary, Poland and Slovenia, and in February 2000 for Bulgaria, Latvia, Lithuania, Malta, Romania and Slovakia (Polish Office of the Committee for European Integration, 22 October 2007).

[2] Section 1.3.1 discusses implementation of the *acquis communautaire*.

[3] The Director of the LTTC, Professor Māris Baltiņš, stated that the English version of Latvian law published by the LTTC was only "informative" and "not officially published in the government journal" (e-mail communication, 29 August 2007). Rather than citing and referencing the LTTC website for each Act, I accept his point whilst giving the official reference in the bibliography.

[4] LTTC, 4 October 2007.

Information and the German Federal Supervisory Authority (BaFin), and the Centre for German Legal Information.

Croatia is, at the time of writing, the Member State that most recently acceded to the EU – on 1 July 2014. Its neighbouring countries are Slovenia and Hungary to the north, both of which acceded to the EU 10 years previously, and Bosnia & Herzegovina, Serbia and Montenegro to the south and east, none of which are currently Member States. The English translation of the Croatian financial services laws comes from the Regulatory and Publication Service (RIPE) of the Croatian Financial Services Supervisory Authority (CFSSA).

Sections 5.1, 5.2 and 5.3 consider a selection of provisions of the financial services laws from Latvia, Germany and Croatia, respectively, as to their compliance with the EU's free movement of capital rules. Section 5.4 is reserved for comment.

5.1 Latvia

The Latvian financial services laws are straightforward. After each section of the relevant Act, the dates on which the relevant provision was updated are stated. Each Article in a Latvian law is clearly labelled – for instance, in the Law of Investment Companies 1997, Article 11 is accompanied by the title 'Provisions for Issuing a Licence'.

One Latvian Act is selected, the Credit Institution Law 1995 (CIL), and a Chapter that includes cross-border provisions analysed – 'Chapter II Licensing of Credit Institutions'. This Chapter comprises sections 11 to 27^1 of the CIL.

Credit institutions may start their activities in Latvia only after they have received a licence from the Latvian Financial and Capital Market Commission (LFCMC), and they register their activities in the commercial register in accordance with the procedures that the law specifies.[5] The

---

[5] s.11(1), CIL. A 'credit institution' is a company that accepts repayable funds from clients, issues credits on its own account, and supplies other financial services (s.1(1), CIL). 'Financial services' comprise the taking of deposits and other repayable funds, financial leasing, payment services, the "issuance and servicing of non-cash means of payment" that is unrelated to the supply of payment services, trading in one's own name or in the name of a client with financial instruments or currency, "fiduciary operations" as a trust, the supply of "investment services and non-core investment services", the issuance of binding obligations that create a duty to be liable to the creditor for the debt of another person, the safekeeping of valuables, consultations with clients that concern issues of financial nature, the provision of information that is related to the settlement of the debt obligations of a

LFCMC is entitled to specify in the licence the conditions under which the credit institution must perform its activities – including the provision of financial services.[6] The LFCMC shall issue the licence for "an unspecified period of time".[7] A credit institution may only be established in Latvia as a joint-stock company.[8]

Credit institutions must be granted a permit from the LFCMC, in order to establish a branch in a foreign state.[9] A credit institution that is registered in Latvia shall found a branch in another Member State in accordance with the procedures that section 12^2 of the CIL specifies.[10] The credit institution shall notify the LFCMC in writing that it would like to found a branch in another Member State.[11] In this application, it shall indicate the name of the host Member State, the address of the branch, and the name and personal identification number of the head of the branch.[12] The credit institution shall append to the application documents that present a true and fair representation of the planned activities of the branch, the financial services to be provided in the host Member State through the branch, and the branch's structure and organisation.[13] The LFCMC shall inspect the application for the establishment of a branch in another Member State within 30 days of receipt of all the necessary documents "processed in conformity with the requirements of regulatory enactments", and shall inform the host Member State's financial supervision authority and the applicant credit institution in writing of the decision (as to whether the applicant will be permitted to open the branch).[14] The LFCMC shall notify the host Member State's financial

---

client, other financial services that are similar to the financial services mentioned above, and the production of electronic money (s.1(5), CIL).

[6] s.11(1^1), CIL.

[7] s.11(6), CIL.

[8] s.3(2), CIL.

[9] s.12(1), CIL. A 'branch of a credit institution' is a territorially (or otherwise) separated structural part of a credit institution, which is not a legal person, and which acts in the credit institution's name (s.1(2), CIL). A 'foreign state' a country that is not a Member State (s.1(45), CIL). A 'Member State' is an EU Member State or an EEA state (s.1(44), CIL).

[10] s.12^2(1), CIL. All individual branches that a credit institution establishes in a single Member State shall be deemed to be one branch in the relevant Member State (s.12^2(8^1), CIL).

[11] s.12^2(2), CIL.

[12] s.12^2(2), CIL.

[13] s.12^2(3), CIL.

[14] s.12^2(4), CIL. Subsection 12^2(4) of the CIL is different from the procedure in Directive 2013/36/EU, Article 35(3) of which requires the home Member State's

supervision authority about the amount of own funds of the credit institution and the indicators of capital adequacy, and provide a view on the suitability of the designated appointee for the position of head of the branch.[15] A branch of a credit institution shall be founded, and commence activities, in the host Member State, if the financial supervision authority of that Member State has provided the credit institution with a certification, or two months have passed from the day on which the financial supervision authority of the host Member State has received the notification from the LFCMC that the applicant credit institution will be allowed to establish a branch.[16]

A credit institution that is registered in Latvia shall begin to supply financial services in another Member State without establishing a branch there.[17] The credit institution shall inform the LFCMC in writing that it would like to commence the supply of financial services in another Member State without founding a branch there.[18] In this submission, the credit institution shall indicate the Member State in which it intends to provide financial services, and the financial services that it wishes to supply there.[19] The LFCMC shall examine the submission with 30 days of its receipt, and shall inform the applicant credit institution and the financial supervision authority of the host Member State of the decision thereof in writing.[20]

A credit institution that is registered in a Member State, its branches, and branches of a foreign credit institution, have the right to provide financial services in Latvia.[21] Credit institutions that are registered in

---

financial supervision authority to forward the information from the applicant credit institution to the host Member State's financial supervision authority, unless it has reason to doubt the sufficiency of the administrative structure or the financial circumstances of the credit institution; see section 2.2.2.

[15] s.12^2(5), CIL.

[16] s.12^2(7), CIL.

[17] s.12^3(1), CIL.

[18] s.12^3(2), CIL.

[19] s.12^3(2), CIL.

[20] s.12^3(3), CIL. Subsection 12^3(3) of the CIL is only partly in accordance with Article 39(2) of Directive 2013/36/EU, which states that the home Member State's financial supervision authority should send the notification to the host Member State's financial supervision authority within one month, i.e. the home Member State's financial competent authority is not empowered under the Directive to take a decision; see section 2.2.2.

[21] s.3(1), CIL. The CIL does not define 'foreign credit institution'. Given the definitions of 'foreign state' and 'Member State' (see note 9), a foreign credit institution is (probably) a credit institution that is established in a third country

another Member State may found branches in Latvia without the licence that the CIL specifies, only after 1) the LFCMC has received a notification from the financial supervision authority of the relevant home Member State that includes the following items: a confirmation that the applicant credit institution has a valid licence,[22] a programme of the branch's activities,[23] the branch's address,[24] the name of the branch's director,[25] information concerning the amount of the credit institution's own funds and indicators of capital adequacy,[26] information about the capital adequacy of the credit institution's parent company (if a financial holding company or a credit institution),[27] and information concerning the investment guarantee system of which the applicant credit institution is a participant,[28] 2) the LFCMC has received from the financial supervision authority of the applicant credit institution's home Member State a written confirmation that it will notify the LFCMC in a timely manner regarding the examination of branches, will not impede the participation of representatives of the LFCMC in these examinations, and will (at the end of this examination and without delay) submit to the LFCMC a notice concerning the results of this examination,[29] and 3) the LFCMC has

---

Subsection 3(1) of the CIL does not mention the possibility of a foreign credit institution providing cross-border services in Latvia.

[22] s.12^1(1)(1)(a), CIL.

[23] s.12^1(1)(1)(b), CIL. Documents are to be submitted that provide "a clear idea" concerning the branch's operational strategy, the financial forecasts for the next 2 years, the plan of market research, the organisational structure – with precisely specified and separated tasks of units and responsibilities of heads of units, the procedures and policies for the management of significant risks, the main principles of the accounting policy and the record system, a description of the management information system, provisions for the protection of the information system and of assets, the procedure and policy for internal audits, and the procedures to identify suspicious financial transactions (Article s.12^1(3), CIL).

[24] s.12^1(1)(1)(c), CIL.

[25] s.12^1(1)(1)(d), CIL.

[26] s.12^1(1)(1)(e), CIL.

[27] s.12^1(1)(1)(f), CIL. A 'parent company' is a commercial company that controls a second commercial company (s.1(10),CIL). A 'financial holding company' is a financial institution that is not a mixed-activity financial holding company and the subsidiaries of which are either exclusively or primarily financial institutions or credit institutions, at least one of which is a bank (s.1(21), CIL). A 'subsidiary' is a commercial company that is controlled by a second commercial company; any subsidiary of a subsidiary shall also be considered to be a subsidiary of latter's parent company (s.1(11), CIL).

[28] s.12^1(1)(1)(g), CIL.

[29] s.12^1(1)(2), CIL.

informed the financial supervision authority of the credit institution's home Member State of the Latvian "regulatory enactments" which "protect the public interest", and that it is ready to start the supervision of the credit institution's branch, or two months have elapsed since the day on which the LFCMC received the notification from the financial supervision authority of the applicant credit institution's home Member State.[30]

A credit institution that is registered in another Member State shall, within 30 days of its submission of a notification concerning the provision of financial services in Latvia to the financial supervision authority of its home Member State, start to provide financial services in Latvia without establishing a branch.[31] If, within 30 days of receipt of this notification, the financial supervision authority of the applicant credit institution's home Member State does not send a written refusal to the LFCMC, then it is deemed that the former does not object to the provision of financial services by the credit institution in Latvia.[32]

A financial institution from another Member State, which at least one credit institution controls, may supply financial services in Latvia (with or without establishing a branch), if it satisfies all of the following conditions: the credit institution(s) that control the financial institution have been granted a licence for operation in that home Member State in agreement with its laws,[33] the financial institution provides financial services in accordance with the laws of its home Member State,[34] the credit institution(s) that control the financial institution own at least 90% of the financial institution's voting stock,[35] the credit institution(s) that control the financial institution ensure prudent management of the financial institution in compliance with the requirements of the financial supervision authority of the country of domicile of these credit institution(s),[36] the credit institution(s) that control the financial institution have publicly disclosed information concerning the fact they are ordinarily liable for the financial obligations of this institution – and the relevant credit institution(s) or the financial supervision authority of the country of

[30] s.12^1(1)(3), CIL.
[31] s.12^1(4), CIL.
[32] s.12^1(5), CIL.
[33] s.12^4(1)(1), CIL.
[34] s.12^4(1)(2), CIL.
[35] s.12^4(1)(3), CIL.
[36] s.12^4(1)(4), CIL.

domicile of these credit institutions has not "objected against it",[37] and the financial institution's activities are subject the consolidated supervision of the controlling credit institution(s) – especially in relation to large risk exposures, capital adequacy, and ownership of other commercial companies.[38] A financial institution that is registered in another (i.e. non-Latvian) Member State is entitled to start to provide financial services in Latvia in accordance with section 12^1 of the CIL, after the LFCMC has received a notice from the financial supervision authority of home Member State of the controlling credit institution(s) that includes the following documents: the information that sub-clauses (a) to (e) of clause 12^1(1)(1) of the CIL specify,[39] documents that contain information concerning the amount of the financial institution's own funds and its group's capital adequacy,[40] and a statement that certifies the conformity of the credit institution to the conditions to which subsection 12^4(1) of the CIL refers.[41] If the LFCMC receives a notification from the financial supervision authority of the Member State of the domicile of the financial institution concerning the fact that this institution no longer satisfies the conditions in subsection 12^4(1) of the CIL, then it shall immediately send a notification to the institution.[42] This notification shall state that, from the day of its receipt, the financial institution has forfeited the right to supply financial services in Latvia according to the procedures that section 12^4 of the CIL specify.[43] In order to provide licensed financial services in Latvia, the financial institution may submit an application to the LFCMC to provide a licence "according to general procedures".[44]

A financial institution that is registered in Latvia is entitled to start to provide financial services in another Member State, by the foundation of a branch in accordance with section 12^2 of the CIL, or by the suppliance cross-border services in accordance with section 12^3 of the CIL.[45] A

[37] s.12^4(1)(5), CIL. It is not clear from the quoted language of the translation of clause 12^4(1)(5) of the CIL, whether the home Member State's financial supervision authority and the credit institution(s) must not object to the latter being ordinarily liable for the debts of the financial institution, or whether they must not object to the latter disclosing information stating liability for these debts.

[38] s.12^4(1)(6), CIL.

[39] s.12^4(4)(1), CIL. See above in this section, for clause 12^1(1)(1) of the CIL.

[40] s.12^4(4)(2), CIL.

[41] s.12^4(4)(3), CIL. See above in this section, for subsection 12^4(1) of the CIL.

[42] s.12^4(5), CIL.

[43] s.12^4(5), CIL.

[44] s.12^4(5), CIL.

[45] s.12^4(2), CIL.

financial institution that is registered in Latvia is entitled to supply financial services in the territory of another Member State, if the financial supervision authority of the home Member State of the controlling credit institution(s) has received a notification from the LFCMC that certifies the financial institution's conformity with the conditions to subsection 12^4(1) of the CIL refers.[46] If the financial institution has commenced its provision of financial services in another Member State according to the procedures that section 12^4 specifies, but no longer satisfies the conditions in subsection 12^4(1) of the CIL, then the LFCMC shall immediately inform the financial institution and the host Member State's financial supervision authority of the former's non-compliance with the conditions to which subsection 12^4(1) of the CIL refers.[47]

If the LFCMC receives an application for a licence to provide financial services in Latvia (as a newly-founded credit institution) from a subsidiary of a foreign financial credit institution or (foreign) financial institution,[48] then the LFCMC has the right not to issue a licence to this subsidiary, if "laws have not been complied with" in the establishment of the new credit institution,[49] a close relationship of the credit institution with third parties may threaten the financial stability of the former or limit the right of the LFCMC to conduct the supervisory functions that "the law" specifies,[50] the legislation and regulation of other countries that apply to persons who have close links with the credit institution (to be established) limit the LFCMC's right to conduct the supervisory functions that "the law" specifies,[51] the documents that the credit institution submits to the LFCMC

---

[46] s.12^4(3), CIL. See above in this section, for subsection 12^4(1) of the CIL.

[47] s.12^4(6), CIL.

[48] See note 21, for a comment the meaning of on 'foreign credit institution'. The CIL does not refer to 'foreign financial institution'.

[49] s.14(1)(1), CIL. The quoted phrase probably means relevant provisions of Latvian law.

[50] s.14(1)(2), CIL. The quoted phrase probably means relevant provisions of Latvian law. The CIL does not define the phrase 'close relationship'. 'Close relationship' may mean 'close links', which note 51 defines.

[51] .14(1)(3), CIL. The quoted phrase probably means relevant provisions of Latvian law. 'Close links' are a mutual relationship between at least two persons as a type of participation or control, or if these persons are linked with another person "by control" (s.1(40),CIL). 'Participation' is the right to a commercial company's shares, which, in establishing a long-term link with this company, are used in order to participate in the management of the company, or a (direct or indirect) holding that contains at least 20% of the number of voting shares or the equity capital of the company (s.1(15^1), CIL).

contain information that is untrue,[52] at least one of the persons to which section 24 of the CIL refers does not satisfy the requirements of "the law",[53] the LFCMC determines that the funds that are invested in the credit institution's share capital "have been acquired in unusual of suspicious financial transactions" or there are no documents to show that these funds have been lawfully obtained,[54] the (third) country in which the parent credit institution or financial institution is registered does not have supervision that is equivalent to the requirements that Member States accept,[55] or the financial supervision authority of the third country in which the parent credit institution or financial institution is registered does not have an agreement with the LFCMC for co-operation and information exchange.[56]

The LFCMC shall consult with the financial supervision authority of the relevant Member State prior to issuance of a licence to a credit institution to be newly established, which is: a subsidiary of a credit institution, investment firm or insurance company that is registered in that Member State,[57] a subsidiary whose parent company has another subsidiary that is a credit institution, investment firm or insurance company that is registered in that Member State,[58] or which is controlled by a natural or legal person who also controls the credit institution, investment firm or insurance company that is registered in the other Member State.[59] Prior to the issuance of a licence, and during the course of supervision of a

---

[52] s.14(1)(4), CIL.

[53] s.14(1)(5), CIL. The quoted phrase probably means relevant provisions of Latvian law. The persons to whom section 24 of the CIL refers are the chairperson of the board of directors, members of the board of directors, the head of the internal audit function, the company controller, the director of a foreign credit institution's branch, and (other) persons who take necessary decisions in the credit institution's name and generate contractual obligations for the credit institution (s.24(1), FSMA). These persons must have a higher education, be competent in issues of financial management, have the required education and (at least) three years of professional work experience in an organisation "of relevant size", have an excellent reputation, and must "have not been deprived of the right of" conducting commercial activities (ss.24(1) and 24(2), CIL).

[54] s.14(1)(6), CIL.

[55] s.14(1)(7), CIL.

[56] s.14(1)(7), CIL. Other than clause 7, subsection 14(1) of the CIL applies to applicants for authorisation as a credit institution in Latvia that are not subsidiaries of a foreign credit institution or a foreign financial institution.

[57] s.19^1(1)(1), CIL.

[58] s.19^1(1)(2), CIL.

[59] s.19^1(1)(3), CIL.

licensed credit institution, the LFCMC shall request and evaluate information from the financial supervision authority of the other Member State concerning the suitability of the credit institution's shareholders and the reputation and experience of persons designated to manage the credit institution who are involved in the management of other companies of the group in which the credit institution is or will be included.[60]

A foreign credit institution may establish a branch in Latvia, if the minimum initial capital of this company satisfies the requirements of section 21 of the CIL, and the credit institution's period of operation is at least three financial years.[61] The 'period of operation' requirement does not apply to credit institutions that are registered in a foreign country that is a member of the WTO.[62]

The LFCMC may revoke the licence of a credit institution, if this entity has not started to function with one year of the day on which the licence was issued,[63] "it is determined that" the credit institution has presented false information in order to receive the licence,[64] the credit institution has suspended its operations for a period of more than six months,[65] the credit institution has gone into liquidation,[66] the credit institution waives the licence "in case of reorganisation",[67] a court has confirmed a decision that is taken in accordance with procedures that the CIL specifies on commencement of the credit institution's bankruptcy proceedings,[68] for more than two months following a warning by the LFCMC concerning the cancellation of the licence for the operation of a credit institution, this entity has not made payments to the Investment Guarantee Fund voluntarily or in full,[69] the credit institution does not satisfy the requirements of the CIL and other laws that regulate the operation of credit institutions – and the LFCMC's regulatory provisions and orders,[70] and/or a prohibition has been set for the use of the voting

---

[60] s.19¹(2), CIL.

[61] s.20(1), CIL. A credit institution's minimum initial capital is 5 million EUR (s.21(1), CIL). A credit institution's own funds may not become less than the minimum initial capital that section 21 of the CIL specifies (i.e. 5 million EUR) (s.21(3), CIL). Subsection 21(2) of the CIL was repealed in December 2010.

[62] s.20(2), CIL.

[63] s.27(1)(1), CIL.

[64] s.27(1)(2), CIL.

[65] s.27(1)(3), CIL.

[66] s.27(1)(4), CIL.

[67] s.27(1)(5), CIL.

[68] s.27(1)(6), CIL.

[69] s.27(1)(7), CIL.

[70] s.27(1)(8), CIL.

rights of stocks that belong to stockholders of the credit institution who have a qualifying holding – which lasts for more than six months.[71] If the LFCMC has withdrawn a licence, then it shall not be renewed.[72] Subsection 27(3) of the CIL is as follows.

> "An appeal of an administrative act issued by the Financial and Capital Market Commission regarding the cancellation of a licence (permit) shall not suspend the execution thereof."

Within 30 days from the day on which a decision to issue or to cancel a licence for the operation of a credit institution was taken, the LFCMC shall notify the European Commission and the European Banking Authority of this decision.[73] The LFCMC shall inform the European Commission and the European Banking Authority concerning the refusal of a credit institution registered in Latvia to establish a branch in another Member State, and regarding the refusal of a credit institution registered in another Member State to found a branch in Latvia, and of measures that the LFCMC has taken in accordance with subsections 108^1(3) and 108^1(4) of the CIL.[74] The LFCMC shall inform the European Commission concerning

[71] s.27(1)(9), CIL.

[72] s.27(2), CIL.

[73] ss.27^1(1) and 27^1(2), CIL.

[74] s.27(3), CIL. The requirements that subsections 108^1(1), 108^1(2) and 108^1(3) of the CIL specify shall not prevent the LFCMC from applying measures in order to rectify contraventions, which are at variance with the laws of Latvia that "safeguard the interests of society", and to apply sanctions for these transgressions (s. 108^1(3), CIL). The English translation of the CIL does not contain a subsection 108^1(4) of the CIL. If the LFCMC determines that a branch of a credit institution that is registered in another Member State, which provides services in Latvia, or a credit institution that supplies financial services in Latvia without opening a branch, performs activities that breach the laws of Latvia, then it shall without delay request this credit institution to terminate these activities (s.108^1(1), CIL). If the branch of a credit institution that is registered in another Member State, which provides services in Latvia, or a credit institution that is registered in another Member State without founding a branch, does not discontinue its activities that are in breach of the laws of Latvia, then the LFCMC shall immediately notify the financial supervision authority of the home Member State – whose duty it is to act in such a way that the contraventions are rectified (s.108^1(2), CIL). In situations of emergency, without complying with the procedures to which section 108^1 of the CIL refers, the LFCMC may apply measures "in order to protect the interests of depositors, investors and other recipients of the services of a credit institution", whilst informing the home Member State's financial supervision authority, the

problems that a credit institution registered in Latvia encounters in commencing or conducting activities in a foreign state.[75] The LFCMC shall notify the European Commission and the European Banking Authority about the regulatory enactments that regulate the establishment and operation of credit institutions in Latvia.[76]

The foundation of a branch or a wholly-owned subsidiary is a 'capital movement' in Title I of the nomenclature in Annex I. Cross-border financial services are 'capital movements' in Titles V, VI, and XIII of the nomenclature in Annex I.[77] If the LFCMC refuses to issue, or revokes, a licence for the provision of financial services across a national border, then it contravenes the free movement of capital.

To be justified under Article 65(1)(b) of the TFEU, the restrictive measures must be necessary for the protection of interests that they are intended to guarantee, be proportionate (i.e. not attainable by less restrictive measures), and satisfy the requirements of legal certainty (i.e. be specific, objective and known to the parties beforehand); in addition, the persons whom the measures affect must have access to legal redress (i.e. intervention must be accompanied by a formal statement of reasons and be subject to review in the national courts).[78] For the most part, these interests are not stated – although in subsection 108¹(3) of the CIL, the measures are imposed in order to rectify breaches of Latvian provisions that are contrary to the laws of Latvia that protect the public interest, and in subsection 108¹(6) of the CIL, the measures are introduced in order to protect the interests of the recipients of a credit institution's services.[79] These subsections of the CIL state neither the measures that the LFCMC may take, nor the circumstances in which the CIL may apply each measure, and, therefore do not fulfil the requirements of legal certainty. In addition, the grounds on which the LFCMC may refuse to issue a licence or to withdraw one may provide it with discretion as to whether or not to apply the restrictive measure – for instance, clause 27(1)(2) of the CIL states that the LFCMC may withdraw the credit institution's licence if "it is determined that" the credit institution has provided information that is

---

European Banking Authority and the European Commission about these measures (s.108¹(6), CIL).

[75] s.27(5), CIL.

[76] s.27(6), CIL.

[77] See note 5, for the list of financial services.

[78] See the subsection '*The requirements for a successful public policy/public security derogation*', in section 2.1.3.

[79] See note 74, for subsections 108¹(3) and 108¹(6) of the CIL.

untrue to the LFCMC, in order to obtain the licence.[80] The existence of this discretion does not fulfil the requirements of legal certainty, and creates the possibility of a situation in which the LFCMC's withdrawal of the licence is disproportionate. Subsection 27(3) of the CIL permits a credit institution to appeal against a decision of the LFCMC to cancel a licence.[81] However, Chapter II of the CIL does not provide a right of appeal against a decision of the LFCMC to refuse to issue a licence. Furthermore, the CIL does not require the LFCMC to support a decision that it takes to refuse to issue a licence, or to revoke a licence, by a statement of reasons. Consequently, the applicant credit institution does not have sufficient access to legal redress. Thus, Article 65(1)(b) of the TFEU does not justify the restrictive measures.

For those restrictive measures that limit the free movement of capital between Latvia and third countries to be justified under Article 64(2) of the TFEU, the EU institutions must carefully take account of the objective of the free movement of capital whilst enacting the relevant legislation, and the domestic rules must not restrict the free movement of capital more than do the equivalent provisions of the relevant Directive.[82] On the second point, the relevant Directive (Directive 2013/36/EU) contains equivalence provisions for the suppliance of financial services in the EEA by credit institutions that are founded in third countries.[83] However, Directive 2013/36/EU does not refer to the provision of services to third countries by credit institutions that are authorised in the EEA. On the first point, whilst Recital 13 of Directive 2013/36/EU states that supervisory decisions and processes should not hinder the functioning of the internal market in respect of "the free flow of capital", the Directive's Articles do not refer to the free movement of capital. Thus, although the EU institutions were aware of the effect of Directive 2013/36/EU on the free movement of capital, they may not have carefully taken account of the

---

[80] See above in this section, for the grounds on which the LFCMC may revoke the licence of a credit institution. If this (Latvian) credit institution is a wholly-owned subsidiary of a non-Latvian company, then the LFCMC contravenes the free movement of capital if it refuses to issue this subsidiary with a licence or withdraws this licence.

[81] See above in this section, for subsection 27(3) of the CIL.

[82] See the subsection '*Derogations that apply only to capital movement to/from third countries*', in section 2.3.2.

[83] Articles 47(1) and 48(1) of Directive 2013/36/EU contain these provisions. See Chapter 3, note 815, for Article 47(1) of the TFEU. See the subsection '*Chapter 2: Authorisation of credit institution (including passporting)*', in section 3.3.1, for application of Articles 47(1) and 48(1) of the TFEU.

objective of this free movement, whist enacting the Directive. Thus, Article 64(2) of the TFEU does not justify those measures that limit the free movement of capital between Latvia and third countries. Consequently, the restrictive measures (including those that limit the free movement of capital between Latvia and other EEA states) contravene Article 63 of the TFEU.

Further to section 4.6, some recommendations can be made in order to bring the above restrictions to the free movement of capital closer to the justification in Article 65(1)(b) of the TFEU. First, each restrictive provision should be accompanied by an objective that is within one of the heads of this derogation, including 'overriding requirements of the general interest'.[84] The interest stated in subsection $108^{1}(6)$ of the CIL[85] is within overriding requirements of the general interest, because it is significant to each country's economic welfare and stability that the interests of consumers of the services that financial institutions provide are carefully and thoroughly considered. Nevertheless, other provisions that limit the free movement of capital, such as subsection 27(1) of the CIL,[86] should be accompanied by an objective that falls within one of the heads of the derogation.

Second, the discretion that some of the restrictive measures provide to the LFCMC should be reduced as much as possible. Given that a system of post-hoc declarations which leads to the revocation of a licence or other measures (such as a fine or a prohibition of specified financial services that the licence authorises the credit institution (or other financial entity) to provide) would not work,[87] the LFCMC should lay down guidelines as to how it will be exercising its discretion in case in which the Latvian legislation provides it with this. For example, the CIL should provide for secondary legislation to be enacted, which lays down the procedures with precision that the LFCMC is to follow (pursuant to clause 27(1)(2) of that Act), in determining whether a particular item of information is untrue.

Third, there should be regulations that lay down the measures that the LFCMC may take under the CIL or other Latvian financial Acts, and the specific circumstances in which it may take these measures. For instance, subsection $108^{1}(6)$ of the CIL should be accompanied by secondary legislation, which states specific circumstances that amount to situations of emergency, and lays down the precise measures that may apply in

[84] See sections 2.1.3 and 4.6, for the use of this additional head of justification in the case law.

[85] See note 74, for subsection $108^{1}(6)$ of the TFEU.

[86] See above in this section, for subsection 27(1) of the CIL.

[87] See section 4.6.

particular cases e.g. withdrawal of the licence of the bank to be able to accept deposits if it is demonstrated (probably beyond all reasonable doubt – the criminal standard of proof) that the interests of at least 100 depositors have been adversely, materially and demonstrably affected by the actions of the bank – and that an associated 'emergency' is present, for instance that the total funds of these depositors sums to (say) at least 1 million EUR, thereby threatening the liquidity of the bank (if all of these depositors quickly withdraw their funds).

Fourth, a provision should be added to the CIL (or at least to Chapter II of the CIL) that requires the LFCMC to provide reasons for a decision which adversely affects one or more credit institutions, and a right for the credit institution(s) to appeal to the Latvian courts against any decision of the LFCMC that adversely affects its interests. Although subsection 27(3) of the CIL provides a right of appeal to the Latvian courts in the case of a cancellation of a licence,[88] this right should be broadened to include any decision of the LFCMC that is against, or may be against, the interests of at least one (natural or legal) person. In order to limit the number of cases that might be filed pursuant to this a wide-ranging right of appeal, there should be strict time limits – such as that an appeal must be made within 20 working days from the date on which a person receives information concerning a decision of the LFCMC, and the person should be required to demonstrate standing before the appeal court – i.e. that the person's interests are materially affected by the decision.

Some of the Articles in Chapter II of the CIL require further ordering for clarity in reportage and analysis. Of particular concern is section 12^4 of the CIL, in which subsections (1), (4) and (5) concern financial institutions that provide services in Latvia and are registered in another state of the EEA, whilst subsections (2), (3) and (6) regulate financial institutions that are registered in Latvia and provide services in another EEA country. The short accession period for Latvia[89] may be partially responsible for this apparent disorder – the national laws needed to be constructed quickly, because the EU required Latvia to implement the *acquis communautaire* in order to take up its status as a Member State.[90] The Latvian legislature should calmly rework the CIL and the other Latvian financial services legislation, so as to order it as well as possible.

---

[88] See above in this section, for subsection 27(3) of the CIL.

[89] See the opening paragraph to this chapter (Chapter 5), for a succinct description of the accession period for Latvia.

[90] Section 1.3.1 discusses implementation of the *acquis communautaire*.

5.2 Germany

The German financial services legislation contains long sections and paragraphs. The English in the translated Acts is good. Each Article in a law is titled – for example in the Payment Services Supervision Act 2009, Section 2 of Part I (Definitions, Scope, Supervision, Payment Systems) is entitled 'Permitted and prohibited transactions for payment institutions'.

Part 5 of the Payment Services Supervision Act (PSSA) is to be the sample legislation of German financial services law, for investigation as to contraventions of Article 63 of the TFEU. Part 5 of the PSSA is entitled 'Cooperation with Other Authorities, Branches, Cross-border Services'. It contains sections 24 to 27 of the PSSA.

In the supervision of payment institutions that supply payment services or issue electronic money in another Member State of the EU or another Contracting State to the Agreement on the EEA, the BaFin and the Deutsche Bundesbank shall co-operate with the competent authorities of these countries.[91] An institution[92] that is licensed under subsection 8(1) or

---

[91] s.24, PSSA. 'Payment services' comprise 1) services that enable cash to be placed on a payment account or enable cash withdrawals from a payment account ('deposits and disbursement business'), 2) the execution of payment transactions, including direct debits, credit transfers and transactions with payment cards, without the extension of credit ('payment transactions'), 3) the execution of payment transactions that involve the granting of credit ('payment business involving the extension of credit'), 4) the issuance of payment authentication instruments, and the settlement of payment transactions that are initiated by these instruments ('payment authentication business'), 5) the execution of payment transactions in which the payer's consent to a payment transaction is communicated by means of a digital, information technology or telecommunication device, and the payment is made to the operator of this device, provided that this operator is acting only as an intermediary between the payment service user and the supplier ('digitised payment business'), and 6) services in which funds are received from the payer (without a payment account being opened) for the sole purpose of transferring a corresponding amount to the payee or to another payment service provider who acts on the payee's behalf, or services in which the amount is received on behalf of, and made available to, the payee (money remittance business) (s.1(2), PSSA). Payment institutions are those that provide the payment services in 4) above (i.e. payment authentication business) (ss.1(2a) and 1(2)(4), PSSA). Electronic money institutions are enterprises that carry out the business of electronic money issuance, other than credit institutions and specified public bodies that issue electronic money (ss.1(2a) and 1a(1)(5), PSSA). 'Electronic money' is all monetary value that is stored electronically, as represented by a claim on the issuer, which is issued on receipt of funds for the purposes of making

subsection 8a(1) of the PSSA,[93] which intends to found a branch in another Member State of the EU or another Contracting State to the Agreement on the EEA, shall promptly notify the BaFin and the Deutsche Bundesbank of this intention.[94] The notification must include the name of the country in which the branch is to be established,[95] a business plan that sets out the nature of the planned activities, the branch's organisational structure, and whether the institution intends to use agents (in the host country),[96] the address in the country "in which the institution maintains a branch" from which its documents can be requested and to which correspondence can be directed,[97] and the name of the branch's director.[98] The BaFin shall forward this information to the competent authorities of the state in which the institution is to found the branch, within one month of its receipt of the notification.[99]

An institution that wishes to provide payment services or to issue electronic money in another Member State of the EU or another Contracting State of the EEA without establishing a branch (i.e. by supplying cross-border services) shall swiftly notify the BaFin and the Deutsche Bundesbank of this intention.[100] This notification shall indicate the country in which the cross-border services are to be provided, a business plan that sets out the intended activities, and information as to whether agents (or electronic money agents) are to be used in the host

---

payment transactions, and which a natural or legal person (other than the issuer) accepts – (s.1a(3), PSSA).

[92] For the purposes of the PSSA, an 'institution' is a payment institution or an electronic money institution (s.1(2a), PSSA). See note 91, for the definitions of 'payment institutions' and 'electronic money institutions'.

[93] A person who wishes to provide payment services in Germany as a payment institution on a commercial basis, "or on a scale that requires a commercially equipped business operation", requires a written licence from the BaFin (s.8(1), PSSA). A person who wishes to carry out the business of electronic money issuance in Germany as an electronic money institution requires a written licence from the BaFin (s.8a(1), PSSA).

[94] s.25(1), PSSA.

[95] s.25(1)(1), PSSA.

[96] s.25(1)(2), PSSA.

[97] s.25(1)(3), PSSA. The quoted phrase (probably) refers to the country in which the new branch is to be established. Article 25 of Directive 2007/64/EC does not mention the request for documents and the address for correspondence. See section 2.2.8, for paragraphs 1, 2 and 4 of Article 25 of Directive 2007/64/EC.

[98] s.25(1)(4), PSSA.

[99] s.25(3), PSSA.

[100] ss.25(2) and 25(1), PSSA.

state.[101] The BaFin shall forward this information to the competent authorities of the country in which it is to provide cross-border services, within one month of its receipt of the notification.[102]

The BaFin and the Deutsche Bundesbank shall have the rights that section 14 of the PSSA provides directly in respect of foreign branches, and in relation to outsourcees, agents and electronic money agents that a German institution uses in other states of the EEA.[103] The BaFin or the Deutsche Bundesbank (via the BaFin) shall obtain the consent of the competent authorities of the host state in advance – in the case of on-site inspections.[104]

An institution that is domiciled in another Member State of the EU or another Contracting State to the EEA Agreement may provide payment services in Germany without a licence from the BaFin, through a branch or by way of cross-border services, if the institution has been authorised by

---

[101] s.25(2), PSSA.

[102] s.25(3), PSSA.

[103] s.25(4), PSSA. On request, an institution, the members of the institution's governing bodies, the institution's employees, branches and outsourcees, and the agents (and electronic money agents) acting for the institution, shall provide information on all business issues, and submit documents, to the BaFin, the agencies and persons that the BaFin uses to perform its duties, and the Deutsche Bundesbank (s.14(1), PSSA). Without being required to provide reasons, the BaFin may conduct audits on institutions and their branches, agents, electronic money agents and outsourcees, and delegate the execution of these audits to the Deutsche Bundesbank (s.14(1), PSSA). The staff of the BaFin and of Deutsche Bundesbank, and any other persons whom the BaFin uses to carry out the audits, may, for this purpose, enter and inspect the business premises of the institution, its subsidiaries, agents, electronic money agents or outsourcees during normal office and business hours (s.14(1), PSSA). Although this sentence of section 14(1) of the PSSA in the English translation of this Act refers to "subsidiary", it may mean 'branch' – a term that is mentioned in the first two sentences of section 14(1) of the PSSA. The BaFin and Deutsche Bundesbank may send representatives to the general meetings or shareholders' meetings of the institution, and to meetings of the institution's supervisory bodies; who may address them (s.14(2), PSSA). At the BaFin's request, institutions shall convene the above meetings, schedule meetings of the supervisory and administrative bodies, and announce items on which resolutions are to be taken (s.14(3), PSSA). The BaFin may send representatives to the scheduled meetings, who may address these gatherings (s.14(3), PSSA). A person who is required to provide information may refuse to answer questions that might expose him/her, or one of his/her relatives, to the risk of criminal prosecution, or to proceedings pursuant to the Administrative Offences Act (s.14(4), PSSA).

[104] s.25(4), PSSA.

the competent authorities of the other country, the payment services are covered by the licence, and the institution is supervised by the competent authorities under provisions that correspond to those of Directive 2007/64/EC or of Directive 2009/110/EC on the taking up, pursuit or prudential supervision of the business of electronic money institutions.[105] If the BaFin possesses “factual evidence” which shows that, in connection with the intended foundation of a branch or engagement of an agent, money laundering or terrorist financing is taking place, has taken place or has been attempted, or that the establishment of the branch or the use of the agent increases the risk of money laundering or terrorist financing taking place, then the BaFin shall inform the competent authorities of the country of origin.[106] In consequence, the competent authority of the country of origin may refuse to register the branch or the agent in the register of payment institutions or the register of electronic money institutions (as appropriate), or, if a registration has already been made, may expunge this registration.[107]

If the BaFin ascertains that an institution that is domiciled in another Member State or another Contracting State to the EEA Agreement and which provides payment services in Germany through a branch or by way of cross-border services, is not fulfilling its supervisory obligations, then the BaFin shall request the institution to rectify the deficiency within a specified period.[108] If the institution does not comply with this request, then the BaFin shall inform the competent authorities of the home country.[109] If those competent authorities do not take measures, or if its measures are insufficient, then the BaFin may “take the necessary measures” – having informed the competent authorities of the home state.[110] If necessary, the BaFin may forbid the institution from initiating new business in Germany.[111] “In urgent cases”, the BaFin “may take the necessary measures” without initiating the procedure described in this paragraph.[112]

Having informed the BaFin, the competent authorities of the institution’s home country may verify the information that is required for

---

[105] s.26(1), PSSA.
[106] s.26(2), PSSA.
[107] s.26(2), PSSA.
[108] s.26(5), PSSA.
[109] s.26(5), PSSA.
[110] s.26(5), PSSA.
[111] s.26(5), PSSA.
[112] s.26(5), PSSA.

the supervision of the branch in Germany.[113] At the request of the home state's competent authorities, the staff of the BaFin and of the Deutsche Bundesbank may support those authorities with the verification, or may conduct it on their behalf.[114] If this request is made, then the BaFin and the Deutsche Bank assume the rights under section 14 of the PSSA,[115] and also under section 5 of the PSSA – if this is warranted by the facts or if it is settled that foreign enterprises are supplying unauthorised payment services, issuing electronic money without authorisation, executing unauthorised transactions under the Banking Act, the Investment Act or the Insurance Supervision Act, or contravening comparable provisions in the home country.[116]

---

[113] s.26(6), PSSA.

[114] s.26(6), PSSA.

[115] s.26(6), PSSA. See note 103, for section 14 of the PSSA.

[116] s.26(6), PSSA. If it is established that an enterprise is supplying unauthorised payment services or issuing electronic money without authorisation, or is (or has been) involved in the initiation, settlement or conclusion of unauthorised payment services or the unauthorised issuance of electronic money, then the members of this enterprise's governing body, the enterprise's shareholders and its employees, shall, on request, provide information about its business activities, and submit documentation, to the BaFin and the Deutsche Bundesbank (s.5(1), PSSA). The BaFin may conduct inspections on the enterprise's premises, and on the premises the persons who, and the enterprises that, are required to provide information and submit documentation under subsection 5(1) of the PSSA (s.5(2), PSSA). The BaFin may charge the Deutsche Bundesbank with the task of conducting these inspections (s.5(2), PSSA). For this purpose, the staff of the BaFin, and of the Deutsche Bundesbank, may enter and inspect these premises during normal office and business hours (s.5(2), PSSA). In order to prevent imminent risks to safety and to public order, these staff shall be authorised to enter and inspect those premises outside normal office and business hours, and may enter and inspect premises that serve as living accommodation (s.5(2), PSSA). The staff of the BaFin, and of the Deutsche Bundesbank, may search the enterprise's premises, and the premises of the persons who, and the enterprises that, are required to provide information and submit documentation under subsection 5(1) of the PSSA (s.5(3). PSSA). During this search, the staff may, for the purpose of seizing items that could be significant as evidence in determining the facts of the case, also search the persons who are required to supply information and submit documentation (ss.5(3) and 5(4), PSSA). This search shall be ordered by the court, other than "in the event of imminent danger" (s.5(3), PSSA). Searches of premises that provide living accommodation shall be ordered by the court (s.5(3), PSSA). The competent court is the local court in whose district the premises are situated (s.5(3). PSSA). The court's decision is subject to appeal (s.5(3), PSSA). A written record shall be made of the search, which must specify the responsible official agency, the place and time of the search, the reason for the search, its outcome and, if no court order was

If an enterprise which is domiciled outside the EEA operates through a branch in Germany that provides payment services or issues electronic money, then this branch shall be deemed to be an 'institution' within the meaning of the PSSA.[117] The PSSA shall apply to these 'institutions', subject to the following limitations.

First, the third country enterprise shall appoint two or more natural persons who are resident in Germany and are authorised to manage the business of the enterprise and to represent it "in respect of the institution's field of business".[118] These persons shall be deemed to be directors (of the institution), and be entered in the commercial register.[119]

Second, the institution shall be required to maintain separate books, and return separate accounts to the BaFin and the Deutsche Bundesbank in respect of the business that it carries out and the assets of the enterprise that serves its (i.e. the institution's) business activities.[120] The provisions of the Commercial Code that concern commercial books of account for financial services firms and credit institutions shall apply accordingly.[121]

Third, a balance sheet to be drawn up at the end of each financial year in accordance with clause 27(2)(2) of the PSSA,[122] a statement of income and expenses, and notes to the annual financial statements, shall be

---

issued, the facts on which the presumption of imminent danger was based (s.5(3), PSSA). Section 5 of the PSSA applies to "other enterprises and persons", as long as facts are known which justify the assumption that these parties are involved in the initiation, settlement or conclusion of payment services, or the issuance of electronic money, which are being provided in another country contrary to a prohibition that applies there, and the competent authority of the other country "files a corresponding request" with the BaFin (s.5(6), PSSA).

[117] s.27(1), PSSA. See note 92, for the definition of 'institution'. If this enterprise operates several branches in Germany, then these branches shall be deemed to be one institution (s.27(1), PSSA).

[118] s.27(2)(1), PSSA. The quoted phrase refers to the business that the German branch of the enterprise conducts as a payment service provider and/or an electronic money institution.

[119] s.27(2)(1), PSSA. One director shall suffice for a small institution with a low volume of business (s.27(2)(1), PSSA).

[120] s.27(2)(2), PSSA.

[121] s.27(2)(2), PSSA. The amount of working capital that the enterprise makes available to the institution, and of operating surplus that remains with the institution in order to contribute to its own funds, shall be shown separately in the annual balance sheet (s.27(2)(2), PSSA). The excess of assets over liabilities, or of liabilities over assets, shall be shown in aggregate, and separately, at the end of the balance sheet (s.27(2)(2), PSSA).

[122] See the previous paragraph, for clause 27(2)(2) of the PSSA.

deemed to be the institution's annual financial statements.[123] The directors of the institution shall select and appoint the auditor of these financial statements.[124]

Fourth, the institution's own funds shall be deemed to be the sum of the amounts that are shown in quarterly reporting under subsection 12(4) of the PSSA, as the current working capital that the enterprise makes available to the payment institution, and of the operating surplus that stays within the institution in order to add to its own funds, less the amount of any credit balance on the inter-branch account.[125]

The nomenclature in Annex I does not mention 'payment services'. Nonetheless, Title XIII(F) of the nomenclature refers to 'Miscellaneous' capital movements. Furthermore, the CJEU has held that the list of capital movements in the nomenclature in Annex I is "not exhaustive".[126] In addition, Article 63(2) of the TFEU prohibits restrictions on payments between Member States, and between Member States and third countries, unless these barriers are justified by the framework of provisions in this chapter of the TFEU.[127] Thus, the suppliance of cross-border payment services is a 'capital movement' by virtue of Article 63(2) of the TFEU, and also within Title XIII(F) of the nomenclature in Annex I. The establishment of a branch is a 'capital movement' in Title I(1) of the nomenclature in Annex I.

---

[123] s.27(2)(3), PSSA.

[124] s.27(2)(3), PSSA. Subject to this proviso, section 340k of the Commercial Code shall apply to the auditing of the institution's annual financial statements (s.27(2)(3), PSSA). The annual financial statements of the enterprise and those of the institution for the same financial year shall be submitted together (s.27(2)(3), PSSA).

[125] s.27(2)(4), PSSA. Payment institutions shall submit the information required for the audit of their capital adequacy to the BaFin and the Deutsche Bundesbank every quarter (s.12(4), PSSA). When evaluating capital adequacy on the basis of an assessment of the business organisation, risk management, internal control mechanisms, "loss database", and risks of the payment institution, the BaFin may require the payment institution to hold an amount of own funds that differs from the principles of solvency by up to 20% (s.12(4), PSSA).

[126] See, for instance, *Trummer and Mayer* [1999], ECR I-1661, at paragraph 21. Section 2.1.1 considers how capital movements are defined. See also Chapter 3, note 1877, and the accompanying text.

[127] See the opening paragraph of section 2.1. 'This chapter of the TFEU' is Chapter 4 (Capital and payments) of Title IV (Free movement of persons, services and capital) of Part III (Union policies and internal actions) of the TFEU. The chapter contains Articles 63 to 66 of the TFEU.

The refusal to enter a branch of a payment service provider in the register of payment service providers, the removal of the details of a payment service provider from this register, and the taking of measures that impede the provision of payment services in Germany (either through a branch located there or across the national border), limit the free movement of capital.

To be justified under Article 65(1)(b) of the TFEU, the restrictive measures must be necessary for the protection of the interests that they are intended to guarantee, be proportionate (i.e. not achievable by less restrictive measures), and observe the requirements of legal certainty (i.e. be specific, objective and known to the parties beforehand); furthermore, the persons whom the measures affect must have access to legal redress (i.e. intervention must be supported by reasons and be subject to review by the national courts).[128] According to subsection 26(2) of the PSSA,[129] the home EEA state's competent authority may refuse to register the German branch of the payment service provider or electronic money institution, or may delete this registration, if the BaFin possesses proof of money laundering or terrorist financing; the interests are therefore the protection of clients' funds and the reputation of the payments services sector. Under subsection 26(5) of the PSSA,[130] the BaFin may take restrictive measures, including a prohibition from commencing new business in Germany, in response to a payment institution that is domiciled in another EEA state that does not fulfil its supervisory obligations – either if the measures that the home country's supervisory authority imposes are insufficient or if the case is an urgent one; the interests are therefore the need to ensure that a payment service provider or electronic money institution satisfies its supervisory duties (or is penalised for not doing so), especially if there is urgency. The restrictive measures that subsection 26(2) of the PSSA provides are not disproportionate, and provide legal certainty – as these measures are clearly stated and rely on 'factual evidence' (rather than on the opinion of the BaFin). By contrast, subsection 26(5) of the PSSA empowers the BaFin to 'take the necessary measures', without specifying what these measures are (with one exception – prohibiting the payment service provider or electronic money institution from initiating new business in Germany); consequently, the restrictive measures that the BaFin imposes pursuant to this subsection do not observe the requirements of legal certainty, and may be disproportionate. Although the PSSA

---

[128] See the subsection '*The requirements for a successful public policy/public security derogation*', in section 2.1.3.

[129] See above in this section, for subsection 26(2) of the PSSA.

[130] See above in this section, for subsection 26(5) of the PSSA.

provides a right of appeal against some of the provisions of the BaFin,[131] there is no (explicit) right of appeal against measures that the BaFin takes pursuant to subsections 26(2) and 26(5) of the PSSA. Furthermore, the PSSA does not require the BaFin to provide reasons for any of its decisions. Hence, the persons whom the restrictive measures affect do not have access to legal redress. Consequently, Article 65(1)(b) of the TFEU does not justify the restrictive measures in subsections 26(2) and 26(5) of the PSSA.

Section 27 of the PSSA is the only provision in Part 5 of this Act that concerns capital movement between Germany and third countries.[132] Although the establishment of a branch (in Germany of a firm that is domiciled in a third country) is a 'capital movement' in Title I(1) of the nomenclature in Annex I, the limitations that subsection 27(2) of the PSSA imposes on this branch are not onerous, and therefore, do not restrict the free movement of capital. Consequently, the justification in Article 64(2) of the TFEU is not considered in respect of Part 5 of the PSSA. Thus, subsections 26(2) and 26(5) of the PSSA contravene Article 63 of the TFEU.

Subsection 26(2) of the PSSA almost reaches the *Commission v Belgium*[133] standard for the successful application of the derogation in Article 65(1)(b) of the TFEU.[134] There is a legitimate interest – the protection of clients' funds and the reputation of the payment services sector in the presence or probability of money laundering and/or terrorist financing; the restrictive measures are necessary to protect this interest; these measures are proportionate, and they satisfy the requirements of legal certainty. The only missing requirement of the derogation in respect of subsection 26(2) of the PSSA is that the persons whom the restrictive measures affect do not have access to legal redress. Although subsection 26(5) of the PSSA is farther from this standard that is subsection 26(2) of the PSSA, this analysis demonstrates that the German legislation has the potential for adjustment so as to be compliant with the EU's free movement of capital rules.

[131] Section 23 of the PSSA provides a right of appeal against measures that BaFin takes on the basis of sections 4, 5, 10(2), 14(1), 15, 16, 17a(1), 19(3) and 30(2) of the PSSA.

[132] See above in this section, for section 27 of the PSSA.

[133] [2002] ECR I-4809.

[134] See section 4.6, for an analysis of *Commission v Belgium* [2002] ECR I-4809, and the successful application therein of the derogation from Article 63 of the TFEU in Article 65(1)(b) of the TFEU.

The reluctance that the German legislature, and the law-makers of the countries studied earlier in this chapter and in previous chapters, have to requiring their financial supervision authorities to support their decisions with a formal statement of reasons – upon which an appeal in the national courts may be based – may be due to a perception that these authorities exist to regulate the firms who report to them, and, therefore, their decisions should be final (unless these decisions are grossly inaccurate or negligent). These legislatures should insert a provision into each of their country's financial services acts, to the following effect.

1. "All decisions of the [financial supervision authority name] must be supported by a formal statement of reasons, which clearly explain the basis or bases on which the relevant decision was taken."
2. "Any applicant who is materially and adversely affected by a decision of the [financial supervision authority name] and who is sufficiently closely connected with the issues involved in the decision may lodge an appeal in the [name of the national civil court] against the decision, which is based on one or more of the reasons that the [financial supervision authority name] provides for it."
3. "This appeal must be made within [specified time period] of the date on which the applicant receives it or [specified time period], whichever is the earlier."
4. "The [name of the national civil court] will publish the results of the appeal, and the reasons on which these results are based, in [specified source] within [specified time period] of the close of the appeal."

5.3 Croatia

The English translations of the Croatian financial services Acts and Ordinances contain clear wording and short sentences. Whilst the chapters and sections are titled, the individual articles are not. For example, the Ordinance on Organisational Requirements for Providing Investment Services and Conducting Investment Activities and Ancillary Services of 7 January 2009 is divided into titles (e.g. 'II. General Organizational Requirements for Conducting Activities of Investment Firm'), subtitles within the titles (e.g. 'General organisational requirements'; 'Monitoring of compliance with relevant regulations'; 'Risk management'), and one or more Articles within the subtitles (e.g. the first of these subtitles contains Article 4, the second Article 5, and the third Articles 7, 8 and 9).

The sample from the Croatian financial services legislation is an extract from Title III ('Carrying on of Insurance Business') of the Insurance Act 2006 (IA). The subtitles of Title III of most relevance to the free movement of capital are III.6 ('Carrying on of insurance business operations outside the territory of the Republic of Croatia'), III.7 ('Freedom of insurance companies from Member States to provide insurance services and reinsurance companies from Member States to provide reinsurance services'), and III.8 ('Conduct of insurance business operations by insurance companies from third countries'). The provisions in these subtitles are considered in turn.

5.3.1 Subtitle III.6 of the IA: Carrying on of insurance operations outside Croatia

A Croatian insurance company[135] may conduct insurance business operations[136] in respect of which it has received authorisation from the CFSSA, in another Member State[137] or via a branch directly (i.e. by the provision of cross-border services), provided that it satisfies the conditions the Articles 77 and 78 of the IA contain.[138] An insurance company shall be

---

[135] An 'insurance company' is a legal person with its head office in Croatia that has been authorised to carry out insurance business operations by the CFSSA (Article 2(1), IA).

[136] Within the meaning of the IA, 'insurance business' is the conclusion and performance of life assurance and non-life assurance contracts, other than compulsory social insurances (Article 3(1), IA). 'Non-life insurance business' consists of the following classes of insurance: personal accident insurance, health insurance, insurance of land motor vehicles, insurance of railway locomotives and rolling stock, insurance of aircraft, insurance of vessels, insurance of goods in transit, insurance against fire and natural disasters, other lines of property insurance, motor vehicle liability insurance, aircraft liability insurance, insurance of liability that arises from the use of vessels, other lines of liability insurance, credit insurance, suretyship insurance, insurance of miscellaneous financial losses, insurance of legal protection, and travel insurance (Article 3(2), IA). 'Life assurance business' consists of the following classes of insurance: life assurance, annuity assurance, supplementary insurance that is connected to life assurance, and other life assurance lines (Article 3(3), IA). 'Other life assurance' includes tontines, assurance with paid-up sum assured, marriage assurance, birth assurance, and the management of group pension funds in cases in which these are accompanied by insurance that covers the conservation of capital or the payment of a minimum interest (Article 3(3), IA).

[137] Within the meaning of the IA, a 'Member State' is a Member State of the EU or a member of the EEA (Article 4(1), IA). As the Contracting Parties to the EEA Agreement are the 28 Member States of the EU, plus Iceland, Liechtenstein and Norway, 'Member State' in the IA means a Contracting Party to the EEA Agreement. 'Home Member State' means the Member State in which the head office of the insurance or reinsurance company is situated (Article 4(4), IA).

[138] Article 76(1), IA.

deemed to be conducting insurance business operations in a Member State, if it concludes contracts that cover risks which are located in that Member State.[139]

A Croatian insurance company or reinsurance company[140] that intends to carry out insurance or reinsurance business operations[141] in a Member State, shall notify the CFSSA, specifying the Member State in which it intends to conduct these operations.[142] This notification shall contain the following information: the name of the Member State in which the Croatian insurance company intends to open a branch,[143] the types of risks that the branch is to insure or reinsure,[144] a scheme of operations pursuant to Article 63 of the IA,[145] a statement by a certified actuary that the

---

[139] Article 76(2), IA.

[140] A 'reinsurance company' is a legal person with its head office in Croatia that has been authorised to carry out reinsurance business operations by the CFSSA (Article 2(2), IA).

[141] Within the meaning of the IA, 'reinsurance business' is the conclusion and performance of reinsurance contracts, whereby the part of the risk that is in excess of that retained by the insurance company is transferred to a reinsurance company, i.e. the activities that comprise the acceptance of risks which an insurance company cedes (Article 3a(1), IA). Unless the IA states otherwise, its provisions that concern joint-stock insurance companies also apply to reinsurance companies (Article 3a(2), IA).

[142] Article 77(1), IA.

[143] Article 77(2)(1), IA.

[144] Article 77(2)(2), IA.

[145] Article 77(2)(3), IA. This scheme of operations shall include 1) information that concerns fundamental business policies, 2) a list of individual classes of insurance within which the insurance company will conduct insurance business, 3) a forecast balance sheet and profit and loss account, 4) the calculation of the capital of an insurance company in accordance with Article 93 of the IA, and of the guarantee fund to which Article 100 of the IA refers, 5) the computation of required solvency margins to which Articles 98 and 99 of the IA refer, 6) estimates of the costs for establishing administrative services, "the organisation for securing business", management expenses, and the financial resources that are required to meet these costs, 7) the planned reinsurance or retrocession programmes, with tables of maximum cover for all business lines, 8) the estimated financial resources and liquidity that will be available to cover liabilities and ensure capital adequacy, 9) a detailed projection of expected operating results for a period of three years or more – including, in particular, expected premium income, expected insurance premiums and claims, expected commission expenses (and other expenses), and estimated levels of technical provisions and other reserves (Article 63(1), IA). If an insurance company intends to carry out travel insurance business, then the scheme of operations shall also contain the description of funds that are required to meet the liabilities that arise from this business line (Articles 63(2) and 3(2)(18), IA).

insurance or reinsurance company satisfies the prescribed capital adequacy requirements (which depend on the insurance classes and the business volume of the branch),[146] the address of the branch in the host Member State from which documents may be obtained, and to which all communications may be sent,[147] and the names of the persons who are responsible for the management of the branch.[148]

Provided that the CFSSA finds that "there is no reason to doubt the adequacy of the administrative structure of the financial position of the insurance or reinsurance company", or "the good repute and professional qualifications or experience of persons responsible in the branch", it shall, within 3 months of receipt of the notification, forward the information received to the competent supervisory authority of the host Member State – and notify the insurance or reinsurance company accordingly.[149] In addition to the notification to which Article 77(4) of the IA refers, the CFSSA shall also submit to the competent supervisory authority of the host Member State a statement to the effect that the insurance company satisfies the prescribed capital adequacy requirements,[150] and information that indicates the insurance classes for which the CFSSA has granted the company authorisation to carry out insurance or reinsurance business operations.[151] If the CFSSA finds that "there is reason to doubt the adequacy of the administrative structure or financial position of the insurance company or reinsurance company, or the good repute and professional qualifications or experience of persons responsible in the branch", then it shall, within 3 months of receipt of the notification to which Article 77(2) of the IA refers,[152] issue a decision to refuse to deliver the information to which Articles 77(2) and 77(4) of the IA refer to the host Member State's competent supervisory authority.[153] The insurance or reinsurance company has the right to commence an administrative appeal against this decision.[154]

Before the branch of a Croatian insurance or reinsurance company may start its insurance or reinsurance business operations, the competent

[146] Article 77(2)(3), IA.
[147] Article 77(2)(4), IA.
[148] Article 77(2)(5), IA.
[149] Article 77(3), IA.
[150] Article 77(4)(1), IA.
[151] Article 77(4)(2), IA.
[152] See the previous paragraph, for Article 77(2) of the IA.
[153] Article 77(5), IA. See note 152. See the previous sentence, for Article 77(4) of the IA.
[154] Article 77(5), IA.

supervisory authority of the host Member State shall, within two months of receipt of the information to which Articles 77(2) and 77(4) of the IA refer,[155] notify the CFSSA of "the conditions under which, in the interests of the general good, that business must be carried on" in the host Member State.[156] Upon receiving this notification, or if it is not received within the two month period, the branch may be founded in the host Member State, and may commence business.[157]

A Croatian insurance or reinsurance company that wishes to conduct insurance business operations in another Member State directly (i.e. by the provision of cross-border services) shall notify the CFSSA of this intention in writing, indicating the classes of insurance or reinsurance that it intends to cover.[158] Within one month of receipt of this notification, the CFSSA shall forward it to the host Member State's competent supervisory authority,[159] together with a statement to the effect that the insurance company fulfils the prescribed capital adequacy requirements,[160] a description of the insurance classes over which the CFSSA has authorised the insurance company to carry out insurance business operations,[161] and a description of the insurance classes that the insurance (or reinsurance) company proposes to provide in the host Member State.[162] The CFSSA shall immediately inform the insurance or reinsurance company that it has forwarded this information to the competent supervisory authority of the host Member State.[163] If the CFSSA does not forward the information to the host Member State's competent supervisory authority within the period stated (i.e. one month of receipt), then it shall issue a decision to refuse to communicate this information to the latter.[164] The insurance or reinsurance company has the right to lodge an administrative appeal against this

[155] See above in this section, for Articles 77(2) and 77(4) of the IA.
[156] Article 77(6), IA.
[157] Articles 77(7) and 77(6), IA. The branch of a Croatian insurance company may initiate the business of compulsory insurance within the transport sector in the host Member State according to the conditions that Article 77 of the IA states, after it has submitted a statement to the host Member State's competent supervisory authority that the insurance company has joined the national guarantee fund or the national insurance bureau of the host Member State (Article 77(9), IA).
[158] Article 78(1), IA.
[159] Article 78(2), IA.
[160] Article 78(2)(1), IA.
[161] Article 78(2)(2), IA.
[162] Article 78(2)(3), IA.
[163] Article 78(3), IA.
[164] Article 78(4), IA.

decision.[165] The insurance or reinsurance company may start to provide insurance or reinsurance services in the host Member State, as soon as it receives the notice from the CFSSA (to which Article 78(3) of the IA refers) that the latter has forwarded the notification to the competent supervisory authority of the host Member State.[166]

The home Member State shall be responsible for the financial supervision of an insurance or reinsurance company, including that of the business that it conducts either through branches or by the provision of cross-border services.[167] If the competent supervisory authority of the host Member State "have reason to consider that the activities of an insurance or reinsurance company might affect its financial soundness", then they shall inform the home Member State's competent supervisory authority.[168] The host Member State in which a branch of an insurance or reinsurance company is situated shall provide that the home Member State's competent supervisory authority may, having already informed the host Member State's competent supervisory authority, conduct on-the-spot verification of the information that is "necessary to ensure the financial supervision of" the insurance or reinsurance company.[169] The host Member State's competent supervisory authority may take part in this verification.[170]

If a Croatian insurance or reinsurance company continues to conduct business operations in another Member State, after the competent authority of that Member State has informed the company that it is breaching that country's regulations, then the CFSSA shall "take supervisory measures pursuant to" the IA.[171] The CFSSA shall, without delay, notify the host Member State's competent authority of the measures that it is taking.[172] If the CFSSA withdraws the insurance or reinsurance company's authorisation to carry out insurance business operations, then it

---

[165] Article 78(4), IA.

[166] Article 78(5), IA. See above in this paragraph for Article 78(3) of the IA.

[167] Article 79(1), IA.

[168] Article 79(1), IA.

[169] Article 79(2), IA. 'Financial supervision' in Article 79(2) of the IA includes verification of the insurance company's whole business, its state of solvency, and the "establishment of technical provisions" and of the assets that cover these provisions, in accordance with the rules that the home Member State lays down or the practices that it follows pursuant to these rules (Article 79(6), IA).

[170] Article 79(2), IA.

[171] Article 79(3), IA.

[172] Article 79(4), IA.

shall immediately notify the host Member State's competent supervisory authority of this revocation.[173]

A Croatian insurance company is allowed to carry out insurance business operations in a third country via a branch, provided that it complies with that state's legislation.[174] In order to establish a branch in a third country, the CFSSA must authorise it to do so.[175] The CFSSA may refuse to grant this authorisation if, taking account of the legislation of the country in which the company intends to open a branch, "it may be reasonably assumed that the exercise of supervision pursuant to the provisions of this Act is likely to be difficult".[176]

The foundation of a branch and the provision of cross-border services are 'capital movements' in Titles I(1) and X of the nomenclature in Annex I, respectively. If the CFSSA refuses to forward information concerning the Croatian insurance or reinsurance company to the financial supervision authority of the host Member State, revokes the authorisation of a Croatian insurance or reinsurance company (due its contravention of the law of the host Member State), or refuses to authorise a Croatian insurance company to establish a branch in a third country, then it restricts the free movement of capital.

For Article 65(1)(b) of the TFEU to justify the restrictive measures, they must be necessary for the protection of interests that they are intended to guarantee, be proportionate (i.e. not attainable by less restrictive measures), and observe the requirements of legal certainty (i.e. be specific, objective and known to the parties beforehand); furthermore, the persons whom the measures affect must have access to legal redress (i.e. a formal statement of reasons must accompany the intervention, and the latter must be subject to review in the national courts).[177] Articles 77(3), 77(5) and 78(4) of the IA each provide the CFSSA with a discretion in the decision as to whether to forward, or to refuse to forward, the relevant information

---

[173] Article 79(5), IA.

[174] Article 81(1), IA. For the purposes of the IA, a 'third country' is a country other than Croatia and other than a Member State (Article 5(1), IA). As a 'Member State' is a Contracting Party to the EEA Agreement (see note 137), a 'third country' is a state that is not a Contracting Party to the EEA Agreement; i.e.it is outside the EEA. The IA does not (explicitly) provide for a Croatian insurance or reinsurance company to provide cross-border services in a third country. Article 81 of the IA does not apply to reinsurance companies (Article 81(4), IA).

[175] Article 81(2), IA.

[176] Article 81(3), IA.

[177] See the subsection '*The requirements for a successful public policy/public security derogation*', in section 2.1.3.

to the financial supervision authority of the host Member State. Consequently, although the applicant should know that the CFSSA may refuse to forward this information, it is not certain as to the precise grounds on which this decision to forward or refuse to forward this information is to be taken.[178] Furthermore, Article 79(3) of the IA gives the CFSSA a broad discretion as to which measures to apply to an insurance or reinsurance firm that contravenes the law of the host Member State; the boundary to the action(s) that the CFSSA may take is that the measures are pursuant to the IA.[179] Hence, Article 79(3) of the IA does not fulfil the requirements of legal certainty, and may be disproportionate. In addition, Article 81(3) of the IA provides some discretion to the CFSSA in deciding whether or not the third country's financial supervision authority is able to effectively supervise the branch of the Croatian insurance undertaking in its territory.[180] This discretion is narrowed by the use of an objective test (i.e. it may be assumed that), and the insertion of the word 'reasonable' into the test. Nevertheless, Article 81 of the CFSSA does not set out the ground(s) on which the CFSSA will take this decision. Therefore, the test is not specific enough to satisfy the requirements of legal certainty. With respect to legal redress, Articles 77(3) and 78(4) of the IA provide the applicant with the right to appeal in the administrative courts against a decision of the CFSSA to refuse to forward the information that it has provided to the CFSSA to the financial supervision authority of the host Member State.[181] Nevertheless, Articles 79 and 81 of the IA do not provide the applicant with a right to appeal against an adverse decision of the CFSSA. Furthermore, there are no provisions in the IA that require the CFSSA to provide reasons for any of the decisions that it takes pursuant to the provisions of subtitle III.6 of this Act.[182] Hence, the persons whom the measures affect do not have sufficient access to legal redress. Thus, Article 65(1)(b) of the TFEU does not justify the restrictive measures in subtitle III.6 of the IA.

---

[178] See above in this section, for Articles 77(3), 77(5) and 78(4) of the IA.

[179] See above in this section, for Article 79(3) of the IA.

[180] See above in this section, for Article 81(3) of the IA.

[181] This right of appeal is pursuant to Articles 146(2) and 148(3) of Directive 2009/138/EC. See section 2.2.3, for Directive 2009/138/EC.

[182] Articles 146(2) and 148(3) of Directive 2009/138/EC require the financial supervision authority of the home Member State to provide reasons to the applicant insurance company for refusing to forward the relevant information to the financial supervision authority of the host Member State (see section 2.2.3). The IA does not transpose these Articles.

As Article 81 of the IA affects the free movement of capital between Croatia and third countries, the justification in Article 64(2) of the TFEU is considered. According to this Article, the EU may limit the free movement of capital between Member States and third countries, if its institutions carefully into account the objective of the free movement of capital whilst enacting the relevant legislation, and if national rules do not restrict the free movement of capital more than do the equivalent provisions of the relevant Directive.[183] Directive 2009/138/EC is the relevant Directive. Recital 72 of Directive 2009/138/EC states that Member States should not require insurance or reinsurance firms to invest their funds in particular categories of assets, as this requirement may be incompatible with the liberalisation of capital movements for which Article 63 of the TFEU provides. However, the Articles of Directive 2009/138/EC do not refer to the free movement of capital. Thus, although the EU's legislators have considered the free movement of capital whilst enacting the Directive, it is debatable whether or not the statement in the recital is sufficient to establish that the legislators had carefully taken account of this objective.[184] In addition, over the area of provision of insurance services to third countries, Article 81 of the IA restricts the free movement of capital more than Directive 2009/138/EC does, because the latter does not specifically empower the EU institutions to make agreements with third countries in order to provide insurance services from the EEA states to the those countries.[185] Consequently, Article 64(2) of the TFEU does not justify Article 81(3) of the IA. Hence, the restrictive measures in subtitle III.6 of the IA contravene Article 63 of the TFEU.

5.3.2 Subtitle III.7 of the IA: Freedom of insurance companies from Member States to provide insurance services

An insurance company or reinsurance company that has the right to conduct insurance business operations or reinsurance business operations in specific classes of insurance or reinsurance in a Member State, may also carry on insurance business operations or reinsurance business operations in these insurance classes or reinsurance in Croatia, either directly or via a

[183] See the subsection '*Derogations that apply only to capital movement to/from third countries*', in section 2.3.2.

[184] See the subsection '*Chapter 2 Division 2: Activities of Estonian Insurance Undertakings in Foreign States*', in section 3.4.

[185] See the comments in the penultimate paragraph of the subsection '*Chapter 2 Division 2: Activities of Estonian Insurance Undertakings in Foreign States*', in section 3.4.

branch.[186] The insurance company to which Article 82(1) of the IA refers, or its branch in Croatia, shall be subject to the provisions of Article 13,[187] Articles 89 to 91,[188] and Article 258 of the IA.[189] A reinsurance company may carry out reinsurance business operations, after the competent authorities of the Member State have approved it to do so.[190]

---

[186] Article 82(1), IA. 'Member State' means a Contracting Party to the EEA Agreement – see note 137. A 'person from a Member State' is a natural person that has permanent residence, or a legal person with its head office, in the territory of that Member State (Article 4(2), IA). An insurance company or a reinsurance company from a Member State is a legal person with its head office in that country, whose competent supervisory authority has granted it authorisation to conduct insurance or reinsurance business there (Article 4(3), IA). See notes 136 and 141 for the definitions of 'insurance business' and reinsurance business', respectively.

[187] Lines of compulsory insurance within the transport sector are lines that are regulated by the Act on Compulsory Insurance within the Transport Sector (Article 13(1), IA). Article 13 of the IA has no further provisions.

[188] Article 89 of the IA contains the information that an insurance company must communicate in writing to the policyholder, before the insurance contract between them is concluded. Article 90 of the IA concerns the information that the insurance company must convey in writing to the policyholder during the term of the insurance contract – which mainly concerns changes in the information that it provides pursuant to Article 89 of the IA. Article 91 of the IA requires the communication to which Articles 89 and 90 of the IA refer, to be drawn up clearly and accurately in Croatian, and to be addressed to the insured person or the policyholder.

[189] Article 82(2), IA. An insurance company shall not permit insurance representation activities, or insurance and reinsurance brokerage activities, to be conducted by persons other than those to whom Articles 250 and 253 of the IA refers (Article 258, IA). Insurance representation business may be taken up and pursued by an insurance agency with a head office in Croatia whom the CFSSA has authorised to carry out insurance representation business, an insurance representation craft founded in Croatia which the CFSSA has authorised to conduct insurance representation business, and an insurance agency from a Member State which has the right to conduce insurance representation business in Croatia (directly or via a branch) pursuant to the IA (Article 250(1), IA). The insurance and reinsurance brokerage business may be conducted by an insurance and reinsurance brokerage company with a head office in Croatia which the CFSSA has authorised to carry out insurance and reinsurance brokerage business, and an insurance and reinsurance brokerage company from a Member State which has the right to conduct insurance and reinsurance brokerage business in Croatia (either directly or through a branch) pursuant to the IA (Article 253(1), IA).

[190] Article 82(3), IA. A reinsurance company's head office shall be located in the same Member State as its registered office (Article 82(4), IA).

An insurance or reinsurance company from a Member State may start insurance business operations or reinsurance business operations in Croatia on the date on which the competent authority of the insurance or reinsurance company's home Member State notifies the CFSSA of the information to which Article 78(2) of the IA refers, subject to the conditions that Articles 78(5) and 78(6) of the IA stipulate.[191] A branch of an insurance or reinsurance company from a Member State may commence insurance business operations or reinsurance business operations in Croatia upon the expiry of a period of three months from the date on which the CFSSA receives the notification from the home Member State's competent supervisory authority to which Articles 77(2) and 77(4) of the IA refer, under the conditions that Articles 78(7) and 78(9) of the IA provide.[192] By way of derogation from Article 83(2) of the IA,[193] in so far as it is necessary, "in order to safeguard public interest", to impose additional requirements for the conduct of insurance business operations or reinsurance business operations through a Croatian branch, the CFSSA shall notify the home Member State's competent authority within the prescribed period of two months, and, at the same time as it gives this

---

[191] Article 83(1), IA. See section 5.3.1, for Articles 78(2) and 78(5) of the IA. Article 78(6) of the IA concerns the requirement for the insurance or reinsurance company to provide written notice to the competent supervisory authorities of the home and the host Member States, in the event of a change in any of the information to which Article 78(2) of the IA refers. By way of derogation from Article 83(1) of the IA, an insurance company from a Member State may start to provide compulsory insurance in the transport sector, only if it informs the CFSSA of its general and special conditions and terms of insurance (Article 83(7), IA). If the CFSSA establishes that the conditions and terms of insurance to which Article 83(7) of the IA refers are contrary to "the legislation in force", then it shall take any measure that is necessary to ensure that the insurance company modifies these conditions and terms, in order to "bring them into line with the legislation" (Article 83(8), IA). 'The legislation in force' probably means the relevant provision of Croatian legislation and regulation. If the insurance company does not comply with the measures that the CFSSA imposes pursuant to Article 83(8) of the IA within the prescribed period that each of these measures stipulates, then the CFSSA shall inform the competent authority of the insurance company's home Member State of the non-compliance (Article 83(9), IA).

[192] Article 83(2), IA. Article 78 of the IA does not contain paragraphs 7 and 9 – there are only 6 paragraphs therein. As Article 83(2) of the IA refers to Article 77 of the IA, this English translation of the IA may contain the following typographic errors: '78(7)' should read '77(7)'; '78(9) should read '77(9)'. See section 5.3.1, for Articles 77(2), 77(4), 77(7) and 77(9) of the IA.

[193] See the previous sentence, for Article 83(2) of the IA.

notice, inform the insurance or reinsurance company.[194] After the company has received this information, or if this notification has not been received within the two month period, its (newly established) branch may carry out insurance business operations or reinsurance business operations.[195]

An insurance or reinsurance company from a Member State shall cease to conduct insurance business operations or reinsurance business operations in Croatia, if any of the following circumstances arise. First, the competent supervisory authority of the home Member State has concluded that the insurance or reinsurance company does not possess the prescribed capital, in order to continue to conduct insurance business operations or reinsurance business operations;[196] Second, the authorisation of the insurance or reinsurance company to carry out insurance business operations or reinsurance business operations is no longer valid.[197] Third, the Croatian branch of the insurance or reinsurance company does not satisfy the requirements to which paragraphs 2 to 4 of Article 83 of the IA refer.[198]

Supervision of an insurance or reinsurance company from a Member State that conducts insurance business operations or reinsurance business operations in Croatia shall be exercised by the (non-Croatian) Member State's competent supervisory authority.[199] This authority may examine the insurance or reinsurance company's conduct of business operations in Croatia.[200] On the request of the competent supervisory authority of the insurance or reinsurance company's home Member State, the CFSSA shall exercise supervision of the business operations of the Croatian branch of the insurance or reinsurance company.[201] The home Member State's competent authorities may, having first informed the supervisory authority of the Member State of the branch (i.e. the CFSSA), conduct on-the-spot

---

[194] Article 83(3), IA.
[195] Article 83(4), IA.
[196] Article 83(6)(1), IA.
[197] Article 83(6)(2), IA.
[198] Article 83(6)(3), IA. See the previous paragraph, for Articles 83(2), 83(3) and 83(4) of the IA.
[199] Article 84(1), IA. In respect of supervision in Croatia, the home Member State's competent authority shall have the same powers as the CFSSA (Article 84(3), IA).
[200] Article 84(2), IA.
[201] Article 84(4), IA. By way of derogation from Articles 83(1) to 83(4) of the IA, the CFSSA may carry out an examination of the branch's business operations pursuant to Articles 158b to 158h of the IA, for the purposes of supervising the operations to which Article 82(2) of the IA refers (Article 84(5), IA). See above in this section, for Article 82(2) of the IA. Articles 158b to 158h of the IA state the procedure for the examination of the operations of insurance companies.

verification of the information that is "necessary to ensure the financial supervision of the company".[202]

The CFSSA may issue a decision to "eliminate any irregularity or breach of the legislation" if an insurance or reinsurance company from a Member State breaches in Croatia breaches any provision pursuant to Article 82(2) of the IA.[203] If the company does not comply with this decision within the time period that the latter stipulates, then the CFSSA shall inform the home Member State's competent authority of this non-compliance.[204]

If the conditions that Article 161(2) of the IA are satisfied, then the CFSSA may impose an additional measure on the insurance or reinsurance company for irregularities or contravention of "the legislation" within Croatia that prevents it from continuing to conclude new insurance or reinsurance contracts.[205] Before the CFSSA takes this measure, it shall inform the home Member State's competent supervisory authority accordingly.[206]

By way of derogation from Article 85(4) of the IA,[207] the CFSSA may impose upon the insurance or reinsurance company a temporary prohibition to the latter's conclusion of new insurance or reinsurance contracts, without giving prior notice to the competent authority of the home Member State, "if postponement of the measure would be

---

[202] Article 84(6), IA.

[203] Article 85(1), IA. Provisions of Article 85 of the IA shall apply to the Croatian branch of the insurance or reinsurance company of the Member State, if it contravenes Article 82(2) of the IA (Article 85(7), IA).

[204] Article 85(2), IA.

[205] Article 85(3), IA. An insurance company shall, within the specified time limit, remove the contraventions and irregularities that have been established, and submit to the CFSSA within this time limit (unless the decision explicitly provides otherwise) a report that describes the measures taken to eliminate these contraventions and irregularities (Article 161(1), IA). The company shall enclose with the report, any evidence that shows that the breaches and irregularities have been eliminated (Article 161(1), IA). If this report and the enclosed evidence show that the contraventions and irregularities have been removed, then the CFSSA shall issue a decision in which it shall certify that these breaches and irregularities have been eliminated (Article 161(2), IA). The CFSSA may, before issuing this decision, conduct another examination of the insurance company's operations, to the extent that is necessary to check whether the contraventions and irregularities have been eliminated (Article 161(2), IA).

[206] Article 85(4), IA. 'The legislation' probably means the legislation and regulations of Croatia.

[207] See the previous paragraph, for Article 85(4) of the IA.

prejudicial to the interests of insured persons".[208] The CFSSA shall promptly inform the home Member State's competent authority and the European Commission of this temporary prohibition.[209]

The establishment of a branch and the provision of cross-border services are 'capital movements' in Titles I(1) and X of the nomenclature in Annex I, respectively. If the CFSSA requires an insurance or reinsurance firm from another Member State to stop providing insurance or reinsurance services in Croatia (either through a branch or by the provision of cross-border services), or imposes a temporary or permanent prohibition on an insurance or reinsurance company from another Member State or its Croatian branch, on its entry into new insurance or reinsurance contracts, then it restricts the free movement of capital.

For the restrictive measures to be justified under Article 65(1)(b) of the TFEU, they must be necessary for the protection of the interests that they are intended to guarantee, be proportionate – i.e. not achievable by less restrictive measures, and satisfy the requirements of legal certainty – i.e. be specific, objective and known to the parties beforehand; in addition, the persons whom the measures affect must have access to legal redress – intervention must be supported by reasons and be subject to review in the national courts.[210] The imposition of a permanent restriction under Article 85(3) of the IA on the insurance or reinsurance undertaking or its Croatian branch to conclude new insurance or reinsurance contracts,[211] in order to prevent further contravention of Croatian law, may be disproportionate, and does not provide the applicant with legal certainty – because the CFSSA has a discretion as to whether or not to impose this measure. The imposition of a temporary restriction under Article 85(6) of the IA on the insurance or reinsurance firm or its Croatian branch to conclude new insurance or reinsurance contracts in order to mitigate or prevent prejudice to the interest of insured persons is not disproportionate;[212] however, it provides the CFSSA with a wide discretion, which does not provide the applicant with legal certainty. The grounds in Article 86(3) of the IA for the CFSSA to require an insurance or reinsurance company that is registered in another Member State to stop its provision of insurance or reinsurance services in Croatia are not disproportionate,[213] and satisfy the

[208] Article 85(5), IA.
[209] Article 85(6), IA.
[210] See the subsection '*The requirements for a successful public policy/public security derogation*', in section 2.1.3.
[211] See above in this paragraph, for Article 85(3) of the IA.
[212] See above in this paragraph, for Article 85(6) of the IA.
[213] See above in this section, for Article 86(3) of the IA.

requirements of legal certainty – as these grounds do not provide the CFSSA with broad discretion. The IA contains no rules that require the CFSSA to provide reasons for its decisions that are taken pursuant to the provisions of subtitle III.7 of the Act. In addition, the IA does not provide an applicant insurance or reinsurance firm with the right to appeal against a decision of the CFSSA in the Croatian courts. Hence, the persons whom the restrictive measures affect do not have access to legal redress. Thus, Article 65(1)(b) of the TFEU does not justify the restrictive measures in Articles 85(3), 85(6) and 86(3) of the IA.

As subtitle III.7 of the IA does consider capital movements between Croatia and third countries, the justification in Article 64(2) of the TFEU is not considered. Therefore, the restrictive measures contravene Article 63 of the TFEU.

5.3.3 Subtitle III.8 of the IA: Conduct of insurance business operations by insurance companies from third countries

An insurance company from a third country may carry out business operations in Croatia via a branch only[214] – i.e. the IA does not permit the company to provide cross-border insurance services in Croatia. A branch of an insurance company from a third country must fulfil the following requirements: the branch's operations must be managed by two persons who have the authority to represent the founders to whom Articles 25 to 29 and Article 31of the IA apply (as appropriate);[215] the branch must

[214] Article 86(1), IA. See note 174, for the definition of 'third country'. Within the meaning of the IA, a 'person from a third country' is a natural person that has permanent residence outside Croatia and the Member States, or a legal person that has its head office outside Croatia and the Member States (Article 5(2), IA). A third country insurance or reinsurance company is a legal person that has its head office outside Croatia and the Member States, which has been authorised by the CFSSA or competent supervisory authority of its home Member State to conduct insurance or reinsurance business operations, or to engage in insurance or reinsurance activities, other than those that have already been authorised (Article 5(3), IA). 'Member State' means a Contracting Party to the EEA Agreement – see note 137, which also contains the definition of 'home Member State'. See notes 136 and 141 for the definitions of 'insurance business' and reinsurance business', respectively.

[215] Article 86(2)(1), IA. Articles 25 to 29 of the IA concern the procedures and qualification for the appoint of members to the management board of an insurance company, and the obligations of these members. For instance, the position of member of the management board of an insurance company may be taken by any person who satisfies the following requirements: 1) a university degree, 2)

employ sufficient staff and be "technically equipped" to carry out its insurance business operations;[216] the branch shall have "adequate funds" of at least one half of the share capital that Article 19 of the IA prescribes;[217] the branch must have assets in Croatia of at least one half of the capital that Article 100 of the IA stipulates,[218] and must deposit these funds as security for payment of the liabilities under the insurance contracts concluded in Croatia (or the insurance contracts that cover the

---

adequate professional qualifications, experience and competence to be able to manage an insurance company's operations in a sound and prudent way, 3) he/she has not held a management position in a financial institution or (other) company against which bankruptcy proceedings have been commenced, or in respect of which the authorisation to carry out its business has been withdrawn; 4) he/she has not been dismissed as a member of the management board on the basis of a decision of the CFSSA under Article 162(3) of the IA, 5) he/she fulfils the requirements for the position of member of the management board that the (Croatian) Companies Act contains, and 6) he/she is not a member of the management board, or procurator, of another company (Article 27(1), IA). Article 31 of the IA states the conditions under which the CFSSA will revoke its approval of a member of the management board of an insurance company.

[216] Article 86(2)(2), IA.

[217] Article 86(2)(3), IA. The share capital of a joint-stock insurance company must be at least 17.5 million Kuna if the company is active in one non-life insurance class, 26.25 million Kuna if the company is active in all non-life insurance classes or one of the classes to which Articles 3(2)(10) to 3(2)(15) refer (i.e. motor vehicle liability insurance, aircraft liability insurance, insurance of liability that arises from the use of vessels, other lines of liability insurance, credit insurance and suretyship insurance – see note 136), and 26.25 million Kuna if the company is active in life assurance (Article 19(6), IA). The minimum amount of a reinsurance company's share capital must be at least 26.25 million Kuna (Article 19(7), IA).

[218] Article 100 of the IA contains the level of the guarantee fund, the essence of which is as follows. The guarantee fund shall comprise the items of the core capital to which Article 95 of the IA refers, and the supplementary capital to which Article 96(1) of the IA refers, subject to the CFSSA's approval of the terms of computation of supplementary capital (Article 100(1), IA). The guarantee fund must be at least one third of the required solvency margin that Article 98 (life assurance) or Article 99 (non-life assurance and reinsurance) of the IA specifies (Article 100(2), IA). An insurance company's guarantee fund must be at least 17.5 million Kuna if the company is active in one non-life insurance class, 26.25 million Kuna if the company is active in all non-life insurance classes or one of the classes to which Articles 3(2)(10) to 3(2)(15) refer (see note 217), and 26.25 million Kuna if the company is active in life assurance (Article 100(7), IA). A reinsurance company's guarantee fund shall be at least 26.25 Kuna (Article 100(8), IA).

risks that are located in Croatia), to amount to one quarter of the branch's capital.[219]

An insurance company from a third country may found a branch in Croatia, provide that the CFSSA authorises it to do so.[220] The application for the issuance of an authorisation for the establishment of a branch must be accompanied by the company's memorandum of association,[221] an excerpt from the court (or other comparable) register in the country in which the insurance company has its head office,[222] the insurance company's articles of association and/or its internal regulations,[223] the insurance company's audited annual financial statements for the most recent three years,[224] an excerpt from the court (or other comparable) register in the country where the insurance company has its head office for the legal persons who have a shareholding in excess of 10% in the insurance company that entitles them to "the corresponding participation" in the company's management,[225] a scheme of operations whose contents are those that Article 63 of the IA sets out,[226] a statement that the branch will keep and file, at its head office, all of the records that relate to the business that the branch transacts,[227] a document that contains proof of the insurance company's capital adequacy and security deposit,[228] and documents on the basis of which it is possible to establish whether the branch is capable of providing the services to which the application for issue of authorisation refers – in terms of staff, technical equipment and organisational support.[229]

---

[219] Article 86(2)(4), IA.

[220] Article 87(1), IA.

[221] Article 87(2)(1), IA.

[222] Article 87(2)(2), IA. If the extract to which Article 87(2)(2) of the IA refers does not show the (required) information about the insurance company's owners, then the applicant shall enclose a document that provides an authentic record of the company's owners and "the level of their participation" in the company's management (Article 87(2)(5), IA). Article 87(2)(5) of the IA couples 'participation' in the company's management with shareholding, which suggests that participation means voting rights.

[223] Article 87(2)(3), IA.

[224] Article 87(2)(4), IA. See note 222.

[225] Article 87(2)(6), IA.

[226] Article 87(2)(7), IA. See note 145, for Article 63 of the IA.

[227] Article 87(2)(8), IA.

[228] Article 87(2)(9), IA. In the authorisation, the CFSSA shall lay down the way in which the security deposit is to be provided (Article 87(3), IA).

[229] Article 87(2)(10), IA.

Articles 59 to 61 of the IA shall apply, as appropriate, to decision-making that concerns the issue of an authorisation to an insurance company form a third country to establish a branch in Croatia.[230] These Articles are as follows.

An application for authorisation to conduct insurance business shall be accompanied by a scheme of operations,[231] the insurance company's articles of association,[232] the company's name and head office,[233] a list of the company's shareholders, the total nominal value of the shares and the amounts of their respective shareholdings expressed as percentages in the insurance company's share capital,[234] further specified information for shareholders that are legal persons[235] and those who are natural persons,[236] and contracts on any of the insurance company's operations that are (or are to be) outsourced.[237] An application for the issue of an authorisation to conduct insurance business shall be accompanied by an opinion of a certified actuary on whether the insurance company will be able to satisfy its capital adequacy requirements, given the nature and the volume of its activities.[238]

The CFSSA shall determine the issue of authorisation for each class of insurance in which the insurance company intends to provide services.[239] The CFSSA shall grant authorisation to conduct insurance operations in a particular class of insurance, if, in its opinion, the insurance company fulfils the requirements for conducting these operations in the insurance class concerned.[240] In the authorisation's wording, the CFSSA shall state the insurance operations to which this permission relates.[241] If the authorisation concerns all business lines within a certain insurance class, then the CFSSA may specify this class in the authorisation's wording.[242]

---

[230] Article 87(4), IA.
[231] Article 59(1)(1), IA.
[232] Article 59(1)(2), IA.
[233] Article 59(1)(3), IA.
[234] Article 59(1)(3), IA.
[235] Article 59(1)(4), IA.
[236] Article 59(1)(5), IA.
[237] Article 59(1)(6), IA.
[238] Article 59(2), IA.
[239] Article 60(1), IA. See note 136, for the classes of insurance.
[240] Article 60(2), IA.
[241] Article 60(3), IA.
[242] Article 60(3), IA. By way of derogation from Articles 60(1) to 60(3) of the IA, the CFSSA shall determine whether to issue authorisation to write reinsurance business in respect of all insurance lines, and shall specify in the authorisation's wording that it is valid only in respect of reinsurance business (Article 60(4), IA).

The CFSSA shall refuse to grant an authorisation to carry out insurance business, if the applicant's shareholders do not have the approval to which Article 21(1) of the IA refers,[243] the members of the applicant's management board have not been approved for the performance of the obligations of a member of the management board,[244] the applicant's articles of association and other documents show that the requirements that the IA, and the regulations adopted pursuant to the IA, lay down have not been satisfied,[245] "the documents and other known circumstances" divulge that the insurance company will be unable (in terms of personnel, organisation and technical issues) to generate the volume of business that the scheme of operations forecasts,[246] provisions of the applicant insurance company's articles of association contravene rules of the IA or of regulations adopted pursuant to the IA,[247] the computed technical provisions and premiums are insufficient for a full, permanent coverage of the company's liabilities under the insurance contracts in force,[248] the insurance company does not satisfy other requirements that the IA, and regulations adopted pursuant to the IA, specify – which refer to the conduct of insurance operations in the class of insurance to which the application for the issue of an authorisation relates,[249] and/or the general and specific conditions and terms of insurance are at variance with the Act on Compulsory Insurance within the Transport Sector.[250]

The CFSSA shall refuse to issue an authorisation for the foundation of a Croatian branch of an insurance company from a third country, if, taking into consideration the legislation of the country in which the insurance company has its head office, or that state's practice in respect of application and enforcement of its legislation, the exercise of supervision

---

[243] Article 61(1)(1), IA. The acquisition of shares in an insurance holding, whereby a person (directly or indirectly) acquires a qualifying holding in the insurance company, shall be subject to the CFSSA's prior approval (Article 21(1), IA). For the purposes of the IA, a 'qualifying holding' is direct or indirect ownership of shares or other rights in a company, on the basis of which the holder acquires at least 10% of the capital or voting rights of a legal person, or a holding of less than 10% if the holder "exercises influence over" that person's management (Article 9(2), IA).

[244] Article 61(1)(2), IA.

[245] Article 61(1)(3), IA.

[246] Article 61(1)(4), IA.

[247] Article 61(1)(5), IA.

[248] Article 61(1)(6), IA.

[249] Article 61(1)(7), IA.

[250] Article 61(1)(8), IA.

pursuant to the IA "could be dimmed or made difficult",[251] or, taking into consideration the legislation of that third country, insurance companies whose head office is in Croatia would be prevented from conducting insurance business operations in the non-EEA state or from carrying out these operations on the same terms as those accorded to insurance companies from that third country.[252] "On an exceptional basis", Article 87(5) of the IA shall not apply to decision-making that concerns the issue of an authorisation to an insurance company from a third country whose head office is in a member state of the WTO, to establish a branch in Croatia.[253]

The foundation of a branch is a 'capital movement' in Title I(1) of the nomenclature in Annex I. If the CFSSA refuses to grant an authorisation for the applicant insurance third country insurance firm to establish a branch in Croatia, then it contravenes the free movement of capital.

For the restrictive measures to be justified under Article 65(1)(b) of the TFEU, they must be necessary for the protection of the interests that they are intended to guarantee, be proportionate (i.e. not attainable by less restrictive measures), and observe the requirements of legal certainty (i.e. be specific, objective and known to the parties beforehand); in addition, the persons affected by the measures must have access to legal redress, i.e. intervention should be supported by reasons and be subject to review in the domestic courts.[254] Some of the provisions in subtitle III.8 of the IA provide the CFSSA with discretion: Article 86(2)(2) of the IA gives the CFSSA the authority to decide the required number, and specify the necessary skill set, of the branch's staff, and the opportunity to assess its technical needs;[255] Article 60(2) of the IA (to which Article 87(4) of the IA refers) empowers the CFSSA to assess whether the third country insurance undertaking is able to provide services in each class of insurance through the branch to be established in Croatia;[256] Article 87(5)(1) of the IA enables the CFSSA to decide whether or not it is possible to supervise the branch on the basis of the IA, in the light of legislative and enforcement practice in the applicant insurance company's home

---

[251] Article 87(5)(1), IA.

[252] Article 87(5)(2), IA.

[253] Article 87(6), IA.

[254] See the subsection '*The requirements for a successful public policy/public security derogation*', in section 2.1.3.

[255] See above in this section, for Article 86(2)(2) of the IA.

[256] See above in this section, for Articles 60(2) and 87(4) of the IA. See note 136, for the classes of insurance.

country;[257] Article 87(6) of the IA grants the CFSSA a discretion to decide what amounts to 'an exceptional basis', in deciding whether to disapply the requirements of Article 87(5) of the IA to applications for authorisation from insurance firms whose head office is in a WTO state outside the EEA.[258] Hence, the measures that CFSSA takes do not provide the applicant with legal certainty, and may be disproportionate. The IA contains no provisions that require the CFSSA to give reasons for the decisions that it takes pursuant to Articles 86 and 87 of the IA. Furthermore, the Act does not provide the third country insurance firm with the right to appeal against a decision of the CFSSA to refuse to grant it an authorisation to establish a branch in Croatia. Thus, the persons whom the restrict measures affect are unable to obtain legal redress. Hence, the restrictive measures in Articles 86 and 87 of the IA are not justified by Article 65(1)(b) of the TFEU.

For Article 64(2) of the TFEU to justify the restrictive measures, the EU institutions must carefully take account of the objective of the free movement of capital whilst enacting the relevant legislation, and the national rules must not restrict the free movement of capital more than do than the equivalent provisions of the relevant Directive.[259] Directive 2009/138/EC is the relevant Directive. Recital 72 of Directive 2009/138/EC states that Member States should not require insurance or reinsurance firms to invest their funds in specified categories of assets, because this requirement might be incompatible with the liberalisation of capital movements for which Article 63 of the TFEU provides. However, none of this Directive's Articles mention the free movement of capital. Thus, the EU's legislators have considered the free movement of capital whilst enacting the Directive; it is a point for discussion whether or not the statement in Recital 72 is sufficient to establish that these legislators had carefully taken account of the free movement of capital as an objective.[260]

---

[257] See above in this section, for Article 87(5)(1) of the IA. The Estonian financial services legislation, including the EIAA, provides a similar ground for refusing to authorise Estonian firms from providing services to third countries, and for refusing to authorise organisations from third countries from supplying services in Estonia. See, for instance, subsections 33(5) and 44(3) of the EIAA, in section 3.4.

[258] See above in this section, for Article 87(6) of the IA.

[259] See the subsection '*Derogations that apply only to capital movement to/from third countries*', in section 2.3.2.

[260] See the comments in the antepenultimate paragraph of the subsection '*Chapter 2 Division 2: Activities of Estonian Insurance Undertakings in Foreign States*', in section 3.4.

Chapter IX of Title I of Directive 2009/138/EC contains detailed authorisation requirements for the foundation of a branch in an EEA country of an insurance or reinsurance undertaking whose head office is located in a third country.[261] Whilst these requirements are more onerous than those that Articles 86 and 87 of the IA impose upon insurance companies from third countries that intend to obtain an authorisation from the CFSSA to establish a branch in Croatia,[262] Article 87 of the IA imposes grounds upon which the CFSSA may refuse to grant this authorisation – for which there is no equivalent provision in Chapter IX of Title I of Directive 2009/138/EC.[263] Thus, the restrictive measures in Articles 86 and 87 of the IA may restrict the free movement of capital more than do the provisions of Chapter IX of Title I of Directive 2009/138/EC.

Hence, Article 64(2) of the TFEU does not justify the restrictive measures in Articles 86 and 87 of the IA. Consequently, these measures breach Article 63 of the TFEU.

5.3.4 Concluding thoughts

Given Croatia's recent accession to Membership of the EU, one would expect its legislators to have given more attention to the free movement of capital – if the sample provisions considered above are representative of all of its financial services legislation and regulations. This expectation arises because the free movement of capital is a significant part of the internal market,[264] and because the *acquis communautaire*, which all Member States are required to apply in their territories as a condition for

---

[261] See the antepenultimate and preantepenultimate paragraphs of the subsection (*Chapter 2 Division 3: Activities of Foreign Insurance Undertakings in Estonia*), in section 3.4, for a description of these requirements.

[262] See above in this section, for Articles 86 and 87 of the IA.

[263] Article 170 of Directive 2009/138/EC provides one ground on which a financial supervision authority of a EEA state must withdraw an authorisation of a branch in that territory of a third country insurance firm – if the financial supervision authority of the EEA country that is to "supervise the solvency of the entire business of the branches established within the Community" has withdrawn its authorisation, due to the "inadequacy of the overall state of solvency" (Articles 170 and 167(2), Directive 2009/138/EC). If the latter financial supervision authority has withdrawn its authorisation on other grounds, then the former authority may revoke its authorisation of the branch on its territory of the third country insurance company (Article 170, Directive 2009/138/EC).

[264] See section 1.2.3, for the free movement of capital's place in the internal market.

accession to Membership,[265] contains an increasing number of cases in which the CJEU has declared provisions of national law to be incompatible with the provisions of Article 63 of the TFEU.[266]

As there are several further candidate countries for EU Membership,[267] it may be appropriate for the European Commission to publish a statement

---

[265] See section 1.3.1, for a description of the implementation of the *acquis communautaire* – the Treaty provisions, Regulations, Directives and case law of the EU as a whole.

[266] Section 2.1 shows a steady reportage of cases that concern the free movement of capital.

[267] Candidate countries for EU Membership include Albania, Iceland, Macedonia, Montenegro, Serbia and Turkey. In June 2014, the EU, the EURATOM and their Member States signed Association Agreements with Georgia, Moldova and Ukraine. Amongst other objectives, EU/EURATOM Member States and Georgia aim "to achieve Georgia's gradual economic integration into the EU Internal Market, as stipulated in this Agreement, notably through establishing a Deep and Comprehensive Free Trade Area which will provide for far-reaching market access on the basis of sustained and comprehensive regulatory approximation in compliance with the rights and obligations arising for the WTO membership" (Article 2(h), EU/EURATOM – Georgia Association Agreement). The corresponding objective in the EU/EURATOM – Moldova Association Agreement requires more work of integration from the Moldovan leadership and economy into the EU framework, as follows: the Association aims "to establish conditions for economic and trade relations leading towards the Republic of Moldova's gradual integration in the EU Internal Market as stipulated in this Agreement, including by setting up a Deep and Comprehensive Free Trade Area, which will provide for far-reaching regulatory approximation and market access liberalisation, in compliance with the rights and obligations arising out of WTO membership; and to the transparent application of those rights and obligations" (Article 2(g), EU/EURATOM – Moldova Association Agreement). The EU/EURATOM – Ukraine Association Agreement requires considerable adjustment in the Ukrainian economy, in order to fulfil the following corresponding objective: The Association aims "to establish conditions for enhanced economic and trade relations leading towards Ukraine's gradual integration in the EU Internal Market, including by setting up a Deep and Comprehensive Free Trade Area as stipulated in Title IV (Trade and Trade-related Matters) of this Agreement, and to support Ukrainian efforts to complete the transition into a functioning market economy by means of, *inter alia*, the progressive approximation of its legislation to that of the [European] Union" (Article 2(d), EU/EURATOM – Ukraine Association Agreement). Although these Association Agreements do not expressly address the free movement of capital, its importance in the internal market requires that barriers to capital movements between the EEA and Georgia, the EEA and Moldova, and the EEA and Ukraine are monitored, raised as little as possible during economic

that strongly advises accession countries to take account of the free movement of capital, whilst drafting their financial services legislation in preparation for accession to Membership. In this communication, the Commission might quote examples of provisions in which the free movement of capital has been restricted – such as examples from this book or the author's earlier publication.[268] The communication could also provide candidate countries with guidance as to how to avoid such breaches, or to bring them under the scope of the derogations from Article 63 of the TFEU.

5.4 Comment

The financial services legislation (and regulations) of all of the countries analysed in this Chapter and the previous two, for contraventions to Article 63 of the TFEU, contains many instances of non-compliance with this provision. This result is inevitable, given the wide definition of 'capital movements',[269] the low threshold to be reached in order for an inhibitory factor to be classed as a limitation to the free movement of capital, [270] and the narrow scope and paucity of the derogations to the restrictive measures that EU law provides.[271]

The issues that emerge throughout the financial services laws of these countries are consistent. These matters include 1) legislative discretion provided to the financial supervision authority of the home country, which contributes to a lack of legal certainty and the possibility of the imposition by this authority of disproportionate measures, 2) lack of access to legal redress for applicants that are adversely affected by decisions of the financial supervision authority of their home state, 3) the absence or imprecision of objectives upon which measures that restrict the free movement of capital are based, 4) a raft of requirements to be satisfied in order for the relevant financial supervision authority to be empowered to issue an authorisation (if an authorisation is required), and 5) a plethora of grounds on which the financial supervision authority may refuse to issue an authorisation or may withdraw one. On the basis of these observations, there is no reason to believe that the financial services legislation of other

transition in these three countries, and lowered in instances in which can reasonably be done.

[268] Baber (2010), *The Impact of Legislation and Regulation on the Freedom of Movement of Capital*.

[269] See section 2.1.1.

[270] See section 2.1.2.

[271] See sections 2.1.3, 2.3.2 and 4.6

EEA states will differ substantially with respect to the free movement of capital.

One interpretation of the observations might be that the free movement of capital only exists in so far as it does not interfere with the other fundamental freedoms of the internal market – i.e. the free movement of goods, of persons, and of services. As seen in the analyses in this book and in the publication of four years ago,[272] the single market Directives impose mild restrictions on the right to establish a branch in another EEA state, and, if they legislate over the area, considerable requirements for the issuance of an authorisation for the provision of financial services to and from third countries. Nevertheless, the free movement of capital is equal in importance in the internal market to the other fundamental freedoms,[273] which, is not immediately apparent from the content of these Directives.

---

[272] Baber, *The Impact of Legislation and Regulation.*

[273] See section 1.2.3.

CHAPTER SIX

IMPLICATIONS OF THE FINDINGS

The analysis demonstrates that a considerable number of the cross-border provisions within the financial services laws of the Member States studied contravene the EU's rules on the free movement of capital. Since the free movement of capital, as stated in Article 63 of the TFEU, is a legal measure of such clear and definite language and meaning, it is not surprising that these breaches of EU law exist.

The derogations that the TFEU and the EU's case law provide are limited in both quantity and scope. Furthermore, the CJEU interprets derogations from the fundamental freedoms narrowly, as a consequence of which they are not often applied. This is exemplified by the application of the public policy/security head of the derogation in Article 65(1)(b) of the TFEU,[1] which, to date, has only been applied to one case from many attempted claims.[2]

In addition, the EU has been fairly slow to recognise the implications of the principles of the free movement of capital. In particular, some of the Directives contravene the free movement of capital, in the sense that they impose measures that limit it, especially with regard to capital movement between EEA states and third countries. It is even more worrying that a minority of EU instruments do not cater for the movement of capital between EEA states and third countries – Directive 2002/92/EC, for example, does not mention the latter states at all.

Member States may attempt to take action, in order to justify national measures that restrict the free movement of capital. In the law as it stands at the time of writing, this probably means that they would need to carefully put in place all the required elements for a derogation under Article 65(1)(b) of the TFEU. This would necessitate considerable additions to the current content of national financial services legislation – although some of the measures that Article 65(1)(b) advocates would be

---

[1] See section 2.1.3.

[2] This case is *Commission v Belgium* [2002] ECR I-4809, which section 4.6 considers in depth.

beneficial to financial institutions, such as requiring the financial supervision authority of the relevant EEA state to provide a formal statement of reasons for a decision that adversely affects the interests of an applicant institution for the foundation of a branch or the provision of cross-border services.

The difficulties in respect of frequent transgression of free movement of capital rules by the national legislation of EEA countries, may be addressed by a co-ordinated effort by the EU institutions and the governments (and, in particular, the financial supervision authorities) of EEA states to co-ordinate the free movement of capital, the free movement of services and the freedom of establishment in the financial services sector. In particular, the paucity of EU laws on the supply of financial services between EEA states and third countries leads to difficulties in co-ordination of such provision with the free movement of capital. This may change, as passporting requirements are extended to financial firms that are authorised to provide services in countries outside the EEA – on the basis of equivalence between regulation of the financial services sector in each of those third countries and that in the EU. Nevertheless, a co-ordinated approach is required, preferably before there are extensive passporting and equivalence requirements in the EU Directives and Regulations that govern banks, investment firms, investment funds, pension funds, insurance companies, insurance intermediaries, and payment service providers.

One feature that is regularly noted from the studies in earlier chapters is that the relevant Directive mentions the free movement of capital in its recitals, but does not do so in the substance of its Articles. For example, Recital 72 of Directive 2009/138/EC states that Member States should not require insurance or reinsurance companies to invest their funds in specified categories of assets, as this requirement might be incompatible with the liberalisation of capital movements in Article 63 of the TFEU. However, the free movement of capital is not mentioned in any of the Articles of Directive 2009/138/EC. One wonders, therefore, the extent to which the EU legislators are serious about the principle of the free movement of capital over the area of the cross-border provision of insurance services – and of financial services in general.[3]

[3] An analogous issue is the extent to which the parties to a cross-border contract can base that contract on general principles of law (by specifying this in the contract), rather than on the rules of a particular national legal system. Recital 13 to Regulation (EC) No 593/2008 of the European Parliament and of the Council on the law applicable to contractual obligations (Rome I) states "This Regulation does not preclude parties from incorporating by reference into their contract a non State

In respect of the free movement of capital between Member States and third countries, if there is agreement on co-operation and exchange of information in place between the EU and a particular third country, then there should be scope for negotiation between these two countries as to reducing the requirements for authorisation for the foundation of a foreign branch in either location. To an extent, this is an issue of trust between the jurisdictions, their governments, and, in particular, their financial supervision authorities. Whilst such trust is lacking, especially in the wake of the financial crisis, there is a need for it to be re-established in order for countries to work together in Europe and across the world. The financial services sector is well placed amongst the various sectors of the global economy to lead the way in this trust-based negotiation.

Trust-based negotiation between EEA states and third countries as to the removal of obstacles to the free movement of capital in respect of the establishment of a branch of a foreign financial institution, should be extended to the provision of cross-border financial services between these jurisdictions. In Estonia, Latvia and Poland, the number of firms that provide banking services in these countries via the cross-border movement of services exceeds the number of banks that have founded a branch there under the freedom of establishment. On this basis, it is reasonable to claim that the cross-border provision of banking services to these countries by entities that are registered in third countries would be at least comparable with the number of banks that are registered in third states that wish to establish a branch or found a subsidiary there (through the authorisation of an Estonian, a Latvian or a Polish bank). Whilst Estonia has taken this step – often going beyond the requirements of the relevant Directives with respect to the provision of cross-border financial services to and from third countries, other countries have been slower to do so. It is not necessary to wait for the Directives to be changed accordingly – national legislators should follow this constructive trend, and amend their financial services laws.

To attempt to provide integration in financial services law, not only within the EEA, but also further afield, the free movement of services and of capital should apply equally to movements between the EEA and third countries as it does within the EEA. From the point of view of maximising trade in the sector, this is the ideal model – limitations of capacity for

body of law or an international convention.". By contrast, Article 3(1) of Regulation (EC) No 593/2008 states "A contract shall be governed by the law chosen by the parties.". Thus, parties must select a national law to govern the contract, although they are able (unofficially by virtue of the recital) to supplement this choice with general principles of law.

supervision of financial institutions in various third countries hinders the applicability of this optimal standard, but does not invalidate it. Consequently, co-operation agreements, and elements of a passporting regime as appropriate, should be pursued between the EEA and its trading partners for financial services.

The rate of introduction and change in both EU and national financial services legislation makes it difficult to obtain a thoroughly integrated financial market, within the EEA and beyond. In the banking sector, for instance, there has been substantial new legislation in the form of Regulation (EU) No 575/2013 and Directive 2013/36/EU. The Regulation is part of a trend within the financial services sector of the production of EU legislation that is directly applicable, and, therefore, leads to a greater degree of harmonisation amongst EEA states than there is currently. Regulation (EU) No 575/2013 is the EEA's implementing instrument of the Basel III Accord – equivalents of which are coming into effect in different jurisdictions throughout the world. Directive 2013/36/EU contains the authorisation and passporting requirements for the provision of banking services, Articles that relate to prudential regulation of credit institutions – including their governance and risk management, and aspects of the Basel III Accord that are difficult to harmonise in the short run – such as the countercyclical buffer requirement. This is the part of the changing financial climate against which the free movement of services and the free movement of capital in the sector are to be maintained and extended.

In the long run, the legislation that corresponds to the anticipated greater financial integration may contain fewer restrictions in the free movement of capital. If this legislation provides a stable framework, then the free movement of services and the free movement of capital will be sustained, not only within the EEA, but also between EEA states and third countries. Whilst this trend is a good thing, it must not be fragile – in the sense that political or economic difficulties within countries should not be able to reverse the trend towards the harmonisation of financial markets. If difficulties arise in respect of a state's relations with its neighbours, then the EEA must be ready to re-extend a favourable environment for the establishment of subsidiaries and branches, and the provision of cross-border services within the financial sector, to and from this country, once the difficulties have passed.

The ability of the Commission, with the assistance of the European System of Financial Supervision of European Systemic Risk Board, European Banking Authority, European Securities and Markets Authority, European Insurance and Occupational Pensions Authority, Joint Committee of the European Supervisory Authorities and the financial regulation authorities of EEA states, to enact informed Regulations and Directives without the need to submit them to the ordinary legislative procedure in Article 294 of the TFEU, enables it to produce sector-specific technical requirements. If appropriate, these requirements help to provide legal certainty to participants in the financial markets within the EEA and, therefore, foster both the free movement of services and the free movement of capital. The latter should be seen in this context, and its derogations in the TFEU developed accordingly, so that capital and services work together. This excellence of standard could potentially be extended to the provision of financial services to and from third countries, on a case-by-case basis. Thus, since the introduction of the European System of Financial Supervision in January 2011, the EU has had a framework that can support harmonisation in the financial sector, within which the internal market should flourish. At the time of writing, it is too early to comment upon the extent to which this process has taken place.

The EU has been remarkably capacious in its ability to accommodate the expanding number of Member States – from 6 in 1958 to 28 today. By 2025, it is possible that the Union will contain at least 35 Member States, all contributing to the operation of a thriving internal market – a remarkable and unprecedented success story. In addition, the organisation has provided for additional integration processes, such as the Euro project, which operate concurrently with the enlargement programme. International frameworks provided by organisations such as the WTO, the IMF, and the International Labour Organization, strengthen the EU's global political and economic influence – as other regions of the world are able to interact with it constructively within those international settings. Thus, the global and regional environment is currently benign, with prospects for further improvement.

This environment generates substantial opportunities for financial market integration, of which the free movement of services and of capital are integral components. Financial laws in countries follow high standards that are set by organisations such as the Financial Stability Board, the International Organization of Securities Commissions and the Basel Committee on Banking Supervision. This sets up a framework for equivalence amongst the legal provisions of countries, who tend to follow the principles that these international bodies set. Thus, the financial services sector can lead the way in integration and harmonisation both within Europe and beyond. The free movements of services and capital are an essential part of these developments.

Further contributions to this benign international environment may be made by burgeoning regional organisations, such as the African Union and the Organization of American States. The African Union, in particular, is determined to follow a path of intra-continental integration, which follows the development of the EU but with its own regional flavour. The Union's Vision is of an integrated, prosperous and peaceful Africa – which is substantially closer today than it was in the days of my earliest memories. A strong, integrated, balanced African Union will create a framework for an internal market within this region, in which the free movement of services and the free movement of capital may be pursued. If standards rise to become similar there to within the EU's internal market – an ambitious but feasible objective – then the free movement of services and of capital between the two regions will be supported, and the supply of financial services across the borders of these regions will flourish.

Thus, EU's internal market, and the financial services sector, in particular, are gradually providing a model on which the free movement of services and of capital can grow and spread. It is important that the EU institutions, especially the European Commission and the CJEU, perceive this integration as extending beyond the boundaries of the EU, thereby fitting into a dynamic global economy. The cases in Chapter 2 mainly concern the free movement of capital within the EEA. Nevertheless, there is room for the CJEU to develop the rules for the free movement of capital between EEA states and third countries, pursuant to its judgment in *Skatterverket v A*.[4] The Court should show as much assiduousness in pursuing the free movement of capital between the EEA and third countries as it has within the EEA, even if governments and financial supervision authorities of those states are required to demonstrate, at least informally, that they are capable of similar standards of supervision to those of the financial supervision authorities of long-standing EU Member States.

Thus, as the title of the book suggests, it is necessary for the free movement of capital to be an integral part of the provision of financial services, both within the EEA and between the EEA and third countries. To achieve this aim, restrictions to the free movement of services and the freedom of establishment need to be as few as is realistically possible, both in the passporting rules of the EU, and in the legislation of Member States that apply these rules. Third countries are to be incorporated into the passporting system in two main steps: first, a dynamic co-operation agreement between the financial supervision authority of the relevant state and the European System of Financial Supervision; second, integration of the third country's financial sector into the passporting structure of the

[4] [2007] ECR I-11531. See the subsection '*Skatteverket v A.*', in section 2.3.2.

EU. It may not be possible to achieve this result simultaneously for all of the constituent parts of the financial sector. For instance, passporting may apply between banks, in (say) Australia and the EU, but not between insurance companies in Australia and the EU, if the financial supervision of banks in Australia is more reasonable and effective than that of insurance firms there.

If the free movement of capital can be extended to third countries, especially within the financial sector, then it may become possible to check that the financial services laws within selected third countries comply with this free movement. The provision of financial services across borders is best served by the free movement of capital and of services throughout the world. There is no better way to start to engage in this project than to check how legal provisions in various jurisdictions promulgate these principles of free movement, and how national rules can be modified to promote such principles without giving rise to any loss of territorial identity and financial market integrity.

BIBLIOGRAPHY

Books, Articles and Reports

Baber, G. S. (2010), *The Impact of Legislation and Regulation on the Freedom of Movement of Capital in Estonia, Poland and Latvia* (Newcastle upon Tyne: Cambridge Scholars Publishing).

Barnard, C. (2010), *The Substantive Law of the EU*, 3rd edn. (Oxford: Oxford University Press).

Cardoso, E. A., and Dornbusch, R. (1989), 'Foreign Private Capital Flows', *in* Chenery, H., and Srinivasan, T. N. *eds.*, *Handbook of Development Economics, Volume II* (Amsterdam: Elsevier Science Publishers B.V.).

Channell, W. (2005), 'Lessons Not Learned: Problems with Western Aid for Law Reform in Postcommunist Countries', *Carnegie Working Papers, No.57* (Washington D.C.; Carnegie Endowment for International Peace).

Charmaz, K. (2008), 'Grounded Theory as an Emergent Method', *in* Hesse-Biber, S. N., and Leavy, P. *eds.*, *Handbook of Emergent Methods* (New York: The Guildford Press).

Commission on European Contract Law (2004), 'The Principles of European Contract Law'.

Cuddington, J. (1986), 'Capital Flight: Estimates, Issues and Explanations', *Princeton Studies in International Finance No.58*, 1–40.

Cypher, J. M., and Dietz, J. L. (2004), *The Process of Economic Development*, 2nd edn. (Abingdon, United Kingdom: Routledge).

Dashwood, A., Dougan, M., Rodger, B., Spaventa, E., and Wyatt, D. (2011), *Wyatt and Dashwood's European Union Law*, 6th edn. (Oxford: Hart Publishing Limited).

Eaton, J. (1989), 'Foreign Public Capital Flows', *in* Chenery, H., and Srinivasan, T. N. *eds.*, *Handbook of Development Economics, Volume II* (Amsterdam: Elsevier Science Publishers B.V.).

Edwards, S. (1985), 'Stabilization with Liberalization: An Evaluation of Ten Years of Chile's Experience with Free-Market Policies, 1973–1983', *Economic Development and Cultural Change*, 33, 223–254.

European Commission Directorate General for Economic and Financial Affairs, 'The EU economy: 2003 review', No.6/2003.

Ewald, W. (1995), 'Comparative Jurisprudence (II): The Logic of Legal Transplants', *American Journal of Comparative Law*, 43, 489–510.

Frankowski, S. *ed.* (2005), *Introduction to Polish Law* (The Hague: Kluwer Law International).

Glazer, B. G. (2014), 'Applying Grounded Theory', *The Grounded Theory Review*, 13(1), 46–50.

Glenn, H. P. (2006), 'On the Use of Biological Metaphors in Law: The Case of 'Legal Transplants'', *Journal of Comparative Law*, 1, 124–130.

Legrand, P. (2006), 'Comparative Legal Studies and the Matter of Authenticity', *Journal of Comparative Law*, 1, 365–460.

McFarlane, G. (1984), *The Layman's Dictionary of English Law* (London: Waterlow Publishers Limited).

Mountjoy, A. B. *ed.* (1987), *Readers Digest Guide to Places of the World* (London: The Readers Digest Association Limited).

Palmer, V. V. (2005), 'From Lerotholi to Lando: Some Examples of Comparative Law Methodology', *American Journal of Comparative Law*, 53, 261–290.

Pearsall, J. *ed.* (1998), *The New Oxford Dictionary of English* (Oxford: Oxford University Press).

Pilbeam, K. (2006), *International Finance*, 3rd edn. (Basingstoke, United Kingdom: Palgrave Macmillan).

Roberts, J. M. (1996), *The Penguin History of Europe* (London: Helicon Publishing Limited).

Twining, W. (2006), 'Diffusion of Law: A Global Perspective', *Journal of Comparative Law*, 1, 3–26.

Weatherill, S., and Beaumont, P. (1999), *EU Law*, 3rd edn. (London: Penguin Books).

Yasmin, B., Hussain, A., and Chaudhary, M. A. (2003), 'Analysis of Factors Affecting Foreign Direct Investment in Developing Countries', *Pakistan Economic and Social Review*, 41(1)–41(2), 59–75.

Zweigert, K., and Kötz, H. (1998), *An Introduction to Comparative Law*, 3rd edn. translated by Weir T. (Oxford: Clarendon Press).

Legislation

European Union legislation

Association Agreement between the European Union and the European Atomic Energy Community and their Member States, of the one part, and Georgia, of the other part (2014).

Association Agreement between the European Union and the European Atomic Energy Community and their Member States, of the one part, and Moldova, of the other part (2014).

Association Agreement between the European Union and the European Atomic Energy Community and their Member States, of the one part, and Ukraine, of the other part (2014).

Commission Regulation (EC) No 809/2004 of 29 April 2004 implementing Directive 2003/71/EC of the European Parliament and of the Council as regards information contained in prospectuses as well as the format, incorporation by reference and publication of such prospectuses and dissemination of advertisements.

Consolidated Version of the Treaty on the Functioning of the European Union (2008).

Council Directive 88/361/EEC of 24 June 1988 for the implementation of Article 67 of the Treaty.

Council Directive 90/434/EEC of 23 July 1990 on the common system of taxation applicable to mergers, divisions, transfers of assets and exchanges of shares concerning companies of different Member States.

Council Directive 90/435/EEC of 23 July 1990 on the common system of taxation applicable in the case of parent companies and subsidiaries of different Member States.

Directive 2002/92/EC of the European Parliament and of the Council of 9 December 2002 on insurance mediation.

Directive 2003/41/EC of the European Parliament and of the Council of 3 June 2003 on the activities and supervision of institutions for occupational retirement provision.

Directive 2003/71/EC of the European Parliament and of the Council of 4 November 2003 on the prospectus to be published when securities are offered to the public or admitted to trading and amending Directive 2001/34/EC.

Directive 2004/39/EC of the European Parliament and of the Council of 21 April 2004 on markets in financial instruments amending Council Directives 85/611/EEC and 93/6/EEC and Directive 2000/12/EC of the

European Parliament and of the Council and repealing Council Directive 93/22/EC.

Directive 2005/56/EC of the European Parliament and of the Council of 26 October 2005 on cross-border mergers of limited companies.

Directive 2007/64/EC of the European Parliament and of the Council of 13 November 2007 on payment services in the internal market amending Directives 97/7/EC, 2002/65/EC, 2005/60/EC and 2006/48/EC and repealing Directive 97/5/EC.

Directive 2009/65/EC of the European Parliament and of the Council of 13 July 2009 on the coordination of laws, regulations and administrative provisions relating to undertakings for collective investment in transferable securities (UCITS) (recast).

Directive 2009/110/EC of the European Parliament and of the Council of 16 September 2009 on the taking up, pursuit and prudential supervision of the business of electronic money institutions amending Directives 2005/60/EC and 2006/48/EC and repealing Directive 2000/46/EC.

Directive 2009/138/EC of the European Parliament and of the Council of 25 November 2009 on the taking-up and pursuit of the business of Insurance and Reinsurance (Solvency II) (recast).

Directive 2011/61/EU of the European Parliament and of the Council of 8 June 2011 on Alternative Investment Fund Managers and amending Directives 2003/41/EC and 2009/65/EC and Regulations (EC) No 1060/2009 and (EU) No 1095/2010.

Directive 2013/36/EU of the European Parliament and of the Council of 26 June 2013 on access to the activity of credit institutions and the prudential supervision of credit institutions and investment firms, amending Directive 2002/87/EC and repealing Directives 2006/48/EC and 2006/49/EC.

Proposal for a Directive of the European Parliament and of the Council on markets in financial instruments repealing Directive 2004/39/EC of the European Parliament and of the Council, COM(2011) 656 final, (recast).

Proposal for a Regulation of the European Parliament and of the Council on markets in financial instruments and amending Regulation (EU) No 648/2012.

Regulation (EC) No 593/2008 of the European Parliament and of the Council of 17 June 2008 on the law applicable to contractual obligations (Rome I).

Regulation (EC) No 924/2009 of the European Parliament and of the Council of 16 September 2009 on cross-border payments in the Community and repealing Regulation (EC) No 2560/2001.
Regulation (EU) No 1093/2010 of the European Parliament and of the Council of 24 November 2010 establishing a European Supervisory Authority (European Banking Authority), amending Decision No 716/2009/EC and repealing Commission Decision 2009/78/EC.
Regulation (EU) No 1094/2010 of the European Parliament and of the Council of 24 November 2010 establishing a European Supervisory Authority (European Insurance and Occupational Pensions Authority), amending Decision No 716/2009/EC and repealing Commission Decision 2009/79/EC.
Regulation (EU) No 1095/2010 of the European Parliament and of the Council of 24 November 2010 establishing a European Supervisory Authority (European Securities and Markets Authority), amending Decision No 716/2009/EC and repealing Commission Decision 2009/77/EC.
Regulation (EU) No 575/2013 of the European Parliament and of the Council of 26 June 2013 on prudential regulation for credit institutions and investment firms and amending Regulation (EU) No 648/2012.
Treaty establishing the European Economic Community (1957).

Croatian legislation

Insurance Act 2006, Official Gazette 151/05 and 87/08.
Ordinance of the Croatian Financial Services Supervisory Authority of 7 January 2009 on Organisational Requirements for Providing Investment Services and Conducting Investment Activities and Ancillary Services.

Estonian legislation

Commercial Code, RT I 1995, 26, 355. Amended by RT I 1996, 40, 773; RT I 1996, 51, 967; RT I 1996, 52, 993; RT I 1997, 16, 258; RT I 1997, 48, 774; RT I 1997, 77, 1313; RT I 1998, 2, 48; RT I 1998, 23, 322; RT I 1998, 30, 410; RT I 1998, 36, 552; RT I 1998, 59, 941; RT I 1998, 91, 1500; RT I 1999, 10, 155; RT I 1999, 23, 355; RT I 1999, 24, 360; RT I 1999, 57, 596; RT I 1999, 102, 907; RT I 2000, 29, 172; RT I 2000, 49, 303; RT I 2000, 55, 365; RT I 2000, 57, 373; RT I 2001, 34, 185; RT I 2001, 56, 332; RT I 2001, 56, 336; RT I 2001, 89, 532; RT I 2001, 93, 565; RT I 2002, 3, 6; RT I 2002, 35, 214; RT I 2002, 53, 336; RT I 2002, 61, 375; RT I 2002, 63, 387; RT I 2002, 63,

388; RT I 2002, 96, 564; RT I 2002, 102, 600; RT I 2002, 110, 657; RT I 2003, 4, 19; RT I 2003, 13, 64; RT I 2003, 18, 100; RT I 2003, 78, 523; RT I 2003, 88, 591; RT I 2004, 86, 582; RT I 2004, 89, 613; RT I 2005, 15, 85; RT I 2005, 57, 449; RT I 2005, 57, 450; RT I 2005, 57, 451; RT I 2005, 61, 478; RT I 2005, 63, 481; RT I 2005, 68, 525; RT I 2006, 7, 42; RT I 2006, 25, 186; RT I 2006, 55, 407; RT I 2006, 55, 412; RT I 2006, 61, 456; RT I 2007, 12, 66; RT I 2007, 58, 380; RT I 2007, 65, 405; RT I 2007, 67, 413; RT I 2008, 16, 116; RT I 2008, 27, 177; RT I 2008, 52, 288; RT I 2008, 59, 330; RT I 2008, 60, 331; RT I 2009, 5, 35; RT I 2009, 12, 71; RT I 2009, 13, 78; RT I 2009, 27, 164; RT I 2009, 29, 175; RT I 2009, 30, 178; RT I 2009, 51, 349; RT I 2009, 54, 363; RT I 2009, 57, 381; RT I 2009, 62, 405; RT I 2009, 67, 460; RT I 2010, 9, 41; RT I 2010, 20, 103; RT I 2010, 38, 231; RT I 2010, 77, 589; RT I, 30.12.2012, 2; RT I, 14.03.2011, 1; RT I, 25.03, 2011, 1; RT I, 02, 11, 2011, 1.

Credit Institutions Act, RT I 1999, 23, 349; consolidated text RT I 2005, 8, 32. Amended by RT I 2004, 86, 582; RT I 2005, 13, 64; RT I 2005, 39, 308; RT I 2005, 59, 463; RT I 2005, 61, 473; RT I 2006, 28, 208; RT I 2006, 63, 467; RT I 2007, 24, 127; RT I 2007, 58, 380; RT I 2007, 65, 405; RT I 2008, 3, 21; RT I 2008, 47, 261; RT I 2008, 59, 330; RT I 2009, 37, 250; RT I 2009, 39, 262; RT I 2009, 61, 401; RT I 2010, 2, 3; RT I 2010, 7, 30; RT I 2010, 9, 41; RT I 2010, 20, 103; RT I 2010, 22, 108; RT I 2010, 26, 129; RT I 2010, 34, 182; RT I, 21.12.2010, 3; RT I, 21.12.2010, 6; RT I, 18.02.2011, 1; RT I, 24.03.2011, 1; RT I, 29.06.2011, 1; RT I, 08.07.2011, 6; RT I, 13.12.2011, 1; RT I, 29.03.2012, 1; RT I, 29.06.2012, 1.

Financial Supervision Authority Act, RT I 2001, 48, 267. Amended by RT I 2002, 23, 131; RT I 2002, 105, 612; RT I 2003, 81, 544; RT I 2004, 36, 251; RT I 2004, 90, 616; RT I 2005, 13, 64; RT I 2005, 59, 463; RT I 2006, 56, 417; RT I 2006, 63, 467; RT I 2007, 44, 316; RT I 2007, 58, 380; RT I 2007, 68, 421; RT I 2009, 5, 35; RT I 2010, 2, 3; RT I 2010, 7, 30; RT I 2010, 9, 41; RT I 2010, 22, 108; RT I 2010, 34, 182; RT I, 21.12.2010, 3; RT I, 21.12.2010, 6; RT I, 24.03.2011, 1; RT I, 08.07.2011, 6; RT I, 29.03.2012, 1.

Insurance Activities Act, RT I 2004, 90, 616. Amended by RT I 2007, 4, 20; RT I 2007, 24, 127; RT I 2007, 55, 368; RT I 2007, 65, 405; RT I 2007, 68, 421; RT I 2008, 48, 269; RT I 2008, 59, 330; RT I 2009, 37, 250; RT I 2009, 61, 401; RT I 2010, 2, 3; RT I 2010, 7, 30; RT I 2010, 9, 41; RT I 2010, 22, 108; RT I, 18.02.2011, 1; RT I, 24.03.2011, 1; RT I, 29.06.2011, 1; RT I, 22.09.2011, 3; RT I, 02.11.2011, 1; RT I, 29.03.2012, 1; RT I, 26.04.2013, 2.

Investment Funds Act, RT I 2004, 36, 251. Amended by RT I 2004, 90, 616; RT I 2005, 59, 463; RT I 2005, 59, 464; RT I 2006, 56, 417; RT I 2007, 58, 380; RT I 2007, 65, 405; RT I 2008, 13, 89; RT I 2008, 48, 269; RT I 2009, 12, 71; RT I 2009, 37, 250; RT I 2010, 2, 3; RT I 2010, 7, 30; RT I 2010, 9, 41; RT I 2010, 22, 108; RT I, 21.12.2010, 3; RT I, 21.12.2010, 6; RT I, 18.02.2011, 1; RT I, 24.03.2011, 1; RT I, 08.07.2011, 6; RT I, 02.11.2011, 1; RT I, 29.03.2012, 1; RT I, 29.06.2012, 1; RT I, 06.07.2012, 1; RT I, 15.05.2013, 2.

Law of Obligations Act, RT I 2001, 81, 487. Amended by RT I 2002, 53, 336; RT I 2003, 78, 523; RT I 2004, 13, 86; RT I 2004, 37, 255; RT I 2004, 75, 522; RT I 2004, 87; 593; RT I 2004, 90, 616; RT I 2005, 39, 308; RT I 2005, 61, 473; RT I 2007, 56, 375; RT I 2008, 54, 304; RT I 2008, 59, 330; RT I 2009, 18, 108.

Payment Institutions and E-money Institutions Act, RT 2010, 2, 3. Amended by RT I 2010, 9, 41; RT I 2010, 22, 108; RT I 2010, 34, 182; RT I, 08.07.2011, 6; RT I, 02.11.2011, 1; RT I, 26.04.2013, 2.

Regulation No. 19 of the President of the Bank of Estonia of 6 July 1999, RTL 1999, 111, 1444.

Securities Market Act, RT I 2001, 89, 532. Amended by RT I 2002, 23, 131; RT I 2002, 63, 367; RT I 2002, 102, 600; RT I 2002, 105, 612; RT I 2003, 81, 544; RT I 2003, 88, 591; RT I 2004, 30, 208; RT I 2004, 36, 251; RT I 2004, 37, 255; RT I 2005, 13, 64; RT I 2005, 39, 308; RT I 2005 59, 463; RT I 2005, 59, 464; RT I 2007, 58, 380; RT I 2007, 65, 405; RT I 2008, 13, 19; RT I 2008, 15, 108; RT I 2008, 31, 193; RT I 2009, 12, 71; RT I 2009, 37, 250; RT I 2009, 61, 401; RT I 2010, 2, 3; RT I 2010, 7, 30; RT I 2010, 9, 41; RT I 2010, 20, 103; RT I 2010, 22, 108; RT I, 21.12.2010, 6; RT I, 18.02.2011, 1; RT I, 23.02.2011, 3; RT I, 21.03.2011, 2; RT I, 24.03.2011, 1; RT I, 29.06.2011, 1; RT I, 02.11.2011, 1; RT I, 22.12.2011, 3; RT I, 29.03.2012, 1; RT I, 28.06.2012, 5; RT I, 29.06.2012, 2; RT I, 26.04.2013, 2.

German legislation

Payment Services Supervision Act of 25 June 2009 (Federal Law Gazette 1, 1506), as amended by Article 2 subsection (74) of the Act of 22 December 2011 (Federal Law Gazette, 1, 3044).

Latvian legislation

Credit Institution Law, 05.10.1995, Latvijas Republikas Augstākās Padomes un Valdības Ziņotājs, 1995, No.23. Amended by Latvijas Vēstnesis, 1996, No.49 (534); LV, 1996, No.100/101 (585/586); LV, 1996, No.183 (668); LV, 1997, No.296/297 (1011/1012); LV, 1998, No.167/169 (1228/1230); LV, 2000, No.223/225 (2134/2136); LV, 2002, No.64 (2639); LV, 2002, No.161 (2736); LV, 2003, No.73 (2838); LV, 2003, No.175 (2940); LV, 2003, No.182 (2947); LV, 2004, No.90 (3038); LV, 2004, No.180 (3128); LV, 2005, No.92 (3250); LV, 2005, No.99 (3257); LV, 2006, No.103 (3471); LV, 2007, No.40 (3616); LV, 2007, No.85 (3661); LV, 2008, No.94 (3878); LV, 2008, No.174 (3958); LV, 2009, No.27 (4013); LV, 2009, No.39 (4025); LV, 2009, No.120 (4106); LV, 2009, No.171 (4157); LV, 2010, No.23 (4215); LV, 2010, No.51/52 (4243/4244); LV, 2010, No.160 (4352); LV, 2011, No.4 (4402); LV, 2011, No.167 (4565); LV, 2012, No.50 (4653); LV, 2012, No.56 (4659); LV, 2012, No.92 (4695); LV, 2013, No.61 (4867); LV, 2013, No.106 (4912); LV, 2013, No.193 (4999).

Law On Investment Companies, 18.12.1997, Latvijas Vēstnesis, 1997, No.342/345 (1054/1057). Amended by Latvijas Vēstnesis, 2000, No.230/232 (2141/2142); LV, 2002, No.165 (2740); LV, 2004, No.54 (3002); LV, 2007, No.51 (3627); LV, 2008, No.94 (3878); LV, 2008, No.104 (3888); LV, 2008, No.174 (3958); LV, 2010, No.51/52 (4243/4244); LV, 2011, No.173 (4571).

Polish legislation

Act of 28 August 1997: Law on the Organisation and Operation of Pension Funds; consolidated text: Dziennik Ustaw 2010, No.34, item 189. Amended by Dziennik Ustaw 2010, No.127, item 858; 2010, No.182, item 1228; 2011, No.75, item 398; 2011, No.106, item 622; 2011, No.171, item 1016; 2011, No.187, item 1111; 2011, No.232, item 1378; 2012, item 596.

Act of 29 August 1997: Banking Law; consolidated text: Dziennik Ustaw 2002, No.72, item 665. Amended by Dziennik Ustaw 2002, No.126, item 1070; 2002, No.141, item 1178; 2002, No.144, item 1208; 2002, No.153, item 1271; 2002, No.169, items 1385 and 1387; 2002, No.241, item 2074; 2003, No.50, item 424; 2003, No.60, item 535; 2003, No.65, item 594; 2003, No.228, item 2260; 2003, No.229, item 2276; 2004, No.64, item 594; 2004, No.68, item 623; 2004, No.91, item 870;

2004, No.96, item 959; 2004, No.121, item 1264; 2004, No.146, item 1546; 2004, No.173, item 1808; 2005, No.83, item 719; 2005, No.85, item 727; 2005, No.167, item 1398; 2005, No.183, item 1538; 2006, No.104, item 708; 2006, No.157, item 1119; 2006, No.190, item 1401; 2006, No.245, item 1775; 2007, No.42, item 272; 2007, No.112, item 769; 2008, No.171, item 1056; 2008, No.192, item 1179; 2008, No.209, item 1315; 2008, No.231, item 1546; 2009, No.18, item 97; 2009, No.42, item 341; 2009, No.65, item 545; 2009, No.71, item 609; 2009, No.127, item 1045; 2009, No.131, item 1075; 2009, No.144, item 1176; 2009, No.165, item 1316; 2009, No.166, item 1317; 2009, No.168, item 1323; 2009, No.201, item 1540; 2010 No.40, item 226; 2010, No.81, item 530; 2010, No.126, item 853; 2010, No.182, item 1228; 2010, No.257, item 1724; 2011, No.72, item 388; 2011, No.126, item 715; 2011, No.131, item 763; 2011, No.134, items 779 and 781; 2011, No.165, item 984; 2011, No.199, item 1175; 2011, No.201, item 1181; 2011, No.232, item 1378; 2012, item 855.

Act of 22 May 2003 on Insurance Activity; consolidated text: Dziennik Ustaw 2010, No.11, item 66. Amended by Dziennik Ustaw 2010, No.81, item 830; 2010, No.127, item 858; 2011, No.75, item 398; 2011, No.80, item 432; 2011, No.106, item 622; 2011, No.112, item 654; 2011, No.133, item 767.

Act of 22 May 2003 on Insurance and Pension Funds Supervision and on Insurance Ombudsman, Dziennik Ustaw 2003, No.124, item 1153. Amended by Dziennik Ustaw 2003, No.170, item 1651; 2004, No.93, item 891; 2004, No.96, item 959; 2005, No.48, item 447; 2005, No.83, item 719; 2005, No.143, item 1204; 2005, No.163, item 1362; 2006, No.157, item 1119; 2006, No.170, item 1217; 2006, No.249, item 1832; 2007, No.82, item 557; 2007, No.171, item 1206; 2008, No.228, item 1507; 2009, No.42, item 341; 2011, No.75, item 398.

Act of 22 May 2003 on Insurance Mediation, Dziennik Ustaw 2003, No.124, item 1154. Amended by Dziennik Ustaw 2004, No.96, item 959; 2005, No.48, item 447; 2005, No.167, item 1396; 2005, No.183, item 1538; 2006, No.157, item 1119; 2009, No.18, item 97; 2009, No.42, item 341.

Act of 20 April 2004 on Occupational Pension Schemes, Dziennik Ustaw 2004, No.116, item 1207. Amended by Dziennik Ustaw 2005, No.143, item 1202; 2006, No.157, item 1119; 2008, No.220, item 1432; 2010, No.18, item 98; 2011, No.75, item 398; 2011, No.171, item 1016.

Act of 27 May 2004 on Investment Funds, Dziennik Ustaw 2004, No.146, item 1546. Amended by Dziennik Ustaw 2005, No.83, item 719; 2005, No.183, items 1537 and 1538; 2005, No.184, item 1539.

Act of 29 July 2005 on Capital Market Supervision, Dziennik Ustaw 2005, No.183, item 1537. Amended by Dziennik Ustaw 2006, No.157, item 1119; 2006, No.170, item 1217; 2007, No.50, item 331; 2009, No.18, item 97; 2009, No.165, item 1316.

Act of 29 July 2005 on Public Offers and the Conditions for Introducing Financial Instruments to the Organised Trading System, and on Public Companies; consolidated text: Dziennik Ustaw 2009, No.185, item 1439. Amended by Dziennik Ustaw 2010, No.167, item 1129.

Act of 29 July 2005 on Trading in Financial Instruments; consolidated text: Dziennik Ustaw 2010, No.211, item 1384.

Act of 19 August 2011 on Payment Services, Dziennik Ustaw 2011, No.199, item 1175.

Regulation of the Minister of Finance of July 6th 2007 on Detailed Conditions to be Met by the Information Memorandum Referred to in Articles 39(1) and 42(1) of the Act on Public Offers and the Conditions for Introducing Financial Instruments to the Organised Trading System, and on Public Companies, Dziennik Ustaw 2007, No.132, item 916.

Resolution No. 389/2008 of the Polish Financial Supervision Authority of 17 December 2008 concerning the list of documents attached to the application to the Polish Financial Supervision Authority on issuing a permit to establish a bank, consent to appoint the members of the bank's Management Board and information about the composition of the board presented to the Polish Financial Supervision Authority by the Supervisory Board of the Bank, Official Journal of the Polish Financial Supervision Authority, 2008, No.8, item 100.

Resolution No. 312/2012 of the Polish Financial Supervision Authority of 27 November 2012 on the Mode of Exercising Supervision over Banking Activity, Official Journal of the Polish Financial Supervision Authority, 2012, No.8, item 43.

Resolution No. 359/2012 of the Polish Financial Supervision Authority of 20 December 2012 on the list of documents relating to business activity of entrepreneurs or foreign entrepreneurs enclosed with requests for authorisation referred to in Articles 6a(1)(1)(m) and 6d(1) of the Banking Law, Official Journal of the Polish Financial Supervision Authority, 2012, No.8, item 33.

Cases decided by the ECJ

Albore, C-423/98, [2000] ECR I-5965.

Almelo, C-393/92, [1994] ECR I-1477.

Amministrazione delle Finanze dello Stato v Simmenthal SpA (No.2), 106/77, [1978] ECR 629.
Analir and Others, C-205/99, [2001] ECR I-1271.
Campus Oil and Others, 72/83, [1984] ECR 2727.
Centros Ltd. v Erhvervs-og Selskabsstyrelsen, C-212/97, [1999] ECR I-1459.
Commission of the European Communities v Belgium, C-478/98, [2000] ECR I-7587.
—. v Belgium, C-503/99, [2002] ECR I-4809.
—. v Federal Republic of Germany, C-112/05, [2007] ECR I-8995.
—. v France, C-483/99, [2002] ECR I-4781.
—. v Greece, C-244/11, [2012] ECR I-, not yet reported.
—. v Italy, C-174/04, [2005] ECR I-4933.
—. v Italy, C-326/07, [2009] ECR I-2291.
—. v Poland, C-271/09, [2011] ECR I-13613.
—. v Portugal, C-367/98, [2002] ECR I-4731.
—. v Portugal, C-171/08, [2010] ECR I-6817.
—. v Portugal, C-543/08, [2010] ECR I-11241.
—. v Portugal, C-212/09, [2011] ECR I-10889.
—. v Spain, C-463/00, [2003] ECR I-4581.
—. v Spain, C-207/07, [2008] ECR I-111.
—. v The Netherlands, Joined Cases C-282/04 and C-283/04, [2006] ECR I-9141.
—. v United Kingdom, C-98/01, [2003] ECR I-4641.
Costa v ENEL, 6/64, [1964] ECR 585.
Eglise de Scientologie and Scientology International, C-54/99, [2000] ECR I-1335.
Konle v Austria, C-302/97, [1999] ECR I-3099.
R. v Secretary of State for Transport, ex parte Factortame Ltd. and Others, C-221/89, [1991] ECR I-3905.
Reisch and Others, Joined Cases C-515/99, C-519/99 to C-524/99 and C-526/99 to C-540/99, [2002] ECR I-2157.
Rewe-Zentral AG v Bundesmonopolverwaltung für Branntwein, 120/78, [1979] ECR 649.
Sanz de Lera and Others, Joined Cases C-163/94, C-165/94 and C-250/94, [1995] ECR I-4821.
Skatteverket v A, C-101/05, [2007] ECR I-11531.
Trummer and Mayer, C-222/97, [1999] ECR I-1661.
Van Duyn v Home Office, 41/74, [1975] ECR 1337.
Van Gend en Loos v Nederlandse Tariefcommissie, 26/62, [1963] ECR 1.
Von Colson v Land Nordrhein-Westfahlen, 14/83, [1984] ECR 1891.

World Wide Web Pages and Other Resources

Latvian Translation and Terminology Centre (2007), 'Strategic plan' (online) (cited 4 October 2007). Available from http://www.ttc.lv/?print=41.

Polish Office of the Committee for European Integration (2007), 'History of the EU: Stepping stones to enlargement' (online) (cited 22 October 2007). Available from http://www1.ukie.gov.pl/WWW/en.nsf/0/D809DBFA2BFB5681C1256ED20047E7C6?Open.

Professor Māris Baltiņš, Latvian Translation and Terminology Centre (2007), Unpublished e-mail: References for laws in Latvijas Vēstnesis.

World Trade Organization (2014), 'Understanding the WTO: The Organization – Members and Observers' (online) (cited 29 June 2014). Available from http://www.wto.org/english/thewto_e/whatis_e/tif_e/org6_e.htm.

INDEX